A SHOW OF JUSTICE

'. . . the real history of all mankind is shameful. But there is hope in bits of it.'

George Bernard Shaw

A SHOW OF JUSTICE

racial 'amalgamation' in nineteenth century
New Zealand

ALAN WARD

University of Toronto Press

ISBN 0-8020-2117-4

First published 1974 in Canada and the United States by University of Toronto Press, Toronto and Buffalo

Printed in New Zealand

To my parents

Preface

The subject of the doctoral thesis on which this book is based emerged from the controversy following publication in 1961 of the report on the Department of Maori Affairs compiled under the direction of the then Secretary for Maori Affairs, Mr J. K. Hunn. The Hunn Report helped to intensify discussion about the theoretical goals of policy affecting Maori-Pakeha relations. Concepts such as 'assimilation' and 'integration' were defined, redefined, and examined for their implications. In general Maori people were much less happy with their purport than were Pakeha. The Report also sought on the one hand to pinpoint areas where the Maori people needed additional practical assistance towards socio-economic advancement and, on the other, to indicate where special legal and administrative provisions applying to the Maori could be dismantled, on the assumption that they contributed unnecessarily to the separation of races in New Zealand.

My purpose in the thesis and in this book was to examine the nineteenth century antecedents of Maori-Pakeha relations, both in their ideology and with regard to the practical legal and administrative provisions relating to the Maori. For this purpose I was given unrestricted access to the surviving records of the old Native Department up to 1895. Although there are a number of excellent books and theses on Maori-Pakeha relations leading to the wars of the 1860s, and on particular aspects of administration afterwards (and this book owes a considerable debt to them), a connected and comprehensive survey of civil administration affecting the Maori throughout the nineteenth century, especially as it relates to problems of social control and the practical application of British law, had not previously been attempted. This, and the nature and availability of the records, led me to focus the study around the Native Department, its antecedents, its structure and methods, its aims, the men who staffed it and the Ministers who directed it. The Department (and more particularly its main instruments in the out-districts—the itinerant Resident Magistrates and their salaried Maori Assessors) will be seen to have exercised a very significant role, especially in the formative decades of the 1860s and 1870s which this study discusses in greatest detail. The Native Department, however, proved to be in part complemented and in part rivalled by the Native Land Court. The development and significance of each, and the relations between them, are considered in the context of general government policy.

The role of the nineteenth century Native Department was very different from that of the twentieth century Department of Maori Affairs; its primary purposes were political and judicial—to draw the Maori people under the control of the centralised machinery of state which the British were establishing in the new Colony of New Zealand. The question of the attitudes of the Maori, a 'stateless' people, to the intruding machinery of state proved a fascinating one. This theme has not previously been closely studied in New Zealand either, the assumptions usually being that the value of British-type parliament, law and law-courts were and are self-evident, or that the Maori were simply compelled by force of arms to recognise them and that the question did not seriously obtain after the wars of the 1860s. Neither view adequately describes what happened.

Examination of Maori attitudes to the concepts and to the machinery of centralised law and administration involved firstly some consideration of traditional attitudes to authority and dispute settlement, and secondly a redefining of the sociologists' and anthropologists' 'model' of Maori acculturation. The results form Chapters I and II of the book. The 'model' proposed is that the Maori response to Western contact was highly intellectual, flexible and progressive, and also highly selective, aiming largely to draw upon the strengths of the West to preserve the Maori people and their resources from the threat of the West itself, and to enable them to enjoy its material and cultural riches co-equally with the Westerners. Very early in the establishment of the Colony the aspirations which Erik Schwimmer (in *The Maori People in the Nineteen-sixties*) called 'inclusion' and 'ambiculturalism' manifest themselves.

The book therefore seeks to encompass the underlying values and attitudes of both Pakeha and Maori towards the question of state and law, central policy and administration affecting the Maori, the application of that policy in the out-districts, and Maori initiatives and responses. It seeks to do this on a New Zealand wide scale and over a time span of a century.

Obviously there is scope for detailed work on individuals who appear in the story or local area studies of the complex interaction of Maori and Pakeha described here. Nevertheless, believing that history is an art, and the historian essentially involved (through the selection of his questions and his sense of the relative significance of his innumerable pieces of evidence) in *interpreting* reality, not simply photographing it, I have chosen to paint on a broad canvas. The Maori artist Selwyn Muru has depicted the extension of state power in New Zealand in his moving painting 'Kawanatanga'—that is 'Government'—as it affected the Maori; this book is another interpretation of the same theme. Few New Zealanders will be neutral on the question, especially in the 1970s when the young urban Maori intelligentsia are demanding an honest answer to some questions that have been glossed over. This, like all history, is not intended, and could not pretend, to be a revelation of 'the truth': hopefully it will help to stimulate the current search for more informed valuation.

While final responsibility for this book remains my own, I have been greatly assisted in its preparation by many interested and considerate people, Maori and European. I am particularly indebted to the Australian National University, Canberra, for the opportunity to undertake the initial research and to my principal supervisor there, Professor J. W. Davidson, for his encouragement and guidance. Professor M. P. K. Sorrenson, University of Auckland, has been very helpful throughout the work, and Professor K. Sinclair, University of Auckland, Dr F. West, Australian National University and Dr K. Gillion, University of Adelaide, assisted at important stages. Among others who have kindly offered encouragement and advice are Dr Joan Metge, Dr H. G. Miller, Mrs Mary Boyd and the late Professor J. C. Beaglehole, of Victoria University; Professor W. Oliver and Mr G. Butterworth, Massey University; Mr John Booth, former secretary to the NZ Maori Council; fellow scholars at the Australian National University and, more recently, my colleagues in the History Department and my students in the Pacific History course at La Trobe University. In the lengthy process of revising the original thesis I have relied heavily on the support of Professors A. W. Martin and J. Salmond and, for the typing of the manuscript, on Mrs Barbara Salmond assisted by Mrs Diane Goodwin. Maori scholars who have contributed their viewpoints and supplemented my rudimentary knowledge of the Maori language with their translations of key documents include Dr Pei Jones of Taumarunui, Messrs Koro Dewes and W. Parker, Victoria University of Wellington, Mr B. Puriri, Department of Maori Affairs, Mr Matiu Te Hau, University of Auckland, and Mr Selwyn Muru. Mr D. Bryce, Wellington, kindly supplied information about his grandfather, the former Native Minister, John Bryce.

For making available the archives on which this study depends especial thanks are due to Mr J. M. McEwen, Secretary for Maori Affairs, Mr J. D. Pascoe and the staff of the New Zealand National Archives, Mr A. G. Bagnall and the staff of the Alexander Turnbull Library, Wellington, and the chief librarians and staff of the General Assembly Library, Wellington, the Auckland Public Library, the National Library of Australia, the State Library of Victoria, the Parliamentary Library of Victoria, the Mitchell Library, Sydney, and the photographic section of the Dominion Museum, Wellington. Mr Littlejohn of the office of the Clerk of the House of Representatives, Wellington, was most helpful in assisting me to explore unpublished parliamentary papers in Parliament Buildings, Wellington.

I gratefully acknowledge financial assistance to visit New Zealand libraries from the Social Science Research Council of Australia and the Research Grants Committee of La Trobe University. And I am obliged to Mr K. Mitchell, Canberra, who drew the maps, and Mrs E. Hill and Mr I. MacDonald, Melbourne, who checked footnotes and quotations.

A.D.W.
1972

Contents

Maps

Plates

Abbreviations

For locations of collections see Bibliography.

AG	Archives of the Attorney-General
AGG-A	Archives of the Agent of the General Government, Auckland
AGG-HB	Archives of the Agent of the General Government, Hawke's Bay
AJHR	*Appendices to the Journals of the House of Representatives* (New Zealand)
AJLC	*Appendices to the Journals of the Legislative Council* (New Zealand)
APS	Aborigines Protection Society
CC	Civil Commissioner
CMS	Church Missionary Society
CN/O	Church Missionary Society, Letters and Journals
CO	Colonial Office papers
Col. Sec.	Colonial Secretary (this refers to the official in the New Zealand executive; the Secretary of State for Colonies in the British Government is referred to by name)
CS	Archives of the Civil Secretary
DSC	*Daily Southern Cross*
EC	Archives of the Executive Council
G	Governors' archives
GB	Gore Browne's papers
GBPP	*Great Britain Parliamentary Papers*
IA	Archives of the Internal Affairs Department—formerly the Colonial Secretary's Department
J	Archives of the Justice Department
JC	Archives of the Justice Department Courts
JC-HN	Archives of the Justice Department Courts, Hamilton
JC-WG	Archives of the Justice Department Courts, Wanganui
JR	*Jurist Reports*
MA	Archives of the Maori Affairs Department
MA-NA	Archives of the Maori Affairs Office, Napier
MA-WG	Archives of the Maori Affairs Office, Wanganui
MLC	Archives of the Maori Land Court
MT-CH	Archives of the Maori Trustee's Office, Christchurch
MT-N	Archives of the Maori Trustee's Office, Nelson
NK	Nan Kivell collection
NM	Archives of the Province of New Munster
NO	Native Office; the official prefix to the numbering on all correspondence of the Native Department
NZH	*New Zealand Herald*
NZLR	*New Zealand Law Reports*
PD	*New Zealand Parliamentary Debates*
PM	Archives of the Prime Minister's Department
SC	Select Committee
T	Archives of the Colonial Treasurer's Department
UPP	Unpublished papers presented in the New Zealand parliament

Glossary of Maori Words

These are abbreviated and more usual definitions; fuller explanation of important terms is given in context or in notes.

ariki	a senior ranking chief
aukati	(v.t.) to debar, (n.) a frontier
hahunga	disinterment and reinterment of the bones of the dead
hapu	sub-tribe (principal operative kin group)
iwi	tribe or people
kainga	domestic settlement
kanga	curse or execration
kaumatua	elder
kauri	a species of indigenous conifer (*Agathis australis*)
kohuru	treachery, unprovoked murder
makutu	sorcery
mana	spiritual potency (hence prestige, authority)
marae	meeting place
muru	compensatory plunder
niu	*Pai Marire* ritual pole
pa	fortified settlement (latterly any Maori village)
panui	notice or proclamation
puremu	adultery
rangatira	a chief
raupo	a species of bulrush (*Typha augustifolia*)
runanga	council
tangi	lamentation over the dead
tapu	charged with spiritual potency, under religious or ceremonial restriction, sacred (*wahi tapu*—sacred place, burial ground)
taua	an armed band
tohunga	expert (usually in spiritual matters)
toa	warriors
ture	customary maxims regulating conduct (hence 'law')
utu	satisfaction, compensation, equivalence
whakawa	to judge
whanau	sub-division of *hapu,* an extended family
whare	domestic house
wharepuni	sleeping house
whenua	land

In the case of two place names, Wanganui and Mangonui, which in the nineteenth century were also spelt Whanganui and Mongonui, the modern and generally accepted form has been adopted. The words 'Maori' and 'Pakeha' (a European settler in New Zealand or his descendants) have been regarded as part of accepted New Zealand idiom and not italicised. The term 'Kupapa', originally an adjective meaning 'neutral', was also taken over into settler idiom to describe Maori who fought on the Government side. 'Hauhau' a term derived from the bark-like utterance climaxing a *Pai Marire* incantation, was eventually applied by the settlers and troops to designate almost any Maori considered hostile to the Government.

Part I

I

The Traditional Scene

Any attempt to describe traditional Maori life before the arrival of Europeans is hazardous. The sources of evidence are largely the written observations of early European visitors and settlers, and the Maori oral traditions they have recorded. The fullest of these date from the mid or late nineteenth century, when the pre-contact pattern, and Maori informants' own recollections of that pattern, had already undergone subtle change. Moreover, as Sir Peter Buck observed, several waves of Polynesian migrants, dispersing through as large an area as New Zealand, or even the various 'canoes' of one migration, might be expected to show significant variety in values and institutions from district to district.[1] The very concept 'Maori' itself of course, emerged after the Europeans' arrival. It must also be realised that Polynesian society was not static, but undergoing change during the dispersal through the Eastern Pacific. The migrants to New Zealand, in adapting to a cold climate and a relatively large land mass, passed through considerable social change, and this was continuing when Europeans arrived.

The following generalisations then, should be read in the light of these warnings. Yet it is probably still of value to attempt some description of traditional life, particularly as it relates to the main themes of this study, the building in New Zealand of a bureaucratic machinery of state, and English concepts of law and judicial institutions. There was, moreover, a basic Eastern Polynesian culture underlying local variety, and the various tribes were interconnected by language and through marriage and descent, which was traced through both male and female lines.

Anthropologists, and sociologists of law, have paid considerable attention to methods of social control in so-called primitive societies, part of their discussion centring about whether they can properly be called 'law'. An early view held that an individual had no real freedom of choice, his every action from birth to death being dictated by what has been called an 'iron mould' of hereditary and unchanging custom, reinforced by pervasive fears of the supernatural. Malinowski found, on living among the Trobriand Islands people, however, that this sense of circumscription was patently absent— that people acted with considerable freedom of choice, without an oppressive, ever-present fear of supernatural sanction. The deliberate breach of convention

3

was even undertaken by daring men, as a calculated risk. Licence was prevented, however, and the community held together, by the principle of reciprocity—a sense of the interdependence, for most of the basic needs of life, among its members—which acted as a sufficient constraint on anti-social behaviour. Customary norms regulated social and economic life. Many of these were secular, involving the actions of men, not of deities and spirits, at least not directly; and they were flexible—subject to reinterpretation according to circumstances.

Nevertheless Malinowski came to admit that the need for reciprocity was not of itself sufficient to prevent wayward behaviour, and had to be backed by coercive sanctions. Within a kinship group a defaulter could be punished by withdrawal of community assistance, demand for compensation, beating, banishment, or, more rarely, by execution. Supernatural sanctions could also be invoked through sorcery. Disputes between kinship groups might be settled by payment of compensation, but if payment was withheld blood feud could follow.

Within many traditional African and Pacific societies the right of an injured party to take redress, and the techniques for securing it, were widely recognised and regularly exercised. Adamson Hoebel writes: 'A social norm is legal if its neglect or infraction is regularly met, in threat or in fact, by the application of physical force by an individual or group possessing the socially recognized privilege of so acting'.[2] On this basis it is certainly reasonable to refer to Polynesian techniques of social control as 'law' or 'customary law', and nineteenth century Maori leaders, reflecting on their society in discussions with Europeans, often referred to 'our law' rather than to 'our custom'.

Many stateless societies, Polynesia among them, lacked specialised judicial institutions—courts or chiefs with specific functions—to pass and enforce judgments, and disputes were resolved mainly by the contending parties themselves. In this situation the strength of the parties greatly affected the outcome. Marshall Sahlins has written of Polynesia: 'The general underlying scheme regulating the application of sanctions to "wrongdoers" is not law, in the Austinian sense [of commands from a central sovereign source of power], but collective retaliation. Punishments, by necessity, vary with kinship backing and support musterable by the respective parties involved'.[3] J. A. Barnes makes the important point that normally no one group could dominate the rest because cross-cutting systems of kinship and organisation 'ensure that a man's friend in one context could be his enemy in another; in any quarrel there are some who are friends of both sides'. This limited conflict, as did a general interest in maintaining relative order so that the economic life of the community and its very rich social and cultural activity could continue. Nevertheless Barnes also notes that 'stateless societies lack courts with power to enforce judgments, and are therefore described as lacking law in the strict sense; they are said to have jural not legal institutions'.[4] While the European system of law has its own irregularities (including the fact that the strongest group politically may erect legal disabilities against a minority, and that those with greater wealth are more readily able to resort to the courts), it is still convenient to use the unqualified term 'law' to denote a system in which disputes are adjusted not only by the parties themselves, but through a separate system of legal institutions substantially apart from the contending parties. That was the sense in which the British normally used the term, when they undertook to introduce 'law' in New Zealand and supplant Maori 'custom', and it will normally be used in that sense in this book, although it should be appreciated that British-type law is not necessarily much more regular than customary law in application, nor is its separation from other social institutions total.[5]

M. B. Hooker has ably shown how traditional Maori jural concepts and institutions were based on and derived much of their detail from the fundamental magico-religious beliefs of the society.[6] His account tends, however, to imply rather more regularity and certainty in the jural order than was probably the actual case; traditional Maori society also illustrates the later views of Malinowski, and those of Sahlins and Barnes. The basic structure was a system of major lineages or tribes, named from founding ancestors, possibly mythical, and themselves descended from the deities who created and still acted in the world order. The tribes ramified into *hapu* or sub-tribes, and *whanau* or extended families, a *hapu* being the main functional political and economic unit. In a Maori village, the central storage and defensive position of a *hapu*, low fences divided the compounds of the various *whanau* (see photograph of Koroniti village). Marriage was normally but not exclusively, within the *hapu*. Although the male line was preferred, descent was traced through both the male and female lines—a principle which extended the network of social relations widely and provided great flexibility.

Leadership in Maori society devolved on chiefs, rank and status normally being ascribed to those in the most direct lines of descent from the ancestor-gods and therefore inheritors of spiritual potency, or *mana*, and knowledge of the rituals to make it effective for the well-being of their kin. The chiefly principle was also flexible: the possession of *mana* was deemed to be revealed through efficiency in leadership, both in the peaceful arts—cultivation, fishing, hunting—and in war, in other words success in defending the resources of the lineage and promoting its well-being. Despite seniority of descent, ineffective men could be considered as lacking *mana* and effective chieftainship could pass to a younger brother or near kinsman who proved more resourceful, although the senior descendant might still be called upon to recite the rituals associated with the cycle of cultivation. Genealogies were manipulated to make a claimant to high rank appear close to the senior lines of ancestry.

The actual authority of a chief in a Maori community was subtle and proved very difficult for early European observers to define. Maori society was not so highly stratified as in Hawaii or Tahiti where the *ali'i* (Tahitian *ari'i*)

were a dominant and fairly exclusive social class. In New Zealand the term
ariki was applied to some men of great rank and power but more often meant
simply the first born son of a senior family, heir to the *mana* attained by close
relation to the ancestor-dead. The senior chiefs could not stand back and give
orders. Their lead or opinion was normally accepted, but the *rangatira* (the
active heads of each extended family) and the *kaumatua* (elders) also had considerable authority in their own right. Although senior chiefs were normally
deferred to by their kinsmen they were still dependent for economic and military
strength upon reciprocal services with kinsmen, and they could not take
independent decisions or persistently flout public opinion without risk of
repudiation. In 1820 an English officer recorded that the leading chief of a
hapu sent the daughters of two *rangatira* aboard a visiting ship in return for
trade goods without their fathers' knowledge, but on going about the village
'he had been so severely reprehended for doing so, that he was obliged in his
own defence to withdraw them'.[7] Early observers then, who believed the
chiefs to be despotic, or capable of giving orders or taking decisions for their
people without consultation, were mistaken. There is merit in the observa-
tion that Maori society had only two classes, *rangatira* and slaves,[8] the latter
being prisoners taken in war—though even these were likely to inter-marry
with their captors and their children would be free. Perhaps a better approxi-
mation was attained by an early Sub-Protector of Aborigines, Dr Edward
Shortland, when he characterised Maori society as 'a democracy, limited by a
certain amount of patriarchal influence'.[9]

Yet, while a senior chief's authority over other *rangatira* was limited, it
was never unimportant and English settlers were as wrong to under-rate it
as to over-rate it. Under traditional religion a high-ranking and powerful
chief, a man of great *mana,* especially when recently engaged in his ritual
duties (and more particularly those relating to death and burial) was charged
with powers that made contact with him or his artifacts extremely precarious
for ordinary men: he was *tapu*. The *mana* and *tapu* principles were the
source of both order and dispute in Maori society. Kinship orientation and
the community routine of cultivating, hunting and fighting were focused
upon them. A chief was the recipient of wealth through gifts from his kin, and
he distributed that wealth in feasts on important occasions. A chief's power
was a source of control which could be used to *tapu* property or person, to
make a crop safe from trespass, to set aside a tree for canoe-building, or to
conserve a stretch of forest or shell-fish ground for an important feast. The
burial places of chiefs were highly *tapu*. These prohibitions were generally
well-known to the members of the community whose chiefs created them, and
would not normally be violated for fear of sickness or catastrophe which would
follow as a result of the anger of the spirits and ancestor-dead. But strangers
could unwittingly infringe *tapu* and the community whose sacred places were
violated would be impelled to exact compensation from or even kill the
intruder, lest their own offended ancestor-dead take retribution on *them* for

the unrequited affront. Moreover, possessors of *mana* were impelled to demonstrate it, by boldness and by constant concern for their names and stations. This made chiefs, especially young and aspiring chiefs, enterprising travellers, entrepreneurs, adaptors and innovators when European material wealth and ideas came on the scene. It also made them highly sensitive to insult, slight, or diminution of status. A curse or execration (*kanga*) levelled at a chief (particularly at his head, the most sacred part of his person) was a frequent source of demand for compensation, or bloody retribution.

Theft was a further frequent source of dispute. Although few would dare touch the property of a high-ranking chief, according to early European observers, thefts often appear to have been committed in a spirit of boldness and daring, offenders often readily admitting their actions when challenged. Powerful people deliberately broke rules to prove that they were *toa*—strong men, possessed of great *mana*. The gods who measured conduct were after all, not like the all-good creator of the New Testament but more like the gods of the Old, jealous of name and reputation and concerned with avenging injury. Therefore, although there were widely accepted rights of person and property, it was not unethical to try to advance one's fortunes, or those of one's kin, by tricky conduct, as well as by manipulation of the network of reciprocal obligations. It was perhaps more shameful to be caught out, demonstrably to fail, and impair relations with another group, although some chiefs were indeed righteously indignant at false accusations of theft after European contact.

A greater sense of shame seems to have been felt by chiefs discovered to have committed adultery and this (perhaps the shame of having brought retribution on one's kin from the kin of the offended wife, as much as shame of the offence itself) seems to have been responsible for many suicides. Women were indeed a constant source of contention, taking precedent over land in the proverb 'by women and land men are lost'. There were complex disputes over conflicting claims to the betrothal of young women, over adultery after marriage, and over the future status of widows.

Land rights were also extremely intricate. Constant adjustment was required to accommodate the primary rights of a lineage born and resident on the land, the contingent rights of those who married or were adopted out of the lineage but later returned, the rights of their children who returned, and the rights of those who married into the lineage or were given permissive residence in time of war or migration. The rival claims of conquerors who settled on the land, and the conquered—or more particularly of the descendants of each— were particularly contentious. Although there was no land in New Zealand not claimed by at least one *hapu,* and some boundary marks were well-known and accepted, the extent of territory within which a *hapu* could cultivate and hunt became less well defined the further one drew from the central village. Between many *hapu* lay areas of disputed land left uncultivated.

The belief that the spiritual order constantly interacted with the material order extended to the view that sickness and death were caused by the withdrawal of protection, or the malignancy, of spirit beings. This could be due to some failure in action or ritual of the afflicted person or his kin, but was frequently held to be the result of sorcery by some adversary, and this too was a cause of conflict.

Maori society therefore held to be wrongs a number of actions which were not recognised as such in the English law of the nineteenth century. The imposition of a sharp differentiation between criminal and civil offences in Maori customary law is not helpful, because as we have seen, in the absence of a state or legal machinery, all disputes were adjusted between the parties themselves, and a greater or smaller circle of kinsmen. In this sense they could all be considered civil matters. On the other hand disputes between *hapu,* especially those leading to full-scale battles, had something of the character of war between separate 'states', and many early European observers did consider Maori society to be in a constant state of war.

Nevertheless there was also considerable correspondence between Maori concepts of wrong and those recognised in English law. Negligence leading to damage to person or property was punishable; so were nuisance, trespass, defamation, liability for animal trespass, seduction and other offences categorised as torts in England. Some disputes—about marriage or reciprocation of labour, for example— were clearly 'civil' in character, being normally confined to the parties most directly concerned. But murder and persistent or flagrant theft or adultery could quickly disrupt the whole village, and involve retribution from the community leaders. Indeed, as might be expected, whether an offence tended to become 'criminal' or 'civil' depended not only on the kind of offence but on its degree or the repetition of it. If a wrongdoer made a victim of a chief the denouement might come earlier than if he had confined his attentions to people of low rank. The goal of dispute settlement also varied with the degree of the offence. The dominant purposes in the case of petty or first offences were usually to remove the causes of tension, to reconcile the parties and restore normal social relationships. A just apportionment of responsibility was usually followed by appropriate transfer of goods to the injured party as *utu* or satisfaction. But where the offender was flagrantly or persistently anti-social, the concept of punishment or retribution loomed much larger and could be very swift and severe.

As a normal method of securing satisfaction an offended party would gather his kinsmen in an armed band and set off to *muru* or formally to plunder the offender and his kin. The leading kinsmen of both parties would normally discuss the matter in great detail. The *whakawa*—accusation, investigation and decision or judgment—were often quite formal and structured. Customary maxims or *ture,* enshrining generally received principles, might be cited, but the complexity of rights and prerogatives of all involved and the peculiarities of the situation would be determinedly pursued. For example, it might be considered appropriate that a chief should kill a slave who had seduced his wife, but if it was felt that the chief's bullying or incontinence had caused her to stray, the wife's kin might also *muru* the chief. It was a sort of litigation in which a high sense of equity (according to the mores of the society) was attained. If an offender were plainly in the wrong, his kin might readily offer compensation. Indeed, since the offence, and hence the severity of a *muru,* increased with the rank of an offender, European settlers were astonished to see the wrongdoers and their kin encouraging the plunder party to seize their goods in order to demonstrate their rank. If a charge was considered false or a demand excessive it would be resisted, or might engender a counter claim. This, and the fact that the contending parties probably had some ties by marriage or descent with one another, limited excesses. The mediatory services of men of rank, related to and respected by both sides, were frequently accepted. Thus the naturalist Dieffenbach records that in a continuing feud between the Ngatiraukawa and Ngatiapa tribes in the Manawatu district the chief Hiko, related by descent to the former and by marriage to the latter, 'is always chosen as peacemaker'.[10] Edward Shortland, also noted that before a plunder party set out to secure redress of a grievance, 'the amount of compensation, or, at least, the more considerable items, have probably been agreed on beforehand, through the assistance of mutual friends going between the parties, to learn and report the nature of the terms likely to be demanded by one, or likely to be accepted by the other'.[11] Although it was normally a temporary role, depending upon status and relationship of the disputants, according to the painter Augustus Earle some elderly chiefs were so valued as 'heralds' or peacemakers that they made it a vocation to mediate between contending parties wherever possible, offering explanation and material satisfaction in order to avert fighting.[12]

However, mediation could be effective only if both parties were willing to avoid conflict. As Sahlins observed, relative power did affect the situation. A high-ranking chief could get his way more easily, though *noblesse oblige* did operate and he could choose to disregard minor offences. A low-ranking man, with little kinship backing, might have to resort to sorcery to secure redress against a chief. In a serious conflict of interests, or where an aggressive and ambitious man led one party, might could prevail, obliging the defeated party to nurse its resentment, try to build strength, and await a chance to secure *utu.* In the complexity of relations between all *hapu* there normally existed a catalogue of unrequited grievances, which might erupt from time to time into feuding.

This situation has led many of the early explorers and settlers in New Zealand, and some scholars since, to argue that Maori society was never properly at peace—that when *hapu* were not actually fighting they were only in a state of truce. In a sense this is true. Men did generally carry arms, or were never far from arms; high value was placed on warrior prowess and young men aspired to make a reputation in battle; and oral tribal histories recorded a plethora of battles, some of them, particularly in times of migration or struggle for economic resources, being battles of annihilation. Yet, if not peace, much of the institutionalised feuding, replete with magnificent oratory and dances of defiance, but involving few casualties, was scarcely war either. The oral tradition probably magnifies the scale of battles and telescopes the time span in which they occurred. In any case it also records long periods of peace and men noted for working for peace and the preservation of life.[13] A proverb observes that a warrior's reputation was likely to be short-lived, while that of a cultivator was enduring. There was a mythological justification and an appropriate set of rituals for making a binding peace—the elusive and precious *tatau pounamu* or greenstone door.[14]

These then were some of the features of Maori society as Europeans found it in the nineteenth century. Contrary to the views of some early anthropologists, weary of the turmoil of their own society and anxious to find and preserve Pacific Arcadias, it was not in a state of perfect harmony or equilibrium. Nor, as its critics were inclined to suggest, was it fundamentally corrupt and vicious. Like all societies it had its strengths and weaknesses. Institutions had been evolved to secure considerable order and security. Yet there were factors which promoted antagonism and made conflict difficult to avoid. Feuding, if not warfare, was endemic, but political sense, oratory and debate were highly developed and Maori leadership and kinship principles were flexible, resilient and adaptable. That resilience and adaptability were to be sorely needed, and strikingly demonstrated, as European and Maori society began to interact.

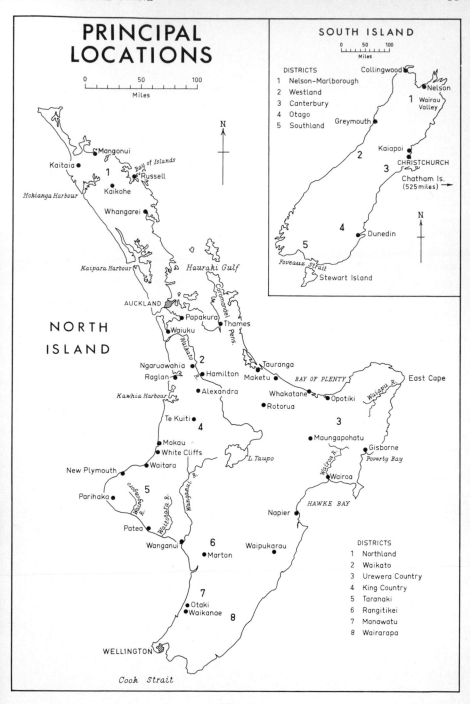

PRINCIPAL LOCATIONS

Miles
0   50   100

N

NORTH ISLAND

Mangonui
Kaitaia
Bay of Islands
Russell
Kaikohe
Hokianga Harbour
Whangarei
1

Kaipara Harbour
Hauraki Gulf
AUCKLAND
Papakura
Coromandel Pens.
Waiuku
Thames
Waikato R.
Ngaruawahia
2
Tauranga
Raglan
Hamilton
Maketu
BAY OF PLENTY
East Cape
Kawhia Harbour
Alexandra
Whakatane
Opotiki
Waiapu R.
Te Kuiti
Rotorua
4
3
Mokau
Maungapohatu
White Cliffs
Gisborne
New Plymouth
Waitara
L. Taupo
Poverty Bay
Parihaka
Wairoa R.
Wairoa
5
HAWKE BAY
Patea
Waitotara R.
Wanganui R.
Napier
Wanganui
6
Waipukarau
Marton
7
Otaki
Waikanae
8
WELLINGTON
Cook Strait

DISTRICTS
1 Northland
2 Waikato
3 Urewera Country
4 King Country
5 Taranaki
6 Rangitikei
7 Manawatu
8 Wairarapa

SOUTH ISLAND

Miles
0   50   100

DISTRICTS
1 Nelson–Marlborough
2 Westland
3 Canterbury
4 Otago
5 Southland

Collingwood
Nelson
1
Wairau Valley
Greymouth
Kaiapoi
2
CHRISTCHURCH
3
Chatham Is. (525 miles) →
N
4
Dunedin
5
Foveaux Strait
Stewart Island

Map 1

II

Maori   and   Pakeha

On 9 November 1769, at Mercury Bay, a Maori trading with Lieutenant Gore of Cook's ship *Endeavour,* made off with a piece of cloth, declining to hand over a cloak he had previously offered in payment; the Lieutenant, already irritated by petty thieving the expedition had encountered, and now incensed by the deceit, shot him dead. The botanist Joseph Banks commented that the man's life was 'forfeited to the laws of England' though he thought Gore's reaction far too severe. Ashore the dead man's kin debated whether vengeance should be attempted, but decided that he had been in the wrong and his death was *utu* for his offence. Trading was resumed, and the Maori felt confirmed in their decision when no further mishap, which would have indicated the spirits' displeasure at their failure to take vengeance, befell the community.[1]

Eleven days later, in the broad estuary that Cook named the Thames, a young Maori stole a timing-glass, whereupon 'The first Lieutenant took it into his head to flogg him for his crime.' When the man was seized the Maori about the ship threatened to attack the crew until the Tahitian interpreter Tupaia assured them that their friend would not be killed but only whipped, 'on which they were well satisfied'. Indeed, when the Europeans had finished with him the culprit was given a further beating by an old man whom Banks surmised might have been his father.[2]

The Maori experienced many other examples of coercive sanctions to enforce European concepts of right during Cook's voyages, and on occasion menaced or attacked the Europeans in defence of their own. The important point about the Mercury Bay and Thames incidents is that once relations had been established, and barter exchanged, the Maori concerned were prepared, within limits, to admit a kinsman's responsibility in a dispute and accept European sanctions against him, for the sake of ending the dispute and resuming trade. Was there in this the basis of a future association of the two peoples? Could there be sufficient agreement as to what constituted offences and their proper punishment? And would the Europeans reciprocate and accept some of the Maori sanctions against *their* wrongdoers?

There was in fact a great deal of violence on the New Zealand coast in the seventy years after Cook's landfall as an increasing stream of explorers, whalers, traders, missionaries and settlers flowed from Britain and New South Wales, from America and France. At times the coastal tribes' desire for European goods led to attacks on ships and shore parties; at times Europeans invited attack by stealing food, molesting Maori women, insulting chiefs or trespassing on *tapu* places. Distrust and aggressiveness on both sides led to some very bloody encounters. The killing of the French explorer Marion Du Fresne in 1772 and the crew of the *Boyd* in 1809, and the retaliations taken against nearby villages by the Europeans in each case, were perhaps the most notorious. The more extreme aggressions and retaliations declined as Europeans learned to respect Maori warrior capacities and numerical superiority, and the Maori to respect naval broadsides and landing parties. Both sides, moreover, increasingly appreciated the advantages of co-operation, and from the early 1800s chiefs sought to locate European whaling or timber cutting stations in their territory and give them protection. They established deserting seamen, escaped convicts, and missionaries in their villages as sources of trade, as armourers and ironworkers, as advisers in the cultivation of crops, as symbols of prestige and, in the 1830s, as teachers of reading and writing. As they acquired new skills the chiefs and their communities launched their own commercial enterprises. By the 1830s some South Island villages, for example, whose men had served aboard European whalers, acquired their own boats and began selling whales to European shore stations.

Concurrently, the Maori died in thousands, as a result of introduced diseases against which they had no immunity. The most careful study suggests that between 1769 and 1840 the Maori population fell from between 125,000 and 135,000 to between 80,000 and 90,000.[3] European observers who knew little or nothing of viruses and immunology, blamed the death toll on Maori eating, clothing and dwelling habits, sexual licence and warfare. Certainly warfare entered a new and bloody era. The acquisition of muskets emboldened the Ngapuhi chief Hongi Hika, of the Bay of Islands, to mount large raids against his traditional enemies far to the south. The intensified feuding which followed over much of the country, coupled with increasing disregard of the traditional controls of the *tapu* system (brought about by inter-action with Europeans),[4] seems to have burst the restraints and conventions of traditional warfare, or at least stretched them to the limits of annihilation, enslavement and cannibalism.

It was this situation that made the question of law a central one in New Zealand for the next half-century. The British authorities, while having no wish to assume further burdens of formal empire in the Pacific, felt increasingly obliged for humanitarian reasons to regulate contact between their nationals and the Maori people. And as a lucrative commerce grew, that too made its claims for protection. The experiments which followed provide an insight into the practicability of the final decision to found a Colony in New Zealand on the principles of English law.

British legislation of 1817 and 1823 nominally extended the authority of

the New South Wales courts to cover offences committed by British subjects
in New Zealand, but with little practical effect. Another device tried, at the
instance of Samuel Marsden, founder of the Church Missionary Society
mission in the Bay of Islands in 1814, was the appointment by the Governor
of New South Wales of one of the initial party, Thomas Kendall, as a Justice
of the Peace, accompanied by the designation of three Bay of Islands chiefs,
Hongi, Ruatara and Korokoro, as his assistants, to help prevent the landing
of alcoholic liquor and to apprehend unruly Europeans. The chiefs and their
kin took satisfaction in their recognition and the swords and letters of authority
accompanying the appointments. They may have used them, as did Moetara,
a Hokianga chief who later enjoyed similar recognition, to bolster the
demands on trading vessels they were already capable of making by virtue
of their physical command of strategic headlands and waterways.[5] Kendall
and his successor John Butler (another missionary, appointed JP in 1819)
were powerless and their magisterial exertions slight and ineffectual. However, Samuel Marsden did have Kendall take evidence against a European
who had assaulted a chief and his wife, and remand him for trial in Sydney.
The promise of punishment implied by these proceedings apparently satisfied
the Maori, who were threatening to take the man's life as *utu* for his offence.[6]

The missionaries had no success at all in mediating between feuding
Maori *hapu* before 1828. To that time they were little more than property
to powerful chiefs like Hongi Hika, obliged even to trade in muskets to secure
subsistence. After Hongi's death from battle wounds in 1828, and his dying
injunction not to plunder or sacrifice the missionaries (as was customarily
done with a dying chief's slaves) they gained a new independence and status.
Significantly it was soon after Hongi's death that their long-standing offers of
peacemaking were first accepted in the Bay of Islands feuds.[7] Thereafter, both
from their knowledge of the language and from the fact that they could
assume the traditional role of negotiators between parties with whom they
were connected but not completely identified, they were frequently called
upon both in disputes between Maori, and those involving Europeans. Henry
Williams, the energetic leader of the CMS party in New Zealand, used the
Maori term *whakawa* (to judge) to describe his function in the settlement of
minor property disputes;[8] the term *ture* (traditional maxims regulating social
conduct) was applied to the laws by which the missionaries sought to regulate
the behaviour of the converts they began to baptise from the late 1820s.

From his periodic visits to New Zealand, Marsden also reported that Bay
of Islands Maori admitted to him the difficulty of preventing disputes about
women and land from leading to violence and expressed considerable interest
in English modes of punishing crime or resolving disputes. Chiefs urged to
give up feuding frequently replied that they would gladly do so but that their
enemies retained arms and there was no law to appeal to or protect them.
Marsden tried to interest them in the idea of a centralised government but
they said that they could not envisage agreement on one man as king since

none would willingly subordinate himself to another.[9] Writing about 1820 Marsden also considered 'that the body of the chiefs would hesitate before they placed their country under the power and government of a foreign nation'. But he did note the concern of many chiefs as feuding intensified and the desire of the tribes without muskets for detachments of English soldiers or English warships to protect them from Hongi's forays. 'It is necessity, not choice,' Marsden added, 'that induces them to solicit this assistance, [but] perhaps this necessity may open the way and lay the foundation for the establishment of a regular government in time.'[10] In 1823 Commissioner J. T. Bigge of New South Wales, reporting on the New Zealand situation, suggested the appointment of more magistrates, with a military detachment and a warship stationed in New Zealand waters to protect trade and quell native warfare. He supported his suggestion by reference to the prompt settlement of disputes and general peace which had prevailed in the district where HMS *Dromedary,* with soldiers aboard, had gathered spars of *kauri* pine in 1820. Marsden in 1830 thought a warship would be useful. He also asserted that a detachment of troops 'would not be objected to or be at all disagreeable to the Natives', but doubted its worth because he feared the soldiers would be seduced from duty and allegiance by Maori women.[11]

There was a persistent tendency among missionaries and officials to confuse their Maori acquaintances' lively curiosity about British institutions and their occasional acceptance of British mediators, with willingness to submit to British direction or control. It was very largely a projection of the Europeans' own values and interests. Missionaries also knew that the recently converted people of Tahiti were framing laws and machinery of administration largely according to missionary direction. The extent to which the Tahitian leaders were manipulating the missionaries and Christianity to serve their own purposes was not then appreciated. After the beginning of 'conversion' and successful mediations in tribal war in 1828, missionaries in New Zealand began to hope they would soon be directors of a new Christian policy in the south Pacific, buttressed by protecting British arms. But many of the Maori chiefs who said they fought only because they had no law to appeal to were certainly speaking tongue-in-cheek and the requests for soldiers arose not so much from an affirmation of peace but from weak chiefs' need of protection and strong chiefs' desire to augment their fighting capacity or to guard their villages while they went on forays. Nor did naval power evoke the respectful co-operation that Marsden and Bigge expected. The *Dromedary's* officers had persuaded chiefs to punish thefts and recover stolen goods not by the threat of force but by the threat to weigh anchor and take their trade to a rival *hapu.*[12] The chiefs in fact extended proprietary rights over the Europeans and goods in their territory and harshly punished lesser kinsmen who infringed them. When two Sydney men established a ship-building yard at Te Horeke on Hokianga harbour 'all the chiefs in the neighbourhood took so great an interest in the work, that any annoyance offered to those employed would immediately be revenged as a personal affront'. Their desire to continue a fruitful trading relationship also led the chiefs, instead of taking instant and bloody retaliation upon Europeans who insulted or injured them, at times to be more tolerant, or to hand offenders over when officials intervened.[13]

But this was a matter of their choice and expediency, not of deference or submissiveness to superior British authority or force. Certainly Maori communities involved in the plunder of European ships did at times make restitution rather than risk bombardment or shore raiding parties, but where they felt substantial right to be on their side, a threat to invoke naval power was just as likely to provoke stiffened resistance. Fortunately, British authorities did not regularly use the naval broadside as an instrument of policy, as they did in the later period of 'commodore justice' in the central and western Pacific. The despatch of warships to New Zealand waters at irregular intervals in the 1830s was as much for the protection of Maori against atrocities by British subjects as for the protection of British commerce. However, in 1834 HMS *Alligator* sought to recover from a Taranaki *hapu* the wife and children of a wrecked British merchantman, held hostage for a delivery of arms. The officers, ignorant of Maori language and customs, failed to establish communication with the chiefs, who, the evidence suggests, were tractable. The settlement was destroyed and many Maori butchered by aggressive and ill-disciplined firing parties.[14] Both the New South Wales authorities and a committee of the House of Commons made the incident the subject of inquiry and it was not repeated.

Not surprisingly, however, the Maori regarded warships with increasing suspicion and reserve. In 1834 the Bay of Islands chief Pomare refused to come aboard HMS *Alligator* to discuss his seizure of a whaleboat in settlement of a debt, until the missionaries pointed out that their own families were hostages for his safety. When he did come aboard he 'stipulated for a complimentary salute similar to that with which he had greeted the British flag'.[15] Although his superiors credited Captain Hobson and HMS *Rattlesnake* with ending the feud in the Bay of Islands in 1837, the chiefs had in fact declined to come aboard the ship for peace talks (except one who said he would do so on payment of a blanket), the feud ending rather through the intervention of the Hokianga chiefs.[16] Like the merchantmen, naval captains generally had to rely on missionary assistance if they wished to take up a contentious issue with the chiefs. Thus when HMS *Pelorus* investigated the plunder of a ship that had gone ashore in the Thames area she spent a week there without meeting any Maori. When appealed to by the commander, the local missionary secured a meeting of the chiefs with the ship's officers, and a promise of restitution.[17]

Debate about the receptivity of Maori society to European ideas, artifacts and institutions is closely related to the question of whether Maori society became disrupted by early contact, or whether borrowings from the West were incorporated into a substantially intact traditional framework. Certainly scholars have been right to reject both the old Eurocentric view that displacement of Maori culture by 'superior' European culture was automatic and inevitable, and the more extreme assertions of functional anthropologists to the effect that change in one area of the traditional culture produced changes in the remainder until traditional society in some way 'collapsed'. It can easily be demonstrated that the Maori adopted artifacts and institutions from the Europeans very selectively and largely within a traditional value scale. Muskets, for example, were acquired both to assist traditional warfare and as symbols of traditional prestige-seeking.

Yet it would be wrong to push the traditionalist view too far. Firstly, there were forces at work which were largely beyond the control of the Maori people. The inroads of epidemic disease have been mentioned; the obverse of that coin was the rapid increase of Europeans in centres like the Bay of Islands. The decline of their people, while the Europeans apparently burgeoned, did not by any means destroy Maori social structures, but it could not help but create deep anxiety. The increased scale of warfare added to that. Economic influences were also at work. Polynesian considerations of power and status at first underlay the prompt adoption of European power and status symbols such as salutes of gunfire, flags, uniforms or pocket watches with heavy chains. And once a chief acquired a weatherboard house, a whaleboat or a trading schooner, other chiefs were impelled to prove their *mana* by acquiring them also. But this sort of selectivity tended to broaden fairly quickly into a powerful appetite for (dependence on is scarcely too strong a term) a variety of imported goods, from guns and gunpowder to clothing and foodstuffs. An inland chief, for example, envying the Cook Strait Maori after the foundation of settlement there in 1840, said 'they do not live on potatoes . . . they have meat, flour, tea, sugar, tobacco, knives and everything they want'.[18] European explorers often commented disappointedly that the proud, independent, hard-bargaining chiefs of the 1820s and 1830s had by the 1840s begun to beg or cadge tobacco or food from them and to squander the resources of their community to acquire European goods. Desire to tap the material wealth of the Europeans in fact tended to erode traditional priorities in the first decades of contact, or at least alter the balance between them. An inconvenient *tapu* that hindered a fruitful trading relationship would, for instance, be set aside, and the engagement of Maori communities in profitable commercial enterprises blunted their readiness to heed a call to assist kinsmen in feuding.

The growth of individual entrepreneurship through wage or contract labour in the whaling or timber industries also affected traditional social relations. Timber cutting and squaring on European shore stations replaced the collecting of whole spars, gathered under the chiefs' direction. Many whaling captains gladly replaced deserting seamen with Maori hands who were considered very reliable. Several became pilots or harpooners; by 1840 a Maori crew rowed the Sydney harbour-master's boat; and it was reported that a 'Mr Bailey', a Maori,

was chief officer of a Sydney whaler and would have been given a command
had he not been a 'foreigner'.[19] Men who made good this way did not usually
wish to break ties with their kin in New Zealand but rather, in order to
cement them, brought presents for their relatives and chiefs when they
returned. But they were no longer bound by the horizons of the village, or its
constraints. This too meant a disturbance (though by no means a total disruption) of the traditional order, and it created new stresses and anxieties.

A second major point which this book is intended to advance, is that once
they had experience of the wider world, the intellectual curiosity, boldness
and willingness to innovate of many Maori was such that they did not want to
cling to an unmodified traditionalism. Perhaps this is only another way of
saying that the traditional Maori social structure and value system were open
and adaptive, not rigid or inflexible; and certainly the rivalry to demonstrate
mana itself stimulated adventurousness and hence change. In any case the
implications for Maori social institutions were very far reaching. The men
who crowded the European ships and engaged in disputations with officers or
missionaries were eager, curious and intellectually adroit. The Maori response
to the West is not to be compared with the rigidity of nineteenth century
China, but with the adaptability of nineteenth century Japan; the younger
Maori chiefs in particular played a role, on a much more localised stage, not
dissimilar to that of the younger, lower-ranking Japanese *samurai* who made
the Meiji Restoration and carried through the modernisation of the 1870s.

The attitudes of the Bay of Islands Maori, as shipping increased in the
1820s, suggest that they were not entirely at ease any more about some aspects
of the traditional culture. Cannibalism, for instance, was at first flaunted
before the eyes of visiting seamen and critical missionaries, but by 1827 the
visiting painter, Augustus Earle, records that some Bay of Islands people
showed a sense of shame about it.[20] It began to be conducted secretively and
then to be abandoned altogether. This tendency preceded widespread adherence to Christianity. It was not that the Maori felt cannibalism to be essentially
wrong; in fact, when pressed they would defend it as perfectly in accord with
Maori custom. They relinquished it partly in order not to deter Europeans
whose trade they desired but also because they were coming to regard it as
primitive, backward and demeaning—something increasingly associated with
'the days of our ignorance', not the actions of men of a new and wider world.

This was even more true for many of the chiefs—and they should probably
be numbered in hundreds—who, from about 1790 onwards, travelled abroad
from various parts of the New Zealand coast as passengers or crew on European ships. They saw not the isolated and often puny representatives of
Europe who came to New Zealand shores but the seaports and capitals of
Australia, England, France and the United States. Similarly the coming of
Europeans to New Zealand in greater strength and numbers inspired increasing respect, as well as anxiety.

This interpretation rests on the view that, following contact with the

Europeans, Maori evaluated their condition and their social institutions, not only on the local scale but in comparison with European culture. This certainly did not mean that they generally regarded everything traditional as inferior to everything European—though they sometimes said things to that effect. Much they saw in European society was downright repugnant. But they were impressed by its wealth, its variety and richness, its apparent orderliness and, above all, by its power. Some became fatalistic about the matter, saying that in time the Europeans would dominate New Zealand; this despondency increased and probably contributed to the increased land-selling of the late 1830s. But most, like the Japanese *samurai*, sought quickly to identify and utilise those European institutions which would give them similar advantages, both for their own sake and to enable Maori society to withstand the potential threat of European power itself. They were of course, still concerned about rank and *mana* and the well-being of their kin, but well-being and *mana* began to be conceived in terms of new material goods, new pleasures and recreations, new ways of doing things, new needs and new threats, and out of all this, as in Japan, a culture—or, more correctly, a variety of sub-cultures—combining elements of the traditional and the European began quickly to emerge.

This development is discernible throughout Polynesia. It is clearly exemplified by men such as George Tupou, the first king of Tonga, who, particularly after a visit to Sydney, selected with the aid of European advisers those institutional changes best calculated not only to enhance his own authority but to enjoy a new richness of wealth and experience, and to create a stable polity which could survive the demands of settlers, backed by their metropolitan governments. In the absence of a single dominant lineage in New Zealand a diversity of experiment followed as a variety of European institutions caught the attention of independent Maori leaders. Hence the invitation by the Bay of Islands chief Ruatara to the missionaries he met in Sydney to bring their agricultural techniques (rather than their religion) to his territory; hence also Hongi's placing of his son in Samuel Marsden's school at Parramatta, and the attempt of Te Waru, of the Waipa district, to inaugurate a new judicial system based on what he saw in Van Diemen's Land. Much depended on the personalities of local chiefs, on their situations and on the nature of their contacts with Europeans. There was, however, an increasing tendency for younger men, particularly chiefs, to engage further with European institutions and values than older chiefs who had a deeper commitment to the old values that sanctioned their power and status. Furthermore, while it is incorrect to suggest two distinct periods of Maori response—a period of borrowing for traditional goals giving way to a period of acceptance of European values—it is probably true that an initial tendency to favour those European institutions or artifacts, such as the musket, which promoted power, was increasingly matched (though by no means supplanted) by an increasing interest in values and institutions favouring peace and stability.

This was a consequence of what the musket itself produced—the intensified feuding of the 1820s and 1830s and of the devastating progress of epidemic disease.

All of this complexity is apparent in the way the Maori people regarded Christianity. The basic reason for their 'conversion' was that the various stresses affecting the Maori people had produced anxiety and wondering about the effectiveness of the old gods and rituals. Sociologists stress man's heavy dependence on his symbolic systems: 'his sensitivity to even the remotest indication that they may prove unable to cope with one or another aspect of experience raises within him the gravest sort of anxiety'.[21] In general, Pacific peoples viewed Christianity as the system of deities, rituals and symbols associated with the wealth and strength of European culture. The relative immunity of the Europeans from epidemic disease, their burgeoning numbers (as well as those of their part-Maori offspring), their material wealth, their imperviousness to any ill consequences for breach of *tapu,* and the inability of the *tohunga* (religious experts) to work sorcery against them, all suggested to people disturbed about their declining numbers incapacity in the traditional deities and strength in the Christian god.

Traditionally Pacific islanders appraised their deities pragmatically, according to their strength and efficacy in the human order. In the 1830s Maori chiefs, like the Hawaiians, Tahitians and Tongans before them, began to test the strength of the rival deities by deliberately carrying food on their backs, or otherwise breaking *tapu*. If unharmed they were prone, not entirely to discard the old gods, but at least to give the Christian god the foremost place among those they recognised. The production of the New Testament by missionary printing presses in the 1830s led to an enthusiasm for literacy and the quotation of scripture, which was seen as a key to the manipulation of Christian deities and the unlocking of the material advantages of European culture. Ex-pupils of the mission schools carried their knowledge to their kin in remote parts of New Zealand, and what they carried was not so much the gospel, as the missionaries hoped and believed, but 'the A and the Z'.[22]

But there were further complexities. As has been noted, missionary mediation in feuding had first been accepted in 1828. This event gave new status to the missionaries and their god, long proclaimed to be a god of peace. Thereafter some Maori quite explicitly began to affirm Christianity in order to escape the obligation to join kinsmen in the destructive cycle of feuding.[23] A rather distorted view of the atonement assisted the process; one prospective convert, for instance, first inquiring whether the Christian god really would exact *utu* for the killing of his brother.[24] A recent historian analysing the rapid progress of 'conversion' in the Wanganui district in the 1840s has observed that 'it is remarkable how often the Maoris, quite simply and directly, contrasted the uncertainties of their former life with the new order they associated with the missionary'.[25]

Once the missionaries' god had been deemed to be strong, however,

Christianity also became involved in traditional Polynesian power-seeking, in which lineages sought to advance their position under the auspices of various gods. Many *hapu* solicited the strength of Jehovah to their cause as their pagan counterparts solicited the aid of Tu or Whiro, and were never more diligent in worship than on the eve of battle. Traditional rivalries and new factionalisms contributed to the otherwise inexplicable divisions within *hapu* and *whanau,* in allegiance to Christian or pagan gods, and Anglican or Wesleyan church membership. When the Catholic mission was founded in 1838 many Maoris experimented with it because it was vogueish. 'We like to try what is new,' a chief told a disgruntled Anglican missionary.[26]

Given the variety of motivations towards Christianity, wide variation in the observance of missionary precepts is not surprising. The most far-reaching 'conversions' were probably in the young chiefs, like Tamihana Te Waharoa[27] and Tamihana Te Rauparaha, who, although heirs of the greatest warriors of the day, saw more advantages for themselves and their people in the principles and techniques of social organisation and production available through the missions than in the ways of their fathers. But generally missionary satisfaction at swelling congregations was modified by an awareness of lack of true 'change of heart', of 'coldness' and 'deadness' in their converts. Of the traditional customs offensive to missionaries the more public ones, such as cannibalism, virtually ceased, but those which could be practised more surreptitiously, such as infanticide or killing of old people suspected of sorcery, continued. Nor did Christian *hapu* entirely foreswear feuding. Chiefs were often obliged to liberate their captives before being admitted to full church membership, but most nominal Christians retained their captives although these now enjoyed rather more lenient treatment and were no longer likely to be sacrificed to pagan gods on the death of a chief. 'Converted' chiefs also found it difficult to observe the missionary demand for monogamy, and despite a battery of regulations and penalties to control sexual behaviour, missionary literature records an endless succession of fallen native teachers and church members debarred from communion for licentious conduct. Relapse into paganism or into a sort of agnosticism was common. And missionaries in every district reported a variety of cult movements, often syncretising Christian and traditional elements, arising simultaneously with the emergence of missionary congregations proper. Of the numberless Maori priests and prophets who led these movements Papahurihia of the Bay of Islands, among the early ones, was only the most notable.[28]

Meanwhile, what was the situation of the Europeans settling in New Zealand? Despite their engagement with them, the Maori's underlying suspicion that the white men, the Pakeha, might reduce them to slavery and take their land and women, remained strong. What they learned about the fortunes of the Australian Aborigines reinforced it. Although missionary assertions that whalers and traders in the Pacific were a particularly villainous lot were biased and extreme, it remains true that from greed or spite, drunkenness or desire to assert their superiority over the coloured and the 'savage', they frequently bullied, insulted and cheated Maori, particularly those travelling on European ships. The early collisions between whalers and Maori and the more spectacular atrocities, such as the assistance lent by the brig *Elizabeth* in 1831 to one of Te Rauparaha's bloody massacres of his tribal enemies, gained the merchantmen in New Zealand waters an evil reputation in humanitarian circles.

Within New Zealand, however, the Maori generally retained physical superiority and remained the dominant party. In the 1830s crews of some vessels wrecked on the New Zealand coast were still killed or enslaved and their ships plundered. The early traders, shore whalers and missionaries who settled in New Zealand experienced varying fortunes. Many, through the trade and employment they offered, and their associations with prominent Maori women, achieved a harmonious symbiotic relationship with a local community and in some cases became virtually absorbed into Maori society. Others were established as the *mokai* (pets) of particular chiefs, who regarded each settler as 'his Pakeha' and jealously, even forcibly, discouraged him from moving to the territory of another chief. Pakeha had to be extremely circumspect in their dealings with their hosts and satisfy their requests for presents of trade goods if they hoped to secure food supplies and protection. Although pilfering of their property declined when a settler was accorded the protection of a chief, Pakeha were still irked by the institution of *muru*. Since Maori tended to see all Pakeha as one kind, innocent settlers were regularly subject to *muru* for offences, or alleged offences, of their neighbours. Shore whaling stations were still being attacked in the 1830s, often because of quarrels about women or because a drunken whaler insulted a chief.

The Maori tended to apply their notions of rank and station to the Pakeha. The naturalist Ernest Dieffenbach in 1839 overheard some Maori categorising them as *mihanere* (missionaries), *hohio* (soldiers), *rewera* (devils—that is, non-missionaries of rank such as ships officers, merchants and 'gentlemen') and 'cookees' (common sailors and labourers).[29] Members of these classes were likely to receive appropriate treatment—*rewera,* for example, to be treated by chiefs as social equals, and 'cookees' as little better than their slaves. Yet a characteristically Polynesian sensitivity in personal relations also affected the issue. A Pakeha who showed hostility or condescension could be made very miserable indeed: but one who showed friendliness, respect and fair dealing could find himself the recipient of a memorable courtesy and hospitality. Once accepted by a community he had some defence against theft and undeserved *muru,* a mere public accusation normally enabling him to shame the offender and secure restitution. Even so a Pakeha's position was often precarious in that some chiefs were moody and hard to satisfy, or were not sufficiently influential to prevent molestation by others in the *hapu*.

It is clear then that the Maori people received Europeans in New Zealand very much on their own rather uncertain terms, including their notions of dispute settlement. Those settlers who could not accept that this should be so were frustrated, humiliated and at times fearful at their dependence upon people whom they considered savages. In his published autobiography Frederic Maning of Hokianga, perhaps New Zealand's most famous early settler, draws a whimsical view of his relationship with the local Maori; but the book also hints at—and Maning's private correspondence makes abundantly clear—the bitter, smouldering resentment he developed towards the Maori during the period of their dominance.[30]

It was out of this situation that Sydney merchants and owners of whaling fleets, such as the Enderby brothers, began to petition for the location of a military force in New Zealand to protect their enterprise; rumours of French interest in the area periodically intensified their concern. But it was, as before, the representations of missionaries and humanitarians that finally moved the British government to increasing official intervention.[31]

III

British Annexation

In 1831, in the midst of alarm about the intentions of the French survey ship *La Favorite* then in New Zealand waters, a number of chiefs, stimulated by the missionary William Yate, petitioned King William IV for protection against foreign invasion and against the improper conduct of British subjects in New Zealand. The petition again spurred official optimism about Maori willingness to accept direction from European administrators and, together with the publicity of the *Elizabeth* affair, led to the appointment of James Busby (a former New South Wales minor official who happened to secure timely patronage in London) as British Resident in the Bay of Islands. Busby was apparently expected to achieve a sort of recognition analogous to that of British Residents in Indian principalities. On the somewhat contradictory assumptions that because the Maori were 'semi-civilised' and well on the way to achieving an ordered polity, and because they were savages they would certainly defer to the direction of 'educated men', it was hoped that Busby would not only be able to check both Maori-Pakeha disputes and Maori tribal feuding, but also to organise some form of settled legislature and executive and system of jurisprudence.[1] Both the segmented and kinship-oriented nature of Maori society and Busby's own officious paternalism operated against any such result.

Moreover, too much had been read into the original petition. Periodic requests for protection against a foreign threat were fired off to various European Heads of State by groups of chiefs in almost every Polynesian group at one time or another during the nineteenth century. Owing to the prior influence of English missionaries the English monarch was the recipient of a good many of these. A further petition for protection was attached to the Declaration of Independence which Busby solicited from a group of northern chiefs in 1835 to counter the claims of the French adventurer, Charles De Thierry, to sovereignty in New Zealand. Others followed in January 1836 and May 1837. These petitions were impulsive attempts to invoke an ally who was understood to be both powerful and disposed to be friendly, and were intended essentially to preserve, not surrender, independence. Furthermore, they were the passing work of a few chiefs in particular localities. In 1831 Yate had stimulated his petition from Hokianga chiefs. Consequently

24

when Busby landed at the Bay of Islands in May 1833, to the accompaniment of a seven gun salute, the local chiefs were confused and disturbed, not knowing what he was there for.[2]

Busby's own attitude, offensive to the Maori, may have stemmed from the intention, which he later claimed, to 'open the way for acquisition and settlement'.[3] He early destroyed his credibility in attempting to impose his decision in a dispute between a Maori and a settler, by a vain bluster about being supported by the guns of a warship. In April 1834 a Maori named Rete and others robbed his house and fired at Busby. The local chiefs were indignant and solicitous about the affront to him—since he was, after all, not just a 'cookee' and they had given him occupancy—and agreed to banish Rete. The banishment was never carried out. Busby had been given no military or naval support and subsequently had to endure the spectacle of feuding Maori actually fighting in the grounds of his Residency and rowing about the harbour in his boat.

On the political side Busby was initially encouraged by the chiefs' readiness to assemble when invited and believed that they could be marshalled into a rudimentary government. Although there was certainly some genuine interest in European forms of organisation the chiefs assembled more from a characteristic Polynesian enjoyment of political discussions and because they regarded an invitation as a mark of recognition of their status. In fact if they were not invited they were likely to arrive, armed and truculent, to make it plain that they should have been. Busby thus had little difficulty in assembling a gathering in March 1834 to select a national flag for the independent New Zealand confederacy he was supposed to be forming. But he failed to notice the acrimony among the chiefs as to who should have been invited first, fed their jealousy by a somewhat cursory selection of thirty out of the assembled multitude to vote on the choice of flag, and finally slighted them all by inviting only the officers of HMS *Alligator* (which had brought the colours) to dinner in the Residency, leaving the chiefs to divide a meagre meal outside.[4]

Following his counterblast to De Thierry in 1835 (the Declaration of Independence by thirty-five chiefs under the designation of 'The United Tribes of New Zealand') Busby proposed an annual legislative congress. A few chiefs showed transient interest. A more concrete result was promised from the Hokianga harbour where the trader, Thomas McDonnell, who briefly held an unpaid appointment as Additional British Resident, secured the assent of the chiefs to a regulation, duly published in the New South Wales government *Gazette,* prohibiting the landing of spirits. But McDonnell's motive was self-promotion rather than genuine concern, and since the chiefs' objections to the demoralising influence of liquor competed with the growing enjoyment of drinking it and the profit of trading it, policing of the regulation soon ceased. In any case the wide dispersal of authority among chiefs and elders worked against enforcement of law, even in a small locality.

Maori interest in the judicial interventions of the British officials was little more promising. McDonnell persuaded a Hokianga *hapu* to be satisfied with the flogging and transportation of a European who had sexual relations with a chief's wife (being 'fairly seduced to the commission of the crime'), a success similar to that of Marsden in 1814.[5] So long as Pakeha methods satisfied their notions of essential justice the Maori were obviously willing to accept them for the sake of continued good relations. Similarly when a Pakeha named Biddle was killed by Kite, the slave of a Bay of Islands chief, Busby persuaded the *hapu* to surrender Kite for trial by a settler 'court', after which he was executed by one of the chiefs. Busby was clear, however, that had the offender been a chief he would not have been surrendered.[6]

In view of his very mixed fortunes Busby concluded that, basically because of their kinship loyalties, the Maori people could not be brought under ordered civil and judicial administration except through the intervention of some outside agency with coercive authority. In 1835 he was relatively cautious; while soliciting British protection for the United Tribes following the De Thierry affair he was also clear that 'any effort to rule the people by the exercise of a power distinct from that which might be exercised through their natural leaders, would make it necessary to overawe them by an Army capable of crushing all resistance that the whole country might be able to offer'. Hence the military establishment that he envisaged should be just sufficient to enforce the law against individuals.[7] By 1837, he was advancing full-blown schemes in which a Maori legislative congress would be subject to the direction of a British officer (he had himself in mind) and its laws enforced by a British military establishment. He still believed a small force would be sufficient because he now considered that not even two tribes could unite in opposing them. 'In theory and ostensibly, the Government would be that of the Confederated Chiefs, but in reality it must be that of the Representative of the protecting power.'[8]

These suggestions were perilous indeed in their smug optimism that the chiefs could be gulled into meek compliance with British direction. However, within twelve months the missionaries in New Zealand had come to similar conclusions. They too were convinced that the Maori would be willing to submit to centralised law and government. After two decades of intensified feuding the northern Maori seemed increasingly to dread both the forays of their enemies and the summonses by their own kinsmen to join them in search of *utu* for insult or injury. By the 1830s some were reiterating the view long put to them by missionaries, that unless inter-tribal fighting ceased, the race would destroy itself.[9] Such a view attributed to warfare a great proportion of the blame for depopulation that rightly attached to disease. Nevertheless it amounted to more than an ingratiating agreement with missionary opinion and led to European settlements being sought by Maori communities for the protection they could afford, as well as a source of strength and trade. 'Do not go to war', a chief is reported to have advised his community which was threatened with involvement in a feud, 'the English do not go to war, and these men [the rival *hapu*] dare not come down, for the English will protect us.'[10] Recently, moreover, Maori Christian communities had begun to pester for codes of law. Certain responses had been considered necessary to placate the traditional gods and now the converts were anxious to know the actions necessary to avoid offending the new god. In particular they wanted to know how to act in a dispute. In 1837 a Bay of Islands Christian documented his needs in a letter to Marsden:

Sir,—Will you give us a Law? 1st, If we say let the Cultivations be fenced, and a Man through Laziness does not fence, should Pigs get into his Plantation, is it right for him to kill them? . . . 2d, Again—should Pigs get into fenced Land, is it right to kill or rather to tie them till the Damage they have done is paid for? . . . 3d, Again—should the Husband of a Woman die, and she afterwards wishes to be married to another, should the Natives of unchanged Heart bring a Fight [*muru* party] against us, would it be right for us to stand up to resist them on account of their wrongful Interference? . . . 4th, Again,—in our Wickedness, One Man has Two Wives, but after he has listened to Christ he puts away one of them, and gives her to another Man to Wife. Now should a Fight be brought against us, and are we, in this Case, to stand up to fight? . . . 5th, Again,—should Two Men strive one with the other. . . . My (Ritenga) Law is, to collect all the People together, and judge them for their unlawful fighting, and also for wrongfully killing Pigs. Therefore I say, that the Man who kills Pigs for trespassing on his Plantation, having neglected to fence, had rather pay for the Pigs so killed . . . Fenced Cultivations, when trespassed on, should be paid for. These only are the Things which cause us to err; Women, Pigs, and fighting one with another. 6th, But here is another,—should a Man who is in the Church come in a Fight against us? . . . Another Thing which we are afraid of, and which also degrades us, is this, Slaves exalting themselves above their Masters. Will you give us a Law in this also?[11]

From such confusion of traditional and new values and apparent strong desire for guidance, the missionaries boldly claimed that 'the natives are not only willing to submit to British laws, but *wish* for them to be enacted'.[12] George Clarke and the Rev. Henry Williams further asserted that the chiefs had made repeated applications for a parliament and that it was only 'for want of power to enforce the laws they might enact' that nothing had been accomplished.[13]

The reference to the lack of power of enforcement reflected the missionaries' despondency about unsteadfastness among Christian Maoris, the heavy tribal fighting of 1836 which led to the temporary abandonment of mission stations at Rotorua and Matamata, the revival of feuding in the Bay of Islands in 1837 in which mission favourites like the young Hone Heke joined, and the failure of Busby's schemes for a confederation. These developments dampened hopes which had welled up during the spread of conversion after 1828, of establishing an ordered administration through the Christian chiefs. In early 1837 therefore, the missionaries joined with settlers in asserting 'that considerable Time must elapse before the Chiefs of this Land can be capable of exercising the Duties of an independent Government'.[14] And in January 1838, in consequence of Maori turbulence as much as in consequence of increasing pressure of settlement, the CMS committee in the Bay of Islands, headed by Henry Williams and George Clarke, recommended as a panacea

> That the whole country be secured under the protection and guardian care of the British Government, for a number of years, with a Resident Governor and other Officers; with a military force, to support their authority and insure obedience to all laws which may be enacted.[15]

As in Busby's scheme the laws were to be enacted by a congress or General Assembly of Chiefs under the 'fostering power' of the governor.

These suggestions, essentially elaborations of the principles urged by Marsden and Bigge in the 1820s, indicate the commitment of missionaries and officials to the use of coercive power in the pursuit of their 'civilising mission' in New Zealand. Although they plainly envisaged that the exercise of coercive power should be in the name of a Maori legislature, and though they initially hoped that British authority might eventually be withdrawn, it is clear that the military garrison was intended to be used to police recalcitrant Maori as well as wayward settlers. A show of strength was considered essential to secure submission to the rule of law. Here lies the fundamental refutation of the myth, still bedevilling interpretations of early British policy in New Zealand, that missionaries and officials were prepared to use only 'moral suasion' in attempting to regulate Maori society.

However, it is true that Dandeson Coates, Lay Secretary of the CMS in London, still held to the view that coercive authority should not be used and quoted the Christian chief's appeal to Marsden for a code of law as evidence not that the Maori needed policing by the British but that they could be led to provide for the internal needs of their society without a British assumption of sovereignty. What they needed, he argued, was the assistance of a stronger figure than Busby, namely a consul supported by a ship of war and with power to conduct assizes on the spot over wayward British subjects. The consul and the missionaries, working through the Christian chiefs, should extend law codes and institutions of government, based on a careful study of 'whatever there may be of Law or Practice' in the several tribes, aiming eventually at a uniform national government.[16] Until such steps were tried, he argued, it could not be said that it was necessary that Britain should assume sovereignty over New Zealand, thereby claiming a coercive power over the Maori as well as British settlers.

Coates has frequently been regarded as a narrow missionary zealot, anxious to preserve the Pacific for missionary theocracies. In fact his concern stemmed basically from his acute awareness of the fundamental dilemma of imperialism. However benevolent and disinterested the intentions of governments or chartered companies towards native peoples, he wrote, 'there is an incompatability between objects so prosecuted, and the exercise of coercive authority in the prosecution of them, which cannot be overcome'.[17] While there was no established coercive power which could be brought to bear against Maori, the settlers and missionaries would continue to bear depredations and alarms, as they had done hitherto, with patience and forbearance. But once a government with coercive power were established, it would inevitably be appealed to by Pakeha injured or threatened by Maori, resisted by Maori jealous of their liberties, and embroiled in a struggle to subjugate the Maori people to its will.

Coates's views, which were shared by the Secretary of the Wesleyan Missionary Society, the Reverend John Beecham, were strikingly prophetic and deserve more consideration from scholars than they have received. In New Zealand, however, the missionaries, in the midst of a turbulent local people, were less willing to be patient and forbearing than Coates and Beecham fondly hoped. Moreover, while their own discomfort and their belief in their civilising mission were in themselves major motives for their paternalistic decision to invoke the aid of the secular arm in bringing the Maori under a European-style rule of law, that decision was considerably vindicated (and Coates's and Beecham's position weakened) by the much greater pressures of settlement after 1837.

The intentions of chiefs who cheerfully signed deeds of sale for large tracts of territory aboard the land-buying ships appearing off their coasts have not yet been fully explained. In some cases it is apparent that, in their eagerness to acquire guns, goods and money offered for land, or to settle small communities of Pakeha beside them as sources of trade or support against tribal enemies, they were careless of the details of transactions. Often they appear to have believed they were granting rights of occupancy as they had granted them traditionally to allies or kinsmen made destitute in war, or, more recently, to isolated settlers. Offers of land made ashore, under the scrutiny of the assembled *hapu*, were likely to be much more exact and deliberate than those made aboard ship, and to include land disputed with neighbouring *hapu* or land recently conquered and tenuously held, rather than choicer land about the principal settlement.

However, younger men in particular, finding that land had a commercial value, also knowingly sold areas of the *hapu's* principal land which they considered surplus to their requirements, often disregarding the rights of kin. This they did, they said, in order to become 'gentlemen'.[18] Kin were not entirely without remedies. Chiefs who signed sweeping deeds of sale were frequently obliged to modify them (thus giving the impression of repudiation which so infuriated early settlers) or else the purchasers were subject to additional claims by right-holders who had not shared the original payment. Yet nothing (save disease) was so difficult to control and so disruptive of Maori society as direct purchase of land, by a plurality of speculators and settlers from individual Maori, in a situation where rights to a particular territory were widely dispersed. A sale by one right-holder resulted in other men, also holders of traditional rights in the land but unable to deny the first seller's right and unable to prevent him selling, hastening to offer land also, for fear it would pass anyway and they would have no share in the return. The prevalence of death and disease probably deepened a growing spirit of living for the day. 'We may perhaps die tomorrow', some were reported as saying, 'and we shall get no payment for it; so, as long as we live, we will sell our land, and derive the benefit of the payment'.[19] In 1839 missionaries in the Bay of Islands attempted to organise widely signed compacts against selling—an early 'land league'—or to have land transferred in trust to the missions, but they felt little hope of either device being effective.[20] Many communities about the Bay of Islands and Hokianga were, at least according to the deeds they signed, becoming landless, while during 1839-40 New South Wales speculators and the agents of Edward Gibbon Wakefield's New Zealand Company secured deeds purporting to give them ownership of the South Island and huge areas of the North Island, measured in terms of latitude and longitude. Offers to purchase land were enormously potent in intensifying traditional rivalries and actual collision. In addition the land buyers such as the New Zealand Company were making plain their wish to enforce their shabby purchase deeds to the letter. A strong centralised native authority, faced with comparatively limited pressure, had some chance of regulating land alienation as did the Tongan king, but in New Zealand the pressure was becoming very strong and Maori society was too segmented to control it even with the help of a British consul and gunboats. There was a very real likelihood that New Zealand, like Australia, the United States or southern Africa, would be the scene of bloody moving frontiers.

For these reasons the benefits for the Maori of a British sovereignty which could permit the scrutiny and disallowance of land claims increasingly appeared to be out-weighing the dangers which, as Coates predicted, would arise from the imperial relationship. The British authorities moved reluctantly to this conclusion. Governor Bourke of New South Wales had objected to Busby's suggestion of a military garrison to police the situation on the very justifiable suspicion that it 'would be open to misinterpretation' by the Maori and 'might eventually be perverted by British subjects to selfish purposes'.[21] James Stephen, Permanent Under-Secretary at the Colonial Office certainly shared this view. But by December 1837 it was accepted in London that, with settlement 'to no small extent' already effected in New Zealand, the only question was 'between a Colonization, desultory, without Law, and fatal to the Natives, and a Colonization organized and salutary'.[22] It was concluded that a consul would have insufficient authority to meet the case and the suggestion of Captain William Hobson, RN, was favoured, whereby there should be annexed to New South Wales those portions of New Zealand where settlers were accumulating in sufficient strength to eschew co-operation with the Maori and assume an independent and aggressive stance.

Hobson, however, had made it plain that his real preference was for assumption of sovereignty over the whole group. Partial annexation would leave the rest of the group open to the encroachment of other powers and leave even the British settlers outside the ceded districts under little control.[23] Stephen too believed that 'British influence or authority' in New Zealand should become 'co-extensive with the limits of the Islands'; but he had no better

success than previous officials in solving the problem of establishing legal
authority in territory not formally under British sovereignty. He did not consider a formal protectorate practicable because the Maori chiefs had little or
no formal authority to vest in the protecting power and could, without any
accountability, withhold support if the British undertook a policy they did
not approve of. Paradoxically, since it also implied the existence of governmental authorities which could be called to account, he contemplated a treaty
relationship with the chiefs outside the ceded districts which would recognise
their sovereign rights and flag (that is the flag which Busby's so-called Con-
federate Tribes of New Zealand chose in 1834) in return for an undertaking
to end war and human sacrifice, and to submit all land sales to the veto of
the governor of the ceded territory.[24] In the event this awkward suggestion
was submerged by concern at the mounting interest in New Zealand by
colonisation companies and speculators, most notably dramatised by the
despatch of the New Zealand Company's first ship in May 1839, to purchase
land in the hitherto sparsely settled Cook Strait area. By July 1839 it was
decided that Hobson, who was to be commissioned both as Consul and
Lieutenant-Governor, would be authorised to treat for the full exercise of
sovereignty over 'the whole or any part' of New Zealand and, in view of the
sparse Maori population there, to declare sovereignty over the South Island
by right of discovery rather than by cession.

To the end James Stephen believed the British Government to be 'embark-
ing on a measure essentially unjust, and but too certainly fraught with
calamity' for the Maori people.[25] Indeed, had he been more clear about the
situation in New Zealand, Stephen would certainly have been even more
reluctant to recommend the establishment of Imperial rule there. The British
authorities' decision was affected by serious misperceptions. Firstly, there was
the long-standing tendency to over-estimate Maori willingness to submit to
government and law directed by benevolent officials and missionaries. Busby's
naive and irresponsible reporting, born of his ambition to secure greater
British involvement and greater prominence for himself, may have contributed
to this. Busby realised that 'It is scarcely to be expected that the chief of a
tribe would be the instrument of apprehending a criminal connected with
himself; but on the other hand,' he added blandly, on no evidence at all, 'he
would never think of affording him protection against a native police which
could fall back on the British troops for support'. And while he was correct in
forecasting that chiefs would welcome the opportunity to enhance their somewhat limited authority by participation in a legislative congress, the Maori
had given him no grounds for saying that they would value membership of
it so highly that suspension from it would soon make a wayward chief submissive.[26] And if Busby's tendentious arguments were discounted in London,
missionary views were certainly influential. The CMS clergy continued to
assert their conviction that the Maori would welcome a British-type rule of
law. Presenting evidence to a Select Committee of the House of Lords which

investigated the New Zealand question in 1838 the Rev. John Flatt of the CMS considered that while some of the elder chiefs might object to laws coercing them 'the young men, I am confident, are anxious for it; they see the Propriety of it; they say there would be no fear of a Party coming and falling upon them, and that unless something was done they would all be dead'. The Rev. F. Wilkinson, Marsden's chaplain in New South Wales, thought the chiefs would be 'very glad' to give up all their territorial and sovereign rights, not to all foreign governments certainly, but to the British government. 'I think they would be very happy to give up what little authority they possess, for they possess very little. . . . They would not know what they were doing but they would take it for granted that they were trusting to an honourable people.'[27] The missionaries had little appreciation of the reluctance the chiefs might have to surrendering the independence they had in a system in which social conflict was adjusted by discussion, bargain and adjustment between the protagonists according to a set of customary norms, to a very different system in which it was adjusted by subservience to an external authority administering a code of laws based largely on another set of norms. They assumed, of course, that through 'conversion' the Maori has adopted another set of norms and that the requests of the Christian Maori for codes of law was evidence of this. In fact the attitude to law was likely to vary with the original motive for conversion. Some Maori Christians were certainly concerned with the ethical principles of their new faith and the laws which embodied them, and had absorbed something of their basic spirit, but those who had given allegiance to the Christian god because he appeared stronger than the old gods or from curious experimenting, were more concerned to know what had to be done to propitiate and manipulate their new deity. This was likely to lead to the observance of the letter, rather than the spirit of law —to the slavishly literal and puritanical sabbatarianism of Christian villages, where travellers found the sullenness at requests to supply food on a Sunday a sad contrast to the Polynesian tradition of hospitality. It did not necessarily lead to a deep acceptance that resort to violence was shameful or that law-enforcement officers should not be resisted.

While it is perhaps not to be expected that the missionaries could make the detached analysis of motives of Maori Christians that scholars may make from hindsight, it is nevertheless evident that they were prone to gloss over the conservative traits plainly revealed among their converts. In the request for a code of laws presented to Marsden in 1837, the last of the reasons given —that slaves were exalting themselves and the chiefs were being degraded— shows that chiefs wanted to use law to bolster their powers and privileges in a situation where old bases of authority such as *tapu* were weakening. This was not a spirit likely to be approved by humanitarians flush with victory in the cause of anti-slavery. But the missionaries' commitment to evangelism, their longing for success, made them too ready to over-look evidence of insubstantial commitment to Christian ethics or, where they could not deny it, to urge petulantly and paternalistically that the Maori ought to accept their standards. They were in fact urging the British government to establish bureaucratic authority in New Zealand at a time when the young Tamihana Te Waharoa was advising his missionary mentor that it would be difficult to enforce a code of law among his people 'until their belief was more firm'.[28] The missionaries' conception of their civilising mission and personal involvement in the success of it led them to propose a British intervention that went beyond the limits necessary to safeguard the Maori from the pressures of settlement. Similar zeal was evident among the humanitarians in London, notably the members of the Aborigines Protection Society, founded in 1837 out of the anti-slavery movement.

Another major misperception obtaining in London was that the Maori were far weaker than was yet the case. Their potential landlessness was seen as a near actuality, their independence was believed 'precarious and little more nominal' and the extent to which they retained physical command in New Zealand much under-rated.

The twin beliefs that the Maori were weak and compliant resulted in Hobson's instructions on Maori policy being inadequate and to a large extent, inappropriate. The most obvious illustration of this was the naive assumption that Hobson could secure a ready acquiescence from the Maori in whatever he wished, with only puny naval and military backing. The historian Ian Wards has further concluded that Colonial Office idealism towards the Maori did not survive the decision of mid-1839 to assume sovereignty quickly over the whole group, a decision which he sees, on tenuous evidence, as stemming from the discovery of official French interest in New Zealand rather than from the despatch of the New Zealand Company's ships to Cook Strait.[29] Wards is certainly right in arguing that the instructions to Hobson of 1839 were first drafted with a view to partial annexation and were not adequately revised to meet the new circumstances. Nevertheless it can be shown that the humanitarian concern of people like James Stephen to find a way of averting disaster from the Maori had not suddenly vanished. If anything it increased with increasing settlement during 1839-40. What had happened though was that the humanitarians' confidence of success had ebbed proportionately. This development (consequent on the despatch of the Company's ships rather than French activity) may well account for the abrupt decision to authorise Hobson to acquire sovereignty over the whole group as the first urgent step. It can certainly be seen over the whole development of Hobson's instructions in 1839 and 1840.

Even when he had contemplated only limited sovereignty Stephen had included in his proposed treaty arrangements with chiefs in the unceded territory provisions for the abandonment of customs repugnant to Englishmen, for right of access for English missionaries and English commerce, and the fostering of Maori participation in industry.

The missions had no desire to preserve Maori institutions, which, in the light of a theology strongly influenced by Calvinism, were seen as pagan and debased, to be uprooted and replaced in the process of Christian regeneration. On the mission stations English food and clothing, English crafts, English etiquette and entertainments, and the gospel of work and individual responsibility, replaced the Polynesian institutions of the Maori village. In that it was intended that the Maori were to be evangelised, educated in English learning, involved in the commercial economy, and subject to certain restraints by civil government, official policy in early 1839 was already broadly assimilationist.

But it was also a gradualist policy. Stephen was concerned to prevent settlement from swamping the Maori before they were equipped to compete with the settlers on equal terms. Stephen would have heartily concurred with the argument of his contemporary, the Rev. Montagu Hawtrey, that nominal legal equality can only lead to actual equality 'between parties who have the same power in the field'. Where one of two parties was unsophisticated in the forms of Western civilisation, 'the only consequence of establishing the same rights and the same obligations for both will be to destroy the weaker under a show of justice'.[30] In line with this view Stephen had included in Hobson's first instructions the direction that purchase of land for settlement was to be 'confined to such districts as the natives can alienate, without distress or serious inconvenience to themselves', and until brought by education 'within the pale of civilised life . . . [the Maori] must be carefully defended in the observance of their own customs'.[31]

However, with the decision to obtain sovereignty over the whole country the instructions gained a much harder edge. It was no longer a question of negotiating for the abandonment of repugnant customs: rather the 'savage practices of human sacrifice and cannibalism must be promptly and decisively interdicted'. Similarly, all notions of a Maori legislative congress disappeared. The pressure of colonisation companies and the despatch of the New Zealand Company ships had shown, to the satisfaction of the Colonial Office, that New Zealand was in process of becoming a settlement colony, no longer a predominantly Maori New Zealand in which the forms of a Protectorate could suffice. Although Hobson's instructions asserted, in the interests of the Maori, that it was impossible to confer political power on the 'indiscriminate body' of settlers then, Stephen, foreshadowing settler self-government, added 'I trust the time is not distant when it may be proper to establish in New Zealand itself a local legislative assembly.' In the meantime the new territory was to be a dependency of New South Wales with legislative and executive power firmly in the hands of the British officials. The Colonial Office felt sure 'that the benefits of British protection and of laws administered by British Judges would far more than compensate for the sacrifice by the natives of a national independence which they are no longer able to maintain.'

Ambivalent and paternalistic though they were the 1839 instructions showed some attempt at balance between concern to avoid dislocating Maori society too abruptly and concern to assist the Maori to participate in the encroaching European order. The Aborigines Protection Society had, meanwhile, taken up a much more forthright approach. On the assumption that the settlers, not the administration, soon became the dominant force in colonies, the Society advocated a boldly assimilationist policy, in order to counter anticipated settler oppression. They envisaged the prompt extension over the indigenous people of the laws of real property and commerce, the assumption by them of the responsibilities of British subjects, such as taxation, and the granting to them of corresponding privileges, including recruitment into local government machinery, enrolment in the constabulary, access to the courts (including appeal to the Privy Council) and full access to education, both literary and technical. Such specific provisions as were necessary (for example the empanelling of mixed juries in lawsuits between Maori and settlers and the acceptance of pagan evidence without oath in lawsuits) were intended only to secure actual equality for Maori and settler in the machinery of state until education, economic interaction and intermarriage should have obliterated the distinction of race.[32]

An express sharing of state power between Maori and settler was also urged by Colonel Robert Torrens, a founder of the New Zealand Company which had sent out ships in a vain attempt to plant a colony in 1825-6. In 1839, the original New Zealand Company having come under Edward Gibbon Wakefield's control, Torrens proposed a colonisation company which would establish a governing council including at least seven chiefs, a joint administration of each province of the colony by a Maori *ariki* and a European High Sheriff, mixed military and police forces, mixed juries and a judiciary including at least two Maori judges.[33] The Rev. Montagu Hawtrey, who was seeking to influence Wakefield's plans, was anxious to secure equal economic opportunity for native and settler. Reflecting on Australian experience, he deplored the policy of trying to preserve Maori institutions in large reserves beyond the settler pale:

> I see them wandering within their narrowed boundaries, a separate and inferior race, without prospect of wealth or impulse to civilization, their numbers dwindling, their spirit broken, their untouched districts standing as melancholy blanks in the landscape of the century's prosperity, till at last these bars to British enterprize are swept away, and the scanty remnants of the old lords of the lands dispersed as menials among the British settlers.

Hawtrey instead envisaged that Maori landholdings should be interspersed among settler holdings where they would rapidly increase in value and provide an income by which Maori might enter 'the same scale of civilization and social order as their European visitants'. Maori land titles were to vest in the chiefs, and descend by primogeniture. The chiefs, while still deriving authority from traditional institutions such as *tapu,* were also to be registered in a sort of Burke's peerage, equipped with coats of arms, and seated in the

Upper House of the legislature, along with landed settlers. With the Maori ranking system brought into line with English class structure it was expected that Maori aristocracy, gentry and labourers would inter-marry with their social counterparts among the settlers. Hawtrey's idea of interspersing Maori landholdings through the settler landholdings was adopted by Wakefield in the New Zealand Company 'tenths' scheme, whereby Maori leaders would draw one section for every ten sections drawn by settlers in the Cook Strait settlements.[34]

About this time too, a Captain George Grey wrote an opportune report from Australia criticising the policy of leaving Aborigines to retain a more or less dislocated version of their own culture provided they did not interfere with settlers, and urged that instead they be educated, given employment and quickly made subject to British laws.[35]

In that these policies—policies of 'amalgamation' as they were generally then called—assumed a high level of capability in Pacific peoples and stood ready to meet their desire to participate in the institutions of the new order, they were liberal and progressive. Their very great weakness was that they were underlain by undoubted convictions of the superiority of English institutions, and conversely by a disastrously limited appreciation of local values, of local peoples' possible preference for their own institutions and of the difficulties they would incur in adapting to new responsibilities and obligations. Though altruistically conceived, amalgamation policies could, in doctrinaire hands, become as oppressive as settler self-interest.

Meanwhile, during 1840, James Stephen had moved closer to the position of the Aborigines Protection Society. With the annexation of the whole country, and the rapid dispersal of settlement throughout the Colony in spite of Hobson's proclamation that land claims were void unless confirmed by the Crown, he became more deeply pessimistic about the ability of government to safeguard the Maori against the effects of colonisation, or of there being sufficient time for them to make their adaptation ahead of the main stream of settler pressure. He was now fully convincing that New Zealand was becoming a thorough-going settler colony in which (as in Canada, where Lord Durham was contemporaneously compiling his famous report recommending the grant of responsible government) state power would ultimately repose with the settlers, not the British officials. In these circumstances Stephen considered a policy of mere protection to be futile: 'whatever unpopular boon we will confer on them [the Maori] will be expiated by persecutions, which no human power will be able to arrest or punish.'[36] Drafting directions to accompany Hobson's new instructions of 9 December 1840, consequent on New Zealand's being made a Colony separate from New South Wales, he wrote:

> It is only in proportion as either respect for the strength of the aborigines, or a clear sense of the utility of their services and cooperation, shall possess the public mind, that they will be placed beyond the reach of those oppressions of which

other races of uncivilized men have been made the victims. Failing these, neither penalties, nor regulations, nor the teachings of Christianity would restrain settlers from oppressing the Maoris.[37]

Stephen was demonstrating rather more than a realistic appreciation of the limits on a government's ability to engineer good race relations. Good race relations do, of course, depend ultimately on the mutual respect of the peoples concerned. But Stephen's lack of confidence in government's efficacy verged upon a dangerous defeatism—in effect, an acceptance that the need to placate settler prejudices must necessarily circumscribe native policy. This lack of confidence was constantly to inhibit officials from granting the Maori a substantial share of state power, for fear of settler hostility. And it was this lack in confidence, rather than a decline in concern among officials in the Colonial Office, that gave the appearance of an abandonment of humanitarian idealism following the decision to extend British sovereignty over the whole of New Zealand.

Yet although from mid-1839 to late 1840 Stephen increasingly modified the protectionist aspects of his Maori policy in favour of rapid 'amalgamation' of the Maori in the settler-dominated polity he retained, not surprisingly, an ethnocentric distrust of the ability of the Maori to share state power in the new Colony at an early stage. Certainly, he appreciated they were not 'mere wanderers' or herdsmen, 'but a people among whom the arts of Government have made some progress; who have established by their own customs a division and appropriation of the soil; who are not without some measure of agricultural skill and a certain subordination of ranks; with usages having the character and authority of law'.[38] But though a superior kind of barbarian the Maori was a barbarian nevertheless, not capable, without tutelage at least, of exercising actual command, co-equally with settlers, of British-style governmental and legal institutions. Hence instead of drafting directions which envisaged speedy offers to Maori leaders of formal places in the executive, legislative and judicial machinery, such as characterised the schemes of Torrens or the Aborigines Protection Society, he made only shadowy suggestions with a view to their occupying only menial roles. The creation of 'a sense of utility' of their services involved pushing ahead with education and the employment of Maori on government projects, to demonstrate that they could be capable workers. Grey's report claiming success with the Australian Aborigines in this field was included by way of example. Settler respect for the strength of the Maori was to be secured by enrolling them in the militia. 'I suppose that they might be trained to act with the same fidelity as so many Seapoys,' Stephen reflected.[39]

In addition, some critical alterations were made in Stephen's draft by Lord John Russell, Secretary of State for Colonies from September 1839 to September 1841. On the question of the rule of law Stephen had carried the gradualism of the 1839 instructions into the 1840 directions, reiterating that, while some customs such as cannibalism must be swiftly interdicted, others,

less objectionable, should be overcome by 'example, instruction, and encouragement', and others again borne with 'and even sanctioned'. But Russell struck
out the last phrase and changed Stephen's suggestion of a declaratory law
'recognising' such customs, to one 'authorising the Executive to tolerate' them.
The 1840 directions therefore did not, as some historians have suggested,[40]
authorise the explicit recognition or codification of Maori customs which
would have the force of law in Maori districts. That had indeed been
Stephen's intention and, in the hands of a governor so disposed, his draft
directions might have had that result. The full consequences of Russell's
alterations seem to have escaped Stephen: there is a significant difference
between the toleration of native customs and the explicit legal sanctioning of
them. Even the direction to enact a toleration ordinance, a point on which the
final draft remained emphatic, was largely contradicted by the inclusion
of George Grey's memorandum which urged the principle, highly disruptive
to traditional authority, that natives aggrieved by the operation of customary
sanctions should be encouraged to appeal to British law. Finally, Russell's one
major interpolation in Stephen's draft read:

> you will look rather to the permanent welfare of the tribes now to be connected
> with us, than to their supposed claim to the maintenance of their own laws and
> customs. The Queen's sovereignty must be vindicated and the benefits of a rule
> extending its protection to the whole community must be made known by the
> practical exercise of its authority.[41]

Russell's alterations therefore weakened the original intention to respect Maori
custom and favoured the speedier extension over the Maori of the regular
administrative and judicial machinery of the Colony and the constraints and
obligations of British law. But, unfortunately as we have seen, suggestions for
granting the Maori a concomitant share in the administrative and judicial
machinery had not been added. To this extent the directions remained
gradualist, as Stephen intended. While it was agreed that the Maori could be
formally acknowledged as entitled to the rights, privileges and obligations of
British subjects, Hobson was not enjoined to admit them to any significant
office.

   This was the worst of all possible worlds. The Maori were to be denied
the advantages of Stephen's original gradualism with regard to the obligations
of a British state, yet not granted a concomitant share of its privileges. Official
policy was basically in line with other 'amalgamation' policies then in vogue
as the best means by which a native people would be saved from extinction.
The 'permanent welfare' of the Maori included the abandonment by them
as soon as possible of their own customs in favour of English law, and the
adoption by them of such European skills as would command the respect and
outweigh the prejudices of the incoming settlers. The saving of the Maori
race involved the extinction of Maori culture. A precise summary of the
problem that had been posed in New Zealand and its proposed solution was

written into the preamble to the first Colonial ordinance specifically aimed at promoting Maori welfare:

> And whereas great disasters have fallen upon uncivilized nations on being brought into contact with Colonists from the nations of Europe; and in undertaking the colonization of New Zealand Her Majesty's Government have recognized the duty of endeavouring by all practicable means to avert the like disasters from the native people of these Islands, *which object may best be obtained by assimilating as speedily as possible the habits and usages of the Native to those of the European population*.[42]

The weakness of this policy was not its lack of idealism. Underlying it was basically the same ideal which today impels the New Zealand authorities to seek the entry of as large a proportion of Maori as possible into skilled trades and professions and high standard homes, the desire to avert the danger of the Maori becoming an economically vulnerable and socially depressed class, subject to all manner of impositions. Nor were its most serious flaws to be found in its Eurocentrism and assumptions of Maori weakness and submissiveness to paternal direction; the Maori themselves could soon remedy that. Its most serious flaw was that it was emasculated by European attitudes of racial or cultural superiority, and by pandering to settler prejudices, which denied the Maori real participation in the European order except at a menial level.

This was doubly unfortunate since, as we have seen, the Maori leaders' intellectual adventurousness, their desire for the material advantages of European culture and their growing sense of need to find new ways of coping with new problems—or even old problems—meant that they were unreceptive neither to a degree of settlement nor to experiments with British concepts of law and government. State-building did have a chance of Maori co-operation. A form of government closely regulating settlement and promptly involving Maori leaders in political and judicial institutions and in the police power which would support them, stood a good chance of acceptance. Unfortunately nothing so subtle was planned in Downing Street.

But the Maori still possessed substantial physical control of the country and initiative in how far they would accept European influences. Whether their values were still mainly traditional, or heavily modified by contact with European institutions, they were in no way inclined to accept subordination to the Pakeha and certainly wished to treat his law and government with the selectivity they had shown his religion and church, reshaping them according to their own wants. A policy of hasty and wholesale assimilation, adopted by the British authorities as a result of their conviction that the settler tide could not be checked, was not likely to prove acceptable. The small bureaucracy and military force sent to New Zealand in 1840 to introduce such a policy on the assumption that the Maori were weak and compliant, was therefore in a false position from the beginning. And in the one critical area where a more thorough-going 'amalgamation' would have made the whole program more palatable—the inclusion of Maori in the machinery of state—the policy fell short. The patchy drafting of Hobson's instructions left the Maori exposed to the impositions of state power without any share in the exercise of state power. All in all the measures intended to avert the danger of collision between them and the settlers went far towards inviting collision between them and the state.

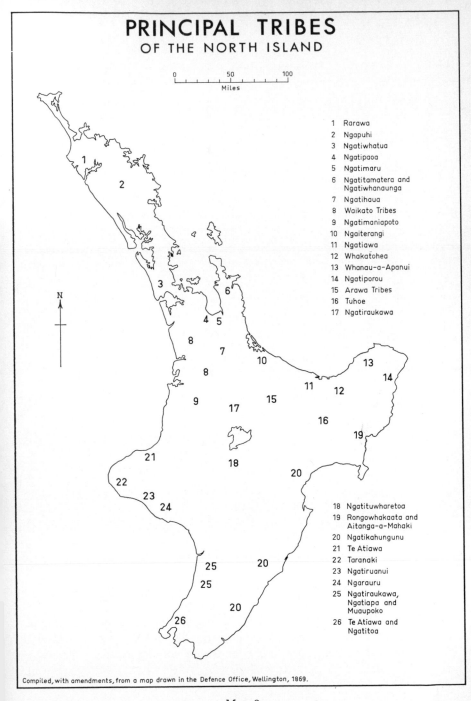

PRINCIPAL TRIBES
OF THE NORTH ISLAND

0   50   100
Miles

1   Rarawa
2   Ngapuhi
3   Ngatiwhatua
4   Ngatipaoa
5   Ngatimaru
6   Ngatitamatera and
    Ngatiwhanaunga
7   Ngatihaua
8   Waikato Tribes
9   Ngatimaniapoto
10 Ngaiterangi
11 Ngatiawa
12 Whakatohea
13 Whanau-a-Apanui
14 Ngatiporou
15 Arawa Tribes
16 Tuhoe
17 Ngatiraukawa

18 Ngatituwharetoa
19 Rongowhakaata and
    Aitanga-a-Mahaki
20 Ngatikahungunu
21 Te Atiawa
22 Taranaki
23 Ngatiruanui
24 Ngarauru
25 Ngatiraukawa,
    Ngatiapa and
    Muaupoko
26 Te Atiawa and
    Ngatitoa

N

Compiled, with amendments, from a map drawn in the Defence Office, Wellington, 1869.

Map 2

IV

The Introduction of English Law

Planning for the administration of New Zealand proceeded on the assumption that the consent of the Maori was virtually a foregone conclusion. It was believed that they made no distinction between proprietary and sovereign rights and that having supposedly alienated the former over much of their land, 'it may be questioned whether strictly speaking the necessity exists for further negotiation with them on the subject'. But the Government's policy of 'frank and open dealing' required that a Treaty of cession be negotiated.[1]

In New Zealand discussions of the Treaty usually began with chief after chief objecting to being placed under a queen or governor, and expressing fear that, like the Australian Aborigines, they would be enslaved or killed and their lands taken by the soldiers. Most of the great interior chiefs, still pagan and both less disturbed and less attracted than the coastal people by influence from the outside world, refused to sign at all. These included Te Heuheu of Taupo, Te Wherowhero of the Waikato, most of the Arawa chiefs of Rotorua district and Tupaea of Tauranga.

As is well known the principal discussion at Waitangi in the Bay of Islands turned in favour of the Treaty after Tamati Waka Nene had declaimed that it was too late to turn back European settlement and urged Hobson to stay to preserve their lands and their customs and to prevent their being made slaves. As each chief at Waitangi signed the Treaty Hobson shook his hand and said, *'He iwi tahi tatou'* ('We are now one people'). The chiefs' signing was taken by the British as a meaningful recognition of the supremacy of the Queen and her agent the Governor. In fact it had almost none of that quality. The Maori leaders had little understanding of the legal concept of national sovereignty as understood by the officials. They had instead a very lively conception of the *mana* of the land and the *mana* of the people embodied in the senior-ranking chiefs of the various lineages. This they had no intention whatever of surrendering; rather they wished to take steps to preserve it. Nene's purpose was essentially to secure the aid of a useful ally to keep in check the settlers and the French. As Te Wherowhero and other senior Waikato chiefs told Hobson's successor three years later, the Maori leaders signed the Treaty 'because that Treaty was to preserve their chieftainship'.[2]

Other reasons for signing included the expectation of material benefits to follow—such as the red blankets issued to each signatory. Some tribes signed because they saw in the British an ally against powerful neighbours. But several chiefs who proposed to sign on that basis also stipulated that soldiers be sent to protect their district, if they were to give up war as requested by the Governor.[3]

Maori interest in social stability and order also entered into the discussion. Nopera Panakareao of Kaitaia saw in Hobson a guarantor of that stability. 'Now we have a helmsman,' he is reported to have said. Formerly 'One said "Let me steer" and another said "Let me steer" and we never went straight.' At the Kaitaia meeting Puipi Riri noted the intractability of adultery disputes. 'Murder and Theft we may subdue but adultery is very common among us. How are we to subdue it, for it often occasions wars amongst us.' Yet the suggestion that the Governor punish such offences raised some unpleasant spectres. 'It would be a strange thing to see ten adulterers all hung up in a row', another chief reflected.[4] In other cases chiefs specifically stipulated before signing that they must have authority over matters internal to their *hapu*. Taraia of Thames said, 'I must be allowed to exercise some influence over my people; if they steal I must punish them.'[5] In general the chiefs considered that the authority of the Governor was to apply to matters involving Pakeha, not internal Maori disputes.

Thus, although Hobson was beginning to collect signatures, there was little ground for the construction he put upon them. Even at Hokianga, Nene's district, Hobson was annoyed on leaving what appeared to have been a successful meeting, when a canoe overtook his boat and a letter from fifty chiefs was handed across 'saying that if the Governor thought they had received the Queen he was very much mistaken and then they threw in the blankets they had received into our boat'.[6] The gulf between Maori and British purposes in 1840 was very great and even on the most optimistic view it would have taken very sensitive statecraft to reconcile them.

Hobson was not possessed of overmuch sensitivity. As far as the actual declaration of British sovereignty was concerned, neither he nor the missionaries were inclined to regard Maori objections and reservations as critical. Hobson had long favoured the annexation of the whole of New Zealand and from the moment of landing began to perform acts of sovereignty.[7] At Waitangi he accepted the signatures of the chiefs, well aware that they were largely signing in trust of missionary assurances as to their future position and without clear understanding of the Treaty's implications. His instructions to officers who subsequently hawked the Treaty about the country also suggest that he saw the task as an exercise in public relations rather than a weighty mission, the issue of which was in serious doubt:

The Koraroes [*Korero*—debates] as they are called will be a great tax on your patience, for probably everyone present will address you in a long speech full of angry opposition, but very little to the purpose; but to secure a favourable termination to the debate you have only to obtain the friendship of one or two of the most influential chiefs, who will probably give a favourable turn to the meeting, and all present will very soon yield to your proposal.[8]

On the question of the chiefs' authority under the British, clearly a vital question to the Maori, Hobson and the missionaries were ambiguous. It has recently been shown that several English versions of the 'Treaty of Waitangi' and the Maori version signed ultimately by nearly 500 chiefs, were each compiled from draft notes by Hobson, his secretary J. S. Freeman and Busby, but that neither English nor Maori versions were direct translations one of the other. By the English versions, which Hobson sent to the Colonial Office as official texts, the chiefs ceded 'all the rights and powers of Sovereignty' over their respective territories and were confirmed only in the 'possession' of their lands and, (by some versions only) their forests and fisheries. In the Maori version they ceded only the 'kawanatanga' (governorship) of their lands and were confirmed in the entire 'rangatiratanga' of their lands, settlements and all their property; 'rangatiratanga' meant at least 'chieftainship' to the Maori and indeed was currently being used by the British to translate 'kingdom', 'independence' and 'sovereignty'. The Maori version therefore went far to justify the conclusion of the Rarawa chief Nopera Panakareao that 'the shadow of the land will go to him (the Governor) but the substance will remain with us'. The missionaries and officials appear deliberately to have avoided translating the concept of sovereign power and authority with the term 'mana' which would have given the chiefs a clearer indication of what they were ceding.[9]

The chiefs were undoubtedly misled, but the Anglican missionaries would probably not have considered themselves as being deliberately deceitful. Although in general they sought to eradicate rather than preserve Maori institutions, they still had ill-formed intentions of using chieftainship, transformed by Christian education and with its more violent prerogatives curbed by British power, as the pivot of local administration in the land. They believed that this regenerated chieftainship, of which Waka Nene was considered a shining example, was what most Maori aspired to, or should aspire to, and that this would be confirmed and strengthened, rather than threatened by the advent of British rule. But they were not at all concerned to press for the establishment of a central legislature of chiefs. That had been appropriate in 1838 when they were envisaging what was essentially a British Protectorate; with the increase in settlement and the establishment of a Crown Colony they no longer saw themselves as bolstering a basically Maori New Zealand. They were, moreover, disinclined to contemplate Maori rejection of British sovereignty and did not put it to the chiefs as a real option. Their over-riding concern was to see established a national authority capable of introducing ordered government and regulating land purchase. Some showed a paramount concern to see English interests, and English missions in particular, safeguarded against the supposed Papist threat represented by the Catholic mission under Bishop Pompallier and the entry of French warships into the Pacific.[10]

The officials, for their part, considered that by recognising customary Maori land claims in the Treaty they had taken all necessary measures to confirm chiefly privileges. Major Bunbury, Hobson's first military commander, proffering the Treaty to Hapuku of Hawke's Bay, stated that 'It was not the intention of Her Majesty's Government to lower the chiefs in the estimation of their tribes, and that his signature being now attached to the treaty would only tend to increase his consequence by acknowledging his title.'[11] In order to avert suspicion of the Treaty, Hobson also issued a circular letter repudiating suggestions that the Maori would be degraded by the advent of British authority, and telling the chiefs that 'the Governor will ever strive to assure unto you the customs and all the possessions belonging to the Maoris'.[12] Finally, missionary George Clarke was appointed Chief Protector of Aborigines and instructed to assure the Maori 'that their native customs would not be infringed, except in cases that are opposed to the principles of humanity and morals'.[13]

Yet it was precisely this power to permit or to forbid that the chiefs had not conceded to the British. Bent on their mission, Hobson and his staff were basically careless of the opinions of the people they had come to save, and cared little that the exercise of their power, unless accompanied by ample measures to engage and compensate the Maori, would appear oppressive and evoke resistance. Hobson took no practical steps to engage the Maori leadership in the formal machinery of state. The Maori were placed in a position of subordination and tutelage from which they have ever since been trying to recover.

In the course of retrieving a whaleboat that the Hawke's Bay chief Hapuku had taken from a settler who had cursed him, Major Bunbury became dimly aware of the dangers of the situation and suggested to Hobson that 'some trifling degree of deference might be paid to their present state and condition, in order gradually to prepare and make them comprehend the more complex and expensive forms of our civil institutions and criminal laws'. He suggested the inclusion of Maori in travelling police detachments. But the degree of deference remained trifling indeed. No local force was organised in which Maori could serve. The reason given by Hobson for declining to raise a militia including Maori, as urged by the Colonial Office in 1840, was that the tension between Maori and settlers would have been aggravated if either or both groups had been formally armed and organised. Actually the officials were reluctant to depend on Maori assistance and were unsure of their ability to control and retain the loyalty of Maori forces. Financial stringency later affected the situation, the Colonial Office in 1842 declining Hobson's request to raise a foot police for this reason.[14]

Moreover, Stephen's failure in 1840 to make sufficiently clear his intention that the Maori might continue to live under their own customs resulted in the local legislation also being unclear on the point. The laws of New South Wales were in force during the year that New Zealand was legally part of that

colony and the first New Zealand ordinances of 1841 and 1842, consequent
on the country becoming a separate Colony, established a system of Justices'
courts, Police Magistrates' courts, a Court of Requests and a Supreme Court
similar to that operating in the Australian Colonies, and applying English
common law modified by local Ordinances. True, the settler Justices of the
Peace had no jurisdiction in Maori cases. Instead George Clarke, Chief Protector of Aborigines, and some of the Sub-Protectors appointed in various
districts, were commissioned as Justices of the Peace and instructed that:

> In your magisterial capacity, where natives are concerned, there are many minor
> offences of disputes which you may compromise or adjust in accordance with
> their custom, which, if brought before a court of justice, and judged according
> to the strict and rigid interpretation of the law, might subject them to grievous
> punishments.

Clarke, however, found this too indefinite to be very helpful. He wrote, 'the
nature of those offences which may be compounded, are not described, and
I am at a loss to conceive how such a principle can be carried out until native
customs have been legalized, or an enactment made to meet the case'.[15] But
no enactment was made to meet the case. Even the declaratory law permitting
temporary toleration of Maori custom, which the directions of 1840 had been
relatively emphatic in requiring, was not considered. In practice of course the
Maori were largely beyond the interference of the embryo administration but
where law enforcement was possible Maori and Pakeha, chief and commoner,
were theoretically open to the same legal constraints, enforceable in Pakeha
courts by Pakeha Police Magistrates. The first court of quarter sessions held in
Wellington in October 1841 discussed the question in relation to a Maori
name Pakewa charged with stealing a blanket from a settler. The Chairman
of the bench asserted that 'the natives were in truth and in fact British subjects
and that they were to be treated in every respect as any of ourselves; and that
they had the same right to the protection of the law and must be held
equally amenable for any breach of it'. Presumably the Maori version of the
Treaty of Waitangi had some common currency for Dr Evans, arraigned to
defend Pakewa, pleaded that the court had no jurisdiction; 'by the Treaty of
Waitangi, all the rights of chieftainship were reserved to the New Zealanders;
and that among these rights was that of administering justice among the
inhabitants of their own tribe'. The Crown Prosecutor objected that the
administration of justice was not one of the traditional attributes of chieftainship (which was correct if Evans' statement was taken to imply a sole prerogative in the senior chiefs) and that in any case this was not an internal
dispute, but one involving a settler. Next day Evans withdrew his plea, stating
that on closer scrutiny of the Treaty (perhaps an English version) he found
it did not bear the construction he had placed upon it. Instead he urged that
the prisoner was not a British subject after all—only an Act of Parliament
being able to make him so—and that he should have the rights of an alien,
in this case a mixed jury, half Maori and half settler. The Crown Prosecutor

rejected this, saying that Maori became British subjects when New Zealand became a British colony. His view was upheld by the court and Pakewa was found guilty by a settler jury and sentenced to seven days' hard labour.[16]

The British authorities tended, in fact, to assert police power over the Maori from the beginning, where the occasion and the opportunity arose. Bunbury records that his small troop was called out for the first time in March 1840, at the Bay of Islands, when a Maori *taua* or war party held up the trial of one of their kin, accused of stealing a blanket.[17] Then in April 1840, 300 armed Maori under the local chief Haratua arrived at the preliminary hearing of charges against Kihi, accused of murdering a Pakeha shepherd at the Paihia mission station. In a panic the magistrate, Willoughby Shortland, landed eighty troops just arrived in the Bay of Islands from Sydney and collision between government and Maori already appeared imminent. But Haratua, infuriated that Kihi, a visitor from Tauranga, had murdered the servant of 'his' Pakeha, had come not to release the prisoner but to demand the right to kill him. The missionaries were able to persuade the *taua* to disperse.[18] Kihi, who became ill and was released to the care of the CMS mission, died before he could be brought to trial in the higher court. Meanwhile, his *hapu* threatened reprisals on the small settler community at Tauranga and Hobson, somewhat shaken by the disclosure of Maori strength, sent HMS *Herald* to the vicinity. Passions died but the incident apparently caused the influential Thames chief Piko to decide against signing the Treaty of Waitangi.[19]

Magistrates arrived in Port Nicholson (now Wellington) in June 1840, together with a detachment of troops under Ensign Best. Within days Best had interceded in a violent adultery dispute in which the principal Wellington chiefs were threatening to take sides. He disarmed the protagonists, and the injured husband was eventually satisfied with a payment of goods as *utu*. Best was probably not exaggerating when he claimed that 'but for our mediation the man would have murdered his wife and a war would have been inevitable'. He went on:

> The same morning a Native chief gave evidence in due form before the bench that 'he had been assaulted by three white men and that part of his fence had been pulled down'. The case was proved and his assailants fined three pounds each. Again a Mauri girl was convicted of stealing a loaf & bit of Soap. The chief of her Pah wished to kill her for said he a Thief is no good. He was told to tie her up in his Wharrey for 24 hours which at last he consented to do but thought it would be better to tie her up longer. On another occasion a Mauri boy was convicted for stealing two axe heads he was sentenced to 12 hours in the Stocks and so delighted were the Mauries when they saw him in that they came in a body to Mr Shortland [the magistrate] to beg that he might not be let out for a week. Who will deny after these instances that the Mauris are easily governed by our law & that it is only necessary to make them understand it in order to ensure their ready obedience to any properly constituted authority.[26]

Best was as enthusiastic about the first signs of Maori receptiveness of the system he represented, and believed implicitly to be superior, as missionaries were about the first converts to theirs. But how far was his optimism justified?

In general, the Maori showed considerable willingness to accept the intervention of the British authorities in disputes between themselves and settlers.
The truculent Bay of Islands chief, Pomare, who seized a whaleboat in
recompense for the drunken provocations of some sailors at his *pa,* gave up
the boat to a magistrate and soldiers who investigated the incident, in return
for assurances of stricter control of the sailors. When settlers desecrated Maori
graves at Cloudy Bay for their greenstone artifacts, Te Rauparaha (conqueror
of the Cook Strait tribes in the 1830s and still master of the district) allowed
the Protectors of Aborigines to settle the matter. Accused Maori also appeared
to value formal inquiries as a means of making plain their values and motives.
Hence a number of Marlborough men attended an inquiry into the deaths
of some settlers they were suspected of murdering, but who had in fact
drowned.[21] Even an elder kinsman of Te Rauparaha appeared in court to
answer a charge of stealing a blanket from a settler and was dismissed with
a caution when he showed he had taken it to square a debt. Chiefs were
usually quick to punish their slaves or kinsmen who stole, or allowed the
authorities to punish them.

In general Clarke, the Chief Protector, found that most petty disputes
between Maori and settler arose out of the misunderstanding of each others
customs and feelings, and that when this was pointed out, Maori were usually
disposed to settle differences amicably. Yet he also thought both sides were
inclined to over-reach themselves in demands for payment for services
rendered or injury received; he instructed the Sub-Protectors that they could
not too often tell the Maori that they would only injure themselves by being
unreasonable and that the Protectors would only help them with just and
equitable claims.[22]

Official mediation was vital in the matter of land claims. Maori and settlers
in the Cook's Strait area were at loggerheads from the beginning. Understandable difficulty in comprehending the intricacies of traditional Maori land
rights was increased by the Maori sellers' tendency to inflate their claims and
compounded by the clumsiness and cupidity of the New Zealand Company's
agents. Purchases had been made from the wrong claimants and freehold
rights assumed over large continuous districts where the Maori had intended
to sell only limited rights within the area. Maori occupants refused to vacate
their existing settlements for the selection of sections the Company planned
for them and surveys were interrupted when the Company began to mark
boundaries. Further complications arose as tribes which had been conquered
or driven out in the inter-tribal wars of the 1830s took the opportunity to
revive claims against their conquerors and cultivate their former territory.
The consequent tendency for a succession of claims to arise once one had
been settled, gave the impression of systematic deceit and extortion by the
Maori. Although this was probably only rarely the case the settlers, driven to
a fury of frustration by the delays and new demands for payment, could not

but believe otherwise and wanted Maori arrested for trespass on areas the Company claimed. Although most Justices of the Peace and some Police Magistrates would have been glad to support the settlers' demand, the Government would not authorise it. At Wellington and New Plymouth settlers tried to force Maori off disputed land. They also moved out to cultivate virgin land in spite of Hobson's proclamation of February 1840 that all claims were void until investigated and confirmed by the Crown, and in violation of the Land Claims Ordinance of 1841 which reserved to the Crown all purchase or leasing of land from Maori.

The Maori were inevitably alarmed by this turn of events. The steady arrival of new immigrant ships brought settlers, including women and children, in unexpected numbers. These were not people to intersperse and inter-marry among Maori communities. And there was a notable shift of attitude in many of the old settlers. Formerly circumspect, they were now inclined to tell the chiefs that Maori could pretend to be gentlemen no longer, and to boast that the Governor and his troops would support the settlers' claims to land. The Maori resisted settler encroachments, destroying fences and buildings erected on disputed ground. Settler retaliation on the pattern of the lawless killing of Aborigines that was occurring in Australia was not initially deterred by Maori strength. Nor was it precluded by the fact that the Wakefield settlers were selected and supposedly superior immigrants. The settlers were very aggressive, believing their claims justified, and considered the Maori to be a cowardly lot who would give way to a show of force.

In this tense and dangerous situation the intervention of officials and troops certainly prevented early bloodshed. In August 1840 the magistrates and Best's soldiers dispersed armed settlers who had invaded Te Aro *pa* in Wellington after a fracas between some Maori and a settler on a disputed allotment. The Maori were glad to see the troops arrive.[23] In 1842 one Francis Leathart was sentenced by the Supreme Court in Auckland to two years gaol for 'shooting at a native'. The offence was described by Clarke as one of several 'assaults' committed against Maori about that time, which were said to have been checked by the sentencing of Leathart.[24]

The defence of Maori rights by the Crown was all the more important since Maori were beginning to feel that the Treaty of Waitangi was a betrayal, a blind behind which their lands would be acquired. In the first three years of British rule, they responded quickly to the officials' efforts, and generally proved more co-operative than the New Zealand Company officials in attempts by the Protectors to adjust claims by negotiation, in most cases being prepared to accept compensation and move to agreed areas. They attended regularly to give evidence in the Land Claims Commissioners Courts established by 1842 and some adapted traditional debating skills to the purpose of artful litigation. In 1842 a prominent Tauranga chief, Kahukoti, showed appreciation of the role of administration by his suggestion that the tribes should send descriptions of their land claims to be recorded 'that the Governor may judge between us and the Pakeha may not say "We have bought the land, it is ours." '[25] Maori in the town grew accustomed to visiting the Protectors incessantly about disputes with settlers over boundary disputes, rights to cultivate, occasional thefts and the vexed question of stock trespass. Stock trespass was a particularly serious problem to both races. As a magistrate later observed: 'So long as Europeans and Maories continue to farm on antagonistic principles—the one fencing their crops and letting their cattle run at large; the other tying up their cattle or driving them to other regions, and leaving their crops exposed—there must be disputes whenever the two races come in contact.'[26] The Maori, understandably reluctant to labour or pay heavily to fence their traditionally unfenced cultivations, were the worst sufferers. When disputes over such questions as these came before the courts the Protectors usually watched the Maori party's interests and acted as interpreters.

Soldiers like Best became popular too when it appeared that they would not be used oppressively. When Best became involved in a dangerous melee with some Ohariu Valley Maori who had been caught stealing in Wellington and resisted the local constable, he greatly enhanced his credit by not immediately taking vengeance when he at last got the upper hand. He reported that the Wellington chiefs told him 'they now know that I loved the Mauries for I had not killed the bad men when I could have killed them all'. He concluded, in another optimistic assessment:

> Laws cannot be forced down the Mauries throats at the point of the bayonet such proceedings would entail hatred and distrust. Let them be persuaded of our good intentions and the wisdom of our laws and in time they will be quietly adopted.[27]

This attitude appeared to be vindicated when the Ohariu chiefs, at his request, returned the stolen goods, with compensation, and promised surrender of the principal offenders.

While the Maori did not consider themselves under any obligation to submit their own internal disputes to British officials there were nevertheless situations in which they did so. Traditional land claims in areas which were the subject of alleged European purchase, were discussed with the Protectors and before the Land Claims Commissioners. In many instances the Protectors were also able to act as mediators and peacemakers in much the same way as the missionaries. For example, Dr Edward Shortland, younger brother of Willoughby Shortland, has recorded how, as Sub-Protector in the Bay of Plenty, he mediated in an adultery dispute. A large *taua,* led by the aggrieved husband, demanded from the adulterer's *hapu* two pieces of land and a canoe; with Shortland's assistance these were quietly made over. Shortland added that he had often known the friendly assistance of strangers to be of service to Maori disputants 'by enabling the weaker party to yield with safety to their honour, on the plea that their doing so was owing to such interference'.[28]

By 1842 a few cases between Maori disputants were coming before the courts. Te Poti was indicted in the Supreme Court for stealing a gun from his nephew. Under cross-examination the nephew admitted that Te Poti had a share in the gun and the jury was directed to acquit.[29] This was a characteristic forerunner of a host of cases that eventually came before the courts about the ownership of movable property. Traditionally such goods as canoes, weapons or cloaks were produced and transferred according to well-defined systems, accompanied by ritual and safeguarded by *tapu*. But goods of European origin were frequently acquired in loose commercial transactions, in which an ill-defined group may have joined, some passing on their rights to kinsmen without informing co-owners. Concepts of individual proprietorship (not absent in traditional society in any case) tended to increase and be asserted, as in Te Poti's case, against the claims of kin. The defining sanctions of *tapu* had lost much of their force, especially among Christian communities, where theft was more common than among pagans. The depredations of wandering stock introduced from Europe, such as pigs, cattle and horses, were a new problem. They were frequently adjusted by payment of *utu,* but stock trespass was so common, and the ownership of stock and value of damage so difficult to determine, that the normal capacity of a *hapu* to adjust disputes was over-strained. Disputes of this kind, usually within a single lineage, began therefore to come before Pakeha officials and courts.

Another straw in the wind was the conviction of a Maori in the Wellington police court in 1843 for the attempted rape of the wife of Moturoa, a prominent local chief. This was an offence which the chief would previously have settled with his club, as less constrained chiefs throughout the country still did. But by 1843, in the vicinity of the main settlements, as Maori became increasingly involved in industry and commerce, warlike habits declined in favour of more moderate adjustment of disputes. Inter-tribal feuding died down. Within two years of settlement Maori in the Wellington area had ceased to carry arms and allowed their fortifications to fall into disrepair. By 1843, except in the heat of the moment, Moturoa would have regarded the clubbing of his wife's assailant as backward and excessive. Moreover his community would probably have lacked the inclination or capacity to face possible retaliation over the matter. Trouble over their women was thus another major issue in which Maori were sometimes willing to allow the intervention of officials.

A most striking example of Maori interest in the rule of law occurred when the first Auckland magistrate, William Symonds, visited the Waipa district in 1841. An elderly chief of the district, Te Waru, a pagan, accompanied Symonds from the coast. On arrival Te Waru announced that his people would henceforth live by British law, and shortly afterwards, in a solemn and deeply moved assembly, handed over to Symonds his only daughter, whom he accused of murder. The girl's brother had committed suicide after the discovery of his adulterous relationship with a female slave and his sister had thereupon killed the slave. Symonds at first proposed to send the girl to Auckland for trial. Te Waru then said he was going to Auckland anyway and asked to be allowed to answer for his daughter. Symonds, however, having found that the act had been done before Te Waru's declaration of commitment to British law, changed his mind about sending the girl for trial.[30] Te Waru's decision seems to have stemmed from a visit to Van Dieman's Land and discussion with Symonds on the journey from the coast. Like other chiefs who had been abroad he seems to have been impressed by a feature of European organisation which he believed gave order and strength to society. Having come to a conclusion, and given his undertaking to Symonds, he apparently sought to drive it home to his community by a dramatic gesture of commitment to it. He would probably not have intended that he and his people should be subject to the unqualified jurisdiction of the police and magistrates, but had a magistrate been permanently stationed in the district, working essentially in conjunction with Te Waru, it is possible that the chief would have sustained his purpose.

A suggestion that chiefs were making an intellectual shift, an altered value judgment, against resort to violence, came from Te Wherowhero of Waikato who, though he had not signed the Treaty of Waitangi, subsequently received officials and offered land for their residence. After Hobson's death in 1842 he wrote to Queen Victoria, pleading for a kindly successor. There was no need, he argued, to send a hard man: 'Formerly we were a bad people, a murdering people—now [we] are settling peaceably. We have left off the evil.'[31] And in 1843 a pagan chief told a Sub-Protector investigating feuding in the Bay of Plenty: 'It is now some years since I took any part in the quarrels of these parts and I find that whilst others become weak I am getting strong. The children of my Pah are not murdered in their youth and the boys are growing into men. I can now raise more fighting men than any Chief of Tauronga and I will use my strength to preserve peace.'[32] The chief's traditional satisfaction in his fighting capacity mingles with a new determination to work for peace, but there is consistency in his seeking the best means of discharging his responsibility for the strength and well-being of his community.

Despite the early interest among some Maori in using Pakeha mechanisms to adjust disputes such mechanisms were generally viewed as alternatives only to traditional methods and the limits of Maori submissiveness either to the concept of the rule of law, or to the machinery of law enforcement, were also very apparent. While they were often willing to accept the intervention of officials in their disputes with settlers few Maori were inclined to refrain from taking redress themselves if no official were handy or if he failed to give satisfaction. Settler property on disputed sections continued to be destroyed and settlers allowed to squat on Maori land in the out-districts naturally had to submit to *muru* if they gave offence, or to have their stock seized if they trespassed on Maori crops or *tapu* places. When magistrates did hear cases they normally had to operate as mediators, rather than authoritarian dispensers of English law, and to take account of Maori values even if these were not recognised in law. In a typical case Symonds, investigating an assault, accepted that the settler complainant had provoked his Maori assailant by cursing him; but Symonds deemed the plunder of the settler's property excessive and secured recompense.[33] Where Maori were accused parties peaceful proceedings often depended on the co-operation of the principal chiefs. In January 1841, some Wellington Maori threatened to release a kinsman arrested over a dispute about a pig. To forestall violence their chief Te Puni secured the prisoner's release, undertaking to be answerable for his appearance in court, and the appearance was duly made.[34] On another occasion the truculent Wellington chief Taringa Kuri was seated on the bench with the magistrate during the trial of two of his people for theft and consulted on various points including the sentence.[35]

Maori compliance with the law was much more likely in petty matters which could be satisfied by a fine, than in serious matters likely to carry a heavy gaol sentence. This was partly because payment of a fine, although it went to the Crown and not to the injured party, came closer to the Maori principle of making over property as *utu*. Because they did not consider themselves to have behaved particularly shamefully, and because they desired to prove boldness and daring, Maori offenders were very ready to admit responsibility and, having been caught out, to offer compensation. But they were not at all ready to submit to the degradation of imprisonment by the British, which chiefs in particular saw as deeply shaming. They regarded it as provocative if officials declined to accept proffered compensation and persisted with talk of gaol sentences. Their views also stemmed in part from differing views about petty offences against property, which the Taupo chief Te Heuheu illustrated when he criticised the Pakeha practice of imprisoning people for pilfering small things of little or no value. A great chief, he said, would take no notice.[36] Knowing their views, officials tended to sentence Maori offenders only to fines or secure payment of redress without a formal hearing in cases where a settler would have been arrested and gaoled. This distinction was deeply resented by settlers and complaint of it became a standard accompaniment of demands for enforcement of law against the Maori for the next twenty years.

Officials believed they had made a breakthrough in 1842 when Maketu, a high-ranking Bay of Islands chief who had killed a settler family and their part-Maori employee, and had to be released from custody because of the menaces of his people, was shortly afterwards surrendered again by them. However, closer investigation showed that this was not so much from any acceptance of obligation to British law, but because Maketu's kin were threatened with bloody retribution from the Maori relatives of his part-Maori victim unless they gave Maketu up. Surrender to the law was seen as a means of avoiding a greater calamity. At the subsequent hanging of Maketu in Auckland Maori excitement was such that Hobson wished he had more troops on hand. News of the event swept through the country producing a mixture of amazed respect for the judge who dared pass sentence of death on a chief, and

resentment of the power assumed by the British authorities. Waka Nene, who
had counselled Maketu's surrender, was taunted as an adulterer, 'because he
allied himself with strangers that is, with a foreign nation'.[87]

British law had little impact outside the main settlements, much of the
country hardly seeing an official. On the other hand, Christian communities
continued to besiege missionaries with requests for guidance on the settlement
of disputes. The Rev. A. N. Brown of Tauranga wrote, 'It is vain to tell them
that you are not a Judge—you must give an opinion and they will act upon it
nor do I know how in the absence of all law any other course can be
adopted.'[38] More and more villages were being regulated by mission rules of
conduct, enforced by the 'native teachers', or in 'church meetings' of the
whole congregation, by means of fines, ecclesiastical penalties such as suspension from communion or by quasi-traditional punishments such as temporary
banishment from the community. In many areas, however, there were clashes
over women, or land or eel fisheries, in the traditional pattern. Clarke believed
that these occurred only in remote places where the Protectors had no influence
but the correspondence and journals of the missionaries show that even in
supposedly pacified areas surreptitious killings for sorcery or adultery were
still common, news of only a small proportion of them ever reaching the
Government's ears.

Moreover, when officials heard of and sought to curb these practices the
chiefs were not very co-operative. In 1840, Wiremu Nera and other chiefs
near Kawhia, prompted by John Whiteley, the local Wesleyan missionary, did
write to the Government in Auckland for assistance in checking a spate of
killings arising from sorcery. But when Symonds visited the area he found
that, although several charges were brought against settlers in the area, none
were brought against Maori. Whiteley reported: 'although they are wishful
for peace and good order, yet they feared to say that murders would cease as
they feared their slaves would not leave off to exercise witchcraft upon them
and to take liberties with their wives'.[39]

Other comments on the first years of British rule in New Zealand give a
similar view of the Maori attitude. The early settler Maning considered that,
'Their intelligence causes them theoretically to acknowledge the benefits of
law, which they see established amongst us, but their hatred of restraint causes
them practically to abhor and resist its full enforcement amongst themselves.'[40]
In 1843 George Clarke, Junior, son of the Chief Protector, reporting on his
experience in the Cook Strait area, drew an important distinction: 'In their
own disputes, they would rather suffer any injury from one another, than
apply to the magistrates for protection, though they frequently submit their
differences to me as a friend.'[41] And Edward Shortland, summing up his
experience of Maori attitudes to British law, wrote: 'the only persons who
professed assent were the suffering party, who were anxious to use our laws
or any other means, to obtain satisfaction; but if, the next day, they had
committed a similar offence, they would have denied the authority before so

anxiously invoked'. Yet he immediately modified this cynical assessment: 'Fortunately, the most certain method of prevailing with a New Zealander is to apply to his reason. Only get him to assent that your proposition is "tika" or straight, and you will soon obtain his consent to it.'[42]

The most experienced observers were agreed then that the Maori's intelligence, sense of equity and need for a basic social stability led them to appreciate many of the principles which British justice sought to purvey. Operating against this was the fact that traditionally 'judicial' matters were imbedded in the wider context of prestige and power seeking. Consequently British courts and law were often resorted to by parties seeking to use them for that purpose and avoided by disputants who could not expect to secure a victory from them over rivals. In addition there was an inevitable suspicion and resentment of alien authority. Clarke believed, as he had since 1838, that a demonstration of military power was necessary to overcome this resistance, 'as it must from the nature of things be a long time ere the Natives yield to the duty of quiet submission to a mere Constabulary force'.[43] The Protectorate Department generally shared Shortland's belief that an appeal to reason would win Maori acceptance of the use of that force, provided of course that it was employed only against manifest aggressors. This belief appears to be supported by an incident Best records where a group of Waikato chiefs, sullen and angry about the execution of Maketu, when fully informed of the details of Maketu's crime, appeared to accept his fate as a legitimate exercise of power, implying no arbitrary oppression which need be feared as an ultimate threat to them.[44]

The chances of extending the rule of law clearly stood to be improved, however, by the modification of strict British legal principles and practices to accord more with essential Maori notions of justice. This was strikingly demonstrated early in 1843 when one Richard Cook, who had brutally murdered a Maori woman and her children at Cloudy Bay in the Marlborough district, was acquitted on the technicality that his wife, who had the crucial evidence, could not testify against him. Though Cook subsequently confessed, this acquittal seriously weakened the prestige of the British courts in the eyes of the local Maori, who had with difficulty been persuaded not to exact *utu* by traditional means.[45]

It was also clear that the overcoming of Maori resentment of unaccustomed state authority must necessarily be a gradual and delicate process, probably best assisted by involving Maori leaders as much as possible in the machinery of state. Since authority was not traditionally concentrated into a narrow elite, this pointed to the involvement of a considerable number of chiefs at the local level, rather than the elevation of a few favoured individuals to office at the centre. The need to involve Maori leaders in government as a whole was also suggested by their restlessness under paternalistic measures intended for their protection. The Crown's sole right to purchase land was increasingly seen as restrictive, especially as would-be private purchasers, themselves seeking to undermine the restriction, tantalised Maori with talk of offers larger than those made by the Crown. Hobson also shelved a plan for prohibiting the sale of arms and ammunition to Maori for fear of their resentment. The involvement of Maori leaders in the official policy-making bodies would not necessarily, of course, have guaranteed Maori compliance with policy; indeed, it carried the danger of detaching the selected leaders from their people. But some involvement of delegates and regular consultation with Maori communities may have both ameliorated policy and diminished Maori ignorance of Government motives.

In a book published in 1843 the scientist Ernest Dieffenbach certainly reflected the opinions of Clarke and the Protectorate, rather than those of his employers, the New Zealand Company, when he argued that to win the co-operation of the Maori it was necessary to show confidence in them, by investing local chiefs, 'formally, and in an impressive manner' with power to act as magistrates over their own people and constables over wayward settlers. He recommended that Maori customs be codified and only gradually supplanted by British law.[46]

The contrary approach to this was to bemoan any dependence on Maori opinion at all and to look simply to the accumulation of sufficient armed force to drive home the dominion of British law. Their desire to secure this outcome led the New Zealand Company settlers to generate the myth that 'In the first instance there was on the part of the natives a disposition to defer with almost superstitious reverence to the authority of the Government' and had 'barbarous customs' been vigorously suppressed and 'the great principles of justice and respect for property' driven home 'no serious resistance would probably ever have been attempted'.[47] Few statements could have been more dangerously misleading but their frustration and prejudice blinded the settlers to any clear appraisal of the Maori attitude.

The sources of antagonism lay deeper even than rancour over disputed land claims. They could be found in the settlers' social, moral and aesthetic values. Settlers took little trouble to cloak from Maori their repugnance at the dirt and vermin of the *pa,* or the skin sores and unwashed smell of the inhabitants. The refusal of the Wellington Maori to vacate several *pa* in the town left the settlers fuming about the pockets of communal 'licentiousness' in their midst, and about the very real fire and health hazard they created. Indeed, half of Te Aro *pa* was destroyed by fire early in 1842 while the owners were away cultivating. Settlers saved the other half and removed five casks of gunpowder from endangered *whare*. A sixth blew up.[48] Not surprisingly an Ordinance of March 1842 placed a tax on existing *raupo* (bulrush) houses in town and forbade the erection of new ones.[49]

The Rev. Montagu Hawtrey's hope for easily accepted and widespread inter-racial marriage also proved illusory. Although settlers in the out-districts frequently had *de facto* Maori wives and sometimes married them, as in the pre-1840 days, in the main settlements a different sexual morality accompanied the arrival of English women. The eighteenth century view of Polynesia as a field of innocent delights was driven out by the prudish Victorian view of Polynesia corrupt and depraved. Nor did attempts to alter Maori habits of life achieve the results hoped for. Edmund Halswell, the New Zealand Company's officer in charge of Maori reserves, wrote:

> I do not think it possible that the present adult race will become, to any great extent, steady in civilized pursuits. There is a constant inclination to fall back and indulge in old associations, and nothing short of breaking up the pahs, and locating their inhabitants in decent huts, in small villages on their own reserves, and by degrees associating them with the white population, would render them fit companions for any, even the lowest of settlers.[50]

Despite the nominal legal equality of races unofficial discrimination rapidly developed in public rooms; most clubs and many public houses, for example, excluded Maori. In New Plymouth the program of 'amalgamation' was frankly abandoned, and something akin to modern apartheid showed signs of taking its place. No selection of rural 'tenths' was made for the Maori, prospective settlers having stipulated against it. Instead, the equivalent of the 'tenths' was to be aggregated into one block, near, but not too near, the settlers' lands.

For their part the Maori continued to regard out-settlers as their tenants-at-will, as in fact they generally were. They were frequently very blunt in asserting that the Pakeha should share property freely with them. Explaining the 'theft' of some potatoes from a settler, the young Bay of Islands chief, Hone Heke, explained simply: 'I asked for them—had they been withheld I should have been angry. . . . When settlers are niggardly I get angry, but when they are generous I say "treat the Europeans well".'[51] The *muru* of the nearest available settler for the offence of another (or of his stock) added to out-settlers' grievances. Most settlers had emigrated in the expectation of quickly acquiring their own freehold farms in the new Colony and wanted to rid themselves of a hated dependence on people they regarded as semi-barbarian and inferior. As early as 1840 Maori in the Wairarapa district had discovered the value of allowing pastoralists to run sheep on their land on payment of rent.[52] The system spread and 'Maori landlordism' promised to become permanent. The Maori's practice of putting bridges and ferries across rivers and charging tolls, sometimes exorbitant, was also deeply resented by the settlers, although they would hardly have been able to traverse the country without such assistance.

Given their attitudes towards the Maori, it was unimaginable that settlers would be eager to see them vested with a share in the machinery of state. Settlers wanted the Maori stripped of power, not confirmed in power. The only chance there was of this pressure being overcome, and Maori included in state machinery, was if the Governor received a strong directive from London to that effect and resolute backing when he implemented it. As we have seen, Hobson's instructions were lacking in any such directive and a chance to found the Colony on the basis of a genuine sharing of power between Maori and Pakeha, and a genuine recognition by either race of the values and institutions of the other, was missed.

Actually Hobson himself shared much of the settler attitude, and believed Maori habits to be 'so inveterately opposed to those of civilized life, and their practices so repugnant to the customs of Englishmen', that he scarcely hoped to preserve peace when the settlers became more numerous.[53] He too looked rather to the simple assertion of his authority, rather than some system of practical co-operation with the chiefs, as the solution to New Zealand's difficulties. In early 1842 the Protectors secured from the powerful Hokianga chief Tirarau, promise of several hundred acres of land in compensation for the *muru* of a settler named Forsaith whom Tirarau's people had wrongly suspected of desecrating a grave. But Hobson saw this as a poor substitute for arresting Tirarau and used the incident to call for more troops in order 'to demand and enforce' the abolition of *muru*.[54] Certainly the practice of *muru* was galling to its unoffending victims and years later Forsaith was claiming that he had not yet got possession of the land he had been promised. But Hobson's desire to arrest a chief of the highest rank, who had not been a party to the original raid on Forsaith, illustrated the dangerous tendency, endemic in imperial situations, for officials to look to a narrow and highly provocative military solution, in a complex problem of inter-cultural relations.

The whole question was highlighted later in 1842 when a long-standing feud between Bay of Plenty tribes revived. The Thames chief Taraia attacked a settlement of Ngaiterangi near Tauranga, killing several (of whom a number were eaten) and taking others captive. The incident may never have engaged the Government's attention more than did other clashes in remote parts of the country but for the fact that the Tauranga Christians, at the instigation of the missionary A. N. Brown, wrote to Hobson formally invoking his protection. The Government's obligation to protect Maori who had, at least nominally, opted for peace and Christianity was added to the obligation assumed, at the foundation of the colony, to stamp out barbarous customs. Clarke told Taraia that his action had been in hostility to the Government as well as to Ngaiterangi and that he would have to accept Government terms. Taraia refused to recognise that the Government had any right to intervene in purely Maori quarrels and was resentful that it had chosen to act then and not in a number of earlier incidents which he recited. Clarke at first felt that troops should be sent to compel the chief's submission, but with insufficient force available he reverted to negotiation, duly securing the release of prisoners and promise of compensation to the Ngaiterangi. Taraia even offered to give up fighting if the Governor would send some soldiers to protect his district.

At Clarke's suggestion a notice was published in the Government *Gazette* that if the Maori 'got up' again, the Governor would 'get up' also. Five months later the Tauranga tribes were again receiving the worse end of feuding, this time from the Ngatiwhakaue people of Maketu village,[55] who killed and ate a number of Ngaiterangi to avenge the loss of their young *ariki* who had disappeared while gathering potatoes from the scene of Taraia's raid, now *tapu* ground. Willoughby Shortland, Acting Governor since Hobson's death in June 1842, proposed to land troops against the Maketu settlement but when Chief Protector Clarke, Chief Justice William Martin and Attorney-General William Swainson voiced doubts about the government's legal position, they were landed instead at Tauranga and used to curb the luckless Ngaiterangi from exacting *utu*. The Ngatiwhakaue proved willing to make recompense and offer peace if the Government stationed troops among them and also at Tauranga to keep the Ngaiterangi in check. When Clarke told them that Edward Shortland would be stationed at Maketu as Sub-Protector, the chiefs were greatly pleased,[56] as the location of an official among them was taken as a mark of recognition and a fountain of the Governor's bounty and attention. It was not long before they were trying blackmail and declaring that they could not guarantee to remain peaceful unless a Protector was stationed among them. Brown and the Tauranga Christians complained that not only had the Government failed to punish the aggressors but had added insult to injury by according them a signal honour. But in view of the long-standing feud, and the likelihood that the Ngaiterangi had indeed killed the Maketu *ariki*, it was just as well that the Government had not taken sides by attacking Maketu. The Bay of Plenty incidents also show that the use of troops to garrison troubled districts, while the Protectors sought to remove sources of contention and secure necessary payments of compensation, was an application of police power which Maori communities were, in certain circumstances, willing to accept.

The question of whether the Government was capable of imposing rather than negotiating terms, had not yet been answered. Meanwhile more feuding erupted near Whakatane, and in the north the Christian chief Nopera Pana-kareao rose in defence of disputed land, claiming 'all the ancient rights and authority' of chieftainship, repudiating the authority of government and defying the Land Claims Commissioners, the missionaries, the Protectors and a threat to bring in troops. Nevertheless both outbreaks were eventually stilled by negotiation and Clarke persisted with the formulation of plans to involve the chiefs of the machinery of justice and administration.

In the Cook Strait area, however, the settlers could wait no longer. Cooped up in coastal pockets, they were irked beyond measure at the lack of finality in land claims, a consequence, they believed, of the Government's supineness, which was allegedly the basis of endless and apparently insatiable demands by the Maori. The dangerous illusion had gained currency that it needed only a show of strength on their part, since the Government appeared unwilling to provide one, to collapse Maori resistance. This belief was fed by the success of the Nelson magistrate, H. A. Thompson, who took a boatload of armed men to Cloudy Bay and by flourishing some handcuffs and threatening arrest, exacted a fine from a minor chief who had destroyed coal-working machinery on disputed ground. In June 1843 the Ngatitoa chiefs Te Rauparaha and Te Rangihaeata, conquerors and suzerains of the whole region, burned some survey huts in the disputed Wairau Valley. Thereupon Captain Arthur Wakefield and Thompson organised a ludicrous attempt to arrest Te Rauparaha for arson. The chief told the armed party that he would be quite willing to appear before 'my pakehas', the Sub-Protector and Land Claims Commissioner, to prove his rights to the Wairau Valley, but he would not submit to arrest, much less to the manacles that Thompson was again flourishing. Crying 'Englishmen forward', Wakefield launched a charge. Before long twenty-two Europeans in the party had been shot and clubbed to death by the enraged Maori.

At Wairau British law had been invoked in a wrong cause and brought into disrepute. In the aftermath, groups of Maori 'openly declared they would have nothing to do with the white man's law'. One settler wrote:

> After the Wairau affair, they seemed to be another race of people. They say they have no occasion to sell their land if they do not like; agree with Rauparaha in almost everything he says; very suspicious, obtrusive, boisterous, thieving, plundering, taking advantage of the white men in dealing; impudent, asking for anything, thinking you will give it them through fear, trying to frighten you, firing off muskets, practising their war dances and songs, eating more pork to make them strong, buying a deal of gunpowder and lead, making tomahawks, laugh at the white people, say they are cowards, the Queen is but a girl; they are ready to fight the people in Port Nicholson.[57]

The settlers, for their part, longed for vengeance. The attempt to found a colony in which the rule of law would guarantee the rights and prosperity of Maori as well as settler appeared to be foundering in a welter of racial animosity and bloodshed.

V

Some Concessions to Maori Viewpoints

During the anxious debate on the Bay of Plenty feuding Swainson and Martin opposed the sending of troops against Taraia and Tangaroa on the ground that English law could not be considered to be in force where chiefs had not signed the Treaty of Waitangi, or had signed it without clear understanding. Swainson subsequently suggested the constitution of such areas as 'Native Districts' where the Maori could live under traditional custom, subject only to the moral influence of the missionaries and Protectors.

The establishment of Native Districts, in some form, was one of the most important alternatives in Maori policy remaining to the British authorities after 1840. But Swainson's plan was opposed by George Clarke. He had decided in 1838 that it was baneful and futile to suppose that an independent Maori New Zealand could be sustained in a country that was being over-run by settlement; in 1842 he argued that Native Districts would be equally vulnerable and urged that tribes which had not yet ceded sovereignty should be prevailed upon to do so.[1]

Actually, circumstances in 1842 were not the same as they were in 1838 and Swainson's proposal did not envisage returning to the pre-1840 position. Although he would have exempted Maori dwelling in them from the obligations of British subjects, at least for a time, the Attorney-General still intended that Native Districts should be regarded as British territory. The Crown would have been in a position to disallow settler claims to land in them, or punish Europeans who committed offences there. Given this support, the Maori would themselves have been more able than the humanitarians appreciated, to control 'designing men', and admit Europeans on their own terms, as they had in the 1820s and early 1830s. The declaration of Native Districts would also have involved a *de facto* acceptance of the Maori social system, and allowed the Maori people to adapt to the Western world, at a pace and manner more of their own choosing. Nor would it have condemned them to backwardness, as humanitarian critics feared, for they had already demonstrated, and continued to demonstrate, when they had the chance, that they had both the aspirations to pursue the material and social complexities of the West, and the skill and energy to engage in the commercial enterprise which would secure them.

The result would have been a very different New Zealand, an essentially

Maori New Zealand, and this was an unpalatable prospect to missionaries, settlers and officials alike, especially with the momentum of nearly three years imperial rule in New Zealand behind them. Clarke's statement discloses the persistent concern of the humanitarians to bring the Maori under the rule of law and propel them into the new order, at a pace dictated by the paternalistic officials, rather than by the Maori themselves. There was thus a coincidence of settler and humanitarian interests, for the settlers were vehement in their opposition both to the entrenchment of Maori authority and the circumscription of settlement implied in the concept of Native Districts. Despite their limited constitutional rights in a Crown Colony it was hard for a governor to ignore the intemperate demands they raised in the press, in correspondence and in public meetings. Indeed earlier in 1842 Hobson, at the insistence of settler leaders, including the unofficial representatives on the Legislative Council, had withdrawn a draft ordinance intended—in the interests not of the Maori but of economical and efficient administration—to confine settlement to selected districts.[2] For his part, Acting Governor Shortland believed, like Clarke, that acceptance of Swainson's proposal would make government impossible. Since it was unimaginable that the tribes who had signed the Treaty would refrain from claiming the privilege of virtual independence if it were accorded to those who had not signed, the officials no doubt feared that recognition of Native Districts in the way Swainson proposed would open the floodgates of total rejection of their authority, sweeping them from the precarious foothold they had gained in the previous three years.

The Colonial Office endorsed Clarke's and Shortland's stand. British sovereignty was deemed to have been established throughout the whole country in 1840, by formal act of state, and whether they had signed the Treaty or not the Maori were all British subjects. Their claim to be able to make peace or war with one another at their own choosing could not therefore be admitted. It was expressly recalled that sovereignty had been assumed as much for the purpose of ending the lawlessness of the Maori as of protecting them from the dangers of settlement, and it was not contemplated that this responsibility should be abandoned.[3] The administration of New Zealand continued then with the Crown retaining the determination not only to persuade the Maori to abandon 'barbarous' customs, but when circumstances permitted, to compel them to do so.

However, Stephen also forcefully refuted the suggestion that 'subjection to British sovereignty and subjection to English law are convertible terms' or that native peoples in British colonies should be subject to 'the yoke of Blackstone's commentaries'.[4] He recollected that Hobson had been instructed to issue an ordinance authorising the temporary toleration of acceptable Maori customs, and wrote irritably, 'I know not what hinders the enactment of such a law'.[5] He later reflected that it was hindered 'by the spirit of legal pedantry from which no English society is ever emancipated, and by the contempt and aversion with which the European race everywhere regard the Black races'.[6]

This certainly showed appreciation of some, at least, of the basic influences shaping Maori policy in New Zealand, although Stephen had clearly not appreciated how heavily the clauses in the 1840 directions favouring recognition of Maori custom had been overlain by those indicating preference for English law.

Lord Stanley, Secretary of State for Colonies from 1841 to 1845, himself believed that in order to induce the Maori 'to be satisfied with our mode of administering justice, and to abandon their own . . . our legislation must be framed in some measure to meet their prejudices'. For example, this might require the authorisation of punishments for desecration of sacred places (*wahi tapu*) that seemed excessive to Europeans. Stanley wrote, 'We must satisfy the natives that what are considered grave offences by them will be punished by us or they will not be restrained from taking the law, or rather vengeance, into their own hands.'[7] 'Amalgamation' was still the main goal, but the immediate aim was to secure Maori acceptance of the *concept* of the rule of law and the regular administration of it through judicial institutions. Only eventually would custom be superseded by the English *code* of law, 'as the natives may learn to understand and to appreciate it'.[8]

Instructions to this effect were sent to the New Zealand officials. After the Bay of Plenty fighting Shortland was informed that except in the matter of feud and other 'barbarous' customs:

> There is no apparent reason why the aborigines should not be exempted from any responsibility to English law or to English courts of justice as far as respects their relations and dealings with each other. The native law might be sustained and the native customs tolerated, in all cases *in which no person of European birth or origin had any concern or interest*.[9]

This seemed clear enough, but, after the Wairau affray, the instructions to Captain Robert FitzRoy, the incoming Governor, seemed to allow exceptional treatment in cases involving settlers as well. It was considered necessary 'to adhere as closely as possible to the general principles of English law' but the detailed application of English legal maxims and procedures was neither possible nor just. It was for the local legislature to make the necessary amendments; that was precisely one of the motives for establishing one. Meanwhile, magistrates were to act with equity and prudence, and settlers who penetrated remote districts were not to be regarded as necessarily entitled to the protection of government.[10] FitzRoy subsequently circulated these instructions to the magistrates to show that, even when not specifically exempted by statute or ordinance, Maori were not necessarily to be treated exactly as settlers in all cases.

Meanwhile in New Zealand George Clarke had analysed the shortcomings of the English legal system from the Maori point of view. There were obvious objections such as unfamiliarity with alien procedures, the tardiness of the law, the rigidities of the law of evidence, the remoteness of the courts from the bulk of the Maori population, and the expense and uncertainty of securing a conviction against a defendant skilful in pleading or in manipulating legal technicalities. Equally serious was a fundamental difference between Maori and European forms of redress. *Muru,* formal retributive plundering, secured compensation for the victim of an offence and his kin; European criminal law merely punished the criminal—a vindictive and largely pointless proceeding in Maori eyes. European civil law did provide a system of securing damages but it was an expensive proceeding and did not cover certain offences serious in Maori eyes, such as *kanga,* or execration.

Some regular provision for adjusting adultery disputes and for legally recognising Maori customary marriages was also needed. The seduction of Maori women by settlers was not uncommon and Clarke quoted the case of a Maori who sought to recover his wife by the traditional method of dragging her off by force, only to find himself charged with assault. He added that to advise the husband to bring a damages claim in the Court of Requests for 'criminal conversation' (the nineteenth century euphemism for adultery) 'would be little better than a mockery of his distress'.[11]

To meet the situation Clarke proposed to legalise appropriate Maori customs and apply them in Native Courts consisting of the Protector of the district associated with the principal chiefs and a jury—all Maori in cases involving Maori only, half European and half Maori in 'mixed' cases. They were to be circuit courts sitting in the villages. The records of their proceedings were to be the guide to legalisation of further custom and by their adjudication on successive land disputes, a 'Domesday Book' of land claims was to be built up. 'Barbarous' modes of securing redress—including *muru*—were to be discussed in the courts so that the chiefs would be fully aware of the reasons why they were considered unacceptable. They would be asked to recommend substitutes and it was hoped that when these were publicised they would be adopted in time without coercion.

The critical part of Clarke's argument concerned enforcement. He recognised that a country 'divided into numerous independencies, each more or less embittered against others by the accumulating feuds of centuries' presented peculiar difficulties. But he argued that, if disputes were adjudicated by a sufficiently wide assemblage of chiefs, and the execution of the judgment left to them, 'their decision in most cases would be tantamount to the enforcement of the sentence'. He speculated that if, for example, Nopera Panakareao's land claims were debated by a court of northern chiefs, 'even though Noble might for a time oppose [the decision], yet eventually he would yield'. Similarly Clarke believed that the recent aggressions of Hone Heke against settlers were disapproved of by most northern chiefs and a formal condemnation of his conduct by them would restrain him.

Clarke's optimism arose partly from his misconception—widely shared among his contemporaries—that the powers of Maori chiefs were formerly 'despotic' but had declined under the influence of Christianity and settlement. He believed that the Native Courts would restore those 'traditional' powers. This view missed the basic point that the chiefs, though normally given deference, were leaders rather than rulers of their kin and had despotic powers only over enslaved enemies. It was true that if the Courts included sufficient men of high rank, fully debating problems in open session as in a traditional *runanga,* their decision would normally be deferred to. Clarke's further answer to the problem, as it had been since 1838, was to bring military force against a chief who defied a decision, the essential point being that the soldiers should appear to operate not as alien British power, but in support of the Maori civil court. If all this seemed unconvincing, Clarke was nevertheless entirely right in saying to those who raised doubts about enforcement, or about the admitted difficulty of finding sufficient money and sufficient 'officers of high character' to service the system, that the only apparent alternative (if Swainson's proposal for Native Districts was excluded) was the even more expensive and bloody solution of conquering the country by force of arms.[12]

Two incidents about this time reinforced the need for some modification of English law. In December 1843 an important Wellington chief named E Waho, arrested for theft, was twice liberated by his people in Pipitea *pa* and secured each time only when the magistrate called out the military detachment in the town. The Maori later disclosed that at E Waho's trial his senior kinsman Wi Tako Ngatata stood ready to sack Wellington if the sentence had been considered too severe.[13] Then in Auckland in February 1844 an over-zealous magistrate refused an offer by the chief Te Kawau to pay compensation for a petty theft committed by one of his kinsmen and sentenced the offender to three months' imprisonment. The enraged Te Kawau and his followers promptly snatched the prisoner bodily from the clutches of court officials and, ignoring shots by pursuing soldiers, carried him off to refuge.[14]

Wi Tako and Te Kawau had both invited settlement in their territory and neither wished for a complete break with the settlers. Indeed when his rage subsided Te Kawau returned his kinsman to custody. But FitzRoy had taken the point. He had already informed the Nelson settlers he would without delay lay before the Legislative Council 'declaratory or exceptional laws in favour of the Aborigines' that would prevent a reckless application of English legal processes such as had produced the Wairau debacle.[15] Now he summoned the Auckland chiefs to a meeting at Government House and rebuked them for being turbulent at a time when 'I and those who understand the law have been engaged in preparing special laws for your good; and particularly to prevent you being dealt with harshly or hastily in cases where you are not sufficiently acquainted with the law'. The chiefs acclaimed this and specifically asked that felons be made to pay compensation to the victims of their offences, according to the Maori principle of *utu,* instead of being subjected to the pointless and degrading European penalty of imprisonment.[16]

When FitzRoy met the Legislative Council in March 1844 he spoke of 'guardedly authorising some of the Native Chiefs to act in a qualified manner as Magistrates in their own tribes, and for granting them small salaries'.[17] To the Waikato Maori, gathering in thousands for a traditional *hui* or assembly at Remuera, Auckland, he said: 'We are preparing a law, by which it will be settled that chiefs of this country shall not be imprisoned, provided that compensation be made according to your own customs, and that two or three chiefs will answer for such compensation being made.'[18]

The measure that finally emerged, the Native Exemption Ordinance, provided that in disputes involving Maori alone no magistrate could serve a summons until two chiefs of the injured party's tribe laid an information, and then the summons or warrant would be delivered to two chiefs of the offender's tribe for execution. In cases where a Maori, living outside the limits of a town, offended against a European, the warrant was likewise to proceed to two principal chiefs, through the Protector of the district. Chiefs who executed a warrant and caused the apprehension of an offender were to receive a small payment. In criminal cases other than rape or murder, a Maori offender was allowed to go free on payment of a £20 deposit, which could be paid to the victim if the offender did not appear for trial. Similarly a Maori convicted of theft could avoid sentence on paying four times the value of the goods stolen, and this could be used to compensate the victim of the theft. Finally, it was provided that no Maori would be imprisoned for a civil offence such as debt or breach of contract.[19]

Three other ordinances of 1844 also modified English law to accommodate Maori needs. The Unsworn Testimony Ordinance, which allowed the evidence of non-Christian Maoris to be received in a court of law without the necessity of Christian oath, was of considerable practical importance, for some magistrates were declining to admit the testimony of pagan Maori seeking redress in the courts against settlers.[20] A Jurors Ordinance authorised the governor to exempt capable Maori from the property qualification for jurors and allow them to serve in a mixed jury in cases involving a Maori plaintiff or defendant. And the Cattle Trespass Ordinance of 1842, which allowed claims for damages in respect of fenced cultivations only, was amended to permit payment for damages to unfenced cultivations as well.[21]

All of these measures were unpopular with the settler community. The Cattle Trespass Ordinance, for instance, touched one of the most contentious issues in the colony. The settlers claimed the right to depasture their cattle freely without having to be responsible for damages except to people who fenced in the English manner. The new Ordinance now obliged stockowners to fence cattle in, rather than cultivators to fence them out.

But most of the settlers' fire fell on the Native Exemption Ordinance, which was regarded as setting the seal on a policy of appeasement.[22] Yet FitzRoy, himself regretting that lack of armed force obliged him to go to extremes of forbearance, had no real alternative to restricting the issue of warrants against Maori, even when the settlers were in the right in a dispute, until he had considered whether he could proceed without embroiling the whole Colony. Unless the Government could concentrate sufficient police power, or win the co-operation of sufficient chiefs, this was only sensible. And although the ordinance appeared to invite Maori to cheat in commercial transactions knowing that they could not be gaoled, or to plunder out-settlers knowing that they could go scot free unless their chiefs handed them over, they knew their strength gave them this freedom anyway. There was a strong case to be made for ratifying this situation, and trying to win the chiefs' co-operation, rather than permitting the Maori a growing sense of having success-fully defied the law.

Moreover, FitzRoy has not been given due credit for the positive aspect of his measure, the incorporation in it of the Maori principle of *utu,* or com-pensation for injured parties, instead of mere punishment of offenders. In 1845 he extended the principle from theft to assault cases, authorising the payment of half the fine for such offences to the victim of the assault.[23] This was a genuine attempt to make English law more acceptable to the Maori by incorporating a useful point of custom and in 1845 Clarke reported that it had given 'very general satisfaction to the intelligent chiefs'. In the town courts the chiefs generally paid compensation for an offence by one of their followers. If the offender was of no account in a local chief's eyes, as was the case with an increasing number of Maori—the so-called 'town rangers' who detached themselves from their *hapu* to live on the outskirts of the settlements —he went to gaol anyway. Clarke also remarked that, despite the readier recognition of the law courts that these provisions had gained from the Maori, they were still seen as appeasement by the settlers and attended by so much unpopularity 'that the magistrates have found their moral courage severely tested in carrying them into operation'.[24] Nor was any attempt made to enrol Maori jurors.

Compared with the original concept of Native Courts moreover, the offer to pay chiefs for the apprehension of an offender in their tribe was a tawdry proposal, amounting to little more than a cheap enticement to sell one of their own race to an alien justice. It made a travesty of Clarke's proposals for salaried Maori magistrates and of FitzRoy's own description of the measure when he introduced it to the Legislative Council. Various reasons contributed to the non-fulfilment of the original conceptions. Wake claims that the Native Exemption Ordinance was substantially a victory for Swainson's policy of Native Districts—an abandonment of any attempt to enforce law in Maori districts except when Maori offenders had been extradited by approaches to their chiefs.[25] This is puzzling since Clarke, an opponent of Swainson's scheme, characterised the Ordinance, soon after it passed the Legislative Council, as a 'very judicious and philanthropic measure', 'admirably adapted' to meet the needs of the situation.[26] Possibly he believed its provisions did allow for the discreet evolution of a system of salaried Maori magistrates, without the need for further legislation, for in September FitzRoy wrote to the Colonial Office for approval of payment of salaries of £1 a month to selected chiefs. Lack of funds in fact frustrated this intention during FitzRoy's governorship, but there were deeper reasons inhibiting the granting of authority and salary to the chiefs. There was widespread distrust, even among the officials, of Maori capabilities. In particular it was believed they did not possess the requisite moderation and impartiality but would use office to promote their private interests. Sub-Protector Edward Shortland described the way Maori mission teachers would mulct their congregations for personal advantage and reported that Maori 'constables' at the South Island whaling settlements who were offered £1 for each deserting seaman they returned to ship, frequently stripped their prisoners of clothing. Rather unfairly (for the Maori resorted to this practice only because they were sometimes denied the promised payment) Shortland argued: 'Similar examples, proving how little scruple the New Zealander has to turn to his profit any circumstance in his power, led me to form an opinion that it would be a dangerous experiment in the present generation, to intrust to him duties of this responsible nature.'[27] If this was how one of Clarke's own Sub-Protectors felt, the hostility of the settlers, jealous and fearful of bolstering Maori authority, may well be imagined. In 1845, Clarke wrote: 'we have been so apprehensive lest any position of the executive power should pass into their hands, that our firmest [Maori] friends have been shaken in their confidence, in our *ultimate* intentions.'[28]

In consequence of the Native Exemption Ordinance and other aspects of FitzRoy's policy which were considered appeasement, a stream of invective against the Governor was sent to London from the New Zealand settler community. Unfortunately FitzRoy also had to bear the responsibility for the rising of Hone Heke in the north. Heke was in fact that bold and enterprising leader whose appearance Clarke had half expected. The substance of his complaint was that the Government, by its customs dues, its pre-emptive right to land purchase and its efforts—weak though they were—at policing the Maori, constituted an intolerable interference in their way of life and threatened a great diminution in their status. Heke and his followers were also concerned at the increasing numbers and self-confidence of the settlers after the British acquisition of sovereignty and his statements had strongly nationalistic overtones. He urged Queen Victoria to confine her attentions to her own country which was made for the English, New Zealand having been made for the Maori. He advised his supporters not to give women to the Pakeha lest 'Before any lengthened period this island will be taken by these half-Pakehas [their offspring]'.[29] His strongest objection, however, was 'to the soldiers, who are enemies to our *mana* of the land and of the people'.[30]

In July 1844 he sought to restore the pre-1840 position by cutting down the British flagstaff at Russell (formerly Kororareka) in the Bay of Islands. FitzRoy tried to allay Maori resentment of paternalism by allowing direct dealings between settlers and Maori for land, while keeping a right of review of the transactions. Direct dealing of this kind was in fact very much in accord with the wishes of the northern Maori who were anxious to raise capital to buy coastal trading schooners. But it could not by itself placate Heke, and it constituted, together with a relaxation of the customs duties, a major change of policy which London considered hasty and excessive, especially as it seriously altered the financial arrangements for the Colony.

But FitzRoy did not mean to deal with Heke by appeasement. Heke's attack on the flagstaff was considered by the officials, including Clarke, to be a perfectly appropriate opportunity to use force in order to compel acceptance of British authority. FitzRoy sent immediately to Governor Gipps of New South Wales for troops and moved against Heke. Before he could land his reinforcements, however, he was prevailed upon by the other Bay of Islands chiefs to accept their guarantee of Heke's future good behaviour. They laid guns at FitzRoy's feet and entreated him to continue patiently his policy of resting British authority on the support of the chiefs. Mohi Tawhai said, 'don't imagine that evil will entirely cease; it will not; you must expect more troubles from us; but when they come, settle them in this way, and not with guns and soldiers.' Anaru said: 'Don't be discouraged Governor.'[31]

This frank pleading was certainly disarming and FitzRoy can hardly be blamed for placing confidence in the good offices of men like Waka Nene and Mohi Tawhai. But he had been led by them to over-estimate their authority over younger chiefs like Heke. Moreover there was widespread sympathy with Heke's point of view, if not with his mode of expressing it. Even the stalwart Waka Nene, smouldering about a government regulation which prohibited the random cutting of *kauri* timber, was saying in January 1845 that he had been over-hasty in signing the Treaty of Waitangi.[32] Te Heuheu Tukino and other great chiefs in the centre of the island also registered their support, as they considered that the chiefs in the settled districts had lost their land, liberty and station, and feared a similar fate.[33] Heke continued his sporadic depredations and resumed his assaults on the flagstaff in early 1845.

This new activity coincided with an alarm at the Wanganui settlement when a large *taua* of Ngatituwharetoa and Ngatimaniapoto warriors under Te Heuheu Iwikau came down to avenge a defeat by the Ngatiruanui in 1839. Under little restraint by Te Heuheu, who claimed that a settler had taken produce from him at Taupo and not paid for it, they pilfered from houses and gardens and postured suggestively at settler women until persuaded by the Taranaki Sub-Protector Donald McLean and the missionaries to restore stolen property and go home. By the beginning of 1845 also Te Rauparaha and Rangihaeata had alienated former sympathisers by not evacuating the Upper Hutt valley for which they had sought and already received compensation. A recent study suggests that Te Rauparaha still had unrequited grievances and was not in fact being unreasonable about them,[34] but numbers of officials were beginning to believe, with the settlers, that they could never reach finality in land claims unless the Government showed itself capable of over-awing the powerful chiefs. Men who had long taken the Maori side against settler pressure—Mathew Richmond, the Superintendent of the Southern Settlements, Edmund Forsaith, the Sub-Protector, and Octavius Hadfield, the redoubtable Anglican missionary at Otaki, together with some of the younger Christian chiefs, all urged that the time had come to subdue Te Rauparaha, hopefully by the display, rather than the exercise, of overwhelming force.[35]

Early 1845 then appeared to be a new point of crisis for British rule in New Zealand and FitzRoy sought to answer it by calling on Sydney again for reinforcements of regular troops. Like Hobson, and with good reason, he feared the provocative effect of enrolling settler militia. He was also too uncertain of the support of the northern chiefs to call upon them to assist him actively against Heke. Beckham, the magistrate at Russell, completely unsure of himself in dealings with Maori, actually declined an offer by local chiefs to help defend the town, which Heke was then threatening. Gipps, not realising the urgency of the situation, was slow in sending reinforcements. Before they arrived Heke and his ally Kawiti attacked Russell, the military officers bungled the defence, and the town was sacked. Waka Nene, with other Ngapuhi leaders, immediately engaged Heke, largely because, as Clarke put it, he saw in him 'a lusting ambition, which, if gratified, would undermine his own and other Chiefs' position and authority'.[36] Chiefs like Nene, and those who had agreed with the authorities on the site for the flagstaff at Russell, also considered themselves as having entered into some relationship with the British which, whatever reservations they themselves had, was not for Heke to disturb. The Kaipara tribes under Tirarau and the Waikato people under Te Wherowhero, traditional enemies of the Ngapuhi and without any particular grievance against the British, pledged themselves to defend Auckland. It was soon clear that Heke's challenge to British rule was precipitating more active support for the British than active antagonism.

Nevertheless the sack of Russell ruined FitzRoy and he was made the scapegoat of settler fury and Colonial Office embarrassment. The tragedy was not just FitzRoy's but that of the future of New Zealand race relations as well. The climax of Heke's depredations was held by the settler community to stem from FitzRoy's pandering to Maori 'bounce'. Consequently the spirit of co-operation and conciliation by which he had sought to win Maori acquiescence in British rule was utterly discredited, along with its protagonists —FitzRoy and the Protectorate Department.

The truth of the matter was that Maori turbulence had occurred in spite of, not because of, FitzRoy's main line of policy. Heke, like many of his fellow chiefs, was reacting against the pressure of European government. The answer seemed to be contained either in the declaration of Native Districts or, alternatively, in the principles applied, albeit ineptly, in the legislation of 1844: firstly, not to press English law too hard upon the Maori; secondly, to modify the provisions of the laws that were applied to suit Maori requirements; thirdly, to give the chiefs an effective role in the machinery of state. Of course this policy needed to be backed—as it was not under FitzRoy—

by an adequate police power and magisterial staff, both incorporating Maori as far as possible, and used with skill and discretion.

Details of the Native Exemption Ordinance reached London about the same time as news of Heke's rising. Stephen's reaction on first reading the Ordinance was: 'this is a wise Law. . . . But it seems much calculated to provoke objection'. When the expected objections from the settlers in New Zealand duly reached London, Hope, the Parliamentary Under-Secretary, suggested that the Ordinance was too favourable to the Maori. Stephen replied that objections were easy to find but that even weightier objections could be found to leaving the law as it was without the Ordinance, but 'Perhaps it might be well in writing to Capn. Grey [who had by then been selected to succeed FitzRoy] to point out the prima facie difficulties . . . that it may appear hereafter that the Law was not unsifted, nor swallowed whole, from any undue bias in favour of the Natives'.[37] Stephen seemed to wish to retain the substance of FitzRoy's measure and make only some gesture to placate settler criticism. However the letter that went out to Grey was a clear statement that FitzRoy's zeal had outrun his discretion. Since 'laws weighted too much in favour of the weaker party will by the sure operation of familiar causes defeat their own ends', Grey was instructed to lose no time in having the Ordinance amended so as to confine its application as far as possible to relations between Maori only and to make no concession in law enforcement 'which can be avoided by any means consistent with the public safety'.[38]

It is possible that Stanley himself stiffened the tone of this despatch for he was noticeably more hostile than Stephen to measures appearing to favour the Maori,[39] but the reference to the liberality of the Native Exemption Ordinance defeating its own ends is entirely in keeping with Stephen's overriding scepticism about the ability of government to protect the Maori from the demands of the settlers. This attitude had caused him in 1840 to favour a policy leaning more towards amalgamation than protection and it now led to his advocating modification of a law he originally termed 'wise' because it was aggravating settler prejudices. Just as officials in New Zealand tended to be discouraged by settler criticism from schemes for Maori constables or Maori magistrates, so also the Colonial Office shrank from giving Maori privileges under the law, even though they were calculated to win eventual Maori support for the rule of law. The replacement of FitzRoy by George Grey, whose memorandum arguing against exceptional laws for native peoples had been singled out for praise by the Commons Committee on New Zealand in 1844, marked the interest, in London, in resuming the policy of pressing amalgamation at a rapid pace. Gladstone, Stanley's successor, hammered home the point. Grey, he wrote, was to stand between the settlers and the Maori, but not, as FitzRoy was considered to have done, in such a way as to cause a separation which aroused jealously and discouraged association between the two races.[40]

VI

Sharing State Power

On the face of it there could hardly have been found a Governor less sympathetic to Maori leaders' concern for traditional prerogatives and values than George Grey. His memorandum on native policy in 1840 had argued that British law should supersede native custom as quickly as possible and that natives afflicted by customary sanctions should be able to appeal to it, and he reiterated this theme early in his New Zealand governorship.[1]

Yet his handling of Heke's rising showed considerable respect for Maori viewpoints. He co-operated well with Nene and the other 'native allies' upon whom success against Heke depended and his decision not to persist with FitzRoy's attempt to confiscate 'rebel' land removed the worst obstacle to the growth of reconciliation between the Government and the northern tribes.

In the south, however, having made some concession to Maori claims to reserves in the Wellington district, he quickly moved over to a not-to-be-trifled-with attitude and ushered settlers into still-disputed areas of the Hutt Valley, to the accompaniment of military demonstration and destruction of Maori property. According to a number of reputable contemporary opinions and the only detailed historical analysis of the question, this wrecked a good chance of settling remaining Maori claims in the area by negotiation.[2] When the excluded Maori replied to the new incursions by plundering settler property and became involved in a skirmish with an outpost of troops, Grey proclaimed martial law and embarked on the 'pacification' of the district, a policy which drove a succession of chiefs, including the upper Wanganui leaders, into active opposition.

As in the north the defeat of 'rebel' chiefs rested heavily on the assistance of other tribes. For example, after the killing of the Gilfillan family by upper Wanganui Maori in 1847 the lower Wanganui chiefs, from long-standing rivalry and from fear of being blamed for the killings, themselves rounded up the attackers. The refusal of Wiremu Kingi and the section of the Atiawa people located at Waikanae, to join the rebellion, was also important to the safety of Wellington. Having compelled the 'rebels' to withdraw to the interior Grey sought to consolidate his hold by extending roads out of Wellington, a policy which also involved the assistance of Maori, working on wage labour under the direction of Captain A. H. Russell of the 58th Regiment.

Grey's policy of imposing British authority by military methods was highly popular with the settlers and with many missionaries and officials. But Grey had brushed aside moral and legal principles in declaring martial law, in seizing Te Rauparaha and holding him without trial, in transporting five Maori to Tasmania after military court martial[3] and in hanging a Wanganui chief named Martin Luther more by way of example than because he was personally guilty of capital crimes. Although having an immediate effect as demonstrations of power, these acts were also widely regarded, and remembered long afterwards among the North Island tribes, as acts of oppression and treachery.

For his part, Grey had seen how the Wanganui 'rebels', through their command of the interior and the operation of wider kinship connections, had obtained arms from the tribes at Poverty Bay on the opposite coast. The resources of the formidable North Island tribes in their inaccessible hinterland disturbed him, and much of his ingenuity was thenceforth spent on the problem of making inroads upon them.

In the field of civil administration Grey soon found himself at loggerheads with the Protectorate Department. Clarke disagreed with the whole tenor of Grey's approach—his proclaimed desire to destroy the authority of the chiefs, supplant Maori custom with common law and force the pace of amalgamation. He also criticised some of Grey's early actions such as his appearance with the troops in the war against Heke. Grey was too autocratic in temperament to bear easily with anyone who was not wholeheartedly in accord with him. Moreover, the Protectorate Department carried an embarrassing legacy of unpopularity with the settlers for its supposed appeasement of the Maori during FitzRoy's governorship. Grey therefore made a scapegoat of it, blaming it for past mistakes, indulging in vindictive attacks on some of its personnel, and finally disbanding it.[4] In so doing he destroyed an organisation which, despite its much-publicised failures, had quietly achieved considerable success in mitigating Maori-Pakeha conflict. The Protectorate had also begun to amass detailed knowledge upon which policy could be based in such fields as Maori land tenure, and the cessation of this development was unfortunate. There was not again to be a department of government so sensitive to Maori viewpoints and the absence of it was to be extremely serious in the next decade.

The office of Native Secretary with which Grey replaced the Protectorate was little more than that of a clerk working under the Governor, mainly in the interests of promoting land settlement. The first Native Secretaries were, successively, J. Symonds and C. A. Dillon. In 1848, after the division of New Zealand into two provinces under the 1846 constitution, Major C. L. Nugent became Native Secretary in the northern province of New Ulster while H. T. Kemp, a former Sub-Protector, became Native Secretary to Lieutenant-Governor Eyre in the southern province, New Munster, with headquarters at Wellington. Of these men, only Kemp had any fluency in Maori language. The Native Secretaries arranged hospitality for visiting Maori, negotiated land purchases and sought to adjust such disputes over land as came to their notice. Kemp also employed himself in making a detailed census of the Wellington district and translating *Robinson Crusoe* and *Pilgrim's Progress* into Maori for use in the church schools.[5] During their land-purchase operations the Native Secretaries frequently made long journeys into the interior, gathering information and settling disputes. The former Sub-Protector Donald McLean, who became an Inspector of Police in Taranaki and Land Purchase Commissioner, also held a magistrate's commission for New Munster and heard cases on his journeys. Even the Colonial Secretary and Surveyor-General on their sporadic visits to out-districts exercised their magisterial commissions. For the regular machinery of local administration and justice among the Maori Grey had introduced, from Australian models, the office of Resident Magistrate.

The Resident Magistrate and his associated machinery were to become the most important institution mediating European law and administration to the Maori. The Resident Magistrates' Courts Ordinance of 1846 gave the Resident Magistrate a summary jurisdiction in disputes between Maori and Pakeha. For disputes involving only Maori, he was to constitute, with two chiefs appointed as Assessors, a Court of Arbitration; no judgment was to be carried into effect unless all three members of the Court were agreed.[6] The Reverend Richard Taylor subsequently claimed that Grey copied the Assessor system from his appointment of leading Wanganui chiefs as 'magistrates' of the missionary congregations, 'to preserve order and put down all open sin and wickedness' and to mollify men of rank who were losing influence to the mission teachers. But in formulating plans for overcoming Heke's rebellion, before he had ever met Taylor or visited Wanganui, Grey had already proposed appointing some chiefs as 'Native Magistrates', with salaries of about £20 a year, payable monthly, in order to attach them to the Government. They were to control their own people, delivering to the European magistrate those guilty of serious offences against settlers, and to report regularly on the state of their districts.[7] Moreover, although Grey condemned FitzRoy's Native Exemption Ordinance, reporting that the Maori had 'not the slightest regard or value for it', (from which it has been generally assumed that Grey repealed it entirely[8]) his Resident Magistrates' Courts Ordinance in fact drew upon it to a very considerable extent. The provision against executing a judgment in Maori cases unless the two Assessors concurred with the Resident Magistrate was an improved version of FitzRoy's requirements that a summons or warrant should proceed only through two chiefs; like FitzRoy, Grey dropped his initial intention of paying Assessors a regular salary, and his provision for payment of £5 for each successful execution of judgment was synonymous with FitzRoy's method of payment by results; Grey's Ordinance adopted FitzRoy's important principle of allowing persons convicted of theft or assault to avoid gaol sentence by paying into court four times the value of the property stolen, which payment could be used to compensate the victim of the offence;

and Maori accused of crimes could not, except within the limits of towns, be apprehended except on the warrant, not now of a Protector, but of a Resident Magistrate. Obviously, although Grey trumpeted loudly about extending English law over the Maori he did not intend to apply it if he was uncertain whether they would submit.

In two important respects, however, Grey's Ordinance was a considerable improvement on FitzRoy's. Previously, Maori could not recover debts or claim damages except through the expensive and inaccessible Court of Requests. Now the authority given to Resident Magistrates to settle minor civil claims summarily created a prompt and flexible machinery for adjusting the disputes constantly arising between Maori and settlers. Secondly the Court of Arbitration in Maori cases, comprising the Resident Magistrate and leading chiefs as Assessors, came close to Clarke's original concept of a Native Court. The Resident Magistrate Courts were also inexpensive. FitzRoy had already authorised the waiving of complainant's fees and Grey now authorised the payment of witnesses' expenses from the justice vote. In Auckland at least the Government retained a solicitor to act for Maori. Interpreters were attached to each court and were frequently the officials whom Maori complainants first approached. Many sons of early settlers or missionaries, who had learned the Maori language from childhood, began a career in Maori administration through the office of Interpreter to the Courts.

The Colony's law-enforcement machinery was strengthened by a Constabulary Ordinance of 1846, authorising the recruitment of an armed police.[9] Numbers of Maori were enrolled in the force under Pakeha officers. In the smaller centres they tended to be young men of chiefly rank who had considerable influence in adjusting relations between Maori and settlers. In the main centres many who were employed constructing roads and barracks for the Royal Engineers expressed a wish to join the police and were duly recruited. They worked with Pakeha constables, making arrests of both Maori and settlers, and served in the courts. Grey reported that the appointments at first 'excited unbounded ridicule' among the settlers, but by 1850 there were a score or more Maori constables in both Auckland and Wellington, and smaller enrolments in New Plymouth, Wanganui and Mangonui. Grey also expressed his intention of creating a native military corps, under Pakeha officers, but did not persist with this, probably because of his doubts about the 'volatile and independent character of the New Zealanders' and the evident reluctance of the settler community to see the Maori officially armed.[10]

The extension of the Resident Magistrate system which followed was well illustrated in the Wanganui River district. During the fighting of 1847 the lower Wanganui *hapu* centred in Putiki *pa* had become closely involved with the government in the joint campaign against the upper Wanganui *hapu*. Major Wyatt, garrison commander in the declining stages of the fighting, reported that the Maori 'had always been in the habit of coming to me to adjust their differences'. Wyatt was then commissioned Resident Magistrate.

He considered that the Maori had dropped the 'bullying, swaggering manner' they had displayed in the period of uneasy relations with the settlers before 1847 and showed a 'reasonable and constructive' attitude in disputes which was rapidly winning the respect of officials and settlers. Wyatt first used his Assessors, principal chiefs such as Mete Kingi and Hoani Wiremu (John Williams) Hipango, as witnesses only in cases between Maori and settler, to prevent 'garbled and magnified' accounts of the proceedings circulating among the local *hapu*. But he soon found their active assistance in hearings to be judicious and effective and began to press for regular salaries for them.[11] This was declined as likely to set a precedent for similar requests which the revenue could not bear and ten shillings a day for important hearings was fixed as the rate of pay. Wyatt was also told that under the Resident Magistrates' Courts Ordinance, Assessors were supposed to take part in proceedings only in cases between two Maori, not in 'mixed cases'.[12] Wyatt henceforth used Assessors as unofficial advisers in mixed cases, but his court in Maori cases consisted of himself and three or four Assessors, formally appointed.

As the up-river *hapu* began to drop their former hostility and trade freely with the town, Wyatt recommended the principal men of each settlement as Assessors. By 1850 Wyatt's successor, J. W. Hamilton, reported a request that a Resident Magistrate be stationed up-river 'that there might be some confidence in the judgments of the Assessors and precedents established by which they might be guided'. Hamilton began a judicial circuit up-river by canoe, accompanied by some of the Maori police and Assessors from Wanganui. In 1851 he extended his circuit to the adjacent Rangitikei district where the people reported 'that they were under great difficulty in settling their small cases, and the Whanganui was too far to go'. In Wanganui itself Hamilton was 'called almost daily' to settle small disputes, which required prompt attention if they were not to rankle and grow.[13]

The extension of the system was greatly assisted by the fact that the authority of powerful and high-ranking chiefs like Hoani Wiremu Hipango and Pehi Turoa was well-established in their districts. (On the nearby Waitotara river the lines of tribal authority were not so well-defined and disputes more frequently gave rise to assemblies where they were discussed, often inconclusively, amidst much jealousy.)[14] There was inevitably some confusion of church and state law in Maori eyes, especially as the state system of justice was represented as based on Christian principles. But many saw the coming of the *ture* (as the officials designated state law) as a new thing and on occasion appealed to the Resident Magistrate against the penalties of the mission magistrates.[15]

The Wanganui Magistrates reported that in 'mixed' cases Maori were most frequently the complainants. Although it had been designed principally to apply to Maori offenders, the principle of levying fines for thefts and assaults and paying the fine to the injured parties was applied to convicted Pakeha as well, since as Hamilton stated, 'it is highly doubtful whether

Maoris would come from a distance [to lay complaints] if they never received any portion of the fines levied'. Civil disputes increased with the increasing flow of trade on the Wanganui river, Maori being complainants in five out of seven cases. Hamilton added that, since many of the up-river Maori were pagan, the Unsworn Testimony Ordinance was an essential part of the judicial system. The principal offence by Maori against settlers was petty theft. In most cases this did not lead to a formal hearing but a mediation, with the accused restoring the stolen goods and offering compensation.[16]

Among Maori themselves the most fruitful source of quarrels was adultery, which was considered to be increasing as chiefs ceased to exact the old penalty of death. It was said to be most common among the wives of Christian converts and despite church law, which usually banished offending males to the bush for a month or two and sentenced offending women to community work, new adultery cases arose week by week. The Resident Magistrates and Assessors usually settled them by ordering payment by the offending parties to the aggrieved spouse. In addition, a wide variety of other disputes of a customary kind was brought forward. Hoani Wiremu, for example, laid complaint against a woman who had, without his consent, tried vainly to save his sick child by the traditional practice of cutting the body with shells. The Resident Magistrate and Assessors concluded that the healer had acted with the best intentions but fined her what was considered to be the heavy sum of £10 in order to discourage the practice.[17]

Wyatt and Hamilton also reported that the Maori always appeared satisfied with the decisions of the courts, even when they were the losers. Civil summonses were rarely evaded, in many cases the amount sued for being paid into court before the day of the hearing. The practice of settling debts through the Resident Magistrate soon became well established in New Zealand. The Resident Magistrates noted, however, that it would be difficult to send anyone for trial to the Supreme Court in Wellington, partly from the fear of prison sentences and partly from the inconvenience to the parties and witnesses involved. A stabbing affray at Wangaehu and other relatively serious matters were therefore dealt with under minor counts that came within the Resident Magistrate's jurisdiction. Yet the Assessors did concur in the sending of a particularly troublesome man, Te Ahuru, to Wellington for trial for a serious felony. J. W. Hamilton reported only one case of outright defiance, not surprisingly involving a kinsman of Martin Luther, the chief executed by Grey.[18]

The role of the Assessors was of critical importance to the system. Their working with the Resident Magistrate helped identify him as part of the local community, particularly where he involved himself sympathetically with the people and treated his Assessors as responsible lieutenants. In such circumstances the taking of disputes before the court did not appear to the local Maori as an appeal *outside* their group; group cohesion, still important to all but a few thrusting and ambitious people, was not impaired.

Some of the chiefs were chosen as Assessors by Grey or McLean specifically because they favoured land-selling,[19] but the men appointed on the Resident Magistrates' recommendations were generally chosen with the principal purpose of promoting law and order. For their part Assessors undoubtedly accepted appointment largely for the enhanced prestige and real power it gave them. Although, strictly speaking, they had no statutory authority to do so, they frequently heard cases on their own. Pehi Turoa, for example, was very zealous, in some cases oppressively so, in travelling about his district to investigate disputes. He pleaded for a salary on account of the time involved (a request with which the Resident Magistrates sympathised) but was not unduly deterred when this was declined. When the Assessors acted alone they were inclined to pass very draconian sentences, particularly for adultery, which were in keeping with traditional values but entirely unsanctioned by law. These the Resident Magistrate had to modify.[20] Hamilton also noted that the inland Assessors 'require some guidance as to the mode of soliciting evidence'.[21] Otherwise the Assessors' sense of equity was remarkable. At least when they sat with the Resident Magistrate, in sifting through the rights and wrongs of often incredibly complex disputes about pigs or horses or debts, they did not appear to favour kinsmen; in fact they could be very severe with them. They often appeared as defaulters themselves in civil suits and accepted the verdict.[22]

The Resident Magistrate system also developed easily in the far north. In the 1840s the small town of Mangonui was heavily frequented by whaling vessels, mostly American. In 1848 W. B. White, the well-educated son of a retired naval officer, having served the Government as Ensign of the militia in the war of 1846-7, was posted to Mangonui as Collector of Customs and Inspector of Police with a detachment of twelve armed constables, some of them Maori.[23] Like Wyatt in Wanganui he was immediately resorted to by local Maori in disputes with settlers; to give him the requisite statutory authority Grey made him a Resident Magistrate and asked him to nominate Assessors. A meeting of chiefs at Kaitaia duly named Nopera Panakareao and Puhipi (Busby), the foremost chiefs of the Rarawa people.[24]

White's records document the persistence of feuding between the *hapu* of the district, over boundary disputes, sorcery, adultery or cursing. A few particularly truculent chiefs were responsible for most of the resorts to arms, which sometimes resulted in two or three people being shot on either side. In many cases, however, White was able to avert fighting, because he could invariably count on the support of Puhipi whose high traditional rank was matched by a steadiness and intelligence which would have made him an outstanding man in any community. The working partnership of White and Puhipi in fact demonstrated possibilities in the Resident Magistrate and Assessor system far richer than the formal duties set out in the Ordinance.

Nopera Panakareao was of much less help. He periodically engaged in feuding himself and on one occasion repudiated White's authority as Collector of Customs, threatening to imitate Hone Heke, kill the Europeans and monopolise trade himself. White sent to Auckland and a man-of-war promptly arrived to over-awe the chief.[25] Nopera was in fact acting almost alone, the small Rarawa tribe too highly valuing the British connection as a support against their powerful neighbours the Ngapuhi to break relations lightly.

In general the system was essential to keep peace between settlers and Maori. The reasonableness of most Maori once it was clear that officials were taking note of their grievances and points of view was often apparent. Near New Plymouth for example, a settler named Brown, mistakenly thinking that a *muru* party from the Puketapu *hapu* had taken his Maori mistress's property, struck the leader of the party, an important chief named Witana, seriously injuring him. Three hundred Puketapu then gathered to attack the town, but other Maori, including Witana himself, urged them to refrain, since the police under Donald McLean had arrested Brown. On the day of the hearing Witana was carried to the court on a stretcher surrounded by eighty or ninety armed Maori. Brown was abject, and the Puketapu agreed to his release on payment of a horse in compensation and the right to war dance through the town. The affair culminated in McLean enrolling some of the chiefs in his police force.[26]

Another Taranaki case illustrates the conflicts and confusions of the time. A settler named Bayley tried to extract half the cost of a boundary fence from his Maori neighbours, but after some dispute the officials decided that the Fencing Ordinance did not apply. Bayley therefore declared that 'he wouldn't fence for natives'. When Maori cattle subsequently came onto Bayley's unfenced wheat he drove them out, injuring some in the process. Their owners asked for compensation but, not getting it, seized goods from Bayley's house and left them with an Assessor until they could receive payment for the injured cattle. Bayley applied for a warrant against the Maori for theft. This the Resident Magistrate, Joseph Flight, declined on the grounds that the Maori were not trying to appropriate the goods but force an inquiry and obtain compensation. However, he told the Maori that no inquiry would be made until they returned Bayley's goods and after some discussion this was done. Bayley then counter-claimed for damage to his wheat and in the eventual settlement received ten shillings damages.[27] Endless variations on the theme of fencing, cattle trespass and theft, were the stock-in-trade of lawsuits on the New Zealand frontier. The necessity for an efficient judicial system taking account of the needs of both Maori and settler was daily apparent.

In declining to charge the Maori with theft Flight had shown an appreciation of their viewpoints. There was a tendency for Resident Magistrates, under constant pressure from settlers, to act legalistically and charge Maori, including high chiefs, with offences which were at most technical and often committed under provocation. The Wanganui magistrate, D. S. Durie, who succeeded Wyatt and Hamilton, was inclined to act this way and impaired relations with his Assessors.[28] Mostly though, this was for the future. In the 1840s and 1850s, the Maori generally held the weight of power and magistrates had to be circumspect. Consequently the Resident Magistrate system generally appeared to the Maori to be helpful but not restrictive and by the end of Grey's governorship there were signs that it could rapidly be extended. The Bay of Islands trader James Clendon was increasingly approached by Maori to settle disputes and by 1853 he too reported that it was 'almost a daily occurrence' for them to write or come to him to adjust their differences.[29] A small community in the Marlborough Sound, troubled by a turbulent shore whaling settlement, whose occupants periodically shot their pigs, requested intervention. At Kawhia, concern at the granting by the Auckland licensing authorities of 'grog licences' to bush taverns in the district caused a meeting of chiefs and settlers to petition for a Resident Magistrate. The chiefs at Rangiaowhia in the upper Waikato asked for the appointment of a Resident Magistrate and Assessors to control disputes between Maori and squatters.[30] Raharuhi Rukupo, a leading chief of Poverty Bay, wrote to Grey:

> We want a law at our place to look into our faults and those of the Europeans . . . we are unacquainted with the wrong trading or dealings of the Europeans of selling rum, and taking our food without payment, of cursing us. The Europeans are also displeased at our . . . taking their horses and property without payment.[31]

The missions' practice of adjusting disputes at regular committees of teachers and chiefs also encouraged judicial proceedings. The Waikato missionary, B. J. Ashwell, reported that Maori of his district tended to 'pity and despise the people of other areas where the Natives are eating one another'.[32] This view (probably exaggerated, though cannibalism may have been still occurring in remote areas) reflected an interest in orderly proceedings as well as traditional pride in being ahead of rivals. In the last years of his governorship Grey was therefore emboldened to make some appointments in the out-districts, in addition to the Resident Magistrates at the main settlements and the new towns like Napier, all of whom had an increasing flow of cases involving Maori. Accordingly, T. H. Smith, a government surveyor, was sent to Rotorua and the Bay of Plenty in 1852 and F. D. Fenton, a settler with legal training, to Kaipara in 1853.

In the Bay of Plenty Smith enlisted support from Tohi Te Ururangi, the leading warrior of Maketu, who took the name of Winiata Pekama (Wynyard Beckham), after the Resident Magistrate of Auckland, just as chiefs accepting baptism took the name of a biblical figure or prominent contemporary Churchman. And as many mission teachers who were concerned largely with their status and advancement frequently acted independently in directions the missionaries could not approve, so Winiata, extremely zealous in scouring the country for disputes to judge, resented having some of his more outrageous judgments or sentences reversed by the Resident Magistrate.[33] Nevertheless the system of British law had been introduced to the district and Winiata remained a supporter of government.

At Rotorua, however, it was revealed that a magistrate unsupported by police or military force was still in a very difficult position. Smith made little headway because of a recent repudiation of British law by Wi Maihi Te Rangikaheke, the ambitious, assertive and inconstant leader of the Ngati-whakaue in that district. Earlier, when Sub-Protector Shortland had been stationed at Maketu, Wi Maihi had agreed that he should have authority to settle all things—'lands and property taken, married women who have been seduced, also men clan-fighting, also the cursing of heads, also the native *tapu*'. When that had been followed by a general peace among the Rotorua, Tauranga and Waikato tribes, arranged by Shortland and the missionaries, 'then for the first time' Wi Maihi wrote, 'the thousands became aware that the spiritual head of the peace was Christ and the head of this world the Queen'. But in 1851 Wi Maihi had asked the police at Tauranga to fetch from a Tauranga tribe a woman whom he said belonged to the Ngatiwhakaue. When the police found she did not want to return and dropped the matter, Wi Maihi threatened to take her by force. Warned that he could be imprisoned for this he angrily disassociated himself and his people from the laws of England, in all disputes affecting Maori alone.[34] Although neither Wi Maihi's acceptance nor his rejection of British law was as thoroughgoing as his rhetoric suggested, Smith's position at Rotorua was thereafter generally limited to that of mediation in disputes between Maori and settlers. The Rotorua people, moreover, continued to scorn the Treaty of Waitangi—'that *pukapuka* [book, document] which the Ngapuhi signed'.[35]

The mixed response of Maori communities to British law was neatly illustrated when Resident Magistrate Beckham of Auckland travelled to the East Cape district by ship to hear charges against local youths who had broken into the home of the local missionary, Ralph Barker. One section of the offending *hapu,* perhaps from a sense of shame, let Beckham take three of the culprits off to Auckland to serve a four months' gaol sentence; but the parents of the remaining four held back their children and built strong *pa,* defying the rest of the community to fetch them.[36]

Despite the progress of the missions, killings continued to occur within Maori society for a variety of traditional reasons. When a high-ranking chief became ill or died someone was likely to be killed for sorcery; women were killed for adultery; infants were killed by mothers to avenge their husbands' infidelities; the host at a feast was killed by guests whom he inadvertently served the hindquarters of a pig still containing faeces. These affairs sometimes gave rise to feuding, especially if they came as sparks to an already smouldering hostility about land or earlier battles. Where the killings were relatively isolated, traditional and terminal events, government interference in them was still resented, even by Assessors who were normally active in assisting Resident Magistrates to secure general stability and suppress feuding. Even Waka Nene, pro-government though he was, told Nugent, when the Native Secretary investigated some particularly repugnant killings in the Bay of Islands, that British law did not suit these matters and that no Maori would assist in securing the surrender of a man who killed a sorcerer or adulterer.[37]

In Auckland or Wellington, although arrests of Maori could now normally be made without forcible release of the prisoner, they often still involved considerable fuss, involving bystanders and soldiers as well as police. After two minor affrays in 1847, Auckland police were instructed not to make arrests for trivial matters.[38] In 1851 the celebrated Ngatipaoa invasion of Auckland caused great alarm. Some Ngatipaoa and Ngatitamatera Maori had attempted the release of one of the latter tribe, arrested for stealing a shirt. In the ensuing scuffle Te Hoera, a high-ranking Ngatipaoa chief, was struck on the head— the seat of personal *tapu*—by a Maori constable. Deeply affronted, Te Hoera rallied his people who arrived in Auckland in six war canoes, seeking *utu*. But, as in the case of Heke's rising, the local Ngatiwhatua and Waikato tribes said they would support the Pakeha and this, together with Grey's deployment of troops and a warship, caused them to depart, along with Taraia and the Ngatitamatera who were coming to join them. Some anti-settler stirrings among the southern tribes, aroused by rumours of a general northern rising, also died.[39]

Despite its military successes against Heke and Rangihaeata, and the partial success of the Resident Magistrate system, the establishment of the rule of British law therefore still remained a primary task for the Government. Grey, rightly, appeared unhurried. The sporadic violence within Maori society was accepted without undue concern. The Native Secretary, on hearing of a killing for sorcery or adultery would simply send a letter to the tribe concerned expressing the Government's horror.[40] Grey reported to London, 'for the next few years collisions will occasionally take place between adjacent tribes, and that no care upon the part of the Government will be able to prevent the recurrence of such events; these disputes, however, will not lead to anything that may be termed a native war'.[41] Although this statement carries an optimistic gloss (illustrating one of Grey's techniques of creating the right impression in London), it is true that, except for the heavier fighting between the Tuhourangi and Ngatiwhakaue divisions of the Arawa people from 1848 through to the mid-1850s, the tribal collisions of the time were generally within the highly institutionalised conventions of Polynesian feuding and did not often produce many casualties.

The Government also appeared unhurried about much of the settler clamour for enforcement of law. The records of Resident Magistrates are filled with settler correspondence inveighing against the weakness of the law and the contempt with which Maori sometimes treated Resident Magistrates' attempts to negotiate redress. There was much talk about the rights of British subjects to protection in a British colony, and demands for strong action. Occasionally the Native Secretary did go with a small party of soldiers to investigate a settler's complaint, but the officials often found complainants to be irascible people who had provoked the Maori to some retaliation. While deeply disliking the necessity to defer to Maori strength they were quite terse in setting aside the demands of settlers 'who have scattered themselves all over the Country in positions where the Government cannot protect them'.[42] However, although the out-settlers were generally leasing land from chiefs in defiance of the Crown's pre-emptive right which Grey had restored with the Native Land Purchase Ordinance, 1846, this was not invoked by the Government except to support a threat to remove a particularly troublesome settler.

Official restraint notwithstanding the very acceptance of a British-style rule of law by part of the population, settler and Maori included, intensified the need to bring the remainder under its restraints. The point was forcefully made in 1849 following the murder of a settler family near Wellington by Maroro, an outcast from the Ngatikahungunu tribe. Maroro had no friends among the Ngatitoa of Wellington, who approved rather than opposed his trial and execution. Shortly afterwards, however, Puaha, a Ngatitoa chief, complained that his brother and other kin who had gone to Wairoa, in Ngati-kahungunu territory, to recover a runaway wife from the whaling station there, had been killed by the Ngatikahungunu because their people had condoned Maroro's execution. Puaha wrote: 'We are the more concerned because it is connected with the carrying out of our New System of Law. Had it been in connection with our own usages, the sun would scarcely set ere our revenge would be obtained; as the case stands now everything remains with you.'[43] Puaha's allegation was open to doubt. There were a great many possible reasons for the death of his kinsmen and it would not have been the first or the last occasion that a chief sought to manipulate the authorities into serving their cause in a tribal dispute. The Government therefore did not act on his complaint. But the kind of situation he depicted undoubtedly supported the official and humanitarian case for bringing the country completely under the rule of law.

The question was, how? The considerable success of the Resident Magistrate system in some districts has been noted, but so also has the continued selectivity with which the Maori treated it. Their objections to troops, police and gaols remained strong: Raharuhi of Poverty Bay, in requesting the intervention of a Resident Magistrate had also stipulated against a gaol. Yet the system as operated in Wanganui and Mangonui did suggest some possible approaches to the problem. Its operation in those districts involved the presence of strong police detachments, with military power not far in the background. Yet this did not seem to have unduly offended Maori sensitivities because the local chiefs were closely involved, as Assessors, in the application of police power and because it was not used in flagrant violation of Maori ideas of right. The use of military power to over-awe even as eminent a chief as Nopera had not created general resentment because Nopera had acted fractiously, not as the representative of his people's general interest.

The critical factor seems to have been not so much the presence of police or the use of the military *per se* but adequate consultation with the people of a district about what laws would apply and what part the chiefs should play in their enforcement. In the case of a district like Rotorua it would probably have been better to have done this in advance, and secured agreement on methods of enforcement, including the stationing of police (including local Maori) and the erection of a gaol. If fractious chiefs had not been willing to accept this it would probably have been better not to have sent Smith as a magistrate at all.

The Government could, moreover, exert powerful leverage on the chiefs through the economic opportunities it could offer or withhold, and through the support it could lend or deny to the chiefs' status-seeking. In a situation of social change there were strong indications that even the independent-minded inland chiefs would welcome Government support in these matters. In a frequently quoted letter Tamati Ngapora, a young Waikato chief of the highest rank, wrote to Grey bemoaning the disobedience of his slaves and complaining that they sullied his name by drunkenness and thieving whenever they went to Auckland. He asked the Governor, 'do you strengthen our hands, so that the many slaves on this land may be kept in awe, and the chiefs enrolled to love and protect you'.[44] Provided government operated to protect the status and authority of the high-ranking chiefs, they would be prepared to co-operate warmly with it. Agreement with this would certainly have carried the danger, if care were not taken, of entrenching favoured chiefs in formal positions with powers much in excess of their traditional prerogatives. Nevertheless Ngapora's approach revealed an area of possible mutual assistance, and the question of finding a place for the traditional leadership simply could not be avoided in the New Zealand context, if a smooth transition to bureaucratic government was to be achieved. It was not too late to buttress the position of the chiefs. Certainly the pressures of culture contact were eroding their authority; that was what Ngapora's letter was about. But Maori society was still remarkably well integrated, with traditional kinship units and leadership based largely on inherited rank, still the vital basis of the Maori social order. Grey could easily have buttressed Ngapora's position administratively, and in so doing given him a vested interest in supporting the state.

His namesake, Earl Grey, Secretary of State for Colonies from 1846 to 1852, thought that he should. Despite his pro-settler and assimilationist attitudes, Earl Grey realised the deep significance of Ngapora's plea and spent much labour on a long despatch aimed at meeting the chief's wishes. He suggested (as others had suggested at various times since the founding of the Colony) that it was necessary to secure for the chiefs the wealth and station they had formerly generated from the exploitation of slaves. This included recognising them as landlords of tribal estates entitled to rent as they had formerly been entitled to tribute, as chief constables empowered to make arrests and, when experienced in English language and laws, as Resident Magistrates.[45] Earl Grey certainly revealed his ulterior purpose when he expressed the hope that chiefs so assured of private estates and position would be all the more disposed to alienate surplus land to settlers. Nevertheless, his policy of recognising the chiefs' concern for status and, by grant of public office, demonstrating that the Maori were not, as a people, to be regarded as inferior to settlers, was very much needed in New Zealand.

As we have seen, Sir George Grey had begun his governorship of New Zealand with the pre-conceived commitment to reducing, not sustaining, the power of the chiefs. He continued to object to them for their tendency 'to draw back the mass of the native population to their old barbarous customs'.[46] Unlike people in London, the settlers and missionaries in New Zealand shared Governor Grey's repugnance at Maori 'barbarism' and had no wish to recognise and reinforce chiefly authority. Nor were they disposed to accept Earl Grey's proposals as the most expedient way of acquiring land: they had a preference for much more direct methods. The Secretary of State's suggestion on Ngapora's letter therefore fell on stony ground. Governor Grey ignored the despatch entirely, neither minuting it nor replying to it.

The reluctance in New Zealand to accord the Maori a real share in state power was further demonstrated in the constitutional developments then taking place. In 1846, as a result of strong campaigning from settler organisations, a constitution for New Zealand had been enacted in the English parliament. Preliminary planning of that constitution, with Gladstone as Secretary of State, had envisaged that the bulk of the North Island (the proposed Province of New Ulster), with its overwhelmingly Maori majority, should remain a Crown Colony. The southern settlements only (the proposed Province of New Munster) with small Maori populations, were to enjoy representative government. This was to be based on municipal elections in which the few Maori holders of the tenement property qualification would participate. The principle of racial equality would therefore formally be preserved. However, Earl Grey, taking office in 1846, was sympathetic to settler demands for wider control and proposed to extend representative government to New Ulster also. Lest this should open the franchise to the Maori majority in the north, a test of literacy in English was added—an effective disenfranchisement since the great proportion of Maori who had become literate were literate in their own language, not English. In order to safeguard the Maori from a settler-dominated legislature, and compensate them in another direction, Earl Grey authorised the temporary demarcation of Native Districts in which Maori custom would be given the force of law and upheld by formally appointed chiefs, backed by the superior courts of the Province.[47]

In New Zealand Governor Grey argued, realistically, that at that stage the Maori were too suspicious and too warlike either to be placed under a settler minority or ostensibly debarred from the franchise. He succeeded in having the 1846 constitution suspended for five years during which time, he claimed, his 'amalgamation' policies would be likely to close the gap between Maori and settler and improve the chances of representative government succeeding.[48] In 1848 the two Provinces of New Ulster and New Munster were created, but both were essentially under Crown Colony government, the latter Province being administered by Lieutenant-Governor Eyre, with an advisory Legislative Council, under Grey's general governorship.

But as part of the same policy, Grey also rejected the proposal for Native Districts, arguing that they would perpetuate 'the barbarous customs of the Native Race'. He feared that a separate system of law, once established as Native Districts, would become entrenched and ineradicable. Accordingly he sought and secured an alteration in his instructions to permit the enforcement of English law, by which he meant the Resident Magistrate system, in Maori districts.

These alterations won the approval of the humanitarians both in New Zealand and in England, for whom the exclusion of Maori from the franchise and the recognition of Native Districts were alike objectionable. They raised the familiar spectres of injustice and danger of oppression from the settlers on the one hand, and, on the other, the perpetuation of the Maori people in backwardness—the twin dangers for which 'amalgamation' was to be the counter.

If Grey's rejection of the Native Districts concept had been accompanied, not by the mere rhetoric of assimilation, but by a genuine attempt to engage the Maori in the main stream of politics and administration, his solution would have been much more satisfactory. But, as in the case of Ngapora's pleas to strengthen the chiefs' hands, a frank inclusion of the Maori leadership in state power was just what Grey and the settlers could not make. Their deep-seated notions of racial and cultural superiority, and the competition for land, persistently worked against it.

Grey's practice therefore became one of trying to draw the Maori into the web of government control by a variety of devices designed to manage and placate them, without open discussion of the fundamental questions about land, law, police power, or political representation. These were subjects about which the Maori remained in the dark, though increasingly suspicious of government intentions.

Although early in his governorship Grey had assailed the missions, along with the Protectorate of Aborigines, for what he considered an overweening influence in government, he encouraged missionary activity in the field and subsidised mission schools teaching in English. Support for the missions, he wrote, 'whilst it is most effective, can neither irritate the pride nor offend the prejudices of the natives; nor does it engage the Government in a course of policy or of remonstrance on which having once embarked, they cannot retreat without an appearance of weakness'.[49] Impatient settlers regarded this as 'moral suasion' and Grey's policy began to be condemned as 'identical with that which in the days of his predecessor was so much reprobated—non-enforcement of the law because it may be in opposition to the native prejudice'.[50] The settlers also heavily assailed his so-called 'flour and sugar' policy —the hospitality given to chiefs visiting the towns, and a stream of presents— of flour mills, livestock, harness, ploughs or food—to chiefs in the out-districts.

Like many autocrats Grey enjoyed the paternalistic role. He used largesse to try to detach the great chiefs from their provincial sources of power and, like Louis XIV of France, to seduce them into seeking honour in his service. He courted leading men like Te Wherowhero, Ngapora and Nene with pensions and shrewd personal diplomacy, attaching them to his entourage and visiting them formally. In response to this Te Wherowhero and Ngapora settled at Mangere, the nearest portion of Waikato land to Auckland. Among the more substantial benefits Grey offered were the large hostelry built for Maori visiting Auckland and hospitals and boarding schools catering for both races in the main centres.

This inclusion of Maori in the social and welfare institutions of the community was indeed valuable and the neglect by succeeding governments of much of what Grey attempted was to be very seriously felt in future decades. Doubtless the leading chiefs gained some reassurance as to their future status and material welfare from Grey's exertions. Yet their doubts and suspicions were not really overcome. The Governor's bounty tended to reach favoured individuals or tribes—increasingly to those who supported land-selling—and there was a spirit of condescension and triviality about much of it which appeared, fairly quickly to some chiefs, to seem demeaning. Neither the missions nor the 'flour and sugar' policy could provide adequate solutions to the problems of population decline, social disturbance, and comparative material want. Enthusiasm for the missions had begun to wane, since Christianity was not providing immediate answers to these problems. Maori anxieties were intensified by the continued settler clamour for land and for political control. Pensions and gifts could not have satisfied the chiefs on these subjects even if carried out on a scale far greater than Grey's meagre resources allowed.

A good deal of Maori resentment centred on the Arms Ordinance and Sale of Spirits Ordinance which Grey had enacted in 1845 and 1846. In the interests of suppressing rebellion and preventing social dislocation there was of course a strong case to be made for preventing Maori from obtaining arms and liquor, but the Ordinances applied to Maori only and the discrimination was greatly resented by them and widely defied. Chiefs who were concerned about the demoralising effect of liquor on their people, sought its prohibition from both races in their districts.

The Government also continued to avoid implementing FitzRoy's Juries Amendment Ordinance of 1844 which provided for Maori jurors to be empanelled when Maori were on trial in the Supreme Court. The question arose in 1849 when one Ratia, wanted since 1843 for killing his wife's lover in the midst of the Wellington settlement, wandered into the town and was arrested. His kin, resentful that he should be brought to trial after such long delay for a killing which was no offence in their eyes, became turbulent. St Hill, the magistrate, hastily suggested that regulations under the Juries Ordinance be gazetted to enable Ratia to go before a Maori jury. But Lieutenant-Governor Eyre abruptly rejected the suggestion in a petulant minute expressing surprise that Maori jurors should even have been considered when the Maori were 'very imperfectly acquainted' with English law.[51] Ratia was acquitted on a technicality and no steps were ever taken to implement the Juries Ordinance. Maori resentment and suspicion of such a remote and alien institution as the Supreme Court, and of a British rule which could hale their people before it, is hardly surprising.

But perhaps the deepest anxieties were created by the vigour of Grey's land-purchase operations. These were intended, in addition to satisfying settler land hunger, to promote 'amalgamation' by making inroads of settlement in Maori districts, increasingly engaging Maori in wage labour, trade, and husbandry of new crops and livestock, and opening them to the restraints of government. Certainly the increased involvement of Maori in commerce and agriculture did promote receptiveness to institutions designed to secure order and protect property. On the other hand the Government's land purchases gravely threatened Maori social stability and generated a powerful reaction against British dominion. Although the passionate advocacy of missionary and humanitarian groups, and awareness of Maori strength, had led Grey in 1846 to uphold Maori claims to the 'waste' or uncultivated lands of New Zealand against settler and colonising lobbies which had won the support of Earl Grey, at heart he, and most of the New Zealand officials, did not believe it just that the Maori should be able to shut settlers out of vast, sparsely populated and uncultivated regions. Clarke and the Protectorate Department had revealed that Maori interests in land were so complex that it was unrealistic to expect the purchase of more than small pieces of land, through careful and protracted negotiations; but Grey pushed through extensive purchases in the South Island, and secured some large blocks in the Wairarapa, Manawatu and Auckland districts with methods that were none too careful or scrupulous. Prices, in the South Island particularly, were nominal; the claims of minority or subject tribes were passed over; blandishment and guile were mixed with bullying and blustering which completely antagonised former friends such as Wiremu Kingi of the Atiawa;[52] boundaries of purchases and reserves were left ill-defined and purchase payments incomplete; former owners huddled on miserable reserves dispirited and resentful. The Native Secretary of New Munster, H. T. Kemp, has recorded the 'dreadful decay' within one year of the *hapu* of Ngairo, a Wairarapa chief who had sold land eagerly enough, but misjudged the terms and consequences of the transaction.[53]

Some of Grey's purchases in Wairarapa and Auckland included provision for the setting aside of a proportion of the profits from the resale of the land (the 'Auckland ten per cents' and 'Wairarapa five per cents') for schools, hospitals, flour mills and annuities to chiefs. Here the principle was excellent, but the percentage allowed was far too low to do more than pay for the basic food and housing of a few Maori. In any case the money was not paid until the Maori had agitated for at least a decade. In Wellington and Motueka Grey offset the good effect of his 1846 enlargement of Maori reserves by taking back some of the reserves (on the ground that there was then insufficient general reserve left) for public schools, hospitals and military barracks. The Maori were supposed to enjoy the benefit of these equally with the Pakeha but were resentful at the loss of their land and never took full advantage of them.[54] Despite the fact that in 1847 he proclaimed his awareness that the Maori were not purely agriculturalists, and needed hunting and fishing grounds, Grey left the Canterbury *hapu* a miserable 10 acres per head of reserve. In 1881 he claimed that he had only just become aware of what his land purchase commissioner had done, and said: 'I feel a sort of humiliation when I think of what has taken place'. Yet the commissioner, Walter Mantell, had reported specifically to him at the time that he had left only 10 acres per head in order that the Maori might not 'continue to live in their old barbarism on the rents of an uselessly extensive domain'.[55] The Otago Maori believed that they had been offered 'tenths' (or reserves of one tenth of all sub-divisions) in the purchase of that settlement, but the provision did not appear precisely in the deed, and in 1881, despite the irritated insistence of the chairman of a committee of inquiry that he must know the answer to such an important question, Grey declined to remember what he had ordered on the subject.[56]

Matters such as these left a legacy of anger and ill-will among Maori for Grey's successor to handle. Moreover, although he acquired most of the South Island, his land purchase officers made relatively little progress in the North Island. Instead he connived at the spread of the squatters into all the more accessible low-land districts in defiance of the Native Land Purchase Ordinance. Despite constant quarrelling with the settlers over payment of 'grass money' and the trespass of stock onto their cultivations, Maori leaders generally welcomed the squatters as a source of revenue and did not want to expel them altogether, but the increase of squatting greatly exacerbated the question of where power and sovereignty were to lie. The settlers were anxious to acquire the title and rid themselves of the dominion of their powerful Maori hosts; the Maori were equally anxious to prevent the squatters from acquiring the freehold and placing them, the original owners, in subordination. The fact that Grey and his officers supported the squatters in seeking to acquire the freehold, made the Maori in districts affected by squatting inclined to withstand all manifestations of the Government's authority. The interior chiefs, like Ngapora, watching the growing social dislocation and antagonism between sellers and non-sellers in the districts where the Land Purchase Officers were operating, grew even more concerned for their authority and the integrity of their communities. As is well known, before the completion of Grey's term of office in 1853, the first emissaries of what was to become the Maori King movement had begun to canvass their ideas to interested audiences through the North Island.

According to his successor, Colonel Browne, Grey knew of this but did not warn him against it.[57] Grey was anxious to wind up his governorship in a blaze of glory, and bombarded London with despatches, compounded of

purblind optimism and a measure of deliberate deceit, about the progress of
the amalgamation policy. It was quite irresponsible to report that 'both races
form one harmonious community, cemented together by commercial and
agricultural pursuits, professing the same faith, resorting to the same courts of
justice'.[58] Only two or three years previously Grey had been playing up the
independence and turbulence of the Maori. Yet his later reports were received
with enthusiasm among official and humanitarian circles all too ready to
believe that the 'great experiment' of amalgamation of Maori and settler was
succeeding, and they were circulated among the British Cabinet.[59] Tamati
Ngapora's earlier pleas were all but forgotten.

Deluding himself that the continuation of his policies would soon bring the
interior tribes under control, Grey passed up his one remaining chance of
allaying the concern of the senior chiefs to prevent the further disturbance of
Maori society and safeguard their own status. Over the protests of the Aborigines Protection Society and contrary to Grey's opinion, the Colonial Office
again took the precaution of providing in the 1852 Constitution Act which
established representative government in New Zealand for Native Districts
wherein Maori institutions could be preserved. But Grey's egotism, self-
deception and paternalistic view of the Maori led him to believe, despite the
evidence of their continued restlessness and defiance, that they could be
placated by pensions and presents—the finance for which would be secured to
the Governor by a small Civil List vote—until the spread of settlement had
encompassed them. He left the Colony without having declared Native
Districts.

Furthermore, trusting his assurances that the progress of 'amalgamation'
was such that many Maori possessed, or soon would possess, individual property
sufficient to qualify them for the electoral roll, the Colonial Office accepted—
erroneously—that 'a very large proportion' of Maori would shortly be enfran-
chised, and did not make any special provision for Maori representation.[60]
Grey's bland and over-optimistic reports had the effect of leaving the Maori
unfranchised.

The period 1845-52 had been a crucial one in New Zealand history; these
were among the last years in which important sections of the Maori people,
particularly the Waikato tribes, showed that they might readily have accepted
the authority of the Queen, and government, and the rule of law, in return
for sufficiently generous provision for their own participation in the machinery
of state. The fruitful association of the Rarawa and Wanganui chiefs with the
Resident Magistrates showed what could be achieved through their recognition and involvement. Unfortunately genuine recognition and involvement
of that kind stopped at the local level; Grey's pursuit of 'amalgamation'
revealed the same weaknesses which had marred it as a policy from the founding of the Colony: while it was used to deny the preservation of Maori institutions in a system of Native Districts, it was not pursued honestly enough to
include them adequately in the general government of the colony. They were,

increasingly, a subject race, with the Government actively acquiring their lands. The British authorities, having failed to meet the needs of the Maori people and win their firm allegiance while they remained an essentially segmented people, were shortly to be confronted with a supra-tribal and separatist movement, as men like Ngapora sought to grapple with their problems in their own way. This was to make the task of peacefully extending the authority of government and centralised law infinitely more difficult.

VII

Crisis in Race Relations

The crisis in race relations developing in the 1850s was intensified by the increasing control which the settlers gained over Maori policy and administration. Colonel Wynyard, Acting Governor following Grey's departure, and his Native Secretary, Major Nugent, were routine administrators, who lacked even the awareness that they were in nominal charge of one of the most conflict-prone situations imaginable. Moreover, Nugent's very office was under attack. The settlers in the first General Assembly, meeting in 1854, recommended the abolition of the position of Native Secretary, for the same reason that they had formerly attacked the Protectorate of Aborigines, namely, that in their view, 'Its principal object has been to persuade the Natives that the Government were their friends and the settlers their enemies'.[1] A motion to strike out the £650 voted for the Native Department was defeated by only fourteen votes to twelve.

The Assembly's grip on finance quickly tightened. The £7000 Civil List vote for native affairs provided under the constitutional arrangements of 1852 was used to subsidise the missionary societies' boarding schools where Maori pupils were taught in English. Other expenditure was dependent on the Assembly's vote and the sum approved paid for little more than the salaries of Nugent and a clerk who printed the tawdry Maori language paper *The Maori Messenger,* a few pensions and presents for chiefs who had assisted the Government, and a contribution to the cost of smallpox vaccination administered to the Maori people by Resident Magistrates and missionaries under the direction of a Vaccination Board.

The Superintendents and Provincial Councils elected by the propertied settlers of the various Provinces into which New Zealand was divided under the 1852 Constitution, had responsibility for education, hospitals, police and charitable aid. Because only one or two Maori in the towns paid rates, and the indirect taxation (to which Maori people contributed heavily) went to the general Government in Auckland, the Provinces declined to assume responsibility for Maori health and education except in individual cases where the general Government transferred funds. A few Maori police in Taranaki and Auckland retained their salaries from funds similarly transferred, but because of settler jealousies and prejudices the Provinces did not continue the policy commenced by Grey of recruiting Maori police. One of the few avenues which had been opened for Maori to enter the machinery of state had been closed off again.

The Maori reserves in the New Zealand Company settlements were supposed to yield a large revenue for Maori purposes but by the Native Reserves Act of 1856 they were placed under commissioners, usually local settlers who let the reserves at cheap rental, in the settlers' interests, often without consulting the beneficial owners. The Maori of course resented the administration of their land in this fashion and, contrary to the General Assembly's hopes, put no more under the commissioners. The small sums raised by the lease of reserves were spent on 'medical comforts', subsidies to church schools and the building of uncomfortable 'hostelries'—usually one or two roomed affairs where people slept on the floor—for Maori visiting the towns to trade.

The position improved only slightly with the arrival of the new Governor, Colonel Gore Browne, in September 1855. Browne made a conscientious effort to search out the needs of the Maori situation, and when, in 1856, responsibility in all other internal affairs was transferred to a Ministry chosen from the General Assembly, Browne withheld Maori affairs from direct settler control. Nevertheless in 1858 the Ministers, while agreeing to pay the subsidies for Maori schools and freeing the £7000 of Native Civil List for other Maori purposes, in return gained the right to approve detailed allocation of that money and of all additional 'Native' votes. It was agreed, moreover, that the Colonial Treasurer, C. W. Richmond, a Taranaki settler with university and legal training, should be designated Native Minister and authorised, along with the Native Secretary, to minute correspondence on Maori affairs. But the settlers deeply resented being denied full responsibility in Maori affairs—the key to the control of Maori lands and thus of the future of settlement in New Zealand. The result was reluctance on the part of the Assembly to vote money to be spent by the Governor and his 'irresponsible' staff, and deadlock and stagnation in the development of Maori policy at a most critical time.[2]

In this confused situation grew the great rivalry of the two colonists most continuously influential in Maori affairs for the ensuing generation, Donald McLean and Francis Dart Fenton. McLean, a Scottish Highlander of humble birth, had established himself early in government service as a Sub-Protector of Aborigines during FitzRoy's governorship; but he laid the real basis of his career as a land-purchase commissioner under Grey, whose strengths and weaknesses he paralleled in many ways. Like Grey he could be very adroit in personal relations with the chiefs and had considerable appreciation of their sensitivities. Indeed he had a genuine sympathy with much of the Maori culture and life-style, which probably came more easily to him than to the cultivated, formally educated Englishmen of the New Zealand Company settlements who increasingly dominated New Zealand politics in the 1850s and 1860s. For example, unlike many of his prudish contemporaries, McLean was inclined to regard Polynesian sexual mores as robust and wholesome, not depraved. Indeed, to his lasting credit he detested the ignorant racism of many settlers who openly wished the Maori had never existed and thought they should be allowed to slip into extinction. But in the last resort McLean was too self-interested and his career too closely identified with the progress of settlement for him to be able to do more than seek to protect the Maori within a basically Pakeha-dominated order and he could not brook their obstruction to settlement. Like Grey therefore, he used his ability to establish personal relations with Maori leaders for the purpose of manipulating them and securing their land. Like Grey also, he was autocratic and could not easily work with people who did not allow him a free hand or follow him sycophantically. Men who openly opposed him, whether Maori or settler, were not readily forgiven. He was industrious and superficially very impressive as an administrator, but he was devious and his work often lacked both real substance and attention to detail. In 1854 a Land Purchase Department of the general Government was formally constituted with McLean as Chief Land Purchase Officer. Subordinate Commissioners were appointed to various districts. These included a little group of McLean's Taranaki cronies—Robert Parris, G. S. Cooper and others —whose fortunes were fixed, in the fashion of the mid-nineteenth century civil service, to their chosen comet. Unfortunately McLean's carelessness of detailed supervision, and his own unscrupulousness, led increasingly to attempts to push through land purchases without sufficient care for the rights of all claimants.[3]

F. D. Fenton, a lawyer, began his rise under Grey, who in 1851 found him among the small settler community squatting on Maori land in the Waikato. Thereafter Fenton served briefly as a clerk in the Registry of Deeds and was appointed Resident Magistrate at Kaipara just before Grey's departure. He brought himself to Governor Browne's notice in 1856 with a series of memoranda on Maori affairs and was appointed Native Secretary. Within a few weeks however, the Native Secretaryship was merged with the Chief Land Purchase Office, McLean being given both posts. This decision was later thought to be highly political, part of Browne's and McLean's desire to grasp control of Maori affairs, and fraught with dire consequences because the Maori saw *all* administration as associated with the desire to acquire their land. In fact, the decision was taken quite casually, Browne and the settler Ministers agreeing that, because the responsibilities of the two offices had never been clearly demarcated, Maori visiting Auckland were already confused as to which officer to see on any subject, and were irritated at being shuttled back and forth between the two. The amalgamation was simply an expedient administrative change.[4] But for Fenton, an ambitious, conceited and fractious man, it was a most untoward set-back, and he never forgave McLean, whom he saw as depriving him of office. Fenton was sent off to be Resident Magistrate at Whaingaroa, south of Waikato heads, from whence he wrote more erudite memoranda.

The nature of the problem with which this cross-gaitered administration had to deal was illustrated by sporadic violence. Feuding from traditional causes sputtered on in various parts of the colony, with heavy loss of life in the Tarawera district. Much more serious, however, was the eruption of feuding in Taranaki, precipitated when the Land Purchase Commissioner, G. S. Cooper, asked a land-selling faction to cut the boundary of a proposed purchase, against the express opposition of some of the non-selling claimants. In feuding of the scale which soon developed, the protagonists were not inclined to wait upon the intervention of the law, while the Government sought to avoid involvement. These events in Taranaki, and also in Hawke's Bay, where feuding broke out for similar reasons, carried ominous implications for thoughtful Maori throughout New Zealand, especially as the settlers inevitably showed sympathy with the land-selling factions. Many were to date 'the evil' which culminated in the Anglo-Maori wars, from the Taranaki feuding, provoked by government land-purchasing.[5]

The issues of law and state power were also brought sharply into focus by a series of fatalities in the Auckland district. During drunken brawling in the town about Christmas 1854, a settler named Huntley killed a Maori from the upper Waikato district, and Kiore, one of a number of Ngatiwhakaue from Rotorua living near Auckland, killed a local Maori. Tension between the various Maori communities and the settlers about Auckland ran high. The Waikato chiefs at first demanded the right to take and kill Huntley, and some were not placated by the arrest and committal of the accused to trial in the Supreme Court. However, when Huntley was found guilty of manslaughter and sentenced to life imprisonment, they told Wynyard they now considered him 'dead' and asked that he be released and sent away.[6] The Ngatiwhakaue, threatened with attack by Auckland tribes seeking *utu* for their kinsman's death, surrendered Kiore for trial by the authorities. Their leader, Te Rangi-kaheke, said, 'Your law says that the guilty alone shall suffer. The law of the Maoris is to punish the innocent, and often the guilty gets free. Your law is better than ours and we submit to it.'[7]

The following Christmas, December 1855, a similar scene was played when a drunken settler, an American named Charles Marsden, killed a Ngatiwhakaue woman named Kerara. The Ngatiwhakaue about Auckland took up arms and were joined by kinsmen from Rotorua and this time Te Rangi-kaheke was not so sure about the advantages of settler law. He wrote to his fellow chiefs, 'There is no recognition of the authority of the native people, no meeting of the two authorities, even up to this murder. Suggestions have been made (with a view to giving natives a share in the administration of affairs), but to what purpose? The reply is, this island has lost its independence, it is enslaved, and the chiefs with it.' He called upon Rotorua leaders to assemble a great council and suggested, 'There are two points for you to consider: whether you will adopt the proposal of Matene Te Whiwhi [of Otaki] to unite with the other tribes and have one system in force over the island, or that of Tukihaumene [of Rotorua] to uphold the separate dignity and independence of the descendants of Rangitihi [the Ngatiwhakaue]: because in the present English system we are mere slaves.'[8]

The reference to Matene Te Whiwhi's proposals reveals the mounting debate among the Maori people which led to the selection of a Maori King. In the end the Ngatiwhakaue did not generally join the King movement but established their own 'Great Council of Rotorua'. This was largely because of traditional rivalry with the Waikato tribes which came to dominate the King movement, but the trial of Charles Marsden also played a part. C. O. Davis, interpreter in the Native Department, persuaded the Ngatiwhakaue to leave their arms aside, in return for places being found for a number of chiefs at the trial. Several were seated in the box for the grand jury and a good many more crowded into the courtroom where the judge spent considerable time explaining English court procedures to them. While the jury was out he became involved in a spirited dialogue with Te Rangikaheke who complained that the 'common people' amongst the settlers were constantly breaking the law and demanded to know 'what amount of influence the natives had in the affairs of the State'.[9] Marsden freely admitted killing Kerara and the settler jury found him guilty, adding a strong recommendation of mercy. The judge, however, did not concur in the recommendation and sentenced Marsden to death. After a delay to receive Governor Browne's confirmation of the sentence (during which the Ngatiwhakaue again came to Auckland and threatened trouble) Marsden was hanged. The revelation that the Pakeha would apply their laws against their own offenders to the extent of hanging them made a profound impression on the Ngatiwhakaue, many claiming to date their attachment to the Queen and to the law from that time.[10] A meeting at Maketu resolved to submit offenders to the Queen's law, asked for the appointment of more Assessors and offered to sell land to the Government for a settlement. Many settlers, however, felt very differently. In the General Assembly a settler politician alleged that a white man 'had been sacrificed to popular fear of the Natives' force'.[11]

In the mid-1850s most Maori shared Te Rangikaheke's dissatisfaction with their exclusion from any real share in a Government which appeared increasingly bent on the acquisition of their land, and increasingly under the control of the settler assemblies. Their principal response was to try to consolidate through tribal and supra-tribal organisations, but there was great difference of opinion as to whether this should be done in association with the Pakeha. Matene Te Whiwhi, the Christian chief from Otaki who visited Ngatiraukawa and Ngatiwhakaue kinsmen in 1853, was said to have sought to 'unite the tribes under the Queen's government'.[12] *Te Hokioi*, the King movement newspaper, later suggested that he had himself in mind as the Maori King, and ceased to support the movement when it was clear that he would not be chosen.[13]

The Government really became aware of the movement after a big meeting at Taupo in December 1856. G. S. Cooper, then Land Purchase Officer in

Hawke's Bay, thought the meeting was to establish an annual Maori parliament to devise a means whereby,

> some check may be applied to the growing influence of the colonists, whilst the power of the Native chiefs . . . shall be restored in so far as possible to its former status. As a principal means towards this end, it is to be proposed to put an immediate stop to all sales of land to the Government, and to use every possible means to induce squatters to settle with flocks . . . in the interior . . . to occupy the position of vassals to the Chiefs under whose protection they may live . . . and to whom they are to afford a revenue, by way of rent for their runs, to assist in maintaining the power and influence of their landlords.

Other important questions for discussion included cattle trespass (which was causing the abandonment of large areas of garden land), the sale of liquor, and the idea of a treaty with the Government whereby the chiefs could settle cases of homicide arising out of adultery and sorcery disputes.[14] The idea of assembling a parliament of leading chiefs from every district at regular intervals certainly gained ground at the Taupo meeting but so also did the idea of choosing Potatau Te Wherowhero as King.

A movement by several tribes and *hapu* to establish regular councils or *runanga* developed concurrently with the King movement and had very similar purposes. These were developments of the traditional *runanga* (meetings where interested parties discussed a problem or dispute) which had persisted much as in pre-contact times. But they tended to assume a more formal structure and sometimes a more defined membership, and were concerned to promulgate codes of law to deal with adultery, cattle trespass, theft and drunkenness. They seem to have been influenced by the *komiti* (committees) of the missionary congregations which performed similar functions. In the 1850s the divisions which had formerly developed between pagan and Christian sections of many villages became blurred as Christianity spread and at the same time, in Maori hands, lost some of the exclusiveness and rigidity which the missions had sought to impose on their early congregations. Pagans increasingly attended the *komiti* of their Christian kinsmen and the term was taken over to apply to quasi-traditional meetings. The Waikato people were also said to be holding 'Christmases'. Biblical influence, and the tendency of the Maori people to see themselves as analagous to the Jews—the suffering people who would eventually be led from darkness—can be seen in the promulgation of laws by the 'Sanhedrin' of the Ngatimahuta tribe.[15] But these terms were generally dropped in favour of the more traditional term *'runanga'*—a trend indicative of the Maori leaders' reassertion of their own culture and their independence of the Pakeha. Secular influences were also apparent, particularly those of the Provincial Assemblies which met in Auckland and Wellington, New Plymouth and Napier and were observed by interested Maori who were, however, debarred by the property franchise from participation in them. The law courts also provided example and the *runanga* frequently began as civil or criminal trials, though kinsmen of the disputants soon involved themselves as in traditional meetings.

Because the *runanga* leaders could not readily enforce their laws against defiant kinsmen some turned to the Government to help establish and confirm their authority. It was possibly the greatest single opportunity lost, that the Government failed to support these spontaneous Maori efforts at social control. McLean was still pursuing Grey's paternalistic system of diplomacy and influence with the chiefs. Of Governor Browne the missionary Robert Maunsell reported that, 'In 1855 I spent a whole evening endeavouring to combat his objections to delegating power to Maori runangas'.[16] About 1855 Wiremu Tamihana suggested to Nugent that Maori leaders be admitted to the House of Representatives, but he received no encouragement. Subsequently—possibly in late 1856 or early 1857—he went to Auckland to seek approval for a Ngatihaua scheme for a separate *runanga* of chiefs in Auckland to provide for the Maori people as parliament provided for the settlers. According to the account he gave the missionary Ashwell, he was kept waiting and slighted at the Native Office while settlers were promptly attended to. 'I said to myself' he related 'We are treated as dogs—I will not go again.'[17] He then threw his influence behind the movement to establish Potatau as King and in 1858 presided over his coronation.

The question was hotly debated among officials and settlers in the 1850s as to whether the King movement was basically a quest for law and order, or an assertion of Maori independence, 'national' in character. More recently historians have debated whether the term 'nationalism' properly applies to the King movement and *runanga* movement. The discussion is bedevilled by disagreement about the minimum definition of 'nationalism' but the practical import of the debate was and is very serious. If the Maori people wanted more law and government then the sending of more magistrates to Maori districts would presumably be appreciated and would allay discontent; but if Maori discontent were nationalistic in character the intrusion of more magistrates, asserting British authority, would only aggravate it. A related question, which quickly excited settlers, was whether it was possible in fact to co-exist peacefully in the same island with a developing national movement.

The King and *runanga* movements were far too complex to admit of an easy answer to these questions, but certainly the Maori were concerned with much more than the control of petty crime. Their real concern was that they were losing control of their own destinies, and being subordinated to the political and economic power of the settlers. The official rhetoric of Waitangi, that Maori and settlers were one people, was increasingly considered false. Paternalistic legislation such as the restriction on sale of arms and liquor was considered discriminatory. Political advancement had included settlers but not Maori. As *Te Hokioi* later put it, 'Look, your attempt to bring us under your rule [*mana*] without authority, is different from what you asserted. It shall not be so, men are of tall stature'.[18] To retain their 'tall stature' the Kingites needed to retain the land which was the basis not only of their economy, but their social order and their freedom of choice. In Tamihana's words, 'the *mana* Maori and holding land . . . These are the real causes of the setting up of the King'.[19]

Were these aspirations which would be impossible to accommodate within the framework of British sovereignty in New Zealand? The powerful inland chiefs were much less prone to see advantages in the British connection than the coastal chiefs. Although they often resented the activities of intruding settlers they considered that the solution Nene had adopted in 1840, of inviting the Governor's support to contain them, had resulted instead in an increase of settlement and the reduction of the coastal chiefs to landlessness and degradation. They were far more inclined to trust to their own considerable strength and traditional authority to control the situation. Indeed they were not only conservative in this sense, but some with more volatile temperaments, such as Te Heuheu Iwikau of Taupo and Rewi Maniapoto of upper Waikato, were inclined to the extreme course of driving the Pakeha into the sea. But an orator who advocated this in the early discussions was answered by another who went about the room blowing out the candles until the meeting was plunged into darkness—a classic illustration of the Maori genius for imagery and symbolism.[20] When Te Heuheu made a violent speech at the enthronement of Potatau in 1858 he was made to sit down by the other leaders, the majority of whom sought to re-establish Maori society on secure foundations the better to control and select, but continue to enjoy the skills, technology, and material resources which settlers were bringing from the wider world. As Cooper observed, the chiefs meeting at Taupo wanted Pakeha to settle among them (but as tenants, not freeholders) and trade with the settlements was not in any way to be inhibited. One of the first fruits of the King movement in the Waikato was a spate of money raising for school building and even an increase in attendance at the mission schools. Moreover, while traditional considerations of genealogical status and *mana* were crucial in the selection of Potatau as king, Tamihana and many of the young chiefs providing leadership for the movement were still Christians, progressives, eager for institutional borrowing from the Pakeha and enthusiasts for peace, stability and law. At the enthronement of Potatau, Tamihana urged that one of his principal tasks was to uphold God's law and suppress the 'foolish customs' which created discord among the Maori people and kept them in backwardness.[21] He later stated that the aim of the King movement was 'to put down my troubles, to hold the land of the slave, and to judge the offences of the chiefs. The King was set up; the Runangas were set up; the Kaiwhakawas [Kingite magistrates] were set up; and the religion was set up. The works of my ancestors have ceased; they are diminishing at the present time.'[22] It is difficult to characterise men like Tamihana as conservative; like many another leader of a threatened community he sought progressive reform among his own people as well as concessions from the ruling power.

However, the task of controlling 'foolish customs' or 'offences of the chiefs' with regard to land (namely, their tendency to assert selfish claims to land and sell recklessly) brought the Kingite leaders into opposition to British authority. For it was now becoming plain that British law was aimed at acquiring Maori land and supporting chiefs or factions who had sold or were wanting to sell land, often in disregard of the wishes of other traditional right-holders. The King movement was a search for 'law' but, as Sorrenson has shown, a law that would uphold Maori social cohesion and restrain land-sellers.[23] It was largely because British law was aiming to do precisely the reverse that the authority of the Crown was resisted, the King's authority asserted over Maori land and efforts made to restrict the Governor's jurisdiction to land already alienated. Kingite emisaries in the late 1850s, including Tamihana, proselytised successfully among aggrieved tribes far from the Waikato. Even if the Maori of Hawke's Bay or Poverty Bay did not recognise Potatau, they were encouraged to establish their own *runanga* and check the authority of the Queen and her magistrates, to prevent Pakeha law from ensnaring the land. The response was often a very explicit rejection of the Queen. A north Taranaki group in 1859 for example wrote: 'send hither your *runanga* to overshadow us, that we may be sacred to you, and that the *mana* of the Queen may fall from us— that your *mana* may exist for us alone for the guidance of the tribes of this island'.[24]

But a complete breakdown in relations with the Government was the last thing wanted by many of the movement's most important leaders—Tamihana, Potatau himself or his nephew Tamati Ngapora. Tamihana's Christianity ran deep. At baptism he had accepted that the missions' laws reflected the Christian God's love and will. He believed, as he had been taught by the missionaries (and as the rhetoric of settlers and officials claimed) that the English settlers and officials also recognised the same God and the same law. All of this blended easily with the Maori concept of *aroha* (care or affection beyond the strict call of obligation), the term with which the missionaries in fact translated the Christian concept 'love'. He furthermore found scriptural authority for the establishment of kings. Putting these concepts together he later wrote that when, in 1856, the Ngatihaua began to make plans to support Potatau,

> their searchings were in accordance with the law, [*ture*] that is to say, to restrain the strong hand of the man who persists in inciting to war on account of his land or his woman, and to refer such matters to investigation . . . that the sin of one man may cease to be visited on the many in cases of murder and to unite tribes which were living apart and in hostility to one another in former times thus making them one body in order to retain the portion of New Zealand that we now possess . . . I consent to the laws, which were sent to this Island by the old missionary society of England. That is to say Belief in God. These are the laws to be worked out by my King. It is by Christianity that we know the troubles of this Island are lessening.

He envisaged that the King would have *mana* over his lands, the Queen over hers 'but that their love [*aroha*] should be one, in accordance with the precepts of God, and that the King should have love for both races and protect them'.[25] On another occasion he said the King was to be in 'close connection' with the

Governor, and the laws which he would uphold were to be 'Your laws, the Queen's laws, they are just and scriptural and we wish to acknowledge them, but do not understand them all, we require instruction.'[26]

There was then, to Tamihana, no basic conflict between King and Queen. Both were doing the same work. Hence he would create symbols such as the two sticks thrust in the ground, representing the King and the Governor, a third across them 'the law of God and the Queen' and a circle about the whole, the Queen, a fence about them all.[27] It was a question of conjoint administrations, mutually applying one law, with the Queen as the protector of both. Subtle though this was, it did not preclude a retention of the Queen's sovereignty in New Zealand, or practical co-operation between King and Governor. There was an opportunity here for a New Zealand Government capable of recognising the constructiveness of men such as Tamihana. The attitude of the more extreme and headstrong Kingites provided a formidable difficulty, which may, in the end, have proved impossible to accommodate peacefully; but the desire of Tamihana and Potatau and their kind to preserve Maori *mana,* while showing many of the features of modern political nationalism was not fully equivalent to it, and the possibility that a *modus vivendi* could have been developed with them was not inconceivable. Maori intransigence was in fact less apparent than settler repugnance at sharing power with 'natives' and accepting the status of tenants under Maori landlords.[28]

Meanwhile settler and official attitudes hardened with the increasing realisation that the Maori were attempting to consolidate against the disruptive pressures of settlement. In early 1855 Nugent had reflected the assurance of Grey's last years of office, that time was on the settlers' side and it was only a matter of quietly waiting before they had their way. Referring to the Taranaki feuds he wrote, 'The sooner our laws are put in force among the natives the better; and as the natives are so rapidly decreasing and the settlers increasing, we shall soon be able to force our laws, but at present we must tacitly acquiesce in some of their customs.'[29]

Early in 1856 Governor Browne appointed a Board of Inquiry to advise him on various aspects of Maori policy. On the question of conferring minor judicial authority on the chiefs, the Board produced a clash of opinion between Fenton and McLean. From his experience as Resident Magistrate at Kaipara, Fenton considered that the chiefs appointed as Assessors had little weight, even among their own *hapu,* independent of the European officer, that they were partial in their decisions and that they should not be given any jurisdiction to act alone. Other members of the Board supported Fenton, arguing that the Assessors' appointments had evoked jealousies, leading to demands for more appointments or attempts to pull down the first appointees by false reports of drunkenness and adultery. It was felt that few chiefs could secure obedience to their decisions, and that what influence they had depended upon their carrying out the wishes of the community; any attempt to enlarge on this, through the authority derived from the government would lead to repudiation and loss of influence. Conversely, it was suggested of the Assessors in the Wanganui River in particular, that they had been overbearing and imposed outrageous sentences on defendants. These sorts of view were reflected in the majority report of the Board which recommended that while more European magistrates should be appointed, with Maori Assessors to assist them, no independent judicial authority should be given to the Assessors. Few Maori, it asserted, were fitted for jury service.

McLean was well aware of all the shortcomings in the system, but unlike the narrow and legalistic Fenton, he was prepared to be tolerant of them. Moreover his perception of chiefly authority was better than Fenton's. He knew the chiefs could not be autocrats but neither were they merely spokesmen of group opinions. They were expected to lead, and, particularly as Maori communities were anxious to find solutions to problems arising from culture contact, intelligent leadership in the judicial field stood a fair chance of acceptance. As we have seen, traditional notions of dispute settlement did not revolve around the notion of 'my kinsman right or wrong', and Maori ideas of right conduct, modified to some extent by Christian influences and concepts of property derived from commerce with settlers, were adaptable to English ideas of jurisprudence. McLean's minority report stated 'In most cases where [chiefs] have acted as assessors they have shown great discretion and equity, based upon natural justice, and have been influenced to a much less extent than might have been expected by tribal jealousies or particularity.' He recommended that a petty authority should be conferred on the Assessors to act alone in Maori cases (which they were doing unofficially anyway) and that Maori should be enrolled on the jury lists as soon as they possessed the requisite individual property qualification in land.

McLean's minority views were not of course acted on, and it is interesting to note where at least one of the missionaries, the representatives of humanitarianism, stood. The Rev. Octavius Hadfield of Otaki, a future Bishop of Wellington, reiterated the basic missionary proposition that the primary task of government was to make the whole Maori populace amenable to English law and added, 'It appears to be highly important, notwithstanding a very general opinion to the contrary, that the government should do nothing towards establishing the influence of the chiefs, but should rather endeavour to lessen this by every legitimate means, and especially by raising the position of inferior men, through the equal action of the law.' The settlers could not have agreed more, and Hadfield was shortly to discover how his principle was to be abused in the case of a chief's rights in land matters.[30]

Reliance on the chiefs, however, necessarily continued and sober calculation found the settlers hard put to prove them unco-operative. The question was raised late in 1856 when Maori from Coromandel Peninsula stole gunpowder from a Government magazine on Kawau Island and their chiefs at first refused to surrender either the gunpowder or the culprits. A Native Offenders Bill was introduced in the General Assembly which proposed to shut off a district that harboured offenders from all trade with the rest of the country as a means of bringing it to submission. But a Select Committee taking evidence on the bill found that few of those involved professionally in Maori affairs believed that the measure would be either effective or necessary. McLean considered that, unless the chiefs were fundamentally disaffected (as in the case of Te Rauparaha after the Wairau affray or the kinsmen of the executed chief Martin Luther), they would, when approached, assist in enforcing the law. Neither attempts at coercion, nor payments 'to sell one of themselves, as it were, like a parcel of goods', would make any difference. Beckham, the Auckland Resident Magistrate, felt that there was no more resistance from Maori than from Europeans to the execution of warrants in the towns and that while there might be difficulty and need for negotiation with regard to the serving of warrants in the interior, he could not recall a previous case when offenders were not eventually given up or at least compensation made. No doubt he had in mind the case of a band of young Maori who in December 1855 had robbed settlers about Waiuku and seriously assaulted a man named Sutton. The Government in this case was not satisfied with offers of compensation, and the immediate chief of the offenders' *hapu* pronounced himself willing but unable to surrender them. However in March 1856, in response to official diplomacy, a big meeting of Waikato chiefs convened under Te Wherowhero and, having been assured that the young men's lives would not be forfeited, arranged for the culprits to be brought in to Auckland by their own *hapu*.[31] The Select Committee reported that there were few cases when measures proposed in the Native Offenders Bill would have been needed to enforce the law—a significant finding to set against the stream of invective about 'Maori outrage' which filled the settler press. Nevertheless the necessity to resort to diplomatic bargaining was regretted by all, and the House of Representatives resolved to ask the Executive to devise some form of municipal institutions for interior districts together with Pakeha magistrates and juries of chiefs, perhaps under clause 71 of the Constitution Act, which authorised the creation of Native Districts.[32]

In late 1856 and early 1857 however, the Government received reports of the developing King movement, and in April 1857 Governor Browne himself visited the Waikato and talked with Kingite leaders including Potatau. There he learned of the desire of the Maori both for laws which would meet their needs and for responsibility in the makng and enforcing of law. He believed that if the Government satisfied them on these scores the determination to elect a king would be given up. Indeed he came away from the meeting believing that he had received undertakings from Potatau to that effect. Probably the old chief had been politely ambiguous to his importunate and high-ranking guest, for the Maori had no intention of abandoning the movement. When in May a further meeting expressed even stronger Kingite sentiments Browne felt that he had been deceived. He was inclined to pomposity and hypersensitivity to slights, real or imagined, to his or his Queen's dignity, and his attitude towards the King movement abruptly hardened. He concluded hastily that 'though they constantly professed loyalty to Her Majesty the Queen, attachment to myself and a desire for the amalgamation of races, they did mean to maintain their separate nationality'.[33] An all-embracing sovereignty of the European type, which would eventually involve all Maori would, he considered, be incompatible with British authority. A second objection was that the King movement would claim powers of administration which it would not in fact be able to exercise, and this would lead to Maori, nominally under the King's jurisdiction, actually being beyond all law. Such a situation was fraught with danger of collision between Maori and settlers. Browne therefore concluded, 'I assume that it would not be safe strictly to permit the election of a King, and the next question is what steps should be taken to render such an election either unsuccessful or nugatory'.[34]

There was then, no move to welcome the Kingites' efforts as constructive. McLean and the Assistant Native Secretary, T. H. Smith (formerly Resident Magistrate at Rotorua) hoped that by ignoring the movement and continuing their personal blandishments of the leading chiefs, Kingism would go away.[35] Fenton, however, involved the government in the support of a counter-movement. In March 1857 he had reported enthusiastically from Whaingaroa of the *runanga* movement in his district. As he found it the younger chiefs were proposing elective councils of twelve for each village, to make regulations for the village. Two or three Maori wardens or magistrates in each village were to enforce the regulations and to meet together to establish district regulations or to settle disputes between villages. Fenton's informant wished to have a European to advise them and preside in the settlement of inter-village disputes, and they proposed to send offenders who defied their rulings to gaol in Auckland.[36] Since variations of this scheme were subsequently to be propounded by a succession of officials as their own brainchildren, it is worth recording that Fenton regarded it as originating entirely from a section of the Waikato Maori themselves. He also rightly observed that the King movement and *runanga* movement sprang from the Maori's recognition 'that the Government of the country is more anxious to obtain possession of their lands for the augmentation of the intruding body, than to elevate the present possessors, and admit them amongst themselves as a competent part of our people'. He was justifiably impressed with their ability to use law as the basis of economic advancement—coping with vexed questions of stock trespass, fencing and noxious weeds. And he tried to anticipate the Governor's and the settlers' dread of a Maori *imperium in imperio* by urging the stationing of statutory circuit court magistrates in the Waikato, to link the *runanga* in a form of indirect rule, overall direction of the movement remaining with the Government.

So far these proposals matched well with the aspirations of some at least of the Waikato Maori, but at this point Fenton's preconceptions and ulterior motives intruded. His dislike of the traditional chiefly system led him to stress the elective principle. He tended to overlook the fact that his young favourites, Waata Kukutai, Takerei Te Rau and Tioriori—were themselves men of high traditional rank, rising in natural succession to their elders because they were better educated and better able to adapt to new needs. Fenton mistakenly thought that the older chiefs like Potatau could easily be won over or brushed aside. He failed even to see how much the young chiefs were themselves deeply worried about their subordination and loss of independence—the fact that, as they put it, the Governor and magistrates 'grew higher and higher, and now they are far higher than we are'. He actually intended that the recognition of the *runanga* would turn them away from ambitions to take a share in the main organs of government, to which he considered they were '*theoretically* entitled' as British subjects but '*actually* not qualified'. Finally he saw his scheme as a means of organising the concentration of settlement in villages, the consolidation and fencing of land holdings, and the growing of pasture for sheep. He hoped that once reassured of title and income by these means, the chiefs' fears of loss of independence would diminish and they would begin selling land. A scheme so paternalistic and underlain by ulterior motives could hardly fail to arouse the antagonism of the suspicious Kingites.

But Fenton's proposals commended themselves to the settler Ministry. In April, when he had first returned from the Waikato, Governor Browne had drawn up proposals which, if implemented, would have gone far towards meeting Maori needs. He had instructed Fenton to draw up a code of law which grappled with problems not well covered in the colonial laws but important to the Maori—questions such as adultery, sorcery, stock trespass, and 'that peculiar form of swearing considered so heinous by the Natives'. To his Ministers he recommended the appointment of a circuit court magistrate and additional assessors, and the transfer of authority to grant 'bush licences' for the sale of liquor from the provincial authorities to the Governor. He advocated the enrolment of a Maori militia, under a European officer, and on the crucial question of land settlement he recommended that settlers choosing to reside in Maori districts should be required to obtain a permit, renewable every two years subject to good behaviour. However, recommendations to limit settlement, to arm the Maori and to strengthen the prerogatives of the Governor were all anathema to the Ministers and were ignored. Instead they took up Browne's suggestion for a circuit court magistrate and recommended that Fenton be sent into the Waikato to pilot the scheme.[37]

Fenton went as C. W. Richmond's protegé, reporting to him. He replaced the ineffectual Dr Harsant who had been stationed at Rangiaowhia in the upper Waikato as Resident Magistrate and medical officer since 1854 but who had scarcely attempted to act as magistrate. The results of Fenton's activity were predictable. He did succeed in winning the co-operation of some of the younger chiefs, in having a number of courthouses built, in hearing a number of cases and in sorting out some disputes with contractors who had built storage sheds for the Waikato Maori at Onehunga wharf, Auckland, where they unloaded grain. But he deliberately polarised opinion between Kingites and those whom he called the Queen party or 'people of law'. These he encouraged to build new settlements, much as the missionaries had earlier founded Christian settlements away from the pagan villages. Although specifically invited by Rewi Maniapoto, one of the most truculent of the Kingite chiefs, he declined to visit any village that did not give prior indication of commitment to obey his judicial decisions; he failed to call on Potatau, whom he wrote privately of as 'a stupid old man' and in his attempts to have some pastures sown, meddled with land to which Potatau had a claim.[38] It was not surprising, then, that Potatau and Ngapora complained to McLean that he was antagonising and dividing the Waikato people. McLean, who had all along considered Fenton's plan far too provocative to the older chiefs, was glad to recommend that Browne withdraw him. Fenton left the Waikato in early 1858, about the time Potatau finally moved from Mangere to be installed as King.

Fenton's mission had had the effect of stimulating not undermining the King movement, and this was largely because he had been so manifestly setting out to build a Queen party. This should not obscure the fact that much of what he offered was considered useful by the Waikato people. It would be wrong to regard the chiefs who accepted assessorships and built courthouses as motivated only by personal ambition and greed, as some of Fenton's critics alleged. Certainly traditional rivalries and factionalism entered into it: Wiremu Nera and his tribe at Whaingaroa were at odds with Potatau over land claims and had entered into negotiations with the Government to sell land. But to young men like Takerei Te Rau, of Potatau's own tribe the Ngatimahuta, Tioriori of Tamihana's tribe the Ngatihaua, and Wiremu Te Wheoro of Kohekohe village, whose father was a King supporter, the King movement appeared retrogressive. Takerei Te Rau was in the grip of an enthusiasm for economic development, declaiming,

> I am weary of poverty—and when I look at the size of my land, and what is growing on it, I say we are a foolish race. But I now have embraced knowledge, and shall strive to put down all Maori ways, and become like the white people. I am also anxious to get a pakeha who can teach us all about agriculture, and prevent us from wasting our labour. Now law and all these good things go together.

He asserted a claim to work his land without hindrance from the King movement: 'I shall not interfere with you in digging fern-root; don't you interfere with me in growing wool'; and he endorsed Fenton's plans for fencing and sowing pasture and for laws to protect sheep from worrying by dogs. But the Kingite spokesmen feared deeper complications—that by the granting of government credits for grass-seed and sheep 'the name of the Queen would stick to all the land covered with grass'. Many Waikato Maori were earnestly seeking to judge between these opinions. One old man named Ruia, had given a pledge of support to Tamihana and would not break it; his son Kipa urged him to support Fenton saying, 'If your wheat is injured there will be no magistrate to seek compensation for you. Living without law, where will be your fence?' He replied 'Why can we not have two roads, and still unite about the law? Why can I not remain attached to the king and still join your plans?'[39] This was a sentiment which Tamihana and Ngapora might have echoed, for they would have welcomed technical advisers and did not even entirely close the door to the Queen's magistrates. It was the adamancy of Fenton's view of the King movement—that it was incompatible with English law and the progress of settlement—that prevented Ruia from getting an affirmative answer.

By its legislation of 1858 the Assembly further demonstrated how it proposed to use the law to promote policies, in regard to land, incompatible with the Maori aspirations that had given rise to the King movement. The Native District Regulations Act authorised local councils—the *runanga* of Fenton's scheme—under a Pakeha chairman, to make by-laws on matters of local concern. The Native District Circuit Courts Act authorised the appointment of Circuit Court Judges, with jurisdiction slightly wider than that of the Resident Magistrates, to sit with Maori Assessors and juries to enforce common law together with the by-laws. The Act also empowered the Governor-in-Council to make regulations giving the Maori Assessors an independent petty jurisdiction of up to £5 in civil cases or a £1 fine in criminal cases. The framer of the Acts, C. W. Richmond, argued that 'there has been no proper adaptation of British institutions to the present condition of the aborigines. It is unreasonable to expect that they should accept our laws without local modification of detail which even British citizens require.'[40] He now proposed to introduce in Maori communities institutions English in spirit if not absolutely in form, to supply the particular needs of the Maori tribes and win their confidence and support. This approach, not dissimilar to the spirit of FitzRoy's and George Clarke's policies of 1843-4, had much to recommend it. Pakeha officers might have proved acceptable, even to the Kingites, provided they went among them to assist their efforts, rather than to promote settler interests or attempt a too rapid reorganisation of society along English lines. Unfortunately the third of Richmond's measures, the Native Territorial Rights Bill, betrayed just those weaknesses. It envisaged the determination of land boundaries by the Circuit Court Judges and Maori juries, and the award of Crown grants totalling up to 50,000 acres a year in individual title as directed by Governor-in-Council. This could then be alienated direct to settler buyers, subject to a tax of 10 shillings per acre. The movement towards individualisation was supported by many officials of humanitarian inclination, who were persuaded by the aggressiveness of settler 'direct purchase' agitation and by the dwindling of the Maori population that the settlers would get the land sooner or later anyway, and that it was better to initiate the process in a controlled way.

Browne, however, objected to the limitations on the amount of land which could be Crown granted; he envisaged granting larger areas to the Maori owners and placing much of it under restriction from sale, a process which the settlers bitterly opposed. Browne also objected to the continued encroachment of the Ministers on his control of Maori policy through the Governor-in-Council clause. The Colonial Office, sharing his views and also fearing the consequences of direct purchase, disallowed the Native Territorial Rights Bill.

In 1859-60 Browne tried again to break the deadlock on the land question, taking up a plan of the moderate politician Henry Sewell to administer Maori affairs through a Native Council. The Council was to include public figures such as Bishop Selwyn and the former Chief Justice, William Martin, and undertake the purchase of large areas of land, substantial portions of which would be returned to the Maori owners on inalienable legal title, other portions reserved for religious and educational endowment (principally for Maori) and the rest sold. It was hoped that the Council would win the confidence of both Maori and settlers.[41] But the settlers wanted full control and mounted a successful lobby in London against the Bill introduced in the English parliament to give effect to the Native Council. Browne in turn reserved a Native Council Bill from the New Zealand legislature which would have made the councillors merely puppets of the Ministry. The deadlock in Maori policy between the Governor and his Ministers remained. In the circumstances considerable initiative passed to the Native Secretary, Donald McLean.

McLean's goals were not substantially different from those of most settlers. He considered that his main task was to acquire land and to assimilate the Maori by inducing them gradually 'to come over from the ranks of their countrymen to those of the Colonists and to change [their] aboriginal right in the soil to one derived from the Crown'. However he criticised the schemes of Fenton and Richmond and proposed to move 'by gradual and almost imperceptible steps' so as not to alienate conservative Maori opinion, particularly that of the chiefs.[42]

This policy he applied to the Resident Magistracy. In 1855 Resident Magistrates had been appointed in several more remote districts and had run into difficulty. A. S. Shand was sent by the Wellington Provincial authorities to the Chatham Islands on the urging of some of the settlers there who had alleged that their previously harmonious relations with the Maori had broken down when the latter acquired several barrels of spirits from a wrecked ship. The local Maori, a branch of the Atiawa tribe, had not been consulted and the larger section under the chief Toenga Te Poki declined to allow Shand to land, saying 'the Governor has no authority over the Maoris'. At a second attempt Shand was accompanied by Carkeek, the Collector of Customs at Wellington, and the Wellington chiefs, Te Puni and Wi Tako. After several meetings these men persuaded Toenga that Shand came 'as an obstacle to disturbances' and the chief admitted that his people were 'quite pleased' with the laws of the Queen and the Church of England. Even so Carkeek had to promise in writing to remove Shand if he 'misbehaved' towards the Maori. Henceforth Shand's relations with the Maori varied astonishingly. Toenga and some other chiefs took office as Assessors and Tidewaiters (or Assistant Collectors of Customs) and eventually received salaries of £50. Disputes were brought and settled in Shand's court, but Shand was frequently in conflict with Toenga and his family. When he remonstrated with the chief at the way the conquered Moriori people were treated by their Maori conquerors (about 200 of this earlier wave of Pacific migrants remaining in Shand's time) Toenga defied him and wrote letters to the Government accusing Shand of drunkenness and supplying liquor to women in order to seduce them. For a time Shand was denied access to his office and books. It was a broken-backed sort of authority that he exercised, but it staggered on until his replacement in 1861.[43]

At Poverty Bay the leading chiefs Raharuhi Rukupo and Kahutia had both at times requested a magistrate to adjust disputes with settlers and to check the unlawful sale of liquor, but the land question as usual intruded. Kahutia had sold land rights to traders and settlers in the 1830s and 1840s but later considered that he had acted foolishly and wished to return the payment. Raharuhi and the others all along denied Kahutia's right to sell. The settlers had threatened that the Government would compel the Maori to respect the sale and the arrival of Herbert Wardell as Resident Magistrate was consequently regarded with suspicion. Nevertheless after a few awkward days Raharuhi did bring a dispute before Wardell and he and Kahutia became Assessors. Wardell's return for his first full year of office showed one prosecution of a Maori for 'armed demands' from a settler, six prosecutions brought by Maori against settlers, mostly for breach of the Sale of Spirits Ordinance, and four charges— three of assault and one of felony—by Maori against other Maori. Civil cases —settlements for debts or claims for damages—included seven between Maori parties and twenty between Maori and settlers. Many more disputes were settled out of court.[44]

In 1858 Wardell's difficulties increased. In May, under Kingite influence, a great meeting established a *runanga* for Poverty Bay. Kahutia subsequently stated, 'I had the *mana* before the Pakeha came and I have it still. We have done with the Queen from today . . . The Queen brings her *mana* here and takes the land.'[45] His view was not unjustified for Wardell was reporting on land claims to McLean, and upholding the Government view that land sold by Maori to settlers in good faith but in breach of the Land Claims Ordinance passed to the Crown. In September Wardell's authority as a magistrate was gravely flouted after he had distrained some cattle from a settler named Wyllie, a sly troublesome man, who had refused to pay a fine for illegally selling spirits. Kinsmen of Wyllie's Maori wife came to the pound and released the cattle, knocking Wardell about in the process. Raharuhi proffered assistance in their recovery and Wardell waited in great agony of mind on the appointed day for him to come, but the chief did not appear. Wardell's position was pathetic. His family also suffered many of the anxieties and deprivations characteristic of frontier life. His wife urged him to leave: 'she says and not without truth—that we are facing a miserable existence—without a Church, without society and no good prospect of any advance—and in constant anxiety on account of the children. We feel so much the want of medical advice.'[46]

Nevertheless the Resident Magistrate did not entirely despair. He believed it was possible to gain considerable influence with the Maori by discussing details of their disputes and offering guidance on their solution, a guidance which they valued. Enforcement of his magisterial decisions was another matter. He did not think the provision for Maori juries in the Native Circuit Courts Act would help much where the defendant was of higher rank or of a different *hapu* from the complainant. He believed some acknowledgment of a common authority was necessary and sought the appointment of some constables to the district. The Government did send some police from Auckland to arrest Wyllie and take him back with them to serve a gaol sentence; but they declined to station police permanently in Poverty Bay for fear of their being defied, which would oblige the Government either to accept humiliation or to send a large force in their support. Instead, in 1859, over Wardell's protests, it was decided to withdraw him.

Even in the Wanganui district the administration of justice deteriorated. This was largely because the Resident Magistrate, Major D. S. Durie, a stiff-necked and self-righteous officer, prosecuted Maori without carefully sifting the accusations of settlers. Moreover he did not get out on circuit as much as his predecessors, but sat in Wanganui. In 1857 some Patea Maori took a horse from a settler who owed them money, rather than lay a complaint before Durie because, they said, 'the Europeans would all be against them in the Town and . . . if the Magistrate liked to come and try the case in the Pah it would all be well and good'.[47] But Durie promptly proceeded against the Maori for theft and sought to arrest the chief Rio as an accomplice. It was hardly surprising that he lost influence in the district. In 1858 feuding broke out on the Wanganui River. This was partly over land and partly over a dispute about a widow between the *hapu* of the *ariki* Te Mamaku (who stood by the customary right of her late husband's brothers to find a new man for her from their *hapu*) and a Catholic *hapu* led by the French missionary Father Lampila (who had married her to a member of his congregation). Durie tended to take the side of Lampila and English law, but custom was too strong and he proved ineffectual. The Rev. Richard Taylor of the CMS was eventually asked by the Government to mediate.[48]

Because of these patchy results, C. W. Richmond and the Ministers felt that Resident Magistrates in Maori districts, unsupported by force, were quite out of place. The Fenton experiment was seen as a failure, a request for a magistrate in Waiapu on the East Coast was not approved, and no replacement was sent to Rotorua after T. H. Smith was removed from there in 1856 to become Assistant Native Secretary. McLean persisted, but more discreetly. In 1858 he asked J. Preece, the son of a Wesleyan missionary settled at Coromandel peninsula, to act as mediator in cattle trespass disputes, and in feuding which broke out near Whakatane in 1858. The Native Secretary observed, 'in reality more good is done by persons acting in that capacity, frequently, when they are not Magistrates than when possessing the nominal powers of that office'.[49] In early 1859 however, he had J. S. Clendon, Resident Magistrate at Russell, and W. B. White, Resident Magistrate at Mangonui, made Circuit Court Judges under the Act of 1858. Clendon had had much success in a visit to Hokianga in 1858 when he heard no less than sixty-seven civil disputes between Maori and settlers, some of ten years standing. McLean did not, however, introduce a *runanga* system under the Native District Regulations Act. On the contrary, Clendon was told to avoid as far as possible any appearance of novelty and change of system but to regard his work as an extension of that already in operation under the Resident Magistrates' Court Ordinance. Clendon and White were favourably received on their first regular round of court sittings and were ordered to keep working quietly and recommend the next steps. It was probably a measure of the success of this cautious approach that the Rarawa for the first time assisted White in sending one of their number for trial in the Supreme Court in Auckland for a serious theft.[50]

Meanwhile, new efforts had been made in the Waikato which threw important light on the attitude of the Kingites. Tamati Ngapora had told Browne that after the excitement caused by Fenton's activities had died down 'we shall be glad to have a judicious person act as magistrate'.[51] Accordingly in April 1859 Hanson Turton, a former Wesleyan missionary who sought employment in the Native Department, was sent on an exploratory circuit of both the Bay of Plenty and the Waikato. He was strictly instructed not to press English law on the Maori but to await their requests to arbitrate. He was to see Potatau as soon as possible, gauge Waikato opinion, but do nothing to widen the breach between those hostile and those favourable to the introduction of English magistrates. Turton eventually reported that the Bay of Plenty people welcomed his coming but did not want gaols. In the Waikato, contrary to his expectation, he found confidence in the Government 'still remarkably apparent' except on the subject of land. He saw no reason for apprehension 'so long as their wants and condition are well enquired after, and their desires or prejudices respected . . . It can only be by some great mismanagement, that their affections, as a body, can be alienated from us. Potatau Te Wherowhero was very strong in some of his remarks on the subject'. The King movement was no more nor less than a league to prevent land sales, but even in this it could not pretend to bind the tribes against land-selling by armed interference. With regard to judicial authority several cases were referred to Turton for judgment 'and at Te Wherowhero's own place, at Ngaruawahia, I was requested to return and afford them general instruction'. Turton did not however think they would welcome a magistrate resident at Rangiaowhia and recommended the appointment of a visiting magistrate at that stage.[52] Consequently Henry Halse, Resident Magistrate and Assistant Native Secretary at New Plymouth, was moved to Auckland from where he made forays into lower Waikato to hear cases. H. T. Clarke (an interpreter and the third son of George Clarke the former Chief Protector) was appointed to the Bay of Plenty and Major Speedy, a retired regular officer, was appointed to the settlement at Patumahoe (or Mauku) south of Auckland.

In 1860 Wardell was moved from Poverty Bay to the Wairarapa; but again he was to visit it from Wellington, lest it appear that a magistrate was being forced on the district; Turton also was moved south, to the Rangitikei-Manawatu district and instructed to 'take no apparent notice of the dis-inclination of the Natives to submit their differences to you' but quietly to hear all cases brought forward.[53]

Further south still A. C. Strode, Resident Magistrate at Dunedin, and James Mackay, Resident Magistrate at Collingwood, near Nelson, were also designated Assistant Native Secretaries. They were to adjust outstanding boundary questions left over from the South Island land purchases of 1848-53 and to arrange medical care for the small South Island Maori population. W. L. Buller, another Wesleyan missionary's son, was made special commissioner to the Canterbury reserves where a sudden demand from sawyers for the limited timber lands of the reserves had given rise to squabbling among the claimants. Buller, with the support of the younger men in particular, supervised a sub-division of the principal reserves into individual blocks.[54] In addition to these appointments doctors in various rural centres were paid annual subsidies of about £100 by the Native Department to treat Maori patients. McLean and Browne wanted to appoint more medical officers and magistrates but the ministry declined funds for them. In relation to a proposed appointment of a Resident Magistrate at Waipukurau in southern Hawke's Bay they revived a long-standing settler demand that Justices of the Peace should instead be given jurisdiction in disputes involving Maori.[55]

Among McLean's new appointees the most noteworthy was another High-lander, James Mackay. Mackay had taken up land in the Nelson district with his father, learned Maori and become noted as an explorer of the alpine passes in the region. He was an energetic officer and needed all his energies to grapple with conflicts and passions caused by the opening of the goldfields in the Collingwood area after 1858. Mackay had some success in securing pay-ment of mining rights to Maori land-holders and enabled Maori to take out miners licences themselves. In the case of the smaller strikes on Maori land, Maori miners, including itinerants from the North Island, seem to have been in the majority. Mackay prosecuted settlers who trespassed on Maori reserves, stealing fruit and shooting pigs, and tried to control the drunken brawling characteristic of mining towns when it threatened to involve Maori—an almost impossible task since he had the assistance of only three rather intimidated Provincial police constables. Working with the principal chiefs Mackay arbitrated and adjudicated in the quarrels of the Maori communities themselves. In two cases of alleged murder he had the assailants referred to the Supreme Court instead of being immediately killed in *utu*. With the gold rush the Maori of the district became a small minority and Mackay's interventions on their behalf were both essential and relatively effective. In the short run they shared the temporary prosperity of the goldfield rather than becoming the victims of it.

Nevertheless the Maori were left little opportunity to preserve a long-term economic independence. This was not entirely Mackay's fault, although he worked diligently to round off the land purchases made in Grey's time and at the best possible bargain to the Government. Grey's initial purchases had included the offer that Maori could buy back the land (now under legal title) at the upset price of 10 shillings an acre before it went to public auction. Mackay tried to give effect to this offer, but by then the Crown lands had been transferred to the Provinces for sale and settlement and he was blocked by the Provincial authorities. Moreover the local Commissioners of Native Reserves (led by Alfred Dommett, erstwhile poet and shortly to be Premier of New Zealand) who frustrated Mackay's efforts to get better leases for the reserves and make more funds available for agricultural machinery which the Maori beneficial owners were anxious to acquire. Despite Mackay's efforts therefore, the Nelson-Marlborough *hapu* were left with a deep sense of injustice at what they considered a breach of faith by the Government on the basic question of land.[56]

In sum, McLean's quiet extension of the Resident Magistrate system had much to commend it, and was securing a not unfavourable response from several districts, including the Waikato. But since officials such as Mackay were in general supporting the settler drive for land, and proved unable even to implement the terms promised to Maori land-sellers, the land question remained a fundamental source of antagonism between Maori and Government. And in promoting the Waitara purchase of 1859-60, McLean himself initiated a 'great mismanagement' which as Turton feared, truly alienated the Waikato tribes and led to open war.

VIII

Resort to War

The root of the Waitara dispute (the intricacies of which have been discussed by Professor Sinclair[1]) was the determination of the authorities, principally McLean, to establish a system of land-purchasing from the sub-chiefs
of *hapu* supposedly with primary rights in the land and actually resident on it,
regardless of the objections of senior chiefs speaking for the wider tribal
group.[2] Although McLean had tried to deal with individual sub-chiefs on
previous occasions he had generally deferred to objections from a senior chief.[3]
The Government's acceptance of the Waitara block from Teira, a minor chief
of the Puketapu, against the objections of Wiremu Kingi, acknowledged leader
of the Puketapu, reflected a new determination in policy. Browne, who had
become increasingly touchy about the Crown's prerogatives since the development of the King movement, was persuaded that, without a hereditary primary
right to cultivate the land, a senior chief had no grounds to interfere—that if
he did interfere he was in effect a bully, an interferer with private rights, an
agent of unlawful Maori land leagues, and an encroacher on the rights of the
Crown.[4] The Taranaki settlers were therefore delighted to hear, in March
1859, the Governor's declaration that, while he would not buy any land where
a minority of owners did not wish to sell, he would not allow Kingi to exercise
the right of chieftainship to deter 'the rightful owners' from selling the land.[5]

Browne believed in fact that his stand would establish the authority of the
Government in a way that had not yet been done in New Zealand, that the
rule of law would prevail, and that purchases of land could thenceforth
be effected without feud between holders and sellers. As he put it, 'I have
insisted on this purchase . . . because had I admitted the right of a chief to
interfere between me and the lawful proprietors of the soil, I should soon
have found further acquisition of territory impossible in any part of New
Zealand.'[6]

The Taranaki settlers also saw much more involved than the possession of
a block of land. They believed a showdown had to come and they believed
both the time and the occasion to be right. 'The great end is . . . to let them
see and feel our power' one wrote. For another the issue was whether 'Her Fair
Majesty or His Dark Majesty shall reign in New Zealand'. They dressed their
ambitions with humanitarian sentiments about the great good that would
follow for the Maori people.[7]

But the occasion was extremely badly chosen. Not only did Kingi have actual cultivations in the block (which McLean and his officers tried to get him to define with a view to partitioning out) but the Government's claim that the Waitara block was the patrimony of two *hapu* of the Puketapu people, with Teira at their head, distinct from Kingi's *hapu,* could not stand close investigation. As Sinclair has shown, four small Waitara *hapu* were closely inter-married. They were sometimes collectively known as the Manukorihi and Kingi, in addition to being acknowledged leader of the group, had essentially similar hereditary standing in it to Teira.[8] Even Ropoama Te One, a Atiawa chief at Marlborough Sounds upon whom McLean greatly relied for evidence in Teira's favour, could only claim, 'The land does not belong to William King *alone,* others have a right to it *as well as him.*'[9] As Fenton stated when he later investigated the genealogy, 'How anyone could think of negotiating for that block from Taylor [Teira] I can't think.'[10]

But although they found their ground shaky and Kingi's resistance unshakable, the Government was not going to back down. The Rev. Samuel Williams of Hawke's Bay, reported the Assistant Native Secretary, T. H. Smith, as summing up their reasoning in three propositions: 'It will never do for the Government to acknowledge an error to a Maori'; 'The natives are so divided by their petty differences they will not be able to resist' and 'There is such a pressure for land'.[11] Following an Executive Council decision to protect the survey of the land by military force, and the interruption of the survey by Maori women who lived on the land, martial law was declared in Taranaki. Smith wrote to Halse to go to Potatau and tell him that the Government was determined that each man should deal with his piece of land as he saw fit, 'that the land had been bought and paid for and will be surveyed and taken possession of' and that the Governor relied on him to contain the Waikato Maori known to be sympathetic to Kingi.[12] In Taranaki, settlers flocked to join the militia and support the regulars and in April a *pa* Kingi had built on the land was attacked. Browne and his advisers had decided to force Maori submission in what they hoped would be a brief but decisive exercise of power. The determined resistance of Kingi and his supporters gave the lie to that hope.

As the war dragged on it became important for the Government to isolate the Taranaki 'rebels'. To this end, in July 1860, Browne and McLean invited to Kohimarama, Auckland, an assembly of chiefs from most districts in New Zealand. Had this come years earlier when Tamihana and others had vainly sought a central Maori council under Government sponsorship it might have appeared a generous act and gained a generous response. But coming after the Government had made war in Taranaki it appeared to the Kingites an act of deception and none attended. Blind to the injustice of his proceedings in Taranaki, Browne put forward the proud claim that

New Zealand is the only Colony where the Aborigines have been treated with unvarying kindness. It is the only Colony where they have been invited to become one people under one law . . . It will be the wisdom of the Maori people to avail themselves of this generous policy . . . Every Maori is a member of the British nation; he is protected by the same law as his English fellow subjects.

Browne admitted there was a difficulty in admitting Maori to the governing councils of the land because they did not understand English. However, the mission boarding schools, receiving Government subsidies, were to overcome this and he urged support for them. Meanwhile the assembled chiefs were offered a new codification of English law written by Sir William Martin and intended to replace the code drawn up by Fenton, which McLean, with justification, considered too elaborate and full of legal niceties. The independent £5 jurisdiction of the Assessors was explained and they were assured of higher salaries. The chiefs were urged to give up customs such as *muru* in favour of resort to law courts, and to seek individual title to land.[13]

The chiefs' replies summed up their view of twenty years of British rule. On the credit side, Waka Nene restated his view that the land had been passing before 1840 and he was glad of the Governor's coming. Paikea of the small Uriohau tribe at Kaipara said: 'I am small and friendless . . . Other tribes threatened to cut me in pieces, but I kept close the Queen, and stooped to shelter under her wings . . . It is now only that I stand as a man.' Others showed their consideration for the technology of the Pakeha. Waka Nene again said, 'Let me remind you that my wife does not know to weave garments. Wherefore I say, let the Europeans weave garments for me.' Te Kihirini said he had no desire to return to eating fern root and *hinau* berries. Paora Tuhaere, chief of the Ngatiwhatua, of Auckland, and chiefs further southward, expressed dissatisfaction with the Treaty of Waitangi, which they regarded as a hastily signed affair of the Ngapuhi that should not be held to bind them; but a conference of the kind then assembled, went far to satisfy them, and some speakers referred to the proceedings as a new pact between Governor and chiefs, the Treaty of Kohimarama.

Several speakers also expressed commitment to settling disputes through the courts of law. The Ngatiwhakaue speakers in particular, expressing satisfaction at the execution of Charles Marsden for the murder of Kerara in 1855, promised to surrender even chiefs to British justice if they committed capital offences. Tamihana Te Rauparaha of Otaki expressed a view much in accord with a widespread settler opinion that the Maori people did not obey their chiefs anyway, and therefore needed to come under the direction of the law. Te Kihirini also spelled out explicit agreement with the principle of individual responsibility for offences: 'Now murder was a cause of contention and fighting in olden times. When the *pa* was captured a hundred persons died for the sin of one man. At the present time the life of the murderer is the atonement of his guilt. I approve of this system.'

But the chiefs were not prepared to swallow the Pakeha system unsifted. Particular exception was taken to a new proposal in Martin's law code to treat adultery no longer as a civil offence with damages payable to the husband, but as a criminal offence with a fine payable to the Crown. Martin's proposal was intended to counter the tendency of Maori husbands, once having discovered this fruitful aspect of English law, to encourage their wives' waywardness as a source of revenue. But it was deeply unpopular with the chiefs at Kohimarama, who said that aggrieved husbands were still likely to extract payment from their wives' paramours. M. P. Kawiti of the Bay of Islands (the turbulent son of Kawiti, Hone Heke's ally) reported that while a *runanga* of his people had agreed to surrender adulterers to the law courts, they would kill sorcerers themselves. He claimed authority from the scriptural injunction 'Thou shalt not suffer a witch to live'. The chiefs also took objection to an attempt to prohibit the making of a dish of steeped or fermented maize (a grain relatively new to the Maori) which was considered by the authorities to be a serious cause of malnutrition. Winiata Pekama (Tohi Te Ururangi) of Maketu expressed the growing interest of the 'modernising' young chiefs in individual land-holdings which they could leave intact to their wives and children. But there were also objections (not made in open speeches but submitted in a letter from the Ngatiwhatua people) that sub-divisions made about Auckland under official auspices tended to favour the chiefs, and that if it was argued that each man's piece was his own to keep under legal title, yet 'he would not be able to keep it, the chiefs would sell it . . . the owner would not be able to retain it through fear of the chief'.

The most fundamental criticism of the official line was expressed by Paora Tuhaere who refuted Browne's contention that Maori and Pakeha were equal under the law. He cited the ordinances against sale of spirits and arms which applied to Maori only, and the failure to provide Crown titles to customary land which would make their land rights equal to those of the settlers. Above all, he said, the Maori leaders were not admitted to the Pakeha councils which made the laws and arranged land questions. He brushed aside Browne's excuse about Maori ignorance of the English language, saying they had plenty of friends to interpret for them. He extended the argument to the law courts: 'I am desirous that the minds of the Europeans and the Maoris should be brought into unison with one another. Then if a Maori killed another Maori his crime would be tried and adjudicated on by the understanding of both Pakeha and Maori. And if one man should interfere with the land of another, then let the same council try him.'[14] Speaker after speaker took up the demand for admission to the institutions of state power: Ngarongomau of Kaipara said that if in days past the Maori chiefs had been taken into the European councils to frame laws for the land 'there would not have been any separation into two sides'. Tamihana Te Rauparaha pointed out that whereas Grey had had autocratic control now 'the Councils'—the Provincial Councils and the General Assembly—had control of revenue, public works and 'all things'. For this reason, he said, the chiefs were most anxious that Maori should take part in the Councils. He also asked for mixed juries in cases involving Maori, arguing that this would make Maori much more willing to surrender offenders to justice. And he wanted Maori enrolled in the militia, and entrusted to defend the settlements, instead of the stockades of troops dotted about the country, obviously directed against the Maori.

The central point made by the chiefs at the conference was clear and unequivocal. They wanted to remain in allegiance to the Crown and to engage with the European order; but they did not want to do so on terms of subordination and contempt for their values. Rather they wanted to be involved, as responsible and well-intentioned parties, in the machinery of state and the shaping of laws and institutions appropriate to the emerging bi-racial New Zealand. On that basis a bureaucratic state and the rule of law could yet be established with Maori co-operation.

But the officials could not overcome their ethnocentrism, their deep-seated view that the Maori were still fundamentally barbarous and immature. To McLean this was an obvious fact that he had no need to cloak. Of the chiefs' claim for admission to the governing councils he said: 'Children cannot have what belongs to persons of mature age; and a child does not grow to be a man in a day.' He admitted that a law had been framed to permit enrolment of Maori jurors but he claimed that tribal particularity meant that Maori jurors would inevitably be partial towards their kinsmen. Since this view contradicted opinions he had expressed in 1856 about the surprising sense of equity shown by Maori Assessors it seems that his rise to precarious eminence had made McLean more conservative.

The Kohimarama conference wound up inconclusively with little gained by Maori or officials. The Governor got a rather lukewarm vote criticising the King movement and Wiremu Kingi but was also told categorically by several chiefs that he should have consulted with them before sending troops to Taranaki. He was urged to appoint a mixed Maori-European commission to investigate the Waitara question.

Once embarked on a military solution, however, the Government, a great majority of the settlers and a considerable number of missionaries were in an uncompromising mood. Attitudes also hardened against the King movement, which was regarded by Browne, amongst many others, as providing a general inspiration to so-called 'land leaguers' like Kingi. Interestingly a call for a more flexible attitude to the King movement came at this time from a high official, Sir William Dennison, Governor of New South Wales. Browne had asked Dennison to supply reinforcements for the war against Kingi. In addition to the troops Dennison sent some forthright advice. He began with the important premise that as British subjects the Maori were entitled to have not only their theoretical rights respected (Browne and the New Zealand officials had their own view of what those were) but their feelings as well. He considered that given the different values and institutions of the two races in New Zealand, 'amalgamation, however desirable it might be, could not be expected to take place for very many years'. This being so, Browne should not ignore or oppose the King movement or object to the title; rather he should suggest to the Maori the necessity of defining the King's power and establishing some system by which the movement could pass and administer local laws. In contrast to the prevailing New Zealand policy of trying to detach Maori individually from their culture and draw them over to the ranks of the colonists by means of individual land grants, Dennison argued that they should be treated as a distinct race, 'a body whose interests you are bound to respect and promote, and . . . give the means of describing what their interests, are, and of submitting them in proper form for your consideration'. Dennison was well aware that 'The first effect, of course, of the new system of policy, will be the cessation of purchases of land from the Maoris. They will decline to sell, and were I in your place, I should be in no hurry to buy.' He believed, however, that the Maori owners would soon want to sell in order to acquire capital, and then they should be enabled to sell direct to settlers in order that they could be satisfied they were getting the best price.[15]

Dennison's despatch, although incautious on the question of direct land purchase, embodied principles which had been lacking from the very inception of British rule in New Zealand: firstly a genuine respect for Maori values and feelings; secondly the offer of a genuine opportunity for Maori leaders to make their opinions effective in government; thirdly an implicit confidence that the Maori would use their opportunities responsibly and constructively within the framework of a bi-racial state. This approach embodied the reasonable expectation that separate development would not become entrenched, but that there would be a continued drawing together of the Maori and settler communities in social, economic and political life. The outcome would be a form of racial 'integration' rather than one-way assimilation of Maori into the settler culture. Certainly, some such approach was essential if the gap between King movement and Government was to be bridged.

In New Zealand Sir William Martin, the former Chief Justice, also argued that the King movement was constructive and should be recognised. He cited Ngapora's advice that this would allow Maori antagonisms to dissipate and encourage the Waikato leaders to again seek a working relationship with the Government. 'Let the waters ooze and drip away', the chief had said, 'do not dam them up.'[16] But recognition of the King movement implied a reversal of the whole emphasis of policy after 1840 and was scarcely conceivable in the face of entrenched attitudes not only of settlers but of officials and missionaries as well.

Settler attitudes were exemplified by C. W. Richmond. In reply to Martin's suggestions that the Government should seek to establish relations with the King movement, he painted an impassioned picture of the settlers' situation in Maori-dominated New Zealand:

> the colonist is exposed to daily provocations. His cattle for example, stray from his paddock; he follows them to a neighbouring Pa, and is compelled to redeem them by an exorbitant payment. In the course of the altercation a musket is,

perhaps, pointed at him, or a tomahawk flourished over his head. On the other hand should he try the experiment of driving Native cattle to the public pound for trespass on his cultivations, a strong party of Maoris, with loaded muskets, breaks down the pound and rescues them. He has to maintain party fences without contribution from his Maori neighbour. Herds of Native pigs break through his crops. The dogs of the Pa worry his sheep. To save his own farm he has to pay for the extirpation of thistles on the neighbouring Native land . . . Redress in the Courts of Law is not to be attained because it would be dangerous to the peace of the country to enforce the judgment. On the other hand, Natives freely avail themselves of their legal remedies against Europeans.[17]

This was a situation which Richmond considered would be perpetuated by recognition of the King movement or any bolstering of traditional Maori values and institutions. McLean gave similar reasons for refusing to contemplate requests from settlers in Hawke's Bay and Taranaki for amendments to the Native Land Purchase Ordinance to permit direct leasing by settlers from Maori—in effect to legalise the many informal leases which squatters had entered into with chiefs since 1840. McLean was adamant that any concession to leasing would entirely preclude the Government's chances of purchasing the freehold. He considered Maori landlordism so capricious and extortionate that 'no Englishman would long submit to it'.[18] All this was very one-sided, of course, and took little account of the fact that the settlers who complained were generally taking up runs illegally, were entirely beholden to the chiefs for permission to reside at all, and in turn materially interfered with Maori society. Nor did McLean appear to consider that putting the leaseholds on a legal basis might end much of the Maori capriciousness of which he complained.

In fact the settlers and the officials (who were now increasingly drawn from the settler ranks) alike had little confidence in Maori administrative competence, even when attempts were made to recognise and formalise it. The tendency for Maori to levy extortionate charges for pasturing cattle, ferrying travellers across rivers or providing food and shelter for them and their horses, was deeply resented by settlers. In 1857, after a settler had his horse seized when he refused to pay pasturage for droving cattle along a beach front, McLean tried to curb capricious demands by paying chiefs for providing rest houses for travellers, and drawing up a fixed scale of fees for paddocking or shelter. But this had had little effect. The *runanga* which had developed in the 1850s were regarded as extortionate, acrimonious, confused—simply a means by which one faction mulcted another by levying fines for breaches of puritanical Christian principles. Nor, apparently, were the chiefs inclined to abide by their own regulations: even a progressive chief like Tioriori of the Ngatihaua tribe, having stimulated a movement to erect a pound for wandering stock, broke the pound down when five of his own cattle were impounded. The official Assessors were often not regarded as much more effective. Sometimes their efforts to mitigate excessive demands were defied by the *runanga*. In other cases the Assessors themselves were known to be over-bearing and extortionate. Few settler judgments were as tolerant as that of G. S. Cooper, who reported that although the Hawke's Bay *runanga* levied exorbitant fines it had been effective in controlling drunkenness, and thefts and assaults on settlers had died away.[19] To a settler population deeply in competition with the Maori and prejudiced against their race and culture, the shortcomings of the Maori always gained more attention than their constructive achievements. There also remained areas of deep disagreement between the two people on the question of what constituted an offence against the law. The *runanga* dealt with sorcery, which the law codes did not recognise; the Maori concept of *puremu*—illicit sexual relations—sometimes extended to unmarried women, but English magistrates refused to treat this as adultery; in Collingwood a man burned down a reed house where his daughter had died (since he regarded it as *tapu* and no longer usable for ordinary habitation) and was charged by Mackay with arson;[20] Maori liked to dam up streams at regular intervals to harvest eels, whereas settlers wanted clear channels and drained ground; Maori claimed particular tribal rights in navigable waterways and tidal ground, but these were Crown demesne in English law. In all of these matters settlers and officials were impatient of Maori viewpoints. That the King movement would tend to entrench them was alarming. Settler objections were, moreover, often unreasoned, blindly racial. Even Fenton's limited efforts to work with some of the Waikato chiefs were denounced by Waikato settlers as likely to foster 'that self-conceit and pride in a race which ought to have looked up to the Europeans as their teachers for many a generation yet'.[21] When, by 1860, squatters in the Waikato began to be summonsed over stock disputes by Kingite *kaiwhakawa* or magistrates, their protests and the hue and cry in the settler press reached new heights.[22]

The clergy and 'humanitarians' in New Zealand, who might have been expected to have more detachment, showed little flexibility in their attitude to the King movement. Martin was exceptional. Although many of the Anglican clergy supported Kingi's claims in Taranaki they generally joined in the litany about the necessity for the Maori to abandon the King movement, sell land and merge with the settlers for their own well-being.

The Government, moreover, had persuaded itself that the King movement would not accept a defined and limited role in the state as Dennison envisaged. In April and May 1860 McLean drew up memoranda admitting that leaders such as Potatau and Ngapora sought to establish order and efficient administration and continue in good relations with the Government, but endorsing the conclusion that Browne had reached in 1857 that their followers could not be vouched for. Potatau's kingship was 'nominal' and simply a focus of disaffection which he and his chief councillors could not restrain. The movement as a whole was 'altogether too distinctive and national in character to admit of its being blended into any form which would recognise European direction or ascendancy'. This being so the Government should give no recognition or encouragement whatsoever to its proceedings.[23] The Governor recited these views in rejecting the possibility of declaring the Waikato a Native District under clause 71 of the 1852 constitution. He added that clause 71 applied only to the recognition of Maori custom in regard to the relations between Maori; it was not intended to authorise the administration by Maori of a mixed legal code to a mixed population.[24] This last argument was a legal pedantry; had there been the will to find a place for the King movement in government the law could have been found, or enacted, to validate it. But the Government's other objections were much more substantial. Was it in fact possible to limit the King movement's jurisdiction territorially? Would not formal recognition of the King movement stimulate Maori nationalism throughout the Colony (whether the Kingite leaders abetted it or not) leaving the settlers in a dreaded subordination to Maori power and virtually ending British rule in the North Island at least? And would the powerful chiefs like Te Heuheu and Rewi Maniapoto, who supported the King as a symbol of opposition to the Pakeha, acknowledge the right of the King's council and magistrates to punish offenders from their tribes? Or would their people rather be able to commit offences with impunity? Browne was entitled to misgivings on these grounds, and the anxiety of settlers, many of whom lived in very real, if unnecessary, fear for the safety of their women and children, is understandable.

Even so the Government had abruptly and inflexibly rejected any hopes of progress on these scores without ever putting them to the test. Their attitude reflected their fears, prejudices and ambitions rather than proven Maori responses. Potatau, Tamihana and Ngapora had constantly shown their desire to be advised by colonists, including officials, in building an effective administration. The limits to which this assistance would have been acceptable were never tested, but it is highly likely that the chiefs at Ngaruawahia, Potatau's capital, would have appreciated Government assistance in shaping legal codes, training a magistracy and equipping a police force. The whole thing would have depended upon whether they perceived the Government's efforts as intended to support them or to supplant them. If genuinely assured of the former it is quite probable that they would have accepted a subordinate role under an over-riding British sovereignty, nationalist sentiment being then ill-formed and ill-organised. Moreover, had the King movement been encouraged to hold land and develop it with Government technical and economic assistance member tribes would have been reluctant to deprive themselves of the resultant prosperity in order to shelter men wanted by the law. In the 1880s the Ngatimaniapoto leaders themselves came to terms with the government for precisely that reason.

Nationalist sentiment certainly gained strength in the King movement following the involvement of Waikato Maori, against the vehement opposition of Tamihana, in the Taranaki war in October 1860. The moderates, however, laboured to maintain relations with the Government. In February 1861 Tamati Ngapora, still living at Mangere, told T. H. Smith that he and his colleagues conceived of the King with authority in his territory, being essentially in

alliance with the Queen and Governor for common purposes.[25] In May Tamihana was still wearily explaining to Pakeha visitors that they should not get
unduly excited about the term 'King', that it implied no emnity to the Queen
but was simply a symbol about which they could rally to prevent disputes about
land and make laws to meet the many new needs of their society. He was
visited by the young Cambridge graduate John Gorst, newly arrived in the
Colony and intensely concerned to avoid collision with the King movement.
Gorst urged on Tamihana the advantages of being under British rule, 'that
they would live in a nation, and that social Institutions would be immediately
granted to them'. Tamihana was recorded as replying 'All this is very good,
we are willing to accept Magistrates tomorrow—we will have but one Tikanga
(rule) one Ture (law) and the Queen is a Fence for us all (Maori and
Pakeha) . . . but leave the King, let him stand . . . If he does any wrong
against the Queen then thrust him down—It is only a name—but let that
name stand.' He then constructed his aforementioned symbol of two sticks
representing the King and the Governor, a third across them, 'the law of God
and the Queen' and a circle about the whole—the Queen, the fence about
them all.[26]

It is indicative of the Government's determination to find justification for
not coming to terms with the King movement that, at this time, Tamihana,
desperately trying to steer a course between the militants of both races and
facing the execration of some of his own people for his efforts, was branded
by the Government as an extremist and not to be trusted.[27] In fact, although
the Government was well aware that the Waikato warriors had gone to Taranaki in defiance of the last wishes of Potatau (who died in June 1860 and was
succeeded by his son Matutaera) and the angry importunities of Tamihana,
although it was known that the moderates had quieted extremists who voiced
wild schemes for an attack on Auckland, and although a truce was achieved
in Taranaki largely owing to Tamihana's mediatory visit to the district in
March and April 1861, Browne resolved to use the involvement of individual
Kingites in Taranaki as grounds for demanding submission from the King
movement as a whole. In June 1861 he sent a proclamation to Ngaruawahia,
accusing the Waikato tribes of violating the Treaty of Waitangi and demanding 'From all: submission, without reserve, to the Queen's sovereignty and
the authority of the law'. This, Browne explained, meant acceptance that
roads and bridges could be taken through the Waikato, wherever the Government—on which the Maori were not represented—so authorised. It also meant
that 'combinations for the purpose of preventing other men from acting or
dealing with property as they think fit' were unlawful—in short a condemnation of 'land leagues' and probably also of the claims of senior chiefs like
Kingi to veto land sales by individuals in their tribes. Browne also demanded
a restoration of plunder taken in Taranaki. As Henry Sewell remarked, 'What
the Governor wants is not peace but to make the Natives submit'.[28] Indeed
Browne made no bones about this, dressing his determination in the now fami-

liar cant about it all being for the benefit of the Maori in the long run.[29] Tamihana's peacemaking in Taranaki had only freed the troops to be used against his own people.

Tamihana wrote a reasoned reply, rejecting Browne's contention that they had been bound by the Treaty of Waitangi and arguing that just as the natives of Europe had separate sovereigns and the Americans had been allowed to separate themselves, the Maori should be allowed their King. The King had done no harm, he argued, the involvement of Waikato warriors in Taranaki being the result of blood relationship and other historic ties. Browne took this reply as proof of extreme Maori nationalism, showing the falseness of Martin's claim that the King movement could be found a defined role in government under the Crown. But again the Governor was reading into Tamihana's statements the justification for war that he wanted to find. Tamihana was only trying to show that it was unreasonable of Browne to assume that the Maori should consider themselves bound by the Treaty of Waitangi; and although they were, in his view, as a separate race entitled to a full and separate sovereignty, Tamihana did not in fact go on to claim one. In a companion letter he reiterated his right to 'overlook my own piece' but repeated that he had no desire to cast the Queen from the whole island.[30] This demand for recognition of their authority, in their own land and lineage, was no more than that which all the great chiefs, 'rebel' and 'loyal' had been making at and since the Treaty of Waitangi negotiations. Although difficult to define and secure in the face of settler pressure, it was conceivably a negotiable demand. At least negotiation should have been attempted if Browne was deeply concerned to avoid war.

Admittedly, negotiation was at this point very difficult to achieve. Tamihana did offer to come to Auckland to discuss matters with Browne, or a conference of the Kohimarama type, but the more bellicose Waikato chiefs restrained him. For his part Browne, claiming that Tamihana's letters were convincing proof that the root of the so-called rebellion was the issue of sovereignty, not the Waitara, began to make plans for the invasion of the Waikato. His efforts were endorsed by the majority of settlers in the General Assembly, including the Ministry of William Fox, who took office in July 1861, although he had, for his own political purposes, condemned the previous Government's policies in regard to the Waitara purchase. The settlers generally hoped for a decisive subjugation of the Maori while the English Government and troops were already so heavily implicated. But there came an eleventh hour stay of execution. The Colonial Office was not fully persuaded that the King movement was incompatible with British rule and felt that Browne was unduly excited by the term 'King'. Accordingly Browne was recalled and Sir George Grey reappointed, at his own suggestion. The man who was believed, erroneously, to have worked wonders in his first governorship in persuading the Maori to accept 'amalgamation', was sent back to try to avert war and achieve a *modus vivendi* with the King movement.

IX

The 'New Institutions'

In December 1861 a group of Ngatiruanui leaders including Erueti Te Whiti (of whom much more was later to be heard) wrote to the Governor refuting charges that they had been among the most heavily implicated in the Taranaki war and stating that 'it was you Pakehas . . . who perverted the laws and made use of them to bring war upon us'. They told the Governor: 'carry out the Queen's law properly . . . and let good come forth like us who properly administer the laws of King Matutaera in order that they may be carefully and well carried out: perhaps we may find a way of joining them together for they are of one tree, the tree of goodness'. This indeed was the essence of the task confronting Grey as he resumed the New Zealand governorship.[1]

In October and November 1861 Grey, Fox, Sewell (the Attorney-General) and Fenton had worked out a policy for the administration of Maori districts which came to be called 'the Runanga system' or alternatively 'the new institutions'. The scheme was simply a variation of the *runanga* scheme suggested by Waikato Maori, elaborated by Fenton and revived in recent memoranda by Browne. Village Runanga[2] under the direction of Resident Magistrates, and District Runanga under new officers called Civil Commissioners would make by-laws; the Pakeha officers, commissioned as Circuit Court Judges, and Maori Assessors would enforce the laws, the Assessors having independent jurisdiction up to £5; in a new effort to grapple with the problem of enforcement, it was planned to appoint paid Maori police—a Warden and several constables—in each 'hundred' of a District; there was to be a British-style separation of powers—members of the Runanga, the legislative bodies, were not supposed to be Assessors (judicial officers) as well.

In addition to grappling with familiar problems of stock trespass, fencing, health and sanitation, the Resident Magistrates and Runanga were to undertake the crucially important duty of defining tribal, *hapu* or individual interests in land and, when these were confirmed by Crown grant, to authorise the alienation of land to Europeans. This proposal envisaged the preservation of corporate tribal authority over land, during both the determination of title and alienation. It therefore contrasted with the alternative view, widely favoured among settlers, that Maori title should be individualised as quickly as possible and direct dealing between individual Maori and settlers permitted.

Legislative authority for the scheme was provided by the Native Circuit Courts Act and Native Districts Regulation Act of 1858. The initial cost of the new institutions, estimated at about £49,000 for the first year and £43,000 thereafter, was to be provided from a £25,000 vote which Ministers agreed to put to the Assembly, and a channelling into Maori administration of some of the Colony's annual contribution to the cost of the Imperial regiments in New Zealand. Subsequently the revenue expected to accrue from land sold or leased would be available for building hospitals, schools and churches, while the Government would provide or supplement the salaries of medical officers, school-teachers and clergy.[3]

For the first time comprehensive machinery was being set in motion to involve the Maori in a substantial measure of legislative, judicial and administrative authority in their own districts. In Sewell's view, 'It is not merely *government* but *self-government* which is to be introduced'.[4] It was the Government's hope that this, together with the cessation of pressure from McLean's Land Purchase Department, would restore Maori confidence in British intentions. Fox and Sewell held to the conclusions of the 'Waikato Committee' of the Assembly which, in 1860, had taken the view that the King movement principally represented a desire for law and official attention and had condemned Fenton's withdrawal from the Waikato. They hoped that if the Government offered them this the Kingites would eventually open their territory to settlement. Through the Runanga system the goal of 'amalgamation' and the settlers' desire for land would both be fulfilled. Although based on an inadequate appreciation of Waikato attitudes the new institutions were therefore an attempt to find a way through conflicting interests without war. They were not, as was suggested by some of Grey's contemporary critics and some historians since, a mere blind put up by Grey to deceive the Maori while he made preparations for a war he had already determined upon. Grey's correspondence with Kingite leaders and his whole conduct of policy up to April 1863 in fact show that he too expected fairly readily to gain the submission of the King movement, though he was prepared to attack it if submission was not forthcoming.

In settling upon this policy Grey and his advisers ruled out several other alternatives which Newcastle, the Secretary of State for Colonies, had asked the Governor to consider. Browne had intended the 1860 conference at Kohimarama to be the first meeting of an annual conference or parliament of chiefs. In addition, a Native Council Bill to create a permanent advisory council of leading settlers and chiefs was still awaiting the royal assent. With characteristic zeal for the goal of 'amalgamation', Grey rejected both alternatives, on the grounds that they would rival the General Assembly for the loyalty of the Maori, and be divisive of the two races and ultimately an embarrassing impediment to the achievement of one law and administration for the country. The Runanga system, he believed, went far enough in the direction of a distinct legislature and administration for the Maori and would train them for ultimate participation in the existing settler legislatures.[5]

It had been appreciated in London that the New Zealand Government would have no easy task bringing the King movement under its control. The heightened passions generated by the war in Taranaki, the threat of a European invasion of the Waikato and Governor Browne's virtual ultimatum of June 1861 had all served to intensify the separatist and nationalist character of the King movement. What had still not been tried, however, was some plan by which the Government would accept the King movement, allow it to operate as best it could in the North Island heartland, offer it assistance and advice but not try to bind it—and wait for time to ease the distrust that had grown up. Realising this, Newcastle had asked Grey to consider whether, in some areas, the establishment of Native Districts, separate from the European Provinces, would not be the best means of promoting 'the present harmony and future union of the two races'.[6] Moreover, it appeared that if the Government were prepared to recognise the King the moderate Kingites at least would have been prepared to co-operate. On 3 December 1861 John Gorst reported from Waikato, where he was assisting the development of Anglican schools, that Tamihana and a *runanga* of the Ngatihaua tribe had expressed a willingness to accept Grey's new institutions, provided that the laws of the Waikato Runanga constituted under Grey's plan went for assent, not only to the Governor, but also to the Maori King. Gorst asked for instructions on how to treat this suggestion.[7] He subsequently reported that, although there were signs that the Ngatimaniapoto were withholding support, the King's Council at Ngaruawahia had also discussed the question fully and concluded that if the Governor would let the King and his flag stand, they would adopt his plans and try to work with him for the common good.[8]

It was possibly in response to Gorst's inquiry that, on 7 December, Fox wrote a memorandum which included these passages:

> If as a Condition in the making or assenting to such laws, the Natives or any part of them, from motives of any kind, chose to recognise a Head or Chief without whose assent no such laws should be introduced we see nothing in principle objectionable to such a Rule. . . . As an experiment at all events, we see nothing which should hinder its being fairly tried; nor in practice would it conflict with the ordinary course of government. . . . So also in the appointment of Magistrates or assessors; if they chose to make the assent of their principal Chief a condition of their appointment, there would be nothing repugnant to the Queen's authority in such a Rule, *provided the punishing power of the magistrates and the ordinary Execution of the law were made to flow from and be dependent on the Governor.*
>
> In this form and to this extent, we see no objection to the recognition of Matutaeri [Matutaera, the Maori King]. On the contrary we see many political uses in having some constant nucleus of organization of the Native race.
>
> The name of King is objectionable but some other may perhaps be found.[9]

This was as near to accepting the principle of the recognition of the King as the Government ever came. Certainly Fox's proviso (italicised above) may have proved difficult for the Maori to accept, but his memorandum might, if acted upon, have provided a basis for discussion with at least the moderate Kingites. However, it seems that it was not handed to Grey in time for his discussions with the Waikato leaders later that week.[10] Instead he was given a memorandum of 6 December (apparently prepared before Fox tentatively rethought the question) stiff and antagonistic in tone, urging that, while no hostilities would be threatened against the King movement unless it molested settlers, it should be treated with indifference. Grey's language to the Kingite chiefs should, it advocated, 'distinctly mark the Governor's disapprobation' of the movement and the folly of preserving a separate nationality.[11]

In fact, for reasons discussed in earlier chapters, very few in the colony were interested in negotiating with the Kingites on any terms which included recognition of the King, under any name. The land-hungry made plain their particular views, the squatter, J. D. Ormond, stating in the Hawke's Bay Provincial Council that 'no final adjustment of the difference of race, and no peace on a lasting basis, would ever be made unless [the Government's] policy was based on resisting the erection of a barrier between the two races by closing the land against the colonization of the British people.' If the Maori were encouraged to stop selling land, Ormond argued, a few years of peaceful institutions would see permanent barriers laid down; 'to settle the king movement and leave the land league behind would be to leave the germ of a greater difficulty and a greater crisis than they had yet seen'.[12] But since the King movement was substantially a land league, any settlement between it and Government would, as Dennison had realised, immediately lead to a cessation of land-selling. This was the root of speculator and squatter antagonism to the 'peace policy' of the Fox ministry, and Fox, knowing it well, must have hesitated, after he had written his memorandum of 7 December, to press a course that implied the establishment of the King movement.

For his part, Grey, because of his autocratic personality and long-standing personal commitment to the policy of 'amalgamation', was disinclined to share power with a semi-autonomous Maori authority in the Waikato. In addition, both he and the Fox Ministry grossly under-rated the strength of Maori nationalist sentiment, and placed too much confidence in their ability to wean the Maori away from the King movement—'miserable mountebanking', 'pitable travesty' Fox called it—in favour of the new institutions.[13] Thus, when he met the Kingite spokesmen in December 1861, Grey sought no agreement with the moderates, but more than fulfilled his Ministers' injunctions to denounce the King movement. He said he considered it dangerous and though he was indifferent to the King himself, through his new institutions he would make many kings in the land. He demanded return of plunder taken in Taranaki and threatened punishment for those who held it. On this point he overreached Fox, who later wrote, 'I think it would have been better if he told them in fact that he would let bygones be bygones . . . I shall not early forget old [Wiremu Kingi Te] Rangitake saying "Don't you say anything about the plunder—I lost plunder also"—and no doubt he did.'[14]

In a situation where flexibility and conciliation were desperately required, and already offered by the moderate Kingites, Grey was stiff-necked and provocative. A critical question was whether he should place troops at Te Ia, on Crown land approaching the Waikato heartland, for the better defence of Auckland. At Taupari Grey walked from his canoe with the gentle missionary Ashwell on one side urging him not to bring troops to the Kingite border as it would destroy confidence, and Ashwell's belligerent colleague, John Morgan, on the other, saying that the troops should be brought down. Grey concurred with Morgan, not simply because he could not trust the moderates to control the powerful chiefs like Rewi Maniapoto, or out of prudent regard for his responsibility to protect Auckland, but because 'he considered it would be the very depth of degradation to be subject to the natives and allow them to say whether the Queen's troops should be placed there or not'.[15] In New Zealand, as in other imperial contexts, decisions were to be made, not simply out of economic competition, or rational calculation of defence needs, but also from irrational motives of national and racial pride. Finally, although Kingite spokesmen politely expressed gratitude to the British for leading them out of 'foolish customs' and having murders and other crimes tried by law, they specifically asked that a Queen's magistrate not be stationed in King territory at that time. Yet Gorst, who naively believed the moderate Kingites from common interest in promoting the rule of law would accept him as a magistrate, was appointed Civil Commissioner in the upper Waikato. There never was any real 'negotiation' with the King movement, with a view to finding it a role in governing the district under the Crown: there was only an attempt to secure Kingite submission, by a refurbished version of Grey's old policy—a mixture of browbeating, 'flour and sugar' and, before long, flattering personal diplomacy with some of the key men. Te Heuheu was greeted as 'the child who has run away from a father who loves you very much'. King Matutaera was urged to return to Mangere, where his father Potatau had lived, 'that I may protect you, that you may dwell in peace in that place and be separated from the faulty teaching you are receiving'. The letter was signed 'from your father, the everlasting friend of the children, G. Grey'.[16] It was all appallingly out of place—slighting the powerful men who stood at the head of a movement heavily tinged with nationalism. Tamihana, the possible mediator, was not approached at all: Grey had dismissed him in conversation with Browne as a 'turbulent and ambitious chief whom he disliked and wouldn't communicate with'.[17]

Other appointments under the 'new institutions' had preceded that of Gorst and many more followed throughout 1862. Grey's choice as Civil Commissioner at the Bay of Islands was the man he had driven from office fifteen years earlier —George Clarke, former Chief Protector of Aborigines. Colonel A. H. Russell, controller of Maori labour employed on public works in Grey's first governorship and, more recently, a squatter in Hawke's Bay, became Civil Commissioner of that district. Edward Shortland, a Cambridge graduate and former Sub-Protector became Civil Commissioner of Hauraki. Fenton declined reappointment to lower Waikato and J. Armitage, a squatter and former associate of Fenton, became Civil Commissioner there. At the request of the chief Poihipi, G. Law, a teacher at the Otawhao mission, was made Civil Commissioner of Taupo. W. B. White at Mangonui, was elevated from Resident Magistrate to Civil Commissioner and Robert Parris of Taranaki, J. Mackay of Nelson and A. C. Strode of Otago were confirmed as Assistant Native Secretaries of their districts.

In consequence of the antagonism that had developed between the Ministry and the Native Secretary during Browne's governorship, Fox was determined to 'sweep McLean and his Department clean out of the Government'.[18] McLean had in fact resigned as Native Secretary in June 1861, shortly before Fox took office, but he remained Chief Land Purchase Officer, while his appointees had remained in the Native Office in Auckland. Now Fox appointed T. H. Smith, the Acting Native Secretary, as Civil Commissioner in the Bay of Plenty and Rotorua, where he had been Resident Magistrate six years before, and shortly almost the whole staff of the Native Office found itself scattered about the North Island, grumbling about the 'change of dynasty' and maintaining a vigorous and nostalgic correspondence with McLean.[19] Thus W. B. Baker became Resident Magistrate at East Cape, John White on the Wanganui River, G. S. Cooper at Waipukurau (southern Hawke's Bay), and Walter Buller in Rangitikei-Manawatu. The ineffectual Henry Halse was retained as Assistant Native Secretary, acting as a mere clerk to the Native Minister.

Other Resident Magistrates, and the clerks who were allocated to each, were found from Maori-language speakers among old missionary families—the Preeces, the Woons and the Clarkes for example—or old settler families such as the Mairs. All in all seven Civil Commissioners and approximately twenty Resident Magistrates—together with their clerks or interpreters—were appointed or confirmed in existing appointments under the new institutions. They were normally constituted as Justices of the Peace, as Resident Magistrates under Grey's 1847 Ordinance or as Judges under the Native Circuit Courts Act of 1858. A Resident Magistrate drew a salary of about £350, a Civil Commissioner about £500—high salaries by the standards of the time, the latter being equivalent to the salary of a permanent head of a government department. The districts of Waimate, Hokianga, Raglan, Waiuku, Taupo, Rotorua, Thames, central Wanganui, East Cape, Manawatu, Wairoa, Waipukurau and upper and lower Waikato, previously never or only briefly attended by a magistrate, were supplied with permanent Resident Magistrates or Circuit Court Judges. At the same time the number of subsidised or salaried Medical Officers to Maori districts was increased from eight to twenty.[20] The new magistrates were despatched with Fenton's efforts of 1857 held up to them as a model, and with rousing injunctions as to the high duty, not only of teaching the Maori the advantages of submission to law, but also of training them in the arts of self-government.

The Land Purchase wing of the Native Department lingered. McLean was still nominally its head, but John Rogan actually controlled the Land Purchase Commissioners and Andrew Sinclair the survey staff, including four Maori cadets in training. Authority to purchase land was also vested in special commissioners such as Isaac Featherston, the Superintendent of Wellington. McLean however, was not a man to be lightly dispensed with. At first he had wanted to resign all appointments and take two years leave overseas but this was declined by both Browne and Grey, who wanted him to settle questions in both islands about reserves and land purchase boundaries, of which he alone had detailed knowledge. Before long he was called upon to negotiate with the Maori over such problems as the acquisition of gold-mining rights in the Coromandel Peninsula and the feud which had developed in Manawatu between the Ngatiraukawa and Ngatiapa tribes, and to use his influence to keep the Hawke's Bay chief Te Hapuku from giving allegiance to the Maori King. He was offered the position of Civil Commissioner in Hawke's Bay but, aware of the unpopularity of the new institutions among the Hawke's Bay squatters, declined. However he did abandon his intention of leaving the Colony and in early 1863 resigned his emoluments (though not his title) as Chief Land Purchase Officer and won election as Superintendent of Hawke's Bay Province.

Of the Ministers, only Fox and Henry Sewell had a very active interest in running the new institutions. Walter Mantell, Native Minister from July to December 1861, was interested only in seeing that promises made to the South Island Maori when he transacted the enormous Ngaitahu purchase were fulfilled.[21] An extraordinarily temperamental person, given to intense flights of passion over supposed injuries, he retired to Wellington in December 1861 having arranged that Dillon Bell would run the Native Office in his stead. Bell, an ambitious but rather superficial man who had come out as a New Zealand Company official at the age of seventeen and moved quickly into political life, established himself as principal adviser in Maori affairs after McLean had resigned the Native Secretaryship.

Direction of policy was still awkwardly divided between Governor and Ministers. In constitutional arrangements of November and December 1861, Grey had given control of the day-to-day running of the Native Department to his responsible Ministers, though he continued to exercise a large measure of authority in Maori affairs. The Ministers, for their part, were anxious to use Grey (with his large resources of Imperial finance and troops) for their purposes. Both sides sought the substance of power while trying to saddle the other party with theoretical responsibility; the issue could never be clearly decided while a man of Grey's nature and ambitions was Governor and while Imperial troops remained in the Colony. The result was confusion in the administration of the 'new institutions'. In Manawatu, for example, the

Resident Magistrate, acting under the Native Minister, made one set of appointments of Maori staff, while Grey, who happened to visit the district, made another, and this could not be sorted out without causing irritation and disappointment.[22] The relationship between Civil Commissioner and Resident Magistrate was also the subject of controversy. Sewell wanted the Resident Magistrate to be the most important officer, communicating direct with the Government. Moreover, the existing Resident Magistrates, already doing duty for the Attorney-General's Department as Coroners, Returning Officers, District Registrars of Births, Deaths and Marriages (to name some of their manifold functions) declined to be supervised by a Civil Commissioner in these matters. Grey, on the other hand, wished the Resident Magistrate to be subordinate to the Civil Commissioner, whom he described as being virtually Lieutenant-Governor of a large Native District.[23] Eventually it was laid down that the Resident Magistrates were to be 'political agents of the Government . . . subject to instructions from the Commissioner, through whom they will communicate', but that in their judicial capacity they would write direct to the Attorney-General, sending duplicates of the letters to the Civil Commissioner.[24] As the distinction between political and judicial functions was not always clear in practice, Resident Magistrates wrote to either the Civil Commissioner or the Attorney-General as they saw fit. On some occasions they wrote direct to the Native Office and, on others (to the great irritation of the Ministers) direct to Grey. Relations between Civil Commissioner and Resident Magistrate were uncertain and sometimes unhappy.

In all districts initial procedure followed the same pattern. The Resident Magistrate or Civil Commissioner toured his district, meeting the chiefs and explaining the nature and purpose of the new institutions. Where they were agreeable a selection of chiefs was made to fill the positions of Assessors, Wardens and *Karere* or Messengers. (The term 'policeman' had been dropped as likely to be alarming to the Maori but the *Karere* did act as constables under the Warden.) Normally there would be one Assessor, with an associated *Karere,* from each village on the Magistrate's circuit, and one man of standing as Warden for the whole magistracy. An Assessor was paid from £30 to £50 per annum, a Warden £20, and a *Karere* £10. Distinctive trappings of office were supplied—a cap with gold bands for the Assessor and a uniform of blue coat and trousers and boots for the Warden and *Karere.* The next steps were to erect courthouses for the magistrate's circuit, and to constitute the Runanga.

The initial Maori reactions to the new appointments were infinitely varied. With much justification, the main Kingite tribes regarded the belated display of salaries and offices as a thinly disguised attempt to deceive the Maori people and reduce them to subservience. As McLean observed, it would have been better to have sent to the Waikato an instructor in agriculture, capable of settling disputes if specifically called upon by the Kingite chiefs to assist.[25]

The sending of Gorst as a fully accredited magistrate was seen for what it was: an attempt to supplant the Maori King entirely. Consequently Gorst was met with determined non-co-operation.

Although some ambitious young chiefs such as Tioriori and Taati Te Waru might have accepted Assessorships they were blocked by the *runanga* of their people, and Tamihana had to retract an offer to let Gorst hear disputes with the aid of a Kingite Assessor. A mixed-race man was forcibly removed from Gorst's court into the jurisdiction of a Maori *runanga*. Thereafter, having thwarted Gorst, the Kingites, apart from one volatile chief who threatened to expel him, tolerated his presence.[26] But it was a rude awakening for Gorst and for the Fox Ministry to find that the discontent in the Waikato was not simply the result of a long-neglected demand for systematic enforcement of law which Gorst could satisfy, but that on the contrary, British law was viewed with the greatest distrust. In rejecting new suggestions that the Waitara dispute be referred to law, in the form of a mixed Maori-European commission, the Waikato chief Aporo had expressed deep-seated Kingite feelings: 'The law is a bad dog [*kuri kino*],' he said, 'it devours many.'[27]

Similarly Armitage made no progress in the Kawhia harbour area and Hunter Brown found the Urewera people's support for the King ('who makes *tapu* our land' against new attempts by the Queen to ensnare it, they said) too strong to warrant his staying. G. Law had little hope of winning converts in Te Heuheu's territory south and west of Lake Taupo: he set up station at the northern end of the lake under the sponsorship of Te Poihipi, a traditional rival of Te Heuheu. A number of other tribes, not necessarily strong Kingites, also held the Queen's magistrates at a distance. The East Cape people were polarised, Kingite sympathies strengthening among some sections in response to W. B. Baker's arrival as Resident Magistrate. The Poverty Bay Maori, Baker observed, 'flatter themselves that they bullied the last magistrate out of the place' and were not seriously courted again. More seriously, the central and southern Hawke's Bay chiefs proved unco-operative.

The major practical grievances which underlay the continued assertion of independence of these tribes (and which also affected, to a lesser extent, the tribes which did accept magistrates) centred upon the related questions of indebtedness and land. The fall in agricultural prices in the later 1850s had left the Maori, after a period of considerable prosperity, with agricultural machinery falling into disrepair and unpaid for, coastal schooners half-purchased, and a habit of taking goods on credit. Storekeepers battened upon their improvidence, frequently foisting goods upon them at exorbitant prices and charging interest on the debt. No tribe was free of debt—every magistrate in the late 1850s and early 1860s reported the problem, though it probably affected coastal trading tribes more than it did those of the remoter interior. Some of the Maori *runanga* made rudimentary efforts to gain better trade terms by withholding produce in order to force storekeepers to lower their prices, but these boycotts usually crumbled quickly.

The Government believed that 'The fear of being compelled to pay their debts, if Queen's magistrates are appointed, is well known to be the sole motive which actuated many natives in refusing to assist in the introduction of the New System'.[28] But although Ministers were irked by the effect the traders had in generating Maori resentment, and instructed magistrates not to press too strenuously for the recovery of debts, they stated that they could not prevent traders from letting Maori customers have goods on credit.[29] The Maori were puzzled and resentful that the Government could interfere to prevent them buying spirits, but would not compel Pakeha storekeepers to lower prices, or Pakeha dealers to pay firm prices for grain.[30] Law, at Taupo, commenced a co-operative store to under-cut the traders and the Government gave him some financial assistance, but it failed within six months and the Government made no further attempt to interfere with the free play of commercial enterprise.

Fears that their lands would be taken in payment of debt—as many creditors had threatened—intensified Maori distrust of what was implied in the advent of magisterial authority. In addition, chiefs in a number of districts had made illegal sales of land to squatters, against the wishes of other owners who feared that the establishment of British law would enable the squatters to complete their bargains (or, because the transactions violated the Native Land Purchase Ordinance, that the Maori title would be held to be extinguished and the land vested in the Crown).

The Fox Government, recognising these fears, sent Crosbie Ward, a member of the Ministry, to Hawke's Bay to try to make the squatters come to equitable terms with the Maori owners through the new institutions, and to confine negotiations for further lands to the same channel. Ward first had to overcome legal objections to Maori bringing actions in the courts about rent for land which they held only on customary title—objections which had long made the law seem useless to the Maori, in the matter which was often of most vital importance to them. He chose to make a test case of a dispute between a squatter named James Shirley who had refused to pay the 'grass money' his Maori landlords had demanded and had his dairy cattle impounded by them. Ward prompted a chief to sue Shirley under the Cattle Trespass Ordinance of the Province. The hearing before a bench which included three leading chiefs whom Ward had enlisted, on doubtful authority, as Assessors, resulted in an award of £30 damages to the Maori claimants. Shirley counter-claimed for damages to his stock, but his suit was dismissed, partly on the grounds that the Maori had been denied any other means of redress. Ward however gave Shirley £30 'compensation' from Government funds. The somewhat contrived nature of these proceedings provoked a wave of indignation among settlers throughout the country.[31]

Fox also ordered the incoming Civil Commissioner, A. H. Russell, to continue prosecutions against squatters, on behalf of the Crown, for breaches of the Native Land Purchase Ordinance, which enshrined the Crown's pre-emptive right to transactions for Maori land. Russell was urged to begin with the former missionary William Colenso, whom Fox had found still occupying for his personal benefit a piece of land given by local Maori for the CMS mission—one of a number of such gifts which, the Maori justifiably claimed, were being misapplied. Russell had to hear Colenso's case himself, as none of the other magistrates was willing. He fined Colenso £5, a sum just below that which would have allowed him appeal to a higher court. There was a wave of popular feeling in favour of Colenso which resulted in his election to the General Assembly, where his case and Shirley's were used as whips to beat the Government.[32] The squatters also raised a furious outcry against Ward's injunctions that they must deal through the Runanga. They desired neither to be tenants of Maori Runanga—for they did not expect them to sell the freehold—nor to assist in the establishment of courts that would treat them as Shirley had been treated. They continued to enmesh the Maori in debt and to agitate for the right of direct purchase of land, rumours of which were in the air.

Nor was the Government greatly compensated by the Maori for having made itself cordially detested among the Hawke's Bay settlers. The principal chiefs had politely assured Ward that they would cease illegal leasing and work out some regular arrangement through a Runanga but, led by the independent old warrior Te Hapuku, they declined to co-operate with A. H. Russell in form-ing one, or to take rent disputes to the courts. The failure of the courts, in earlier years, to give them redress against squatters had generated a distrust that was not easily overcome; meanwhile they had had considerable success in compelling the payment of rent, or compensation for trespass, by impounding settlers' stock, sometimes using force against Pakeha stockmen. Apart from a number of persistent and rancorous disputes with determined squatters, they were fairly much in control of the situation, in some cases extracting rent in advance from several squatters. For this reason, and because of the question of their indebtedness, the Hawke's Bay chiefs preferred to keep control of the situation in their own hands, than to admit the interference of Government officers and courts of law.[33]

Meanwhile, in other districts, magistrates had met with more success. In some cases they gained an initial advantage from the divisions within Maori society. Smaller and weaker tribes (like the Ngaitai, sandwiched between the Whaka-tohea and the Whanau-a-Apanui in the Bay of Plenty) welcomed the Govern-ment officers as the Rarawa had done in the 1840s. Some of the tribes on the borders of the Waikato, traditional rivals of main King tribes, or involved in recent land disputes with them, also aligned themselves with the Government. Moreover, the Maori people were still looking for better means of regulating their society and in many cases their own *runanga* had proved factional, oppressive, and capricious. Where they were dominated by young chiefs who had also become mission teachers their discipline was often fiercely puritanical. For example Turton reported a woman being fined because her child licked a potato before grace was said. He added, 'It is from this kind of thraldom and perpetual interference that so many of the middle and lower class of Maories, would, I believe, delight to be liberated.'[34] About the same time Resident Magistrate J. R. Clendon noted that the young men at Hokianga had tired of the exactions of their chiefs and appealed to him for advice. The steadily increasing engagement of Maori in trade or as farm hands, fencers, and shearers introduced a multitude of contractual disputes. While piece-work was often done by gangs of men from one *hapu,* wage employment increasingly mixed men from various *hapu,* and the leadership in commercial enterprise did not exclusively come from men of hereditary rank. In industries like *kauri* gum digging there was a considerable movement of Maori labour about the country. In these situations traditional mechanisms for adjusting disputes were not always available or appropriate. More recently too, and beginning in the far north where contact with Europeans was oldest, a passion for drinking spirits had begun to sweep through coastal communities, producing utter demoralisation among some traditional leaders, who sacrificed their energies, their property and that of their kin, to acquire liquor. In these circumstances many Maori, as in the previous decades, continued to welcome the assistance of the officials. In many districts where magistrates had hitherto appeared only fleetingly, the coming of 'the law' was hailed as enthusiastically as the coming of the gospel twenty years earlier.[35] T. H. Smith, rejected by the Arawa in the 1850s, now found himself more warmly welcomed, because, he reported, they were fearful of the influence of Waikato, wearied by the loss of their young men in recent feuds, and dissatisfied with their *runanga.*[36] In Northland, northern Hawke's Bay, Rotorua, Manawatu, Wairarapa, the Wanganui River and parts of lower Waikato, the East Coast, the Bay of Plenty and northern Taupo, some form of the new institutions was established.

Inevitably it was not the neat pattern which the Government had outlined. This was particularly true of the Runanga. Grey had looked to the District Runanga to assume real legislative and administrative functions, and hoped that the smaller village *runanga* would die out; the Ministers, on the other hand, regarded the District Runanga as an institution alien to Maori society, and, following Fenton's theory of 1857, proposed to take the existing Maori *runanga* and see if this could 'work itself into form' as a useful instrument of government, but with as few alien procedures as possible. In fact the heterogeneous mixture of tribes in most Districts prevented the assembling of District Runanga. Smith could not hope to unite such virulent rivals as the Arawa, the Ngaiterangi and the Ngatiawa in one assembly. On the East Coast, W. D. Baker at first assembled his Assessors at periodic intervals for instruction and informal discussion but the arrangement petered out largely owing to the inconvenience to the Assessors from far off and the expense to the Maori at Baker's headquarters of providing for them. In other areas, such as Manawatu,

Kingite influence was strong and it was considered sufficient to introduce the Resident Magistrate system without hazarding Runanga.

Only in the relatively homogeneous and stable Districts of Northland were District Runanga assembled, the Bay of Islands Runanga meeting at Waimate under George Clarke, for the Ngapuhi *hapu* and a Runanga of Rarawa chiefs at Mangonui, under W. B. White. These began to meet regularly at about nine-monthly intervals. The Bay of Islands Runanga consisted of two or three representatives selected from each Hundred of the District, by the Pakeha officers in consultation with the major chiefs. Despite the intention to achieve a separation of powers the members of the Runanga were mostly all Assessors. An election of delegates had been avoided for fear that this would have pitted one *hapu* against another, inflamed popular passions, and led to the election of men whom only their immediate supporters would have recognised. However, by the inevitable operation of kinship loyalties and obligations, each representative at the first meeting of the Bay of Islands Runanga, brought a friend whom he wanted to have formally included into the assembly. Clarke had difficulty excluding these without giving offence, and also in keeping out the retinue of warriors that some chiefs insisted on bringing, the throng who came out of curiosity, and the Maori grog sellers who were at this time flourishing in many districts, with the aid of Pakeha suppliers. The Runanga wrangled for two days about salaries and office bearers, each chief being very concerned about his status in relation to other members. They also became preoccupied with procedural matters both because they enjoyed them and because they were anxious to match the settler Provincial Councils in formality and dignity.

W. B. White organised a compact Runanga of seven members at Mangonui but seated the other Assessors of the District as non-voting members. He, like Clarke, had to adjust initial bickerings over office and salary. Both Runanga then settled down and passed resolutions to the effect that land disputed would be brought to the Runanga for settlement, other quarrels taken to the Resident Magistrates and Assessors to be settled by English law, and the traditional system of *muru* abolished. Useful resolutions were also passed with regard to stock trespass and fencing. Finance was raised, with Government subsidies added, for the erection of 'hostelries' (really two or three-roomed wooden huts) for Maori visiting Mangonui and Waimate, and for a small hospital at Mangonui.[37] Early in 1863 the Waimate Runanga began to organise support for secular village day schools, which the Government was increasingly favouring as a means of educating Maori children in English. The first building was erected at Whangape village by mid-1863.[38]

The northern Runanga had certainly revealed the constructive determination of Maori leaders to provide for new needs and solve new problems. Yet powerful traditional values intruded. Grey had told northern chiefs that the Runanga was to be the supreme body, controlling the chiefs themselves through its law-making powers, and that the Maori police could arrest even chiefs if they broke the laws of the Runanga. Chiefs of ancient lineage, not on the

Runanga, were asked to sink their particular ambitions and particular *hapu* interests in loyalty to the Runanga of the whole District.[39] But the officials' dream of securing Maori submission to laws and regulations, even those of the Maori leaders' own making, was not to be attained so easily. The District Runanga were as yet without strong influence over the tribes, their decisions not yet respected as of right. Chiefs valued an invitation to join a Runanga as a mark of the recognition of their chieftainship, but once a meeting had dispersed, many of its members reverted to their traditional function as heads of a *hapu* and could and did, act quite contrary to the rulings they had just joined in passing. Chiefs who were not placed on a Runanga felt obliged to assert their dignity by ignoring or disparaging its proceedings. White's device of seating all important men as non-voting members was, however, a useful means of averting this and he was most successful in working the Runanga system.

Meanwhile, experiments with the small unit in Grey's plan, the Village Runanga, were also having mixed fortunes. In almost every large village there was a *runanga* of a quasi-traditional kind. In many districts each of these eagerly expected that the Resident Magistrate would liberally endow it with salaried officers and pay it for meeting under his chairmanship. This was partly an expression of cupidity and unashamed eagerness to mulct the apparently wealthy but close-fisted Pakeha. It was also an indication of the villagers' disinclination to forego quickly their recent judicial activities— tedious and often unsatisfactory though they were—and submit to becoming mere rule-making bodies, subject to the magistrate and denied executive or judicial functions. On the Wanganui River, for example, mission influence was strong and the *runanga* had been under the control of the Maori catechists, fees and fines exacted in the process of upholding mission morality going to mission funds. A deputation of twenty-five Maoris waited on John White, the new Resident Magistrate, to ask for salary for the Government Runanga, saying that if they did not receive it they would simply continue the *Runanga o te Hahi* (Runanga of the Church) as before. White replied that only the Assessors and Police would be paid, and it would henceforth be illegal for the Church *runanga* to levy fines and fees. 'This was the close of the Runanga idea', he reported.[40] Other magistrates were obliged to point out that the new institutions involved a separation of functions, that only they and the Assessors would receive salaries and exercise judicial and executive powers and that in any case the Government could not possibly afford to pay the *runanga* in every village. Consequently in district after district disappointed Maori withheld their co-operation and hopes of incorporating the traditional *runanga* into the new institutions faded.

In the Hundred of Taupari, however, Armitage got a Runanga to meet by having the Warden of Police give the members five shillings a day each from his salary, and in Kohekohe Hundred, Wi Te Wheoro, an enthusiast for the law and a strong anti-Kingite, also assembled a Runanga. These assemblies passed a number of resolutions: some were simply requests for aid—a black-smith, wheat, seed potatoes; some dealt with cattle trespass, dog nuisance, the clearing of thistles, damages for houses destroyed by fire; others dealt with the erection of courthouses; and others again concerned the question of *puremu* (adultery), that familiar cause of dispute in Maori society of which one European officer reported, '[a Maori] judges law a good deal by the way it grapples that crime'.[41] Magistrates and clergy in the Thames district and the small South Island communities had regulations passed and fines enforced against drunkenness and the bringing of liquor within villages, but this was about the total extent of regulation making under the 'new institutions'.

On the vital question of land, the magistrates, even among the most co-operative tribes, made almost no progress. The Ngatiporou refused to sell Baker a single acre for his courthouse but voluntarily ceded him 120 acres, demonstrating that initiative in the disposition of land clearly remained in their hands. Thereafter, Baker wrote, 'The word *whenua* [land] is banished from my vocabulary. To utter a word having reference to it is to imperil my position and popularity.'[42] It was made plain to Smith by the Bay of Plenty and Rotorua people that as proof of its benevolent intentions, the Government should acquire no more land.[43] Armitage made one effort to introduce the subject of individualisation of land tenure in his Runanga at Taupari, but as this immediately produced a threatened withdrawal of one section of the Runanga he shelved all further consideration of the question.[44]

Only John White in central Wanganui successfully settled a disputed boundary case in formal proceedings. On his first trip up the river he gave judgment in two cases, once for the plaintiff, an Assessor, and once for the defendant, a man of the Assessor's tribe. In each case the disputed boundary was laid off and accepted by the disputants and assembled Maori. These decisions started a ferment of discussion among the Wanganui River *hapu* as to whether the practice of referring land disputes to White should be con-tinued. Most of the pro-Government people were in favour, the Kingites against. White eventually advised against further involving the Crown, as his adjudication would 'in the eyes of the stupid Waikato people touch the very point for which they are making the fuss'.[45]

In June 1862 an affray at Hokianga showed the Maori temper with regard to major land disputes. There an ancient and smouldering quarrel flared up in a series of bloody encounters between followers of the chiefs Tirarau and Matiu. Tirarau flatly refused to submit the case to the Runanga as George Clarke suggested and one prominent member of the Runanga, Arama Karaka (who had lately undertaken never to resort to arms again) joined the conflict. The magistrates were defied and only the intervention of Grey and some of the neutral Ngapuhi enabled the dispute to be referred to the arbitration of a panel of chiefs in Auckland.[46] This event, and Arama Karaka's involvement in particular, was seized on by the settler press as proof of the futility of trying to secure Maori submission to law except by military subjugation. Yet this was unfair. The feud was a deep one, Government offers to purchase the disputed land had aggravated it, and Arama Karaka had a compelling traditional obligation to avenge his father, killed fighting Tirarau twenty years earlier. It was too much to expect these values to be foresworn over-night. Moreover, in a lesser but nevertheless serious dispute in the same district, the 'new institutions' did score a success. The *hapu* of the chiefs Te Tai and Makarena took up arms and built *pa* on disputed land. But they agreed to the suggestion of Resident Magistrate James Clendon, that the dispute be referred to the Runanga. The Runanga decided for Te Tai and he disbanded his 150 men, ignoring Makarena's parting insults, which in earlier times might have precipitated combat. Te Tai told Clendon that as they had submitted to the law they trusted the law would support them should Makarena give more trouble.[47]

Clearly the 'new institutions' were not going to become a ready means of determining land title, facilitating land alienation, as the government hoped, but the Maori people were obviously far from reactionary and continued to make intelligent but selective use of the new modes of social control.

Moreover the ordinary civil and criminal jurisdiction of the Resident Magistrate continued to win support in many districts, the regular progress of the magistrate, accompanied by his principal Assessors and *Karere* becoming an accepted mode of justice and administration. John White, Resident Magistrate of the Wanganui River district, has left accounts of his circuits on the river, which he travelled in a canoe poled by his *Karere*. At each main settlement he held court in a *raupo* courthouse, thronged by all the people of the village, the magistrate flanked by his Assessors, defendants flanked by blue uniformed *Karere,* the whole proceedings efficient and White's judgments respected by the participants.[48] White was careful to work in co-operation with the principal chiefs—indeed the Assessors' concurrence in his judgment was required by the Resident Magistrates' Courts Ordinance and the Circuit Courts Act. Outside the formal hearings he settled a great many more disputes by personal advice and arbitration. Exhilarated by his success White wrote, 'As I find the Assessors would give the New Policy support we grasped the nettle firmly as we ought to do and were not stung.'[49]

In the north Clarke instructed the Resident Magistrates of his district to make regular rounds and patiently hear all disputes brought to them, however trivial: disputes over breach of *tapu* and 'native curses' were to be heard, even though still not formally recognised in New Zealand law; Assessors were to be advised and their decisions reviewed; the magistrates were not to deliver their decisions and sentences peremptorily but give their reasoning fully since the local Maori appreciated the equities of a case.[50] These instructions were amply fulfilled by the Resident Magistrate of Waimate, E. M. Williams, eldest son of the veteran missionary Henry Williams, and one of the most able of the new officials. After a year's work Williams reported that he had a weekly court at his headquarters and a periodical round among five *raupo* courthouses in the villages where people assembled to meet him. He found the patient listening to complex arguments over trifling disputes very wearying, but his earnestness was rewarded in that only one verdict had been disputed to the date of his reporting. His summing up of the situation was a balanced one: it was not immediately clear, he said, that the local Maori had accepted the supremacy of the law—he had had no serious cases—but their general willingness to co-operate was plain.[51]

Down at Maketu, in the Bay of Plenty, Winiata Pekama (Tohi Te Ururangi) continued to impress with his zeal as an Assessor. A traveller reported him, resplendent in gold-laced Assessor's uniform, in a European style house, wallpapered, carpeted and fully furnished, ruling the community with the efficient support of 'Retreat' Tapsell, his mixed-race Warden of Police.[52] Among districts not formerly visited by magistrates, Wairoa in nothern Hawke's Bay gave A. H. Russell a good reception, the Assessors supporting him and allowing him to modify the decisions of their own *runanga*.[53] In all of these situations the flexibility and informality of the Resident Magistrates' proceedings and their working in with the Assessors were important, three times as many cases being settled by mediation as by formal hearing. The principle of levying fines for theft and assault and paying part of this money to the injured party was in constant use.

The *ad hoc* work of the magistrates also assisted in winning Maori co-operation. In their capacity as political and intelligence agents, they established what were essentially diplomatic contacts with the principal chiefs, gauging their allegiance to the King or to the Governor, and sounding their reactions to movements by the Government or the Kingite leaders. The Assessors enjoyed being brought into this process and most Resident Magistrates and Civil Commissioners were fed a stream of information—much of it mere rumour, some of it of great importance—by means of the *Karere,* who became indispensable links between Resident Magistrates and Assessors, and between Resident Magistrates and neighbouring districts. In several districts the *Karere* were engaged to carry the regular mail of the Colony; indeed the overland postal services of the North Island depended upon Maori carriers well into the 1870s. In the absence of organised Runanga such development works as were carried out—for example, the laying out of a new village, the founding of a school or the introduction of stock and crops—were arranged by the Resident Magistrate in informal consultation with the principal chiefs.

The twenty or so doctors subsidised as part of the 'new institutions' gave patchy satisfaction. Though ordered to make regular circuits of the *pa* in their district, they too often waited in the towns for Maori patients to come to them. The loneliness of their life in rural districts led many of them into drunkenness and liaisons with Maori women; the Maori consequently often requested that doctors sent to them be married men, preferably elderly. Preventive medicine, other than smallpox vaccination and general advice on diet and hygiene, was not considered in that age to be part of a government's functions, or within its resources. The sick were frequently unable or disinclined to continue the nursing treatment prescribed by visiting doctors and epidemics continued to take a very heavy toll. Even so, the system of subsidised medical officers represented an advance in the Government's conception of its responsibilities, creditable in a *laissez faire* age. Most Maori living within 15 miles of a township, and visitors from further afield, could be reasonably sure of free medical treatment. Traditional remedies, including the rituals of the *tohunga* or spiritual healers, were still the norm in rural districts, but many certainly appreciated the availability of a doctor at least as an alternative. When epidemic diseases were reported doctors were usually sent to the area promptly. Indeed one of the last acts of co-operation between the Government and the King movement was the sending of doctors to an epidemic in Matamata, Tamihana's district.

As with the Runanga, the judicial side of the new institutions was inevitably affected by the persistence of traditional values. In many districts the *runanga* rivalled the Resident Magistrate and Assessors. The Assessors could not suddenly detach themselves from their people and assume a strict judicial impartiality. In some cases where the Government had declined their requests for salary, the village *runanga* tended to absorb the paid Assessors, share their salaries, and resume their former proceedings. Some officials were inclined to watch the proceedings of the *runanga* from the sidelines, mitigating their severity and actually relying on them in tangled cases involving custom, particularly *puremu* disputes. Others condemned them for their obvious factionalism and partiality, the product of complex local politics. When Fenton (now Assistant Law Officer) asked for suitable Maori to be named for a jury list most officers reported only three or four men in a district as having sufficient impartiality. Once again the participation of Maori in juries was shelved. Yet it might also be considered that the existence of three or four men in each district capable of matching the stringent notions of most of the officials was good progress. A young chief like Te Wheoro of lower Waikato, who had clearly grasped the European notion of the supremacy of law and committed himself to it because he wanted to end factionalism and division among his people, impressed official observers with his decisions as an Assessor. So did Papahurihia, Warden of Police at Hokianga, and formerly head of the *atua wera* cult which had plagued the missionaries in the 1830s. Such men were uncommon, but more were emerging.

Unfortunately settler opinion inevitably focused not on Te Wheoro and his kind but on the plethora of unsuitable Assessors, Wardens and *Karere* whom Resident Magistrates had to appoint to satisfy jealous elders. A return of January 1864 lists some 495 Maori officers with another thirty-five on pensions. The Bay of Islands had fifty-three, the Bay of Plenty and Rotorua eighty-four, and central Wanganui fifty-two.[54] The process of culling the appointments began almost as soon as they were made. Though a man of high birth, Mangonui Kerei, Warden of Russell, had to be dismissed after he had beaten two women, assaulted another Maori and taken his horse, threatened to shoot his brother and defied the magistrate's summons—all perfectly predictable actions in an aggressive Polynesian chief of a somewhat disordered community but not acceptable in an Assessor of the Crown.[55] Others were dismissed because of their Kingite sympathies, for drunkenness, for failing to attend when required on court days, or (by the more intolerant officers) for declining to give up polygamy.

Although many of the Maori police appointed in each district where the 'new institutions' operated had proved to be zealous and resourceful in bringing men of low and middle rank into court, the independent behaviour of many of the leading chiefs meant that the crucial question of law enforcement was still largely unresolved. In December 1862, the Hawke's Bay chief Karaitiana led a party which rescued one of his *hapu* from a lock-up at Clive, where he had been detained for a petty theft, and informed the authorities, 'There is no policeman who had power to take a Maori in charge. You know that our law is that we shall try our own criminals.'[56] The following February a large party of drunken Maori rescued from the provincial police in the streets of Napier, a chief named Paora who had been detained for disorderly behaviour.[57] Even the more co-operative Ngapuhi were not willing to surrender men for offences involving long gaol sentences. Settler indignation flared when a Bay of Islands Maori attempted to rape an English girl named Emily Stephenson. The Assessors, while admitting the man's guilt, declined to surrender him for a gaol sentence and offered instead a payment of £50 which the authorities perforce had to accept.[58] At Whangarei the Resident Magistrate was obliged by an assembly of Maori to release a man whom he had committed to the Supreme Court on a burglary charge. The Crown Prosecutor issued a warrant to the Auckland police for this man's arrest but Bell, then Native Minister, countermanded it and wrote:

> It is an unhappy illustration of the state of things in this country, that even in the midst of the European settlement of Wangerei [sic] the Magistrates dare not put a native prisoner on board a ship and send him up to be tried . . . but there is far less outrage to the administration of justice in admitting this fact than there is in the farce of taking out a warrant here in Auckland which could not be enforced without provoking a serious clash with the Northern Maoris.[59]

A great many offences by Maori were committed while they were drunk and the flow of money to Maori office-holders stimulated drunkenness. Barstow, Bay of Islands Resident Magistrate, appalled at the demoralisation and lawlessness caused by liquor in his district, pleaded for stronger prohibition laws, stating: 'I object to class legislation but not to race legislation. I should no more make the same law for European and Maori than feed my horse and dog alike.' George Clarke, on the other hand, noted the Maori people's strong objection to discriminatory laws, and believed that the wave of drunkenness had passed its climax. He argued that Maori should be permitted to buy liquor but that the laws against intemperance should be strictly enforced.[60] Clarke's was in fact the more practicable course; it was clearly difficult to police a restriction on sale of liquor to Maori once liquor was in the district, and equally difficult to prevent the landing of it on hundreds of miles of coastline with many natural harbours. Nevertheless, for the time being the prohibition school prevailed. The Bay of Islands Runanga, at Grey's request, reluctantly passed a resolution, which was duly gazetted, tightening the restrictions against the acquisition of liquor by Maori. Fines against offending publicans were raised from £10 to £50 or more and the proportion offered to Maori informers. It was of little avail. Would-be informers were few and some were intimidated by gangs of roistering young Maori.[61] The Provincial authorities themselves, frequently heavily involved in the liquor trade, gave the Resident Magistrates little support in their efforts to convict publicans or the itinerant grog-sellers, Maori and Pakeha, who roamed the villages.

Given the refusal of the Kingite districts to accept the new institutions, and the selectivity with which other districts treated them, can it be said that the Government's efforts showed sufficient promise to justify persistence with them? Gorst's opinion—that they were 'everywhere a failure', or supported by the Maori only for the sake of financial gain—has generally been accepted by historians. But Gorst's was a jaundiced view, the embittered condemnation of a disillusioned idealist. Moreover it generalises too widely from Waikato experience. It all depends what one expects. The British officials and settlers generally hoped for a far more thorough-going acceptance of their institutions than was reasonable; of course Polynesian values persisted and spoiled the tidy pattern of justice and administration which they wanted. Looked at thus the impressive feature is perhaps not the Maori rejection of British law and new judicial institutions, but their selective acceptance of them. For the operation of the new institutions in the far north, on the Wanganui River, parts of the Bay of Plenty, northern Hawke's Bay and even lower Waikato shows a serious and thoughtful involvement of Maori people, much more than that implied by mere cupidity. The judicial circuit of the Resident Magistrate and Assessors was a major innovation, widely accepted by the communities in which it operated. Even the Runanga of the north were not without promise.

Maori defiance of the law was also more reasoned than was granted by the colonists, and on occasion the Maori were at pains to explain their reasoning. The day after Paora's kinsmen had released him from the Napier police one of them appeared in court on his behalf and quietly told the not unimpressed officials that it was wrong to put a chief in prison for being drunk: it was quite in order to arrest a common Maori, they would never rescue one of those vagabonds, but intoxicated chiefs should be ignored like the English gentlemen of the town who got tipsy and kicked up a noise.[62] Long gaol sentences were resisted, the punishment being regarded as cruel and excessive in relation to most of the offences for which it was imposed. The implacability and remoteness of the Supreme Court's proceedings was frightening. John White, who did persuade his Assessors not to resist the remand of an offending chief to the

Supreme Court in Wellington was told that the Wanganui River Maori were anxious to have the Supreme Court sit in the up-river district itself since they 'dread the separation of those committed more than the degradation of imprisonment'. Much Maori unco-operativeness about suppressing the illegal liquor traffic was due largely to the fact that the law was discriminatory, the prohibition applying to Maori only.

Of course the question of enforcement of law still had to be squarely faced. John White believed he could police the Wanganui district if he were allowed to enrol thirty or forty Maori police under a Pakeha officer, but this request was declined as too expensive and too risky.[63] The suggestion may indeed have had more merit if White had suggested that a Maori officer be in charge, with a European associate, for he himself put the principal difficulty plainly when he wrote: 'nor can I make myself believe that the Maoris can be led driven or coaxed unless the power used be distinctively Maori; any purely European policy is looked on by them as the shadow of a reality of future aggression'.[64] Indeed it is conceivable that by persevering with efforts to enlist the support of the chiefs, and by further modifying the law to accommodate Maori values, government may in time (and with other circumstances favourable) have established sufficient rapport with Maori communities to isolate recalcitrants and undertake limited police actions, with the support of Assessors and with a substantially Maori police force.

The new institutions were, moreover, gradually making inroads. In most districts bordering the Waikato there was a steady trickle of appeals to the Resident Magistrate's court by Maori aggrieved by the decisions of Kingite chiefs, and sometimes whole *hapu* came over. White's up-river tours brought Kingites into his court (some in their uniforms), swearing oaths on the Bible, giving evidence and accepting judgment. Reports from Manawatu, Bay of Plenty and Poverty Bay suggest a steady decline in Kingite enthusiasm and a blurring of distinction between King and Queen factions. Outside the Kingite heartland, and to a large extent within it, most chiefs and *hapu* were still pragmatic and independent, rather than ideological nationalists. The powerful Pehi Turoa of upper Wanganui was a typical example. He leaned to the King movement from distrust of the Europeans, but resented a direct Kingite demand to keep White out of his territory. After six months White secured his approval to enrol officers and build courthouses in his villages.

On balance then, there was just sufficient encouragement in the Maori response to the new institutions to justify Henry Sewell's optimistic conclusion that 'upon the whole, a work had been begun, which, with time and patience —unless interrupted by external disturbances—might have restored peace to the Colony, and reconciled native self-government with British supremacy'.[65] Had the Government been able quickly to restore the Waitara block and heal the Taranaki sore, had it been able to recognise the King movement along lines acceptable to Tamihana and the moderates at least, had it been able to institute a carefully controlled system of land-trading which would have reassured responsible Maori leaders that they still retained the initiative in land transactions and would not be coerced—had all these things been possible, then Sewell's hopes could conceivably have been fulfilled. But of course none of these necessary pre-conditions obtained. The patient work of the more able magistrates and their Maori associates could not prevail against basic conflicts of interest, fundamental prejudices and the passions of the militant.

X

Invasion of the Waikato

The new institutions had been launched at a time when a large proportion of the settler community wanted the Maori subdued by force of arms. Ignoring Maori consumers' heavy contribution to indirect taxation, William Buckland in the Auckland Provincial Council declaimed that 'They [the settlers] did not come here to pay £50,000 a year for civilizing the Maoris'.[1] Even the subsidising of teachers in the Maori villages was sneered at by some who claimed that there was no way of 'improving' the Maori but by the sword.

Among those who expressed the strongest objections to the new policy was one who had much to do with administering it—Dillon Bell, the Acting Native Minister and Native Secretary. He not only opposed numerous appointments made in the out-districts but dragged his feet over requests for agricultural implements or stock, or grants for flour mills and access roads, sent in by the Runanga or the Resident Magistrates. In April 1862, Fox displaced him and ran the Native Office himself. This, however, only served to increase the fear in settler minds of their old bogey—an irresponsible and nepotistic Native Office. The fact that George Clarke and three of his sons were back in harness was alarming to the many settlers who recalled the Protectorate Department and its allegedly philo-Maori policies.[2] The old Chief Protector's behaviour in 1862 was said to be meddlesome and over-bearing. A. H. Russell was despised in Hawke's Bay for his 'sneaking missionary tendencies'.[3] C. O. Davis's return to the Native Office to revitalise the official Maori language newspaper was widely condemned: he had been dismissed by McLean in 1857 on suspicion of intriguing with the King movement. Armitage, Civil Commissioner in lower Waikato, was despised because he drank heavily and lived with a Maori woman. The reputation the Native Office had gained under McLean for inefficiency and secretive proceedings persisted.

The Runanga system fell into contempt once it was clear that the Maori did not want to decide land-title questions and alienate land through it. Even before this was apparent Ministers had advised Grey that settlers and speculators would be intolerant of circumscribed dealing under the Runanga. Hawke's Bay opinion underlined the point; Ormond wrote angrily of the squatters' dependence upon the chiefs, who, he claimed, could exact what rents they chose by taking settlers' stock or boycotting shearing or other work

147

squatters required done. He asserted that the 'league against land selling etc
in this Province [is] only kept in existence by the terror the runanga poses'.
When Crosbie Ward maintained that the title the Runanga would determine
would be a 'tribal' one the outcry against 'communism in land' reached new
heights. 'All our difficulties in New Zealand arise from the existence of the
"tribal right" ', moaned the *Daily Southern Cross*.[5]

But settlers also objected on racial grounds to sharing authority with local
Maori, even when they gave constructive and conciliatory leads. When the
Mangonui Runanga passed a useful resolution on fencing, *The Aucklander*
exclaimed in horror that 'it only wants the Governor's approval to subject
Europeans settled in that district to Maori law administered by Maoris'.[6]
When Armitage's Runanga wanted to appoint a Pakeha policeman to assist in
disputes between parties of both races, the settlers in the lower Waikato
forced the proposed appointee, a local tradesman, to decline office by threatening to withdraw their custom from him.[7] At Armitage's request, Fox did
secure in the 1862 session of the Assembly an amendment to the Native
Districts Regulation Act to permit regulations of the Runanga to extend to
alienated land and settlers dwelling in predominantly Maori districts. But this
was to be conditional on the consent of a majority of the settlers involved, and
such consent was beyond hoping for.

Once Fox saw the way Pakeha opinion was shaping he lost heart. As
early as May 1862 he told Armitage to postpone questions about gaols, courthouses and hospitals till after the General Assembly session in June.[8] Before
the Assembly met, developments in the Waikato had given the advocates of a
'firm hand' new ammunition. As has been noted, Gorst's going to the Waikato
was resented by the Kingites who had specifically asked that a magistrate
should not be sent at that time. *Te Hokioi* observed perceptively: 'How else
came he [Grey] to send hither a European magistrate among the Maori King
people to excite them, that it may be said, perhaps, that the evil originated
with the Maoris whereas his was the persistence in coming here.'[9] In May
1862, aggrieved by his lack of progress, Gorst went into Auckland with a view
to giving up altogether. The Ministers were depressed; they were inclined to
want to send Gorst to another district and 'shut Waikato up', that is, withdraw all settlers from the district and impose a trade embargo on the King
movement, in the hope that it would then collapse in disillusionment. But
Grey decided, 'it will not do, the Europeans must hold their ground. It would
appear as if we were driven out of Waikato.'[10]

Meanwhile, the devious Dillon Bell, smarting under his recent dismissal
from the Native Office, perceived a way of bringing Fox's 'peace policy' into
disrepute. He had been informed by Gorst that 'My residence in Waikato is
bringing me to look upon vigour and power as the highest qualities in a Government.'[11] Bell therefore joined in urging Gorst's return, not to serve any
more summonses, but to write a report on his recent experiences. This report,
coming from a young intellectual, an idealist, sympathetic to the Maori, and

manifestly not a land-shark, was utterly damning of the King movement. Gorst stated that he now believed that his initial hopes for a reconciliation and alliance between the Government and the leaders of the King party, whereby all the King's officers might be employed in a local Waikato administration to have been illusory from the beginning,

> Because the King subsists entirely upon the feeling of opposition to our Government. It is possible that the King movement originally may have been a movement for law and order; it has altogether lost that character now . . . the King and his Council have not the slightest power to enforce obedience to the law. As a scheme for creating a Government, the King Movement has failed long ago.

Gorst gave many illustrations to show that, while the King provided a rallying point for disaffected Maori, these adherents did very much as they pleased, under cover of the King's name, but were in no way submissive to his authority. In passing, he argued that it was senseless to try to remove the King, without trying to remove the cause of the 'feeling of common danger' (principally the threat to their lands) which provoked the Maori to establish him. This was sound counsel, but it was not the most urgent point of Gorst's argument. He went on to state:

> But there is a danger, which is a very much more serious and permanent source of peril to the Colony than that one the symptom whereof is the Maori King—it is the utter lawlessness and anarchy of the Native population of New Zealand. . . . The great mischief of all is not that the Natives choose to be governed by a King instead of by us, but that they are not in any real sense governed at all.

So long as that state of affairs continued—and here he referred to other districts besides Waikato—'peace and prosperity in Native districts will be an impossibility'. He then stated: 'The great remedy then for the evils of the land is Government—but I mean vigorous Government—I mean authority which is able to protect life and property by enforcing obedience to the law.' Magistrates and laws were in abundance he argued; it was police power that was defective; the task of establishing sufficient police power was fraught with difficulty and danger, 'but there can be no peace in the Colony till it has been fairly met and fully solved'.[12]

To this report Gorst's personality greatly contributed. Morgan commented on his lack of patience and perseverence, his tendency to be 'soon elated and soon depressed';[13] Maunsell described him as 'a talented, pious, but by no means judicious magistrate'.[14] His hopes had been based on false assumptions to begin with because he had not appreciated the depth of Maori distrust of Government intentions; his tidy European conceptions led him to take an unduly pessimistic view of the fortunes of the civil institutions of 1861-3; he was insensitive enough to Maori needs and efforts to regard the resolutions of Armitage's Runanga as simply 'amusing';[15] his observations on the lawless tendencies that obtained in the Waikato under the cloak of the King movement had much justification, but his remedy—to give up further attempts at co-operation with the Kingites in favour of a simple assertion of police power by the Government—involved a wanton condemnation and abandonment of the moderate chiefs who were themselves unhappy about the followers' turbulent behaviour, and was a foolhardy and dangerous policy to boot. Moreover, his report gave great support to those who, for baser reasons than his own, wanted to coerce the King movement. It was called for in parliament by Fox's opponents. When published it was hailed throughout the settler press and greeted by a chorus of I-told-you-so from the long-standing advocates of 'vigorous action', and Grey was 'greatly pleased with its truth telling'.[16]

When the General Assembly met in June, Fox clung rather hopelessly to the central idea of the new institutions. He spoke of the Runanga as the *point d'appui* to which to attach the machinery of self-government, and fore-shadowed a Native Lands Bill which would have confirmed the Runanga's power, under the Governor-in-Council, to determine land title, and permitted alienation to settlers at the rate of one economical farm to each settler, with full freehold title to come only after ten years occupancy. These restrictions were calculated both to satisfy Maori sensitivities and to prevent speculation, but they were dismissed by even a moderate like Sewell as 'preposterous'. Fox soon resigned, convinced that his Ministry had not the support which 'would enable us to carry out those measures which we consider essential cardinal points of our native policy'.[17] The incoming Premier, Alfred Domett, graduate of Cambridge and the Middle Temple and a leader of the New Zealand Company settlement at Nelson, 'did not care to deny that he still believed that, if the Natives had been taught first to respect the power of English arms, the schemes proposed for their benefit would have had much better chance of success'.[18] The new Native Minister was Dillon Bell.

The 1862 Assembly then enacted some important legislation affecting Maori and settler relations. The jurisdiction of the Resident Magistrates and Circuit Court Judges had been found to be too restricted, resulting in un-necessary referrals to the Supreme Court, with the consequent risk of their defiance by Maori accused. The lower courts' jurisdiction was therefore con-siderably augmented. Explaining the changes, Sewell (who remained Attorney-General till September) wrote

> It is necessary in order to establish *some* authority to which the Natives will sub-mit and to which they will look up as a governing power to arm the Magistrate with very extensive Jurisdiction. He must be able to administer Justice on the spot and at the instant, in order to wean the Native from his own barbarous habits of enforcing rights or redressing wrongs.[19]

Moreover, to encourage Maori acceptance of the jurisdiction of the Supreme Court, the Assembly at last passed a Jury Law Amendment Act to permit the enrolment of a Maori jury in cases involving Maori parties only, and the enrolment of a mixed jury in civil cases between a Maori and a settler. Sewell had intended that Maori accused should also have the right to call for a Maori jury or at least a mixed jury in criminal cases where Maori and settler were involved, but the Domett Ministry would not accept this. Bell argued that to go too far in the direction of allowing Maori jurors power over settlers in criminal cases, would be to excite so much animosity from the settler community that racial harmony would be impaired rather than increased.[20] However, the amendments passed were soon brought into operation. One Metane Te Huiki of Wairoa, having been voluntarily surrendered by his relatives to a Maori constable, was indicted before a Maori Grand Jury in Napier in September 1862 for the murder of his wife.[21] Mixed juries were not uncommon in later years, while coroners' juries, empanelled according to very flexible rules, began to be used much more regularly than before in cases of Maori deaths, and they normally included Maori jurors.

The question of Maori reserves also received attention from the 1862 Assembly. Maori distrust of the Commissioners who administered the reserves under the 1856 Act was amply justified. In the review of the Commissioners' accounts and proceedings after McLean's departure from the Native Office many anomalies had been found, including the sale of a reserve by the Taranaki Board to one of its own members—Robert Parris. The Fox Ministry shut down all further transactions under the 1856 Act and lectured the Taranaki Commissioners on the grave impropriety of their act. The reserve was taken from Parris but returned not to the original Maori owners, they being deemed to have received full payment for it, but to the Province.[22] The 1862 Assembly passed a new Native Reserves Act based on the ideas advanced by James Mackay from his experience as Assistant Native Secretary in Nelson. Maori owners no longer had to convey land to the Crown but could simply place it under the administrative control of the Governor, who would administer it through officers of the Native Department. Under this Act a full-time commissioner of reserves, George Swainson, was appointed in Wellington and began the painstaking work of scrutinising deeds, making accurate surveys, ascertaining beneficial owners, arranging for better leases and discussing with the owners the application of the revenue. This was at least the beginning of some attempt to turn theories of trusteeship into reality. But ultimate legal control of the reserves remained with the Governor-in-Council, which meant that leases or sales of reserves could—and in fact would—be made by the Government of the day. High-flown humanitarian theories of how the Maori would benefit from the increased value of their reserved lands could not outweigh the fact that the lands in the 'reserved' category were no longer in Maori control.

Much the most important preoccupation of the Assembly in 1862 was, however, the Native Lands Act. The Waitara purchase had shown the establishment of a competent tribunal to determine Maori ownership to be clearly necessary and disinterested parties in New Zealand, as well as the land-hungry, thought that the Crown must disengage from land purchasing. Newcastle had advised Grey that Her Majesty's Government would be willing to assent to 'any prudent plan' for the individualisation of Maori land title and direct purchase by settlers under proper safeguards.[23] The bulk of Maori opinion after Waitara was probably more concerned to see an end to land-selling altogether; the King movement and Hawke's Bay Maori wanted to receive settlers as tenants, and there were strong movements in Poverty Bay and other districts to return the payments hastily made direct to settlers in earlier years. Nevertheless, there were still many willing to sell and there was also the general resentment evident since FitzRoy's time, that the Crown should make the profit on resale. Many Maori owners entertained the fond hope, assiduously fostered by settlers, that with direct purchase they would receive the full price the Crown was paid. There was therefore some plausibility in Bell's argument that the Native Lands Act might assist in re-establishing confidence between the colonists and the Maori people, by granting the latter firstly, their legal right to all their lands including the uncultivated lands (for settler opinion had not yet conceded that the land rights expressed in the Treaty of Waitangi included the 'waste' lands) and secondly, the full market value of those lands when they chose to alienate them.[24]

But these principles had been well catered for in the scheme—advanced by Grey in his new institutions and Fox in his Native Lands Bill—for alienation of land through the Runanga. They would, however, have greatly circumscribed would-be purchasers and, once Fox's Ministry had fallen, Bell introduced a new Bill more calculated to suit European tastes. Bell was not markedly sympathetic to speculators—indeed he at times bitterly opposed them[25]—but he was a devious man, lacking in principle, who bent easily to powerful pressures; at his elbow in the Domett Ministry were the leading Auckland financiers and speculators of the day, Thomas Russell and Frederick Whitaker. Moreover, in September 1862 Sewell was dropped from the Ministry by Domett at the insistence of Russell and Bell because of his lack of sympathy with the Native Lands Act, and Whitaker became Attorney-General.[26]

The Act established a Native Land Court in the form of panels of important chiefs in each district meeting under the chairmanship of a Pakeha magistrate. This was a sound proposal. It envisaged working through existing Maori leadership, determining, as far as possible, the various customary rights in the land, and agreeing, after exchange and arbitration of claims, who would share in the grant of a legal title. However, machinery to ensure that the Maori owners could carefully control the disposition of their legal estate and receive full market value for such portions as they chose to sell, was not provided. There was, for instance, no requirement that sale be by public auction. Instead the Act provided that once Maori claimants had a certificate of title awarded by the land courts and endorsed by the Governor this could be used as the basis for the transfer of the land to individual purchasers. The Act would simply 'to a great extent convert the Native Lands into transferable paper'.[27] Moreover, it declared that private transactions with the Maori for their lands before the grant of a certificate, would merely be 'void', not unlawful. The way was open for a mammoth spree of land speculation and jobbery, pending the passage of the land through the courts; the Auckland land-sharks openly avowed this intention, while in Hawke's Bay squatters were already making arrangements with complaisant chiefs. Grey accepted the Act on the grounds that it was the best he could get from the Assembly, and that it finally defeated the vocal section of settler opinion which still bitterly opposed the recognition of the Maori right to the waste lands. (Even so, a clause declaring customary lands the 'absolute' property of its Maori owners was struck out;[28] New Zealand legislators and judges held to the view that radical title rested in the Crown, Maori customary rights being recognised as an act of grace.) But Grey also wanted the Maori interior strongholds opened by inroads of European settlement and any scruples he may have had about the legalised jobbery invited by the Act were assuaged by the provision that he could declare reserves, which would prevent complete Maori landlessness.[29] It was to be several years, however, before the Native Land Act received the approval of the Imperial authorities and machinery was established to implement it.

The larger question of the Maori people's place in the political and legal structure was raised in the 1862 Assembly in the form of a series of resolutions moved by J. E. FitzGerald, the educated and erudite leader of the Canterbury settlement. The first of these reiterated the familiar principle that the 'entire amalgamation of all Her Majesty's subjects in New Zealand into one united people', should be the goal of all law and policy; the second stated that the Assembly should assent to no law which did not accord both races equal civil and political privileges; the third, fourth and fifth resolutions asked that Maori be brought into the Government, both Houses of the Assembly, the Provincial Councils, juries and responsible positions in the courts of law, with the least possible delay. Speaking in support of his resolutions FitzGerald said that Grey's Runanga system must be scrapped as trivial and unworkable, but the District Runanga might be converted into Provincial Councils, equal in power and functions with the settler Provincial Councils. The King movement should also be given this dignity. Laws that made a distinction between the races, such as the Arms Ordinance or Sale of Spirits Ordinance, should be abolished in favour of those which applied equally. He summed up with two basic points. Firstly, the rule of law must be shown to be equal for both races even if it took years before the Maori fully accepted it. (At that time, FitzGerald said, a policeman stood for the law in the settlers' eyes only; in Maori eyes he stood as a 'badge of their racial servitude'.) Secondly, it was futile to wait until the Maori were ready for the privileges and responsibility of sharing in machinery of government; they should be given that responsibility and allowed to grow in experience.[30]

Admirable though all this sounded, it is difficult to know how serious FitzGerald's concern was for Maori rights. In the 1850s, when North Island politicians had been enrolling Maori voters with a view to manipulating their votes, he had been to the fore in successfully defending the principle that land held under customary tenure did not entitle Maori claimants to qualify for the franchise. Moreover in 1862, perhaps to disarm his opponents, he privately supported his resolutions in very different language, telling J. C. Richmond (brother of the former Native Minister) that

> He would adopt the King movement and furnish it with means. By this he would reckon better to bring about a reductio ad absurdum of the thing, or if it has enough life to effect any organisation and establish a power, he would hope to rule it by means of the purse strings, and at all events to give some few chiefs such a taste of the pleasures of position as to enter the small end of the wedge in respect of land sales.[31]

Outside the Assembly the FitzGerald resolutions were greeted with scorn and fury. A correspondent to the *Aucklander* challenged the very principle of amalgamation itself:

> Does it mean that we should give our daughters to their sons and take wives of their daughters for our sons? If so what is there to prevent it, except that moral purity cannot descend to the level of animal instincts . . . there can be no companionship . . . between the domestic purity of our wives and daughters and the communism of the native kainga where the females were never taught that chastity was a virtue . . . there can be no such social amalgamation until the inferior race shall stand upon the same level in regard to morality and knowledge as ourselves.[32]

In the end only the first two resolutions passed the Assembly, for members found no difficulty in paying lip service to the doctrines of racial equality. The third resolution, approving Maori representation in the Assembly, was strongly opposed on the grounds that the political system would be debased either by Maori representatives of poor quality or by settler candidates manipulating the Maori vote. Even so it was defeated by only twenty votes to seventeen and the ayes included some of the leading politicians in the Colony —among them Fox, Bell and Mantell. The debate had at least had the effect of keeping the question of Maori political representation alive.

The Domett Ministry continued to administer the new institutions but in half-hearted fashion. District staff was kept up to strength and small sums paid to assist a village school, build a bridge or access road, equip a smithy or supply a village with seed or agricultural implements. But Bell suffered from opthalmia and increasingly confined his attention to the Taranaki question. Mantell was brought into the Government in December 1862 and given direction of Maori affairs in the Wellington Province. He was more hindrance than help. He affected a stiff aloofness from any Maori with Kingite leanings and missed chances to establish friendly relations with waverers; his hypersensitivity about being by-passed led him to meddle unnecessarily in petty matters; and his officers received illustrations of his fancied wit, rather than clear guidance. It was no help to John White, toiling amidst considerable physical hardship and an incredibly complex political situation, to be told 'If you ask me point blank what course to take I say straight on; if you can say that is impossible, I then say take the nearest you can to it. And God speed you.'[33]

Unfortunately, almost all the useful resolution of the Runanga met a cold reception. Many requests for economic aid were treated as grasping; resolutions on the *puremu* question as quaint. The resolutions on stock trespass, fencing, clearing of thistles and sale of spirits was treated as too vague or simply ignored, and the neglect to confirm them was the subject of bitter complaint among the Maori.[34] Only a Kohekohe resolution on wandering cattle and the Bay of Islands resolution on the sale of spirits were confirmed by the Executive Council and gazetted.

The Resident Magistrates were generally left in their enormous Districts, obliged to travel frequently in arduous conditions of terrain and climate,[35] required to do incessant judicial work and political negotiation all day and write reports late at night, specifically told not to expect precise orders as the time lag in communication frequently rendered them redundant, but obliged by a nagging Audit Office to account for every penny of expenditure.

Important opportunities were lost. Wairoa, in northern Hawke's Bay, had waited a full year after the local *hapu* had agreed to accept the new institutions before it received its permanent Resident Magistrate. A. H. Russell reported that he had difficulty keeping the people from wavering, a principal chief, Ihaka Whanga, stating that he was reluctant to abolish their own *runanga* system 'until he saw the law established in its stead'. Russell added: 'the Government cannot know what they lose by not acting more promptly—had their present policy been carried out with spirit from the first mention of it I am of opinion that much greater progress would have been made'.[36]

The question of police power that Gorst had highlighted remained a critical issue. From various parts of the Colony the settler press reported incidents where Runanga or Assessors had ruled in favour of a settler in dispute with a Maori, but had not enforced their decision if the Maori offender was defiant. The obvious place to tackle the problem was in one of the relatively well-disposed districts like the Bay of Islands or Mangonui. There was some chance that in these, a bold decision to enforce the verdict of a Runanga or bench of Assessors, with a mixed police force, would command considerable support, or at least not be widely resisted. In Whangarei, for example, the Assessors under the principal chief Manihera, decided a dispute over a bullock in favour of a settler and against his opponents—some Rotorua Maori digging *kauri* gum in the district. The Rotorua men then became violent and scuffled with the settler, but at that point a young Bay of Islands Assessor named Sydney [Hirini Taiwhanga?] rode up with some Maori police and promptly enforced the Whangarei Assessors' judgment.[37] Admittedly, enforcement against Maori from outside the district was much more likely than if the offenders had been local. Yet the northern districts possessed a number of zealous young Maori officials like Sydney, who might have served as the lynch-pin for the beginning of a more vigorous enforcement of law.

But the Government did not begin in the far north. They began, in, of all places, the upper Waikato. Grey responded to Gorst's plea for 'vigorous' government by suggesting that police barracks be built at Otawhao, Gorst's station, and at Kohekohe, the village of the young 'Queenite' chief, Te Wheoro. Gorst realised that the barracks at Otawhao would be resisted and instead had it established as a trade training school, to recruit a body of young men who would ultimately rival the King's soldiers. As a school it was an excellent institution, the last seriously to undertake the trade training of young Maori until the 1960s, but the Kingites soon suspected its ulterior purpose. The moderate leaders protected Gorst at Otawhao from their angry colleagues but in March 1863 a strong party came down to Kohekohe and in as deliberate and orderly a manner as possible, threw the timber for the proposed barracks into the river and rafted it back to Government land.

Meanwhile a new opportunity for diplomacy between Grey and the Kingites had arisen. At a big meeting at Peria, Tamihana's village, in October 1862, the King tribes agreed on their policy in the face of what they considered to be increasing Government pressure. The Mangatawhiri Stream was declared to be the limit to which the military road, being steadily constructed from Auckland, would be allowed; the armed steamers which the Government was having built to run up the Waikato River were not to be permitted; trouble-some settlers in the Waikato were to be sent back to Auckland, peaceable ones to be well treated; the Governor was to be asked to come to the Waikato for a frank exchange of views; if the discussion went well then the King party would agree to Waitara's being investigated.[38]

In October also, Grey had received a despatch from Newcastle authorising the recognition of the King movement according to the terms Tamihana had put to Gorst the previous December, namely, that a Waikato Native Council should make local laws which would be submitted for assent to the King as well as the Governor.

In response to the Kingites' invitation then, Grey again visited the Waikato. The most important discussion occurred between the Governor, Tamihana and Taati Te Waru at Taupiri on 8 January 1863. According to the *Daily Southern Cross* summary:

> the natives said that hitherto they had employed all their energies to establish the [King movement], and had no time to devote to the making of laws; that, now the thing had obtained a position among the people, they would elect from among their chiefs those who were most learned, to frame rules and laws for the good government of the people; these laws will be handed by Matutaera to the Governor for his sanction, and, if assented to by the Governor, they should become law.[39]

Pressed by Tamihana for agreement to this, Grey replied that although he understood that Tamihana and the moderates meant well, they could not control their followers, and nothing but evil would result from the King move-ment. He quoted the case of a Maori called Wirihana in the Rangitikei district who was believed to have attempted to rape a young English girl named Lind and been forcibly released from custody by Kingite 'soldiers' and carried off into sanctuary. Tamihana fell silent at this, for the question of the

limited authority they could exert over turbulent tribes was of grave concern
to the idealists at the head of the King movement. *Te Pihoihoi,* a newspaper
Gorst had lately begun printing, reported Grey as concluding with the statement that the recognition of the King could not be the work of a day, of
months or even of a year 'but perhaps three years or ten'. In the meantime, the
Kingites should send a deputation to Auckland to discuss the matter with
him and the 'Pakeha runanga' and if the two agreed he would confirm the
arrangement.[40]

Shortly after the meeting Grey sent to London the press reports relating
Tamihana's offer, with a covering note saying that the King tribes had subsequently withdrawn from the 'agreement', on the ground that they had been
grievously wronged over Waitara 'and that they would therefore not again
come under the authority of the Queen'.[41] Six years later, in answer to a
charge by Sir William Martin that he had missed an excellent chance of
establishing good relations with the King movement, Grey elaborated his
account of this important exchange:

> I . . . with the full assent of my Responsible Advisers, offered to constitute all
> the Waikato and Ngatimaniapoto country a separate province, which would have
> had the right of electing its own Superintendent, its own Legislature, and of
> choosing its own Executive Government . . . the Waikato tribes would within their
> own district . . . have had the exclusive control and management of their own
> affairs. This offer was, however, after full discussion and consideration, resolutely
> and deliberately refused, on the ground that they would accept no offer that did
> not involve an absolute recognition of the Maori King, and his and their entire
> independence from the Crown of England, terms which no subject had power to
> grant, and which could not have been granted without creating worse evils than
> those which their refusal involved.[42]

The account somewhat surprised the Colonial Office, as well it might, for
there is not a shred of contemporary evidence to support Grey's claim to have
made such an elaborate offer. His Ministers had made it quite clear they were
reluctant to approve Grey's going to Waikato at all, and consented only in the
hope that the Kingites might make a submission; they were certainly not in
favour of the recognition of a Waikato Province, which would have shut up
Waikato lands and (in their view) left the question of law and order
unsolved.[43] All the contemporary settler press reports show Grey to be disparaging and evasive on 8 January.[44] The Kingite newspaper, *Te Hokioi,*
reported that the *korero* (debate) began after breakfast and lasted till evening;
'great obstinacy' prevailed on both sides 'and nothing favourable to the King
party was favourably received by the Governor, not in the least, none whatever'.[45] Maunsell, who was interpreter at the meeting, wrote that the King
people were extremely suspicious of the Governor's intentions: 'With great
eagerness they laid upon an unfortunate remark casually dropped by Sir G.
Grey to the effect that he would not wage war on the King party, but he
would "dig around" it (by his Institutions etc.) till it fell.'[46] In May the Ngatimaniapoto expelled Gorst from the Waikato for building his barracks, publish-

ing virulent attacks on the King movement in his Maori language paper, and pulling up a boundary peg on the Mangatawhiri Stream. Several clergy and settlers went with him. The Ngatimaniapoto said they were driving off the Governor's 'spades'.

After the Taupiri meeting the situation developed rapidly towards war. Grey, rejecting offers of assistance and words of caution from Tamihana, reoccupied Tataraimaka, a block of Crown land in Taranaki seized by the Ngatiruanui during the war of 1860-1. Now, when a concession by the Government was urgently called for, the divided responsibility in Maori affairs had a fateful effect. Grey wanted to return the Waitara; some of the Ministers favoured an amnesty for the events of the Taranaki war. Each wanted the other to approve the step and share the expected opprobrium from the settlers. While they haggled, Ngatiruanui Maori, incited by Rewi Maniapoto and other Kingite extremists, ambushed troops supplying Tataraimaka, near the village of Oakura. War in Taranaki resumed.

It was not yet clear that the war must spread to Waikato. Amid great tension the Government sent John Rogan to Ngaruawahia (no Maori guide daring to accompany him) to demand that the King movement openly dis-associate itself from the Oakura killings or be held liable for punishment also. Rogan found the Kingites bitter about Grey's refusal to accept Tamihana's assistance in reoccupying Tataraimaka, and inclined to blame what followed on that. After a lengthy conclave of the King's *runanga* Rogan was told that the chiefs could not agree on an answer, but that Matutaera had spoken once, to say '*Waikato takoto*' (Waikato, lie still).[47] Rewi was known to have urged an attack on Auckland; the moderates to have blocked him. After a flurry of panic among the settlers in the out-districts, a calm returned as powerful chiefs with Kingite sympathies—Wi Tako of Otaki, Pehi Turoa of upper Wanganui, and the Hawke's Bay chiefs—all repudiated the action at Oakura. On 8 May Grey had received a despatch from Newcastle informing him that he should generally accept the policies recommended by his Ministers except that he should act on his own judgment if the policies proposed were 'marked by evident injustice towards subjects of the native race' or involved the use of Imperial troops. He still had to have good grounds for an invasion of Waikato.

Maori extremists gave him just sufficient justification. From mid-June reports began to come in of plots being hatched for a general rising, of purchases of arms and lead nails and marbles for ammunition. The Waikato people began to exhume their dead from the vicinity of Auckland. On 24 June Grey put before Ministers his detailed plan to

> throw forward military posts . . . to Paetai and Ngaruawahia, taking permanent possession of those places . . . At the same time to clear out all hostile Natives at present residing between the Auckland isthmus, and the line of the River and fortified post . . . Lastly to confiscate the land of the hostile Natives, part of which would be given away and settled on military tenure to provide for the future security

of the district near Auckland, and the remainder sold to defray the expenses of the war.

Of this 'bold policy' Domett stated: 'You may suppose *I* was always for this—the difficulty of course was to get over Grey's horror (by anticipation) of the possible condemnations and ululations of Exeter Hall and Co'.[48]

In late June Tamihana warned Ashwell of a plan 'by the false [Maori] friends of the Governor about Auckland' to attack the out-settlers; he promised to frustrate their design.[49] Tamati Ngapora, still living at Mangere in token of the King movement's desire for peace, warned that turbulent warriors might disregard him and leave him to his fate. He said that if there were no murders by 12 July all would be well, as it would mean that Tamihana and the advocates of peace would have prevailed.[50]

But Grey waited no longer. Bell wrote to Mantell:

> The certainty of the existence of a conspiracy to commence the work of murder on our own frontier has determined the Governor to make the first move . . . The Governor's mind has been very much influenced, as well as ours . . . by accounts similar to Ashwell's relating to a general rise throughout the Country . . . he has come to the same conclusion that we all did in 1860-61, that fighting at Taranaki did nothing, and that the real issue must be tried in Waikato.[51]

Grey's reluctance to accept the risk of having out-settlers killed is understandable. Yet he did not take the last chance of contacting Ngaruawahia, supporting Tamihana's efforts, or at least receiving accurate intelligence as to how they were progressing. Had he done so he would have found that Rewi had already abandoned his design for an attack in the direction of Auckland and gone off to Taupo for the interment of the bones of Te Heuheu Iwikau who had died the previous year. It did not appear that the Governor was anxious to avoid war. On 9 July warships turned back canoes coming into Auckland harbour (for some Waikato Maori were still trading with the town) and the *hapu* south of Auckland were asked to swear an oath of allegiance and surrender their arms. Tamati Ngapora and his kin took this to be an act of war and hurried off to King territory. A proclamation was issued stating that because the King movement was 'unwilling or unable' (the last two words being added at Gorst's suggestion) to control its turbulent followers, the Government would take posts in the Waikato. Those who resisted would forfeit the right to their lands. On 12 July, before the proclamation could reach Ngaruawahia, General Cameron had crossed the Mangatawhiri. To the Maori, the only possible conclusion was that the Government had begun the war to subjugate them and seize their lands. Tamihana, Taati Te Waru, Tioriori, Tamati Ngapora and other moderate Kingites therefore joined in the general resistance.

The invasion of the Waikato gave vent to half a century of mounting impatience among the British in New Zealand with the independent-mindedness and selectivity of the Maori people. A major military subjugation of the

Maori was indeed likely from the time the decision was taken to acquire sovereignty and establish the authority of centralised law and administration in New Zealand, in the mistaken belief that the Maoris were weak and compliant. From the beginning the chiefs had made plain their concern for their *mana* and the *mana* of the land, and the only conceivable way their suspicion and hostility could have been overcome was to have allowed them to take reassurance that their values and aspirations would be recognised by involving them promptly and fully in the developing political, judicial and administrative institutions. As it was, some chiefs like Nene were satisfied with the relationship Government established with them, others like the Te Heuheu brothers, never had their suspicions overcome. More seriously, others like Paora Tuhaere of Auckland, initially warm towards the British, were becoming increasingly disgruntled at their continued exclusion from effective power in the state; the King movement leaders, almost all of whom at one time or another had warmly sought co-operation with the Government, were, of course, deeply disillusioned.

Most of the tentative efforts to engage the Maori people in the machinery of state, like the new institutions of 1861-3, were too belated, too circumscribed, too sullied by ulterior motives, to be really effective. Moreover, from the 1850s, it would have been necessary to recognise in some form the King movement which the disillusioned young progressives had established in somewhat uneasy alliance with the more narrowly conservative inland chiefs. But a bold course of this kind had to overcome both bitter settler hostility and a defeatist official line, laid down in 1839-40, that New Zealand was destined to be a settler colony and that policies favourable to Maori interests should not be pursued if they flew too strongly in the face of settler wishes. Accommodation between Government and King movement might have had a better chance if Browne had been replaced in 1861 not by Grey but by Dennison, who did advocate recognition of the King movement and at least a temporary check on the spread of settlement. But we cannot know what a year in office among colonists already largely self-governing and with powerful supporting lobbies in London, might have done to Dennison. The fate of FitzRoy, who did make some attempt to accommodate Maori viewpoints was a stark warning. Grey knew better how to trim his sails to the winds of settler ambitions and prejudices.

If the economic conflict for land and official alignment with the settlers gave a particular impetus to the policy of suppressing Maori independence, the Maori were in a deeper sense the victims of British ethnocentrism and racial prejudice. For the former of these qualities at least was as evident among the humanitarians as among the settlers. 'Amalgamation'—that is assimilation—of the Maori people into contemporary English social patterns was most earnestly desired by the missionaries even before the settler influx gave the concept new urgency, and to the end the missionaries and humanitarians, with few exceptions, upheld it against Maori selectivity and separatism. When the

Tamati Ngapora, from the painting by G. Lindauer, Cowan Collection, Alexander Turnbull Library, Wellington, New Zealand. Reproduced by permission of the Library.

Tamihana Te Waharoa. Reproduced by permission of the Dominion Museum, Wellington, New Zealand.

The village of Koroniti (Corinth) on the Wanganui River, about 1885. Reproduced by permission of the Dominion Museum, Wellington, New Zealand.

invasion of the Waikato appeared imminent many missionaries welcomed it for reasons that lay deeper than revulsion at the Oakura massacre and other aggressions Rewi was believed to be inciting. Not only the virulent anti-Kingite, John Morgan, but the moderate and scholarly Maunsell, increasingly angry at the continued 'worldly-mindedness, self-will and pride' of his Waikato congregations, felt the invasion to be necessary, hoping only that the Lord be pleased to 'chasten and humble' not destroy the Maori in the forthcoming conflict.[52]

But British ethnocentrism, at the same time as it denied the Maori people the independent use and development of their own institutions, also denied them full and prompt participation in the new order. For the Englishman's pride in his institutions also involved a notion of high standards, of a degree of excellence which must be reached before non-Englishmen could be admitted to the prerogatives of the club. Thus Englishmen who could not strictly be called racialists firmly believed that the Maori were far from ready to exercise judicial or political power, though it was rather vaguely hoped that in time they would be.

In this sense, ethnocentrism was the ally of a more rabid race prejudice, which held that the Maori people were innately inferior. Some like Domett, who repeated the pseudo-scientific nonsense of the craniologists, thought the Maori biologically inferior; most colonists simply confused cultural and biological features and used infanticide or the persistence of sorcery, or the slaughter of settler families in Taranaki, to argue that the Maori were essentially brutish. This attitude produced its poisonous fruit in the form of increasing segregation of public facilities in the towns and in the increasing use of the term 'nigger' in reference to a Maori. Another consequence was the refusal to take seriously the ideas and enterprises of the young Maori leaders, including possibly the most sensitive, subtle and conciliatory man of either race, Wiremu Tamihana.

The aggressiveness of the colonists in New Zealand also stemmed from a very real sense of insecurity. Certainly the settlers had themselves contributed heavily to this by scattering throughout Maori territory in defiance of the Native Land Purchase Ordinance and inviting Maori reprisal by letting their stock roam or behaving boorishly. But it was extremely difficult for Government to prevent the mingling of both races in the interior since both Maori and settler saw advantages in it. Once scattered, settlers understandably found extremely irksome the practice of *muru* and the occasional casual bullying to which they were subject. More tragically they did not trust, nor would they co-operate with, Maori efforts to establish more regular methods of law and order, as in the *runanga* system, official or unofficial. This was largely because their ethnocentric pride and their racialism made them unwilling to subordinate themselves to Maori authority at all, and led them to regard the inevitably patchy results of Maori efforts to achieve social control as evidence of their fundamental lawlessness. The *Daily Southern Cross* expressed the growing racialist conviction of many settlers that 'The Maori is by habit, by instinct, by immemorial custom, by race—by blood itself—an anarchist. He is a pirate by nature.'[53]

Objective analysis would today reject this nonsense, but there is another and more substantial difficulty. Was Maori society too kin-oriented to permit chiefs to exercise impartial justice and too segmented to permit reliable law enforcement against defiant offenders supported by powerful *hapu?* This problem underlay the most powerful objection that the Government had adduced against recognition of the King movement—the argument that the King movement had been unable to police its followers, and King territory had become a refuge for criminals beyond its borders. Although the release of the Lind girl's attacker was the most widely discussed among the settlers it was not the only case of its kind. According to the *Southern Cross,* even a settler who escaped from the custody of a Maori constable in Taranaki had been sheltered in King territory.[54] 'The real question at the time was this', wrote Grey later, 'was our jurisdiction or that of the so-called Maori King to prevail even in the security of our own settlements?' Like Browne he feared that to allow the heartland to set up an independency would be to abolish all law among the Maori, even those interspersed in the settled districts, since Maori offenders would claim their nationality and be supported as Wirihana was supported, by the heartland.[55] Even equable missionaries such as Maunsell shared Gorst's view that the King tribes were too heterogeneous and disjointed to submit to a central authority at Ngaruawahia.

Perhaps this was so, and since the law and order question had to be solved if Maori and settler were to co-exist in New Zealand, it is likely that, regardless of the land question, the Government may have ultimately been forced to undertake a para-military police action against known offenders like Wirihana, if the King movement had been unable or unwilling to punish them. But the fact remains that the chiefs at Ngaruawahia—young men like Tamihana, now joined by former Queenites like Taati Te Waru—were never given a proper chance to show what they could do. They were not narrow, uncooperative nationalists but had shown that, while undoubtedly concerned with the protection of Maori *mana,* they would have felt that this was assured by recognition of their views on land alienation and by a grant of local governmental responsibility within the framework of British sovereignty. Even without this recognition they were working to develop administrative and judicial institutions that would allow for fruitful co-existence of Maori and settler in the island. They had restrained extremists, as Gorst admitted, and despite their much-publicised failures there were cases of Kingite magistrates and police recovering debts for a settler where a Queen's Assessor had failed.[56] Moreover, Tamihana had justification for his plea that 'Maori law was in its infancy—they had no money, no prisons etc.'[57] It is just conceivable that had the Europeans recognised and assisted the moderates' aspirations, offering them technical assistance and encouragement instead of constant denigration and harrassment, a patient and long-sighted government might have seen a regular administration of law in the interior achieved. Certainly the segmented nature of Maori society was such that it was most unlikely that Tamihana's group could have established a stable administration without the assistance of government, including, probably, its police power. But once assured of official recognition of their basic anxieties and aspirations they might well have accepted government police actions against defiant law-breakers whom they could not themselves control. Furthermore the particularly defiant behaviour of the Ngatimaniapoto was very much a product of the wider political situation. Before 1860 Maori communities had not often remained adamantly defiant about a genuine claim to redress, firmly pressed home through chiefs of rank; when they did, adroit diplomacy could, as in Heke's case, quickly isolate them. Non-co-operation and more extreme nationalist sentiments had gained ground in the King movement largely because the Tamihana group's aspirations had not been recognised and because of the Government's aggression in Taranaki. In 1861-3 it was difficult to undo this damage but it is just conceivable that had the Government settled the Waitara issue quickly, recognised the moderates and been generous with technical and economic assistance they could have isolated the racalcitrants again. Subsequent events were to show that the leaders of recalcitrant tribes—even Rewi Maniapoto himself—would find it difficult to sustain a long antagonism with the Government if it meant declining opportunities for economic advancement which other tribes seemed to be enjoying.[58] At least it is a policy that a government single-minded about law and order might conceivably have tried, if only to limit the conflict, before resorting to a massive assertion of British power against the whole King movement.

In fact, of course, real though it was, the Government's concern for law and order was imbedded in the wider context of the establishment of a settler colony in land held by the Maori and defended in particular by the King movement. This meant inevitably that other, less worthy, considerations were involved, considerations which made no fine distinctions about the types of men and kinds of principles involved in the King movement. When plans were agreed upon for the confiscation and settlement of the Waikato lands in the wake of Cameron's advance, thus making conquest and colonisation simultaneous, Dillon Bell wrote to Mantell: 'This has never been done before since the time of the Romans, and we may preserve the remnant of the New Zealand race by forcing upon them a civilization which they will not accept as a peaceful offer.'[59] Here was a full statement of imperialism in all its arrogance and exhiliaration. Its implacability and cruelty was evidenced in the comment of the Taranaki leader, A. S. Atkinson: 'I find one lies in wait to shoot Maoris without any approach to an angry feeling—it is a sort of scientific duty.'[60] Its greed was apparent in the early request of the missionary John Morgan that land be found for two of his sons-in-law and three of their brothers on confiscated land in upper Waikato.[61]

The dominant themes in all of this were ethnocentrism and self-interest. The *New Zealander* bluntly stated the general war aim:

> The Maori will not be able to say to the Pakeha 'Thus far shalt thou come and no further'; the Maori and the Pakeha will become the joint occupants of the same territory. But it is impossible that the two races should continue to live in neighbourly amity whose laws and usages in no wise coincide. Both races must be persuaded to give in their allegiance to the same laws; the same usages must pervade them both . . . And since it is also very certain that this state of happiness cannot be obtained by the white race conforming to the usages of the Maori, it is plain that the Maori must be made amenable to the higher civilization of the white man.[62]

Quod erat demonstratum! British bayonets, introduced into New Zealand from 1840 for the purpose of establishing the rule of law, were now employed in making them 'amenable' to their prescribed salvation. It was a ruthlessly adamant logic compared with Maori schemes for the joining of the two systems.

Amidst the barbarism of all this there was, however, one ray of hope for the Maori; racialism as distinct from ethnocentrism was more muted. It was certainly not muted in the more rabid settler press and in the actions of the rabble about Auckland and other North Island towns, where in July 1863 *any* Maori, whether of 'rebel' or 'loyalist' connections, was likely to be subject to abuse and harrassment. But it was opposed by the officials, clergy and more thoughtful settlers, many of whom held the view that the subjugation of Maori separatist organisations like the King movement was necessary to prevent 'race war'. Thus Frederick Maning wrote: 'If the natives were once subject to the law and reduced to the condition of peaceable subjects I would be the first to protect them from any unnecessary or vulgar tyranny'.[63] And Barstow, Resident Magistrate at Russell, angrily took issue with the racialist *Daily Southern Cross* for implying that only financial considerations should prevent the Government making war on the Northland Maori 'at the present'.[64]

It remained to be seen whether the 'humanitarian' and ethnocentric purposes of the war—that is the desire to establish the rule of British law and promote racial 'amalgamation'—would be carried through consistently into the peace settlement, to the extent that the Maori, denied the semi-independent evolution of their own political, administrative and judicial institutions, would be genuinely included in those established by the Pakeha.

Part 2

XI

Early Effects of War

Cameron's advance up the Waikato River was resisted by the King tribes in pitched battles at Koheroa and Rangiriri. In December Tamihana arranged that the occupation of Ngaruawahia, the King's capital, would not be resisted, in the expectation that the Government would then make peace. But the settler Ministers wanted a complete subjugation of the Maori: they wanted from the 'rebels' a cession of land, the surrender of arms and an oath of allegiance. So while they haggled with Grey over the extent of the proposed land confiscation and the terms to be announced, the advance continued. Tamihana then drew the fighting men to Paterangi and sent the women and children to Rangiaowhia. By Maori custom Cameron should have attacked Paterangi;[1] but both the military and the politicians wanted to drive towards Ngatimaniapoto territory and in March 1864 Cameron struck through Rangiaowhia. Rewi Maniapoto then defied the British at the exposed Orakau *pa*. Most Ngatimaniapoto disapproved of his bravado and sought rather to draw Cameron further up the Waipa, where they waited in formidable positions,[2] but Rewi was joined by Kingites from Ngatiraukawa and Ngatituwharetoa and from as far away as the Urewera district, East Cape and Wairoa, Hawke's Bay. They suffered heavy losses when the *pa* fell on 2 April. Meanwhile the Government had made landings at Tauranga. They were repulsed with heavy losses at Gate Pa in April but defeated the Ngaiterangi at Te Ranga in May. The Arawa, meanwhile, joined the Government side against their old enemies in the Waikato and Bay of Plenty.

The rise of the *Pai Marire* cult brought a new bitterness to the war. The movement, initially peaceful, began in late 1862 in South Taranaki, under the leadership of a former Wesleyan catechist, Te Ua, who appeared as a medium of supernatural assistance to redress Maori social and economic deprivation in relation to the intruding settlers. By 1864 under the stress of Government military advances and the threat of land confiscation, it had taken a violent turn and its adherents, from the short barking climax to their chant, become known as Hauhau. Elements of the faith included prophecies that when the head of a slain soldier, Captain Lloyd, had been carried round the island, the Pakeha would be driven out and pro-Government Maori made slaves of the believers; that men would then come from heaven to teach the arts of the

167

Pakeha to the believers; and that meanwhile the English tongue could be learned in ritual circlings of a sacred pole, the *niu*. Te Ua spoke of the Maori as the lost tribes of Israel, signed himself 'a peaceable Jew' and referred to the building of the 'new Canaan'. In August and September 1864 Matutaera and the Kingite leaders met Te Ua in South Taranaki. The Kingites adopted the *Pai Marire* form of worship and exchanged their baptismal names for non-Christian ones. Matutaera henceforth became Tawhiao and sealed his letters with the seal given him by Te Ua.

Although after a defeat at Moutoa in May 1864 Te Ua gave up Lloyd's head to one of John White's police, and lost influence after about January 1865, there were other soldiers' heads and new leaders who were even more militant. During early 1865 the movement swept through Waikato and into the Bay of Plenty, the Urewera and the East Coast from East Cape to Wairarapa, bringing new attacks on settlers and conflict with Government forces.

But the point has been forcefully made that the war was not simply between Maori and Pakeha, but in a very real sense, civil war among Maori.[3] The division between 'rebels' and those who came to be called 'Kupapa' (neutral or pro-Government Maori) followed the lines of traditional enmities to a considerable extent, but the pattern was by no means clear-cut. Some lower Waikato *hapu* fought on the Government side; some Arawa *hapu* joined the Kingites. Moreover, many *hapu* were divided. The young chief Wi Te Wheoro, who had lent his support to Gorst, became an officer in the auxiliary forces the Government recruited; his father, after an impassioned and poignant final debate with him, joined the Kingites at Rangiriri and was killed there.[4] The ramifications of kinship, descent and marriage made their conflicting pulls on individual allegiance. A section of Ngapuhi, led by Mangonui Kerei whose sister married Potatau's brother in 1861, tried to ship gunpowder to the Kingites. Christianity provided no reliable indication of pro-Government sympathy, most of the Kingites themselves remaining fairly orthodox Christians until the clear-cut alignment of the missionaries in support of the Government policies alienated them almost irrevocably from the missionary churches. The *Pai Marire* movement added new complications. When upper Wanganui Hauhaus struck down-river, the lower Wanganui *hapu,* both 'loyal' and Kingite, for whom command of the navigable river was a traditional goal, met and defeated them at Moutoa.

But the *Pai Marire* began to rival the King movement as a focus of Maori resistance to Pakeha dominion. Outside the Waikato former Kingites converted the flagstaffs from which they had flown the King's flag into *niu,* ritual poles flying *Pai Marire* pennants. Some even pronounced themselves ready to take the oath of allegiance to the Queen, relying on their new faith to preserve their essential interests. Indeed the Government was for some time divided on the question of whether allegiance to *Pai Marire* was of itself an offence which legally justified military suppression. Prophets like Te Ua tended, sometimes explicitly, to challenge the authority of hereditary chiefs, often with considerable effect. In Hawke's Bay for instance, many of the kin of the chiefs Tareha and Takamoana joined Te Hapuku, who had welcomed *Pai Marire* emissaries, even though they had been in bitter feud with him in the 1850s. There was a good deal of changing sides, most chiefs in fact being pulled by conflicting emotions and trying pragmatically to gauge which side to support to secure or advance their own position best. Thus the Ngatiporou chiefs Henare Potae, Mokena Kohere and Ropata Te Wahawaha, having fought the Kingites among their own people, decided, with Government encouragement, to attack the 'rebels' at Poverty Bay. By 1868 Wikiwhiri, a Ngatiporou Kingite, had decided to support the Government against the *Pai Marire* on the west coast. Pehi Turoa, in the middle reaches of the Wanganui River, supported the *Pai Marire* in an attack on the coast in 1865, largely because Hori Kingi of lower Wanganui was offering to sell land in which Pehi claimed an interest; but by 1868 Pehi was an auxiliary officer supporting the Government against Te Kooti. Nineteenth century imperialism, in New Zealand as elsewhere, triumphed largely because its subject peoples were divided.

Pakeha society displayed its own provincial loyalties and factions in the bewildering series of ministerial changes resulting from shifting coalitions in the General Assembly. However, while there was often division over the means, there was general agreement that Maori resistance to the spread of coloni-sation must be crushed. In the 1863 Assembly the Domett Ministry introduced, and the Whitaker-Fox Ministry carried, the necessary legislation. The Suppression of Rebellion Act permitted trial by court martial and the suspension of *habeas corpus;* the New Zealand Settlements Act authorised the confiscation of 'rebels' land'; and the New Zealand Loan Act authorised borrowings of £3 million for the recruitment and location of military settlers, and development work, in the conquered districts. A Provincial Compulsory Land Taking Act, which authorised Provincial Councils to take any land for public works, was intended to remove any legal quibbles about the settlers' right to build roads or telegraphs through Maori customary land. It was disallowed by Edward Cardwell (who had replaced Newcastle at the Colonial Office) on the principle of reserving control of Maori affairs to the General Government. The Public Works Land Act of 1864, however, gave the General Government power to take Maori land compulsorily with compensation payable only to 'loyal' Maori. As was often the case the great argument used to justify British imperialism—that it introduced the rule of law—was brought into disrepute by the prostitution of that law to the interests of the colonising race.

The question of Maori prisoners also gave rise to legal confusion and contradiction. The first Maori prisoners taken in Taranaki and the Waikato and shown to be directly involved in the killing of soldiers were sentenced to death for murder, but it was plain that their actions were those of subordinates in war and their sentences were commuted. Thereafter captured Maori were generally treated as prisoners of war and put in prison hulks—from which they repeatedly escaped. Those involved in the killing of civilians, for example the murder of the missionary Carl Volkner and the mixed-race government interpreter, James Fulloon in 1865, were hanged after trial by a civil court (court martial proceedings having been questioned both in New Zealand and London). In the closing and most savage stages of the war the Government offered rewards for the delivery of the principal 'rebel' leaders, dead or alive. This drew a protest from Granville, then Secretary of State. He was silenced by Prendergast, the New Zealand Attorney-General, who claimed that the common law on 'fleeing felons' gave ample authority, and asserted that in any case the English were doing worse things to their Irish subjects.[5] In fact New Zealand governments throughout the war generally did what they found expedient and covered subordinates with annual Acts of Indemnity.

In one important particular, however, the Maori people did derive some benefit from the rule of law. While successive governments were sweeping in their classification of who were 'rebels', they maintained fairly consistently that they were not making war on the whole Maori people, and were prompt to institute proceedings against settlers who shot Maori manifestly not involved in war. When some youths fired on a party of Maori innocently passing near a house where a woman settler had recently been murdered, even the rabid *Daily Southern Cross* urged that they should be punished with 'the utmost rigour of the law'. The difficulty, in this and subsequent cases, was to get a verdict of guilty from prejudiced settler juries.[6] Nevertheless the fact that prosecutions were initiated in these cases was vitally important in preventing an already brutal conflict from sliding further into the racialist abyss, to the utter degradation of both oppressors and oppressed.

In the divisions and shifting allegiances of Maori society the work of the civil officers of the Native Department assumed a new importance and urgency. The Whitaker-Fox Ministry was anxious to secure a firm grasp of Maori affairs, and Fox, as Colonial Secretary and Native Minister, ran the Native Office as a branch of the Colonial Secretary's Department. Edward Shortland became Native Secretary, but this had once more become little more than a clerical post and Shortland resigned after a year. The ubiquitous Henry Halse again became Acting Native Secretary. Isaac Featherston, the Superintendent of Wellington Province, was accredited as General Government Agent in place of Mantell to give more rigorous direction to Native Department officers in that district. Gorst, who had left for Sydney with Bell to recruit military settlers. went off to England apparently dejected when the Ministry declined Bell's request to give him a place in the Legislative Council.[7] Armitage was restored to office in lower Waikato only to be killed by a Ngatimaniapoto war party within a few weeks. George Law was then withdrawn from Taupo on account of his exposed position. But in the wake of the advancing troops, R. O. Stewart became Resident Magistrate in lower Waikato; R. C. Mainwaring (who had come out on the same ship as Gorst and been his assistant at the Otawhao school) was appointed in upper Waikato, and W. G. Mair at Taupo. Exempted from militia service, the Native Department officers were ordered to be active in their districts until driven out by hostilities. They were to present the Government's case on the need for war, to refute the teaching of Kingite or *Pai Marire* emissaries, make gifts and offer pay, plunder and promises of support in traditional rivalries in an effort to prevent *hapu* from joining the 'rebellion' and, if possible, to attach them to the Government side. They were to inform the Maori of government victories, explain proclamations, take submissions or oaths of allegiance and send back detailed information on the fluctuating attitudes of the chiefs and the movements of war parties. The refutation of rumour was a particularly important duty. Extravagant rumour was rife in Polynesian societies since the claim to special knowledge was a traditional mode of bidding for influence.[8] In the early months of war officials had frequently to refute the most extravagant stories of Maori victories over the British troops; later they countered among neutral *hapu* alarming tales of the sweeping subjugation the Pakeha intended for the Maori. Unfortunately, there was too much substance in the latter rumours for the officials to be entirely convincing, but it was notable, if pathetic, how Maori leaders anxious to escape involvement snatched at assurances of peace and non-molestation.

It was not possible to say that this work was the most important influence that decided a chief or *hapu* for peace or war—a Government victory or defeat, the presence of a large 'rebel' force or European population, the confiscation of land or the effect of traditional rivalry were more fundamental factors—but it did determine whether the Government could make the most of its advantages. Wavering chiefs like Pehi Turoa were considerably influenced by the attention of officials and the information they brought. Chiefs who felt themselves neglected soon developed anti-Government inclinations; left alone there can be little doubt that 'rebel' emissaries, who were also very active, would have over-persuaded many of them. Moreover, chiefs who had joined the 'rebels' and suffered loss could be persuaded, in a mood of disillusion, to make peace. Pehi Turoa again provided an example.

On the other hand, a tactless or ineffectual Resident Magistrate in a critical district was a disaster and, as the events of 1868 were to prove, could allow whole districts to go into rebellion. Noting the appointment of Major Edwards to Otaki, in 1865, Sewell congratulated himself that the Government had found a man of judgment adding 'the presence of a good man in a district is the best safeguard. The difficulty is to find them.'[9]

The civil officers worked closely with the military. They were involved in organising the people of their districts into commissariat corps to carry food and supplies, in inducting some Maori into the militia, and, later, in organising Maori contingents. The Resident Magistrates' clerks, designated 'Interpreters to the forces', became important intermediaries in this work.

While the advice of the civil officers based on the stream of information they gathered from their Maori contacts was invaluable to the military, relations between civil and military authorities throughout the war were awkward, ill-defined and at times exceedingly bitter. With much justification the civil officers prided themselves on knowing better than anyone else the true sentiments of Maori communities in their districts, and the weight of their official interest was generally in organising a stable polity, not in widening the conflict. Some, moreover, had come to have a genuine personal respect for the Maori. Usually, therefore, they reacted strongly to rabid anti-Maori outcries in the press and blanket charges of Hauhauism against all the Maori in their district. They did a service to the Maori by ascertaining precisely which *hapu* were indeed strongly in rebellion and which were only reluctantly so or in fact pro-Government. Thus T. H. Smith intervened for the people west of Tauranga in 1864 when they were generally condemned as rebels; fortunately Grey listened to him and supported him against the Ministers who had wanted to attack the district. James Mackay, Smith's successor in the Bay of Plenty (despite a temporary arrest by Colonel Greer, the stiff-necked military commander of the area, for his alleged 'interference'), gave Grey detailed information about Tamihana's inclination to make peace and refuted the charge that the Kingmaker had become an out-and-out Hauhau. This information contributed largely to the averting of a campaign, much desired by the settlers, against the Matamata area and the upper Thames.

Robert Parris's hidebound official mind had been shaken by Maori chivalry in 1862, when his horse fell on him and the north Taranaki Maori, victims of Parris's irresponsible proceedings in the Waitara negotiations of 1859-60, carried him 25 miles into New Plymouth on a stretcher.[10] He was much affected by the incident, and although he never attained the view that the Maori people were justified in resisting the progress of settlement and the over-riding authority of government, fought a running feud with successive Ministers and military commanders to try to prevent the worst despoliation of the Taranaki tribes.

After the occupation of the Waikato the Resident Magistrates were instructed

> to superintend the interests of friendly Natives, as well as those who have surrendered, to settle any disputes which may arise between them and the soldiers; and to see that no injury be done Natives without redress being obtained. You will also investigate any complaints of Native property being plundered, or their persons molested.[11]

They were also to take a census of the *hapu* in their districts, and try to revive agriculture and improve the health and sanitation of their people. Army commanders were instructed early in the war to hand looted horses and cattle to the Resident Magistrates to dispose of 'according to law', with 10 per cent payment to their captors. Theoretically the commissariat was supposed to buy them if it wanted them, while Maori whose stock was looted were to lay an information with a Resident Magistrate and have offending soldiers summonsed.[12] In practice Resident Magistrates found great difficulty in according the Maori the protection implied in their instructions, and the Government which issued them was not particularly wholehearted about the matter. The looting of Maori property (by British soldiers, settler militia and Maori auxiliaries alike) generally followed each Government victory.

If settler militia did the plundering the Maori were not encouraged to expect redress since, the Native Office argued, settlers had lost horses and other property at Maori hands. Moreover, 'rebel' Maori were officially said to be to all intents outlaws and if they applied to the courts for the return of cattle or other redress 'it is not likely they would meet with any'.[13] Although the Resident Magistrates did institute some prosecutions, with occasional success, looting continued to be wide-spread throughout the war.

Nevertheless the coming, in the wake of the soldiers, of a civil authority instructed to restore normal relations as soon as possible did prevent continued depredations once the lawlessness and depravity of a battle situation had passed. While extreme settler opinion favoured a result similar to that which occurred in Australia and North America, where native populations were eliminated entirely from whole districts, governments acceded to this policy on only one occasion in New Zealand—namely with regard to parts of south Taranaki in 1868-9. The war was nominally fought to extend the rule of law and civil authority did establish itself remarkably quickly. The Resident Magistrates moving into the Waikato began immediately to appoint Maori Assessors and police and began to hear cases on the frontier posts that were established. They found it much more difficult to control military settlers—often a raffish and drunken lot—than the remaining Maori. The British regiments, however, were subject to a harsh discipline and their commanders more inclined to co-operate with the civil officers after a campaign than they were before one.

Reconstruction consisted largely of settling returned 'rebels' on small reserves of land—their old cultivations or the land of 'loyal' or Kupapa kinsmen. Returned 'rebels', and some Kupapa *hapu* as well, were frequently quite destitute, for war completely dislocated agriculture. Crops, stock and trading schooners had been sold to pay for arms, and destroyed in battle or looted; planting seasons had been lost while tribes were fighting; agricultural implements and mills had fallen into disrepair. Only the minimum of subsistence cropping was practised, and a flood, a drought or a blight could, and did, result in starvation. Once again the Fox-Whitaker Government was at first very cold about the need for aiding surrendered 'rebels', believing apparently that once a Maori had been placed on a patch of ground only indolence prevented him from fending for himself. At first they did not even supply seed potatoes, but the pressure of magistrates, army doctors and friendly chiefs persuaded them to supply, first the women and children of 'rebels' and then the 'rebels' themselves. Food and seed potatoes were given in increasing quantities, sometimes coupled with demands that the recipients work on roads and bridges in return, lest they become dependent and pauperised. The need for Government food supplies generally lastd for about twelve months in each newly subjugated district before the Maori cultivations began to revive. Disturbance and demoralisation persisted for longer near the permanent military posts, largely because the Kupapa in the transport corps received both the army rum ration and regular pay which they spent on liquor much as the soldiers did.

Another form of assistance administered through the Resident Magistrates was the granting of pensions to Maori auxiliaries wounded while fighting on the Government side, and to the widows of those killed. This began apparently at Grey's suggestion and was readily acceded to by the Government after the spontaneous display of gratitude and respect—unique in its way—shown by settlers and officials of Wanganui for the brilliant and heroic defence of the district by lower Wanganui *hapu* at the battle of Moutoa.

Meanwhile, in the districts not subject to military campaigns, the machinery of government continued to function. Resident Magistrates and Assessors still travelled their circuits; their *Karere* continued to serve summonses, help make arrests and keep order in court. The records of the Taupo court show that for three years after George Law had left his station the Assessors under Hohepa Tamamutu continued to hear cases (usually about *puremu* or horse stealing), and recorded their proceedings in the books.[14] In districts such as Northland the immediate effect of Cameron's victories was to quell some initial stirrings in favour of the Waikato tribes. Some Waima chiefs frankly stated that, despite traditional rivalry with Waikato, they felt as Maori, and could not think warmly of the Government.[15] A senior missionary claimed that in the first months of the war, when the Kingites had some small victories, they had to use all their influence to keep their congregations calm, and that had the Government been defeated at Rangiriri some of the Ngapuhi 'would have become troublesome'.[16] In 1864 W. B. White took a party of Rarawa and Aupouri chiefs to the Waikato to convince them of the reality of Government victories; they witnessed the battle of Orakau and returned duly impressed with the power of the Pakeha. The Government consolidated its advantage by increasing the pensions of Ngapuhi chiefs like Waka Nene, and offering employment to considerable numbers of Maori on road contracts. In the Manawatu, Buller reported a considerable increase in the number of cases brought to his courts and the request of former Kingite *hapu* for appointments of Queen's Assessors from their ranks.[17] In November 1863, the Civil Commissioner in Hawke's Bay noted that, 'The submission to law shown during the past week is new to the Province'. In one criminal case a single policeman arrested a Maori from amidst a large concourse of his friends and conveyed him to gaol without an attempt at rescue.[18]

Yet *Pai Marire* soon swept sections of Hawke's Bay and Manawatu into defiance again, and even in Northland magistrates were by no means assured of regular submission, the Maori continuing to show much of their pre-war selectivity about when to surrender men to Pakeha justice. In December 1863, however, following the murder of a European woman and child by Ruarangi, a man of some rank at Kaipara, the Government, asserting that they 'didn't intend to put up with this sort of thing any longer', sent 100 armed men to make the arrest.[19] They were not needed. Paul Tuhaere, a principal chief of the Ngatiwhatua at Kaipara as well as Auckland, persuaded Te Otene, the chief of Ruarangi's *hapu,* to surrender him to a single policeman. He was tried and executed, and though there was some excitement when his body was returned to the *hapu* in 1866, Te Otene angrily refuted a newspaper suggestion that revenge would be taken for his death.[20]

There was more difficulty about the surrender of a mentally ill man named Nicotema Okeroa after he had killed a chief who had ordered him from his village. The chief's relatives caught Okeroa, beat him and would have killed him, but some informed the Resident Magistrate, William Barstow, who with only one Pakeha and six Maori police to help him had great difficulty in getting Okeroa away. Barstow urged his superiors to show no leniency to Okeroa or the Ngapuhi would never surrender another man in similar circumstances again. Indeed, although too demented to plead, Okeroa was sentenced to death and executed after a travesty of a trial.[21]

A few months later at Waimate a well-connected young man named Tarawau gathered a *taua* to shoot a man from a neighbouring *hapu* who had committed adultery, not with Tarawau's wife, but with his chief's wife. Although he had been mate on a ship and lived in England with an English wife, Tarawau stated plainly that now he had returned to live among his Maori kin, Maori laws would prevail. Tarawau succeeded in wounding one of the adulterer's kin, and though his people conceded that he might pay the court some small penalty for his impetuousness, they would not surrender him to serve a prison sentence for wounding. Waka Nene and the principal chiefs being firm on this, the Government did not press the matter.[22] Nor did it press even the case of Hohepa Whare who had assaulted Emily Stephenson in 1863. Hohepa's kin had offered to pay Mrs Stephenson £50 and banish him from the district to satisfy the law, but the banishment was not carried out and Mrs Stephenson refused the money. When the case was discussed in the Resident Magistrate's court Hohepa broke away from the gathering, took a gun, and hunted for the Stephensons' boy Albert until restrained by his people. The differing Maori responses in these four cases reveal conceptions of justice which, except perhaps in Ruarangi's case, did not accord very closely with Pakeha conceptions. There was usually some willingness to accommodate the demands of Pakeha law but it was still expected that the Pakeha should acknowledge Maori standpoints also. In general there was a marked falling off in the number of cases brought to the Northland Resident Magistrates in this period.

The official Runangas of Waimate and Mangonui however, continued to meet, and a new magistrate in the Chatham Islands, W. E. Thomas, actually inaugurated a new Runanga among the six small *hapu* there.[23] The Mangonui Runanga, in its third session, shared some of W. B. White's concern at an increase in robbery, usually associated with drunkenness. White felt that the system of paying four times the value of goods stolen was having a bad effect;

it enabled a thief to go scot-free while his kin bore the cost. He urged that thieves should be imprisoned, as the chiefs already permitted for more serious offences. The proposition was earnestly debated. One chief, Ruinga of Whangaroa, was still in favour of surrendering kinsmen only for murder, but Karaka voiced the general opinion that henceforth thieves should be imprisoned. Speakers stated that from the great love they bore their kin they found difficulty 'in keeping to what we approve of'. But they too now felt that the traditional principal of *utu* (which the fines for theft principle embodied) involved the innocent suffering for the guilty, and that traditional notions of rank had led to men of no standing being killed for theft, while chiefs were able to steal from low-ranking men with impunity.[24] Although it was clear that traditional values would persist, the English judicial concepts of individual responsibility for an offence, and equality before the law, were continuing to gain ground.

The Mangonui Runanga also spent some time discussing White's proposals for village day schools. Maori parents had objected to their children being taken away from their own homes to work in the gardens of church boarding schools. But money for development works was not forthcoming from Government at this time and White's request for funds, like those from Wairarapa for a hospital and from Waiuku, Rotorua and the Chatham Islands for more 'medical comforts' for the Maori of those districts, was declined. The first year of full-scale war, under the hard-line Government of Whitaker and Fox brought mainly destruction and austerity for the Maori; but general policy on reconstruction, together with the genuine interest and zeal of individual civil officers in the out-districts, offered them some hope and relief.

Paora Tuhaere's house, Orakei, Auckland, about 1885. Reproduced by permission of the Dominion Museum, Wellington, New Zealand.

Sir Donald McLean. Reproduced by permission of the Alexander Turnbull Library, Wellington, New Zealand

Francis Dart Fenton, photograph from the Schmidt Collection, Alexander Turnbull Library, Wellington, New Zealand. Reproduced by permission

XII

Moderates in Office

The Weld Ministry replaced that of Whitaker and Fox in November 1864, on a policy of 'self-reliance' which meant, in essence, that in return for full responsibility in Maori affairs the Colonial Government would accede to the withdrawal of the British regiments at an early date. Confiscations of Maori land were quickly agreed upon by Grey and Ministers, including Sewell, returned to office as Attorney-General, and Mantell, the Native Minister, both previously strong opponents of the Settlements Act of 1863 and the confiscations planned by the Fox-Whitaker Ministry. The amount taken in the Waikato, about 1.2 million acres, was certainly far less than the more extravagant confiscations planned by the previous Ministries, but probably not less than Fox and Whitaker would have settled for at the end of their feuding with Grey on the subject. The Ministry and General Cameron agreed that it was inexpedient, for military and financial reasons, to advance further into the rugged hill country of the Ngatimaniapoto, who consequently escaped the brunt of the war they had done much to precipitate and the subsequent confiscation. Sewell and Mantell agreed to the confiscation of the fertile lower Waikato plain and down-land—including about one-third of the Ngatihaua people's land—in the expectation that liberal portions of it would be returned under Crown title to Kupapa and surrendered 'rebels' and that the Waikato district would then quieten.

Confiscation in Taranaki was first intended to include a 10-mile wide coastal strip from Wanganui to White Cliffs in north Taranaki, in order to open communications between these places and give the confined settlers some room to expand. Sewell and Mantell seemed to agree readily with this too, and the Taranaki members of the Government were pleased and surprised at their co-operation. However, partly owing to the larger ambitions of the settlers, partly to Cameron's insistence on moving his whole army to Taranaki, ponderously and expensively, and partly to Grey's desire to keep as many Imperial troops in the field as possible in order to retain his maximum prerogatives as Governor in the now self-governing Colony, the Taranaki operation became not a minor expedition in support of road parties but a massive campaign which threw the Maori and the peacemakers into greater despair than ever, drove more *hapu* into active rebellion and made nonsense of Weld's plan to

177

send the Imperial troops home.[1] Confiscation, with Grey's ready acquiescence, widened to include another 1.2 million acres from White Cliffs to Wanganui, extending inland up to 30 miles from the coast, and embracing all the best coastal land including the disputed Waitara and Waitotara purchases.[2]

As part of his self-reliant policy Weld entrusted greater responsibilities to local civil officers. The foremost of these was Donald McLean. In the absence on leave of Whitmore, Civil Commissioner for Hawke's Bay, Weld commissioned McLean as General Government Agent with wide powers to control the *Pai Marire* movement on the East Coast. He was told to by-pass the standing military authorities if necessary and raise and direct the militia and the Kupapa auxiliaries himself. Weld wrote: 'If you can find a dashing clever young fellow Native or European, make much use of him these are not times for routine. If your commanding military officer is likely to be any obstruction call your cavalry corps "mounted police" & don't let him have anything to do with them.'[3] He was authorised to offer pay, plunder, pensions and shares in confiscated land to Maori allies he could enlist on the Government side and to remove *Pai Marire* agents 'or actively disloyal persons' without benefit of trial. The abuse of this power in the case of Te Kooti Rikirangi was to prove disastrous.

McLean soon demonstrated what J. D. Ormond called 'his peculiar ability'. In his absence on a visit to Wellington the Hawke's Bay chiefs began to be swayed by *Pai Marire* emissaries, but, returning, McLean 'worked them all round again' by his familiar mixture of blandishments, promises and thinly disguised threats.[4] From the Poverty Bay tribes, who under Wardell's old Assessor Raharuhi Rukupo, had defiantly flaunted their adherence to *Pai Marire* and fortified a *pa* at Waerenga-a-Hika, McLean demanded a total submission. Though anxious for terms, Rukupo could not meet McLean's demands with dignity, and when his submission was not promptly forthcoming McLean unleashed upon Waerenga-a-Hika both the Pakeha forces in the district and their Ngatiporou allies who had been convinced by McLean's promises that there was much to be gained by supporting the Government.[5] McLean's leadership was ruthless and devastating to the Poverty Bay tribes, but it won him much admiration among the colonists, and the East Coast campaign of 1865 became a by-word for efficiency and economy in comparison with the lengthy and expensive proceedings of the Imperial troops on the West Coast.

In the Bay of Plenty, H. T. Clarke, who had replaced T. H. Smith as Civil Commissioner, was given powers similar to McLean's. Another intelligent and energetic officer, he both raised, and at times directed in combat, Arawa auxiliaries and Pakeha militia.

The direction of military operations by able civil agents, with the regular military officers clearly subordinate to them, usually worked well. Alternatively, military men were appointed Resident Magistrates, Major Edwards in Otaki and Major Noake in upper Wanganui both replacing civilians; later Major

Biggs became Resident Magistrate in Poverty Bay. In Taranaki, however, largely because of the continued presence of large numbers of Imperial troops, civil officers never gained the preponderance of authority over the military that McLean and Clarke enjoyed. Parris's feud with military commanders intensified but Parris gained no advantage in the struggle.

In general, however, the civil machinery of the Native Department was strongly supported by the Weld Government. Mantell did not share the popular hostility to the office of Civil Commissioner. He appointed Hunter Brown, Wairoa Resident Magistrate, as Civil Commissioner in Canterbury, Otago and Southland to report on boundary questions and promises to the Ngaitahu people of education and medical care left unfulfilled after the great South Island land purchases. John Rogan became Civil Commissioner of Kaipara, a populous district left without a resident judicial officer since Fenton had been Resident Magistrate there in the early 1850s. The transfer of the seat of government from Auckland to Wellington in 1865 necessitated the appointment of an able officer in the former district and James Mackay was appointed Civil Commissioner there. With the successive Resident Ministers representing the Government at Auckland, he directed the Native Department officers in the Auckland Province.

A further important appointment by Weld and Mantell was that of William Rolleston as Under-Secretary of the Native Department (the term 'Native Secretary' now being dropped). A Cambridge graduate, formerly Provincial Secretary in Canterbury, Rolleston served from June 1865 to May 1868 when he resigned to become Superintendent of Canterbury. Rolleston exercised more influence on policy than any subsequent Under-Secretary and had much to do with the shaping of legislation affecting Maori schools, land, and parliamentary representation.

Even the Runanga system enjoyed a brief Indian summer. W. B. White, through his Runanga and circuit courts, was virtually administering the far north as a semi-independent Native District. W. Thomas's Runanga in the Chatham Islands met for a second time and passed regulations providing for the branding of cattle and registration of dogs. These regulations, vitally important in a pastoral society, were to be policed by the Maori Assessors, who could authorise the shooting of stray dogs or cattle. The regulations were gazetted and remained in force for some years.

Mantell was prepared to spend quite liberally on the machinery of the Native Department, framing estimates of £40,400, some £9000 higher than the estimates of the previous year. The Government also showed a certain liberality and respect for the principle of racial equality with regard to Maori losses in the war. When the commissioner appointed to investigate settlers' claims for war damage asked if the claims of 'friendly' Maori should be entertained, Weld and Mantell minuted that 'of course' they were.[6]

But a far more important development at this time was the start of work by the Native Land Court. Some preliminary moves had been made by the Whitaker-Fox Ministry. After the 1862 Native Lands Act had been approved in London, the aging George Clarke, Civil Commissioner of Waimate, was asked to suggest regulations for the Court and to name chiefs who could form a panel of Assessors under Clarke's chairmanship, as envisaged by the Act.[7] But already, in June 1864, John Rogan, then Land Purchase Officer at Kaipara, had invoked the Native Land Act and assembled the Assessors of the district to determine the title of some land for which Maori claimants had already accepted payment from a settler. The newspaper report commented that 'the Native Judges appeared well suited for the important task they had to perform. They well know that all responsibility will fall on themselves should they award certificates to any but the rightful owners—hence the examinations are extremely minute, and well and ably conducted.'[8] It was this sort of court, the key role being played by the Maori leaders of the district wherein the land was situated, that the Weld government sought to constitute in December 1864 when it proclaimed the Act to be in operation and appointed as Judges in their specific districts George Clarke, W. B. White and J. Rogan, and as Land Court Assessors, a number of chiefs.[9]

However, in January 1865, Weld and Mantell selected as Chief Judge the man who was eventually to have a fateful influence on the whole future of Maori land legislation—F. D. Fenton. Fenton was to head both the Native Land Court, and the Compensation Courts set up under the New Zealand Settlements Act to apportion confiscated land. His work was not expected to be arduous; it was actually envisaged that he would be able to continue his private legal practice. He later told Mantell that he expected to lose financially and only accepted the position because he 'wanted to show that the land of New Zealand could be judicially dealt with'.[10] He was given virtually a free hand in reorganising the Court and making appointments, and promptly used it. The 1862 Act, in accordance with principles first suggested by Fenton himself in 1858-60, and already put into practice by Rogan, envisaged the chiefs of a district meeting with the local Resident Magistrate and threshing out agreement on boundaries in that district only. Now that he was Chief Judge, Fenton abandoned this idea and set about creating a tribunal along the lines of the Supreme Court, whereby a roving Judge could sit in any centre, summon witnesses, hear evidence and hand down a judgment with due pomp and formality. On 11 January 1865 all existing districts proclaimed under the 1862 Act were cancelled and the Colony was made one district subject to the jurisdiction of one Court. Fenton's view that Land Court Judges should not also hold 'political or diplomatic' functions as Resident Magistrates and Civil Commissioners was accepted.[11] Accordingly White and Clarke lost their Judgeships while John Rogan and T. H. Smith (who was appointed Judge in December 1865) gave up the office of Civil Commissioner. James Mackay was also made a Land Court Judge but he disagreed with

Fenton about the manner of apportioning interests among recipients of Court awards and, placing most value on his work as Civil Commissioner, shortly resigned his Judgeship. Finally Frederick Maning of Hokianga, a popular figure in the North, became a Judge allegedly at the insistence of the Northland politician, Hugh Carleton, to keep his popular rival from entering politics.[12] The transformation of the Native Land Court and the elevation of the status of the Judges stemmed partly from Fenton's own ambition and vanity. It also stemmed from the belief, now advanced most strongly by Fenton but also widely held among the settler community, that only a solemn legal tribunal would be respected by contending Maori claimants. There was some apparent justification for this view. The demarcation of the territorial claims of two or more *iwi* or *hapu* was rarely clear-cut, there frequently being an area of territory between them which was disputed ground (*kainga tautohe*), often left vacant after years of intermittent warfare. There were also small sections of cultivable land, hunting and fishing spots and fruit trees within the general territory of one *hapu,* over which members of another had been accorded rights. It was argued by those who sought to elevate the status of the Land Court that given this confusion of intersecting claims contending Maori parties could never agree on boundaries, especially if interested chiefs formed the tribunal, and that the only way to gain a quick determination of the issue was for a Pakeha Judge to hand down an authoritative decision, which the defeated parties would be obliged to accept by the peacekeeping forces of the Colony.

There was certainly some justification for an authoritative tribunal, backed by police power, because any disentanglement of claims for the marking of distinct boundary lines involved some arbitrariness, but Fenton's view took too little account of the fact that it was not impossible for contending Maori parties to come to an agreement on boundaries without compulsion. The process was not simple. It involved some give and take with regard to long-disputed areas. It involved parties meeting with the idea of compromise, not winner take all, much to the fore. It may have required the presence of a neutral chairman to lift the question from the plane of traditional politics; purely Maori committees which later adjudicated upon land boundaries were sometimes obstructed by contending claimants on the ground that they included interested and self-seeking parties.[13] An official's presence would also have set the seal of legal ratification on the agreement that was reached. He and the panel of local Maori leaders who comprised the 'court', would thus have acted as arbitrators of a public discussion, making sure that traditional rights were respected, and deterring and exposing—by their authority and knowledge of the district concerned—false claims and false evidence. As T. W. Lewis, Under-Secretary of the Native Department in 1891, observed, 'the truth would be more likely to prevail' before an open Runanga of chiefs than before Pakeha Judges for whose benefit contending claimants made the fabrication of evidence a fine art.[14]

There were several indications that a tribunal of this kind could have worked well. Apart from the apparently orderly determination of boundaries under Rogan at Kaipara in 1864, there were several reports from the Hokianga District about this time of large meetings being held, under the stimulus of the new method of direct sale to settlers, by chiefs wanting to determine their boundaries. In relation to the specific areas of land for which the meeting was called, these assemblies reached a decision in quiet and orderly proceedings; only when new areas were brought into the discussion without notice did they become acrimonious.[15] Throughout the 1870s and 1880s moreover, Maori leaders, anxious to forestall the sort of adjudication likely to be given by the Land Court, increasingly met in conference with the leaders of the neighbouring tribes and *hapu,* and frequently came to clear agreement upon boundaries which they wanted only to be formally ratified by the external authority. In the King Country adjudication in the mid-1880s, when the Native Land Court did little more than register the boundaries agreed upon between contending *hapu,* the award was highly successful and gave rise to little friction. In the case of the Tauwhareparae block, when the Court was deadlocked over the claims of seven contending groups, the case was referred to a Maori committee which held an orderly investigation, produced 100 pages of evidence and a decision which a reviewing Court could not fault.[16]

That an arbitrating commission rather than a court could work was also proved in practice by the commissioners who heard the claims of Bay of Plenty tribes to confiscated lands near Tauranga, and by other commissioners who negotiated for the sale of mining rights. In 1867 for instance, James Mackay treated for the cession of mining rights in which four tribes had intermingled claims and at least fifty proposed boundary lines were disputed. After an eighteen-month long process of open discussion and negotiation with all the principal men on the disputed ground itself, Mackay had agreement on all points. The decisions on claims to mining rights did not in fact give rise to the serious dissatisfaction among the Maori people that the Native Land Court decisions did, and during many years of subsequent public debate Mackay rightly advanced this as evidence in favour of remodelling the Native Land Court along the lines of the Wardens' courts of the goldfields.[17]

But the securing of agreement in this way had to be unhurried, not made under pressure, and would-be purchasers of Maori land were in no mood to delay. The pontifical decisions of Fenton and his brother Judges were expected to follow quickly from a hearing of evidence and alienation of land could ensue. Settler politicians were no doubt actuated by this consideration in supporting Fenton's view of the Court. After all, as Lewis was eventually to admit, 'the whole object . . . was to enable alienation for settlement. Unless this object is attained the Court serves no good purpose, and the Natives would be better without it, as, in my opinion, fairer native occupation would be had under the Maoris' own customs and usages without any intervention whatever from outside.'[18]

As the 1865 session of Parliament approached, the Weld Government shaped its legislative program. Besides a new Native Lands Bill, the Government also proposed to introduce legislation for Maori representation in parliament. This, said J. C. Richmond, was a corollary to the Native Lands Act. 'The two were essentially the abandonment of the system of protectorate, or dry-nursing . . . They were throwing the Maori on the world to take his lot with other subjects, and they must remove all disabilities.'[19] Richmond's statement was indicative of the strongest currents in Maori policy for the remainder of the century; a reaction alike against the control of Maori affairs by the Governor, against the provision of special machinery for Maori affairs in the form of an elaborate Native Department, and against such centres of residual Maori authority as the Runanga.

Before the 1865 session was fairly under way, Mantell, who had recently shown some willingness to make special provision for Maori needs, had ceased to be Native Minister. For some time the Otago Provincial Council had been urging the General Government to transfer to it a valuable 3-acre reserve in Princes Street, Dunedin. This reserve, on the waterfront adjacent to the city centre, had been made by Mantell himself in 1853 as a canoe-landing and central market for the local Maori, but it had been over-run by miners camping on it before proceeding to the Otago goldfields in the rush of 1861. General Governments had resisted the Otago politicians' pressure until July 1865, but when the Assembly met Mantell announced his resignation, 'on account of the sudden conversion of a colleague to a different opinion from what he held with me a short time previously on the question of the Princes Street Reserve'.[20] Mantell spent the next decade in the Legislative Council fighting for the rights of the South Island Maori.

After a fortnight's interregnum in which J. C. Richmond, the Colonial Secretary, acted also as Native Minister and assisted in shaping Maori policies for the parliamentary session, Mantell was succeeded on 12 August by a man who was widely believed to be even more 'philo-Maori' than his predecessor— J. E. FitzGerald of Canterbury. FitzGerald, who had lately been declaring the invasion of the Waikato to have been unnecessary, intended and expected that peace should shortly be concluded with the 'rebels', except for a number of *Pai Marire* involved in the murder of civilians. He had already written to Tamihana, who in May 1865 had laid down his arms in the belief that further conflict was futile and the hope that an investigation into the origins of the war might win the Waikato Maori some redress. FitzGerald was also well remembered among the settlers for his 1862 resolutions advocating political and legal equality for Maori and Pakeha. The announcement of his taking office was greeted in the House with a painful silence. J. D. Ormond wrote: 'there is a general feeling of consternation at this news. To my mind nothing so dangerous to the interests of the Northern Island could possibly have happened.' A few days later, angered by FitzGerald's statement 'that Thompson and those brave men who have fought for their liberties are those he wants to meet and talk with', Ormond attacked both the Native Minister's negotiations with Tamihana and the Government's proposals for Maori representation.[21]

Yet when FitzGerald announced his policy, Ormond concluded, with relief, that 'FitzGerald is a different man as Minister'.[22] FitzGerald's policy included the measures on Maori land and Maori representation already planned and a Native Rights Bill. It also included an Outlying Districts Police Bill to punish by confiscation of land those tribes which sheltered men guilty of crimes such as the recent murder of Volkner. Moreover FitzGerald soon proceeded to sully his more high-minded postulations of Maori rights with a weak-kneed adaptation of them to policy.

The Native Rights Act stated firstly that the Maori were deemed to be natural-born subjects of the Crown, thus re-enacting in statute law the provision in the Treaty of Waitangi that the Maori were to have the rights and privileges of British subjects. This pleased liberal groups in the Assembly, especially as it removed one possible objection to enfranchising the Maori. But it also pleased those who wished to see the Maori in arms treated more stringently, since it implied that they should definitely be regarded as rebels, not as foreign belligerents. FitzGerald's main intention was, however, to remove the long-standing prohibition of Maori claimants from taking questions affecting customarily held land before the Supreme Court. He had argued since 1862 that it was futile to demand that the Maori people come under English law and at the same time to debar them from the use of the Supreme Court in questions affecting the bulk of their lands.

However, FitzGerald was compelled by Richmond, Sewell and others to admit that decisions on ownership according to Maori custom should be made by a more specialised body. The Native Rights Act, therefore, while establishing the right of Maori claimants to bring actions affecting their persons and property in the Supreme Court, provided that cases should be referred to the Native Land Court when a decision was required on who were the owners of disputed customary lands. FitzGerald at that time still intended that the Land Court should only be a Commission of Inquiry, an auxiliary of the Supreme Court, rather than a full court.[23] But Fenton's influence and the obvious inconvenience of referring customary lands to the Supreme Court only to have them immediately referred to the Land Court, meant that adjudication on title to customary lands almost always originated in the latter. The Supreme Court consistently declined to go behind or alter the decision of the Native Land Court and could be resorted to effectively only in connection with disputed dealings between Maori and Pakeha after a Land Court decision. Access to the Supreme Court in fact proved a privilege of dubious value to the Maori, who, though they were able at times to win favourable verdicts against settlers, were subject to ruinous costs.[24] Moreover, it was subsequently ruled in the Supreme Court that the Native Rights Act had not improved the legal standing of Maori customary tenure. It was held to be 'merely a declaratory Act' setting out more clearly the Maori people's existing rights, not creating a right where none had existed before. Insofar as it required the Supreme Court to refer all disputes concerning customary title to the Native Land Court, the Native Rights Act, it was stated, 'excludes the idea that tenure of lands according to Native custom is to be equivalent to, or have the incidents of tenure of land according to English law'.[25]

The Native Lands Act, 1865, like that of 1862, was shaped largely by the pressure of speculator interests in the Assembly. Before the session, at the request of Sewell and Mantell, Sir William Martin had given his ideas on the subject, but in the end little account was taken of them. Martin wanted a court along the lines of the 1862 Act—essentially a panel of local chiefs. But Fenton's formal Court comprising Pakeha Judges was already established and was ratified by the new Act, although provision was added for the empanelling of a Maori jury at the Judge's discretion. Martin wanted the land, once awarded, to be sold only under public auction and some of the payment compulsorily invested.[26] FitzGerald however, did not adopt this provision or the proposal of Fenton, who, to his credit, had proposed making private dealings with Maori land prior to the Court's award, not merely void, but illegal.[27] On the contrary, FitzGerald stated that the Bill was to repeal the Native Land Purchase Ordinance and let speculators risk their money in prior dealings if they wished. To the objection of Mantell (who had supported Fenton's proposal to make prior dealings illegal) FitzGerald frankly stated that the Bill was a compromise and in bringing it forward 'he had to give up some of the views he had held'.[28] In other words he was surrendering to speculator pressures. A move by John Hall and others in the Legislative Council to include Martin's proposal for sale by public auction only, was defeated, J. C. Richmond, the Colonial Secretary, voting with the majority.[29]

With the inauguration of the new system the Land Purchase Department was disbanded and the Crown began no new negotiations for land. The setting up of the Land Court was accompanied, however, by a spate of dealing between Maori and settlers who sought to secure their claims ready for the Court's first sittings. Whitmore, who had the ear of the Government, warned McLean to 'Close all bargains with Natives so as to be as little hurt by [the] new Native Land Act and when it is proclaimed get hold of all you can'.[30] Even before the 1865 Act had been finally passed Rolleston, the observant Under-Secretary, noted that agents were advertising themselves to negotiate for Maori land, including reserves, and urged that the Act be amended to prohibit speculation. FitzGerald wrote: 'I think it best not to interfere.'[31] Fenton urged the Stafford Government, which took office later in the session, to re-enact the Native Land Purchase Ordinance, but was told that it was too late.[32]

The Maori people were consequently exposed to a thirty-year period during which a predatory horde of storekeepers, grog-sellers, surveyors, lawyers, land agents and money-lenders made advances to rival groups of Maori claimants to land, pressed the claim of their faction in the Courts and recouped the costs in land. Rightful Maori owners could not avoid litigation and expensive surveys if false claims were put forward, since Fenton, seeking to inflate the status of the Court, insisted that judgments be based only upon evidence presented before it.

The introduction of the new form of Native Land Court was also to have grievous effects on Maori society. It set up a body of self-proclaimed experts who had to try, and frequently failed, to interpret Maori custom. One of the Judges subsequently admitted that the Court was not uniform in its practice —that each Judge 'sails along serenely', either trusting to his Assessor for guidance or interpreting Maori custom according to his own ideas.[33] The system invited not co-operation but contention between parties who—although the Court frequently divided the land—could win all, or lose all, on the Judge's nod. It ushered in an era of bitter contesting, of lying and false evidence. The legalistic nature of the Court also instituted a costly and tedious paraphernalia of lawyers, agents, legal rules and precedents—a morass in which the Maori floundered for decades, frittering away their estates in ruinous expenses and still all too often not getting equitable awards.

One further unfortunate consequence of the 1865 Lands Act must be considered. This is the question of succession. Under Maori custom, rights to the use of land descended, generally patrilineally but not exclusively so, to children who retained their basic ties with their parent *hapu* and resided on the land. Traditionally, although children could trace descent through either parent, they inherited rights to the use of land only in the village where they lived and were active members. Their rights to land in the village of the other parent lay dormant unless they chose to live there, and the rights of absentees were usually lost after three generations of absence. Children did not inherit in equal shares from both parents, regardless of where they resided. Essentially the land remained in the control of the elders of a village community and rights to its use descended to those who resided among and made their primary identification with that community.[34]

But to the majority of settlers, and to Fenton in particular, the application of these principles to land which had been awarded by the Court to individual owners suggested a reversion of the land to Maori 'communal' title again, and the frustration of one of the main purposes of the land legislation. It had been intended hitherto that Crown granted land should devolve according to the principles of English law. In 1865, however, professedly paying some deference to Maori viewpoints, the General Assembly adopted the vague formula that the land should succeed 'according to law as nearly as can be reconciled with Native custom',[35] and left the interpretation of this to the discretion of the all-powerful Fenton.

The Land Court Judges considered that:

> it would be highly prejudicial to allow the tribal tenure to grow up and effect land that has once been clothed with a lawful title, recognised and understood by the ordinary laws of the Colony . . . it will be the duty of the Court in administering

this Act to cause as rapid an introduction amongst the Maoris, not only of English tenures but of English rules of descent as can be secured without violently shocking Maori prejudices.[36]

English law (and mid-Victorian values) favoured inheritance of intestate estates by widows, but Fenton amended the English rule, again professedly to accommodate Maori values, to include children. He therefore divided the estates of Maori deceased, male or female, in approximately equal shares to all children of either sex, resident or absent. The result was that titles soon became divided into an infinite number of shares, smaller and less economic with each succeeding generation, until they were soon so over-crowded and fragmented as to put the actual land almost beyond efficient use. Moreover, the whole Maori population was encouraged to indulge in the pursuit of inheritances from both sides of their ancestry and in districts remote from where they lived.

FitzGerald, Richmond and the Stafford Government which finally passed the Act all, therefore, bear a share of the responsibility for making it so hazardous to the Maori and so suitable for speculators. Richmond produced some pearls of rhetoric to describe the new mode of colonisation. The Maori people's desire to close their land to settlement was a perfectly natural one he agreed:

At the same time, the settler was, quite properly, anxious to extend settlement, nor could his desire for land be properly called greed. It was not individual wealth he was grasping; he was indulging in the healthy wish for the spread of civilization.[37]

As for the Maori, free trade in land, would in Richmond's view, expose them to the healthy play of individual competition:

Deprived of the superficial gloss of which mere independence gives, the ordinary savage Maori would sink below the uncultivated European, whilst others possessed of more real force of character would rise to a higher level, from the great power of wealth which was put into their hands.[38]

If the Maori did not accept this challenge, the *Daily Southern Cross* later stated, 'they must be ground to dust between the forces which a vigorous and progressive civilization will bring to bear upon them'.[39] A tooth-and-claw system of ruthless competition was to be thrust upon a people whose social polity was traditionally organised in extended family and village co-operatives. The greater tragedy was not simply that the utter disruption of Maori social relations was deliberately initiated but that it was initiated through a system of land purchase that encouraged cupidity and unscrupulousness among Maori landholders rather than thrift and responsible use of land. At the same time as they had thrown down their demand for Maori self-advancement the settler politicians had placed well-nigh insuperable obstacles in the path of well-founded Maori enterprise.

Maori representation was introduced as part of Weld's drive for a rapid pacification. Weld and J. C. Richmond stated that they did not expect that the

Maori would, in practice, gain very much from parliamentary representation, but it was intended to remove a disability and to provide an opportunity for Maori people to place their grievances. More generally it fitted into the context of 'amalgamation'.[40] Ideas on the form that Maori representation should take, were, however, very confused. In 1863 a Select Committee chaired by Stafford had recommended that the Maori elect two European representatives.[41] The Weld government was divided on the subject. Sewell, and possibly Richmond, had some idea of calling chiefs such as Tamihana and Wi Tako to the Legislative Council. Mantell opposed this and all 'special' representation (in contrast to enfranchisement on the common electoral roll) as inferior, and bound to curtail the Maori people's due influence in the Assembly; he wanted Maori voters placed on the common roll on a £50 property qualification based on the Certificates of Title awarded by the Land Court, together with a recasting of electoral boundaries to give Maori voters a preponderance in at least three electorates.[42] In addition, there were fears that the Kupapa chiefs would be offended if ex-Kingites were called to the Legislative Council, while to have admitted both sections would have introduced more Maori members than Pakeha opinion was prepared to accept. During the 1865 Assembly, George Graham, an Auckland member, moved for Maori representation by five European members, three to come from the Auckland province. But Richmond and FitzGerald were inclined towards Maori representation by Maori members, and the need to balance Provincial strengths in the House frustrated Graham's attempt. These complications prevented the Government from bringing down concrete proposals but led to the introduction of the Native Commission Bill under which Weld proposed to assemble 'a kind of constituent assembly' of chiefs, including Tamihana 'and perhaps Matutaera' provided they took the oath of allegiance.[43] The Bill passed despite the opposition of romantic paternalists such as Colenso, who wanted the chiefs to 'meet the Great Father [the Governor] as the American Indians met the President of America'.[44] But Tamihana recalled that his request that Maori representatives be included in the General Assembly had been ignored in the 1850s, and declined to be drawn.[45] Some Kupapa chiefs were named for the commission, but the Weld Government fell before it could be assembled. Nevertheless the vote in favour of the Native Commission Act was a further step towards acceptance of Maori enfranchisement in principle.

FitzGerald's Outlying Districts Police Act was, in essence, an attempt to relieve the southern Provinces of the expense of suppressing the *Pai Marire*.[46] It provided that the chiefs of tribes harbouring men wanted for the killing of civilians should be called upon to surrender the fugitives, failing which land would be taken to pay the cost of police action and police garrisons in the district. Ironically, since FitzGerald had opposed the Settlements Act of 1863, the Act added a new and sweeping ground for confiscation. It drew the opposition of Mantell and Sir William Martin and the condemnation of the

Colonial Office, which let it pass into law only because London had officially surrendered complete responsibility in Maori affairs to the Weld Government. The Act also included provision for the voluntary surrender by the Maori of tracts of land to maintain police forces in their territory. This idea was founded on FitzGerald's hope that the chiefs, regretting the decline of law and order among their people, would welcome the chance of re-establishing it by means of Government police. In the prevailing climate it was a vain hope and Fitz-Gerald had apparently realised it by the time the Native Department officers were circularised to implement the Act. The Resident Magistrates were told that the Government had no sanguine expectations but to try cautiously in friendly districts for the cession of land—the title to remain with the Maori—to be leased to settlers to provide revenue for the support of police, gaols, hospitals and schools. The Runanga were offered a share in the management and expenditure of the revenue.[47] At a more favourable time these might indeed have been useful principles and won some Maori support, but there was no response before FitzGerald left office.

Late in the session FitzGerald introduced a Native Provinces Bill which envisaged the creation of semi-autonomous Maori provinces. This revived suggestions which FitzGerald had advanced in his speech of 1862, but may have stemmed more directly from Sir William Martin who was then pressing for the declaration of Native Districts to be governed by Maori committees and courts (with jurisdiction in all cases except homicide and serious assault) and a much larger Maori police force under the guidance of the Civil Commissioners. Martin regarded White's administration among the Rarawa as a promising model.[48] The Rev. T. S. Grace, formerly of Taupo, who was then denouncing the 'amalgamation' philosophy as the cause of much of the trouble in New Zealand, may also have provided some inspiration. The Bill had much to commend it. FitzGerald proposed to offer the 'rebel' chiefs (the Ngatimaniapoto in particular) authority and finance to administer and police their districts, under the *mana* of the Queen as manifested by the presence, not of a magistrate, but of a Resident. (Here FitzGerald referred to the error of sending a magistrate, Gorst, to upper Waikato in 1861).[49] The Bill recognised that the Government could not then impose its rule in the King's territory without reviving the war in the Waikato, but it sought to establish some lawful authority which the interior tribes might, in time, accept. Settlement meanwhile was to be kept out of the Maori provinces.

Sewell, a long-standing supporter of the Runanga system, described the scheme as a worthwhile attempt to 'organise the Natives into a self-governing people', but the Bill raised all the objections that had been levelled at earlier proposals to recognise the King movement. Stafford voiced a more general sentiment when he protested at FitzGerald's audacity in suggesting that settlers must wait while the Maori were first trained to peace and obedience. As usual he threw in the additional moralising argument that recognition of Maori provinces would perpetuate 'that 'Maori communism . . . that cursed *wharepuni* [sleeping-house] . . . and the communism of the sexes' which were allegedly the ruin and destruction of the race.[50] The *Daily Southern Cross* denounced what it called the plans for Maori Superintendents and a Maori army, to whom settlers in the Maori Provinces would be subject, as a surrender of all the points the war had been fought for.[51] The Bill was regarded as a serious issue, especially by the Auckland members who stood to lose most by the making of three Maori Provinces within the existing Auckland Province. It was defeated by a formidable display of 'log-rolling', Auckland gaining the support of Wellington and Otago in return for agreeing to a clause in the Native Lands Act reserving to Wellington monopoly rights of purchase in the Rangitikei-Manawatu block, and (for Otago) the transfer of the Princes Street Reserve to that Province.[52] Thus was policy made in the Parliaments of the 1860s.

FitzGerald's administrative record was as mixed as his legislative program. He sent Mainwaring, Resident Magistrate in upper Waikato, to meet the long-neglected Tamihana and ask him to throw his influence fully on the Government's side in exchange for the return of Ngatihaua land not already promised to settlers.[53] Tamihana, however, was not to be bought. He had already told George Graham, the Auckland politician who had induced him to lay down arms, that he held to his principles which underlay his support for the King movement: 'If you mean that I shall agree to the *ture,* that will be well; but if you mean that I am to give up my *mana* to the Queen I say no, I will not give up my *mana* no not one particle of it. I have told you the King and Queen will stand together and the *ture* shall be over both of them'.[54] Still trusting in his elevated concept of the law as a means of determining equity and justice he demanded of Mainwaring an inquiry by 'just judges' into the whole origin of the war, and the consequent return of all the Waikato land. With FitzGerald's support he also petitioned the General Assembly. His petition was a ringing manifesto rather than a plea but, after furious debate, and a division of twenty-seven to sixteen, it was received, 'on the broad principle that the rights of petitioners ought not to be circumscribed, especially in the case of the Native race'.[55] But Tamihana gained little from his petitions either then or on a second occasion in 1866 and returned to Waikato a bitterly disappointed man.[56]

Meanwhile, FitzGerald ordered the military commanders to leave the Hauhau alone unless they actually committed crimes, and sought to confine operations to the arrest of Volkner's murderers in the Bay of Plenty and Waiapu districts. On 2 September the Government issued two proclamations. One was a proclamation of peace and amnesty, without the requirement of an oath of allegiance or surrender of arms, to all but a few 'rebels' whose deeds were most reprehensible in European eyes; the other made extensive new confiscations in Taranaki. The Government was 'ending the war by proclamation' according to FitzGerald and the Resident Magistrates were circularised to tell their people that a final settlement of the country was being made. But Fitz-

Gerald's hopes were illusory and more hard-headed men knew that the whole performance had the appearance of hypocrisy. Clearly renewed confiscation together with the Outlying Districts Police Act, the expedition to Opotiki against Volkner's murderers and Weld's promises of vigorous action against *Pai Marire* recalcitrants, meant not an ending but a revival of the war. Moreover the *Daily Southern Cross* rightly pointed out that the 'rebels' were by no means all war-weary and anxious for peace, and predicted that if the Native Minister were in office for a further six months he would go down in history as 'Fighting FitzGerald'.[57] The newspaper editor had read his man well. When a Government interpreter was killed while negotiating under flag of truce with a *Pai Marire pa* near Patea and two Kupapa emissaries carrying FitzGerald's Peace Proclamation to Waikato were killed on the way, FitzGerald, demonstrating the violent reaction of the spurned idealist, wrote to McLean: 'The late conduct of Weraroa Natives in shooting our messengers of peace has sealed their doom I will have them utterly destroyed.'[58] And H. T. Clarke in the Bay of Plenty was instructed that, if captured, Volkner's murderers were to 'be tried by Court Martial on the spot and executed after a fair trial'.[59] The handling of the confiscated lands in Taranaki showed FitzGerald at his most inconsistent. In a letter appointing Parris as Civil Commissioner in Taranaki the Native Minister set out the Government's intentions:

> It is proposed to confiscate the whole of the lands to a distance of 20 miles or thereabouts from the Coast lying between the Waitotara River and the White Cliffs, not with a view to holding or occupying the whole of it, but in order to enable the Government to clear away all disputed titles and at once to settle down upon sufficient blocks of land the whole of the Native population of that district, who may be willing to come in, accept Crown Grants and promise to live peaceably under the law. . . . The Government wants to see a speedy and final settlement made of the whole matter and however it may regard as of importance the acquisition of land for sale so as to reimburse the Treasury for the expenditure upon Military operations, it regards the final settlement of the Natives upon the lands under Crown Grants, and their consent to the arrangements you make of so much higher importance, that they do not wish to limit your discretion in dealing liberally in the disposition of the land, if by so doing you can win their final acquiescence in the settlement of your whole district.[60]

But the wide discretion given to Parris alarmed the rapacious Taranaki politicians who feared his growing tendency to act protectively towards the Maori. FitzGerald's ministerial colleague, J. C. Richmond, therefore went to FitzGerald and persuaded him to alter Parris's instructions.[61] Parris was told that the settlement of the Taranaki confiscation should be 'not only so as to win the acquiescence of the Natives but also the Europeans' and that in all cases where settler interests were affected Parris must 'act in concert with the Superintendent of the Province'.[62] Here was the familiar theme which had ruined Maori policy since the foundation of the colony: no beneficent or protective act towards the Maori should be undertaken if it antagonised the settlers. Inevitably this meant more confusion, and more injustice. Within a month the loyal Ngatirahiri *hapu* was being pushed off its cultivated land near Waitara to make way for a military settlement. Parris, in defence of the Ngatirahiri, went to Wellington to see Weld and Atkinson—the Defence Minister and a Taranaki man—but was told only that the land of loyal Maoris would not be taken 'if it could possibly be avoided'.[63] The Provincial authorities then brought in their own surveyor and the most Parris could do, at the cost of bitter unpopularity, was to secure a reduction in the number of military settlers located on Ngatirahiri land.[64] FitzGerald was reduced to making a plaintive minute on Parris's report: 'I despair of any settlement of our Native difficulties if we persist in taking the lands belonging to Natives who have been friendly to us all through the war.'[65]

In the matter of the confiscations (as with the Native Lands Act) Fitz-Gerald was largely the victim of settler pressures. With the Weld Ministry holding power by a slim majority and Richmond and Atkinson, his Taranaki colleagues, pressing him to give way the Native Minister was in an unenviable position. Yet FitzGerald himself could take a hard line. In 1864 Hunter Brown made the first of many recommendations by subordinate officers, that the South Island Maori should either be liberally provided with schools, hospitals, churches and technical assistance as they anticipated when they sold their vast hinterland in the 1850s, or that they should receive enlarged reserves or compensation payments. Secure in his framework of English values FitzGerald wrote complacently:

> my friends at Kaiapoi say we have got all their land and promised to give them Schools and Hospitals and so on . . . Explain to them that as to the land, all land is worthless . . . till man adds his labour to it . . . and if the Maoris worked as hard as Europeans they would be as rich. Next tell them that when I was Superintendent I went to them with Bp of N.Z., and we told them that to put a clergyman, a School, a Hospital, in each small village of 10 or 12 inhabitants was utterly impossible but that if they would all come together in one place, all these things should be provided, but they would not. It is entirely their own fault that we have not been able to do more for them. Tell them moreover that when the Government provides schools for the English it expects the English to pay and they do pay so much a week for their chn. . . . If the Maori people do not pay the shilling a week for their chn. the School must be removed altogether . . . If they got the School for nothing they would not value it. If they pay for it they will love it and honour it.[66]

This was in keeping with the spirit of the age, and certainly carried no risk of subjecting the South Island Maori to pauperisation, but it showed an insensitivity both to Maori values and needs, and to the spirit of promises made at the time of the land purchases.

Meanwhile, violent objection had been made in the Assembly both to 'the rottenness of the Native Department'—the number of supposedly useless Resident Magistrates and Civil Commissioners remaining from Grey's 'new institutions' of 1861-2—and to the extent to which the officers in Northland had supported the Runanga system, thus allegedly placing European settlers in a condition of dependence similar to that obtaining in the days before 1840. Faced with this attitude, and with the pressing need for economies owing to the depression into which the Colony had fallen, FitzGerald dismissed some clerks and interpreters, reduced Civil Commissioners' salaries, ordered the Resident Magistrates not to fill vacancies in their staffs, and asked for returns showing the degree of usefulness of Maori Assessors and police, pending a reorganisation of the whole Native Service.

On this note FitzGerald's brief and hectic three months charge of the Native Department ended. Vogel, the emergent Otago capitalist, had moved a vote of no-confidence in him early in the session for the 'wild visionary' nature of his Maori policy, for his too flagrant assertions that the Maori rebels were as right from their point of view as the settlers were from theirs, and for his attacks on the 'financial bubbles'—the inflationary speculations—of Auckland and Otago financiers. Vogel's attack was too personal and failed, though Mantell's reason for opposing it was that he wanted FitzGerald to stay in office so that the Maori people and the humanitarians in England could see that he was not the great stalwart for Maori rights that they thought him to be. A few weeks later Colenso pushed through a motion of censure on the Government for FitzGerald's proclamation of amnesty to various Maori rebels—a subject always likely to raise settler passions, particularly at a time of considerable *Pai Marire* activity.[67] Weld's Ministry finally fell in mid-October on a question of finance, but FitzGerald's unpopularity contributed very greatly towards this result. Weld and FitzGerald were so depressed by their experiences that they left politics, Weld immediately and FitzGerald the following year, to the position of Auditor-General. They gave place to men who would be even less troubled by scruple in riveting settler control upon the Maori people and their lands.

XIII

The Native Department Reduced

The early policies of the Stafford Ministry were largely in reaction to what was regarded as the leniency or pro-Maori inclination of FitzGerald's administration. Stafford determined that: 'We mean taking the oath of allegiance . . . to mean something substantial, and all who take it and break it, and all prisoners in future will either be executed, transported or put to hard labour.'[1] Any further outbreaks of rebellion, he declared, were to be severely punished, and sufficient land would be taken to pay for putting them down. The Government was pleased to have a new instrument to hand for a ruthless policy in General Trevor Chute who had replaced the relatively humane Cameron, and Grey—whose continued authority depended upon the retention of the Imperial troops in New Zealand—supported Stafford in planning a new campaign. Chute's army marched from Wanganui to Taranaki, behind Mount Egmont, and back again down the coast, killing, burning villages, destroying crops, looting, and occasionally shooting prisoners.

One result of the campaign was the serious dislocation of Parris's negotiations with the 'rebels', the unsettling of chiefs such Te Ua and Hone Pihama, who had submitted and were settling on reserves, and the alienation of others like Wi Kingi Matakatea who had not previously taken up arms against the British. If the military were not curbed, Parris urged, the country would drift into that 'war of races' which many colonists considered had not so far occurred. 'Never since the war began have I been so disheartened as I am at the present time.'[2] Parris's efforts to restrain the military served to spur some officers, resenting his 'interference', to greater ruthlessness. Colonel McDonnell opened negotiations with the Pokaikai *pa*. But when the inhabitants said they had sent a messenger to seek Parris as well, McDonnell, who had for many months resented Parris's proceedings, treated this as prevarication and, without warning, attacked the *pa* in the night. Although the Maori had only three killed, this act was regarded by them all, including McDonnell's Kupapas, as one of the outstanding examples of treachery committed by the British during the war. It was smoothed over by a Commission of Inquiry but the Government admitted that McDonnell might have 'made a mistake'.[3]

Parris's pleas to the Government to check indiscriminate looting and burning of crops also met little response. Colonel A. H. Russell, late Civil Commissioner of Hawke's Bay, had taken office as Native Minister 'to fill the gap', he said, when Stafford had difficulty in forming a Government in October 1865.[4] He brought a stiff-necked, insensitive attitude to the administration of Maori affairs. Parris was told to assure the Taranaki *hapu* that it was only by misadventure inseparable from civil war that non-rebels suffered disturbance and loss of property, and to make gifts in recompense to important chiefs, but not to raise the question of compensation generally. When Parris persisted Russell replied that rough measures were the work of soldiers 'smarting under the loss of their officers and comrades', that the Maori had a remedy at law 'and he [Russell] cannot doubt that in an English community it will be fairly and impartially administered'.[5]

Stafford and Russell also dealt vigorously with Hauhau prisoners. The Weld Ministry had convicted a number of them before a military court martial of complicity in the murders of Fulloon and Volkner; Stafford, arguing that the Maori people were amenable to the civil law, had the prisoners retried in the Supreme Court. Thirty-five were convicted and five hanged. This was much the largest single act of judicial retribution in the war, only two prisoners besides these five being executed on charges arising out of the war.[6] Russell and McLean arranged that in future *Pai Marire* prisoners would be deported to the Chatham Islands.

Meanwhile Russell set about the dismantling of the Native Department which had been heralded in the closing stages of FitzGerald's tenure of office. The Stafford Ministry planned a vigorous retrenchment and reorganisation of the civil service generally and, immediately upon taking office, appointed a commission to make inquiries and recommendations for that purpose. But there were special reasons why the Native Department came under attack. Russell himself took office believing that the civil institutions established by Grey in 1862-3 had been only bribes to buy allies and avert war. They had failed, and now served no useful purpose, though Maori office-holders continued to harvest allegedly undeserved salaries. On principle, Russell argued, 'true policy requires that all exceptional law should gradually cease and the Natives be encouraged to conform to that of Europeans'.[7] In accordance with this general policy he proposed to settle quickly the confiscated lands question and set the Compensation Courts working to determine which Maori claimants were 'rebels' and should lose land within the confiscation boundaries; he proposed to spend £2000 on finally settling outstanding questions in regard to the South Island reserves; he proposed to introduce Maori parliamentary representation—six Maori members in the House of Representatives and three in the Legislative Council, to inaugurate a system of village schools where Maori children would learn English, and to abolish all discriminatory legislation such as the Sale of Spirits Ordinance. In short, he intended to bring the elusive policy of 'amalgamation' to a rapid consummation and thereafter to drop all special consideration of Maori affairs. The Weld Ministry's estimates for the

Native Department were slashed from £53,000 to £33,000, and Russell began his policy of excision, intending the total abolition of the Native Department by the end of the Parliament then elected.[8]

The remnant of the Runanga system was an early victim. Russell's lack of success with it as Civil Commissioner in Hawke's Bay in 1862 had convinced him that:

> [The Runanga system] was not desired by the Natives and was incapable of being worked . . . as a rule it has utterly failed and . . . what the Natives appear to desire and respect is a calm but determined enforcement of English law . . . they could not understand and did not believe in the decisions of their own Runangas, they established them in the absence of any law, but they constantly appealed to him against their own decisions and gladly seized upon his reversal of their judgments . . . The object of the Government must be to identify the Natives with ourselves, to become one people and to realise their expressed desire for, one law, one Queen, and one Gospel.[9]

Russell was in fact weighting the evidence to suit his case. Undoubtedly the unofficial Maori *runanga* had run into many difficulties and the participants were frequently glad to appeal to a local government official, but this is not to say that they still did not value them and wish to have them supported and guided rather than supplanted. Moreover, the Native Minister was simply passing over the promising efforts of the chiefs and magistrates in Northland and the Chatham Islands who were co-operating in local self-government through the official Runanga. White, Thomas and Clarke were instructed to close down their Runanga, and James Mackay, who was wanting to start one in the Hauraki district, was declined permission. Thus was closed a fruitful avenue for the development of Maori responsibility in the machinery of government. It was symbolic of the transition to more direct rule that the Runanga building at Waimate was taken over as a courthouse and office for the Resident Magistrate.

Some 300 out of 450 Maori recipients of Government stipends—Assessors, Wardens, police and pensioners—had their salaries stopped or heavily cut. Russell wanted only four Assessors and four police in each Resident Magistrate District and, if he could not secure the necessary reduction immediately, he ordered that no vacancies should be filled till numbers had fallen to that figure.[10]

Russell found it more difficult to dispense with European officers. Certainly, with the Runanga gone he was able to reduce the number of Civil Commissioners. W. B. White (Mangonui) reverted to the status of Resident Magistrate that he had enjoyed from 1848 to 1862. Since Williams was Resident Magistrate at Waimate, the aging George Clarke was dispensed with altogether. Rogan (Civil Commissioner, Kaipara) and T. H. Smith (Civil Commissioner, Eastern Bay of Plenty) became Land Court Judges, and Russell expressed the hope that 'before long the office of Civil Commissioner will cease altogether in the Colony'.[11] But given the slowness of communications and the troubled state of the out-districts, Russell saw some advantage in leaving in office three Civil Commissioners—J. Mackay (Auckland), H. T. Clarke (Tauranga), and Parris (Taranaki) in order that these districts could be administered without the need for frequent reference to the Native Minister in Wellington. He hoped that as the war situation eased these men could be dispensed with also, and meanwhile he largely negated the value of retaining them by requiring the Resident Magistrates to communicate directly with Wellington, not through the Civil Commissioners.

Reduction in the number of Native Department Resident Magistrates eluded him entirely. He claimed that his experience in 1862 proved that a good Resident Magistrate, by spending half his time in the saddle and half in his office, could easily cover a district the size of the Bay of Plenty. But that was in time of peace, and Russell soon realised that the political work of a Resident Magistrate in conditions of war more than made up for the falling off in the number of civil disputes that had to be heard. He dispensed with J. R. Clendon of Hokianga, and warned Resident Magistrates who had no knowledge of the Maori language to learn it within twelve months in order that interpreters could be dispensed with, or face a cut in salary. On the other hand he appointed J. H. Campbell to Waiapu and W. G. Mair to Taupo to re-establish a civil power in those districts.

It was easier to make reductions in the number of Native Department medical officers in Maori districts. Russell dismissed several on the grounds that they were doing no work, and that in any case, the Maori, who seemed to have plenty of money to spend on liquor, should be induced to pay their doctors' bills like the colonists. The program of smallpox vaccination now ceased to be a Native Department responsibility. Russell also cut down the £2000 or more being spent annually on presents and entertainment for Maori visiting the towns or by officials in the course of their visits to chiefs. All in all he succeeded in reducing expenses in the Native Department from about £60,000 in 1864-5 to £48,000 in 1865-6 and £34,000 in 1866-7.

In many cases the man dismissed in these retrenchments had ceased to do effective work and could well be spared, but several effects of the reductions were unfortunate. The withdrawal of subsidised medical care meant, not that the Maori spent less on liquor and more on medicine, but, as modern social welfare legislation recognises, that many who were without money either for squandering or for medicine had less chance of treatment. The reductions in Resident Magistrates' salaries bore hard on them since hospitality to chiefs was in accord with Maori custom and the basis of meetings where much of importance was discussed freely and frankly. Now they had to curtail this hospitality, pay for it out of their own living expenses, or submit food bills for the uncertain approval of the Native Office, as 'contingencies'.

Removal of the Civil Commissioners and the by-passing of those who were left meant that the Resident Magistrates were left largely unsupervised, since the Native Minister himself could not keep up close supervision of the out-districts. When there was an energetic Civil Commissioner, like James Mackay, this was unfortunate. Mackay described the situation in the Waikato, as he saw it, to Rolleston:

> he [Captain Hamilton, Resident Magistrate, Raglan] is continually making a fool of himself, picking up all sorts of paltry cases and making mountains out of them. His temper also is anything but good. Stewart [Port Waikato] is very slow—and not worth much. The fact is none of them are worth much. Old Searancke [middle Waikato] is the most straightforward and willing. I never hardly hear anything of Mainwaring [upper Waikato]. If Russell had left me alone I would have made something of them before now.[12]

The Runanga system, as White, Clarke and Thomas had proved, was not by any means valueless, and before many years were out Maori leaders throughout the country were agitating for representative local councils. The Resident Magistrates had also opposed heavy reductions in their Maori staff, especially of Assessors. Rogan wrote that if he dismissed all that Russell asked him to, 'Why Sir this would leave me no where. The people hold very little communication with me personally. The Chiefs rule them and I rule the Chiefs.'[13] Williams of Waimate informed Russell that his Assessors worked hard, travelling at his request without extra pay, and said that he could suggest the names of none he wished to see dispensed with. When ordered, he reduced his staff by about one third, very reluctantly, and reported that he still had to consult, on important cases, some of the chiefs whom he had dismissed.[14] Other Resident Magistrates, especially those in troubled districts, reported their embarrassment at not being able to continue salaries to chiefs whose allegiance they were trying to win or retain for the Government. The Kaipara Maori held a meeting about the loss or reduction of the salaries and most of the Ngapuhi were reputed to be disgruntled at the loss of what they deemed to be marks of their chieftainship.[15]

At the same time as the Ngapuhi were protesting, Russell's parsimony provoked a row with the Arawa. He offered them for their services to date, besides the £3000 already paid in rations, only £1500 in cash, which worked out at about £2.5.0 per man for three months active service. By contrast, a British expedition to catch Volkner's murderers, considerably less successful, cost about £40,000. The Arawa and their white officers were not slow to raise a fuss. They asked Russell that they be kept on a regular military payroll or that Pakeha troops be paid off also; they asked for sections in the towns then being laid out in the confiscated lands, for employment on public works, for schools, for a definition of their land boundaries and for an Arawa member in the House of Representatives. Russell approved the requests for roads, schools and public works provided that the Arawa would sell some of their land to pay half the cost of them, and told them they would soon be allowed to vote for a Pakeha member of the Assembly.[16]

The possibility of discord with the two great 'loyal' tribes of the North Island, owing to Russell's proceedings, aroused alarm among many of the settlers. The Native Minister had never been a popular figure in the Colony, and now his actions formed one of the grounds on which the Assembly of 1866 passed a vote of no confidence in Stafford's Ministry—though not in Stafford himself.

Russell resigned readily, informing Stafford, 'You are aware that I took office only to keep out the Weld ministry and that object having been accomplished I am quite ready to give place to any one else'.[17] He went unmourned by his staff. In six months he had antagonised them all, not only by pushing through his retrenchments, but by inhibiting their initiative or influence on policy. He had tried to restrict Rolleston, the Under-Secretary, to giving advice on matters of detail, not of policy, and Rolleston had gone to Stafford to have him over-ruled.[18] James Mackay commented to Rolleston:

> I note what you say about writing less savagely—it is quite true. I fear another six months under Russell would have made me hate the whole service. I know what you have gone through, and God forbid that any of us ever go through another such ordeal.[19]

Direction of the Native Department was then taken over by J. C. Richmond, lately Weld's colleague, but now willing, after a suitable interval, to serve under the man who had turned Weld out. Mackay commented: 'I am glad we have got a gentleman at the head of the Department in lieu of the ex-sergeant major.'[20]

But Richmond was not designated Native Minister. Despite Russell's realisation that it was premature to wind up the Native Department, the Civil Service Commission appointed by Stafford reiterated the popular prejudice against its authority. Reporting in June 1866, the Commission recommended still heavier reductions, and restriction of Resident Magistrates to purely judicial duties rather than the general political duties they then performed. It recommended that matters involving Maori lands should be placed under the Crown Lands Department and the Resident Magistrates' general correspondence handled by a Judicial Branch of the Colonial Secretary's Department.[21] In announcing his Ministry in August Stafford stated:

> There would be no Native Minister in the present Government. The state of Native affairs had so much improved that there would appear to be no longer any speciality in dealing with them. As long as there is a line of demarcation between the management of European and of Native affairs, so long would there be causes of dissatisfaction and irritation between different parts of the colony. It appeared therefore a step in the right direction to do away with the office of Native Minister. Native affairs, would, like other affairs, be conducted by the Colonial Secretary or by some other Minister.[22]

XIV

Main Lines of Policy and Practice

The ruthlessness and the expense of the West Coast campaign of 1866 led to renewed suggestions in the General Assembly, especially from South Island politicians whose Provinces provided the bulk of the colonial revenue for the war in the North Island, that the Maori people could be brought under English rule more readily and more cheaply by the provision of schools and hospitals than by wholesale military expeditions which only united them in resistance. Moves by Auckland politicians either to make their Province a separate colony, or to make Maori affairs a Provincial responsibility—both moves designed to allow them to pursue a strong Maori policy—were defeated. The Government took steps to damp down the war, placing the warlike Arawa auxiliaries more firmly under the control of the civil officers and shelving plans for the military occupation of the Taupo district. Grey made a useful tour of the North Island receiving the submission of *hapu* whose *Pai Marire* enthusiasm had subsided. He had also hoped to meet King Tawhiao and Rewi Maniapoto at Kawhia harbour but they avoided him.

In 1867 he was replaced, after a long controversy with the Colonial Office over his relations with commanders of British regiments in New Zealand, and his delay in arranging the return of those regiments to England. His successor, Sir George Bowen, was the first of a new type of Governor—fond of ease, good living and race-horses. It was a sad commentary on the fragility of Maori rights, however, that the horses he brought with him were stabled in the out-buildings of the Maori hostelry in Wellington.

After 1867 the British regiments did begin to go home, being replaced by the Armed Constabulary, a force of full-time settler volunteers. The Armed Constabulary was open to Maori recruits too, but most of those who fought on the Government side were organised into special Native Contingents sometimes under their own officers such as Ropata of the East Coast, or Kepa (Kemp) of Wanganui, or Pakeha officers such as W. G. Mair.

Meanwhile the situation in the Waikato became more settled. Tamihana had accepted the adjudication of the Compensation Court established to determine the awards to Kupapa tribes and former 'rebels'. Large groups of Ngatihaua came in, rather defiantly; Tamihana quietened them and the civil officers tried to settle them and assist them to begin cultivating. Much of the best Ngatihaua territory was, however, leased to the run-holder J. C. Firth. In mid-1866 the Kingites beyond the confiscation boundary established an *aukati,* or frontier, between their territory and that of the Pakeha. They sought to draw into the 'King Country' all the Maori whom they could influence, and to discourage their return to Pakeha territory. Large numbers of ex-'rebels' and many Kupapa *hapu,* disgruntled with awards of the Compensation Court, flocked to Hangatiki and Tokangamutu, the principal King Country villages. In December 1866, Tamihana, worn and depressed, died. More Ngatihaua abandoned the policy of co-operation enjoined by their late leader, killed Firth's cattle and menaced his men, and retired beyond the *aukati.* This mood lasted for about a year when many began to drift back again and resume cultivations within the confiscated lands. By 1867 William Searancke, Resident Magistrate in middle Waikato, had two flour mills in operation to grind their wheat. In order to prevent their people from trading with the settlers and possibly exposing the King Country to settler encroachment, the Waikato Kingite chiefs held meetings to harden the *aukati.* As a result of one of these the neutral Maori and a few Europeans who had clung to Kawhia harbour throughout the war, were expelled and the harbour closed. But King Country Maori visited and traded in the frontier towns; the *aukati* was in practice enforced only one way.

The same Kingite meetings that established the *aukati* also called on *Pai Marire* throughout the island to cease fighting. In response to this the Government at last made formal contact with the still-resisting Kingite leaders. In October 1867 Resident Magistrate Searancke took to Hangatiki letters from Grey and Richmond welcoming the King's move to establish peace, explaining recent legislation regarding Maori representation, Maori schools and the Native Land Court, and urging the familiar argument that the two peoples should unite under one law. Grey asked Tawhiao if he would care to confirm the peace with the Duke of Edinburgh, Queen Victoria's son, who was shortly to visit New Zealand.[1] A press report later claimed that Grey had also offered Tawhiao a large salary 'if he would consent to keep order in his territory as a stipendiary of the late Government'.[2] Tawhiao and Tamati Ngapora, (now called 'Manuhiri', the visitor, in reference to his position in Ngatimaniapoto land) formally declined to reply.[3] However, in November 1867 C. O. Davis met Manuhiri at the home of Louis Hetet, a Frenchman who had dwelt among the Kingites throughout the war. Soon afterwards, Hetet told Searancke that Tawhiao was going to send a *Tekau-ma-rua* or 'Twelve' (so named from the *Pai Marire* fashion of identifying its picked bands with the twelve apostles of Christianity) through the Waikato. If it was unmolested, Tawhiao would make peace. Searancke arranged that the *Tekau-ma-rua*—actually about 100 men—was given food as it paraded and danced *haka,* in full war accoutrement, through the Waikato townships. In February 1868 after a big meeting attended by chiefs from most districts of the North Island including the 'loyal' districts, the Kingites wrote to C. O. Davis announcing the new order.

Weapons were to be put away; but the King's territory was closed to lease or sale, to roads and gold prospecting, and the King movement would not recognise the confiscation of the Waikato. The Government and settlers were disposed to accept this situation and rely on trade and friendly contacts to eventually break down the *aukati*.

Richmond also sought to bring the confiscated lands question to a final settlement in Taranaki and the Bay of Plenty by returning large reserves, mostly their original territory, to former 'rebels'. His efforts were complemented by the non-violent policy of the prophets Te Whiti and Tohu who were increasingly making their influence felt from the village of Parihaka in South Taranaki. The Government actually began to feel that the war was over.[4]

The Government's effort to bring the war to a conclusion was accompanied by further consideration of the role of the Native Department, and renewed attention to the questions of Maori parliamentary representation, education, and land. Richmond continued Russell's policy of withdrawing the subsidies paid to medical officers to treat Maori patients free of charge. He also closed the hospital at Mangonui, built by the District Runanga in 1862. The hospitals built during Grey's first governorship on Maori land in New Plymouth and Wanganui and since taken over by the military, were handed over to the Provincial authorities, the General Government paying a subsidy for the few Maori patients still admitted. Special medical services, such as they were, had not entirely ceased, but whereas the subsidised rural doctors, specially designated to care for Maori patients, had often been readily approached by them at all hours of the day and night, Maori people were reluctant, for cultural rather than financial reasons, to approach the private practitioner surrounded by wealthy white patients in his town surgery. Ailing Maori had to make do with the 'medical comforts' dispensed by the Resident Magistrates or the sporadic attention of an idealistic private practitioner or army doctor. But it was an age in which traditional ritual healing by *tohunga*, based on the concept that illness was caused by malign spirits, still flourished, with some of the *tohunga* adding to their cures a variety of European products believed or alleged to have some potency.

The Government did not, however, accept the recommendation of the Civil Service Commission that Resident Magistrates be confined to judicial duties. On the contrary, Richmond requested that they report regularly on all matters of importance in their districts, a duty he considered essential, 'as long as there is a department of political agents'.[5] With the spread of telegraph lines from 1868 the Resident Magistrates were asked to make a regular practice of telegraphing short summaries of passing events to Wellington. The Native Office in effect functioned as a clearing house for an island wide intelligence network. Richmond considered that eventually the Native Service might be allowed to wither through vacancies being left unfilled, but only Mainwaring of upper Waikato and Nesbitt of Maketu, who had got into financial difficulties

(Nesbitt having borrowed from a local *runanga* against an order on his salary) were dropped. On the other hand, Captain Biggs of the Armed Constabulary was made Resident Magistrate at Poverty Bay. Richmond also proposed to continue spending fairly liberally to allow Government officers to repay Maori hospitality, to make presents to chiefs as courtesy and diplomacy required, and to appoint important ex-'rebels' as Assessors.

A consolidating Resident Magistrates Act was passed by the General Assembly in 1867. The debate brought forth settler hostility to the provisions of the Grey's Resident Magistrates' Courts Ordinance of 1847 and of the Native Circuit Courts Act 1858, which reserved the administration of justice among the Maori people almost exclusively to the Resident Magistrates and provided for certain variations from the ordinary operations of the law. A majority in the Assembly, backed by the press, sought to have the Maori made subject to the same legal code and courts as the settlers, including the petty jurisdiction of the Justices of the Peace. But, because of the continued uncertainty of enforcing law in the out-districts, the Government included in the Resident Magistrates Act a number of special sections retaining most of the earlier exemptions and satisfied the Assembly by reserving their application to districts proclaimed by the Governor-in-Council. Sections 103 and 115 together prohibited the apprehension of a Maori, outside the main towns, save by the order of a Resident Magistrate or of a Superior Court (i.e., a Maori could not be apprehended, outside the towns, on the order of a Justice of the Peace, or by a policeman on his own initiative); sections 105-6 (re-enacting Governor FitzRoy's attempt to embrace the principle of *utu*) stated that thefts should be punished by a fine of four times the value of goods stolen—instead of imprisonment—and that a proportion of the fine would be paid to the victim of the theft (FitzRoy's extension of this principle to assault cases was now dropped); sections 107-10 re-enacted the clauses of the 1858 Native Circuit Courts Act (and its Amendment Act, 1862) providing for the appointment of Assessors and the hearing of all civil disputes between Maori, save those affecting land title, by a Resident Magistrate with the Assessors, whose concurrence would be necessary to the execution of a judgment; section 111 gave the Resident Magistrates in Native Districts a jurisdiction of £100 in cases between Maori and European—a larger jurisdiction than that generally enjoyed by urban Resident Magistrates; section 112 forbade the serving of a distress warrant for debt, without the approval of a Resident Magistrate; section 113 provided that a Resident Magistrate might delay the execution of any judgment; section 114 provided for the payment of Assessors according to the number of warrants executed, rather than by salary; section 115— reflecting the bid by the settler Assembly to break the virtual monopoly of Maori jurisdiction by the Resident Magistrates—gave Chairmen of Petty Sessions the same power as Resident Magistrates in any case affecting Maori.

Richmond circularised the Resident Magistrates for their views on the necessity of special provisions, noting that:

The feeling of the Legislature appears to have been decidedly opposed to the introduction of any exceptional legislation of the character contained in the above-named Sections and the Government is averse to exercising the power of bringing them into operation unless special circumstances seem to render it necessary.[6]

The response of the Resident Magistrates, however, was decisive. H. T. Clarke later wrote: 'Officers in Native Districts have to deal more with facts than with policies enunciated in the General Assembly.'[7] Certainly their opinions as to the relative value of each of the special provisions varied. A growing number of Resident Magistrates thought the principle of punishing theft by fines instead of imprisonment aroused too much jealousy from settlers and encouraged feckless Maori to steal, relying on their community to bear the fines. But others thought the principle essential and all in all the Government was left in no doubt of the necessity for most of the special provisions. In February 1868 sections 105-13 were proclaimed as applicable at the Resident Magistrates' discretion in all rural districts of the North Island and sections 107-13 (omitting the fines instead of imprisonment for theft principle) in the urban districts. In the South Island the special provisions were applied only to the Nelson-Motueka district, the scattered Maori communities further south being brought under the authority of the regular petty courts and police. Even so' Maori Assessors and constables were appointed in Canterbury and Otago and assisted the Resident Magistrates. Sections 104 (which authorised payment of Assessors according to the number of warrants they served rather than by salary) and 115 (giving Chairmen of Petty Sessions the same authority over Maori as the Resident Magistrates) were not proclaimed. In the North Island the system of Resident Magistrates taking circuit court among the Maori villages assisted by about six salaried Assessors and six Maori police in each district was to operate for another twenty-five years.

There were, however, significant changes. The Maori Assessors' independent £5 jurisdiction was dropped. Resident Magistrates were expressly debarred from hearing disputes involving land title; these were to be referred to the Native Land Court. The provisions for civil cases between Maori disputants to be heard before a Maori jury were repealed, no doubt to the regret of James Mackay, who had begun to use the system in the Hauraki district and frequently found Maori jurors 'a great deal sharper than some of the twelve good and lawful men occasionally seen in the box in the Supreme Court'.[8]

These points, together with Russell's closing down of the Runangas in 1865-6, meant that the comprehensive system of Maori local self-government envisaged in the legislation of 1858 and in Grey's civil institutions of 1861-3, was now abandoned and the opportunity for Maori leaders to exercise a wide range of local legislative and judicial powers virtually closed. Nor could the Resident Magistrates any longer be mediators in the sense of helping the Maori to evolve and administer a pattern of by-laws compounded of English elements and local customs, to suit local requirements. Essentially they could now only be mediators of English law to the Maori—cautiously and flexibly and with the co-operation of the Assessors—but nevertheless, in the end, substantially the same pattern of law as regulated the affairs of the settlers.

English law inevitably fitted ill with Maori values. This remained particularly true of the problem of *puremu* or adultery. Before 1867 *puremu* had sometimes been treated by the courts as 'criminal conversation', then punishable by fine or gaol sentence, and in Hawke's Bay a Supreme Court Judge, anxious to inculcate the sanctity of a marriage contract, sentenced two or three Maori offenders to heavy sentences of hard labour.[9] However, the Divorce and Matrimonial Causes Act, 1867 abolished the offence of 'crim.con.', providing instead that the aggrieved husband would sue the adulterer for damages. Most Native Department Resident Magistrates in fact treated Maori *puremu* this way, but some of the new appointees refused to consider the question on the ground that Maori customary marriages were not recognised in English law. For this and other reasons most Maori communities continued to meet in unofficial *runanga* and to levy traditional *muru* on offenders. Chiefs, including Assessors, continued to exercise a quasi-magisterial authority, in many cases (though now illegally) levying fines.

On the other hand, Maori disputants continued to resort to the Resident Magistrate's courts freely with regard to disputes over the ownership of stock or damage to property. High-ranking men, who were usually Assessors, often initiated these actions, but sometimes lower-ranking men went to Resident Magistrates about chiefs who had abused a traditional prerogative, or exercised it in a way which was no longer acceptable.

The resort to Pakeha law caused the eminent Karaitiana Takamoana of Hawke's Bay to lament: 'In olden times disputes could be settled by discussion; now in these days of civilization everything is settled in courts of law.'[10] But modernising tendencies were also strong; one of McLean's officers considered that the principal chiefs of Hawke's Bay 'were anxious to have European laws carried out in every way [;] they want us to give them grog like other people but have police and lockups; they find the runanga cannot manage to keep the peace'.[11] These diverging views reflected an inevitable concern for traditional values, combined with a desire to be treated as equals of the Pakeha, fully able and willing among other things, to run an ordered society. The Resident Magistrate and Assessor system continued to bridge these aspirations to some extent, since the Resident Magistrates in practice continued to adapt English law to the quasi-traditional situation, settling a great many disputes through informal discussion, encouraging Assessors to act alone, or even fostering an informal Runanga system to regulate matters which courts would either have deemed frivolous or treated too heavy-handedly.

The experience of J. C. Campbell, appointed Resident Magistrate at Waiapu in 1866, illustrates some of the possibilities in the system at that period. Campbell found petty crime rampant. Maori *runanga* of a kind were meeting every month, but were dissatisfied with their own efforts, largely owing to drunkenness of important chiefs. Within six months the Ngatiporou had built Campbell a court house, office, and lock-up, making the bricks themselves out of local material. After consultation with the chiefs he quelled a rash of horse-stealing and house-breaking by shipping several offenders to gaol in Auckland. He extended hospitality to the chiefs when, as was frequent, they visited him from all parts of the district, took them into his confidence, and was continually solicited by them to arbitrate in community disputes.[12]

By the late 1860s the problem of enforcement of law had eased. Largely because the Resident Magistrate worked with Maori Assessors and police, acceptance of their decisions, in petty matters at least, was general. Thus White reported that fines in his district were readily paid and the Maori constables not resisted even if they were obliged to escort a prisoner to gaol outside the district.[13] Between 1863 and 1866 there had been several breaches of the peace among the powerful and independent-minded Ngapuhi for which no arrests had been made, including two offences against Pakeha, one of rape and one of serious assault, which had been officially condoned after the payment of a fine. But in 1866, on two separate occasions, Ngapuhi charged with robbery and released from custody by a *taua* were surrendered again after negotiation with the Assessors. In one of these cases a threat to deny the guilty party a hearing in the Land Court unless they accepted the law in the robbery case, was used to produced submission.[14] Maori wanted for the murder of settlers (other than in the context of war) were surrendered by their kin, as had been usual from the founding of the Colony. The confidence of the people in their Resident Magistrate sometimes helped; the Rarawa for instance surrendered a man who had killed a settler near Kaitaia on condition that W. B. White tried the offence.[15]

With regard to tribal feuding in which Maori were killed, the Government and the settler public began to be more insistent that the law be vindicated. In 1866-7 three separate cases of tribal feud in Northland resulted in at least eight killed and seven wounded, the Maori refusing to surrender any involved in the affrays. In one case a Government Assessor led a *taua* which shot a chief with whom he had had a quarrel over a woman. The officers inquiring disclosed two other previously unreported killings—one of an old man and his son for alleged *makutu,* another of a girl killed by a jealous lover. The Government declined to take an expedition against the parties involved in these cases for fear of provoking wider resistance, but it also declined officially to admit the claim of Tamati Waka Nene 'that the murder is confined to the Maoris and is a matter for them to arrange'.[16]

In mid-1868 a formally arranged battle, arising out of a land dispute result-ed in the shooting of one Nuku, a Ngapuhi, by Te Wake, a Rarawa. The Ngapuhi threatened wider reprisals and the Government, anxious both to avert a major clash and to please their great northern ally at the expense of the smaller Rarawa tribe, pressed the Rarawa to surrender Te Wake. After intensive negotiation by J. C. Richmond, James Mackay (Civil Commissioner, Auckland), and Barstow (Resident Magistrate, Bay of Islands), Te Wake was handed over to the magistrates. He escaped, was recaptured, and tried in the Supreme Court for murder. Chief Justice Arney held the case to be something of a landmark—the first in which the consequences of tribal feud were brought before English law. But the court recognised the truth of Te Wake's plea that he was only a tribesman acting at the behest of a chief. Mohi Tawhai, a Ngapuhi and a Government Assessor, had in fact appointed the day of Nuku's death as a day of fighting, and strictly speaking he should have been on trial as an accessory to the murder. Te Wake was sentenced to death but the sentence was commuted. Shortly afterwards the fleet-footed prisoner again escaped, this time from Mount Eden gaol, and found his way back to his people.[17]

One outcome of the Te Wake incident was a petition to Parliament from the Ngapuhi for more gaols and Maori police and schools to inculcate and enforce the Pakeha order of things. The petitioners wanted all previous killings forgiven and the next aggressor handed over to Pakeha law. This enthusiasm proved not wholehearted—the gaols, for instance, were not established—but it did mark an awareness among the Ngapuhi that tribal warfare was becoming anachronistic.

Over and above their political and judicial work the Resident Magistrates did a good deal to ease the stress of culture contact in New Zealand. James Mackay's work on the Thames goldfield illustrates this. He toiled constantly to negotiate mining rights from the chiefs sufficient to satisfy the miners' demands and arranged terms which brought a considerable revenue to the Maori people of the district. Until all claimants were satisfied he held back miners from land not subject to agreement, expelling defiant diggers who infiltrated Maori territory with a troop of armed Maori police assisted by special levies of local Maori. The Government was of course concerned to avert war with formidable chiefs such as Te Hira of the upper Thames, who threatened to attack if his land was interefered with, but there is also evidence that men like Mackay and some of the Ministers, were genuinely sympathetic towards the Maori and unsympathetic towards the brash mining populace. The ready use of Maori police and auxiliaries, not a Pakeha force, is perhaps an indication of this. Mackay was also instrumental in securing an amendment to mining legislation in 1869 that had threatened to reduce the scale of mining rights payable to the Maori land-owners.[18]

The situation at Thames was always tense. Scufflles between Maori and Pakeha in the town frequently threatened to assume dangerous proportions. In such a situation a man like Mackay was invaluable. On one occasion a Kingite *hapu* alleged that one of their number had been murdered by Pakeha flax-cutters, but they declined to allow Mackay to inspect the body for the wounds they claimed were made. Mackay, having held the flax-cutters on a minor charge, surreptitiously entered the forbidden territory, dug up the body, and, finding no wounds, was able to dispel a mounting crisis. Mackay was cynical about his work and rather contemptuous of the people in his charge.

'I have been very busy,' he wrote to Rolleston, 'working night and day to try to satisfy Messrs. Nigger and Digger, two as troublesome specimens of humanity as ever were brought together.'[19] But the value of his work brought him considerable recognition. When, in 1868, he began to show a preference for private work as a land agent in the towns he was laying out on the goldfields, the Government was constrained to keep him on at the very large salary of £800 a year, plus extra Maori police to help him, and the right to transact private business as well. Mackay was in fact becoming the rival of McLean as a man capable of 'managing' the Maori.

Although Richmond did not want Resident Magistrates to engage in land-purchase operations, they were asked to assist the progress of the Land Court. With the aid of the Assessors they were to distribute copies of the Maori version of the official *Gazette*—the *Kahiti*—which had been commenced in September 1865 to advertise the hearings of the Land Court; they were to see that surveys were ready and that the claimants had trustees for reserves selected; they were to collect Crown Grants when they were issued and give them to the Maori owners on payment of Court fees; they were frequently asked to act as agent for the Crown to support the Crown's claims to land or the claims of individuals who had bought from the Crown. Other Resident Magistrates assumed responsibility for reserves. Alex Mackay, brother of James, was the first to bring the needs of the South Island Maori communities within the regular surveillance of Government. He sought to enlarge existing reserves by using revenue from them to make discreet purchases of Crown land, and he was effective in commencing schools and improving housing.

The main tenor of all this activity was of course paternalistic and tending towards 'amalgamation'. In a grandiose phrase Richmond characterised the Resident Magistrates as 'lay missionaries converting the Maoris to civilization'.[20] But in what was in fact a nakedly imperialist situation the concern of some local officers to secure the Maori a fair share in the new order of things was often notable; they did gain some appreciation of Maori rights and values and protected them to some degree from the impact of general settler attitudes.

In 1867 McLean took a new initiative on Maori representation. The Governor's speech of 9 July, setting out ministerial policy, made no mention of the subject, though it did mention extra representation for the mining population of the West Coast of the South Island. On 28 July, J. E. FitzGerald, probably at McLean's request, sent McLean a draft of a Bill on Maori representation and advised him to show it to Bell, Richmond, and others before introducing it, to allay opposition. He wistfully added:

> I wish I could fight the question under your lead; but I always had a difficulty to contend with which you avoid—They looked on me as a dreamer and a theorist. With the great prestige of your practical acquaintance with the subject I have hopes that you may carry the measure.[21]

It was generally expected that the enfranchisement of Maori voters on the common roll already provided for in the 1852 Constitution Act would proceed as the Land Court individualised Maori titles and so provided them with the necessary property qualifications. But, because this would take time, and the Stafford Government wished to capture Maori support for its pacification program, Stafford accepted as a temporary measure McLean's Bill, which provided for special Maori representatives (who might be Europeans) elected by Maori manhood suffrage.[22] The exact form of the representation—four seats, three in the North Island and one in the South—and its successful passage through the Assembly was determined largely by the fact that it preserved the distribution of seats between the North and South Islands which would otherwise have been unsettled by the grant of increased representation to the West Coast goldfields. On the other hand it was largely because the South Islanders were unhappy at the prospect of three additional Pakeha members in the North that the Government accepted an amendment making it mandatory that the Maori representatives should themselves be Maori.[23]

In this way, an important feature of the New Zealand constitution, remaining to this day, stumbled into being. Despite some grumbling by members who objected to exceptional legislation for Maori at a time when all special provisions were supposed to be ended, and despite a strong plea by Mantell that wider Maori enfranchisement on the common roll would give them more effective representation, the Bill passed the Assembly with little difficulty. Press comment generally approved the measure in principle but waxed sarcastic about the Maori members' likely abilities. It was feared that they would be captive voters for the government of the day, and the principle of granting universal suffrage without the incentive to acquire personal estate was also deplored.[24]

Initially the Native Department treated Maori representation rather as a matter of public relations and goodwill than a serious attempt at democratic representation. Rolleston proposed arrangements to prevent a general poll, which he feared would excite tribal antagonisms and allow the votes of commoners to swamp the influence of the chiefs. He intended rather that a meeting of chiefs in each electorate should agree on a single candidate. 'I would have a good feast and a good talk and I think there would be little doubt of the thing going off well,' he wrote.[25] The Resident Magistrates were instructed to this effect. Many Maori treated the Act with indifference. Most of those in the disturbed districts were in fact unaware of it, while the Northland and Bay of Plenty Maori were angry and disappointed that there were to be only four representatives, because each tribe could not choose its own representative and none had confidence in a representative from another tribe within the same vast electorate. Consequently, on nomination day at the Bay of Islands only a few Ngapuhi attended and F. N. Russell, a mixed-race man connected with Waka Nene, was the only nominee. Paora Tuhaere of Auckland, already disenchanted with the Treaty of Waitangi, promptly stated that the Ngatiwhatua would not recognise Russell 'lest we should be twice put into a false position by that nation the Ngapuhi'.[26]

On the East Coast Campbell organised the Ngatiporou into nominating Mokena Kohere, a man of high traditional rank and an increasingly important leader of Kupapa auxiliaries. But the nomination arrived in Napier too late and at the open poll a desultory crowd showed thirty-four hands for the chief Tareha and thirty-three for Karaitiana.[27] In the Western Maori electorate Mete Kingi Paetahi, a chief among the lower Waikato people was the only nominee. As an Assessor, a civil servant, Mete Kingi was technically disqualified, but the Assembly passed a special act to validate his election and prevent a technical restriction from spoiling the spirit of the new move. In the South Island nomination, held at Kaiapoi, three Kaiapoi men were nominated and Patterson elected by the 8 per cent of voters who bothered to record a vote at the subsequent poll.[28]

In the 1868 session of the House of Representatives settler members discovered somewhat to their surprise, that the Maori members wished to speak in debate and an interpreter was brought belatedly into the chamber. Three of the members were unimpressive but Mete Kingi showed intelligence, judgment and force of character that made an impression. He angrily refuted suggestions that the Maori members could be bought. Indeed when McLean moved a vote of censure on the Government's Maori and defence policies, two Maori members voted with him and the Government was saved only by the Speaker's casting vote. This revealed, to Pakeha members' annoyance, that the Maori members could not be regarded as unimportant, though it was still believed that they were mere pawns, ignorant and easily manipulated by leaders of the parties in the House. Nevertheless a self-effacing motion by F. N. Russell that Maori representatives need no longer be Maori was defeated on the grounds that the experiment had not been fully tried, that it gave an incentive to Maori people to learn English and identify themselves with the general framework of government, and that the exclusion of Pakeha candidates from Maori electorates would prevent the 'carpetbagging' of Maori votes. During the debate both Stafford and Fox (leading the opposition), needing Maori votes, claimed to be in favour of appointing Maori nominees to the Legislative Council and Executive Council. Meanwhile a trickle of Maori voters were placed on the common roll after securing Crown Grants to their land and in Northland and East Coast electorates it became a standard practice for European candidates to enrol them and try to purchase their votes.

A Native Schools Act was the third important measure of Maori policy passed by the 1867 Assembly. Experiments with village day schools, teaching in English, had been made from 1862 and apart from a few South Islanders, jealous of the revenue their Provinces generated being spent in the North, few members in 1867 baulked at voting £4000 a year for seven years to expand the program. A condition of government aid was that the people of a school district organise themselves into a committee, offer land for the school and make an annual contribution to the teacher's salary. This was not merely to minimise government spending but arose largely from concern at the uncertain interest which the Maori at that time showed towards education; it was hoped that the requirement that they contribute would both indicate and capture their genuine interest in the schools. The spirit behind the Act included a fair measure of genuine altruism; many settler politicians and officials, including Resident Magistrates, were ashamed that most Maori children were not given an opportunity for education. But it also derived from both the best and the worst features of the 'amalgamation' philosophy. Its worst aspect was revealed in a characteristic passage in the *Wellington Independent*:

> but scrape a Maori, the most civilised, and the savage shows distinctly underneath. The 'Haka' [war dance] is an *exposé* of the evil which really lies at the root of their present prostrate condition, an exhibition of the substratum of utter immorality, depravity, and obscenity, which forms the ground work of their race; and in spite of the veneering with which we clumsily cover the rough wood, we shall do nothing until we alter their entire character, by taking in hand the education, *per force* of the young growing saplings.[29]

The missions' boarding schools had been intended, by separating the Maori child from the so-called communal squalor of the *pa,* to create a highly trained youth who was then supposed to lead his people into English ways. This policy was believed to have failed. The boarding schools had often proved shoddy, ill-managed, epidemic-ridden institutions, and even when very well-managed, had not proved popular with Maori parents, who disliked the long separation from their children and considered such features of the system as corporal punishment degrading. Moreover, when a boarder returned home, he seemed to resume the mores of his community, not to change them. In 1867 the Government determined to start quietly at the village level, teaching English and using English as the medium of instruction. Meanwhile many of the boarding schools established before 1863 had foundered during the wars or been diverted to the education of settler children. Although they were entitled to limited assistance under the 1867 Act and about seven struggled on, the cessation of liberal government grants prevented the revival and expansion of the system. William Rolleston, Under-Secretary of the Native Department, believed in principle in a secular state system of education, not a sectarian one. His influence behind the 1867 Act had been considerable, and survived the attacks hurled upon him by the church leaders, especially the Catholic Bishop, Pompallier.[30]

The better aspect of the 'amalgamation' philosophy which pervaded the village schools system, was the determination of the Government to prevent it becoming a racially segregated one. Maori villagers in Northland, the Bay of Plenty and lower Waikato, though hard put to find cash for their share of the teachers' salaries, had been quick to offer land for a school and by 1870 thirteen village schools had been established. All were also open to settler

children in their vicinity and with the continued decline in the Maori population and the increase in settlement, such children often formed a significant
minority or eventually a majority in many of the schools. Conversely, although
the education of settler children was a responsibility of the Provinces, the
General Government made some effort to prevent segregated systems from
being founded. Thus A. H. Russell approved the request of the Superintendent
of Taranaki that educational reserves be made in the confiscated lands only
'on the understanding that such reserves were always to be available for both
races'.[31] When Richmond was considering the needs of the scattered South
Island Maori communities, Alex Mackay was instructed that 'the Government
is more desirous of promoting the attendance of Native children at the
ordinary European schools than of establishing Native schools for Maori
children exclusively'.[32] In carrying out this instruction Mackay met with difficulty from local education authorities who objected to Maori children in their
schools 'consequent on their filthy habits and their being afflicted in most
instances with an incurable itch'.[33] Mackay was successful only in establishing
side schools for Maori children financed from General Government funds and
with the voluntary aid of missionaries and teachers working after hours. But
although the General Government had only limited success in having Maori
pupils admitted to Provincial schools, its firm advocacy of the principle of
integrated schooling was to bear invaluable fruit when the Provinces were
abolished and a national system of education replaced the Provincial system
in the late 1870s.

Matters relating to Maori land provided the fourth area of important legislation in 1867-8. Many Maori claimants, stimulated by the direct offers from
settlers and speculators, had begun to resort to the Native Land Court which
was soon adjudicating on customary land at the rate of three-quarters of a
million acres a year. The Judges claimed that their work signalled an end to
an era of violence in Maori society and laid the bases of individual small
holding. With sublime English ethnocentrism, Governor Bowen boasted that
what was being done would be as beneficial for the Maori as he believed the
destruction of clanship and chieftainship to have been for the Scottish High-
landers after the Rebellion of 1745.[34]

But the evidence of this period points more to the social evils than the
social benefits of the operations of the Land Court and direct purchase. Professor Sorrenson has shown how the long drawn-out court sittings, attended by
contending Maori claimants and their families, and frequently adjourned,
disrupted normal life and hastened the spread of epidemic or endemic disease.[35]
At a Court session in Taranaki for example, an observer noted that the proceedings were barely audible for the coughing of most of the 200 assembled
claimants.[36] Fenton chose to hold sittings at central localities and attending
claimants either bled the local *hapu* dry or ran up huge accounts with local
storekeepers. Court sittings were not always well-advertised and Fenton

stuck to the principle that only evidence presented in court would be taken into account. Sometimes Maori villagers actually resident on the land under adjudication might not have heard of the court sitting and on occasion the first intimation they received of it was when settlers appeared to occupy it, having purchased from those the Court found as owners.[37] The claims of lawyers, land agents and surveyors, in addition to the store debts run up during a Court hearing, generally obliged Maori claimants to sell far more of the land to defray expenses than they had reckoned.[38]

The worst consequence of the new system, however, was probably the marked decline in responsibility and trust between members of a kinship group, formerly bound by reciprocal ties. The principles upon which Judges opted for one line or another of conflicting evidence were never very clearly elucidated and the Land Court's Maori Assessors, being bound by Fenton's ruling that only evidence presented in court would be taken into account, were not adequate guarantors of a sound decision. A local Maori jury, provided for by the 1865 Act, was requested only in the Wairarapa and because the necessary regulations had not been issued was even then not summoned.[39] With community scrutiny of Court proceedings so inhibited greater opportunity was given to unscrupulous claimants to acquire and sell as much land as possible by false evidence.

This was also fostered by the 'ten-owner' system. Under the 1865 Act the Court was supposed to subdivide blocks with many owners into smaller portions with no more than ten owners to each. Fenton arbitrarily adopted the practice of awarding whole blocks, unsubdivided, to ten of the principal owners. Moreover they were named as absolute owners, not as trustees. The chiefs naturally welcomed this process and traditional values inhibited rank-and-file kinsmen at this time from pressing themselves forward to be added to the list. Maori communities were also anxious to avoid the expenses of sub-division surveys. They did not then realise that the ten nominated owners would soon be drawn into mortgaging or selling the patrimony of their *hapu* who were without legal means of redress. Sometimes the chiefs were downright extravagant, living in flashy imitation of the settler gentry; some wanted cash to provide traditional feasting and hospitality for the large and frequent political meetings which developed through the nineteenth century; others stocked up sheep and cattle runs. Karaitiana Takamoana exemplified the desire to share in urban sophistication by having contractors build a large house outside Napier—the so-called 'Maori Club'—with sleeping accommodation and reception rooms for Maori and settler visitors and by hiring a Pakeha married couple to run it.[40] This scale of expenditure made the chiefs easy prey for speculators who went into collusion with them or deliberately entangled them in debt in order to shame them, under threat of court proceedings, into selling huge areas of land.

The major public figures in Hawke's Bay did little about this. J. D. Ormond boasted to McLean of the ease with which he could get reserves alienated because of their owners' need for ready cash.[41] McLean did not interfere and Fenton, making a bid for his friendship, wrote: 'They say you are an enemy of the act. All I can say is that I wish I had a few more such enemies to deal with as Superintendents.'[42] However, some of the local Native Department officers, particularly G. S. Cooper, Resident Magistrate at Waipukurau, and Rolleston, the Under-Secretary, pointed to the need for reform and persuaded Richmond to introduce amending legislation.

The Native Lands Act Amendment Act, 1866, made it incumbent upon the Judges (when it had been optional before) to take note of the needs of Maori claimants of land for their present and future use and, if necessary, to recommend restrictions on the alienation of blocks awarded to them. It further declared that Maori reserves could only be alienated by lease of up to twenty-one years except with the consent of the Governor-in-Council and empowered the Government to suspend the operation of a Land Court in cases where the pressing of a disputed claim threatened to disturb the peace of the district. But as the Judges still placed very few blocks under restriction, section 17 of the Native Land Act, 1867, went much further. It required the Court to determine all the owners of a block brought before it, whether or not they put in a claim and, while it could still enter only ten names on the Certificate of Title, to enter all the owners on the Court records. As in the case of reserves, the ten nominated owners could not alienate the land save by lease of twenty-one years, except with the consent of the Governor-in-Council. The office of Inspector of Surveys was also established to bring some order into the chaos of unco-ordinated and amateurish surveying of land, which was giving rise to a host of boundary disputes. In addition, whereas in 1866 he had had no objection to Maori adults selling the interests of minors,[43] in 1867 Richmond secured the passage of the Maori Real Estate Management Act, which provided that the interests of Maori minors should be vested in trustees, either adult Maori or Europeans involved in Maori administration, and that the trustees could not alienate, other than by twenty-one year lease, without the consent of the Governor-in-Council.

These restrictions were highly unpopular with considerable sections of the settler community, and Richmond and his colleagues were charged with over-protecting the Maori. The usual maxim of 'one law for both races' was produced and pseudo-humanitarians argued that the preservation of reserves was perpetuating communism and slothfulness and that the sooner the Maori dispensed with their land entirely in order to necessitate their working for a living the better.[44] Richmond stuck to his policy with some vigour. He had discovered, in office, that a literal application of the dogma of 'equal laws for both races' would bear very cruelly on the Maori and defended his 1866 and 1867 amendments as 'a sort of cushion upon which the Native race might be let down more gently into perfect self-reliance'.[45] John Hall, a prominent Canterbury politician, in reply to a complaint that difficulties were being placed in the way of 'capitalists' seeking to buy Maori land, noted that too much was being said about the Maori being British subjects and having the right to sell land as they liked; they had not, he said, become accustomed to the responsibility of individual property rights, were imprudent, and needed restraint.[46] The Native Office took the unusual step of issuing a press statement regretting the lack of good relations between it and the public and explaining the purpose of the 1866 Amendment Act: 'It is not meant to restrict permanently the alienation of any native land, but only to retard the alienation of some small portion till the Maori race have taken their ultimate position in the colony, and can be relied on to provide for themselves as the European does.'[47] Requests for the removal of restrictions imposed against Maori land by the Acts of 1866-7 were normally handled by the Native Office and Rolleston proved a firm watchdog for the Maori owners. A precedent was set by an early decision to decline the alienation of sections in the Pipitea and Te Aro *pa* in Wellington, despite the continued hostility of the settlers to the Maori communities in their midst. In this and most subsequent cases Richmond accepted Rolleston's advice.[48]

Nevertheless the security of reserves and restricted lands was still most uncertain. The Provincial Compulsory Land Taking Act 1866 relating to the taking of land for public works, while still not applied to Maori customary land, was applied to Maori lands which had passed the Land Court, including reserves. The Stafford Government had come into office dependent upon support from Otago members, secured by promises to give the Otago Provincial Council a grant for the Princes Street reserve. In 1867 it was disclosed that the Princes Street reserve had in fact been alienated to the Council. When one of the Maori owners petitioned the General Assembly, Stafford informed the Petitions Committee that he had 'inadvertently' passed up to Grey (the then Governor) a Crown Grant making over the land to Otago, and Grey claimed to have 'inadvertently' signed it with others in the bundle![49] Such was the dismal absence of probity of the nation's leaders. From his lonely position as Commissioner of Audit, J. E. FitzGerald performed a late act of service to the Maori by blocking the transfer of accumulated back rents for the reserve to Otago, and toyed with the idea of having Grey prosecuted for the misuse of property of which he was trustee.[50]

A further illustration was provided by the use of Maori reserves in Wellington, taken over by Grey in his first governorship for the principal public hospitals, school and military depot in the town. In 1868 Rolleston drew Richmond's attention to these reserves, arguing that their alienation was in contravention of engagements, expressed or implied, with the local *hapu,* and a constant source of grievance which poisoned Maori-Pakeha relations well beyond Wellington itself. Richmond adopted Rolleston's minute entirely and enlarged upon it in an impassioned draft memorandum to the Cabinet calling for the payment of compensation 'for the sake of justice and our national honour'.[51] But no compensation was paid. Richmond wrote of Maori reserves that:

> At present they are almost absolutely in the hands of the Executive, who are subject to heavy pressure on political grounds from friends and foes . . . The public morality is not delicate on such points, and a trust property which stands at all in the way of a public improvement or a public desire would be summarily dealt with by the public if they had the chance.[52]

Whether the restrictions on alienation which Richmond had secured in his 1866 and 1867 Lands Acts were maintained, depended upon the doubtful integrity of the government of the day.

Reform in Maori land law was also frustrated to a considerable extent by the wilfulness and self-aggrandisement of Chief Judge Fenton. There was truth in Fenton's contention that the prestige and acceptability of the Court depended upon its being entirely independent of governments. But Fenton extended this to independence from parliament also, to the extent of deliberately trying to frustrate legislation. He not only objected to the power accorded to the Government by the 1866 Act to postpone Court sittings if they threatened the peace of a district; he objected to the whole attempt by Richmond in 1866 and 1867 to place legislative restrictions on alienation. While admitting that the location of Maori owners on individual farms was not taking place as expected and that intemperate land-selling prevailed, he submitted officially that:

> it is not part of our job to stop eminently good processes because certain bad and unpreventable results may collaterally flow from them, nor can it be averred that it is the duty of the Legislature to make people careful of their property by Act of Parliament, so long as their profligacy injures no one but themselves.[53]

As for section 17 of the 1867 Act, requiring all owners to be listed on the Court records, Fenton claimed that he had a 'discretion' whether or not to apply it and continued to issue Certificates of Title to ten owners as if they were the only claimants. He made no effort to explain section 17 to Maori applicants and as late as 1871 Hawke's Bay *hapu* did not even know of its existence.[54] In Parliament Richmond reported that 'the Government, finding themselves foiled by the unwillingness of Mr Fenton to cooperate with them, had sent hurriedly round to discover cases where the 17th Section had been overleaped by the Court and to obtain declarations of trust on the part of those Natives who had received grants for their tribes'.[55] Fenton himself later claimed that when he perceived that the ten nominated owners were alienating the patrimony of their *hapu,* he urged upon the Government the necessity of getting trust deeds executed.[56] This was a barefaced lie. He had known of the excessive alienations in 1867 and opposed the introduction of restrictions; he continued to foster the ten-owner system, publicly expounding the view that the principal men of each *hapu* should be established in property and allowed to live as gentry, while the remainder were compelled to labour for a living; and in 1880 he was still resisting the argument that the ten owners should be regarded as trustees, stating: 'The whole theory of the Native Lands Act, when the Court was created in 1862, was the putting to an end to Maori communal ownership. To recognise the kind of agency contended for would be to build up communal ownership, and would tend to perpetuate the evil instead of removing it.'[57] A fair assessment of Fenton's complex and contra- dictory behaviour was given by a colleague: 'That man's life is one constant scheme [;] what might once have been Utopian enthusiasm has turned into scheming for self-advancement & specious toadying.'[58] Richmond, Mackay and other officials still thought that the Court should be only a board or commission, its sitting and even its decisions subject to review by the executive if they threatened to provoke a breach of the peace, but a majority of settlers were either unaware of Fenton's high-handed behaviour or found it served their interests, and were inclined to support his view of the Land Court.

In comparison with that of many of his contemporaries Richmond's record with regard to certain aspects of the Maori land question was a creditable one, but it was by no means uniformly in favour of Maori interests. In contrast to his protective measures he had, in the 1867 Land Act, made it easier for surveyors and speculators to secure mortgages over Maori lands; in response to the claims of the Canterbury Maori (the Ngaitahu) to enlarged reserves he approved their being extended from a pitiful 10 acres per head to an equally pitiful 14 acres per head and closed off further consideration of the question by an act of the Assembly;[59] and unless a grievance was constantly and forcefully brought before him by a zealous and determined local official, or by Maori petitioners, it escaped remedy. In summary, Richmond shared the settler determination to acquire and hold the great bulk of the Maori lands, but tempered it by a paternalistic concern to preserve to them their last acres and remedy some of the most glaring frauds and injustices, so long as it was not politically disadvantageous to do so.

By 1868 the main lines of policy and the main framework of institutions which were to dominate Maori administration and affect race relations for the next hundred years had been laid down by settler politicians. It had been a con- fused process when, as Bowen wrote, 'almost every leading member of both Houses has a Native Policy of his own, and is swayed by various kinds of personal and local feelings and interests'.[60] The most formative years were 1865-7, when J. C. Richmond, as a member of both the Weld and Stafford Ministries, McLean and Rolleston, the Native Department Under-Secretary, had co-operated. The fundamental settler demand that the Maori people had to be brought into submission and the bulk of their lands opened to coloni- sation appeared to have been attained despite continued centres of resistance. And although the rule of British law had not been fully attained even among Kupapa tribes the balance of power seemed now to be so decidedly in favour of the settlers that they were willing to approach complete dominion more slowly.

Certain alternatives had been rejected. The denial of Tamihana's requests for recognition of the King movement, the defeat of FitzGerald's Native Pro-

vinces Bill of 1865 and the winding up of the Runanga system had ruled out
the possible development of a semi-autonomous native protectorate or a
separate native administration such as developed in Fiji. Nor were native
tribunals to be used to determine land titles as they subsequently were in
Tahiti under the French or the Gilbert Islands under the British. On the
contrary, effect had been given to policies aiming at racial 'amalgamation':
the Maori had been granted theoretical legal equality with the settlers by
act of parliament; the era of missionary domination of education had been
ended and Maori children were being taught English in state schools; there
were four Maori representatives in the House of Representatives; the Polynesian
system of land-holding was supposedly being reduced by English judges to an
individual English-style tenure; the Maori were generally subject to English
common law, administered by settler magistrates and judges.

Having achieved the substance of their goals, settler legislators were willing
to make some concessions to special Maori needs in order to permit a more
gradual, though more certain, adaptation to the new order. Hence the legislation of 1866-7 to curb the total despoliation of Maori land, protect Maori
reserves, and continue the circuit court and Assessor system. The Juries Act
of 1868 provided that Maori accused could be tried before a Maori jury if
they requested it. Variations in the conservation laws affecting native birds
and fish and special Acts affecting sections of the tidal foreshores (otherwise
the property of the Crown by common law) enabled a few traditional hunting
and fishing rights to be preserved. These deviations from 'one law for both
races' rouse criticism from the selfish and doctrinaire. Some politicians grumbled at the excessive number of special Maori acts in 1867 and the *Daily
Southern Cross* editor, criticising expenditure on Maori Assessors, wrote:
'we had rather see £50,000 a year spent in making them like ourselves, than
£20,000 spent in keeping them apart.'[61] But the doctrinaire sometimes changed
their views on closer contact with Maori administration. Thus A. H. Russell
proved the forerunner of several who came into office expecting to abolish all
special laws and administrative provisions for the Maori but, as Native
Minister, defending their retention. These men were considerably influenced
by officials, such as Rolleston, who had permanent and detailed contact with
Maori affairs and better appreciated Maori needs.

Because they had supposedly provided both the benefits of full equality
with the Pakeha and additional privileges and protective measures as well, it
became axiomatic for New Zealand politicians from the late 1860s to boast of
how magnanimously they had treated the Maori and how wonderfully well
they had provided for them. One considered that 'it would be admitted by
impartial observers outside the Colony, that there had never been any action
on the part of the colonists which was intended to injuriously affect the
Native Race. On the contrary, the whole course of the legislation of the Colony
had been devoted from its very commencement to the preservation of the
race, and to inducing them to embrace the arts and habits of civilization'.

Idealists wrote of 'opening to the Maori people such a prospect of renewed social and political life as shall outbid Pai Marirism'.[62] Officials boasted that they had ended Polynesian violence and war, and introduced the Maori people to unprecedented material prosperity. This was the genesis of a national legend and in the 1870s Vogel and Grey were to base a claim for New Zealand to annex the central Pacific islands on the colonists' supposedly excellent record in Maori administration.

In fact, as in the pre-war period, neither the proposed recognitions of special Maori needs nor the inclusion of the Maori in the privileges of the settler order were properly carried through. For example, such special provisions as the clauses of the 1868 Juries Act providing for Maori juries were again not followed up by the necessary regulations to give them effect, and an order of the Legislative Council for sessional paper and Bills affecting the Maori to be translated into the Maori language was almost entirely neglected. Conversely, where real 'amalgamation' implied the appointment of Maori local officials capable of independent contributions to policy and administration, they were restricted to the rank of Assessor; where real 'amalgamation' implied giving Maori owners a substantial voice in the administration of reserves which they had vested in the Crown or made over to the churches as education trusts these were entirely under the control of Pakeha trustees; where real 'amalgamation' implied that Maori leaders be given a responsible role in the determination of land titles, they were reduced to the position of litigants or, at best, Land Court Assessors. The concept of 'equal rights' was strangely distorted in practice. Thus when all payments of claims for war damages, to which 'loyal' Maori as well as settlers were entitled, had ceased, it was found that all but £1957 of £55,765 awarded to Europeans had been paid; not only had many of the Maori claims not been heard, but they had received only £927 of the £2412 awarded them.[63] When the Military Pensions Act of 1866 to provide gratuities for soldiers wounded in the war and widows or children of those killed was passing the Assembly, it was, at McLean's suggestion made applicable also to wounded Kupapa or their dependants. But the *rates* of pension for Maori chiefs, although they often bore officers' rank and did much more effective work than most Pakeha officers, were equal only to those for Pakeha NCOs and privates, and the rate for Maori rank and file considerably lower still.[64] The prevailing notion of the inferiority of native peoples was clearly still undermining the 'amalgamation' policy. The dominant tone was patronising, as in Governor Bowen's complacent approval of efforts being made to preserve the 'surviving remnant of a most interesting race'. The Maori people were being treated rather as museum pieces to be preserved for the greater renown of their custodians rather than as intelligent and resourceful people capable of constructive contribution to their own and the general community's well-being.

Unfortunate results also flowed from the limited view prevailing in the nineteenth century, of the functions of the state. By 1868, largely owing to the efforts of a Dr Cusack who treated a measles epidemic in the Nelson district and had his conclusions published in the *New Zealand Gazette,* the notion that the Maori were an inherently weaker species of mankind, doomed inexorably to barrenness and extinction, was officially—though not popularly—discarded. It was recognised that the very high Maori death rate, especially the infant mortality rate, could be checked by good diet and medical care.[65] But though the Government still subsidised a number of resident Native Medical Officers and almost invariably sent doctors to provide food and 'medical comforts' to areas affected by epidemic, officials assumed that they could do no more than coax and admonish the local Maori with regard to needful reforms in diet, clothing, hygiene and housing though without much hope. Thus Barstow, Resident Magistrate in the Bay of Islands, lamented: 'It may be that when but a few, a handful, of survivors remain, our control over them shall be so direct and absolute, that we may be able to enforce sanitary and dietary regulations, and as it were compel them to exist in spite of themselves.'[66]

With regard to their much desired goal of producing individual Maori small farmers nineteenth century governments had little appreciation of the need for sustained and detailed guidance by men sympathetic both to the values of the old society and to the economic needs of the new. In rare cases where sub-division surveys were made for a Maori community, as at Kaiapoi in the South Island and Putiki near Wanganui, officials were discouraged by the owners' tendency to disrupt or ignore the arrangement soon after they had left. Generally the owners were expected to arrange and pay for surveys, pass the land through the Court and make a most complicated social adjustment virtually unaided. Consequently titles were rarely individualised even on paper. When the owners of the Arowhenua reserve in Canterbury attempted individualisation they were so discouraged by the heavy bills for surveys and Crown Grants that early enthusiasm gave way to bitterness and the remaining South Island communities were discouraged from following the example of Arowhenua.[67]

Nor, despite its valuable efforts to prevent segregation in the state school system, was Government very active in combating the fervid racialism which denied Maori people opportunities which they sought in the private sector. In a Waikato hearing of the Land Court, for example, a settler objected to a Maori 'lawyer' (actually an agent) appearing on his behalf, allegedly because 'the spirit of an Englishman could not brook the degradation of being represented in Her Majesty's Court by a Maori'. The newspaper report added, 'the time may yet come when an Englishman will receive legal assistance from a Maori; but thank Goodness, it won't be in this generation'.[68]

Urban settler communities in particular were increasingly inhospitable to the Maori, who were often denied public facilities or insulted when they used them. By the end of the 1860s Maori who had hitherto dwelt, contentedly enough, on urban reserves, had largely left them. The New Plymouth people left their *pa* in the town in 1860 and did not return. The Greymouth people in 1869 asked Alex Mackay to set apart a block of land for them in the Arahura valley and moved in a body from the town that had grown about their old village. Wellington Maori increasingly left for the Hutt Valley and Porirua, though Te Aro *pa* in the city continued to be occupied by a remnant until the 1890s.

In general Maori people felt that government and law were not helping them to overcome their problems but catching them in further toils. Thus Te Rangikaheke, in an address to the Duke of Edinburgh in 1867, spoke of their sense of loss and bewilderment under the flowing tide of settler government; Te Wheoro petitioned Bowen about his frustration at not being able to live on terms of equality under the law with the Pakeha 'because these things have not yet been carried out'; and the first speech by a Maori representative in the General Assembly, that of Tareha Te Moananui of Hawke's Bay, was a criticism of the Native Land Court and a confused objection that the chief's wandering cattle were impounded by Pakeha law, but that when he impounded settlers' cattle trespassing on his land he was taken to court.[69]

The social and economic conditions of Maori people varied enormously, even within a single district. The lower Thames *hapu* drew about £2000 a year in miners' rights and a similar sum in rents, but possibly as much as 50 per cent of this went to the chief Taipari who employed European surveyors to lay out a town on his land and built a large English-style house overlooking it. At Kaipara the principal chiefs received £5000 a year from timber and *kauri* gum royalties. At the Bay of Islands, M. P. Kawiti heralded an exciting bicultural life-style that could, had it been enabled to flourish and develop, have been the glory of New Zealand; his house was multi-roomed but had carved barge-boards and woven patterned lining in the Maori style; at his formal gatherings guests, Pakeha and Maori, were announced by a doorman and turned away if their standard of dress was wanting; the food combined traditional and European dishes; the entertainments included European dances and Maori *haka* and top-spinning competitions; there was no drunkenness.[70] Lower-ranking kinsmen shared to some extent in their chiefs' provision of feasts and gifts, as in the traditional system. Up to 1000 at one time were employed in the defence forces at four shillings a day, the same rate of pay as the settler Armed Constabulary,[71] and more took advantage of the road contracts offered by both Provincial and General Governments in 1868.

But these things favoured only some districts and only some Maori within those districts. In areas most affected by war and confiscation, 'loyal' and 'rebel' Maori alike cultivated mainly for subsistence and at times still depended upon Government doles. In other areas land sales were beginning to produce, after a flush of wealth, indebtedness and confinement to shrinking reserves, only partly used owing to the confusion of the non-traditional form of multiple ownership introduced by the Land Court, and constantly subject to trespass from settlers' cattle. The South Island Maori formed a prototype of what was to be the fate of many in the North Island. Most dwelt on reserves that were far too small for economic farming even if the problem of multiple ownership had been overcome, the soil in some cases already exhausted by repeated subsistence cropping, the forest behind the reserves where the people had hunted increasingly restricted by settlement and the swamps which had been sources of eels increasingly drained. In 1864, at the height of the liquor craze in the South Island H. T. Clarke had found the Canterbury Maori, far from exemplifying the benefits of European rule, to be 'squalid, miserable and lifeless' and subject to a very heavy mortality rate.[72] By 1868 most of the South Island communities had thrown off drink, almost entirely. But depressed and resentful at the immensity of the social dislocation they had experienced, they only toyed with economic enterprises and lived a hand-to-mouth existence, compounded of a little subsistence cropping, a little return from reserves let to settlers and a little wages from seasonal work such as shearing. They dwelt in wooden cottages, usually said to be an improvement on stuffy *raupo whare*, but in fact cold and draughty 'coffins above ground'.[73]

Generally oblivious to the part they had played in this process, settlers held the Maori in increasing contempt, railing at them for being lazy, sulky and dishonest. Those who did appreciate the shock produced by colonisation advocated little more in the way of practical assistance than the provision of elementary education, hoping that some few enterprising Maori would, of their own initiative, make the adjustment to confident participation in the new individual order, and that the rest of Maoridom would follow their example.[74]

Amidst the confusion and bleakness of the Maori situation under British dominion and British law there were however, some important ameliorating factors. The rule of British law in general involved a respect for individual life probably greater than old Maori society had known, and few Maori seemed to regret the passing of infanticide, the casual killing of secondary wives by chiefs displeased with them, or the repeated obligation to engage in blood feud often precipitated by their own 'wild men'. Moreover, statements of principle about the equality of Maori and Pakeha were not quite worthless. The evidence in fact suggests that they contributed materially to the fact that the Maori were not to be butchered as were Australian Aborigines or American plains Indians. Thus, a few weeks after FitzGerald's Native Rights Act had been passed and his Peace Proclamation made, a surveyor in Taranaki who allegedly shot at a Maori was arrested by an official who stated: 'The Maories are British subjects and we are no longer at war with them. Any person killing another except in self-defence is liable to be hanged.'[75] Arrests for similar offences occurred in Taranaki in 1868 and 1869.[76] Such actions kept alive the concept that the war was for the enforcement of law against specific rebels, not a war against the Maori race. The survival of the Native Department also meant that the enforcement of law at the local level was in the hands of Resident Magistrates who, though often limited in vision, were nevertheless a good distance ahead of the rabid anti-Maorism of many settlers, and were formally associated with the Maori leaders who were Assessors and police.

It remained to be seen how far the Maori could feel confident enough in their own abilities, and in Pakeha protestations of racial equality, to find their feet in the new order of things and make increasing accord with it, or how far conservative values and Pakeha mismanagement would impel them to increasing antagonism and separation from the main stream of New Zealand life.

XV

McLean Resumes Power

The formative legislation of 1867 had been passed during a period of comparative peace. However, Government assertions that the wars were nearly over involved turning a blind eye to the movement of armed Hauhau *Tekau-ma-rua* in Hawke's Bay and the Bay of Plenty and sporadic fighting in the latter. In 1868, moreover, the Government's land confiscations provoked renewed full-scale hostilities.

On both East and West Coasts confiscation extended to areas claimed by Maori who were not at all or but little implicated in the rebellion; awards of the Compensation Court to loyal and ex-rebel Maori were frequently not followed up by survey and location on the ground; and in each area a hard core of rebels refused to accept the confiscations, interrupted surveys and stole stock from the farms of military settlers. A feature of the administration in each of the confiscated areas was the corrupt, overbearing and incompetent behaviour of the occupying military authorities. Militia officers, finding themselves in situations of unaccustomed power, frequently abused their authority, spending more energy in illegal trading in commissariat stores than in seeing to the good order of their districts. In some districts, drunkenness and ill-discipline were prevalent among officers as well as men.[1]

On the West Coast Parris continued his tussle for control of Maori policy with the military, with the Provincial authorities and with Fenton and the Land Court. Despite Rolleston's belief that it should be ended lest the injustice that it occasioned should provoke renewed hostilities, the conflict of authority was not resolved.[2]

In early 1868 Parris approved the extension of military settlers further into confiscated territory in south Taranaki. Ngatiruanui warriors responded by stealing settlers' horses and, in April, by driving off two settlers who cut timber on a Maori reserve. Richmond utterly failed to appreciate the cause of increasing tension and ordered James Booth, Resident Magistrate at Patea, to investigate an alleged Maori liquor still which he believed might be responsible for the Maori's 'recently altered demeanour'.[3]

Now the division of authority had its worst effect. Parris, as Civil Commissioner, was nominally responsible under the Minister, for Maori affairs in the whole Taranaki district but since his denunciation of Colonel McDonnell for the Pokaikai affair, was reluctant to involve himself in south Taranaki where McDonnell was still military commander.[4] Booth and McDonnell gained Richmond's direct approval to recover stolen horses from Maori *pa;* McDonnell, proceeding quietly, recovered some of the horses and was successfully negotiating with Ngatiruanui chiefs for the recovery of the remainder, but Booth, apparently anxious to assert himself, did not wait for the result of McDonnell's negotiations. Without consulting McDonnell he took a detachment of troops to a village which he believed to harbour horse thieves and arrested three men, two of whom proved to be innocent parties. Regarding this as extreme provocation the Ngatiruanui began killing out-settlers.[5] Despite Richmond's efforts to brush the affair off as one of individual crime, in six months most of the West Coast Maori, seeking to recover their lands, were in arms. Their leader was Titokowaru, a warrior-prophet who revived cannibalism with the bodies of militiamen, and preached the deliverance of the Maori from the Pakeha yoke.[6]

On the East Coast Richmond wanted land to plant colonies of military settlers or of Ngatiporou and Ngatikahungunu auxiliaries among the Hauhau as he had recently planted a colony of Arawa among the Whakatohea at Ohiwa in eastern Bay of Plenty. Stafford and McLean were by now sceptical of the effect of confiscation but agreed to demand a cession of land from the Wairoa and Poverty Bay Maori, which amounted to much the same thing. At Wairoa, northern Hawke's Bay, in discussing the cession, Richmond took occasion to lecture the people about avoiding drink, sending their children to school and farming their land. Kopu Pitiera, an able though aging Assessor, who had long supported the Government in northern Hawke's Bay, replied that they understood all about that but wanted the Government to stop hunting the *Pai Marire* on the East Coast and cease pressing for land. He also referred to greedy Europeans who tempted the Maori to lease land before it had passed through the Native Land Court. 'I have withstood these things, but have received no assistance in doing so from the Government from whom the prohibition emanated.' The Anglican deacon Tamihana Te Huata, supported Kopu, arguing that as Ngatikahungunu Kupapa who had fought their Hauhau relatives were prepared to forgive them, the Government had no cause to interfere further. An angry Richmond said that the land had to be taken, and despite a plea from Te Huata to prove him wrong, not just contradict him, over-bore the Kupapa chiefs. At the end of the meeting Kopu died of pleurisy. The officials gave him military honours and acted as his pall-bearers, then took 71,000 acres of land including land in which the Kupapa had interests.[7]

At Poverty Bay Biggs, the local military commander and Resident Magistrate, was a zealot for confiscation and pressed demands which even the local squatters considered 'too unyielding'.[8] While Biggs haggled (and the local tribes petitioned parliament that government officers never visited them except 'for the purpose of teazing us into handing over our land to them without any recompense')[9] it was deemed expedient by Biggs and McLean to keep in exile some of the Poverty Bay people who had been deported to the Chatham Islands during the campaigns of 1865 and 1866, lest they return to stiffen resistance to the cession.[10] In the Chathams, Te Kooti Rikirangi, deported without trial in 1866 for allegedly supporting the Hauhaus, fostered a new religious cult and talked about exacting vengeance on the *momo kino*—the bad breed—of settlers and Kupapa Maori. In July 1868 he organised a mass escape in a government vessel and shortly afterwards attacked Poverty Bay, killing sixty Maori and thirty-four settlers, Biggs and his family among them.

The dual onslaught of Titokowaru and Te Kooti threatened to engulf the island in full-scale war again. The settlers particularly feared Te Kooti's proposed junction with the King movement, especially as circulars had recently emanated from Tokangamutu, Tawhiao's principal village, to all the '*pooti*' (posts) in 'the land of Canaan', suggesting that a '*waea*' (telegram) from the Lord had appointed October as the month in which the island would 'arise'.[11] Settler bitterness and ruthlessness in turn reached new depths; Richmond himself, furious at the ruin of his peace policy, permitted Kupapa troops to kill prisoners after the capture of rebel *pa*.[12]

Nevertheless the Government, now practically bereft of the aid of Imperial troops, was desperately concerned to localise the new risings as far as it could, and the military commanders were ordered to confine their operations strictly to the *hapu* and territory of the leading 'rebels'. Even Parris was supported by Richmond when he opposed Colonel Whitmore's proposal to take an expedition against Titokowaru through the remaining territory of Wiremu Kingi and the Atiawa, peaceful since 1864.[13] By early 1869 the Government commanders had won important victories on both coasts. In south Taranaki the pacificism of Te Whiti emanating from Parihaka, weakened Titokowaru's influence. And whatever King Tawhiao's obscure symbolism meant it apparently did not mean violence; although the missionary Whiteley and some other settlers were killed at White Cliffs in February 1869, this was known to have been the work of a Ngatimaniapoto *taua* which had escaped the efforts of the anxious Kingite leaders to restrain them.[14]

Richmond had indeed strengthened contacts with the King movement. A request by Kupapa chiefs to erect a counter-*aukati*, to debar movement from the King Country to government territory, was declined.[15] In April 1869, through the mediation of Te Wheoro and the Anglican deacon, Heta Terawhiti (a kinsman of Manuhiri), Richmond proposed a meeting with Governor Bowen and a treaty of peace. The basis of this was to be 'the return of the unsold or alienated lands in Waikato, the establishment of regulations as to trade and intercourse similar to those in the Indian Territory in America, and the subsidising of the Tokangamutu Government. On their side the chiefs to withdraw the *aukati* and openly and public[ly] disavow and excommunicate the murderous tribes of Hauhau, to allow needful roads and royal rights over the territory etc., etc.'[16] Rewi Maniapoto showed some interest but the Waikato chiefs were reluctant to accept anything short of full recognition of

Tawhiao's Kingship over the interior districts and the return of all Waikato lands as far as Mangatawhiri creek. These things Richmond would not concede though Stafford was apparently inclined to weaken, especially as there was some pressure from England, believed to have been prompted by Sir William Martin, to restore confiscated land more generously.

In a characteristic memorandum to his Cabinet colleagues Richmond argued against concession:

> We ought not to be too yielding. I have been meditating the return of confiscated land question and cannot see my way in it, whilst I do see immense advantages in holding to the land as the one great means of inducing immigration now or shortly hereafter. Of course much must depend on success against [Te Kooti in] the Urewera . . . Population is our main want . . . I hope you will take my view on this, and if success attends Whitmore, harden your hearts a little to Sir W. Martin and Tawhiao. It is for their good.[17]

This is the Richmond that one New Zealand historian has characterised as the 'gentle philosopher'.[18]

Meanwhile the Stafford Government was enjoying only a precarious tenure of office. In difficulty over the economic crisis and the mounting struggles between provincialists and centralists, it was hit hard by the dual rising of Titokowaru and Te Kooti. McLean helped it survive one vote of no confidence then fled the sinking ship to join the opposition group that Fox had organised in August 1868. The partnership of Richmond and McLean, which had had so much influence in Maori affairs in 1867, was severed. Although McLean was thought to be indispensable on the East Coast and retained the office of General Government Agent in that district, relations between him and the Government were very strained. Richmond himself went to the East Coast to superintend measures against Te Kooti. He became alarmed at McLean's influence on the East Coast and at the system of patronage he had built up whereby many old friends and subordinates from the days of the Land Purchase Department had found public office and formed the habit of communicating with McLean in Napier rather than the Native Office in Wellington. Richmond dismissed two of McLean's protegés, Deighton of Wairoa (who had already proved incompetent in the Te Kooti crisis) and Campbell at the East Cape. Deighton was replaced by W. S. Atkinson, a member of the Richmond-Atkinson family alliance. Campbell, however, appealed directly to Stafford and was temporarily reinstated in order to retain his considerable influence in the East Cape area which Te Kooti was then menacing.[19]

In early 1869 the final break came. McLean asked for semi-independent authority as Commissioner for three years to direct the defence of the East Coast, with a steamer and some £56,000 to spend on militia, Maori contingents and public works. Such a concentration of power the Stafford Government rightly suspected to be for the aggrandisement of Donald McLean as much as for the good of the East Coast settlers, and a dangerous infringement of responsible government. They offered to give him the money and command if he joined the Cabinet as a fully responsible Minister but McLean did not respond. In February 1869 the Government sought to move some Ngatiporou troops from the East to the West Coast; McLean, pleading greater danger in the East, held them at Napier in open defiance of the Government; he was therefore dismissed as General Government Agent and his place taken by a Stafford supporter.[20]

The Assembly met in June 1869 with Te Kooti still active and about to effect his junction with the King movement. Richmond advocated the planting of military forces at Ruatahuna and Taupo to command the centre of the island, and Government estimates included a substantial increase for the 'conquest of a permanent peace'. But the prospect of expensive campaigns was alarming, particularly to the South Island members, and since few had much confidence in it any longer Stafford's Government quickly fell. McLean came into office in Fox's cabinet to assume an almost unbroken seven-year control of Maori affairs.

Circumstances were very favourable in 1869 for the cessation of hostilities. Te Kooti's junction with the King movement in August caused a flurry of agitation in the Waikato, upon which the Government enlarged in a vain effort to prevent the departure of the last regiment of British troops but the crisis quickly passed.[21] Of the Kingite leaders only Rewi, humiliated by Te Kooti's bitter oration on the battle of Orakau where East Coast *hapu* had suffered heavy losses while the Ngatimaniapoto rested in their fastnesses, was inclined to respond to a call to arms.[22] Te Heuheu Horonuku and some of his Taupo people supported Te Kooti but he antagonised the upper Wanganui chiefs and Topia Turoa joined the pursuit as the guerilla leader withdrew to shelter in the Urewera.

Despite Te Kooti's declaration that if left in peace he would attack no more settlers, and despite the urging of Kupapa chiefs and some influential settlers that this should be accepted, Fox considered: 'I had rather the war went on for ten years than that we should come to any terms with Te Kooti other than hanging . . . it would be as weak and unstatesmanlike to think of any compromise with the cold-blooded murderer of Wilson and Biggs and their poor wives and infants.'[23] Native Contingents, drawn from Ngatiporou, Arawa and Wanganui *hapu* and led by European officers, scoured the Urewera. Batches of Te Kooti's and Titikowaru's captured followers were tried, not for murder, but for high treason under the Summary Trials in Disturbed Districts Act, 1869. This measure was based on the principle that the full force of their position as British subjects must be impressed upon the Maori and that the time had passed when their unfamiliarity with the law and its obligations could be pleaded in their favour.

Newspaper reports welcomed the trials as a new era in the history of the Colony, extending over the Maori in fact as well as theory the sovereignty of the Queen.[24] About a hundred of the prisoners were sentenced to death—

the first batch to hanging, drawing and quartering, the only penalty applicable according to the then state of the law of treason, before it was hastily amended. However, all but two of the sentences were commuted and the prisoners shipped off to varying terms of imprisonment in Dunedin. The only other Maori executed for events during the wars was Kereopa, Volkner's killer, who was captured in 1871.

These proceedings considerably hindered peacemaking. Even the Kupapa viewed them not so much as just retribution but as vindictive anti-Maorism. The Arawa resented the execution of Kereopa because the Hauhau leader was of the Ngatirangiwewehi branch of that confederation; the Hawke's Bay Kupapa also commented that because Kereopa had killed a Pakeha he was hanged, while a Hauhau who had killed a Hawke's Bay chief escaped scot free.[25]

In 1872 Te Kooti, eluding capture, again entered the King Country, this time to ask, and receive, sanctuary. Not considering his capture worth a new campaign against the King movement the Government at last gave up the pursuit. Meanwhile, in other ways, pacification had made considerable progress. McLean and the Colonial Treasurer, Julius Vogel, fully apprehended that continued war increased the Colony's debt and retarded its development to an extent that the confiscation of land could never offset.[26] Appreciating the provocative effect of confiscation McLean in 1869 persuaded the still somewhat reluctant Fox not to take land from Te Heuheu Horonuku of Taupo, for his recent participation in Te Kooti's rising. McLean also abandoned his scheme of taking a portion of Ngatiporou land in expiation of that tribe's partial involvement with the King movement and Hauhauism in 1863-5. This appearance of magnanimity was McLean's greatest asset in the negotiations which were to follow. McLean wooed the rebel chiefs by a variety of tactics. He took care to write personally to numbers of important men, announcing his coming to office at Native Minister, and toured disaffected areas, meeting rebel chiefs, assuring them that they would be allowed to dwell in peace as long as they did not molest settlers, and making them gifts of food, seed potatoes, wheat and agricultural implements, to help them settle to farming.

An important instrument of his diplomacy was a revitalised and extended Native Department. Vacancies were filled in important districts such as Taupo, upper Wanganui, the Bay of Plenty and Poverty Bay. The men appointed were instructed that their duties were of a political rather than a judicial nature. They were to confirm the friendly and wavering in allegiance, and to try to wean the Hauhaus and Kingites from their beliefs and assist them in assuming peaceful pursuits. Samuel Locke, appointed Resident Magistrate of Taupo, was to develop communications with the King tribes and learn their history and traditions. The Government was to be kept constantly informed of details of the political, social and economic position of the tribes. McLean's officers generally worked effectively and diligently, keeping in close correspondence with McLean, who for his part was always willing to be guided by their opinion. The Maori valued the presence of a magistrate to whom they could go with requests for material assistance and inquiries about Government intentions.

McLean also used the Kupapa chiefs such as Major Kemp and Mete Kingi, to negotiate with 'rebels', and supported the arrangements they made. A number of surrendered 'rebels' were located on reserves under the eye of Kupapa tribes and obliged to remain there, some until the amnesty of 1883.[27] The influence of Te Whiti was assessed and, once it was known that his half-yearly meetings had a pacific effect, the attendance at them of Titokowaru and chiefs from all over New Zealand, was tolerated and even encouraged.

McLean and his officers took time over the work of diplomacy, never pressing the disaffected tribes too hard, but ensuring that every advantage was taken of their disenchantment with war, Hauhauism or the King movement. Over a period of twelve months Locke and McLean secured first the laying aside of arms by a majority of the Taupo and Ngatiraukawa people, then their acceptance of arbitration in disputes and finally their consent to admit roads and telegraphs. The effects of pacification were cumulative, success in one district encouraging Maori in others to resume friendly relations with Government and settlers. Between 1870-3 most of the leading 'rebels' outside Ngatimaniapoto territory made their peace.

It could not fairly be alleged that McLean bribed them into submission. He rebuked Woon, Resident Magistrate on the Wanganui River, for encouraging 'rebel' chiefs to expect office merely by giving their submission. They were to embrace 'peace and order' for its own sake, and could expect aid with agriculture, but office would come only after 'adequate services' had been rendered.[28] Thus while Te Mamaku, the *ariki* of upper Wanganui made peaceful overtures in 1870, he did not receive a pension until 1873, when the award set the seal on the district's submission to the Queen's authority.

It was plain that the main element of McLean's success was simply that he was able to tell the 'rebels' meaningfully that the Government intended to leave them alone and take no more land. For example Tamaikowha, a leading Whakatohea 'rebel' of Waimana, in the Bay of Plenty, agreed to cease hostilities and to allow troops through his territory in pursuit of Te Kooti but stated plainly that if his cultivations were interfered with or his land forcibly taken he would begin fighting again.[29] The assurances given by McLean and his officers were unlikely to be undermined by the action of other Ministers and departments, for McLean secured an aggregation of authority far greater than that of any previous Native Minister. It had been recognised in 1868 that the separate action of Native and Defence Department officers had contributed largely to causing Titokowaru's rising, and J. C. Richmond had stated that it was the intention of the Stafford Government to shut down the Defence Office and place the Armed Constabulary under the Native Department.[30] The amalgamation was never carried that far but McLean became the first to assume both Native and Defence portfolios. He amalgamated both head office staffs and ran them essentially as one. The remaining settler militia corps were disbanded in 1870 as were the smaller provincial police forces. The Armed Constabulary took over their duties and henceforth assumed more the character of a police force than an army, curbing crime among the settler populace as well as making roads and doing garrison duty in recently fought-over districts. With the transformation in 1875 of the remainder of the Native Contingents—about ninety men on garrison duty in the Bay of Plenty—into a branch of the Armed Constabulary the last standing forces of a purely military nature disappeared.

Usually McLean saw to it that in the out-districts the civil authority was supreme. Fox would have preferred to see the military commanders have supremacy in the disturbed districts,[31] and in south Taranaki where Major Noake was made Resident Magistrate in place of Booth, his views had some effect. But in any case McLean kept a close watch on all his officers, civil and military, for signs that they were provoking the Maori to renewed belligerence and succeeded in stopping the systematic looting of Maori horses and cattle.

Finally McLean assumed supervision of land-purchasing and public works as well. The various means of extending colonisation were thus co-ordinated; there was to be no more 'patch-work'. McLean regarded the Crown's power of taking roads compulsorily through Maori customary land as in abeyance and extended roads into Maori territory only with the owners' consent. (The Public Works Act 1876 ratified this policy in respect of customary, though not of Crown-granted lands.) Under an arrangement between McLean and the Minister of Public Works, surveyors and engineers, unless specially accredited by McLean to act alone, were to wait upon the Native Department officer of the District for permission to proceed with their work.[32] Frequently Native and Defence Department officers themselves both negotiated permission to make a road in Maori territory and supervised the making of it.

The extension of roads and telegraphs depended considerably on respect for Maori values, usually more readily found in a Native Department than a Public Works Department officer. Thus H. T. Clarke spent much time negotiating the passage of road through a range of hills long made *tapu* on account of its association with battles between the tribes on either side of it, and when the road was negotiated the terms included an assurance that workmen would not be allowed to trespass or hunt pigs away from the line of road during the Maori pigeon-spearing season. Contracts were let to the *hapu* through whose land the road passed. In the vast expansion of the road network throughout the North Island in the 1870s Maori workmen were almost invariably the pioneers. Pakeha engineers frequently complained at the difficulty and delay of having to organise new gangs as the road moved through the territory of successive *hapu,* but McLean insisted on giving the preference to Maori labour as part of his pacification program.[33]

In 1870 the Crown resumed land-purchasing to provide for the vast public works and immigration program undertaken at the urging of the Colonial Treasurer, Julius Vogel. The Land Purchase Officers were first appointed to the Public Works Department, but most of them—James Booth, James Mackay, C. O. Davis and S. Locke, for example—were past or present members of McLean's staff and worked under his scrutiny. In 1873 they were organised into a Land Purchase Branch of the Native Department. McLean also exerted his authority over private purchase operations and those of local government authorities. Few were too powerful to avoid censure if their ambitions threatened to cause a breach of the peace or complicate McLean's negotiations with important chiefs.

McLean's approach stemmed in part from a genuine liking for the Maori. He mixed easily with them and had little sympathy with the rabid anti-Maorism characteristic of many settlers. Moreover, he had come to regard hurried assimilation as impracticable. In 1869-70 he revived and expanded views regarding the authority of chiefs which he had first expressed as Governor Browne's Native Secretary.

> If we had fully recognised the chiefs of the country, and reposed confidence in them, I believe they would have reciprocated that confidence and we should have had a power ready to work with us . . . Our tendency has been too much to break down existing institutions amongst the Natives, instead of aiding and helping those institutions, to the benefit of both races.[34]

He further regarded as fallacious and dangerous the view that because the Maori were British subjects no exceptional laws should exist for them. The only effect of such a view, he asserted, 'has been to induce Europeans on the one hand to expect the enforcement of the Queen's writ throughout the country and on the other of exasperating a large section of the aborigines who emphatically declare national independence and deny the right of any foreign power to exercise jurisdiction over them'. He noted that European laws and customs were the product of a long and gradual evolution, that the various sections of the British Isles still had different local laws, and that a proud and tradition-minded people like the Maori could not make the transition to settler institutions in one generation. He contemplated dealing with Maori districts as territories similar to those in the Western United States, where Maori usages would prevail and where colonisation would not be permitted freely to extend, and to establish local councils of chiefs with limited powers of self-government. Contacts between Maori and settlers were to be eased by McLean and his specialist staff, who would pave the way for the extension of settlement. Meanwhile the provision of education for the Maori would bring about their gradual adaptation to European institutions.[35]

The limits of McLean's concessions can, however, be seen in his handling of the King movement. In 1869-70 recognition of the King movement in some form was still being urged by Sir William Martin, by Lord Granville at the Colonial Office and by Rolleston, who had retired from the position of

Under-Secretary in the Native Department to become Superintendent of Canterbury Province and a Member of the House of Representatives. Martin suggested that the Waikato be constituted a separate Province, linked by some form of treaty relationship with the rest of the country, and the Kingite chiefs granted authority to make regulations and govern within their borders, admitting only such Pakeha as they chose to invite among them. But McLean viewed this as a 'very pernicious proposal' going much too far, and raised the familiar objections that a virtually independent Maori Kingdom would command the allegiance of declared Kingites outside its borders. He wrote:

> The recognition of an organisation now which would draw the native race together . . . would be dangerous to madness. Nothing that can be done now will restrain the European race from overrunning the Island. With a recognised *active* Maori government complications would be seen to arise which would inevitably lead to a war of races. I use the word active because my objection does not apply to allowing to the King an imaginary state and power. I do not object to his being called King so long as the allegiance he can claim is only . . . the allegiance under another semblance which a chief may claim but this is very different from recognising and legalising his right to exercise independent authority.[36]

In the House of Representatives Rolleston, supported by the Maori members, moved for a commission of inquiry on Maori-Pakeha relations with a view to restoring confiscated lands. This was contemptuously dismissed by Fox.[37] McLean also opposed any large return of confiscated land. He was prepared to agree to Martin's proposal that the Kingites should be given a block of land within the confiscation as well as sections in the Waikato towns if the land had not yet been allocated to settlers, but he well knew that not much of value was left. He was also prepared to allow the King and his councillors powers of local government in the King Country and the right to exclude settlement from their territory, but only so long as they admitted a Pakeha Resident (thus acknowledging that their laws and powers derived from the Queen), agreed that Maori fugitives from the law be surrendered for trial, and admitted the over-riding right of the Government to 'maintain order'. Clearly this sort of submission from the King movement, which would have eliminated its capacity to shelter Maori militants was more important to McLean at that stage than immediately opening the King Country to roads and settlement. Failing agreement with the King movement McLean hoped that continued trading and visiting by King Maori within the settled territory would enable settlers and Kingites to 'glide into a state of peace without any specific terms'.[38]

McLean had put his terms to Rewi and Manuhiri (now the principal spokesmen for the Waikato tribes) in November 1869. They agreed on minor points; McLean undertook to release some Kingite prisoners on Manuhiri's assurance of their good behaviour and ordered certain lands on the confiscation boundary in which Rewi had an interest to be withdrawn from the Land Court.[39] But to the Kingites, the fugitives in their territory were patriots rather than murderers and they would not contemplate surrendering them to the Pakeha. The exiled Waikato chiefs also knew that McLean's offer to return unallocated blocks in the confiscation was specious; in any case they viewed the whole confiscation as unjust and wanted it all restored. Jealousy between Waikato and Ngatimaniapoto also complicated the position. The Waikato Kingites were interested in a grant of authority provided it was not too circumscribed; the Ngatimaniapoto chiefs, on the other hand, did not want Tawhiao confirmed in any Government-sponsored position while he was in Ngatimaniapoto territory, since that implied giving him permanent authority over them and their lands.

The inconclusiveness of these negotiations left a frontier situation of considerable tension in the Waikato. In 1871 the Kingites expelled some traders who sought to open a store at Kawhia and a Maori mission teacher who had been sent to Aotea. On occasion settlers were killed near the *aukati*, and the King Country continued to offer refuge to Maori fugitives wanted for crimes committed in the settled districts. Thus in 1870 Lyons, a fencer, was murdered for his coat, and a surveyor, Todd, killed on land claimed by Kingites. In April 1873 a labourer, Sullivan, was killed while working across the Kingite side of the *aukati* on the Pukekawa block—a block in which Waikato Kingites had a good traditional claim but which had been awarded by the Land Court only to Maori on the Government side of the *aukati* and leased. In 1876 a Maori named Winiata killed his employer at Epsom, an Auckland suburb, and fled to sanctuary in the King Country. There was also at least one case of an alleged sorcerer being put to death and his killers retiring to the King Country, besides a number of instances in which men summonsed for theft or lesser offences were given sanctuary. The killing of alleged sorcerers within the King Country itself was also reported.[40] Moreover, in 1871 it was alleged that one O'Connell, reputedly a Fenian organiser among the Irish at the Thames goldfield, was intriguing with Te Kooti and the Kingite chiefs.[41]

Incidents such as Sullivan's murder were the occasion of great flurry among the settlers who were very edgy and feared a repetition of the events of 1868. Its real or alleged connection with conspiracy and murder caused many of the North Island settlers to take the line advocated by the Auckland politician, Cracroft Wilson, that the King Country be opened by force of arms ('a little scrimmage which in the Western States of America they would think very little about') and its leaders, along with Te Kooti and other wanted men, hanged.[42] Partly because he viewed such fanaticism with repugnance, and partly because the Government desired neither the trouble nor expense of deviating from its peace policy, McLean firmly withstood such arguments. He continued to operate his policy of friendly communication with the Kingites through the Native Department officers on the frontier and Wi Te Wheoro and by a steady stream of letters and telegrams. He met Rewi and Manuhiri on several occasions and Tawhiao in 1875. He made them gifts of seed wheat and agricultural implements and tried to entice Manuhiri to return to ancestral lands at Mangere which had been preserved for him by Richmond.[43]

His policy was partly successful. Despite the murders tension on the frontier steadily eased over the decade. Adamant non-co-operation was hard for the Kingites to sustain against the attractions of engagement with the Pakeha economic order—attractions adroitly dangled by McLean but not pressed too hard. The King movement began to crumble as a 'land league'. Most of the Ngatiraukawa and Ngatituwharetoa accepted roads and offers of land purchase after 1871; in 1875 Te Hira of the upper Thames who with King movement support had closed his land to gold mining in 1862, gave way. In 1876 at an important meeting in the Tuhua country, south-west of Taupo, Rewi announced to the Tuhua and upper Wanganui chiefs, that as far as the King movement was concerned, they were free to deal with their land as they wished—they would not be advised or restrained by the King movement any longer.[44] In 1876 also Rewi and Tawhiao visited frequently across the *aukati* and the Ngatimaniapoto chief Wetere Te Rerenga leased land to a settler. Tawhiao himself would probably have weakened and accepted McLean's proposals for recognition, under the Crown, of his authority over his immediate followers, and for a return of a limited portion of the confiscated lands. But his stern-principled advisers Manuhiri and Te Ngakau were not readily inclined to compromise their claim for the return of the whole confiscation. McLean's tenure of office ended with Kingite and settler relations greatly eased but with no conclusive agreement achieved. The Kingites allowed European police across the *aukati* in 1873 in pursuit of a Pakeha fugitive,[45] but there was no entrée in 1876 for the pursuers of Winiata.

On the West Coast McLean wanted the ex-'rebels', about a hundred of whom were in gaol in Dunedin and hundreds more dwelling with other tribes in inland Taranaki and Wanganui, to be allowed to reoccupy defined areas within their former territory. But Fox, supporting the bitter south Taranaki settlers, debarred the district south of the Waingongoro river to ex-'rebels' by means of armed patrols. The West Coast thus remained for some time in a state of sullen tension. When some displaced Maori interfered with a settler's ploughing a Wanganui newspaper commented:

> This is a pretty state of things! We are assure however, that if there is any further interference, the Maoris will be shot down like dogs, as a number of determined men are armed and ready to act. This is the best argument in such a case with savages, if the Native agents and Native office cannot maintain the indubitable right of the settlers. This argument is a potent one with the Australian blacks.[46]

In September 1872, however, the Fox Government was defeated in the General Assembly by Stafford, who was himself over-turned a month later by Waterhouse and McLean. In the lobbying both groups, seeking the votes of the Maori members, promised to redress the situation on the West Coast. In 1873 McLean was able to return the prisoners and exiles to defined reserves.

Yet the difficulties of the West Coast were far from ended. A variety of rumours abounded as to the extent of the confiscated land Stafford and McLean had promised to restore; certainly the West Coast tribes came to expect too much. McLean in fact made reserves totalling only about 50,000 acres, including the Compensation Court awards of 1866;[47] moreover he sought immediately to buy up many of the awards, some of which were already occupied by squatters. Among many of the ex-'rebels', gratification at their return from gaol and exile gave way to dissatisfaction and increasing support for Te Whiti, dwelling north of the Waingongoro.

Te Whiti, Parris soon found, while standing for principles of non-violence, also stood firmly for resistance to roads and land sales and non-recognition of the confiscation. He poured scorn on Wi Parata, then member for Western Maori, who helped McLean define reserves in 1873.[48] In 1870 Parris had summed up the problem he posed for the Native Department:

> What I am afraid of is, that he will dictate action independent of the Government which sooner or later must lead to collision, unless by patience and conciliatory measures they [Te Whiti and his followers] are gradually . . . restored to confidence in the Government a process difficult to administer in opposition to popular feeling and the progress necessary for the advancement of the country.[49]

McLean did not define reserves north of the Waingongoro (an omission for which some politicians subsequently held him blameworthy) mainly because Te Whiti would not have recognised them. Instead he instructed the officers on the West Coast to make payments to those both north and south of the Waingongoro who declined to recognise the confiscation, in order to get them to relinquish the bulk of their lands. He did not admit that the confiscation was abandoned; the payments were to be regarded as compensation in consideration of the 'rebels'' former claims.[50] Parris handled the matter somewhat clumsily, paying a price per acre and having the Maori sign deeds of cession, an implication that they were selling the freehold. Charles Brown, a former Superintendent of Taranaki, who succeeded Parris as Civil Commissioner of Taranaki in 1875, took no deeds and talked not in terms of price per acre, but made offers of lump sums and insisted on the Crown's claim to lay out reserves and take the rest of the confiscated territory.[51] The 'purchase' operations proceeded slowly, accompanied by surveys and roads between the Waitotara and Waingongoro Rivers. Surveys were resisted several times and Maori claimants occasionally refused to vacate the land, but, by the exercise of all the weapons of diplomacy, guile and blandishment, and by buying off the chief men, including Titokowaru, government officers seduced potential leaders of the resistance.

But north of the Waingongoro River was Te Whiti's territory. The prophet gave no indication that he was willing to permit roads and surveys and McLean forebore to press him. He held his officers in check and, emphasising to his colleagues the need for caution, stated that he was prepared to wait many years, until Maori opinion had ameliorated before he could open up the whole of the West Coast.[52]

XVI

The McLean 'System'

In the uncertain 1870s, with the settlers pressing to complete the colonisation of the North Island, with Maori objectors interrupting surveys every few weeks, with *hapu* still periodically taking up arms over land or *puremu* disputes, McLean's revised and extended Native Department clearly played a central role. McLean required of his senior staff a sense of the need for resolute and decisive intervention between Maori and settler, and a willingness to absorb the criticism from both sides that such interventions drew. G. S. Cooper, former Land Purchase Officer and later Resident Magistrate at Waipukarau, who succeeded Rolleston as Under-Secretary in 1868, did not possess those capacities and was soon moved to the safely Eurocentric post of Under-Secretary in the Colonial Secretary's Department. He was succeeded by H. T. Clarke a long-serving officer who carried a permanent limp from a wound received while acting as interpreter during Hone Heke's rising. He had been an energetic administrator of the Bay of Plenty during the wars; and from 1869 to 1873 had succeeded James Mackay as Civil Commissioner of Auckland, Waikato, and the Bay of Plenty. At Wellington McLean entrusted him with all routine work and the handling of most minor disputes.

McLean also retained Parris as Civil Commissioner in Taranaki. Fox had wished to dismiss him to placate the settlers who were violently critical of his alleged over-protection of the Maori. He agreed, however, to McLean's suggestion of surrounding Parris with a 'Taranaki Board' of five local settlers and five Maori chiefs, with Parris as executive officer, but not chairman, of the Board. The Board, carefully picked by McLean, soon developed views very close to those of Parris, and ceased to meet after about two years. Parris, however, viewed its creation as a betrayal by McLean and relations between the two men were never thereafter cordial.[1] In 1875 Parris retired from the Civil Commissionership in favour of Charles Brown, sometime Superintendent of Taranaki, lately chairman of the Taranaki Board, and an old friend of McLean.

James Mackay, the former Civil Commissioner of Auckland, Waikato and Thames, quarrelled with McLean over the terms of his appointment and resigned. For some time he intrigued with the Stafford faction in the expectation that in the event of their victory he would be made Native Minister but when, in 1872, they did briefly hold power, they feared that he would become a dominating and semi-independent figure, as McLean had, and did not encourage him to seek election to the Assembly. In 1873 he wrote to McLean, patching up their quarrel and offering to contest a seat in the Assembly on behalf of McLean's party, or to take the Land Purchase Department off McLean's hands.[2] McLean, however, carefully kept him in more subordinate positions as Land Purchase Officer, as special commissioner in the Waikato at the time of the Sullivan killing, and in difficult negotiations such as adjustments to the King Country border and the opening of the Ohinemuri goldfield. These tasks he performed with customary boldness and skill and, in the case of the Sullivan killing, at the cost of an attack on his life.[3]

McLean also created the position of 'Native Officer', which, like that of Civil Commissioner was non-judicial, and mainly concerned with land questions and political relations between Maori and settler. However it avoided much of the public hostility towards the plenipotentiary powers associated with the latter title. The most important Native Officer was W. G. Mair, who in 1871 was moved from his Resident Magistracy at Opotiki to the frontier post of Alexandra, on the King Country border, to handle relations with the Kingites.

Besides building up the staff of Resident Magistrates McLean appointed about twenty-four Medical Officers in Maori districts and required of them regular circuits and monthly reports. The number of Maori office-holders was also greatly increased. Men of rank such as M. P. Kawiti, who had been retrenched by A. H. Russell and had since hindered administration, growling about 'children of slaves' being allowed to judge in his district, were restored to office. Assessors and police were appointed from each *hapu* that gave its adherence to the Government and vacancies were filled as they arose.

In the early 1870s, then, for a population of just under 50,000 Maori (and 220,000 settlers) there was a staff of twelve at head office, sixteen officers in rural posts, ancillary staff of interpreters, clerks, and medical officers, 150 Assessors, 180 Maori police and sundry others. Total salaries amounted to £16,000. In addition the rapidly increasing staff of village school-teachers, the Land Purchase Officers and other officials administering the land acts, also came under the Native Department.

Unlike J. C. Richmond who accepted an extensive Native Service as a somewhat undesirable necessity, McLean worked his little empire with verve and considerable attention to detail. Whereas in the 1860s officers had often complained of inadequate guidance and supervision, they were now constantly hounded, by letter and telegraph, to get out among the villages, talk with the principal men and report frequently on all aspects of Maori life and opinion. The Native Office in Wellington acted as clearing-house for these reports, making great use of the newly extended telegraph service to relay the essence of them to McLean, who spent more time touring the out-districts or on his farm in Hawke's Bay than he did in Wellington. On the basis of these detailed reports McLean was able, without having to visit the area concerned, to shape a policy with confidence. He reputedly worked very hard, up to fourteen hours a day, replying to reports.[4] A stream of letters and telegrams flowed back through the Native Office to the out-districts. Chiefs were chided, placated, warned, reassured or bribed as the occasion demanded, while Native Department officers were instructed whether or not to press or restrain a survey, make an arrest, or, as was most usual, negotiate and report again. In 1873 McLean handled entirely from Napier a serious armed confrontation between the Ngatiraukawa and Muaupoko in the disputed Rangitikei-Manawatu purchase, sending out and receiving streams of telegrams until both parties had been persuaded to retire.[5] At less troubled times the telegraph was used to direct movements of staff, arrange details of Land Court sittings, direct vaccinators and medical officers to an epidemic, or authorise the delivery of food or seed or agricultural implements to needy communities.[6]

McLean rarely relied on the use of constabulary either to coerce or make a demonstration of force. He was lenient with people who interrupted surveys when his colleagues would have made arrests, knowing that in many cases the interrupters were only asserting a claim to share in future payments. If the 'moral influence' of his officers failed, his favourite weapon was a personal visitation; the chief clerk informed Woon, when the latter struggled to keep the peace on the disputed Waitotara block, that there was nothing to be done 'except *management* and sliding over matters as well as you can' pending the visit of 'our chief'.[7] When McLean did use force he used it discreetly. Thus an Arawa party who obstructed a survey in 1871 were quietly disarmed by the constabulary and the surveyors warned off the ground.[8]

Diplomacy was strongly supplemented by gifts and payments, known generally as 'contingency expenditure'. Much of this was simply repayment of the lavish hospitality usually extended by chiefs, gifts of food or seed to tribes hit by drought or flood or blight, gifts of stud stock, draught animals or agricultural machinery, loans for the purchase of whaling gear, subsidies to the old or indigent, medical care and food in times of epidemic, and places for chiefs' sons in boarding schools. These reflected some appreciation of Maori needs. Other gifts and awards were for services rendered—hence Te Wheoro's promotion to Major for help at the time of the Sullivan killing and cash payments to a chief who secured the recovery of stolen property.[9] Other payments were simply to procure compliance; thus McLean's diary records that H. M. Tawhai 'brought some grievance over land for which I gave him £10'.[10] As far as they had funds or influence, McLean's officers in the field observed similar practices. Contingency expenditure formed a large proportion of the annual Native Department vote, which under McLean, rose from about £27,000 in 1869-70 to between £32,000 in 1870-1 and £34,000 in subsequent years, a level not reached since the retrenchments of 1865-6.

Insight into the work of the Resident Magistrates in the 1870s and their relations with the Maori people is provided by the records of Richard Woon.
The son of a Wesleyan missionary, Woon became an interpreter in the
Wanganui district in the early 1860s and was Resident Magistrate for the
Wanganui River from 1870-80, administering the affairs of 2000 Maori along
the 250-mile waterway. After a series of meetings with ex-'rebels' Woon had,
by 1871, brought most of the river under the regular purview of his circuit
courts though he did not hold courts in the high reaches of the Tuhua country
until 1876. The principal men of the district such as Mete Kingi, Major Kemp
and Topia Turoa were usually made Assessors or policemen or, like Topine
Te Mamaku in upper Wanganui, were granted a Government pension. One of
Woon's Assessors had been appointed as early as 1851 during Grey's first
Governorship, others in 1863 during John White's magistracy, and others
again during the 1870s. The police had a similar range of service. There was
generally an Assessor and a policeman in each principal village. Some
Assessors accompanied Woon on circuit, others awaited him in the village and
sat with him on the bench as he held Court (first in the village *runanga*
houses, later in the Government schools and special courthouses) or assisted
him in unofficial arbitrations. The police paddled and poled him up the long
river, served summonses, checked drunkenness at meetings, kept order in
court, and carried messages to officers in other districts.

Woon tried, on average, only about six criminal cases and eighteen civil
cases annually. The complexity of ownership of stock underlay a lot of
disputes. For example a man whose crops were destroyed by cattle might seize
a horse from the owner of the cattle to compensate himself. The owner of the
cattle might not object, but others who claimed rights in the horse would.
Inconclusive wrangling about this sort of question was likely to lead to one of
the parties charging another before Woon, and argument of the case before
the Resident Magistrate and Assessors could take most of the day. Questions
relating to custom often arose. For example, one Heketua gave his son's wife
a bullock as a marriage gift when they wed, but took it back again when the
son died and the girl's kin declined to allow Heketua to find her another
husband. The dispute centred on whether a marriage gift, formally accepted,
could be retrieved by the giver. On another occasion Rotohiko gave maggoty
food to some men who were building a house for him. One of them, Anakereti,
likened it to the putrid remains of Rotohiko's kin. The enraged chiefs of the
village demanded payment from Anakereti's chief, a powerful figure in the
district, and when it was declined took it from Rotohiko, his current employer,
instead. Rotohiko in turn took Anakereti before Woon to secure recompense
and Woon awarded him £5.

Traditional custom usually determined these sorts of decisions to a considerable extent, Woon relying heavily on the Assessors for guidance. But custom
was rapidly becoming inappropriate in many disputes. For example when
Reneti Tapa took part in an expedition against the Bay of Plenty Hauhau in

1867 he returned with two prisoners who had been given into his charge much as tribal enemies had been enslaved in pre-contact times. In traditional fashion he married one of them, Nepia, to an unmarried kinswoman and gave them timber and *totara* bark to build a house. In 1874, with peace well-established, Nepia decided to move to the district of another Wanganui Maori and to take the house with him. Reneti asked Woon to restrain Nepia from leaving him, 'his parent and master'. Woon did order that the house be left, but did not, of course, feel empowered to restrain Nepia.[11]

As Rotohiko's case indicates, *muru* was still resorted to very frequently by Maori disputants. Woon sought to extinguish it by punishing it as theft but awarding damages freely to people aggrieved by customary offences as well as offences under common law. He admitted that he strained the letter of the law in trying to make it appropriate to the needs of the district. He frequently awarded the injured party part of the fines levied for theft or assault, although FitzRoy's Fines for Assault Ordinance had been repealed.

As was usual with the Resident Magistrate system, a great part of Woon's work was unofficial mediation, especially over land disputes. He arranged for some land disputes to be referred to his court then adjourned proceedings pending a decision of the Native Land Court, a method which allowed passions to abate and agreement sometimes to be reached. Although Woon urged his people to take their land disputes to the Land Court he also encouraged their many *runanga* discussions over land boundaries and was one of several Native Department Officers who urged the Government to give formal recognition to these preliminary discussions and merely have the Court ratify them.[12]

Woon's judicial authority was not entirely unchallenged. From 1873 he reported a movement among his people, prompted by the visit of a Hawke's Bay leader named Henare Matua to refer cases to a *runanga* selected from among themselves. This move was encouraged by Woon's action—deemed excessively harsh—in gaoling a first offender for assault. In 1875 there was a confrontation between Woon's authority and that of the *runanga*. A man named Rupuha quarrelled with a member of the *runanga* and exchanged *kanga* with him. He was thereupon 'summonsed' by the *runanga* and having ignored the 'summons', had some of his property seized by Hiroki, a paid 'policeman' of the *runanga*, armed with a warrant. This was a *muru* modified by European forms. Rupuha laid an information with Woon against Hiroki for larceny and Woon sent one of his constables to recover the goods. When they were not surrendered Woon prompted Rupuha to press his action in the Circuit Court and fined Hiroki £5 with the option of six months hard labour. After a week of negotiations during which Hiroki remained in custody, the leaders of the *runanga* paid his fine.[13]

Nevertheless, the *runanga* persisted. It enjoyed favour because it embodied Maori, not alien, authority, because its proceedings and decisions in some respects were more appropriate than English law (even as modified by Woon) to traditional Maori offences and Maori notions of justice, and because the fines and fees it levied remained in the district instead of going to Wellington. In fact Woon's court and the *runanga* tended to alternate in popularity owing to the influence of faction and according to whether a somewhat fickle local opinion believed one or the other to be giving the more satisfactory judgments. Because the *runanga* was inclined to be faction-dominated and oppressive, Woon thought the trend favoured him, but his returns show a decline in the number of civil cases brought before him over the decade.[14]

About one third of Woon's time was taken up with non-judicial duties such as the promotion of agriculture and the founding of schools. Three schools were started on the river in the 1870s and experienced fluctuations of fortune. Woon assisted the chiefs to raise money and repair their flour mills. He also arranged for a supply of hops, mulberry and tobacco seedlings and for some instruction to be given in the culture of these plants. McLean encouraged him in this work, but Government aid did not extend to the provision of the plant nursery and paid instructor which Woon requested. A combination of spasmodic interest, the inherent difficulty of cultivating the crops, unsuitable climate and uncertain market caused the new ventures on the Wanganui River to dwindle by the end of the 1870s.

Woon's other important duties included intensive diplomacy during times of crisis such as the Todd and Sullivan killings on the Waikato frontier, and the sending of intelligence on the attitude of the Kingites and followers of Te Whiti in his district. Miscellaneous work included arranging mail contracts, distributing pensions awarded to elderly Maori and wounded Kupapa or their dependents, issuing arms and ammunition permits, recovering arms issued to Kupapa during the Wars, distributing rents to Maori owners on behalf of the Reserves Commissioners, assisting in the election of members for the Western Maori electorate, witnessing deeds, arranging for the care of destitute and elderly Maori, collecting subscriptions for the Government newspaper (the *Waka Maori* of Napier, which McLean had made the official publication), negotiating the passage of roads and telegraphs, taking censuses and administering the liquor laws in the district. Woon frequently toured his district with the missionary Richard Taylor until the latter's death in 1875 and with the Native Department doctor, J. Earle. In Wanganui he was often host for Maori visitors.

Although he was instructed not to engage directly in negotiations for land, Woon, like other Resident Magistrates, was asked to lend his influence in support of the work of the Land Purchase Officers. However, he had little sympathy with the guileful and pushing methods of Booth, principal Land Purchase Officer of the district, and several times reported that Booth, by recklessly advancing surveys with the support of only a fraction of the owners, was endangering the peace. Booth on the other hand charged Woon with obstructing land-purchase operations.[15] In fact Woon was as anxious as any Pakeha to see settlement enter the district, provided always that the local people were not pressured into selling and that they were able to retain ample reserves. Because he was anxious that his official role should not be confused with that of the Land Purchase Officers, he arranged in 1872 to have a separate office in Wanganui from that of George Worgan (another Land Purchase Officer) with whom he had previously shared.

Woon was also frequently called upon to report whether land purchases by private individuals conformed with the anti-fraud legislation of 1870 and to recommend on the advisability of removing restrictions on land reserved for 21-year lease. Acting usually on the advice of Major Kemp and other leading Assessors he did approve certain transactions if he was satisfied that the price was fair and that all owners consented to the sale, but he vehemently declined to approve the sale of such vital reserves as Putiki near Wanganui and expressed concern that the idea should even be contemplated.[16]

Woon passed up—and frequently supported—representations by men of his district who were involved in disputes with settlers over boundaries, or rents or purchase money, although these were not frequent until the late 1870s when extensive sales of up-river land first took place. He represented his people strenuously and with some success in their claim for a canoe landing place and market centre on the Wanganui foreshore when their original landing place was taken for harbour reclamation work.[17]

The pattern of administration developed by Woon was fairly representative of that of Resident Magistrates in the more remote districts. Only in the King Country, the Urewera and Te Whiti's domains did Maori leaders not, by and large, welcome the work of the magistrates. There was a tendency for young men, with some experience or even formal education in the Pakeha order to lead in this direction. At meetings in the Bay of Islands in 1873, for example, young Maori spokesmen moved that elderly Assessors be struck off pay and replaced by young men competent to sift judicial matters, and called on Williams, the Resident Magistrate, to be firm in the discharge of his duty, not leaving disputes to be settled by the older chiefs.[18] As a result, although the older and more conservative chiefs were consulted in all important matters, young men frequently became the Assessors who sat on the Bench with the Resident Magistrates or assisted them as police. The missions, struggling to re-establish themselves, grumbled at their young Maori teachers being drawn off into Government service.

The inexpensive and peculiarly flexible jurisdiction of the Resident Magistrates' court made it possible for disputants, at the risk of a few shillings, to gain a speedy decision. An amazing variety of complaints was brought by Maori litigants. Thus Williams, Resident Magistrate at Waimate, awarded £2 damages against a man who called a meeting, which many Maori went out of their way to attend, and then failed to arrive himself.[19] Hamlin in Maketu prosecuted the local medical officer on behalf of local people who complained that he had interfered with the bones of their dead, and was even obliged to ask the Attorney-General whether his jurisdiction covered the case of a Maori who lost a side bet on a horse which was 'pulled' at the local races.[20]

In every district the Resident Magistrates were involved as mediators in threatened outbreaks of feuding. Von Sturmer at Hokianga described a typical situation at Waima. Wi Totoia and his wife Haua, a woman of rank, invited Rawiri Te Tahua, from a neighbouring settlement, to dig kauri gum on their land. Arama Karaki Pi, perhaps the highest ranking chief in the district, objected and asked Von Sturmer to prevent the land from being dug without his consent and to take charge of the gum already collected. At a meeting arranged through the aging Mohi Tawhai (also of very high rank) it was agreed that a portion of the gum would go to Pi and no more would be dug there. But Haua, Wi Totoia and Rawiri apparently did not keep their word, so Tawhai built a pa on the land and plundered Haua. Von Sturmer found 150 armed men on each side. Mohi Tawhai said that he did not really intend to fight but only 'chastise his children', and indeed the confrontation was largely a traditional display of strength, bravado, oratory and diplomacy. But there was a danger that people from outside the district with old scores to settle who joined either side would open fire. Knowing that Hongi Hika's daughter was in Tawhai's pa, Rawiri himself was inclined to forget about kauri gum and recall the unavenged death of a kinsman at Hongi's hands, several decades earlier. In the event the Resident Magistrates persuaded Totoia and Pi to refer the disputed land to the Native Land Court and leave the kauri gum in their charge until the decision.[21]

A single turbulent chief could give a Resident Magistrate a great deal of work. Thus within twelve months H. Brabant at Opotiki had quelled a dangerously tense puremu dispute involving Tamaikowha, the restless ex-'rebel' chief of the Waimana valley, settled another quarrel with Tamaikowha about alleged under-payment for road works and intervened between Tamaikowha and a faction inclined to lease land to settlers, advising the would-be lessors not to take the money and the would-be lessees to leave the district.[22]

Another frequent source of trouble was the testy or truculent type of settler who commonly made a frontier home in a Maori district and was constantly engaged in a running feud with his neighbours over stock trespass or other grievances, real and imaginary. About half of Hamlin's cases at Maketu for instance, involved charges and counter-charges between T. H. Smith[23] and his neighbours, many of them highly coloured by the participants' imaginations. The Resident Magistrate's Court provided a ready outlet for such feuds and prevented them from assuming ugly proportions. There was a dangerous tendency, where Maori committed petty crime in districts not under a Resident Magistrate's special jurisdiction, for the more aggressive settlers to assemble under a local leader, possibly a Justice of the Peace, in order to 'discipline' the offenders. When this happened in New Plymouth, after a Maori had stolen a shawl, the Native Department considered extending to the town the sections of the Resident Magistrates Act which reserved Maori cases to the Resident

Magistrates.[24] This did not prove necessary, however, it being generally considered that cases involving Maori were for the Native Department officers to handle, rather than the local Justices of the Peace and police.

Given the constant sense of crisis and need for care and tact in their work, it is not surprising that the Resident Magistrates placed a high value on their presence in a district. When it was rumoured that he was to be retired, White of Mangonui wrote: 'I venture to say that it would be a very serious blunder . . . one misunderstanding would cost the Government much more than the salary of a responsible officer.'[25] White was retained.

The Resident Magistrates constantly paid tribute to their Maori associates. A few of the older Assessors were still inclined to be self-assertive and domineering but this was not usual. Jackson of Papakura, South Auckland, noted that in arbitrating or adjudicating on disputes, 'Assessors, when their own people were not involved, act very fairly, are good reasoners, and some are remarkably clear and shrewd'. Woon so valued his Assessors' ability and influence that he asked the Minister of Justice to consider granting the Resident Magistrates discretionary power to invite Assessors to assist them on the bench in mixed cases as well as purely Maori cases. This concession, which in the settlers' view would have made them subject to Maori judicial authority, was not granted, but Woon nevertheless usually had an Assessor on hand when hearing mixed cases.[26]

Aubrey in Whangarei, noted that his principal Assessor, Taurau Kukupa, assisted him in every case involving a Maori and he was greatly respected by Europeans in the town.

Assessors, for their part, regarded their positions as offering status among both Maori and settler communities. They frequently asked Resident Magistrates to ensure that they were supported in this regard. A Hawke's Bay Assessor, for example, asked for a supply of official paper and two paid policemen, as he was ashamed of sending unpaid messengers about on official business. Another asked for a broadcloth suit so that he could sit on the Resident Magistrate's bench with due dignity. On the other hand Maori communities were quick to request that an Assessor who became drunken or too over-bearing be replaced.[27]

Maori policemen were sometimes regarded by Assessors as *their* policemen, but they often exercised an independent authority and initiative that gained the respect of all sections of the local community. In south Taranaki their recovery of stolen property from Te Whiti's and Titokowaru's district greatly contributed towards the checking of settler demands for subjugation of the prophets' sanctuary.[28] Some of the most effective policemen were men already prominent in their districts—the mixed-race Tapsell brothers at Maketu, for example, or Papahurihia, who served as Warden of Police at Hokianga until his death in 1875 'and was a useful officer'.[29] In remote districts such as upper Wanganui the Resident Magistrate relied almost entirely upon Maori police, but in districts interpenetrated by settlement Maori police and members of the Armed Constabulary usually worked in co-operation.

Crime among Maori was, as could be expected, most frequent where social dislocation was most severe. It could frequently be associated with the drunken sprees that followed the completion of a land sale; it was also more common among tribes suffering from the aftermath of war, such as the ex-'rebels' of Poverty Bay, who were supposed to be in exile in the Bay of Plenty, but who kept drifting back to their own district to find their land ceded and their people dispersed. Otherwise the annual reports of the Resident Magistrate almost invariably complimented the local tribes on their law abiding ways. For example, of 2000 Maori in the Hokianga district, Von Sturmer noted only one assault and three burglary cases in one year. In cases of disputes between Maori and settler, Native Department officials generally laid much of the responsibility upon the Europeans.[30] Social control through the elders and men of rank in the kinship system was still clearly very strong.

Where petty crime was blatant, Maori communities now made little objection to the enforcement of law. W. B. White, Resident Magistrate at Mangonui, reported: 'Warrants are issued on the information of Natives, and culprits are apprehended by Native constables without difficulty, no one attempting to interfere.' And in 1877 Williams in Waimate reported that he had imprisoned for larceny two young men, the sons of chiefs, 'whose tribes would, a few years back, have offered strenuous opposition, and tendered any sum of money rather than that they should be sent to gaol'. Von Sturmer at Hokianga sentenced a number of people to gaol for not paying store debts, and for petty theft (instead of allowing their kinsmen to compound the penalty) and claimed that this had a very salutary effect.[31]

With regard to crimes of violence the magistrates' authority was also increasingly accepted, though more uncertainly. Having secured the surrender of one Paapu, accused of murder, Williams remarked that although submission to Pakeha law was still not automatic, each case was now easier.[32] The authorities punished more leniently the killings which arose out of a breach of Maori custom and were not therefore *kohuru,* or unprovoked murder, in Maori eyes. This encouraged compliance with the law although the victim's kin usually grumbled about the inadequacy of Pakeha retribution against offenders. The grant of a full pardon (after his formal submission at the gates of Mount Eden gaol) to Te Wake, who had been gaoled for killing an opponent in a land feud in 1868 and then escaped, removed a source of grievance in the north and increased the northern tribes' confidence in European justice. By the late 1870s even the Urewera surrendered a Ngatiawa Maori who had killed a kinsman for sorcery and fled among them, while the independent Turoa family of upper Wanganui gave up one of their number who had killed a settler in a drunken fracas in the town.[33] Unpunished killings for adultery and sorcery were, however, reported from Taranaki, Waikato, Tauranga and Eastern Bay of Plenty, and probably more remained undisclosed.

In most cases involving land the parties submitted to arbitration and in only one instance during McLean's administration was loss of life reported. In this case, a clash between two *hapu* of Ngatiporou in 1871, resulting in one man shot dead, the killing went unpunished and led to continued retributive raids by the victim's relatives as late as 1882.[34]

Muru were reported to be declining in frequency throughout the 1870s and in at least one district the use of them led to requests for circuit courts and the appointment of Assessors.[35] Nevertheless *runanga* persisted in every district, and as Woon had found, formed an alternative tribunal at which Maori could adjust differences. The Resident Magistrates usually let them work unless they came under the control of an oppressive faction and their victims appealed to the European court for redress. The chiefs of a district, including the Assessors, were often leaders of the unofficial *runanga,* but were normally discreet and worked against judicial excesses or over-frequent resort to *muru.*

Throughout the 1870s there was a persistent demand from Maori leaders that the *runanga* be given official status and power to make and enforce regulations, such as had been offered under C. W. Richmond's 1858 legislation or Grey's Runanga system. Because of the encroachment of the Land Court and Land Purchase officers, this demand centred increasingly on requests for authority to determine land boundaries and control land alienation, as well as to regulate community relations and control petty crime. Rolleston also raised the idea in the House in 1869, Sir William Martin put it to McLean in 1870 and several of the Resident Magistrates supported it warmly. In 1872, therefore, McLean drafted a Native Councils Bill proposing to allow local councils under a Maori president to pass and enforce appropriate by-laws regulating the familiar problems of *puremu,* sanitation, drunkenness, noxious weeds, dogs and trespassing stock. The councils were also to investigate and determine disputed land boundaries, their decisions to be ratified by the Land Court.[36] The Bill promised to give Maori leaders a much-needed recognition and responsibility. Moreover in 1872 Maori communities were more amenable than they had been in 1862 to adopting some system of local government under central government direction, while their community structure was still sufficiently intact to allow local councils to work effectively.

The Bill was introduced late in 1872 after the out-districts had heard rumours of it and numbers of Maori communities had elected committees in preparation for its passage. The Premier, Waterhouse, claimed that 'so firm a hold on the Native mind has this question obtained, that it has now risen to the prominence that the King Movement did some years ago'. Although the Native Minister recalled that Fenton's attempt to introduce a Runanga system in 1857 had aroused chiefly jealousy he said he would try to introduce it cautiously in a few districts. However the Bill roused the same objections that had greeted Grey's 'new institutions' of 1861-3. Gillies said that the measure gave the Maori too much authority over important matters which affected settlers and that it destroyed the authority of the Land Court. Wi Parata, member for Western Maori, said that he knew that settlers feared that through the councils Maori would regain control of their lands.[37]

Having withdrawn the Bill until the 1873 session, McLean urged Campbell, Resident Magistrate at Waiapu, to establish an experimental council among the Ngatiporou. The council met twice and showed a tendency to discuss matters of wider than local concern.[38] Meanwhile, McLean tried to make his Bill more palatable to European tastes by restricting its application to Maori customary land and by allowing settlers to opt to come under it and elect members to the council. It was to no avail. The House objected to granting the decision on land title to 'a set of outside Republics, presided over by Government officials'. Fenton too, had expressed his jealousy and contempt of the measure. McLean again and, finally, withdrew the Bill.[39]

McLean's failure to secure legal recognition and power for them meant that any *runanga* subsequently sponsored by Government officers at McLean's encouragement soon collapsed, its members preferring a more traditional, unofficial *runanga* to a powerless Government one. Thus Hamlin, Resident Magistrate at Maketu, reported: 'The Native Assessors' Court at Ohinemutu, which I took much trouble to establish for the purposes of trying cases . . . has been neglected since September last, in consequence of which a runanga has since been established, to which the Assessors give their support.'[40] The unofficial *runanga,* not authorised to compel adherence to their decisions against defiant offenders, continued to form, break up and reform throughout the 1870s and 1880s.

McLean's inability to re-establish a system of Maori local councils was to some extent offset by the participation of Maori leaders, as Assessors and police and on School Committees and Licensing Benches. The School Committees, working under the guidance of the Resident Magistrates, varied widely in ability and interest, but in general they provided a valued outlet for constructive work, an outlet of which the younger leaders especially took advantage.[41] McLean encouraged the system by an amending act of 1871 which authorised the Government to assist schools without the Maori having had to make a cash contribution as required by the 1867 Native Schools Act. Maori schools grew in number from thirteen in 1870 to thirty-three in 1873-4 and sixty-six by 1880.

Maori participation on the Licensing Benches was McLean's solution to the liquor question. It was clear that not only was enforcement of the 1847 Sale of Spirits Ordinance impracticable but also that the Maori resented a prohibition that applied to them and not to Europeans. The alternatives were to legalise drinking for both races or to enforce prohibition on both. McLean therefore resolved to give this choice to local districts and to ensure that the Maori population had an effective voice. The Outlying Districts Sale of Spirits Act, 1870, provided that in districts of at least two-thirds Maori population applicants for liquor licences must obtain the written consent of the Assessors of the District. Legislation in 1873 established a general system of

Licensing Courts, usually under the chairmanship of the local Resident Magistrates and amendments to the Outlying Districts Sale of Spirits Act provided that a leading Assessor must sit on the Court with power to veto any application for a new licence or renewal of an existing one. The Sale of Spirits Ordinance was not repealed as regards the towns until 1881, but it remained unenforced.[42]

In a number of districts the hoped-for results followed. In Mangonui for example, the two principal Assessors allowed the granting of licences to accommodation houses only when strictly necessary, and when the houses were well away from Maori settlements. A licensee who had established himself at Ahipara and abused his privileges, was closed down by the Assessors' veto. From about 1874 local officers reported that the Rarawa leaders were drawing their people into increasing sobriety.[43]

But an unexpected result of the 1870 Act was a flood of requests by Maori, including Assessors, to take out liquor licences themselves. The Native Office succumbed to the long-adduced argument that 'We drink for the profit of the Pakeha, why should not the Maoris too make some of the money by the sale?'[44] Resident Magistrates were informed that Maori of good character might take out 'bush licences'. The manner in which this privilege was exercised depended upon the firmness and good sense of the Resident Magistrate and Assessors, especially the former, since some Assessors were inclined to petition for prohibition one day and apply for a licence the next. Officials such as Woon at Wanganui, White and Kelly at Mangonui, and Brabant in the Bay of Plenty, gave a clear lead and supported very few Maori applicants. But on the East Coast, Campbell allowed fourteen licenced and an estimated forty-eight unlicenced Maori grog-houses to flourish so that the district became a by-word for drunkenness and tumult.[45]

The Outlying Districts Sale of Spirits Act did not prevent drunkenness, especially in the towns or when a *hapu* was flush with cash after the conclusion of a land sale. Nor did it entirely prevent publicans selling adulterated liquor to Maori customers. (Wi Te Wheoro claimed that the Pakeha police did not adequately test liquor supplied to Maori, and asked fruitlessly that this become a duty of the Maori police.[46]) Nevertheless, it did permit greatly increased control of the supply of liquor to most Maori communities and local officers throughout the 1870s and 1880s reported themselves much impressed by the steadily increasing sobriety. The Maori leaders' own efforts were assisted by the Good Templar temperance movement. By 1876 the movement was active in the King Country—virtually the first Pakeha organisation to be allowed there freely—and both Rewi and Tawhiao had become members, although the latter, to the deepest embarrassment of his supporters, was an erratic observer of his pledge until the late 1880s.[47]

Subsequent legislation did not seriously alter the power of the Maori Assessors on the Licensing Benches. Unpopular though it was with many Pakeha it was supported by the powerful temperance forces in parliament and the system remained in force into the twentieth century. In response to periodic demands from Maori leaders other Native Ministers—Sheehan in 1878 and Bryce in 1881—while retaining McLean's system, again took power to prohibit liquor to Maori, in specific districts, on petition from a majority of Maori residents. But when, in some districts, prohibition was proclaimed it was not effective for long because it did not apply to settlers and was usually withdrawn within a few years.

The operation of the Outlying Districts Sale of Spirits Act, disclosed principles which appeared best to meet the needs and aspirations of the Maori people. They were resentful of being placed under any legal disability even of a protective kind. Rather they wished to share the opportunities and institutions of the settlers, particularly if those were modified to take into account special Maori needs and values and included Maori leaders in responsible roles. In the 1870s McLean's administration went quite some distance towards accommodating these aspirations. In the revived and extended Resident Magistrate system, in School Committees and Road Boards, in the Licensing Courts and the police, Maori leadership and Maori community opinion were brought into association with, and permitted to modify, the general machinery of administration. Had McLean been able to carry his Native Councils Bill this trend would have gone much further. His failure showed how the struggle for land over-rode the otherwise healthy development of a racially integrated local administration.

XVII

Land Legislation

Land legislation in the 1870s was heavily influenced by the resurgence of the long-standing rivalry between Fenton and McLean which had been temporarily buried by McLean's retirement to Hawke's Bay in 1861. The rivalry was a personal matter as before but also a consequence of Fenton's efforts, already begun under J. C. Richmond, to gain for himself and his Court as much influence over Maori policy as possible. This involved collision with McLean's ambitions for himself and the Native Department.

In 1869 the Assembly considered further measures to prevent direct purchase from reducing Maori to landlessness. J. C. Richmond introduced a Bill to restrict advances of credit to Maori to £5, in order to curb the now familiar practice of entangling them in debt in order to oblige them to sell land. This, an essential point in control of alienation, was accepted by Fox and McLean for the Government, as 'necessary', and Richmond and McLean were authorised to prepare the Bill. A fortnight later McLean succumbed to a powerful lobby by speculators and the Bill was withdrawn.[1] An alternative measure was passed making any alienation of interests in a block conditional on the consent of a majority, in value, of the other owners. But this did not prevent the piecemeal acquisition of rights until the majority in value had been purchased, a process which was facilitated by Fenton's continued practice of awarding title to ten owners only.

Meanwhile Fenton, who had been called to the Legislative Council by Stafford in 1869, introduced a Native Reserves Bill which would have given the Land Court the right of setting aside reserves, administering them as trustee and permitting or restricting their subsequent alienation. He also sought trusteeship of all the interests of Maori minors. There was considerable merit in Fenton's claim that reserves and restricted lands should not be under the control of the government of the day. However, members felt that Fenton was acting not out of altruism but self-aggrandisement. Government speakers opposed the Bill, pointing out that the Court had a bad record hitherto for neglecting to create reserves and, though the Bill passed the Council, it was not proceeded with in the House.[2]

The following year, probably at McLean's insistence, Fenton was excluded from the Legislative Council because of his official position.[3] William Gisborne, the Colonial Secretary, reintroduced Fenton's Bill but a Select Committee of the Assembly concluded that the Land Court should not assume such large powers as Fenton contemplated, independent of Government. Some of the phrases of the Select Committee's report—the suggestion that Fenton's proposals would 're-establish the old protectorate system' and 'interfere with the [Maori owners'] free right of disposal of their lands'—show that the self-interest of the land-sharks had as much to do with the defeat of Fenton's bid for enlarged powers, as disinterested concern at the possible abuse of those powers.[4]

Meanwhile McLean had made two counter moves. He appointed Charles Heaphy, a Victoria Cross winner from the wars, to be Commissioner of Native Reserves, with wide powers. Gisborne had expected him to work with the Chief Judge, but McLean kept him firmly under his own control. Secondly the Government passed a Native Lands Frauds Prevention Act, under which were appointed Trust Commissioners (officers of the Native Department, not the Land Court), authorised to disallow any transaction in Maori land if contrary to equity or in contravention of any trusts, or if liquor or arms formed part of the consideration. This measure was only partially effective. It was not retrospective and when H. R. Russell, leader of a rival faction to that of McLean in Hawke's Bay politics, in order to strike at McLean's own dubious dealings, secured an amendment in the Legislative Council to make it retrospective, McLean had it deleted in the House of Representatives.[5] The five Trust Commissioners appointed were all part-time officials and could not possibly investigate all transactions thoroughly. Although they reported optimistically that they were having a salutary effect, and certainly did deter some of the more blatant frauds, the records show that some were either careless or downright unscrupulous. Thus Hanson Turton, Jr, McLean's appointee as Trust Commissioner in Hawke's Bay, passed deeds signed by minors, took care to warn his patron, McLean, to cover flaws in his transactions, and used his powers cavalierly to reject a transaction by McLean's rival, H. R. Russell.[6] Both Haultain and Parris (Trust Commissioners in Auckland and Hawke's Bay respectively), whether deliberately or inadvertently it is impossible to tell, passed sales of land the restrictions on alienation of which had not been removed.[7] The stream of petitions to parliament by Maori claimants left out of transactions or deliberately gulled supports the opinion of a later Native Minister that 'It is notorious that the Frauds Commissioners in the past have performed their duties in the most perfunctory manner, and passed transactions when the consideration was a mere bagatelle'.[8]

Heaphy and the district reserves commissioners undoubtedly did some extremely useful work in saving reserves, such as the sections on which the town of Greymouth was built, from the demands of settler politicians to transfer them, as the Princes Street reserve had been transferred, to settler ownership. They secured redress for some grievances, such as payment of compensation for the Wellington reserves taken for public purposes in Grey's first governorship. And they were usually efficient in securing the best possible revenue from reserves under their control. At Greymouth, for example, where the reserves yielded some £21,500 between 1869 and 1879, the ninety beneficiaries (approximately) gained good quality housing, regular food in times of crop failure, and medical and educational assistance.[9] But this was exceptional, as the reserves were usually not sufficient to yield the revenue for even an average living standard.

Efforts to bring more land under the reserves commissioners in trust failed. Early in his appointment Heaphy did secure 31,000 acres in Hawke's Bay, before settlers found that by paying deposits to two or three lesser owners they could block the completion of a trust. Moreover, Maori owners were deeply suspicious of the system.

The proneness of many Maori owners to succumb to offers of purchase in order to clear the stigma of indebtedness (or the threat of gaol) led reserves commissioners to adopt a strongly paternalistic attitude to the beneficial owners of such reserves as were vested in the Crown. They willingly discussed the administration of reserves with meetings of owners but were not inclined to grant them legal powers. This exclusion was deeply offensive to Maori owners. With reference to the consolidating Native Reserves Act, 1873, Renata Kawepo of Hawke's Bay wrote, 'This law resembles the law for Pakeha children, drunkards and lunatics. And we are compared by this law to infants, inebriates and idiots.'[10]

That the administrators could see no answer to Maori inexperience and cupidity other than a rigid paternalistic control which entirely inhibited the growth of Maori responsibility, remained one of the weaknesses in Maori land administration until the twentieth century. The Maori landowners' response was to decline to place under the Crown any more reserves than they were obliged to. The fact that reserves occasionally did pass out of the trustees' hands through compulsory acquisition under the Public Works Act, seemed to justify their distrust.

In 1870-3 McLean considered further remedial legislation affecting the central problem—the working of the Native Lands Acts. The Maori people's principal grievances were the ruinous cost of surveys, the fact that application by one claimant obliged all to join the scramble if they were to have any hope of appearing on the title and the ten-owner system worked by Fenton. From his experience as commissioner of confiscated lands in Tauranga, H. T. Clarke urged that the Land Court should meet on the land itself, exclude all parasitic lawyers and agents and have its own surveyors; if land was to be sold, the Court should make inalienable reserves (at a minimum rate of acres per head) and supervise the distribution of payment. At McLean's request, Sir William Martin, assisted by Dr Edward Shortland, former Civil Commissioner and Native Secretary, submitted a draft which endorsed these principles and added important provisos in favour of sale by public auction only, compulsory invest- ment of purchase moneys, succession strictly according to Maori custom, and a preliminary investigation by the judges (to show that applications came from a substantial proportion of the *hapu* likely to be found the rightful owners, not from an isolated individual pressed by a would-be purchaser).[11]

Fenton, smarting under his defeats of 1869-70 and resenting interference with his Court, responded with a violent denunciation of Martin's 'ridiculous' principles as likely to destroy the judicial authority of the Court and reduce it to the role of negotiator, land broker and auction room (which might indeed, were it true, have been the most honest thing to have done with the Land Court). He also claimed that it would frustrate the purpose of the Land Acts as he saw them—the creation of a leisured class of chiefs with the rest of the Maori race obliged to work at wage labour for a living. Claiming that, apart from the matter of excessive survey charges, Maori owners were not dissatisfied with the system, Fenton forwarded his own draft bill which strengthened the rights of mortgagees over Maori land and increased the powers of the judges —for instance making the presence of Maori Assessors dependent on their discretion.[12] T. M. Haultain, appointed by McLean to conduct a commission of inquiry into the subject, also reported that survey costs, mortgages and the ten-owner system were anomalous, but claimed that Maori witnesses desired no major transformation of the Court. C. W. Richmond, heading another inquiry, secured by McLean's political opponents, into the by then notorious Hawke's Bay land transactions, reached similar conclusions. He recommended the appointment of subordinate officers to make the preliminary inquiries into the genuineness of an application for determination of title and to decide upon reserves; but as the Court had established a judicial authority among the Maori, Richmond argued that it would be retrogressive to reduce it to the status of a commission. It was indeed true that the Court, backed by the police power which the Pakeha were now capable of, did have authority in Maori eyes. Moreover, it was resorted to readily enough by many claimants who sought the victory in long-standing land disputes with their tribal rivals in the new arena, or who wished to secure the cash payments being touted by land purchasers before some other claimant headed them off. But a close reading of the evidence before Haultain's commission suggested that many Maori witnesses, including Wi Te Wheoro and Paora Tuhaere, favoured settling titles among themselves through a form of traditional *runanga* and bringing their decision to the Court to secure the requisite confirmation and authoritative support.[13]

In the event, although McLean adopted much of Martin's draft as the basis of a new Bill, parliament agreed with the views of Fenton, Haultain and Richmond, and the Native Land Act of 1873, re-established the Land Court and Fenton's powers much as before. Certain definite reforms were made. Surveys became the responsibility of Government surveyors acting under the Native Department, and mortgages could no longer be enforced against undivided interests in Maori land. 'District Officers' were to be appointed to make preliminary inquiries into the good faith of a claimant, to arrange for the setting apart of inalienable reserves at a fixed ratio of 50 acres per man, woman and child, and to compile genealogies and maps of tribal boundaries. The Judges were required to take cognisance of the facts the District Officers produced in Court, and numbers of other safeguards were erected to prevent such abuses as forgery of signatures or mistranslation of deeds.

But while he wanted to guard against fraud and total Maori landlessness, McLean had sought to place no real restriction on direct purchase. Martin's principle of sale by public auction was shelved as it had been in 1865. McLean's own land-purchase agents in fact led the way in the system of 'laying ground bait'—advancing payment to some owners to secure a foothold in the title and completing the purchase over a period of years. One further great change was introduced by the 1873 Act, namely the requirement that every Maori owner be listed in the 'Memorial of Ownership' and the signature of each be obtained before a purchase could be complete. This made it easy for agents to begin to purchase a title but hard to complete the purchase and in fact slowed the rate of alienation of Maori land. It has been contended—and many contemporary statements support the view—that the provision marked a new stage in the drive towards individualisation of Maori land titles,[14] and, hopefully, of Maori society. But though this was certainly in the minds of some Ministers it does not seem to have been McLean's main intention. He sought rather to end Fenton's ten-owner system, define interests by *hapu* or family, with each one of a limited number of owners named, in order that they should not be at the mercy of irresponsible trustees. Further individualisation of interests he saw only as a long term goal. Indeed the 50 acres per head of reserves which the District Officers were to make were intended, in McLean's expressed view, to allow Maori communities to continue their traditional village order relatively cushioned from the demands of Pakeha society.[15] Yet there is little doubt from the way McLean used his Land Purchase Officers, that he felt that if the listing of all owners facilitated the purchase of the remainder of their estate, so much the better, since half to three-quarters of the North Island was said to be still in Maori ownership.

Unfortunately, most of McLean's safeguards broke down. Before the 1873 Act was passed McLean was warned that Fenton 'may neutralise the best Act that can be passed, if it does not originate in his brain'.[16] This indeed proved to be the case. Fenton produced a long document claiming to show that many of the clauses of the Act were contradictory and unworkable, and he made no effort to make them work.[17] Soon he was back to his high-handed ways with Maori land, playing fast and loose with requirements about succession and reserves. Te Wheoro gave up his position as Land Court Assessor angry and disgusted, later claiming: 'It would appear, when a block was going through the Native Land Court, as if the land was owned by the Court itself, and not by the litigants'.[18] A Judge who quarrelled with Fenton, asserted that the Court tended to ask 'not what is right or is Constitutional but "what does the Chief Judge say" '.[19] Many of Fenton's brother Judges were no better than he; Maning, for example, despised the Maori and thought 5 acres per head was ample reserve for them.[20]

The District Officers also had little success, enjoying the confidence neither of Fenton, who resented their 'interference', nor of the Maori people, who were reluctant to tie their land up into inalienable reserves at the request of a Government official.[21] Before long the District Officers' only effective role was to make preliminary inquiries and advise the Court whether it could safely hear a claim without the danger of rival claimants disturbing the peace. This was not unimportant work; it is significant that the number of obstructed surveys and armed confrontations between claimants was very high in Ngatiporou territory where there was no District Officer and many Maori learned of a pending claim and transaction only when the surveyors appeared on the ground.[22] But without the strict creation of the 50 acres per head of reserve, the 1873 Act did little but prolong the passing of the land. Indeed, in a sense, it made things very much worse. Since all owners were listed, such chiefs as were still good trustees of their people's land, were powerless to stop surreptitious sales by rank and file owners. Consequently those chiefs who had long resisted now tended to sell in their old age because the land was passing anyway and they sought to share the proceeds before they died.

Hundreds of examples could be given of the dubious traffic in Maori lands at this time; one must suffice. The Crown and a private purchaser, Robert Graham, were contenders for the small but important Wairakei block, containing hot springs and geysers. At the Land Court hearing the Judge spent five days hearing the case of one of four sets of Maori claimants—the group with whom Graham had been negotiating. Then he announced that he would return to Auckland the next day and the remaining three groups rushed their cases through. One of them employed an agent and interpreter, J. C. Young, but their case seemed a little hopeless in view of the fact that Young had his fee and expenses paid by Graham. At 4 p.m. on the sixth day the Judge ruled in favour of a list of five names handed in by the first group of claimants—but he did not read the list for fear of disorder. By that evening Graham had worried the five into signing a deed of sale for two shillings and sixpence an acre.[23]

One important feature brightened an otherwise sombre picture. About one-twelfth of all land passing the Court was placed under restriction. Head Office referred all requests for removal of restrictions to the local Resident Magistrate for advice on whether all owners consented to the sale and had other lands adequate for their support, or whether minors' interests had to be protected. This gave the men most cognisant of Maori needs a chance to resist the encroachment of land agents. Woon's angry reply opposing the sale of Putiki reserve, near Wanganui, was typical. Outright refusal was normally given in the case of town sections, South Island reserves, fishing stations, or any Maori's last acres. At other times the Native Office would withhold consent until the price was raised to the minimum value of unimproved land in the vicinity.[24] Control was not watertight. For example, Te Aro *pa* in Wellington was considered a nest of immorality and sale of Wellington sections was from time to time approved; much rested on the perception of the local officer; and McLean was not very respectful of the interest of non-sellers until Sullivan was killed on Pukekura block, from which restrictions had only shortly before been lifted.[25] But refusal was more often given than consent and the alienation of many key areas was at least long delayed. Thus much must be set against the sordid trafficking in land which characterised the period.

Despite the failings of the 1873 Act McLean was reluctant to depart from its principles until pressed in 1876 by Vogel, then Premier, who proposed to abolish direct purchase altogether and take up the principle of sale by public auction, the Crown to act as agents on commission and the Maori vendors to state what areas of a block should be exempted from sale and what minimum price they wanted. But a Bill to this effect did not get beyond the introductory stage in the 1876 parliament; its principles lay in abeyance until the 1880s.[26]

McLean's record with regard to the land laws reveals something of the ambivalence and deviousness of his character and his policy. As has been shown he was resolute in preventing the more blatant intrusions into Maori land by Public Works officers or Provincial politicians and earned the Native Department a rich harvest of unpopularity. Clarke commented wryly when asked by the Public Works Department to assist in negotiating a telegraph line: 'They know whom to come to to help them out of their difficulties—and then abuse them soundly afterwards.'[27] Awareness of settler hostility to their intervention was one reason why the Native Department did not do more to protect Maori interests. Discussing a *hapu's* efforts to prevent a stretch of fishing water from being drained, Clarke added: 'It is a great pity the Natives have not someone to advise them in this matter. It would never do for a Government officer and especially for one of this wretched Native Department to tender such advice. It would directly be stated that we were opposing the opening up of the country.'[28] McLean too, was inhibited at the political level, from going far to redress Maori grievances. Spurred by his officers he did, for example, pay £4600 for the Wellington reserves taken for public purposes by Grey in 1853, and further cash compensation to Kupapa *hapu* aggrieved by the taking of land in Wairoa, Poverty Bay and Taranaki. But more far-reaching questions received less consideration. When a Select Committee recommended a moderate enlargement of the miniscule reserves in Canterbury McLean replied that the Government would not consider the forfeiture of so large a part of the public estate.[29] Although he secured payment of £5000 to the Maori owners of Princes Street Reserve this was made not in recognition of their claims but to stop litigation, and it was many years before the owners were granted the £6000 accrued back rents. Above all, he could not, in the face of settler demand, seriously restrict land purchase operations.

Yet while these were matters in which McLean was largely a prisoner of public opinion as reflected in Cabinet and Parliament, there were also a great many other matters in which he held direct responsibility. In the course of his diplomacy McLean made a great many promises of redress, usually verbal, which were never followed up and remained to plague his successors after his death. His apparently good staff work and furious concentration at moments of crisis did not extend to supervising the implementation of routine adminis-trative decisions. Reserves were promised and not marked out; interminable delays hung over question after question and unless aggrieved Maori or their sponsors made a persistent fuss McLean was content to let them lie.

He was not above bluster and deceit. A familiar gambit was to urge Maori land-holders to put their lands through the Court, saying that the settlement of title in no way involved alienation, blandly rejecting Maori protestations, which he well knew to be true, that once ownership had been awarded the designated owners were open to pressure from land agents and creditors and beyond the control of the *hapu* as a whole. He would assure Maori communi-ties protesting at a survey that it was only a trial line; he would purchase from a minority and try to brush aside the remainder, though he was now quick to draw back if they stood firm; he would hint that Crown-granted land might be taken under the Public Works Act for road or other public purposes—but give the owners a chance to sell freely if they chose; he would respect the objections of powerful groups but complaints of injustice by unimportant individuals were ignored; though his system of rewards and gifts brought considerable advantage to the compliant, he also used it in reverse and threatened with loss of office Assessors who opposed the purchase of land.[30]

The ambivalence of McLean's character and policies reached down and affected his whole Department, so that it is difficult to generalise about the attitude of his officers. Many were a good distance ahead of the settler com-munity at large in freedom from racial prejudice and respect for the Maori as individuals. Thus when a Pakeha jury acquitted a settler manifestly guilty of wounding a Maori, a Native Department officer in the Waikato expressed concern, writing 'we were under the impression that the d—— nigger theory was thoroughly exploded in our island'.[31] Yet W. G. Mair still habitually wrote of the Maori as 'niggers' and Maning continued to breath rancour about them in his private correspondence.

Moreover, even those who liked Maori personality and character did not usually respect Maori institutions. Thus Woon wrote proudly: 'The race is, from increasing contact with the Anglo-Saxon (the greatest colonizers of the earth) advancing every day in the scale of civilization, and soon all Maori customs and habits will become a thing of the past.'[32] Perhaps it was his sense of imperial mission that caused Woon to be among the most earnest of Native Department Officers in introducing new skills and crops on the Wanganui River. But he like others, was quickly discouraged by lack of progress and inclined to fall back on the idea that the Maori would be better off when they had no surplus lands and were compelled to work for settlers as labourers or take up trades—a notion that conflicted with and generally overrode alarm at the possibility of Maori landlessness and concern that larger reserves should be made.[33]

The Native Department was also affected by personal rivalry and factionalism. This was not uncommon in a Civil Service which depended heavily upon patronage for promotion, but in McLean's department the weaknesses of the system were multiplied by his liking for and tendency to attract flattery and subservience. All of McLean's officers reported confidentially to him as well as officially, advancing their own claims to favours and reporting adversely on their colleagues—'cat and dog' behaviour, as Clarke put it. Jealousy and tale-telling sometimes flared into public scandal (as in the row between James Wilson, Land Purchase Officer, and Rogan, Judge of the Land Court).[34] McLean's tendency to give office to sycophantic cronies led to bad appointments, such as those of George Worgan and James Grindell—men already dismissed for dishonesty and drunkenness respectively. While briefly running the Native Office in McLean's absence, Fox discovered that Worgan was supposed to be buying land for the Government at £1 an acre, but was paying the lesser Maori owners only ten shillings and splitting the remaining ten shillings between himself and the principal chief.[35] The power that McLean had accumulated for his Department was easily misused by men in the out-districts. Aggrieved Maori—and some settlers—usually had to put up with this. A Maori complainant recalls being ordered out of the office of H. T. Clarke, then Civil Commissioner of the Bay of Plenty. 'Of course,' he added, 'I did as I was ordered, without a murmur; for in those days officers of the Native Department were almost despotic.'[36]

There seemed to be a fateful tendency for land purchase work to corrupt those involved in it. Unfortunately McLean was not so determined as his predecessors to keep Resident Magistrates' duties clearly distinct from those of Land Purchase Officers. By the end of the 1870s it was apparent that Resident Magistrates such as Woon, Barstow, Williams and Brabant, who were careful to disassociate themselves from land-purchasing, still retained the confidence of their people even in the midst of bitter controversy over land. But one or two, such as Campbell of Waiapu, became involved in dubious land deals, impaired their impartial status and frittered away their authority. The result in Campbell's case was a steady demoralisation to the point where he was suspected of trade in illicit liquor and of defalcation of Assessors' pay, while a spirit of lawlessness and drunkenness spread among the Ngatiporou.

An epitome of the McLean spirit was provided by the conduct of his officers on the West Coast—most of whom he had known from the pre-1860 period. Partly because they genuinely liked them, and partly to secure Maori compliance with the survey of the West Coast confiscation, McLean's men, from time to time, took Maori mistresses. The liaison was usually preceded by bargaining with the girls' kin, who valued the alliance with a Government officer. Brown, Civil Commissioner in Taranaki, noted that the relatives of the mistress of Captain Blake, another of McLean's officers, were vexed with Blake for some reason 'and wanted to take her from him and give her to me'. Brown, a widower, was not disinclined, adding 'For if it is necessary for the acquisition of the plains, no woman shall be left out in the cold, only they must catch me before I get another wife.' He delayed taking over the girl because he was contemplating marriage with a Pakeha woman, but decided not to propose because 'She told me that she "hated Maoris and everyone who likes them" and other playful remarks that went against the grain.'[37] These were the very hall-marks of the administration of McLean and most of his staff—a certain raw liking for the Maori people, combined incongruously with the use of a variety of immoral and amoral tactics to gain their 'surplus' lands. Divided motives, self-interest, even corruption marred their administration but at least it generally avoided the most arrant racialism and subservience to the more ruthless settler attitudes.

McLean's methods generated much heated opposition. In building his Department he had tipped out of office men like W. S. Atkinson, the appointees of his political adversaries, and reinstated many who were his cronies from the days before the wars, or satellites of his new appointees. Thus H. T. Clarke, when appointed Under-Secretary, brought with him to Wellington his brother Marsden, who became interpreter and front office man, greeting the stream of Maori visitors to the Native Office, and his clerk, Richard Gill, who eventually headed the Land Purchase division of the Department created in 1874. The deposed factions of course searched for and found plenty of sticks in the form of petty scandal with which to beat the Native Department.

In parliament there were heated annual objections to McLean's extensive and allegedly unnecessary staff and to his heavy contingency expenditure, which was given the familiar designation of a 'flour and sugar' policy. It was held that McLean secured Maori acquiescence in Government policies only by liberal gifts, payments or grants of office, that such a policy exhibited weakness and encouraged Maori opposition, or alternatively was pauperising in effect. It was further alleged that McLean had built his system of influence, his 'personal government', primarily for his own aggrandisement, and was using his departmental machinery to damage his political opponents. There was substance to these charges. McLean did use his officials to influence Maori electors especially against the Stafford party in 1872, the faction of H. R. Russell and John Sheehan in Hawke's Bay and, after 1875, against the party formed about Sir George Grey, who had retired in New Zealand and entered colonial politics. The Maori-language newspaper *Waka Maori* became a focal point for opposition attack because it too was used by McLean for party purposes. There were also some inevitable abuses of contingency expenditure, such as the use by several Ngatiporou chiefs of a ton of seed potatoes, not for planting, but to redeem a store debt largely accrued in liquor.[38]

For some years McLean's adversaries had little success, for it was manifest that his tactics were not only keeping the peace but gradually opening more and more territory to colonisation. South Island members in particular, were well aware that renewed war would cost them more than McLean's Department, so were content to allow him a liberal purse and to be patient with recalcitrant chiefs. Relying on their support McLean was able, in supply debates, to brush aside criticism of himself and his officers with a few brief words—which in itself served to further enrage his opponents.[39] Moreover, since he controlled defence and land purchase funds as well he had little difficulty sidestepping minor restrictions on his expenditure. When he proposed to lend money for a flour mill and the Commissioners of Audit declined on principle to 'allow public money to pass on loan to Natives' McLean simply issued the money from one of his many funds as a final payment for land and credited it again as it was repaid.[40] Native affairs came to be regarded as McLean's speciality, a subject where the uninitiated could not trespass, while McLean himself was accorded a position almost above party and, except during Stafford's month-long government in 1872, was included in every Ministry between 1869 and 1876.

But by 1876 his position was becoming precarious. This was partly a product of his success. He had kept the peace long enough for the war-weariness of the early 1870s to fade. Settlers had become impatient of his cautious waiting policy towards the King movement and Te Whiti. When Winiata, who killed his European employer in Auckland, reached sanctuary in the King Country there was a violent debate in the Assembly, condemning the Kingite *imperium in imperio*.[41] Once again the familiar cry of 'law and order' provided the emotional cutting edge to the broader thrust towards settlement of Maori lands.

McLean's Pakeha opponents were joined by Maori supporters. In 1875 Karaitiana Takamoana won the Eastern Maori seat for the Repudiation movement. This movement, among the Hawke's Bay Maori in particular, to challenge the shabby land transactions of the previous decade, had been taken up by H. R. Russell, and the lawyer John Sheehan, largely as a means of striking at McLean and his Hawke's Bay associates. Taiaroa, Southern Maori, voicing the grievances of the South Island communities, also joined the opposition, while petitions began to come from small communities of the North Island, who had become aware of the speciousness of many of McLean's promises, that he be 'overthrown'.[42]

In 1876 with McLean absent from the Assembly, Grey and Sheehan succeeded in reducing the Native Department vote, especially contingency expenditure, and the vote for McLean's newspaper, the *Waka Maori*, was specifically struck out. The first inroads were also made into the structure of McLean's empire by the transfer of responsibility for confiscated lands and surveys of

Maori lands to the Department of Crown Lands. Exultant opponents forecast the end of McLean's political life.[43] When in fact McLean abruptly retired in December 1876 his opponents rejoiced at the fall of 'the New Zealand Wolsey'. But their victory was hollow; McLean was a very ill man and within a month he was dead.

McLean does indeed invite comparison with Wolsey—or with Grey. Like them he amassed power, resented rivals, was egotistical, could write a plausible despatch, and was not particularly scrupulous. But McLean surpassed Grey in ability to like and understand Maori people and he was subsequently to be remembered by them, in a time of colder personalities, with some nostalgia and warmth. Moreover, his Native Councils Bill 1872 was an attempt to secure recognition of their rights, aspirations and abilities.

How much credit should accrue to McLean personally for the years of peace during his tenure of office? It is certainly true that he was able to pursue a peace policy mainly because with the withdrawal of the Imperial troops settler opinion had come to appreciate that Maori resistance could not be brushed aside without a considerable cost in blood and treasure—that the Maori were not people to be meddled with lightly. But McLean personally bore a considerable responsibility during the periodic outbursts of settler demands for the enforced opening of the King Country, or carrying of roads through Te Whiti's territory. Not all of his colleagues (Fox for instance) or his successors showed the same patience and forbearance with Maori opposition and the same resolution to withstand settler pressure, as McLean at the height of his career. His opponents caricatured his tolerance as appeasement, but McLean at least had recognised that the settlers, not the Maori, were the intruders.

It can nevertheless be stated—as it was bluntly stated by the astute and principled Te Whiti—that McLean's policy was still largely bent on the subjugation and subordination of the Maori people. The limits to his willingness to support their values and aspirations soon showed through. His withdrawal of the Native Councils Bill, for example, and his persistent turning aside of requests from junior officers to implement the sections of the 1868 Juries Act providing for Maori juries, indicated his greater respect for settler prejudices than Maori needs and wishes.

McLean believed it inevitable that settlement must spread and was too much the settler politician not to support, in the main, his fellow settlers' drive to extend colonisation. His protestations of respect for Maori rights and values, and of their claim to a share of state power, were not the expressions of a man detached, principles to be defended at all costs. It was Martin, not McLean, who would have recognised the King movement and restored much of the Waikato land. But McLean, the politician, did not have Martin's freedom. His career was a course steered between settler pressure and Maori resistance. Because the former was the stronger McLean's policy was largely a continuation of that which Grey and he himself had evolved in the 1840s and 1850s, namely one of 'managing' the Maori people to permit the extension of settlement at the greatest rate possible short of provoking renewed violence. In this somewhat limited aim he was highly successful.

XVIII

Maori Initiative and Frustration

Previous chapters have argued that the Maori people, including both Kupapa and 'rebel' tribes, engaged very positively with the institutions promoted by McLean in their districts. The point must be heavily stressed owing to the persistence of the myth, founded by anthropologists and largely demolished by historians, that after the wars most of the tribes, demoralised by defeat and confiscation, lapsed into a 'dark age', a period of apathy, the Kupapa tribes allowing themselves to be fleeced of their land and the ex-'rebels' dwelling in sullen defiance and isolation within their boundaries; from this attitude, the traditional account runs, they were rescued in the late nineteenth and early twentieth centuries, the 'renaissance' being led by the Ngatiporou, a tribe which suffered little in the wars, and by several leading figures—Ngata, Buck and Pomare—trained in the Western tradition and able to straddle, in masterly fashion, both Maori and Pakeha worlds. Alternatively, the honour of leading the Maori emergence into self-respect and confident grappling with the new order has been given to the movement of the prophet Ratana in the 1920s.[1]

In point of fact, as even a cursory reading of contemporary published reports of the Native Department officers reveals, among many tribes the cessation of fighting was accompanied by an upsurge of determination to come to grips with the now apparently unshakable Pakeha world and to succeed in it. Not only were there requests from Kupapa tribes such as the Ngapuhi for settlers, gaols, doctors, schools and communications, but, as has been stated, McLean's officers also received a warm reception from former 'rebels' such as the Ngati-raukawa, and most of the people in the Taupo, Bay of Plenty and upper Wanganui districts. Maori leaders asked for magistrates to come amongst them to teach them the law and build schools; they asked for appointment as Assessors and policemen; they asked for roads and townships in order, they said, that they might widen their markets and sources of employment and purchase goods competitively.[2] For some communities these were fairly new requests, but for many they were only a resumption of the drive of the pre-war years to engage with the incoming Western order and share its advantages equally with the Pakeha. The renewed engagement was a conscious adaptation, but not an acceptance of total assimilation to the Pakeha mould. Of the 1870s and 1880s Sir Apirana Ngata, one of the most eminent scions of the age, was later to write: 'The old men did send us forth as were the Japanese nobles after the West had forced its way into Japan, to learn the material culture of the West in order to prepare the people to take the impact of [Western] civilisation with the least harm to essentials.'[3]

Europeans officials expected that the cessation of hostilities would see a revival of the cultivation of grain that Maori communities had developed in the 1850s and encouraged them as before with gifts of seed wheat, ploughs and grants for flour mills. Indeed, from 1870 grain was again cultivated in all districts including the King Country, some Maori-owned schooners began again to trade with Auckland, flour mills were refurbished and used in several North Island districts for most of the century, harvesting machinery was purchased, and the hostelry and grain store built by Waikato tribes at Onehunga on the head of the Manukau harbour in 1853 was again in use. However production of grain (which increasingly included oats and maize rather than wheat) did not usually reach more than 50 per cent of pre-war levels, largely because many Maori leaders turned to pastoral farming along with the settlers. Much has been written about the Ngatiporou leading the way in sheep farming in the 1880s and 1890s. But by 1870 they already had six or seven thousand sheep scattered in small flocks along the East Coast. By the mid-seventies some chiefs in Hawke's Bay, Rangitikei and the Chatham Islands were also running flocks of several thousand, in some cases employing Pakeha shepherds. Hapuku had 5000 and Renata Kawepo gave 2000 from his large flocks to Mete Kingi of Wanganui when Kingi started sheep farming in 1877. Small herds of cattle were also carried in most districts.[4]

Northern communities relied heavily on the pre-war extractive industries of *kauri* gum digging, timber milling and flax-dressing because land was either not suitable, or not available for farming. Several coastal *hapu* built boats or financed them through government loans, to resume whaling. Contract labour was also popular as whole communities could camp near the place of work, the women and children foraging and cooking, the men working long hours. Contract work included road making, bush-clearing, fencing, harvesting and shearing. A traveller in the 1870s noted that most shearing gangs were Maori, a situation which persists today.[5]

It is clear from the variety of economic enterprises which Maori entered into immediately after the wars that they were far from supine. From at least as early as 1872 the Kingites too were trading increasingly across the *aukati* in wheat, hops, pigs and other commodities and using cultivating machinery obtained through government officers. A considerable portion of them moved close to the confiscation boundary to secure the advantage both of better soil for grain cultivation and easy access to the Pakeha towns. A 'native store' was built by the Government at Alexandra to encourage this trade.[6]

The Ngatiporou have also been credited with establishing the first marketing and retail co-operatives, in 1885-95. In fact co-operatives grew very early as an extension of kinship organisation and needs. Campbell reported from the

East Coast as early as 1875 that, 'Several stores, some on the co-operative principle, have been established, and appear to be doing well.'[7] But the Tauranga people were reported to be experimenting with a co-operative in 1869 and the Raglan and Waikato Maori Company was inaugurated in 1872 to issue 5000 shares at £10 per lot of 500 (no Pakeha being permitted to buy), build a vessel, buy up Waikato grain for sale at Onehunga, and retail goods purchased in Auckland.[8] These early enterprises failed for want of managerial experience among the organisers, and the difficulty that treasurers had in resisting pressures to spend funds among kinsmen. But intermittent attempts at co-operative ventures continued to be made until experience, and stronger legal protection of trust monies, made greater success possible about the turn of the century.

In the late 1870s some Maori communities began to benefit from tourism. Rotorua people began working as guides in the thermal districts and in 1879 the first Maori concert party went to Sydney, under a Pakeha entrepreneur, to become forerunners of a major industry on Australia's east coast.[9]

Despite the impressive amount of enterprise the Maori people's place in the New Zealand economy was precarious. They depended heavily on extractive industries which were declining and on labouring which was unskilled and seasonal. Wages and contract pay were soon spent but meanwhile traditional planting or bird-catching seasons could be missed. When potato crops—the staple—were ruined by blight, Maori communities, their traditional ecological relationship with the bush or sea seriously disturbed before they had achieved true integration into the commercial economy, actually faced malnutrition or dependence on government doles.

Moreover, many of the spectacular developments in pastoral farming centred on a single chief, who had been successful both in manipulating Government and Land Court, and in persuading his *hapu* to support or at least acquiesce in his efforts. For example, the Ngatiruanui chief, Hone Pihama, an ex-'rebel', had gained from a succession of Governments anxious to placate him the sole rights to 2000 acres of first class land, interests in numerous other land titles, stipends as Assessor and as guard to the Cobb and Co. coach between Wanganui and New Plymouth, contracts for mail carrying and numerous small cash payments and presents, the whole calculated to be worth about £5300 during McLean's tenure of office. Hone was sufficiently wealthy to build a hotel with stables and put it under a Pakeha manager.[10] Other chiefs did well out of road contracts, which they sub-contracted to men of lesser rank to get the work done, and in the 1870s the bases of substantial and lasting fortunes were laid by a number of fortunately placed Maori. But many were less secure. Hapuku, for example, was in debt to H. R. Russell for most of his 5000 sheep. And although the *hapu* of a prospering chief usually shared in some measure in his prosperity, they also shared his downfall. Even *hapu* that achieved a more solidly based community enterprise, often declined in fortune after the death of leaders who held the group to its initial sense of purpose.

The worst destroyer of consistent enterprise was the operation of the Land Court and subsequent land purchasing. It was exceedingly difficult for the owners listed on multiple titles, their shares increasingly fragmented through the introduced system of succession, to organise effectively to farm their land; on the contrary it was all too easy for owners to gain a ready penny by signing a deed of sale or lease or grant of timber rights to one, or several, of the land agents prowling the out-districts or lounging in the city hotels. Under these temptations chiefs betrayed their people and commoners betrayed chiefs. Nothing, save perhaps epidemic disease, was so disruptive of Maori life as this. It was the sordid, demoralising system of land-purchasing, not war and confiscation, which really brought the Maori people low.[11]

The same early positiveness, followed by increasing frustration and bitterness, can be seen in other fields, such as education. Many Maori parents, expecting that Pakeha education would enable their children to share in the benefits of a clearly Pakeha-dominated order, badgered for schools, insisted on their children's attendance and demanded that they be instructed in English. In recent years the fact that Maori children were punished for speaking Maori in the government schools and playgrounds is recalled with bitterness, as evidence of enforced assimilation; but in the 1870s Maori parents themselves petitioned that this should be so.[12] Many schools failed, partly from the shortcomings of teachers who did not show sufficient sensitivity to cultural differences but the steady increase in the number of schools, and the interest of Maori communities in them, pleased and surprised official observers.

However, village school education was too elementary to make Maori children readily employable. Various people—Governor Bowen, several Resident Magistrates and Maori spokesmen—urged McLean to provide more facilities for secondary education and trade training. In a forward-looking statement, Te Matenga of the Bay of Islands stated his people's needs:

> we have been taught three things—reading, writing and arithmetic. What we want is, that education should be progressive, and that schools should be established for children of two years up to twenty-one . . . We want more than these three things to enable our descendants to cope with the Europeans.[13]

McLean did approve grants to the few church boarding schools being established, or revived in the 1870s, and paid the fees for the sons of several chiefs attending them. Some of the wealthier Maori leaders also raised money to send their children to secondary school, so that by 1877 there were 220 Maori pupils in secondary schools, particularly Te Aute and Stephen's Colleges (Anglican schools for boys), Hukarere and St Joseph's (Anglican and Catholic girls' schools respectively) and Auckland Grammar School. These provided an elite of well-educated young Maori, many of whom became leaders of their people by the turn of the century; but the majority of Maori children had no opportunity for more than elementary schooling. This was also true, of course, for the majority of settlers' children, but they had many more opportunities to join parents' enterprises or become apprentices. Maori parents themselves, however, were reluctant to see their children apprenticed, regarding the long and arduous indenture as a form of exploitation—which in fact it often was. As one of McLean's officers had pointed out, special trade training schemes for Maori youths could easily have been provided out of endowments of Crown land or land offered by Maori communities themselves,[14] but such training was in fact neglected between 1863—after the closure of Gorst's school at Otawhao—and 1945, when Maori Members of Parliament such as Eruera Tirikatene began to prod the state towards a new appreciation of its special responsibilities in the matter.

The other major vehicles of European culture, the organised churches, were still largely avoided by the 'rebel' tribes because of their association with government and conquest. But there was a revival of church-building and requests for resident clergy in Northland and the East Coast, parts of the Bay of Plenty and lower Waikato, Manawatu and along the Wanganui river. Where the CMS kept their stations manned, a fairly constant congregation was retained. It was also highly significant that where Maori teachers and clergy were still employed, they could build congregations and win over former Hauhau.[15] The involvement of Maori laity in support of the local church through Native Church Boards was also said to be effective in Northland.[16] But the CMS, depressed by the catastrophe of the 1860s, withdrew from New Zealand, and the metropolitan churches, while retaining the land Maori communities had given for CMS stations, found almost no place for Maori representation and leadership. This situation was a far cry from the years before 1870 when Anglican synods had been dominated by missionary and Maori clergy and conducted in the Maori language, and was a source of grievance to Maori clergy and people.[17]

Nevertheless, the churches were unlikely, even if they had tried much harder, to have regained the influence over Maori life that they had enjoyed in many communities before 1860. For the causes of disillusionment went far beyond the involvement of the churches with government and army in the 1860s; 'loyal' tribes as well as 'rebels' were turning away because of the Christian churches' apparent inability to assist them to overcome the problems resulting from culture contact. Thus, when Anglican clergy at Waiapu urged the local Maori to stop spending heavily on *tangi* and give their money to the church, they remarked to the Resident Magistrate that they had 'had quite enough of that in former years'.[18] Maori Christianity assumed a pattern closer to that of the surrounding settlers. There was a good deal of nominal church adherence and an increasing vogue for church weddings, but the week-day life of Maori communities was detached and secular. Ashwell regretted that many young chiefs, formerly zealous mission teachers, now spent their time as Assessors or policemen—and in the public house.[19] Meanwhile, much of the traditional order endured in the form of persistent belief in *makutu,* continued polygamy by pagan chiefs, the resort to *tohunga* or spiritual healers, and the rise and fall of prophetic movements.

The 1870s, as has been noted, saw the Maori people heavily involved in local administration. However, their roles as Assessors, police and members of school committees were almost entirely within the system of administration built by the Native Department. They had almost nothing to do with the machinery of settler local administration—the Highways and Harbour Boards, the Provincial Councils, or their successors (following the abolition of the Provinces in 1876) the County and Borough Councils. Their relations with these bodies were in fact generally antagonistic, partly because of the local authorities' encroachment on Maori land for public works, and partly because the Maori were unwilling and generally unable to pay rates. Maori land was rateable under the Highway Boards Empowering Act, 1871, only if leased to settlers and traversed by roads. A few Ngapuhi chiefs, such as Wi Katene, and resourceful mixed-race people, such as Retreat Tapsell, paid rates and participated on local County Councils but these men were exceptional in the nineteenth century. Generally, Maori owners were too heavily indebted to pay rates. A wider levy of rates would in fact have amounted to a compulsion to sell land—although settlers, observing heavy spending by Maori people when flush with cash, were unsympathetic.

McLean passed a Native Districts Road Board Act in 1871, to enable Maori communities to form Road Boards and rate themselves, but few did so. McLean fell back on urging local European Road Boards to include Maori leaders, but generally he regarded the contribution of Maori land and labour for road works, as sufficient for the time being.[20]

Appreciation of the need to tread warily with the still formidable tribes, together with the opposition of the Native Department, meant that prosecution of Maori land-owners by local authorities for non-payment of rates was rare. A similar picture emerges with regard to fencing, noxious weeds, and impounding laws. In any case, by the Constitution Act, local bodies had no jurisdiction over Maori customary land and attempts in the Assembly to amend the Act failed.[21] The fact that Maori land grew thistles and rabbits, which the Maori said *they* had not brought to New Zealand, and that Maori owners were beyond the sanctions which could be brought against Pakeha farmers, remained a serious source of friction in pastoral New Zealand society. Clearly the Maori land-owners' freedom from compulsion in these matters could be but short-lived.

In the meantime local authorities, pleading that the Native Department had placed the Maori in a sheltered position and assumed responsibility for them, were inclined to do very little on their behalf. The issue was raised in 1870 when the Auckland Provincial Council asked to be relieved of charges they had been paying for ten Maori and part-Maori children at a private orphanage. McLean argued that the Provinces should provide aid for destitute Maori as for Pakeha but local bodies in fact did not assume the responsibility.[22] Such indigent or destitute Maori as gained relief received it by General Government payments through the Resident Magistrates.

In contrast to their lack of involvement with local bodies, Maori interest in the General Assembly mounted rapidly. Maori leaders were quick to grasp where the realities of power lay, a Ngapuhi spokesman stating in 1870: 'The only way of accomplishing the object of uniting the two races is, in regulating the Parliament of New Zealand . . . , The only power in the Island is the meeting of the Assembly at Wellington.'[23] Whereas in 1868 the Maori were ill-prepared for the elections, the 1871 and subsequent elections were preceded by large meetings, and all four Maori seats were contested at the polls. By 1879 it was estimated that some 7000 of an eligible population of about 14,500 were voting.[24] Ineffectual members were generally quickly replaced by intelligent and determined spokesmen, such as Wi Katene for Northern Maori and H. K. Taiaroa for Southern Maori. Tribal loyalties still tended to dominate the voting patterns, but not exclusively.[25]

Maori elections were of considerable importance to settler parliamentary factions. Stafford's taking of office in 1872 and his defeat a month later depended upon Maori votes;[26] in the bargaining for their support Wi Katene and Wi Parata were appointed to the Executive Council, and Maori nominees called to the Legislative Council. However, Stafford said the Executive Council members were 'not, of course, to take their places as ordinary Ministers, for it would be absurd that they should enter into a Cabinet and take part in the administration of the ordinary affairs of the Colony'. They were rather to be 'Ministerial Assessors'.[27] McLean and Fox also consulted them only on particular occasions as at the time of the Sullivan murder.

Elections for the Maori seats also saw settler factions backing rival candidates. Thus the Hawke's Bay member Takamoana was a protegé of McLean's rivals, H. R. Russell and the 'Repudiation' group, while McLean and Ormond backed Porourangi of Waiapu. Maori voters were also put on general electoral rolls, in varying numbers (usually under the householders qualification), largely according to how much money the candidates were prepared to spend and how far they controlled the machinery for registering voters and conducting elections.[28] Attempts to alter Maori representation also reflected factional interests. In 1875 a move by Reynolds to abolish the special Maori seats and one by Taiaroa to increase them both failed. Pakeha members desired neither to increase Maori representation on the common roll, least they swamp it, nor, by adding more Maori seats, to give Maori members greater facility to make and break governments than they already possessed. In 1872 and 1875 McLean supported an increase of one seat, but when, by 1876, it was clear that the Maori members were supporting Grey, he spoke rather of eventual abolition of special Maori electorates.[29] In the event the Assembly agreed to continue the four-member system indefinitely but in 1879 began to cut down the Maori entitlement to join the common roll by removing the householder franchise.[30]

The Maori people's own preference, with regard to the manner of their representation, was overwhelmingly for an increase in the number of special seats. The Ngapuhi pressed for more members and tribes such as the Arawa and

Ngatiporou who were not winning elections, pressed persistently for a member of their own.[31] Some of the more confident leaders did seek an enlargement of the Maori franchise on the common roll, but most were discouraged from this course by the fact that they were used by Pakeha candidates in elections and virtually ignored by the successful members thereafter.[32] Seeing that common roll representation was being quoted to block requests for more special seats, Hoani Nahe, in 1876, asked that it be abolished.[33] Occasionally a venturesome Maori stood for a common roll seat, but these efforts were quite ineffectual, although Wi Katene did poll third out of four candidates in the Bay of Islands in 1879.[34]

Maori members in the Assembly were generally to be found with the opposition and were vehement critics of Government Maori policies. Their efficacy is hard to gauge. In the major questions such as the Native Land Acts they had little immediate effect. But Taiaroa's persistence kept the Ngaitahu claims before public attention and this, in the long run, was to bear fruit. Maori members could also secure redress for small grievances by asking questions of Ministers.

Aggrieved Maori also sought redress by petitioning the Assembly, while the Native Affairs Committee set up after 1872 to handle the flood of petitions became an important part of New Zealand's constitutional machinery. It included the four Maori members and Opposition representatives, although the Government normally kept a majority on it and before 1879 the Maori members' votes were split as often as they were united. Here too redress could not be gained on the large questions such as return of confiscated lands but in a variety of small questions, especially if Government members were absent, petitioners were able to obtain favourable decisions.[35] The Committee received scores of appeals from the Land Court and although it declined to review judicial decisions, from time to time reported that it considered there were grounds for a rehearing, or urged correction of a faulty survey. It then rested entirely with the Government and the Land Court whether action was taken, but a favourable decision by the Committee (as in the case of back rents for the Princes Street reserve) especially if taken up by Opposition, could embarrass the Government or cause a well-disposed Minister to act.[36] The Native Affairs Committee was one institution which helped create just sufficient flexibility to prevent the Maori from quite despairing of the parliamentary system.

The Maori people's own political organisation showed great variety and vitality in the 1870s. Local councils or *runanga* were of continuing importance. *Hapu* and inter-*hapu* meetings increased in frequency and complexity, accompanied by a spate of building of elaborate and finely decorated 'meeting houses'. *Tangi-hanga* (burial rites) for important chiefs were widely attended and were the occasion of much social and political debate. Semi-permanent committees or elected councils were established both at *hapu* and tribal level. These were often encouraged by officials and by temperance workers to deal with a variety of social problems, but they were primarily concerned with the basic problem of settling land claims and preventing alienation, by individual members, of tribal land. With the failure of McLean's Native Councils Bill in 1872-3 they were without legal standing and tended to break up and reform, but some remained firm. At a large meeting of Tuhoe *hapu* in June 1872, 'All the Urewera boundaries were joined into one' and a *Hokowhitu* or council of seventy was elected to prevent applications to the Land Court or for survey or disposal of land in any way, and to control disorder 'so no crime might be charged against them'.[37] The Urewera boundaries remained firm through the 1870s and 1880s against the blandishments of government officers.

Several centres aimed at creating a supra-tribal organisation. The Ngapuhi opened a building named Te Tiriti o Waitangi at the Bay of Islands in 1875; it proved the forerunner of a larger building and a wide-spread demand for a separate Maori parliament.[38] The tradition of the Kohimarama 'parliament' of 1860 was also strong. In early 1869 a number of Kupapa chiefs, including Matene Te Whiwhi, Tamihana Te Rauparaha, Paora Tuhaere and Hone Mohi Tawhai, attended the big meeting at Tokangamutu where the King movement shaped its post-war policy. Having failed to bring about a meeting between King and Governor they proposed in a circular letter, to revive the Kohimarama conference as a regular Maori council which would present to the General Assembly requests for necessary reforms in law.[39] In 1879 Paora Tuhaere in fact assembled what his group designated the first Maori parliament, at Orakei (Auckland). The meeting resolved that the confiscated lands should be restored, the Land Court's powers curtailed in favour of Maori committees, and traditional claims to fisheries or tidal land recognised; it objected to levies of rates but on the other hand opposed discriminatory provisions such as the requirement that Maori, but not Pakeha, must obtain permits before they could purchase arms.[40] Although the Ngatiwhatua had welcomed the coming of the British in 1840, Paora Tuhaere at Kohimarama in 1860 had voiced his discontent with the position of the Maori under British rule; his discontent, and his sympathy with the 'rebel' tribes, had increased in subsequent decades.

In Hawke's Bay the loss and distress caused by devious land-purchasing produced a leader in a young chief named Henare Matua, who sought to stop lands being put through the Land Court and to upset 'fraudulent and deceitful purchases, mortgages, signing names . . . wrong leases, unfair payments', 'that we may be united in holding the land' and 'that it shall be left for the Natives themselves to name the conditions and terms for the Leases'. He also sought to change extravagant traditions and desires in Maori society which led to improvidence and land-selling, and he opposed violence. Matua enjoyed somewhat precarious relations with the senior chiefs of Hawke's Bay such as Renata Kawepo, Takamoana, and Henare Tomoana. H. R. Russell and John

Sheehan also supported the 'Repudiation' movement but their own self-interest was fairly apparent to Matua and his committee, who never fully trusted them. Matua at first hoped to gain results from petitions to parliament, and pressed for more Maori members to be elected there, but grew disillusioned with that course. The main thrust of his organisation, through visits, letters, and a round of meetings, reached into Poverty Bay, Wanganui, Taupo, Rotorua and the Bay of Plenty, where his efforts assisted the tribes of those districts to withstand land purchase operations until the late 1870s. His ultimate goal was 'That all the tribes of this island should unite . . . in "the bond of love" '; the word 'kotahitanga' or 'unity' appeared frequently in his writings. Organisationally, he increasingly favoured the withdrawal of the Maori members from the General Assembly, the establishment of a separate Maori parliament, and an end to the Native Department and the Native Land Court.[41] The *Kotahitanga* movement was to link with the efforts of the Ngapuhi and Ngatiwhatua in an island wide organisation by the early 1890s, several of the most important meetings being held in Hawke's Bay.[42]

The King movement continued to proselytise and receive delegations from as far afield as Canterbury and the Chatham Islands, but particular attention was centred on capturing the support of Wi Te Wheoro and other Waikato men on the Government side of the *aukati,* in a *whakakotahitanga* of the Waikato tribes. But though many saw Tawhaio as a symbolic focus for their aspirations they did not take readily to requests to cut ties with their home district and live at Te Kuiti, in Ngatimaniapoto territory. In addition the Waikato Kingites were embarrassed by worsening relations with their Ngatimaniapoto hosts who, for their part, were increasingly disenchanted of semi-isolation behind the *aukati* and inclined to lease land and participate more fully in the Pakeha order. In 1875 the Waikato Kingites moved from Te Kuiti to Hikurangi, Kopua and Kawhia where they were increasingly visited by Hone Te One, the principal Kupapa chief expelled from Kawhia in 1868, and by Wi Te Wheoro. In 1879 Te Wheoro was elected member for Western Maori, largely on the votes of Waikato Kingites and Kingite sympathisers in Wanganui and Hauraki. The *whakakotahitanga* of the Waikato tribes was indeed becoming a reality.[43]

Maori religious movements, part-Christian, part-traditional, complemented and inspired much of their political activity. The Maori, whose traditional world view did not make such a separation between the earthly and spiritual order as the missionaries, considered that the Christ of the mission churches had not saved them from sin and misery. Tawhiao himself was increasingly regarded as an *atua,* in direct communication with the deities, though young Kingites visited Ashwell to obtain the whole Maori translation of the Bible and Church of England prayer book, and used them in the construction of their *Tariao* or Morning Star ritual.

From exile in the King Country, Te Kooti fostered his *Ringatu* (upraised hand) faith in the Urewera, upper Wairoa, and Poverty Bay districts, and from

1876 it spread through Tauranga, eastern Bay of Plenty, and northern Hawke's Bay.[44] In Taranaki Te Whiti's influence increased with the increasing landlessness of the West Coast *hapu*. He stressed that the Maori people should be guided by the elect, the prophets and their apostles, not by their traditional chiefs and *tohunga,* who were failing them. Minor prophets flourished briefly in numberless small communities in both Islands. Although Te Whiti and many of the prophets led their people in a repudiation of Government-sponsored institutions, boycotting elections and declining to receive schools, they were not sullen reactionaries. They sought mainly to save their land, and within its confines, to restore their people's self-respect, enable them to shape their own destinies, curb drunkenness and disorder, and promote economic enterprise. In these matters Parihaka, Te Whiti's village, was to become a model.

The overall view of the 1870s then shows that Maori communities, far from being apathetic, were engaging in a wide variety of experiments designed to improve their situation. Initially, these involved a considerable determination to engage with and succeed in the economic, cultural and political aspects of the European order. Even the strongholds of the King and the prophets grew cash crops and traded across their boundaries. The tragedy of the time was not that the Maori were crushed and supine, but that they did not receive the assistance and encouragement in higher education or political and administrative responsibility that their interest and abilities warranted. The limited conception of the role of the state, settlers' disinclination to vote money for Maori purposes when the Maori were not ratepayers (notwithstanding their substantial contribution to indirect taxation), racial prejudice with regard to employment, and the desire to deny the Maori real power if that were likely to be used to block settler acquisition of Maori lands—all these combined to keep the Maori in subordination and frustrate their progressive ambitions. For these reasons, and especially because of the insidious encroachments of the Land Court and Land Purchase Officers, Maori disillusionment increased. By 1876 when some, such as the Ngatimaniapoto, were beginning to engage more fully with the Pakeha order, others, such as Wi Te Wheoro, who had engaged with it eagerly a decade or more earlier, were withdrawing into quasi-nationalist activity. The tendency to separation was marked by a continuance of the retreat from the towns, in the face of discouragements such as the closure of the traditional Maori market at the foot of Queen Street, Auckland, because it was supposed to be dirty and squalid.[45] There was a general movement in the country from the more to the less settled districts; in 1875 the Turanga people left the town of Gisborne that had grown about them, and moved inland to Waerenga-a-Hika, and the remaining Atiawa at Waikanae moved to the upper Waitara valley.[46] Though the opportunity had been there, the settlers had not followed up their military successes with a clear-cut capture of the 'hearts and minds' of the Maori people. Certainly, many Maori were not dissatisfied; some had prospered and others gained experience which was to bear fruit later in the century. But the later 1870s had seen a revival of separatist political and religious activity, which competed with continued efforts to progress within the main stream of settler-ordered society.

XIX

Mismanagement

McLean's immediate successor as Native and Defence Minister, Daniel Pollen, recalled that when he took office it had been felt that administration of Maori affairs should no longer be a speciality:

> the people of both races having become amenable to the law of the land—the function of the Native Department might be confined to that of . . . interpreter of thought and necessary medium of instruction between the two races not speaking the same language; that its political character should be taken away, and . . . the idea that the Native race was to be governed by the Native Department might no longer be entertained.[1]

Pollen continued the reductions in the Native Department's powers begun in 1876, transferring superintendence of most road contracts to the Public Works Department and beginning retrenchments of staff. A number of Maori staff such as ferrymen at the important estuaries and mail carriers were dismissed, their places being taken by County Council and Post Office employees. Several requests for free medicine, for aid with flour mills, and for supplies for meetings or districts devastated by flood, which McLean would have granted, were declined. A further sign of the trend was the cancellation of subscriptions to a variety of provincial newspapers which the Department had taken to supplement its information on Maori-Pakeha relations throughout the Colony.

In land legislation the initiative was taken not by Pollen but by Attorney-General Whitaker, presumably with the approval of Atkinson, who had replaced Vogel as Premier in 1876. Whitaker and J. D. Ormond, both land speculators, introduced a Bill which aimed at curtailing Crown land purchase-operations and permitting unrestrained free trade by private purchasers. Restrictions on Maori land were to be substantially removed and Maori owners allowed to mortgage freely for survey and Land Court expenses. The Bill raised vehement opposition from Maori leaders who recognised its rapacious tendencies, and from small settlers. Both groups were championed by Grey's party in the House and Ballance secured an amendment to the effect that any land act should aim at close settlement. 'Then,' wrote Ballance, 'confusion reigned and it was evident the most unprincipled combination the colony had yet seen was doomed.'[2] The Bill was withdrawn and shortly afterwards the Atkinson Ministry fell. Grey then formed a Government, with Sheehan as Native, but not Defence, Minister.

It was to be expected that the principal attackers of the Native Department in McLean's time would continue to reduce its powers. Indeed, in his opening policy speech Sheehan, while maintaining that some sort of intermediary between the two races was necessary (because 'the difference in point of intelligence' was so great) proposed to 'lop off' some of the ramifications of the Native Department and reduce it 'to a useful skeleton department, concentrated here in Wellington'. In land policy, quickly divesting himself of the role of advocate for the Maori which he had assumed in the Repudiation movement, he announced several proposals of doubtful equity to facilitate the completion of purchases in which the Crown was engaged. He gave as one of his reasons for pruning the Native Department that it hindered settlement, and undertook progressively to withdraw the Crown from Maori land-buying and leave the field to private purchasers.[3]

This program was well received but, to the settlers' disgust, instead of withering, the Native Department burst into an unnatural flowering. Sheehan followed the now familiar practice of replacing a number of McLean's men with his own appointees, dismissed some Maori Assessors only to appoint others, and reappointed some Medical Officers retrenched by Pollen. The only bold measure of reduction was the transfer of Native Schools to the newly founded Education Department, responsible for the national system of education after the abolition of the Provinces in 1876. But this came late in Sheehan's term of office and as the Education Department continued to work through the Resident Magistrates in establishing and administering Maori schools, these were still regarded as being part of a special machinery of Maori administration.

Sheehan's 'contingency' expenditure rapidly mounted. It included payments for useful items such as a hostelry at Patea, food and clothing for the indigent and tarpaulin coats for Woon's boatmen; other expenses—for champagne, jewellery and personal photographs, and shares in a coastal vessel for Rewi and Wetere Te Rerenga—were incurred during negotiations with the King movement; but a bust, costing £200, of the Hawke's Bay chief Te Hapuku, a personal orderly for Te Wheoro and a much-discussed £578 on cab-hire by Sheehan himself, indicated downright extravagance. A committee of investigation after Sheehan's fall found that he had exceeded the Native Department vote by about 16 per cent.[4]

This might have been tolerated if Grey and Sheehan had met with greater success. They abandoned McLean's patient waiting policy and inaugurated a series of personal meetings with Tawhiao and the Kingite leaders, feted them as much as they could and reiterated McLean's terms—notably a salary for Tawhiao and authority for the Kingites to rule their own territory, including the right to debar communications.[5] All began well; Rewi visited Auckland and Manuhiri accepted a pension. But in May 1879 Grey found the Kingite leaders, Tawhiao in particular, suddenly hostile, apparently angered by Government road-works near Raglan and on the Waimate plains (Te Whiti's district) and aware of the divisive tendencies of Government policy. Grey responded with a mixture of pained anger and condescension, reminiscent of his attitude in 1861-3. 'I look on Tawhiao as my own child,' he said, and deplored the 'evil counsel' which, he alleged, had hardened the King's attitude. Then he withdrew the proffered terms and said that such favourable ones would not be repeated.[6]

In the Assembly Grey and Sheehan faced biting criticism. There were many jibes at Grey's handing out sweets to Maori children and dancing polkas to the music of a Jew's harp and concertina.[7] In defence Grey and Sheehan argued that their having seized the opportunity to withdraw McLean's terms would enable them to get better ones in due course. This was true. Already some of the Ngatimaniapoto were becoming disgruntled at having missed an opportunity to enjoy the favour of the Government and closer engagement with Pakeha money and trade.[8] But the benefits of Grey's strategy were to be reaped by a later Government; Grey had only failure to record.

Nor was this all. Throughout the country a series of crises had arisen, each seemingly more serious than the last. In two separate cases in Hawke's Bay, Maori villagers resisted sheriff's officers seeking to execute Supreme Court orders to eject them from land claimed—unjustly in fact—by settlers;[9] in Canterbury a large party of Ngaitahu deliberately trekked inland from a coastal reserve to lay claim to land in the upper Waitaki valley which they considered had never been purchased;[10] at Ohinemuri (upper Thames) an old Kingite *ariki,* Tukukino, threatened force to block a road through his district;[11] at Waitara a disturbance occurred in a local hotel between a drunken Pakeha and a party of visiting Ngatimaniapoto, one of whom was arrested but forcibly released from gaol by his friends;[12] at Maketu an armed party of Arawa occupied the Land Court, repelled the police and forced the Court to adjourn the hearing of a disputed claim;[13] two *hapu* of the Ngatiporou took up arms and some *kainga* were burnt.[14] Worst of all, in 1879, a clash between two Ngapuhi *hapu* resulted in four dead and three wounded,[15] and at Ohinemuri a Maori ambush fired on a Pakeha survey party wounding one man and escaping arrest.

By no means all of these disputes were of Grey and Sheehan's making— several had arisen from problems shelved by McLean. But the fact remains that in McLean's last years of office disputes of this nature were remarkably rare, and nothing as serious as the Ngapuhi affray or the Ohinemuri shooting had occurred since Sullivan's murder in 1873. The Government's policies, moreover, clearly contributed to the disorder. Far from curtailing the dubious activities of Crown land purchase agents the Government had pressed ahead with large-scale land-purchasing under the cover of proclamations debarring private purchasers from blocks in which the Crown was heavily engaged.[16] Surreptitious purchasing of signatures from sections of the many owners named on a title had always been possible; Sheehan's officers engaged in the practice freely. In March 1879 the land-purchase branch of the Native Department was constituted a separate sub-department, with R. J. Gill, its *de facto* head since 1873, as first Under-Secretary. This meant that land-purchase operations were once again not within the regular purview of the Under-Secretary of the Native Department and no longer so closely related to Maori policy as a whole. At the same time private buyers stepped up their activity.[17] Sheehan's amendments to the land laws (while tightening the provisions against mortgage of Maori land) empowered trustees, with the consent of the Chief Judge, to sell the interests of minors, enabled the Court to compel the attendance of witnesses in order to assist the Crown to complete titles, and dispensed with the District Officers and preliminary inquiry required by McLean's Act of 1873. Proposals for a Court of Appeal, above the Land Court, came to nothing.[18] Not surprisingly, Sheehan was able to boast that he had first doubled and then trebled the quantity of land passing through the Native Land Court.[19] The number of blocks purchased also trebled.[20] But this increased pressure on Maori land, unrestrained by the vigilance and veto of a McLean, had much to do with the clashes in Hawke's Bay, Thames and Northland.

Finally, the Grey Ministry found itself involved in a crisis with Te Whiti. Impelled by need for revenue and by heavy settler demand for land the Government at last carried surveys north of the Waingongoro River. Sheehan relied on the advice of Brown, the Civil Commissioner, that resistance could be bought off.[21] Responsibility for surveys having been transferred from the Native to the Crown Lands Department in 1877, he did not himself closely supervise the progress of the survey, though McLean would certainly have scrutinised progress into such tricky territory very closely, whichever Department was nominally responsible. Above all, Sheehan failed to see that reserves were marked out for the Maori residents. After several provocations from the survey party, such as taking lines through gardens and shooting Maori pigs, a follower of Te Whiti, named Hiroki, shot the surveyors' cook and found refuge at Parihaka.[22] Supporters of Te Whiti came in to the village from several districts of the North Island as the survey advanced and tensions mounted. Some months later Sheehan demanded the surrender of Hiroki but Te Whiti refused and next day his followers removed the survey parties south of the Waingongoro. Soon afterwards he sent parties of ploughmen to cultivate the land of settlers in various parts of the confiscation, an action imitated by aggrieved Maori in other parts of the North Island, including Poverty Bay. The settlers, especially on the West Coast, inflated this to mean not simply the pacific assertion of a right, which it was, but the beginning of a new campaign by a seditious fanatic, likely to produce war. Grey and Sheehan, to their credit, at first resisted demands for military preparations and the arrest of the ploughmen;[23] but when the settlers themselves began to arm and 'arrest' ploughmen the Government's hand was forced. Soon Te Whiti's men began to be taken and held without trial, under draconian legislation of the 1879 Assembly.

In the Assembly the Government was blamed for bringing the Colony to the verge of another 'Native war'. Sheehan was attacked for his broken pledges about reduction of Native Department expenditure. In defence Sheehan claimed that McLean had only left affairs 'quiescent' and that personal government in Maori affairs was inescapable.[24] But, in the settlers' view, McLean's administration had generally kept the peace and permitted private settlement to advance quietly whereas, despite Sheehan's heavier spending, he and Grey appeared only to have been humbled by the defiant and cocksure Maori. R. C. J. Stone has shown that the large investors inside and outside of the Grey 'party' were doubly incensed by the Government's policy. Speculators with interests in Maori lands were antagonised by the Crown's heavy purchasing, under cover of proclamation, to constitute a public estate for sale to small settlers on the open market. Secondly, in a situation of deepening economic recession they feared that the troubles which had arisen with Maori protestors would further diminish confidence.[25]

It has been suggested that Sheehan has been unjustly maligned by his political opponents[26] and certainly it is true that his most vehement critics were generally land-sharks and dismissed officials from the McLean period. But though his adversaries may have been prejudiced or disreputable Sheehan deserves little sympathy. His land-purchase activities had been, to say the least of it, unguarded and provocative and for all his vaunted industriousness and travelling he was less sensitive to the danger signals than McLean had been, sitting in Hawke's Bay and reading his officers' innumerable reports. Some of his actions appeared generous to the Maori—the appointment of a commission of inquiry into the Ngaitahu claims, for instance—but he too declined to implement the provisions of the 1868 Act for Maori juries.[27] In fact he had little genuine respect for the Maori people and their sensitivities. Nor did he always keep his attitude masked. Although recounted through his political adversaries, the accounts of his philandering with Maori women do seem both to have substance and to suggest that he had breached the conventions acceptable to the chiefs. It was reported that, during his negotiations with the King movement, 'Even Rewi remonstrated with him regarding his conduct with women, while the natives themselves say it is useless to apply to him unless they are accompanied by their women. He has long promoted immorality to be a branch of the science of Government.'[28]

In July 1879 conservative propertied interests, already at odds with the Grey Government over questions of tariff and electoral reform, found in its Maori policy additional material with which to secure its defeat in a vote of no confidence. In the subsequent general election which led to the formation of a new Ministry under Hall, candidates promised retrenchment, a firm policy with recalcitrant Maori and abolition of the Native Department.

XX

Maori Administration Transformed

The new policy in Maori administration found a fitting instrument in John Bryce, Native Minister in the Hall Government. The son of a Glasgow carpenter, Bryce was employed in a variety of rural occupations before managing a family property near Wanganui and entering politics. Self-educated and severely practical, he was concerned to advance the fortunes of earnest settlers. He had little sympathy for speculators but even less for Maori values and aspirations, especially—after his experience of Titokowaru's rising—those of prophets. He was peppery and frugal, kindly in a very paternal way, but not to be crossed lightly.[1] He proposed to end 'the system of personal government which obtains in the Native Department', dispersing its functions to other Departments and reducing staff and contingency expenditure to within the £7000 of Civil List voted for Maori affairs since 1852. He proposed a vigorous enforcement of the law against resisting Maori in Taranaki and Thames; and he proposed to end the shabby jostling for land between Government and private agents by reviving Vogel's scheme of 1876 for Government boards to act as agents for the Maori, selling land by public auction.[2]

Over the next three years Bryce achieved much of his program. The transfer of Maori schools to the Education Department and road works to the Public Works Department was completed. In 1881 Charles Heaphy, Commissioner of Native Reserves since 1870, died and the Maori reserves vested in the Crown were soon afterwards transferred to the control of the Public Trustee. The remaining Civil Commissioners, Brown (Taranaki) and Kemp (Auckland) were retired and the New Plymouth office closed. A number of Resident Magistrates and Native Officers, including Woon, were dismissed or promoted to Land Court Judgeships. The subsequent amalgamation of districts left Thames, Raglan, Marton, upper Wanganui, Wairarapa and the South Island without permanent Native Department Officers. A number of medical officers, clerks and interpreters were dismissed and, on the retirement of H. T. Clarke, T. W. Lewis, McLean's former private secretary, became Under-Secretary. Lewis was destined to serve no less than six Native Ministers and was a competent and loyal staff officer to each, but nothing more.

Bryce slashed the number of Maori Assessors, police and pensioners by between half and two-thirds, and reduced the stipends of the remainder. After

1882 the remaining Maori police were transferred to the Defence Department (in 1886 to the newly established Police Department) and were henceforth subordinate to the local constabulary rather than the Resident Magistrates. The Assessor system was not entirely destroyed, however, for although it was considered that Assessors were no longer needed in the Resident Magistrate's Court, the retention of able men was considered desirable to 'influence the general conduct of the Natives and indirectly assist . . . in maintaining order and peaceful habits in their localities'.[3] About 150 Maori still drew stipends and leading Ngatimaniapoto chiefs such as Rewi and Wahanui, whom Bryce was trying to influence, were granted large pensions.

Grants of aid—contingency expenditure—were also heavily reduced, though Bryce still paid relief to some indigent Maori and subsidies for farming equipment if the Maori applicants had also raised money themselves. The Maori hostelry system was curtailed, the Wellington hostelry in Molesworth Street being taken over as offices for the Native Land Court, the Napier hostelry let and the Onehunga hostelry, which had been damaged by fire, sold.

In financial terms Bryce cut Native Department salaries from £21,164 in 1879 to £13,453 in 1880; about £6000 of remaining charges were for the salaries of Pakeha staff—Maori salaries and pensions coming within the £7000 Civil List vote for Maori affairs. Contingency expenditure fell from the £8000-£12,000 spent by McLean and Sheehan, to a mere £2500—about £800 on gifts and entertainment for Maori leaders, £800 for medical care and £800 for travelling expenses.[4] Against this it should be observed that a steadily rising expenditure for Maori schools came under the Education Department vote.

In contrast to the declining Native Department, the Native Land Court steadily grew. Bryce, in accordance with his general policy, transferred it to the Justice Department, with the idea of putting it on the same footing as other courts. But within a year he became so irked with its ill-co-ordinated and scandalously protracted hearings that he brought it again within the control of the Native Department and supervised its operations more strictly than before.[5] More Judges were appointed—former Native Service officers like Mair, Puckey and Alex Mackay, and for the first time, solicitors such as Brookfield, O'Brien and MacDonald. The vote for the Court rose from about £10,000 in 1879 to £13,000 in 1881 and £16,000 in 1883, by which time it had well over-taken that for the Native Department proper. In other words the Court had clearly become the most important special institution in Maori administration.

Bryce's retrenchments were greatly regretted in the out-districts. Apart from the loss of office and salary, at which Pakeha magistrates and spoilt Maori favourites like Ropata alike grumbled, the Resident Magistrates reported a serious loss of contact with Maori communities.[6] In parliament a Pakeha member stated:

The present Government, in using the pruning-knife, not merely pruned but amputated the outlying districts: they dismissed the Native Assessors and police-men, who were doing good service and had the confidence of the Maoris; and, in place of a Magistrate resident, a peripatetic Magistrate was appointed, whose duty it was to gallop through the country once a month to hear any case which might happen to be set down for hearing, and be off again the same day.[7]

The loss of Maori staff also meant that close association of Maori leaders with the machinery of government was curtailed, detailed comment about the life in the village no longer reaching magistrates' ears. Bryce adopted a sug-gestion by Lewis that Justice Department Resident Magistrates communicate with the Native Office in matters affecting the Maori, but they were mostly town-dwellers and saw little of Maori communities. Paora Tuhaere's second 'parliament', meeting at Orakei in 1880, complained not only of the want of compassion by the Government in stopping the supply of goods, refusing loans and closing hostelries, but at their 'ending the work of administering the laws by Maori chiefs', and expressed their sadness 'that it stops the two races uniting under such a system'. The practice of McLean and his officers of constantly using the chiefs in informal arbitration was recalled with nostalgia, and the Government was charged with keeping authority entirely in Pakeha hands.[8]

The Government's apparent 'want of love' was increased by Bryce's refusal to mediate between Maori and local bodies or private settlers in land disputes; Maori petitioners were simply told to use the courts—cold comfort indeed![9] The placing of reserves administration under a remote official like the Public Trustee exacerbated the Maori owners' feeling, already strong under Heaphy and Mackay, that their fortunes were being determined by a remote and imperious authority no longer accessible to them.[10]

Whereas in the 1870s there had been a machinery of administration actively linking Maori communities with government and, in some measure, serving the interests of the Maori, in the 1880s, government seemed once again to come to them only when it wanted something. The Resident Magistrates' Courts came to be used infrequently to arbitrate disputes in the villages, but increasingly as agencies for enforcing the payment of debts to Pakeha creditors. In 1887, for example, J. Preece in Napier, heard 111 civil claims by settlers against Maori and three by Maori against settlers. After 1880 also, Maori villages began to be visited by dog-tax collectors from the local bodies, parliament having decided, with much justification, that the unregulated hordes of ill-kept Maori dogs were an intolerable menace to New Zealand's sheep flocks, not least to those of the Maori. But the tax was seen as an imposition and dog-tax collectors were frequently defied and threatened with violence. In some districts prosecutions followed; in others the Government stayed collec-tion of the tax.

In 1882 also, by the Crown and Native Lands Rating Act, Maori lands within five miles of a highway became liable for rates.[11] The Crown in fact paid the rates to local bodies and made the debt a first charge on the land.

Lewis discovered in 1883 that the Property Tax Department had been valuing Maori land for rating purposes at up to three times its market value and that, like the dog-tax, collection of rates threatened to provoke breaches of the peace. The Native Department thereafter exercised a supervisory control over the rating of Maori land and much of it that was legally liable under the 1882 act, continued to be exempted. Nevertheless Maori lands were charged with some £10,000 of rates by 1890. Other measures which bore increasingly upon the Maori included a sheep-tax (to provide a fund for the eradication of scab) and river and harbour control programs.

Most of these measures fulfilled a genuine public need, and the Maori people themselves shared in the benefits. It is difficult to see how the Maori minority could have been allowed to stand in their way without incurring an opprobrium very damaging to their chances of achieving genuine equality in the community. It is rather in the abrupt manner in which they introduced the measures that the Government may be criticised. There was little effort to discuss patiently the necessity for a sheep-tax or control of a dog population with local Maori leaders—an approach which, because it would have indicated recognition both of their sense of responsibility and intelligence, and of economic and cultural disadvantages which made the requirement especially difficult for them, would very likely have won qualified Maori co-operation. Nor was the loss of an eel-fishing weir during river or harbour works regarded by the authorities as a serious matter, warranting careful prior investigation and generous compensation. The works were often simply carried out and traditional food traps, used for generations, ruined. It is through such small things, indicative of disregard for their values and sensitivities, that Maori people have possibly derived the greatest sense of grievance against Pakeha authority.

Meanwhile Bryce was pursuing his aim of bringing the Maori more firmly under the rule of settler law. It should be appreciated that at that time, the settler community was still insecure and easily panicked. When, in February 1881, a Maori was murdered at Thames by a settler named Procoffy, the Maori community, though fearful of his acquittal by the white jury, was content to await the trial; but the Thames settlers for a time lived in fear, quite unwarranted but very real, that the local tribes would exact vengeance on the town.[12]

The greatest tension, however, existed in south Taranaki where Te Whiti's men were still opposing the government road and challenging the confiscation. Bryce, arguing that Te Whiti was a semi-demented fanatic whose demands were insatiable, strongly favoured taking him at once by force. More moderate members of the Hall Ministry, however, decided that a liberal demarcation of reserves, combined with a resolute pushing of the road through the confiscation, would overcome Te Whiti's opposition.

Bryce resigned on the issue in January 1881, William Rolleston, former Native Secretary and, more recently, Minister of Justice in the Hall Government, taking over the Native Department. However, by October 1881, Rolleston found that Te Whiti could not be placated by reserves; he was leading a campaign for the recovery of the whole of the confiscation. This the Government would not concede. Te Whiti's men were still fencing across the road and ploughing on settlers' claims; this was pacific in intention but tempers began to rise among both settlers and Maori. When it was apparent that Te Whiti was not going to call off the campaign, Rolleston began preparations for the investment of Parihaka village.

Bryce resumed office to actually superintend the policy he had long advocated, but by this stage the Ministry was agreed on the course proposed. A large armed force arrested Te Whiti, his lieutenant, Tohu, and the fugitive Hiroki who was tried and executed for murder. The Parihaka community— which consisted largely of Maori from distant tribes—was dispersed. Fairly liberal reserves were made for the Maori in the confiscation but most of them were placed under the Public Trustee and let by him to settlers on terms over which the Maori owners had no control. Hans Tapsell, a mixed-race leader from the Bay of Plenty who had long co-operated with the Government, was later moved to write that 'while the Government professed with one hand to give the lands to the Natives, with the other hand they took them back and placed them beyond the Natives' control'.[13]

The whole Parihaka affair added renewed bitterness to Maori-Pakeha relations, but the majority of settlers applauded Bryce for having introduced 'a little backbone in the Native Department' and taken the first steps towards its eventual abolition.[14] Grey and Sheehan, observing the popularity of the Hall Government's actions, did not join the minority in the Assembly who refused to support the Act of Indemnity passed to cover them. Maning derived amusement from the thought of 'old Grey being dragged behind Bryce's Gun Carriage and making believe he is pushing'.[15]

Other Maori fugitives from settler law were also overtaken by Bryce's stern policy. Winiata, wanted for murder since 1876, was kidnapped from near Te Kuiti by paid agents, tried and hanged. The Thames Maori who had wounded a surveyor in 1879 were arrested and imprisoned. Road and river-clearing works were pushed through the Thames district with strong forces of Armed Constabulary nearby.

With regard to the King movement the Government passed, in 1880, a Waikato Confiscated Lands Act to reopen offers of land grants to ex-'rebels' within the confiscation (at the rate of 50 acres per man 'or less where the quality of the land is good or the position desirable'[16]). Few took advantage of it. Next, Rolleston, while briefly replacing Bryce, initiated a new negotiation with Tawhiao through W. G. Mair. His telegram stated that 'if question of opening land and railway comes up you would ascertain how far his mind goes in this direction. Another point is the harbouring of malefactors this is the great obstacle to friendly intercourse and you could perhaps impress him with this.'[17] In August Tawhiao rode into Alexandra and laid guns at Mair's feet in confirmation of peace. Soon afterwards he and Manuhiri accepted a payment of the accumulated back rents for their lands at Mangere, although at the moment of transfer the King slipped quietly out of the room, 'an indication', in the opinion of an official observer, 'that he is *nearly,* but not quite, ready openly to receive the gold of the Pakeha'.[18]

Parliament then passed an Act of Amnesty giving full pardon to those sheltering from European law in the King Country, including Te Kooti, Wetere Te Rerenga (implicated in the murder of Whiteley in 1869) and those involved in the latest killing, that of Moffat, a disreputable gold prospector, in 1880. The Government had clearly decided that since the Kingites would not solve the law and order issue by surrendering the wanted men, and since the King Country could not be coerced as Te Whiti had been coerced, they would remove the issue by issuing pardons to men they had execrated for years. Yet it should not be concluded from the way it had been disposed of that the law and order issue had never been a real one—merely a pretext for making war on the Maori for their lands. The impassioned address to the grand jury by Chief Justice Gillies at the opening of the Supreme Court session of 1879, on the subject of crimes unpunished and insecurity of settlers' lives and property is evidence of real strength and feeling.[19] So too was the bitter opposition to the Amnesty of Te Kooti by many of the settlers, especially the Poverty Bay settlers who, despite his pardon, were arming in preparation to kill him when he proposed to return to his home district in 1889. Nevertheless the cynicism of the Amnesty is apparent when contrasted with the ruthless treatment of Te Whiti and the execution of Hiroki. Principles counted for little when the prize of success was the opening of the King Country.

But when Bryce met Tawhiao his usual 'take it or leave it' style of diplomacy precluded agreement. According to the Premier

> Bryce made liberal proposals, but insisted they should at once be either accepted or rejected. With due deference to his better knowledge of Maori matters, I think this was a mistake in tactics. Donald McLean would have allowed the niggers to talk on for days if they so pleased, and then probably would have got what he wanted.[20]

Whether an outcome more favourable to the Government was possible is not clear, however, for there were many adherents of the King movement who did not want compromise terms with the Pakeha.

Bryce now turned his attention to the Ngatimaniapoto. He offered the increasingly influential leader Wahanui a pension, a house and a seat in the Legislative Council and urged him and his kinsmen to lease not sell their land.[21] After decades of pursuing freehold purchase, this was a new government policy, and one much closer to Maori inclinations. It had recently been inaugurated in Rotorua; the Crown acting as agent had leased the land at public auction and the Rotorua people had received high rentals. The Ngatimaniapoto were intrigued by this experience and since the King Country had been specifically excluded from the Crown and Native Lands Rating Act there seemed to the chiefs to be no serious disadvantage in opening their lands. In 1883 Wahanui and Rewi agreed to allow a survey for a railway route to enter the King Country. Although the survey party was soon seized by the prophet Te Mahuki (a zealous follower of Te Whiti who had renamed his *hapu,* south of Te Kuiti, the *Tekaumarua* or Apostles), they were rescued by Wahanui and the lately pardoned Te Kooti and ushered through further obstructions in the upper Wanganui district by Major Kemp and Pehi Turoa.[22] Legislation in 1883 incorporated Wahanui's conditions for further opening his territory—the exclusion of private purchasers from the King Country and prohibition of the sale of liquor. Bryce also agreed to his request for survey and award of title only in respect of tribal and then *hapu* boundaries—not yet going on to individual awards, which could too easily be alienated.[23] Wahanui was leading the Ngatimaniapoto in a new bid for an intelligent, controlled, selective engagement with the Pakeha order. In 1883 Bryce occupied a location on Kawhia harbour said to have been purchased years before, and used Armed Constabulary to deter threatened resistance from Tawhiao. The Ngatimaniapoto made no objection, apparently regarding the troops as a safeguard against Waikato pretensions;[24] it appeared that the King Country would be opened.

But it was not to be so easy. In 1884 David McBeth, a settler deeply concerned about the effects of land-selling on Maori society, and Hirini Tai-whanga, a disaffected Ngapuhi leader, visited the King Country to persuade Tawhiao and Te Wheoro to visit England and plead that the King Country, before being opened to the railway, be made a self-governing Native District under clause 71 of the 1852 Constitution Act. Tawhiao and Te Wheoro concurred in the proposal, seeing it as a chance to save the King movement. Tawhiao wrote to Bryce, 'You grant the Maoris local self-government and control of their own lands and we will grant you a railway and also throw open the greater portion of our lands under the leasing system.'[25] The letter was probably drafted by McBeth or Taiwhanga but it nevertheless asserted no more than the chiefs had asserted at the Treaty of Waitangi and subsequently through the King movement and other organisations—namely, a willingness to engage with the Pakeha order provided they could maintain the *mana* of their lands and kin.

The characteristically volatile Rewi supported the new move. Swayed by Kingite oratory to the effect that in agreeing to Bryce's survey he had 'left the canoe', he sprang to his feet and amidst applause announced that he would rejoin it. He wrote to Bryce withdrawing from their agreement and rather shamefacedly told Wilkinson, the new Native Officer at Alexandra, to call him henceforth '*kopikopiko*'—'backwards and forwards'.[26] Wahanui was not interested in a move that would rivet control by Waikato chiefs over Ngatimaniapoto territory, but he was alarmed by the spread of trigonometrical stations and at rumours of negotiations for sale of land and cooled to the whole arrangement. Bryce's successor had virtually to renegotiate the survey.[27]

In land legislation generally, as in his arrangement with Wahanui, Bryce showed that, while he was anxious to extend settlement rapidly he was willing to support measures to rid land acquisition of its worst evils. The Bills he introduced in 1880 to reform abuses have been described as a sham, merely devices to provide opportunities in debate to denounce the Crown land purchases of the Grey Government and to withdraw from them leaving the field clear to private speculators upon whose political support the Hall Government depended.[28] But as Chairman of the Native Affairs Committee from the late 1870s Bryce had come genuinely to detest the scramble of direct purchase with its attendant confusion and fraud.[29] Hall too, seemed to approach the question dispassionately though unenthusiastically. In March 1880 he wrote to Whitaker, the Attorney-General and the financier of much Maori land purchasing:

> I understand from Bryce that you still think free trade the best principle to go upon, but that it having been tried & rejected [in Whitaker's Native Land Court Bill of 1877] you are willing to help in putting his plan, of Government selling for the Natives, in the way of having a fair trial . . . I am not very sanguine as to the success of such a plan, but it is about the only thing which has not been tried.[30]

The new principle, neither free trade nor Crown pre-emption but the Crown auctioning land publicly as agent for the Maori, was embodied in the Native Land Sales Bill, 1880. But Whitaker was not in favour and the Bill met vehement opposition from the speculators who feared that to leave it to the Maori *voluntarily* to offer land for auction would effectively shut up the country. For their part the Maori members, distrustful of Government paternalism and alarmed at the 10-30 per cent commission and roading expenses proposed to be deducted from profits, also opposed it.[31]

Realising that persistence with it would alienate their supporters the Government withdrew the Bill and sought instead to apply its principle in local areas. The Thermal Springs Act 1881 ratified an arrangement between the Government and the Ngatiwhakaue tribe, administered by Chief Judge Fenton, whereby a planned township was to be established in the Rotorua thermal region and the land alienated on long lease, at public auction. The Native Reserves Bill of 1882 also incorporated the principle of lease by public auction in respect of the land wrested from Te Whiti's control, and any other land Maori owners might care to lease through the Public Trustee. In Rotorua initial auctions of land were wildly successful, rents being offered far in excess of those the Maori usually received. But within a year the system had begun to fail. The lessees began to default on payment of rents, and organised a lobby for the repeal of the Thermal Springs Act and the right to purchase the freehold. As usual the more feckless and imprudent Maori owners, tempted by promises of high prices, abetted them, while the Supreme Court decided that the Ngatiwhakaue tribe was not a body corporate and could not sue for rents.[32] The whole Rotorua scheme began to founder in acrimony. What should have been a thoroughly beneficial system broke down, not only because lessees found they could not pay inflated rentals in the intensifying economic depression, but also because they had a great repugnance to being tenants of Maori landlords at all, and because the Government was not prepared to oblige tenants to fulfil their contracts, or even negotiate between parties for an economic rental.

In a number of other respects Bryce's policy on land questions was constructive, aiming to end wastefulness and fraud. His Native Land Laws Act, 1883, at long last made dealings prior to Land Court awards not only void, but illegal, and punishable by a £500 fine.[33] On the question of removal of restrictions, he was hostile to any proposed transaction that had a hint of deceit about it, several times over-ruling local officers or the Under-Secretary if he thought some Maori owners' interest had not been considered.[34]

The Land Court had come under heavy criticism for some enormously protracted hearings at Cambridge and Marton, as a consequence of which Fenton was at last exposed and denounced as incompetent and an antagonist of the Maori people.[35] He retired in 1882 but unfortunately his successor, J. E. MacDonald, proved equally careless of Maori interests and duller witted into the bargain. He even later recommended that since restrictions on alienation were imposed merely to 'prevent natives denuding themselves of all land before they have learned to maintain themselves by work', as long as it could be shown that Maori vendors had some other land, 'prior illegalities in a transaction leading to removal of restrictions should not debar their removal'. Fortunately the Minister judged this reasoning to be 'morally unhealthy' and did not implement MacDonald's recommendation.[36] But given MacDonald's propensities it was unfortunate that Bryce's policy involved granting to the Court powers which McLean had long denied it. The power to grant rehearings, previously exercised by the government on the advice of the Court, was vested solely in the Chief Judge, who considered applications in private and did not publish reasons for his decisions. All Judges were made Trust Commissioners, with authority to make the inquiries against fraud which had previously been vested in special officers; and the Native Succession Bill, 1881, gave the Court power to award succession to Maori personal estate, as well as land. Bryce also sought to give the Court authority to order removal of restrictions, a power hitherto reserved to the Government, but speculators, who preferred to lobby a minister rather than a judge, were opposed. From time to time scandalously unjust decisions by the Court were revealed, but the only appeal was to parliament. Special legislation was often required, even to order a rehearing, if the Chief Judge had declined one, and members were often reluctant to over-rule a court in this way.[37] The Court remained in a privileged position—with the full autonomy of a legal tribunal and with sufficient independence to perpetrate gross errors and injustices unchecked.

Meanwhile the agitation to authorise local Maori committees to adjudicate on land titles had revived. 'The Committee of Ngatipikiao who nurse the law' and similar groups all over the North Island petitioned parliament.[38] The Maori members pressed home the attack and in 1882 Henare Tomoana, member for Eastern Maori got a Bill through to the second reading. Acceding to the pressure Bryce, in 1883, secured the passage of a Native Committees Empowering Act giving regional committees authority to discuss disputed land claims and advise the Land Court, and to arbitrate between Maori disputants in a variety of questions if the contending parties had given prior agreement to accept such arbitration. But whereas the Maori sought local committees at *hapu* level and, as in 1862 and 1872, eagerly set them up in anticipation, Bryce had in mind only seven or eight committees for the whole North Island. All the Bay of Plenty and Rotorua tribes were, for instance, to be included in one district. Consequently committee activity throughout most of the 1880s consisted largely of squabbling between tribal groups for control of the committee elections and requests for more committees representative of smaller units.[39] Probably the most active committee was the Kawhia committee, representing many of the Ngatimaniapoto and chaired by the extremely able part-Maori John Ormsby, which assisted in negotiating terms for the opening of the King Country with Bryce's successor. Other committees, such as that on the East Coast, investigated and secured agreement about title to a number of blocks; but the Land Court Judges, instructed only that the Committees' reports on land claims 'should be taken for what they are worth',[40] and highly jealous of their own authority, in fact took little notice of them and this side of the Committees' work lapsed.

The official Committees did little to out-bid the mounting movement in Maori society to establish institutions of local self-government. The reduction of the Resident Magistrate and Assessor system, the pressures of rates and dog-tax, the Government's seizure of Te Whiti, the continued passing of the land and the decline of timber and *kauri* gum industries all contributed to a mounting bitterness. The striking feature of the early 1880s was the movement of previously 'loyal' tribes and outstanding 'loyalist' leaders of the 1860s into vigorous political co-operation with the ex-'rebels'. Even such an amicable tribe as the Rarawa sought to disengage from Pakeha administration and set up committees of twelve in each village to hear all disputes and regulate such perennial problems as worrying of stock by dogs.[41] Of the Ngapuhi, it was said that 'A feeling of sullenness and distrust of Europeans appears to be spreading among them'.[42] In 1881 a new and larger version of their meeting house Tiriti o Waitangi was opened and regular 'parliaments' began to meet there. The Ngapuhi established links with southern movements through the active leader, Hirini Taiwhanga. Hirini, the son of Rawiri Taiwhanga, first convert of the CMS in New Zealand, had been educated at Bishop Selwyn's school, St John's College, and had some experience in surveying. He had contested unsuccessfully every election for Northern Maori since 1871; with government assistance he had founded a boarding school at Kaikohe in 1877 but aggrieved over a land dispute, neglected it for political agitation. He began to attend Paora Tuhaere's 'parliaments' at Orakei and meetings in the King Country and Hawke's Bay.[43] In the 1870s, Hirini had seemed too excitable and radical for the Ngapuhi, but in the 1880s, as their sense of grievance and frustration increased, Taiwhanga's passionate demands for redress seemed increasingly to represent their aspirations better than did those of the higher-ranking and more conservative leaders who had relied on co-operation with the Pakeha.

But many of the previous generation of leaders had also been alienated, among them Major Kemp of Wanganui. Bryce became embroiled in a bitter quarrel with Kemp over a Government survey of land in the upper Wanganui district claimed by the chief. Kemp occupied the land with an armed force and turned back all travellers in the vicinity. He also established a 'Council' of chiefs to govern the Wanganui River and, with the aid of Robert Stout, politician and partner in the legal firm of Sievwright and Stout, sought to establish a 'trust' to recover and withhold from sale, lands in respect of which government and private agents had paid advances to some owners. This alliance of lawyers, politicians and leading chiefs was not untypical of the period. Another such alliance developing about the same time was that of W. L. Rees, a lawyer in Grey's 'party', and the Poverty Bay leader Wi Pere. These arrangements promised to put much land into the hands of their pro-genitors but they did offer both to Maori owners and potential settlers an improvement on existing modes of alienation. Kemp and his associates, for example, proposed to open the bulk of their land to settlers on the leasing system. But despite his own support for that principle and his own specific criticism of the way Crown agents had advanced money on the upper Wanganui land before title had been decided, Bryce reacted violently against a scheme in which political adversaries like Robert Stout were involved. The immediate results were that the Wanganui River was closed to Pakeha travellers above a point 80 miles from its source, and that Kemp began to interest himself in the developing Kotahitanga movement.[44]

Perhaps most significant was the adherence to the King movement of Major Te Wheoro. A young progressive leader, Te Wheoro had supported Fenton in the late 1850s and Gorst in the early 1860s and showed himself to be possibly the most able and impartial Assessor in the country, genuinely convinced, it appeared, of the value of the rule of British law; he had parted in sorrow from near kinsmen when the Waikato was invaded and fought with the Queen's armies; he had co-operated eagerly with government policies at the close of the 1860s, believing that the Maori were to be enabled to share as equals with Pakeha in the new society. But through the 1870s his disillusion-ment had increased and he turned to the King movement, supplanting Manu-hiri as its principal adviser. He later related:

in 1866 I was appointed Assessor of the Native Land Court, but when I saw the
corruption of that Court I left it in 1872 . . . in 1875 I was made a Maori Commissioner,[45] and then I saw more clearly the unfair dealing of the government
towards the natives, and I gave up the post in 1879; and in the same year I was
made a member of Parliament, thinking that there, perhaps, the rights of the
Maoris would be respected, but when I saw the Maori members were ignored, and
that the whole Maori race was under oppression, I came to England with
Tawhiao to lay our wrongs before Her Gracious Majesty, for we are tired of
laying our complaints before the New Zealand government.[46]

The tactic of taking petitions personally to London had been initiated by
Hirini Taiwhanga who in 1882 presented a petition to the Queen, through
the Colonial Office, embodying the demands of the Tiriti o Waitangi movement and referring to the case of Te Whiti and the confiscated lands. In 1883
he sponsored a further petition from all North Island tribes, to similar effect;
and in 1884 he and McBeth had visited the King Country and persuaded
Tawhiao and Te Wheoro to petition Queen Victoria for the establishment of
the King Country as a self-governing Maori district under clause 71 of the
1852 Constitution Act.[47] These petitioners were all referred back by the Colonial
Office to Wellington, as entirely within the province of the Colonial Government. The Government refuted the allegations of injustice and claimed,
speciously, that clause 71 was outmoded since it authorised the establishment
only of Native Districts where *custom* could obtain, not introduced forms of
law and government. With the failure of this tactic the King movement leaders
associated themselves with the *Kotahitanga* demand for a separate Maori
parliament in New Zealand.

The Hall Government's policy had wrought a transformation in Maori-
European relations. Its 'strong' policy towards Te Whiti and others had
enabled the settlers to consolidate their dominion. Resistance to settlement was
still offered in the King Country and the Urewera but it was felt to be
isolated and likely to be overcome with little difficulty. Bryce was the first
Native Minister both to have assumed office advocating a curtailment of the
powers of the Native Department and to have left it still holding to that policy.
In fact in 1884 he wrote: 'with such success has that course been pursued that
I am prepared to advise the Cabinet and Parliament that the Portfolio may
now with safety be abolished'.[48] Not all his colleagues agreed; Rolleston, for
example, in his brief tenure of office in 1881, had concluded that 'a policy of
ignoring the speciality of Native Affairs won't wash'.[49] But Bryce had dealt the
death blow to the Native Department in its old form, and although it was
retained for a further eight years, its power and influence were but a shadow
of what they had been in the 1860s and 1870s.
Bryce himself left a reputation that was not entirely enviable. His own
colleagues found him ill-tempered and unapproachable. Hall felt that his
success in policing recalcitrant Maori had 'given him an undue sense of his
own importance'.[50] It was in fact an open quarrel with Bryce,[51] coupled with

his own illness, that led Hall to resign in favour of Atkinson; this dissension also contributed to the Government's defeat by Vogel's party in 1884.

If Europeans found Bryce unlikable, the Maori detested him. For his raid on Parihaka he was deemed a persecutor and a tyrant; for his retrenchments he was deemed mean and parsimonious; for his inaccessibility—his refusal to tour and meet and talk with Maori leaders—he was considered cold and indifferent. In fact, as his land legislation shows, Bryce was not an unqualified land-grabber. Most of the Maori people's problems derived not from Bryce but from the thrust of settlement as a whole. Bryce was a willing enough instrument of that thrust but his policies in some important respects ran counter to those of Whitaker and the advocates of free trade in land. He was able enough to see the necessity for reform in land law and resolute enough to retain the restrictions against alienation of much reserved land. Moreover it was Bryce who implemented the long-neglected provisions of the 1868 Juries Act whereby Maori defendants could claim trial by a Maori jury, and the system was soon in use.

But since he was unable to carry through his major proposals for land reform, few of the Maori people were aware of Bryce's virtues. What they did know was a brusque, ill-tempered man ruthless with opposition. Whatever his strengths Bryce was throroughly paternalistic, insensitive and unsympathetic towards the deeper Maori aspirations. As Chairman of the Native Affairs Committee, he had found Maori plans for increased powers of local government 'original and amusing'.[52] It was therefore hardly likely that as Native Minister he would give much consideration to the claims of a Te Whiti or a Taiwhanga, people he saw as semi-barbarian upstarts, dangerous to peace and order and to what he believed, in his complete Eurocentrism, to be the best interests of the Maori themselves. Bryce's tenure of office saw the rule of British law and central state power pushed vigorously forward.

XXI

The End of an Era

John Ballance, a self-educated and able settler who had founded the *Wanganui Herald,* was Native Minister in the Stout-Vogel Government of 1884-7. He offered some respite from the stringency of Bryce's retrenchments and revived McLean's practice of touring the out-districts to discuss policy and hear grievances. Important chiefs such as Kemp and Ropata regained their pensions; the Chairmen of the Native Committees established under Bryce's Act of 1883 were granted £50 each for running expenses; a memorial was erected to Hongi Hika to appease Ngapuhi unrest. When Mount Tarawera erupted in 1886, killing ninety-seven Maori and seven Pakeha, parliament voted £400 for feeding and housing destitute Maori and £2000 for the settlers; Ballance exceeded the vote for the Maori by £800.[1] Such activities led him to be called 'Ngawari'—'soft man'—in contrast to Bryce who was designated 'Maro' or 'hard man',[2] but it was trivial expenditure and Ballance did not fundamentally reverse the trend towards reducing expenditure and special machinery relating to Maori affairs. Most requests for aid with housing, food, seed, and fencing material continued to be declined. Maunsell, Native Officer, Wairarapa, and several Native Department clerks were paid off; Scannell, Resident Magistrate, Taupo, and Von Sturmer, Resident Magistrate, Hokianga, became Land Court Judges; the Auckland office was closed, Wilkinson, the remaining Native Officer, moving to Otorohanga in the newly opened King Country; requests for appointment of Medical Officers were declined, unless the Maori community paid half the doctor's subsidy. In 1887 Ballance was obliged by parliamentary pressure to reduce the list of Assessors and pensioners again and to curtail the payments to Chairmen of Native Committees. In 1886 the Native Land Purchase Division was abolished, the functions formerly exercised by its Under-Secretary again being assumed by the Under-Secretary of the Native Department. But the latter was now much more concerned with land transactions than with political or judicial matters, while the remaining Native Department Resident Magistrates themselves were involved in making inquiries about land on behalf of the Crown.[3]

As Defence Minister, Ballance also ended the system evolved to establish settler dominion over the Maori frontier. Under the Defence Act and the Police Force Act of 1886 the para-military Armed Constabulary were disbanded and their redoubts and block-houses scattered over the North Island left unmanned. A small military garrison was kept at Auckland and a reserve militia enrolled, but civil order was now mainly the responsibility of a new Police Force. The remaining Maori police of the old Resident Magistrates' establishments became part of it. The effect of these changes was revealed in 1886 when Te Whiti, released from exile in the South Island, launched a new 'ploughing' campaign. His smart re-arrest was effected by the local police Inspector, Pardy, with about six men, in a lightning raid on Parihaka which barely ruffled the surface of Taranaki life. This time, moreover, Te Whiti was given the privilege of a trial before being sentenced to six months' gaol. Admittedly, there was more of a fracas when Titokowaru and other 'plough-men' were arrested at 'the battle of Hastie's farm' about the same time, but it still involved only civil authorities, and truncheons rather than firearms.[4] Inspector Pardy was a diligent, patient and even-tempered officer, whose enforcement of the liquor laws, quiet suppression of petty misdemeanours by local Maori and determined quashing of alarmist utterances by either race did much to preserve south Taranaki in tranquility.

In 1892 a King Country prophet named Te Kere turned back a boatload of photographers travelling on the Wanganui River, for fear they were spying out land for purchase. A flurry of angry demands from the settler community for a punitive raid was damped down by Pardy who advised that there were insufficient grounds either for serious alarm or a prosecution.[5]

Rather more serious was an affray at Hokianga where a prophet named Eruera Rapana had evolved a ritual involving the use of a sacred enclosure and white robes. He attracted some notice by allegedly seizing the followers of a neighbouring but rival sect led by a prophetess, Ani Koro, and holding them until receipt of payment from their kin. In July 1887 a settler named Hearn, wearing dark clothing apparently offensive to the cult, stumbled into the sacred enclosure during a fog. He was subject to some ritual and released after the payment of £1. Unfortunately Bishop, then Resident Magistrate at Mangonui, succumbed to the characteristic settler over-reaction and barged into the area with armed police wearing their dark uniforms. Rapana's alarmed followers resisted with axes and spears; the police fired a volley which wounded Rapana and the community was dispersed. It was quite needlessly brutal. Even so it remained essentially a police matter and caused little stir outside the district.[6]

In land policy Ballance offered a number of reforms, hearing Maori griev-ances and correcting them through an annual Special Powers and Contracts Act. The rankling dispute between a Hawke's Bay *hapu* and the settler Harding was ended, for instance, by Harding's being obliged to surrender claims to the disputed acres and take compensation.[7] Other clauses settled claims to reserves or compensation outstanding since McLean's time, and set aside the mutton-bird islands in Foveaux Strait for Maori use exclusively. Responsibility for advising on the removal of restrictions on land was given to a special commissioner, G. Barton, who made diligent inquiries as to the needs of Maori owners and was supported by Ballance against the pressure and contumely of speculators.[8] With regard to the West Coast reserves, Ballance reduced the commission charged by the Public Trustee and directed that no liens be placed against the land without the owners' consent. In negotiations with the Ngatimaniapoto he offered payments above the usual rate for 'waste land' and agreed that large areas be taken on perpetual lease. With regard to perpetual lease Vogel considered that Ballance had gone further than the settler electorate would approve; parliament had voted £1,500,000 for the railway and expected a substantial return in freehold. 'We should be beaten into a cocked hat if we stood against this', he wrote.[9] For the time being however, Ballance held to his policy and was able to overcome the hesitancy the Ngatimaniapoto leaders had shown towards the end of Bryce's adminis-tration. A start was made with the railway, prospectors were admitted under strict licence, and by 1887 schools, stores—even a police station—were estab-lished in the King Country. With some prompting Te Heuheu gave the great mountain heartland about Ruapehu to the Government as a national park, not to the satisfaction of some Maori who wrote irritably of the 'tourists who howl and shout over our once eloquently silent country, who unsettle things of old, and cause depravity amongst our young people'.[10]

Meanwhile, relations between the Ngatimaniapoto and the Waikato Kingites became acrimonious, and Tawhiao moved to Pukekawa in Te Wheoro's terri-tory near Mercer, lower Waikato. In the 1887 election, although Tawhiao called for support for Te Wheoro, Ngatimaniapoto voted for Hoani Taipua who polled 1158 votes to Te Wheoro's 516.[11]

A further important aspect of Ballance's policy was his vigorous attempt to inaugurate the system whereby the Crown sold or leased land as agent for the Maori. Bills to this purpose failed in 1884 and 1885 but in the Native Lands Administration Act 1886, the principle was accepted by the Assembly. The Act also took up an important idea being advanced by the lawyer W. L. Rees and the mixed-race leader Wi Pere, then partners in a scheme for land settlement on the East Coast. Rees argued that instead of listing a multiplicity of names of owners, fragmenting title even further through succession and allowing dealing with individual owners (as under the 1873 Native Land Act) the principle of tribal title and tribal dealing should be preserved by the incor-poration of owners of a block as one legal entity. The 'incorporated' owners would then elect a 'block committee', with executive powers.[12] Ballance's 1886 Act empowered the block committee to decide on the terms of a sale or lease and place their land with a District Commissioner (a Government official) for auction. Direct purchase by settlers was prohibited. Wi Pere also recom-mended that the block committee be empowered to meet with five chiefs from other districts and a Land Court Judge in the determination of title—a pro-position very close to the demands of the *Kotahitanga* groups—but this was not acceptable to the Government or Assembly.[13]

By dint of strenuous tours of the North Island, by incorporating amendments suggested by Wi Pere and Wahanui, and by allowing minorities of
owners to partition out their share of land, Ballance thought he had won Maori
acceptance of his proposals.[14] Yet he was to be disappointed. In prior discussions Maori communities seem to have believed that the *mana* of the land
would be returned to them, without any significant interposition of officials,
but, following the passage of the 1886 Act, an observer of the latest *Tiriti o
Waitangi* meeting reported that 'it appears to them as an instrument working
solely for the benefit of the Government, against the interests & very independence of the Maori race . . . whilst professing to put an end to Land
Sharking, it virtually creates the Native Department into the most dangerous
and greatest Land Shark that ever existed in New Zealand'.[15] This view was
not accurate of course, for it over-looked the power granted to the block committees. But Maori owners did not care to put land under Government Commissioners, no matter how carefully the terms of alienation were prescribed;
furthermore the propriety of tribal leaders had been seen to crumble so disastrously when they controlled Land Court awards that rank-and-file owners
were reluctant to vest authority even in block committees.[16] Ballance had
mostly consulted with chiefs on his tours and was not fully aware that men
like Wi Pere were distrusted for the accumulation of land rights and political
influence they had achieved over the previous twenty years. Ballance's Commissioners waited in vain for land to be vested in them.[17] Perhaps the fairest
attempt to balance the interests of settlement and Maori landholders that
the Colony had yet seen was a dead letter. Speculators and free traders who
had fed Maori suspicions of Government intentions, were jubilant.

The unpopularity of the 1886 Act also contributed to the defeat of the
Stout-Vogel party in the 1887 election. The idea of incorporation of owners
and block committees was, however, kept alive by Wi Pere and others on the
East Coast. Pere was one of the first Maori leaders—ante-dating the better-
known Ngata by a decade—to urge that the Maori people were not indolent
but that such problems as fragmentation of title frustrated men who wanted to
put their land to efficient use. Indeed as early as 1876 succession had reduced
some inheritances to fractions such as 0.4 of a 52nd part of an estate.[18] Pere
intended incorporation to permit the Maori to use land, and indeed it has done
so, in the twentieth century, with respect to extensive pastoral farming and
timber milling in the North Island.[19]

With the failure of his 1886 Act, Ballance had little else to offer the
Maori. He rejected their claim to full powers over their land including adjudication of title, and the Land Court retained its position. He insisted that they
should pay rates, and supported an Impounding Act which removed their
privilege, first granted in Governor FitzRoy's Cattle Trespass Ordinance of
1844, of claiming for damages to unfenced cultivations.[20] Tawhiao on his
mission to London, and others in New Zealand, were still demanding a separate
Maori parliament or the right to set up separate self-governing Native Districts

under the 1852 Constitution Act. But Ballance replied that the Constitution Act had intended these only to be temporary expedients and that the time for them had long passed.[21]

The hiatus in land-purchase operations caused by Ballance's 1886 Act, invited a redoubled onslaught on Maori lands following the replacement of the Stout-Vogel Ministry by that of Atkinson in 1887. Candidates in the election raised new demands for the total abolition of 'that humbug . . . that mischievous appendage', the Native Department.[22]

The Native Land Act, 1888, restored the system of direct purchase, providing that, subject to fraud control, the Maori might dispose of their land as they saw fit. Ministers claimed that this was what the Maori themselves had sought, since three of the four Maori seats were won by candidates campaigning specifically for the repeal of Ballance's Act of 1886 and for full control of their lands. But these candidates included Hirini Taiwhanga, at last victorious in the Northern Maori electorate, and Taiwhanga vigorously opposed the 1888 Act. He introduced a succession of alternative Bills which embodied the *Kotahitanga* demands for an end to the insidious encroachments of the Land Court, and the restoration of control over lands to the lineages primarily interested in them so that individual owners could not sell their community's patrimony on the open market.[23] In the Legislative Council Major Ropata told Ministers, 'Do not say, or pretend to say, that these clauses [in the 1888 Act] do fulfil that [aspiration of the Maori] and that they do return to the Maoris the *mana* of their land.'[24] Major Kemp was also in Wellington, conducting a vigorous lobby in support of Taiwhanga's Bills.

The rapacious character of the 1888 legislation was also revealed in its relaxing of the restrictions on alienation that J. C. Richmond had enacted in 1867. Restrictions could now be removed by the Land Court on the simple application of a majority of owners; adequacy of consideration, proof that the vendors had other land for subsistence, and consent of the Native Minister were no longer required. Hoani Taipua, Western Maori, stated, 'It seems to me that the present Government are sweeping away the whole of the safeguards which have . . . prevented the Natives from pauperising themselves.'[25] J. C. Richmond in the Legislative Council said that the Government was abdicating a trust it had assumed for the Maori.[26] Their protests were in vain; in the next three years land-purchase operations made very heavy inroads into Maori land, and numbers of important areas long under restriction, such as the New Zealand Company reserves in Wellington or the Otago Heads reserve, passed into Pakeha hands. Roading and drainage projects continued to erode favoured reserves and fishing grounds, compensation often being evaded.[27] The Maori owners had not simply been dog-in-the-manger about these lands. For example, chief Piripi Te Maari and an able committee had fought a long campaign to prevent the draining of much of Lake Wairarapa, a valued eel-fishery which depended on an annual flush of water, but they offered to let the lake be drained except for the two or three months of the traditional eel-catching season. However, this was not acceptable to the farmers and authorities of the district and Te Maari lost his campaign—as he also lost a campaign to stop settlers slaughtering wild duck on the lake with punt guns. This was a not untypical case of settler barbarism triumphing over Maori civilisation.[28]

In the King Country, despite the original decision to define *hapu* interests only, disputes among claimants had led to individuals being listed on the titles. However, the chiefs and community opinion at first restrained individuals from selling their interests and the sheep farming projects that Wahanui and others had envisaged were begun. Government officers gave no encouragement whatsoever to these, but waited cynically for them to fail. A typical comment from one Land Purchase officer to another reads: 'they have sheep on the brain and this makes them quite unmanageable and until the mania passes away, or until they overdo it, or quarrel amongst themselves over the sheep and where they should run they will not think of selling'.[29] In 1890, however, Wilkinson reported gleefully that he had succeded in breaking through the opposition and made the first freehold purchase in the King Country; the secretiveness of the deal amply displayed the cynicism and fundamental immorality of the government agents' activities;

> the two who just disposed of their interests . . . were fully a fortnight after discussing the matter with me, before they could screw up their courage to sell, and, instead of coming to me in the day time they waited upon me at 9 p.m. . . . having ridden 12 miles since sundown (they would not leave their own settlement until dark) and returned that night least any of the local natives should see them and surmise that they had been selling land.[30]

Before long, news of the sale leaked out, the familiar process of jealousy and distrust convulsed the Ngatimaniapoto and more land was sold.

Meanwhile Edwin Mitchelson, who had succeeded Ballance as Native Minister when the Atkinson Ministry took office, though protesting that he could not complete the abolition of the Native Department in a day, had made a very good start. While the Native Land Court vote continued to rise from £17,000 in 1869 to £18,938 in 1890 and £20,967 in 1891, Native Department expenditure, including the salaries of Pakeha staff as well as Maori, was reduced to within the £7000 Civil List vote for Native Affairs.[31] This was a far cry from the £16,000 of salaries and £12,000-£13,000 of contingencies spent by McLean. Few chiefs, except those such as Wahanui whom the Government was trying to influence, continued to receive stipends. Contingency expenditure was down to £800; requests from indigent Maori for aid were normally declined. In 1888 Mitchelson, seeking to reduce contingency expenditure further, circularised local and charitable aid boards asking them to assume care of sick and indigent Maori. Few responded, and those who did declined on the ground that few Maori were paying rates.[32] The Native Department continued to pay a beggarly subsidy to about eight doctors and small pensions of a few aged Maori, but, as Lewis wrote, 'To make anything like adequate provision for the medical wants of the Natives or for the destitute among them, would mean . . . a large special vote.'[33] Medical care for the Maori was at its lowest ebb since Grey spread his new institutions over the Colony in 1861. The Native Department still handled a few outstanding land disputes, usually at the behest of the Native Affairs Committee of the House, but most questions affecting land were referred to the Public Works Department or Department of Crown Lands.

The functions of the remaining Resident Magistrates in the out-districts—Clendon, Bishop, Bush, Booth and Preece—were also transformed. They had more to do with settlers than Maori and their salaries were paid by the Justice Department. They were made 'Recorders' of the Land Court to hear simple succession cases, which were inundating the Judges. In Mangonui the Resident Magistrate still reported that his Court was used by Maori disputants in preference to the *runanga* and that the whole community greatly enjoyed a day's litigation, employing solicitors and taking a great interest in their ingenuity;[34] but since Resident Magistrates were now mostly remote townsmen, Maori communities had generally to sort out their own problems or go to the police. In some cases it began to appear to be a disadvantage, to the Maori as well as the settlers, that the Resident Magistrates Act of 1867 debarred Justices of the Peace and local police from acting in Maori cases, without a Resident Magistrate's consent. For example, in 1880 a Maori woman of the Thames district sought to lay an information against her husband who was being extremely violent to her. But the Resident Magistrate was touring his district and the Justice of the Peace she approached could not issue a warrant for the husband's detention since it was a Maori case, outside the confines of the town. Two weeks later the man shot his wife and committed suicide.[35] An under-staffed, badly worked Resident Magistrate system was probably worse than no Resident Magistrate system at all.

While most reports continued to refer to the extremely law-abiding conduct of Maori communities and serious violence rarely disturbed Maori life, armed parties occassionally took the field in land and other disputes, though they were generally easily placated. However, in 1888, at Poroti, near Whangarei, two *hapu* of Ngapuhi fought a formal traditional battle over a land dispute caused, once again, by a Pakeha attempt to purchase from one of the claimants. *Pa* were built, a day was fixed for fighting, arms were prepared, a vigil kept with the sentries of either side singing the ancient chants associated with their duty; in the subsequent clash—probably the last in the long tradition of Maori warfare—four were killed and four wounded, before the dispute was settled, in traditional fashion through the mediation of ranking men connected with both sides.[36] The following year, at Omahu, Hawke's Bay, another feud, similarly aggravated by Pakeha offers of purchase, resulted in the shooting of one man and a conviction for manslaughter against his assailant.[37]

The Government continued to have difficulty with the politico-religious leaders. Te Mahuki and his armed *Tekaumarua* occupied a store at Te Kuiti whose proprietor had refused to grant them further credit, whereupon a party of fifty police from Auckland led, incongruously, by Lewis the Native Department Under-Secretary, made a dramatic attack on the store from a special train which pulled in at dawn on the recently constructed line. But Te Mahuki's people had already retired and surrendered peacefully to the arresting officers.[38]

Te Kooti was the subject of a considerable stir. Since his pardon in 1883 he had stated his intention of returning to Poverty Bay, the scene of his birth, his arrest and his subsequent revenge at the Matawhero massacre. Successive Native Ministers had dissuaded him, but claimed no authority actually to prevent him. In 1889 he moved to Opotiki, gathering a large cavalcade behind him. But memories were bitter in Poverty Bay among both settlers and Kupapa Maori and violence threatened if Te Kooti moved through the mountain pass to Poverty Bay. Atkinson visited the district and, while concluding that 'everyone here . . . seem to have lost their heads', decided to order the arrest of Te Kooti for unlawful assembly.[39] A force of settler volunteers and Maori under Ropata was sent to Opotiki but Te Kooti, deeply distressed and drinking heavily, had already started back to the Waikato.[40] He was captured by Ropata's men, ordered to pay sureties of £1500 to keep the peace and, not having that sum, gaoled until some Pakeha sympathisers paid it for him. A lawyer concerned for civil liberties then appealed to the Supreme Court against the order. The appeal was upheld, the Judge, Mr Justice Connolly, asserting that as a pardoned man Te Kooti had every right to go to Gisborne and go in company, that he had committed no unlawful act, and that although the Gisborne settlers 'chose to be alarmed', he had not intended to disturb the peace. The Crown, however, went to the Court of Appeal where Connolly's judgment was reversed, the Judge this time stating that 'the eruption of this drunken fanatic, with all the instincts of a savage, and the prestige of a prophet, with his turbulent following, in the scene of his former, if amnestied, outrages' was 'sinister' and 'in itself a menace to the peace of the district'.[41] Whatever its standing in law, this can scarcely be described as a dispassionate judgment.

But despite these alarms and continued settler panickiness the authorities now considered Maori disturbances to be easily within their control. Offenders sought by Pakeha justice were now almost invariably surrendered (as in several instances of murder on the East Coast in the 1880s)[42] usually after considered discussion by the tribal leaders. Even feuding chiefs of eminent rank such as Tuta Nihoniho and Te Hati Haukamau of the Ngatiporou allowed themselves to be taken and incarcerated for a few weeks for carrying arms. In 1890 an incident in the Waikato graphically revealed the King movement's want of physical power. Since his move to Pukekawa, Tawhiao had continued to oppose surveys of Maori land. On his orders his 'magistrate' and secretary, Kerei (Grey) Kaihau pulled down a trigonometrical station on the Piako block. Kerei declined to accompany the Maori constable who served a warrant upon him and a party of King Maori turned back the constable and two others who came to Pukekawa to arrest him. Despite pleas by Kerei's brother Henare Kaihau, an Assessor, that the Government negotiate with

Tawhiao, Mitchelson said that the days of negotiation had passed and a party of armed police and part-time militia from Auckland, under the direction of the Native Secretary, Lewis, plodded through seven miles of swamp and clay track from the Mercer railway station to Pukekawa. They found King Tawhiao and the Kaihau brothers waiting in the ferny clearing of the *kainga,* with only one other Maori—an old woman who shouted abuse at the police. Tawhiao asserted that his *mana* was on the land and that he wanted matters investigated to the root—to Waitara. Lewis replied that 'There was only one sovereignty—that of the Queen—and there was only one law, the law of the Queen.' Kerei Kaihau was then taken from the protection of the man who once had thousands fighting for his standard, and Tawhiao's distress was very evident.[43]

These events demonstrated that the once crucial political role of the Native Department was over. It had not generally been intended to provide a separate and lasting machinery of administration tailored to Maori requirements. By most settlers it had been treated as a necessary expedient to draw the Maori under the rule of Pakeha law and it had served its purpose. Ballance's party, now called the Liberal Party, returned to power in 1891. Although in some senses this was to be the beginning of a period of considerable change in New Zealand life, Alfred Cadman, the Native Minister, merely brought to a logical conclusion the trend of the previous twelve years in Maori administration. Resident Magistrates' courts in historic localities such as Waimate were closed and Bishop, Resident Magistrate, Mangonui, moved to Auckland.[44] The list of Maori stipendaries were trimmed to about twenty Assessors. These and about ninety-six aged pensioners, some of them wounded veterans of the Kupapa forces, took only about £2300 of the Civil List vote and their numbers dwindled rapidly by the end of the century. There were also about 113 Land Court Assessors but of these few were active members and they were paid only on days of attendance at Court.[45]

In December 1891 Lewis, Under-Secretary in the Native Department since 1879, died while on leave in Australia. Morpeth, the Chief Clerk, took charge but the following December the Native Department was dismantled. The Land Court was transferred to the Justice Department, and land-purchasing and the settlement of recurring disputes about lands were taken over by the Department of Crown Lands and the Justice Department. Cadman also decided that 'considering the number of years Native Schools have been in vogue' most correspondence with Maori in the out-districts could be in English;[46] the remaining clerks and interpreters were therefore given positions under the district Registrars of the Land Court. The Justice Department administered official policy on such matters as still required special notice—Tawhiao's funeral in 1894, for example. Remaining Resident Magistrates became simply Justice Department magistrates and the sole remaining Native Officer, Wilkinson, lingered on at Otorohanga, distributing pensions and reporting cases of indigence, until his death in 1906.

The dispersal of the Native Department was accompanied by the removal of the legal basis that had underlain it. The Native Districts Regulation Act and Native Circuit Court Act, 1858, on which Grey had built his 'new institutions' were repealed in 1891. In 1893 the Magistrates Court Act repealed the Resident Magistrates Act, 1867, abolishing the office of Resident Magistrate and replacing it with that of Stipendiary Magistrate (the modern SM) with strictly judicial functions. As the special provisions of the 1867 Act were not re-enacted the Maori people became amenable to the ordinary legal machinery of the land, including the local Justices of the Peace and constables. The remaining Maori Assessors lost the right to assist the bench in cases affecting Maori. When the Magistrates Court Act was passing the Assembly two Maori members, Kapa (Northern Maori) and Parata (Southern Maori), objected to the measure because it left Maori litigants to the mercy of magistrates who did not understand their language, let alone their customs and point of view, and deprived Maori leaders of a share in judicial responsibility.[47] Their protests did not even draw a serious reply and one of the most useful roles ever accorded Maori leaders in the Colony was ended.

By 1893 the only important special institutions affecting the Maori were the Land Court, which substantially served settler rather than Maori interests, the Maori schools service of the Education Department, and the four special Maori electorates. In parliament and administratively, efforts were made after 1887 to eliminate these last two, along with the Native Department. The Maori were pressed to accept either a reduction in the number of special electorates or the loss of the extra vote they had on the common roll, if possessed of sufficient property. In 1896—having given every indication of wanting more, not fewer, Maori electorates—the Maori (unless 50 per cent or more part-European in descent) lost their right to membership on the common roll. The four Maori electorates have thus remained a feature of New Zealand parliamentary life.[48] When attempts were made to place Native Schools under the local Education Boards and extinguish their special status, it was found that Maori communities objected to the loss of a school system which was shaped, to some extent, to serve their special needs, and which they had come to value.[49] European parents also objected to their children mixing with Maori children. The reasons given included concern that 'the invincible race-prejudice' of the more unreasoning settlers could cause the mixed schools to fail, the fear that settlers' children in Maori districts 'already have too great a tendency to adopt Maori habits' and that 'Maori children from a very early age not uncommonly possess an amount and kind of physiological knowledge that Europeans do not attain to till they reach maturity; and perhaps, in most cases, not even then'.[50] The Maori schools remained but they did include an increasing number of settler children, and Maori children increasingly attended the ordinary Education Board schools.[51] The teachers in the Maori schools, under the sympathetic and energetic leadership of J. Pope, organising officer for the schools from 1881 to 1904, often took a broad view of their responsibilities;

working with committees of Maori parents they tended to succeed both the missions and the old-style Resident Magistrates as the principal mediators of Pakeha culture to the Maori people.

The advent of the twenty-year Liberal regime has usually been judged to have resulted in much more benign Maori policies than those of previous years, and in many respects this was true from the later 1890s when the association of the mixed-race politician James Carroll as Minister Representing the Native Race and the Premier, Richard Seddon, began to bear fruit. But Liberal benignity was not immediately apparent to the Maori especially in the early 1890s. The Ballance Government specifically undertook to purchase Maori land at an even faster rate than the Atkinson Government had achieved from 1888-90.[52] Moreover their methods were hardly less scrupulous than those of previous years. Cadman ruthlessly forced a survey in the Urewera in 1893, on the consent of only a minority of owners; some Tuhoe who removed surveyors' instruments were arrested, and the situation threatened violence until that 'notorious savage' Te Kooti used his influence to have the survey permitted and the whole dispute referred to the *Kotahitanga* 'parliament', then meeting in Hawke's Bay.[53] The ghoulishness of land-purchase methods was revealed at the death of Tawhiao in 1894; settler politicians noted that 'Land Purchase Officers should be active as many blocks will be offered for tangi expenses'.[54] Moreover, although Seddon curtailed land-purchase operations in 1900, in deference to pressure exerted through the *Kotahitanga* movement, Pakeha opinion obliged him to resume it in 1905.[55] The confusion of titles and constant teasing for land led to a steady decline in the number of Maori sheep farms between 1890 and 1910.[56] The Liberal Government also authorised the reimposition of rates on Maori lands, (which had been suspended by Atkinson pending a re-examination of the problem), a new tax on land under lease, and the requirement that Maori owners pay their share of boundary fencing. Maori land-owners were being pressed to assume the same obligations as Pakeha farmers—a policy which would have been fairer had land-buying and other distractions from steady enterprise been curtailed and the Maori been better assisted to generate the revenue with which to meet public obligations.

The Liberals did indeed make a vigorous effort to reform the Land Court, locating Judges each in specific districts which they were expected to learn to know well, and creating an Appellate Court. The Land Court gained added powers—the right to administer Maori wills and Maori adoptions, and the right (previously with the Governor-in-Council and later with the Supreme Court) of authorising the alienation of minors' interests. It was not immediately apparent, however, that the Court carried out its multiplying duties with much more efficiency and responsibility under the Liberals and their early successors than in previous years. It could hardly be a firm guardian of Maori interests while it included judges like Von Sturmer, who expressed satisfaction at the passing of Maori land into Pakeha hands, and added, 'I have determined never to place restrictions on Native Land where it is unoccupied'.[57]

In the period 1910-20, moreover, it was still attracting the same charges of incompetence and wasteful delay as it had in the nineteenth century.[58] And although a Native Department was recreated in 1906, recognising special Maori needs to some extent, it was paternalistic in character, largely concerned with the settlement of Maori land, and for many years gave very little scope for Maori leaders to exercise responsibility through it.

By 1893 then the Maori people had, in the main, been subordinated to the settler political and legal system and asked to assume its obligations, while being steadily parted from their lands by processes which favoured speculation and deviousness and hindered Maori farmers. The Maori culture itself was widely denigrated. At best it was regarded as a hindrance to Maori participation in the new order; at worst as depraved and obscene. In 1886 the Premier officially informed the leader of a Maori concert party that the Governor could not be present at the performance of war dances in a Wellington theatre because of their alleged depravity.[59] But while their own culture was assailed and disrupted through the land-purchase system, little encouragement was being given to Maori participation in a wide spectrum of Pakeha vocations. Opportunities for skilled employment had not improved over a generation. Despite pleas from Resident Magistrates to apprentice promising Maori boys in boat-building, carpentry or saddlery, only one was having his fees paid in 1889. Maori cadets were not welcome in white-collar occupations, even in the Public Service. The newly-organised labour unions, whose votes the Liberals needed, checked the Government from giving the privileges to Maori labour on road and railway contracts that McLean had given.[60] Economic opportunities everywhere seemed to be closed off to the Maori. Meanwhile discrimination against Maori in public places, accommodation and the real estate trade increased.

As has been shown too, the rule of law was no clear safeguard of Maori rights. It was markedly the rule of the majority, shaped to suit settler convenience (especially with regard to land-purchasing) and set aside altogether, if inconvenient, as during the imprisonment of Te Whiti and his followers without trial in 1879-82. When a Maori tried the same game the outcry was enormous. In 1871 a Thames Maori debarred a settler from floating timber down a small (non-navigable) stream on his land and damaging his eel-weirs, unless a toll was paid; he won an action in the Supreme Court on the question but the jury itself protested piously against the law being made 'the instrument of spoliation and oppression' and the Assembly responded with a Floatage of Timber Act to prevent tolls being charged in such circumstances.[61] The instruments specifically purporting to give the Maori people certain rights and privileges were interpreted narrowly in the courts. The Treaty of Waitangi itself has not been held to have any standing in domestic law and could not prevail against the Crown's prerogative rights, as successive judgments on the subject of fisheries in tidal waters show.[62] FitzGerald's attempt to translate the Treaty provisions into law, through the Native Rights Act, 1865, did seem

to have some effect in recognising the Maori as having the personal rights of
natural-born British subjects, but the Supreme Court ruled in 1881 that it did
not give Maori customary rights in land the force of a legal title, as FitzGerald
had intended.[63] At the turn of the century the Privy Council cast doubts on
this interpretation, even alleging the subservience of the New Zealand Judges
to the Executive, and although the Native Rights Act was re-enacted in 1908
it was repealed by the Native Land Act, 1909, which also specifically stated
that Maori customary title was not to prevail against the Crown.[64]

From about 1893, just when the Government was winding up the special
machinery of Maori administration, the *Kotahitanga* was entering its most
influential phase. The Maori people had become deeply disillusioned by the
'sham' equality they had been offered, particularly by the negligible influence
they had in the machinery of state. Four Maori seats in an unsympathetic
parliament were utterly inadequate and the winding up of the Resident
Magistrate and Assessor system had removed the opportunity for local executive
and judicial responsibility. The *mana* of the land and the *mana* of the people
had clearly passed into Pakeha hands. Both the tradition-minded chiefs and
the progressive young men who had sought to engage in the new order were
affronted and frustrated. A principal goal of the *Kotahitanga* was therefore a
separate council or parliament to handle Maori affairs, with committees of
owners, under the council, to administer their lands (to the total exclusion of
the Native Land Court), to enforce their own game conservation laws, and
to try their own people for crimes arising from breaches of Maori custom. At
first this program was pursued through Bills presented by Taiwhanga and his
successors to the General Assembly. Taiwhanga's plea that the word 'Maori'
replace 'Native' in official terminology also symbolised his demand that the
settlers should cease thinking of his people and culture as primitive and
inferior.[65] The movement was supported by former staunch allies of the Government—Kemp, Te Wheoro, Topia Turoa, H. M. Tawhai, Wi Parata and lately
Mokena Kohere, the anti-Hauhau stalwart of the 1860s who in 1886 resigned
the seat in the Legislative Council he had ultimately been rewarded with.
Meeting no success in the General Assembly, the movement sought to establish
its parliament independently and, after a series of meetings that united majority
Maori opinion,[66] succeeded by 1893 in establishing a fairly effective boycott of
the Land Court.[67]

After its withdrawal from Ngatimaniapoto territory the King movement
also showed a remarkable resilience. 'King Committees' were organised throughout the Waikato to try cases and raise revenue by taxes on stock. Kingite
leaders such as Te Wheoro interested themselves in grievances throughout the
country, and engaged with the *Kotahitanga*. From 1882 efforts had been
made to raise funds for a new printing press, and in 1892 the first numbers of
Te Paki o te Matariki began to appear, from Mangakawa, near Hamilton.
Significantly, one of the leaders of the movement was Wi Tana Taingakawa
Te Waharoa, son of Tamihana the Kingmaker. When Tawhiao died in 1894,

the Ngatimaniapoto were accorded the privilege of guarding the body before burial. Already disgruntled at the way the opening of their territory had got out of hand and resulted in extensive alienation of land, the Ngatimaniapoto were once again re-engaged in the King movement through this act of traditional diplomacy and symbolism. The subsequent coronation ceremonies for Mahuta, Tawhiao's successor, gave further impetus to the King movement.

Prophetic traditions also remained very strong. By the time of his death in 1893, Te Kooti had established his *Ringatu* faith firmly in the Bay of Plenty, Urewera and East Coast districts and had helped the Tuhoe to hold their land. Other prophets arose in their own localities, though none out-shone Te Kooti until Ratana in the 1920s organised the most successful of all Maori politico-religious movements.[68]

XXII

Myths and Realities

What then was the outcome of a half-century of efforts to bring the Maori people within a centralised state, under the rule of law and on the basis of 'amalgamation' with the settlers? About 1901 the lawyer Walter Buller wrote a description of race relations in New Zealand which represented what might be called the 'official' view. It was to the effect that the Maori had accepted their defeat in war without bitterness, that they had full civil rights and that far from being stripped of their land they retained '5,000,000 acres of the *cream* of it'. If the Maori were a dying race, and official opinion was by no means agreed on that question, this was held to be something beyond the control of government and administration. New Zealand race relations were in Buller's estimation an example to the whole world.[1] The Pakeha public has generally believed this view unquestioningly, and reacted with shock and anger when Maori writers, and most Pakeha scholars, have denounced it for what it is—smug, ignorant and hypocritical. The view of a number of today's young Maori intelligentsia is reflected in the painting by Selwyn Muru, which depicts a phalanx of white soldiers, with the Christian cross in the background, trampling the prostrate body of a Maori: the title of the painting is *Kawanatanga*— Government.

Indeed, as the preceding chapters show, the colonisation of New Zealand, notwithstanding the Treaty of Waitangi and humanitarian idealism, was substantially an imperial subjugation of a native people, for the benefit of the conquering race in which the notions of white supremacy and racial prejudice, familiar in other examples of nineteenth-century European imperialism were very much in evidence. 'Amalgamation' had operated to bring the Maori people under as much as possible the same political and judicial system as the settlers, with nominal equality before the law, but with very little assistance to attain a genuine equality in economic and social life. As an astute settler observed in 1861, 'the Native race has been . . . treated from a political, religious or judicial point of view, and not, I think sufficiently from an ethnological or social one'.[2] This tendency increased rather than diminished during the century and by the 1890s it seemed as though, as Montagu Hawtrey had feared, the Maori people, manifestly 'unequal in the field' with settlers who possessed the skills and values appropriate to competitive commercial enterprise, were being 'destroyed under a show of justice'.

In 1870 Earl Grey, well aware of the proclivities of the New Zealand settlers, had written to Henry Sewell that he had no confidence in the permanence of friendly relations between the colonists and the Maori:

> I fear that the same causes which led to the war of 1860 will sooner or later lead to another struggle between the two races, and that an ultra-democratic government, in which the Maoris cannot be allowed their fair share of power, will not long abstain from giving them cause for discontent. Not only the King party, but the most friendly of the Natives are likely to consider themselves aggrieved by the measures of a government constituted like that of New Zealand.[3]

Open war in fact had not again developed, largely because with the Imperial troops withdrawn, the Colonial politicians were forced to face the crippling cost of fighting determined Maori adversaries; especially under McLean they avoided the worst provocations and restrained their more aggressive compatriots. Yet government basically represented a white settlers' electorate whose determination to assure their dominion over the Maori and acquire Maori land on terms they considered satisfactory, could not be denied. Politicians who appeared too tolerant of Maori defiance or who tried to deny the settlers the freehold of Maori land soon found themselves in difficulty—as Sheehan, for instance found. In the last resort the settlers were capable of defying governmental and legal restraints and forcing the issue, as when they armed and began to seize Te Whiti's ploughmen or systematically defaulted in payment of rents for the Rotorua lands. Given this reality Earl Grey's prediction that even the friendly Maori would be aggrieved was well-based and proved very accurate.

In view of the subordinate and unequal position of the Maori in New Zealand society at the end of the nineteenth century, can it then be concluded that the 'amalgamation' policy, conceived as a humanitarian approach to prevent the Maori being left backward and isolated in a white settler colony, had failed? And since the Maori people were seeking to preserve elements of their traditional culture through semi-separatist organisations, can it be argued that 'amalgamation' should never have been attempted?

In fact, despite the distortions and duplicity, the official ideology of racial 'amalgamation' and equality of Maori and European before the law, had not been without benefit to the Maori people. It had limited wanton violence against the Maori by settlers during the wars. It was the basis of the policy of multi-racial schools which on the one hand enabled masters like Mr Morgan of Taeri Ferry public school to 'resist the efforts of those European parents and members of the Committee who wished to oust [the Maori children] from his school' and on the other, kept the Native Schools open to rural settler children. It meant that unofficial segregation in public buildings could never become too blatant. Certainly officialdom was rather inactive about the matter, but it was never quite dormant. In 1892, for example, when a Urewera Maori was refused service in a Whakatane hotel the publican was threatened with prosecution by the local police and criticised in the General Assembly.[4]

Although the emergent trades union movement sought to block employment of non-union Maori as they blocked non-union white labour, the unions themselves were on a non-racial basis, Maori shearers forming a large section of the New Zealand Workers' Union and Maori union organisers emerging at an early date.[5] In the rural situation Maori and Pakeha were regularly associated in work, without stress or incident. District sporting clubs, especially Rugby football, were also normally multi-racial. In other words, although all Maori would from time to time experience slight or discrimination on account of their race their day-to-day experiences would often include much open and equal association with the Pakeha.

Perhaps most important of all, the official philosophy of 'amalgamation' sanctioned racial inter-marriage. Casual liaisons were, of course, common, as in most frontier societies, and numbers of settlers formally took Maori wives.[6] Marriage of white women with Maori men was more rare but Hirini Tai-whanga, for example, had a European wife. Moreover, when in 1879 Leopold Puhipi, eldest son of Timoti Puhipi, a principal chief of the Rarawa, married a Miss Hardiman, daughter of an early settler, the wedding was celebrated in the old mission church at Kaitaia and the local Maori and European com-munities joined in a wedding breakfast that lasted two days.[7] It is a matter for speculation how the young couple fared amidst the prejudice that no doubt existed about them, but the fact that this marriage could be accorded full social recognition by the settler community indicated that the Maori were not going to be held immediately and permanently inferior by virtue of race; pro-viding certain social prerequisites were met—and Leopold Puhipi was an intelligent, personable young man—they would be welcomed into European society. Whether the product of informal or formal marriages between settlers and Maori, mixed-race offspring usually identified more strongly with the Maori side of their parentage; but possessing links with the settler community they formed an important bridge between the two races. Several of the leaders of the Maori people at the turn of the century, drawing them into fuller participation in the new order, were in fact of mixed parentage.

In the economic sphere some Maori were fortunate enough to retain land and even to gain a sufficiently secure title to work it; by 1888 the Ngatiporou had begun the first successful farming incorporation.[8] Others could still get contract work and seasonal labour which provided the income to supplement a basically traditional pattern of cultivating and hunting. It would not be mere sentimentality to suggest that many found this life-style satisfying, although they would usually be quickly frustrated if they tried for rapid material enrichment of it.

Such political power as the Maori possessed provided just sufficient of a safety valve to avert complete despair of constitutional processes. The four Maori members of parliament, if allied with a sufficiently interested European party, could occasionally score a victory on particular issues. Thus, after Te Kooti's threatened visit to Gisborne in 1889, a Government Bill to prohibit

'Maori assemblies' was hotly debated in the Assembly and neatly killed in the Native Affairs Committee when the four Maori members secured the deletion of the word 'Maori'.[9]

These sorts of experience indicate that although 'Government' *was* based on the military subjugation of the Maori as Selwyn Muru depicts it, that was not all there was to it. Humanitarian notions of the rule of law and racial 'amalgamation' had had an important ameliorating effect. It was for these reasons that, in the end, the majority of the Maori people chose to pursue advancement and reform through the framework of state institutions rather than intensifying the separatist tendencies of the *Kotahitanga*. In the 1870s and 1880s numbers of nameless young men had engaged with some success in the Pakeha milieu and were assisting their communities towards the same end, by promoting village schools and engaging in commercial enterprise.[10] In the 1890s too, graduates like Apirana Ngata and Te Rangihiroa were emerging from a background of village school, church boarding school and university. Working with men like the mixed-race politician James Carroll, they were able in 1900 to secure from the Liberal Premier Seddon, a cessation of land purchasing and legislation creating Village Councils and Land Boards which at last gave the Maori some significant control of their land and of local community problems of health and welfare. On the basis of this success they were able to persuade the *Kotahitanga* to disperse. And although the Village Councils were inhibited by lack of official support, although the settler electorate forced a resumption of land purchasing in 1905 and although William Herries, Native Minister in the Reform Government from 1912-20, introduced another gloomy period when the philosophy of 'no special institutions for the Maori' was again the key-note, Ratana too, turned his movement, not into political separatism, but into a vehicle for the social and economic advancement of his people within the main political order.[11]

In an important sense then the policy of 'amalgamation' did match Maori aspirations, apparent from the early years of culture contact, to share fully in the European order as it intruded into New Zealand. Certainly it was much more appropriate to Maori needs than the policy of protections on reservations against which it was largely a reaction. Moreover, both in its compulsion upon the Maori to assume the obligations of citizens, and in its protection, however imperfect, of their rights as citizens, it did, as James Stephen hoped, avert some of the jealousy and antagonism which a privileged and protected minority tends to attract.

Yet there is little justification for Buller's self-congratulation in all of this. Indeed it is largely because the Maori people did seek full 'inclusion' (to use the sociologist Erik Schwimmer's concept) in the economic activity and the state power of the new order, that the settlers stand indicted in their own terms.[12] It was their self-interest and their racialism which checked and frustrated the burgeoning drive of the Maori, most evident in the 1870s, to acquire Pakeha skills, join Pakeha institutions, seek Pakeha assistance, and achieve, for their children if not for themselves, 'equality in the field' with the dominant settlers. Such success as the Maori achieved by 1900 was as much in spite of, as because of, Pakeha assistance. Many settlers were too locked in their stereotyped view of coloured peoples as inferior to appreciate the intelligence and resourcefulness of Maori leaders; others who did recognise it were reluctant to acknowledge the fact because to do so would weaken their political dominion and control of Maori land. Hence Wahanui's attempt to make a careful controlled opening of the King Country to the Pakeha while trying to safeguard his own people's farming enterprises, was subverted by cynical and secretive land-buying, against the known wishes of the Ngatimaniapoto leaders; hence also, as Te Wheoro found, the constant denial to Maori leaders of more than a limited share of state power. In these ways the full program of 'amalgamation' as conceived by the humanitarians, was not applied during the nineteenth century.

Moreover, in another important sense, the 'amalgamation' policy never did match Maori needs and aspirations. Hence, because it generated antipathy among them, it worked *counter* to the aim of genuine unity of the New Zealand people. Schwimmer sees Maori aspirations, in the 1960s as involving 'ambiculturalism' as well as 'inclusion'. By 'ambiculturalism' he means not only tolerance of cultural differences, as in 'pluralism', but the recognition of the validity of the two cultures and the ability of each to make creative use of the other.

This aspiration too has existed from the earliest years of culture contact, Maori leaders and entrepreneurs necessarily moving from a basis in their own institutions, seeking to be selective in their admission of European influences, and to retain self-respect as regards their race and culture. It was an attitude unfortunately not reciprocated by nineteenth-century colonists. Government policy reflected the predominant Pakeha view that the unity of the New Zealand people was only to be achieved by a uniformity of institutions—inevitably the colonists' institutions. And though some like Sir William Martin and T. S. Grace were aware of the fallacy of this view, most humanitarian opinion at that time was firmly in support of settler opinion. Thus there was no humanitarian protest when the Native Department and Assessor system was wound up, allegedly because they kept up 'a measure of separation between the two races'.[13] Had the system remained too long as one exclusive to Maori instead of an alternative one like the Native Schools system, that judgment may ultimately have proved true, but it was not generally true of the system in the nineteenth century. Indeed it will be recalled that Paora Tuhaere's objection to Bryce's retrenchment of the Resident Magistrates and Assessors was that it *stopped* the two races 'uniting under such a system'. Clearly Tuhaere did not see the modification of the main line judicial structure to include the Native Department Resident Magistrates and Assessors as divisive. On the contrary it reconciled Maori leaders to the growth of the state by recognising their aspirations for local judicial and administrative authority, and according them formal salaried office in the structure of the Queen's government. Their subsequent exclusion not only left local Maori leaders without a clear sense of sharing state power but also caused the law and its application to become much more alien to the Maori people. Courts sat in the settlers' towns, with Pakeha magistrates sitting on daises in solid court-houses, the proceedings being marked by formality and technicality. It must have seemed enormously remote and forbidding to Maori litigants and defen-dants—a far cry from the days when 'their' Resident Magistrates came around the villages in company with the leading local men, settling disputes with sensitivity to local values and a minimum of legal technicality. It is often said that Western individualism is in conflict with Polynesian communalism: in this case it was the lack of time and concern for individual nuances in the Western legal system, its apparent cold, machine-like inexorability, that antagonised the Maori. It is hardly surprising that today Maori attitudes to the law appear more ambivalent than they did in the 1870s and 1880s. The *ture* is still spoken of with respect as a source of strength and stability; but its impositions are frequently seen as oppressive and alien.

The extension of the jurisdiction of the Stipendiary Magistrate and Justice of the Peace over the Maori was desirable on many grounds. Indeed, as we have seen, some Maori had themselves found the confining of their disputes to the Resident Magistrates unduly restrictive. With the loosening of the kinship structure many felt less inclined to pay four times the value of property stolen by reckless kinsmen and more inclined to see the offender gaoled—especially if he were prone to abuse the system. But the abrupt curtailment of the whole Resident Magistrate system was another matter, especially as it was not accom-panied by the appointment of Maori Justices of the Peace, let alone Maori Stipendiary Magistrates (even though at that stage it was normal to choose men who were not qualified solicitors). Had some of the personnel, principles and procedures of the Resident Magistrate system been carried over into the Stipendiary Magistrate system and the Justice Department, and made available to both Maori and Pakeha, some genuine 'ambiculturalism' would have been possible. Not only would the Magistrates' Courts have remained more accept-able to the Maori, but the Pakeha might have gained something from a system which had been modified to accommodate Maori values. We now recognise, for example, that nineteenth-century English law and its application, were unduly punitive and not sufficiently directed towards reintegration of offenders into society. This could have been learnt earlier from Maori principles of settling petty disputes. So too could the principle of awarding compensation to the victim of an assault, instead of simply gaoling the offender. Certainly, the Resident Magistrates, whose respect for Maori values and abilities often deepened remarkably from their association with the Assessors and police of their districts, were inclined to urge greater recognition for Maori leaders and Maori institutions in the machinery of state. Their viewpoint was shared by McLean and reflected in the Native Councils Bill, 1872. Self-interest—the knowledge that giving the Maori greater control of their own land would hinder land-purchasing—had frustrated that approach. In 1893 the colonists' racialist attitudes made it unthinkable that a Maori, even a law graduate like Ngata could be granted judicial office that carried authority over Pakeha, and their ethnocentrism did not allow that British law could learn anything from Maori principles and procedures.

Twentieth-century governments, moved both by the protests of those, such as the *Kotahitanga* leaders and Ratana, who had been aggrieved by the 'amalgamation' policy, and by the lobbying of men like Carroll and Ngata who had gained prominence through it but were determined to modify it, did go far to admit the shortcomings of their predecessors. The creation of Maori Councils and Maori Land Boards by Seddon was a partial recognition of Maori abilities and enabled the creative energies of local communities to be brought to bear on pressing problems; Coates's Government in the 1920s admitted the colonists' culpability in the Waitara purchase, the land confiscations and the miserable payment for the South Island, and paid compensation to the descendents of the lineages most affected; state support for Ngata's land development schemes in the 1930s, the Labour Government's full employment policy and social security system established after 1935, and the special assist-ance towards Maori housing and education of the 1960s have enabled many Maori to achieve a genuine 'equality in the field' with Pakeha New Zealanders.

Yet there are important issues in race relations which were swept under the carpet by complacent statements such as Buller's and are only now being dragged out for somewhat unwilling Pakeha gaze by a numerous, educated and forthright Maori urban intelligentsia. These involve a full recognition by Pakeha New Zealanders of the extent to which their forebears' racialism, ethno-centrism and self-interest frustrated vigorous and intelligent efforts by Maori individuals and communities at advancement within the encroaching European order. They involve also a recognition that a basic demand of Maori leaders in the nineteenth century was for ample inclusion in the machinery of state, in terms of equality with the European, not just in minor subordinate positions. This was not, in their view, to depend on qualifying on strict European educa-tional criteria; it was something they sought as of right, as a people; without it Maori *mana* would not be preserved, neither would there be full equality in the land with the Pakeha. In the twentieth century some few Maori have qualified for positions of power by years of education in the European system, and in the early 1970s the first Maori magistrate, first Senior Inspector of Schools, first full Colonel in the army and first Bishop in the Anglican church (apart from the incumbents of the special Maori bishopric) were appointed. Yet the administration of Maori affairs is still heavily marked by paternalism, and a much greater inclusion of Maori leaders in positions of political and administrative authority may be necessary to avert renewed frustration.

Finally, nineteenth-century experience suggests that Maori achievement was also checked by the undermining of traditional institutions which the people valued and sought to adapt to new purposes, and by the constant denigration of Maori character and culture. This too has in part been reversed by such measures as official support for farming and timber-milling incorporations, by the substitution of the term 'integration' for 'amalgamation' or 'assimilation' in official policy, and the increase of courses in Maori language and culture in schools and universities. But the establishment of tribal *marae* in the cities, or the recognition of a form of *runanga* in Maori-populated suburbs to take cognisance of disputes and delinquency, appear, in the early 1970s, still to be frowned upon by responsible ministers and officials as divisive of Maori and Pakeha, rather than received optimistically as a means of helping young Maori to develop a sense of belonging and confidence and of enabling older Maori both to develop improved social control and to enjoy a larger sense of respon-sibility in New Zealand society.

Pakeha fears and prejudices are certainly likely to be inflamed, as they were in the nineteenth century, by marked departures from general New Zealand norms. Some of the more strident young Maori leaders might also note that as an historical fact and continuing reality; although the practical application of prejudice may be curbed, prejudice itself is not usually allayed by frontal political assault alone, but rather by education in the broad sense, in which forthright political demonstration may play a part. But while it is certainly possible that extravagant demands extravagantly stated could jeo-pardise positions already won (and this, in the relatively amicable condition of New Zealand race relations, would be tragic) the threat of Pakeha ill-temper should not be made grounds by government for denying reasonable claims, reasonably argued, for variations from the norm. As the above chapters show, the defeatist aspect of nineteenth-century humanitarian and official policy—that the Maori must assimilate as quickly and completely as possible to the Pakeha order for fear of settler prejudice and reprisals—has not been entirely helpful. Firm support for modifications of main line institutions sought by Maori leaders as socially valuable, optional, (not obligatory) alternatives for Maori—and hopefully, for interested Pakeha as well—would be conducive both to the enrichment of national life and to a genuine unity of races, based on mutual respect.

Appendixes

Appendix A

Native Ministers 1858-93

C. W. Richmond	August 1858 to November 1860
F. A. Weld	November 1860 to July 1861
W. B. D. Mantell	July 1861 to December 1861
F. D. Bell (Acting)	December 1861 to May 1862
W. Fox (Acting)	May 1862 to August 1862
Bell	August 1862 to October 1863
Fox (Colonial Secretary and Native Minister)	October 1863 to November 1864
Mantell	December 1864 to July 1865
J. E. FitzGerald	August 1865 to October 1865
A. H. Russell	October 1865 to August 1866
J. C. Richmond (Collector of Customs)	August 1866 to June 1869
D. McLean	June 1869 to December 1876 (except 10/9/72 to 11/10/72)
D. Pollen	December 1876 to October 1877
J. Sheehan	October 1877 to October 1879
J. Bryce	October 1879 to January 1881
W. Rolleston	January 1881 to October 1881
Bryce	October 1881 to August 1884
J. Ballance	August 1884 to October 1887
E. Mitchelson	October 1887 to January 1891
Ballance (Acting)	January 1891 to February 1891
A. J. Cadman	February 1891 to June 1893

Appendix B

Native Secretaries

(Under-Secretaries of the Native Department) 1856-92

D. McLean	1856-61
H. Halse (Acting)	1861-3
E. Shortland	1863-4
Halse (Acting)	1864-5
W. Rolleston	1865-8
G. S. Cooper	1868-71
Halse (Acting)	1871-3
H. T. Clarke	1873-9
T. W. Lewis	1879-91
W. J. Morpeth (Acting)	1891-2

Notes

Chapter 1

1. Sir Peter Buck [Te Rangi Hiroa], *Viking of the Sunrise,* p. 290.
2. E. Adamson Hoebel, *The Law of Primitive Man,* p. 28. T. Olawale Elias, in *The Nature of African Customary Law,* also argues that the absence of state judicial machinery is not sufficient reason to deny the term 'law' to techniques of adjusting disputes in stateless societies.
3. Marshall D. Sahlins, *Social Stratification in Polynesia,* p. 150.
4. J. A. Barnes, 'Law as politically active, an anthropological view', p. 171.
5. P. Bohannen, 'The differing realms of the law', pp. 33-42. For a useful summary of the above issues see Dennis Lloyd, *The Idea of Law,* chapter 10.
6. M. B. Hooker, 'An enquiry into the function of the magico-religious as a jural mechanism in primitive Maori society'.
7. Richard A. Cruise, *Journal of a Ten Months' Residence in New Zealand [1820],* pp. 152-3.
8. Augustus Earle, *Narrative of a Residence in New Zealand,* p. 186.
9. Edward Shortland, *Traditions and Superstitions of the New Zealanders,* p. 227.
10. Ernest Dieffenbach, *Travels in New Zealand,* I, pp. 80, 100-1.
11. Shortland, *The New Zealanders,* p. 236.
12. Earle, *Residence in New Zealand,* p. 126; see also Earle's portraits of the 'Herald or Peacemaker', in *Augustus Earle in New Zealand,* ed. Anthony Murray-Oliver, pp. 113, 120.
13. See John White, *Ancient History of the Maori;* Pei Te Hurinui [Jones], *King Potatau;* also the speech of Te Irimara at Kohimarama, 1860, MA 23/10, p. 117.
14. Hooker, 'The magico-religious as a jural mechanism in primitive Maori society', pp. 103-9.

Chapter 2

1. Closely matching details of the incident are recorded both in Cook's journals and local Maori tradition. See James Cook, *The Voyage of the Endeavour 1768-1771,* p. 196; White, *Ancient History of the Maori,* V, pp. 121-30; and Wynyard to Gray, 6 December 1852 and enclosures, G 8/8.
2. *The Endeavour Journal of Joseph Banks,* I, p. 437.
3. D. I. Pool, 'The Maori population of New Zealand', pp. 229-32.
4. Hooker, 'The magico-religious as a jural mechanism in primitive Maori society', p. 5.
5. Edward Markham, *New Zealand or Recollections of It,* p. 89, note 14.
6. Samuel Marsden, *The Letters and Journals of Samuel Marsden,* ed. John Elder, p. 119.
7. I am indebted for this point to Miss Lila Hamilton who has recently completed a doctoral thesis with the University of Otago on Christianity among the Maori.

8. *The Early Journals of Henry Williams,* pp. 393, 400.
9. Marsden to Pratt, 11 June 1834, *Historical Records of New Zealand,* I, p. 627.
10. Marsden, *Letters and Journals,* p. 335.
11. Marsden to Governor Darling, 2 August 1830 and Darling to Sir George Murray, 12 August 1830, *Historical Records of Australia,* Series I, vol. xv, pp. 702-4. Marsden no doubt had the example of the missionary Kendall very much in mind.
12. Cruise, *Journal,* pp. 81, 174.
13. Earle, *Residence in New Zealand,* p. 67.
14. William Barrett Marshall, *A Personal Narrative of Two Visits to New Zealand in His Majesty's Ship Alligator, A.D. 1834,* pp. 121 ff; *GBPP,* 1836, 538, pp. 434-54.
15. Marshall, *A Personal Narrative,* p. 23.
16. A. N. Brown, Journal, 29 May 1837, CN/0 26b.
17. William Williams, Journal, 14 November 1839, CN/0 96a.
18. *GBPP,* 1844, 556, Evidence, p. 144.
19. Ibid., 1840, 582, p. 68.
20. Earle, *Residence in New Zealand,* p. 115.
21. C. Geertz, 'Religion as a culture system', in William A. Lessa and Evon Z. Vogt, *Reader in Comparative Religion,* p. 209.
22. Ralph Barker, Journal, 23 May 1852, CN/0 22.
23. Dieffenbach, *Travels in New Zealand,* I, p. 316.
24. B. Y. Ashwell to Society, 31 March 1843, CN/0 19.
25. Janet Murray, 'A missionary in action', p. 203.
26. R. FitzRoy, *Remarks on New Zealand in February 1846,* p. 8.
27. The name Wiremu Tamihana is a transliteration of William Thompson, the name taken by Tarapipipi Te Waharoa on his baptism in 1839. Contemporary spellings include Tamihana, Tamehana and Tamahana. Modern Maori authorities, including descendents of William Thompson, favour Tamehana. However in the only (two) original letters I have seen in his own handwriting, the signature is 'Wiremu Tamihana' and I have accordingly followed that spelling.
28. See Harrison Wright, *New Zealand, 1769-1840: Early Years of Western Contact,* chapters 8 and 9; J. Owens, 'Christianity and the Maoris to 1840,' pp. 18-40 and Judith Binney, 'Christianity and the Maoris to 1840: a comment', pp. 143-65.
29. Dieffenbach, *Travels in New Zealand,* I, p. 369.
30. [F. E. Maning], *Old New Zealand;* F. Maning autograph letters.
31. E. J. Tapp, *Early New Zealand, A Dependency of New South Wales, 1788-1841,* chapter 4.

Chapter 3

1. Bourke (Governor, N.S.W.) to Busby, 13 April 1833, cited in Tapp, *Early New Zealand,* p. 88; Eric Ramsden, *Busby of Waitangi, H.M.'s Resident at New Zealand, 1833-40,* pp. 46-8.
2. William Williams, Journal, 17 May 1833, CN/0 96d.
3. Busby to Sewell, 18 July 1856 cited in Ramsden, *Busby,* pp. 43-4.
4. Marshall, *Visits to New Zealand,* pp. 107-11.
5. For McDonnell's activities see CO 209/3, p. 469.
6. Ibid., pp. 1-11.
7. Ian Wards, *The Shadow of the Land,* p. 14.

8. Cited in Keith Sinclair, *A History of New Zealand* (revised edition), p. 56.
9. *GBPP*, 1838, 680, p. 37.
10. Ibid., 1844, 556, Evidence, p. 111.
11. Ibid., 1838, 680, p. 272.
12. Eric Ramsden, *Marsden and the Missions: Prelude to Waitangi,* p. 183.
13. Dandeson Coates, *Documents Exhibiting the Views of the Committee of the Church Missionary Society on the New Zealand Question, and Explanatory of the Present State of that Country,* pp. 43-4.
14. *GBPP*, 1838, 680, pp. 339-40.
15. Coates, *Views of the CMS,* p. 44. (See also Henry Williams's views, ibid., p. 45.)
16. *GBPP*, 1838, 680, pp. 268-72.
17. Dandeson Coates, *The Principles, Objects and Plan of the New Zealand Association Examined,* pp. 10-11.
18. *GBPP*, 1838, 680, p. 44.
19. Ibid., 1840, 582, p. 65.
20. Richard Davis to Coates, 18 November 1839, CO 209/8, p. 165.
21. Bourke to Glenelg, 9 September 1837, cited in Samuel Hinds, *The Latest Official Documents Relating to New Zealand, with Introductory Observations,* p. 26.
22. Glenelg to Durham, 29 December 1837, CO 209/2, p. 410.
23. Hobson to Glenelg, 21 January 1839, CO 209/4, p. 92.
24. Stephen, draft instructions to Hobson, *c.* 24 January 1839, ibid., pp. 228-37.
25. Normanby to Hobson, 14 August 1839, *GBPP*, 1840, [238], p. 38.
26. Busby [to Bourke?] 16 June 1837, cited in Hinds, *Official Documents,* p. 37.
27. *GBPP*, 1838, 680, pp. 44 (Flatt) and 102 (Wilkinson). The Committee recorded similar views from Watkin and Tawell, two surgeons who visited New Zealand, and a dissenting opinion from Montefiore, a trader.
28. Brown, Journal, 16 February 1839, CN/0 26b.
29. Wards, *The Shadow of the Land,* pp. 15-17 and 28-32.
30. The Rev. Montagu Hawtrey, 'Exceptional laws in favour of the natives of New Zealand', Appendix A, in E. G. Wakefield and J. Ward, *The British Colonization of New Zealand.* Also cited in John Beecham, *Colonization: Being Remarks on Colonization in General, with an Examination of the Proposals of the Association which has been Formed for Colonizing New Zealand,* p. 24.
31. Normanby to Hobson, 14 August 1839, *GBPP*, 1840, [238], pp. 39-40.
32. Standish Motte, *A System of Legislation for Securing Protection to the Aboriginal Inhabitants of all Countries Colonized by Great Britain,* copy filed in CO 209/8, pp. 426-37.
33. Torrens, 'Scheme of Native Government', 6 November 1839, CO 209/3, pp. 296ff.
34. For Hawtrey's plans see Hawtrey to Russell, 30 December 1830, CO 209/7, p. 433; Hawtrey to Stanley, 12 March 1842, CO 209/19, p. 231; 'Exceptional laws in favour of the natives of New Zealand', in Wakefield and Ward, *British Colonization,* and *An Earnest Address to the New Zealand Colonists— with Reference to their Intercourse with the Native Inhabitants.*
35. *GBPP*, 1841, 311, pp. 43-7.
36. Stephen minute, 28 December 1840, CO 209/8, p. 450.
37. Stephen, draft instructions to Hobson, 9 December 1840, CO 209/8, pp. 490-1.
38. Ibid., p. 480.
39. Stephen minute, n.d., on Hobson to Gipps, 15 June 1840, CO 209/6, p. 190.

40. A. H. McLintock, *Crown Colony Government in New Zealand,* p. 67; C. H. Wake, 'George Clarke and the government of the Maoris', p. 347.
41. Russell to Hobson, 9 December 1840 (amended draft), CO 209/8, pp. 480-7.
42. Native Trust Ordinance, 1844, *The Ordinances of the Legislative Council of New Zealand,* Session III, no. IX. (Italics added.)

Chapter 4

1. Stephen draft instructions, *c.* January 1839, CO 209/4, p. 239.
2. Report of conversation at Governor FitzRoy's inaugural levée, *The Southern Cross,* 30 December 1843.
3. Bunbury to Hobson, 15 May 1840, CO 209/6, pp. 438-9.
4. Richard Taylor, Journal, 14 April 1840. This statement has been incorrectly reported as 'It will be good to see all the adulterers hanged in a row', in T. Lindsay Buick, *The Treaty of Waitangi,* p. 149.
5. George Clarke, report, enclosed in Gipps to Russell, 7 March 1841, CO 209/9, p. 96.
6. Taylor Journal, 14 February 1840.
7. Wards, *The Shadow of the Land,* pp. 43-4.
8. Hobson to Major Thomas Bunbury, 29 April 1840, cited in Bunbury, *Reminiscences of a Veteran,* III, pp. 63-4.
9. The points in this paragraph are discussed fully in R. M. Ross, 'Te Tiriti o Waitangi, texts and translations', pp. 129-57.
10. Taylor Journal, 5 and 6 February 1840.
11. Bunbury to Hobson, 28 June 1840, CO 209/6, p. 473.
12. Hobson to the New Zealand chiefs, 27 April 1840, cited in Buick, *The Treaty of Waitangi,* p. 191.
13. *GBPP,* 1844, 556, Appendix, p. 349.
14. Stanley to Hobson, 10 September 1842, CO 209/14, p. 195.
15. Clarke to Col. Sec., 31 July 1843, *GBPP,* 1844, 556, Appendix, p. 349.
16. Edward Jerningham Wakefield, *Adventuring in New Zealand from 1839 to 1844,* II, pp. 146-9.
17. Bunbury, *Reminiscences,* III, p. 52.
18. A. D. W. Best, *The Journal of Ensign Best 1837-1842,* pp. 217-9 and Appendix 3, pp. 405-8.
19. Bunbury to Hobson, 6 May 1840, *GBPP,* 1841, 311, pp. 18, 100.
20. Best, *Journal,* p. 228.
21. Ibid., pp. 251-3.
22. Clarke to McLean, 14 December 1844, 6 January 1845, D. McLean, MSS. 180.
23. Best, *Journal,* p. 239; W. Shortland to Hobson, 29 August 1840, CO 209/7, p. 95.
24. W. Shortland to Stanley, 1 September 1843 and enclosures, CO 209/22, pp. 507-8.
25. W. Shortland to Hobson, 5 August 1842, CO 209/16, p. 136.
26. John Gorst, *The Maori King,* p. 10.
27. Best, *Journal,* p. 275.
28. Shortland, *The New Zealanders,* pp. 238-9.
29. *New Zealand Colonist,* 21 October 1842.
30. W. C. Symonds, MS. Journal, 27 April 1841; Best, *Journal,* pp. 298-9 and plate 7; Dieffenbach, *Travels in New Zealand,* II, pp. 38-9.
31. Maunsell to Society, 2 February 1843, CN 0/64.
32. Best, *Journal,* p. 394.
33. Ibid., p. 298.

34. John Butler, *Earliest New Zealand: the Journals and Correspondence of the Reverend John Butler,* p. 427.
35. *New Zealand Gazette and Wellington Spectator,* 16 December 1843.
36. Lady Martin, *Our Maoris,* p. 59.
37. *AJHR,* 1860, F-3, p. 30.
38. Brown Journal, 3 October 1843, CN 0/26b.
39. John Whiteley, Journal, 16 April 1841.
40. [F. E. Maning], *Old New Zealand,* pp. 110-1.
41. Clarke, Junior, to Chief Protector, 14 June 1843, *GBPP,* 1844, 556, *Appendix,* p. 351.
42. Edward Shortland, *The Southern Districts of New Zealand,* p. 135.
43. Clarke to Col. Sec., 18 March 1843, MA 4/58.
44. Best, *Journal,* pp. 340-1.
45. Clarke, Junior, report, 14 June 1843, CO 209/23, p. 301; Graham Billing, 'The Wairau affray', pp. 449-50.
46. Dieffenbach, *Travels in New Zealand,* II, pp. 152ff.
47. Report of the House of Commons Committee in New Zealand, *GBPP,* 1844, 556, p. 10.
48. J. Halswell, report, 10 February 1842 and W. Wakefield to Clarke, Jnr, 1 March 1843, *GBPP,* 1850 [1136], p. 241.
49. Raupo Houses Ordinance, 1842, *Ordinances of New Zealand,* Session II, no. XVII.
50. Halswell to Secretary, NZ Company, 11 November 1841, *GBPP,* 1844, 556, Appendix, p. 671.
51. CO 209/35, p. 156.
52. Best, *Journal,* p. 269.
53. Hobson to Russell, 15 October 1840, *GBPP,* 1841, 311, p. 113.
54. Hobson to Stanley, 12 March 1842, CO 209/64, p. 90.
55. A settlement on the Bay of Plenty coast, not to be confused with the chief Maketu executed for murder in 1842.
56. Best, *Journal,* p. 395.
57. Clarke to Col. Sec., 4 January 1843, *GBPP,* 1844, 556, Appendix, p. 122.

Chapter 5

1. Minutes of Executive Council, 28 December 1842, *GBPP,* 1844, 556, Appendix, p. 457.
2. Hobson to Stanley, 29 March 1842, CO 209/14, p. 357.
3. Stanley minute, 14 May 1843, CO 209/16.
4. Stephen minute, 28 December 1843, CO 209/22, pp. 252-3.
5. Stephen minute, 19 May 1843, CO 209/16, p. 455.
6. Stephen minute, 26 February 1846, CO 209/35, p. 47.
7. Stanley minute, 23 August 1842, CO 209/14, p. 202.
8. Stephen minute, 28 December 1843, CO 209/22, pp. 247-52.
9. Stanley to Shortland, 21 June 1843, *GBPP,* 1844, 556, Appendix, p. 475. (Italics added.)
10. Stanley to FitzRoy, 10 February 1844, ibid., pp. 171-2.
11. Clarke to Col. Sec., 31 July 1843, ibid., Appendix, p. 347.
12. Clarke to Col. Sec., 31 July 1843, ibid., Appendix, pp. 346-8; 31 July 1844, CO 209/30, p. 108; and 1 July 1845, ibid., 1846, 337, pp. 135-6.
13. *New Zealand Gazette and Wellington Spectator,* 2 and 30 December 1843 and 10 January 1844; CO 209/28, p. 92.

14. FitzRoy, *Remarks on New Zealand*, p. 21.
15. *GBPP*, 1844, 556, Evidence, p. 202.
16. Ibid., 1845, 131, pp. 37-43.
17. FitzRoy to Stanley, 20 August 1844, ibid., 247, p. 30.
18. FitzRoy to Stanley, 25 May 1844, ibid., p. 13.
19. *Ordinances of New Zealand,* sess. III, no. XVII.
20. This was also a source of grievance to Maori deckhands who had been bullied or cheated en route to Sydney; NSW magistrates in some cases declined to hear their evidence when they applied to the courts for redress (*GBPP*, 1836, 538, p. 176).
21. *Ordinances of New Zealand,* sess. III, nos. II, XIV and XVI.
22. The historian McLintock has endorsed this view (*Crown Colony Government,* pp. 181-2), but he erroneously regards the Ordinance as an attempt to pacify restless Maori in the Bay of Islands. This is a speculation based merely on the fact that it was passed in July 1844 when disorder in the Bay was mounting. As has been explained, the origins of the Ordinance lay in Stephen's instructions to FitzRoy, in Clarke's ideas, and in FitzRoy's remarks much earlier in the year to the Nelson settlers, the Auckland Maori and the Legislative Council.
23. Fines for Assault Ordinance, 1845, *Ordinances of New Zealand,* sess. V, no. VII. See also FitzRoy to Stanley, 18 July 1845, *GBPP,* 1846, 337, p. 66.
24. Clarke to FitzRoy, 1 July 1845, CO 209/35, p. 72-3: *GBPP,* 1846, 337, p. 134.
25. Wake, 'George Clarke and the Maoris', pp. 354-5.
26. Clarke to Col. Sec., 31 July 1844, CO 209/30, p. 108; FitzRoy to Stanley, 16 September 1844, CO 209/28, p. 231.
27. Shortland, *Southern Districts,* p. 267.
28. Clarke to Col. Sec., 1 July 1845, *GBPP,* 1846, 337, p. 134.
29. Letter quoted by C. O. Davis, *DSC,* 14 October 1868.
30. 'Ki to tatou mana ki te mana hoki o te whenua me to mana hoki o nga tangata', cited in Clarke to Col. Sec., 24 March 1845, CO 209/34, p. 70.
31. *Southern Cross,* 7 September 1844, cited in *GBPP,* 1845, 247, pp. 150-4.
32. T. Lindsay Buick, *New Zealand's First War,* pp. 52-3.
33. McLean to Clarke, 11 July 1845, in *Epitome of Official Documents,* A-2, p. 126.
34. Wards, *Shadow of the Land,* pp. 214ff.
35. *GBPP,* 1846, 203, pp. 31-3 and 337, pp. 10-18.
36. Clarke to Col. Sec., 1 July 1845, CO 209/35, p. 480.
37. Stephen minute, 1 August 1845, CO 209/29, p. 191 and *c.* 10 August 1845, ibid., p. 199.
38. Stanley to Grey, 13 August 1845, ibid., pp. 214-16.
39. See their respective comments on FitzRoy's instructions to M. Richmond, his Superintendent in the Cook Strait settlements, not to proceed against Maori occupying European sections unless he could do so without provoking a major disturbance (CO 209/28, p. 60).
40. Gladstone to Grey, 31 January 1846, *GBPP,* 1846, 337, p. 160.

Chapter 6

1. Grey to Russell, 4 June 1840, *GBPP,* 1841, 311, p. 43; Grey to Earl Grey, 13 May 1847, cited in McLintock, *Crown Colony Government,* p. 393.
2. See Maunsell to Society, 27 October 1846, CN/0 64 and Wards, *Shadow of the Land,* chapters 7 and 8.

3. One of these prisoners died in Tasmania. The sentences of the remainder were commuted after about two years and they were returned to New Zealand. About fifty Europeans sentenced by the civil courts for serious felonies (as well as about twenty-four soldiers sentenced by court martial) were transported to Tasmania, but though on a few occasions Maori civil prisoners were also sentenced to transportation (see, for example, Wakefield, *Adventuring in New Zealand,* II, p. 149), they do not seem to have been actually transported. Certainly in September 1851 Haimona Pita (Simon Peter) Te Ahuru was sentenced by Henry St Hill, Resident Magistrate Wellington to seven years transportation for a felony and sent to Hobart Town, 'but the authorities there declined receiving him' and he returned to Wellington on the ship which brought him (IA 55/3920). I am indebted to Mr M. Saclier, Principal Archivist, Archives Office of Tasmania, for lists of prisoners transported from New Zealand ports. The five sent after Grey's court martial are the only Maori mentioned.

4. *GBPP,* 1850, [1136], pp. 155-9. See also P. D. Gibbons, 'The Protectorate of Aborigines'.

5. *GBPP,* 1851, [1420], pp. 232-42, and 1854, [1779], p. 110.

6. *Ordinances of New Zealand,* sess. VII, no. XVI.

7. Richard Taylor, *The Past and Present of New Zealand with Its Prospects for the Future,* p. 52 and note; Grey to Stanley, 22 November 1845, CO 209/38, p. 18.

8. Grey to Gladstone, 14 November 1846, *GBPP,* 1847, [837], p. 85. See also J. Rutherford, *Sir George Grey K.C.B. 1812-1898: a study in colonial government,* pp. 211-13 and Wake, 'George Clarke and the Maoris', p. 356.

9. *Ordinances of New Zealand,* sess. VII, no. II.

10. Grey to Stanley, 10 December 1845 and 11 December 1845, CO 209/38, pp. 129, 145.

11. Wyatt reports, 2 May, 3 July and 14 August, 1848, Resident Magistrates' Courts Letterbook, Wanganui, 1847-54.

12. Eyre minute, 21 February 1849, NM 49/141.

13. Hamilton to Col. Sec., New Munster, 6 December 1850 and 22 May 1851, Resident Magistrates' Courts Letterbook, Wanganui.

14. Hamilton to Col. Sec., New Munster, 27 January 1851, ibid.

15. Murray, 'A missionary in action', p. 216.

16. Hamilton to Col. Sec., New Munster, 31 January 1851, Resident Magistrates' Courts Letterbook, Wanganui.

17. D. S. Durie to Col. Sec., New Munster, 23 June 1852, ibid.

18. See letters of Hamilton and D. S. Durie to Col. Sec., New Munster, 11 March 1851, 17 July 1851 and 27 July 1852, ibid.

19. Grey, minute, 27 November 1852, CS 52/157.

20. Murray, 'A missionary in action', pp. 216-17.

21. Hamilton to Col. Sec., New Munster, 9 December 1850, Resident Magistrates' Courts Letterbook, Wanganui.

22. See the Wanganui casebook for the period, JC Wanganui 1.

23. W. B. White, 'Reminiscences 1821-1908'.

24. IA 1850/1826.

25. White to Col. Sec., New Ulster, 19 December 1850, IA 50/2303, and 27 January 1851, IA 51/253.

26. IA 48/1899.

27. Flight to A. Domett, 29 January 1852, JC New Plymouth 1.

28. Janet Ross, 'The missionary work of the Rev. Richard Taylor at Wanganui', pp. 210-13.

29. Clendon to Col. Sec., 14 October 1853, IA 53/2348.
30. Whiteley to Grey, 30 July 1851, Grey MSS.; Sinclair and Ligar to Wynyar₫
    7 December 1852, G 8/8.
31. Raharuhi and others to Grey, c. February 1851, *GBPP*, 1854, [1779], p. 3.
32. B. Y. Ashwell, annual letters, 20 October 1850, CN/0 19.
33. T. H. Smith, Letters, 1852-5.
34. Wi Maihi to Grey, 16 December 1851, G 8/5.
35. Chapman Journal, 1848-55, *inter alia*, CN/0 30b.
36. Barker to Society, 31 December 1852, CN/0 22.
37. Nugent to Col. Sec. (Auckland), 25 November 1847, *GBPP*, 1850, [1002
    p. 98.
38. IA 47/991.
39. George Graham, 'The Ngatipaoa invasion of Auckland, notes taken fro₥
    Makuwhara, a participant'; Halse to Grey, 15 January 1851, Grey MSS.
40. Symonds minute, 13 January 1848, IA 47/182.
41. Grey to Earl Grey, 21 January 1850, *GBPP*, 1850, [1280], p. 109.
42. Col. Sec. (Auckland) to Resident Magistrate, Russell, 2 February 1849, J₵
    Russell, 2.
43. Enclosed in Grey to Earl Grey, 13 October 1849, *GBPP*, 1850, [1280
    pp. 89-90.
44. Ngapora to Grey, c. April 1848, *GBPP*, 1849, [1120], pp. 19-20.
45. Earl Grey to Grey, 27 December 1848, G 1/22, no. 97.
46. Grey to Earl Grey, 13 May 1847, cited in McLintock, *Crown Colony Govern*
    ment, p. 393.
47. Earl Grey to Grey, 23 December 1846, *GBPP*, 1847, [763], p. 71 and Chapte₹
    XIV of the Charter and Instruction, December 1846, ibid., p. 87. For a detaile₫
    and insightful exposition of the course of New Zealand constitution makin₲
    see W. L. Renwick, 'Self-government and protection: a study of Stephen's tw₥
    cardinal points of policy in their bearing upon constitutional development i₥
    New Zealand in the years 1837-1867'.
48. Grey to Earl Grey, 15 December 1847, *GBPP*, 1847-8, [1002], pp. 55-6; Ea₹
    Grey to Grey, 7 and 15 July 1848, ibid., pp. 175-7.
49. Grey to Pakington, 9 October 1852, ibid., 1854, [1779], pp. 162-3.
50. Fox to Secretary, NZ Company, 15 September 1849, ibid., 1851, [1398], p. 3₢
51. Eyre minutes, 7 and 13 August 1849, NM 49/831.
52. Rutherford, *Grey*, pp. 177-86.
53. Kemp's census of the Wellington district, 1850-1, *GBPP*, 1851, [1420], pp. 232 f₮
54. Eyre memo, 23 June 1848, *AJHR*, 1873, G-2B, pp. 14-15; A. Mackay mem₵
    9 July 1883, ibid., 1888, G-1B. p. 2.
55. Grey to Earl Grey, 7 April 1847, ibid., G-1, p. 4; minutes of evidence o₥
    petition of H. T. Taiaroa and others, UPP, Native Affairs Committee, 1881
    Mantell to Grey, 23 March 1851, cited in R. W. Chapman, 'The South Islan₫
    Maoris and their reserved lands, 1860-1910', p. 22.
56. Minutes of evidence in petition of H. K. Taiaroa, UPP, Native Affairs Com
    mittee, 1881.
57. Browne minute, n.d., on ministerial memo, 8 October 1861, GB 4/1; Brown₢
    to Maria Browne, 28 November 1861, GB 2/4.
58. Grey to Earl Grey, 7 February 1852, *GBPP*, 1854, [1779], p. 71.
59. Renwick, 'Self-government and protection', p. 114.
60. See Sir John Pakington's reply to Sir Fowell Buxton in the House of Commons
    cited ibid., p. 157.

Chapter 7

1. *PD,* 1854-5, p. 424.
2. Keith Sinclair, *The Origins of the Maori Wars,* chapter 7; see also B. J. Dalton, *War and Politics in New Zealand, 1855-1870,* chapter 2.
3. The missionary William Williams described McLean's land purchase activities in Hawke's Bay as 'a system of iniquity going on from bad to worse in the face of native remonstrances' (Williams to Bishop of New Zealand, 31 July 1861, Williams MSS., 32. See also Williams to Fox, 31 July 1861, for details of the Akito case of 1855).
4. For details see the exchange of minutes on the subjects, UPP, 1861, no. 23.
5. See letter of Wiremu Tamihana, *DSC,* 23 August 1866. For details of the Taranaki feud see Sinclair, *Origins of the Maori Wars,* chapter 8.
6. *GBPP,* 1860, [2747], pp. 67-8, 86-98.
7. Ibid., p. 68.
8. Te Rangikaheke to Ngatiwhakaue chiefs, 3 December 1855, ibid., [2747], p. 181. The official translation is quoted. A slightly different translation appears in *AJHR,* 1860, F-3, p. 24 which reads, *inter alia,* 'the *mana* of this island is trampled upon by the Pakeha . . . the Maoris . . . are not admitted to share in the Government administration of justice'.
9. *Southern Cross,* 4 December 1855.
10. See T. H. Smith to his mother, 14 February 1856, Smith Letters. Also the speeches of Tohi Te Ururungi and Eruera Kahawai at the Kohimarama conference of 1860, MA 23/10, pp. 46-7.
11. *PD,* 1856-8, p. 277.
12. See statement of Horomona Toremi in 1860, MA 23/10, p. 123; see also the Rev. Thomas Chapman to Society, 2 March 1853, CN/0 30b.
13. *Te Hokioi,* 15 June 1862. (This and subsequent statements or quotations from *Te Hokioi,* are taken from the official translations made in 1863.)
14. Cooper to McLean, 29 November 1856, *AJHR,* 1862, C-1, p. 323-4.
15. Ibid., 1860, F-3, p. 39 and Appendix p. 113; ibid., 1862, E-5A, p. 3.
16. Maunsell to Society, 2 January 1864, CN/0 64.
17. Cited in Ashwell to CMS, 1 May 1861, CN/0 19. The date and important details of the visit are controversial. See B. J. Dalton, 'Tamihana's visit to Auckland', pp. 193-205, and A. D. Ward, 'Tamihana's visit to Auckland', pp. 324-7.
18. *Te Hokioi,* 22 January 1863.
19. Tamihana to the 'Waikato Committee' of the General Assembly, 24 January 1860, UPP, 1860, 'Official Correspondence'.
20. *AJHR,* 1860, E-1C, p. 2, note.
21. See Tamihana's letter in *Te Hokioi,* 8 December 1862.
22. Tamihana to Browne, 7 June 1861, *AJHR,* E-1B, p. 19.
23. M. P. K. Sorrenson, 'The Maori King movement, 1858-1885', pp. 39-40.
24. *Te Hokioi,* 15 June 1862.
25. *Te Hokioi,* 8 December 1862. A similar conceptual view was embodied in the statement of a Urewera Kingite in 1862: 'The King is established by the law, I found him in the Bible', Hunter Brown to Fox, 26 April 1863, Grey MSS.
26. H. T. Clarke report of conversation with Tamihana, 14 January 1861, *GBPP,* 1862, [3040], p. 20.
27. Ashwell to Society, 1 May 1861, CN/0 17.
28. For further discussion of the appropriateness or otherwise of the term 'nationalist' see Sinclair, *Origins of the Maori Wars,* chapter 6; Sorrenson, 'The Maori King movement'; Dalton, *War and Politics in New Zealand,* pp. 62-7; and

discussion between Dalton and Sorrenson in *The Journal of the Polynesia Society,* vol. LXXIII, no. 3 (September 1964), pp. 351-3, vol. 74, no. 1 (March 1965), pp. 70-5 and *New Zealand Journal of History,* vol. II, no. 1 (April 1968), p. 95.

29. Nugent to Col. Sec., 25 January 1855, *GBPP,* 1860, [2747], p. 73.
30. For the reports and evidence of the 1856 Board see ibid., especially pp. 236 ff. For Hadfield's opinion see pp. 233-4.
31. T. H. Smith to Col. Sec., 1 and 13 March 1856, MA 4/2.
32. For report and evidence see *AJHR,* 1860, E-5 and E-5A; for decision of the House see *Votes and Proceedings of the House of Representatives,* 1856, pp. 271-3.
33. Browne to Labouchere, 9 May 1857, CO 209/141, cited in W. P. Morrell *British Colonial Policy in the Mid-Victorian Age,* p. 224.
34. Browne memo, 5 June 1857, G 36/3, p. 60.
35. Smith memo, 15 June 1857, MA 4/2.
36. *AJHR,* 1860, E-1C, p. 2.
37. See Browne's memo to Ministers, 28 April 1857 and Stafford's reply, 6 May 1857, ibid., 1858, E-5, pp. 7-10.
38. Fenton's journal is printed in ibid., 1860, E-1C.
39. Ibid., pp. 25, 40-1.
40. Richmond memo, 29 September 1858, *Epitome of Official Documents,* A-1, pp. 58-9.
41. Dalton, *War and Politics in New Zealand,* pp. 91, 119-21, 141-2.
42. McLean memo, n.d., *c.* 1858, McLean MSS., Folio 9, no. 5.
43. See correspondence and minutes in *Votes and Proceedings of the House of Representatives,* 1856, Appendix C-5, and AG 61/513.
44. T 57/100, 101 and 153.
45. H. Wardell, Diary, 20 August 1850.
46. Ibid., 4 July 1858.
47. R. W. Woon (Interpreter) to Durie, 13 January 1857, T 57/153.
48. J 59/331, 59/333.
49. McLean to Preece, 30 December 1857, MA 4/2.
50. T 58/366; Smith to Clendon, 12 March 1859 and Smith to White, 14 October 1859, MA 4/3; McLean to Brown, 29 December 1860, MA 4/4.
51. Browne to Secretary of State, 13 June 1859, *AJHR,* 1860, F-3, p. 99.
52. McLean to Turton, 25 February 1859, Smith to Turton, 8 April and 17 October 1859, MA 4/3; Extract from Turton report *c.* August 1859, *AJHR,* 1860, F-3, p. 100; H. Turton, Jnr, to McLean, 7 December 1859, McLean MSS., 399; Smith to McLean, 12 September 1859, ibid., 383.
53. McLean minutes, 23 January and 3 April 1860, MA 1/1, NO 60/28; Smith to Turton, 13 February 1861, MA 4/4.
54. *Compendium of Official Documents Relative to Native Affairs in the South Island of New Zealand,* pp. 95ff.
55. Minutes of Richmond and Stafford, 30 January 1860, IA 1859/2106.
56. For details see Mackay's Letterbook, MA Collingwood, 2/1.

Chapter 8

1. Sinclair, *Origins of the Maori Wars,* especially chapter 9.
2. McLean memo, 23 September 1859, McLean MSS., 9.
3. See for example the objection of the Ngatiraukawa chief Nepia Taratoa, to the sale of land in the Manawatu by Ihakara, a sub-chief (Diary of William Searancke, Land Purchase Officer, 31 March 1858, NK 6448).

4. Sinclair, *Origins of the Maori Wars,* pp. 139-45.

5. See journal entry of A. S. Atkinson, 12 March 1859, G. H. Scholefield (ed.), *The Richmond-Atkinson Papers,* I.

6. Browne to Newcastle, 22 May 1860, *AJHR,* 1863, E-2, p. 3.

7. See letters of the Richmond and Atkinson families, *c.* February 1860, Scholefield, *Richmond-Atkinson Papers,* I, pp. 515-24.

8. Keith Sinclair, 'Some historical notes on an Atiawa genealogy', pp. 55-65.

9. James Mackay, notes of meeting, Nelson district, 17 January 1861, MA Collingwood, 2/1, p. 186. (Italics added.)

10. Fenton to W. Rolleston, 1 August 1866, W. Rolleston, MSS., 1. He wrote to Smith, 'We found W. Kingi equally entitled with Teira to his block, only more so perhaps' (Fenton to Smith, 24 July 1866, Smith Letters).

11. *DSC,* 8 February 1861. I am obliged to Dr Harold Miller of Wellington for drawing my attention to this letter.

12. Smith to Halse, 28 February 1860, MA 4/3.

13. Quotations and summaries of speeches are taken from the official record book of the conference, MA 23/10.

14. Similar sentiments were expressed by Wi Maihi Te Rangikaheke to a parliamentary committee investigating the attitudes of the Waikato tribes as revealed by Fenton's activities in 1857-8. Asked what the chiefs principally complained of or principally desired, Te Rangikaheke replied, *inter alia*: 'the Pakeha system is taught to the tribes; the Maoris therefore consider that it is taking away the *mana* and enslaving this island. This is the principal source of the present darkness of the Maoris, they are not admitted to share in the Government administration of justice. The Pakehas say that their regulations alone should be law for both races; the Maori chiefs say that the two should be joined, so that the bodies of the Pakeha and Maori may be joined (or united), and also the thoughts of their hearts. But there is no joining of systems, what is the good of there being one *mana,* one law, one system of administering justice and one King?' The further question was asked, 'Is it the desire of the Natives that there should be a joint mana under one Queen for both races, or one mana under their own King for the Maoris, and another under the Queen for the Pakehas?' Te Rangikaheke replied, 'The Maoris have said let there be one law for the two races; had the administration of justice by the Government been clear, the mana would have been one, but the Pakeha system went contrary to the Maori, the Maori Chiefs proposed to elect a Chief for themselves, but still to have the one law, that of Heaven and the Queen.' He said that if law was administered by Pakeha magistrates in conjunction with Maori magistrates and *runanga* (the tribes to select their magistrates and choose which Pakeha should be their magistrate) 'there would be two manas united in that mode of administering justice' and the chiefs would not feel aggrieved. Land disputes should be settled by the joining of the two systems; if the magistrate and *runanga* could not settle the dispute, influential chiefs and a *tohunga* who had command of the genealogies and history of the land, should be involved (*AJHR,* 1860, F-3, p. 24.)

15. Dennison's despatch is printed in *The New Zealander,* 29 June 1861.

16. Martin memo, 3 May 1861, MA 1/2, NO 61/55.

17. Richmond memo, 25 May 1860, *AJHR,* 1860, E-1B, p. 5.

18. McLean memo, 25 March 1857, ibid., 1862, C-1, p. 330.

19. Cooper to McLean, 12 March 1860, ibid., p. 350.

20. MA Collingwood, 2/1, pp. 320 and 454.

21. Waiuku settlers to McLean, 18 October 1860, McLean MSS., 10.

22. See for example, Robert Ormsby to Col. Sec., 4 April 1860, IA 60/701.
23. McLean memoranda, 30 April 1860, McLean MSS., 2/2/12 and 31 May 1860, MA 4/3.
24. Browne memo, 21 January 1861, G 36/3.
25. Smith memo, 2 February 1861, MA 1/2.
26. B. Y. Ashwell to Society, 1 May 1861, CN/0 17; G. S. Rickard, *Tamihana the Kingmaker,* p. 74.
27. McLean memo, 31 May 1860, MA 4/3.
28. Henry Sewell, Journal, 25 November 1860.
29. Browne to Newcastle, 2 February 1861, *AJHR,* 1862, E-1, p. 10.
30. Tamihana's letters are printed in *AJHR,* 1861, E-1B, pp. 15-17.

Chapter 9

1. Te Whitiorongomai and others to the Government, n.d., *c.* December 1861, MA 1/2.
2. The Government-sponsored Runanga are hereafter distinguished from the unofficial Maori *runanga* by the use of a capital R and no italics.
3. *AJHR,* 1862, E-2, pp. 10ff.
4. Sewell Journal, 20 October 1861, vol. 1, p. 315.
5. Grey to Newcastle, 30 November 1861, *AJHR,* 1862, E-1, sec. II, p. 33-4.
6. Newcastle to Grey, 5 June 1861, ibid., sec. III, p. 4.
7. Gorst to Fox, 3 December 1861, ibid., sec. II, p. 46.
8. Gorst, *The Maori King,* p. 140.
9. Fox memo, 7 December 1861, PM 1/1. (Italics added.)
10. It bears a pencil note to the effect that it was entered into the Ministers' memorandum book and a copy made for the Governor on 4 January 1862, that is, after Grey's return from the Waikato.
11. Ministers to Grey, 6 December 1861, *AJHR,* 1862, E-2, pp. 19-22.
12. *Hawke's Bay Herald,* 14 September 1861. The Waikato missionary John Morgan, wrote: 'Sir George Grey will not be able to secure the peace of the Colony without breaking up the land league' (Morgan to Browne, 18 September 1861, GB 1/2).
13. Fox, notes of journey on the Waikato, *AJHR,* 1863, E-13, p. 6.
14. Fox to Mantell, 22 April 1863, W. Mantell, MSS., 281.
15. Morgan to Browne, December 1861, GB 1/2.
16. Grey to Te Heuheu, 17 January 1862, Grey to Matutaera, 15 February 1862, MA 4/73 (Maori letterbook).
17. Browne, draft comments on a ministerial minute of 8 October 1861, GB 4/1; Browne to Harriet Gore Browne, 19 December 1861, GB 2/4, no. 24.
18. Parris to McLean, 26 September 1861, McLean MSS., 335.
19. J. H. Campbell wrote that he had named a child after McLean; W. L. Buller wrote that he kept McLean's photograph on his desk (Campbell to McLean, 8 January 1862, McLean MSS., 174; Buller to McLean, 13 June 1862, ibid., 161). Such were the responses of civil servants where position and promotion depended largely on connections with men in high places.
20. For returns of officers employed by the Native Department, see *AJHR,* 1863, E-10; 1864, E-7; and MA 1/3, NO 63/34a.
21. Mantell to Fox, 11 July 1861, Mantell MSS., 338.
22. Halse to Buller, 23 February 1863, Mantell MSS., 233.
23. Grey memo, 29 November 1861, G 35/1; Sewell called them 'Prefets a la Francais' (Sewell Journal, 15 December 1861, vol. II, pp. 11, 20).
24. Fox to G. Clarke, 27 November 1861, MA 4/4.

25. Unsigned, undated memo, McLean's handwriting, McLean MSS., 14, no. 35.
26. Gorst, *The Maori King,* pp. 163, 189; Morgan to Browne, 4 March and 2 April 1862, GB 1/2.
27. *DSC,* 7 February 1862.
28. Fox to Law, 21 June 1862, MA 4/5.
29. Halse to Buller, 15 February 1863, ibid.
30. H. Brown report, June 1862, *AJHR,* 1862, E-9, sec. IV, pp. 32-3.
31. *The Aucklander,* 8 July 1862.
32. UPP, 1862, select committee on petition of Hawke's Bay settlers; *Hawke's Bay Herald* special supplement, 28 June 1862.
33. *AJHR,* 1862, E-9, sec. VI; see also correspondence of the Civil Commissioner, October and November 1862, MA-Na 1/2.
34. Turton report, 20 November 1861, *AJHR,* 1862, E-5A, pp. 7-8.
35. Rangikatea and others to Grey, 20 December 1861, *Epitome of Official Documents,* D, p. 39.
36. Smith report, 25 January 1862, *AJHR,* 1862, E-9, sec. IV, p. 12.
37. Ibid., sec. I, pp. 8-12; *The Aucklander,* 7 October 1862.
38. See correspondence, MA Waimate 4.
39. Notes of meetings, Kerikeri, 7 November 1861, MA 1/2, ND 61/150; Fox to Maihi Kawiti, 4 June 1862, MA 4/73.
40. White to Mantell, 11 May 1863, Mantell MSS., 228.
41. Whitmore to Col. Sec., 27 January 1864, MA-Na 1/2.
42. Baker to McLean, 10 November 1862, McLean MSS., 148.
43. Smith to Native Minister, 26 December 1861 and 28 May 1862, *AJHR,* 1862, E-9, sec. IV, pp. 5, 20. Smith gave an equivocal reply to the Bay of Plenty Maori, saying that while all transactions should henceforth be made with the knowledge and consent of the Runanga 'it would not be right to restrict the liberty of any tribe or individual with respect to the disposal of his own property'. This was the doctrine underlying the Waitara purchase.
44. Armitage to Fenton, 6 January 1862, *AJHR,* 1862, E-9, sec. II, pp. 8-9.
45. White to Mantell, 6 May 1863, Mantell MSS., 228.
46. *AJHR,* 1863, E-4, pp. 6-16. Most of the chiefs on Government pay refrained from becoming involved; the chiefs that were left out of Government favour were inclined to be more defiant. Arama Karaka joined Matiu's side to avenge the death of his father, killed fighting Tirarau twenty years before (Maning to McLean, 20 June 1862, McLean MSS., 311).
47. Clendon to Civil Commissioner, Waimate, 2 May 1862, MA Waimate 2, 62/71.
48. White to Mantell, 28 April 1863, JC-WG 4; MA 24/21, NO 63/1995.
49. White to Native Minister, 10 December 1862, MA 24/22, NO 62/118a.
50. Clarke to Resident Magistrates, Bay of Islands District, 3 August 1862 and December 1862, George Clarke, Letterbook.
51. Williams to Civil Commissioner, Waimate, 17 February 1863, JC Waimate 1.
52. 'Travels in the Lake District', *DSC,* 29 April 1862.
53. Russell to Grey, and Russell to Native Minister, 24 November 1862, MA-Na 1/2.
54. *AJHR,* 1864, E-7.
55. Barstow to Civil Commissioner, Waimate, 25 March 1863, JC-Russell 1.
56. Enclosed in Grey to Newcastle, 6 December 1862, *AJHR,* 1863, E-3, p. 4.
57. Russell to Native Minister, 25 February 1863, MA-Na 1/2.
58. *AJHR,* 1863, D-9.
59. Bell to Domett, 17 January 1863, IA 63/118.
60. Barstow to Native Minister, 28 December 1863 and Clarke to Native Minister, 16 and 29 December 1863, Mantell MSS., 135.

61. Barstow to Native Minister, 23 January 1862; Barstow to Col. Sec., 7 February 1863, JC-Russell 1.
62. Taylor Journal, 1 April 1863.
63. White to Mantell, 11 May 1863, Mantell MSS., 228.
64. White to Mantell, 4 March 1863, ibid., 227.
65. Henry Sewell, *The New Zealand Native Rebellion*, p. 14.

Chapter 10

1. *The New Zealander,* 11 January 1862.
2. The three sons were H. T. Clarke, Resident Magistrate at Tauranga, Marsden Clarke, assistant to Gorst, and Hopkins Clarke, assistant to George Clarke himself.
3. McLean to Browne, 8 August 1862, GB 1/2.
4. Ormond to McLean, 23 December 1863, McLean MSS., 326.
5. *DSC,* 28 January 1862.
6. *The Aucklander,* 7 October 1862.
7. Armitage report, 17 January 1862, *AJHR,* 1862, E-9, sec. II, p. 21.
8. Fox to Armitage, 5 May 1862, ibid., pp. 40-1.
9. *Te Hokioi,* 15 June 1862.
10. Morgan to Browne, 4 March and 20 May 1862, GB 1/2.
11. Bell to Browne, 27 May 1862, GB 1/2.
12. Gorst report, 5 June 1862, *AJHR,* 1862, E-9, sec. III, pp. 18-19.
13. Morgan to Browne, 29 September 1863, GB 1/2.
14. Maunsell to Society, 23 May 1863, CN/O 64 b.
15. Gorst, *The Maori King,* p. 161.
16. Bell to Browne, 30 June 1862, GB 1/2.
17. *PD,* 1861-3, p. 477.
18. Ibid., p. 516.
19. Sewell memo, 22 September 1862, PM 2/1.
20. *PD,* 1861-3, p. 502.
21. Te Huiki's wife had been found drowned. The evidence was too scanty to rule out the possibility of suicide and the jury, diligently following the direction of the Judge, acquitted the accused. Nevertheless local Maori opinion was adamant that if Te Huiki did not kill his wife he at least drove her to suicide. He had to be hastily shipped off to Dunedin with a public subscription to start him off in the south lest the dead woman's relatives kill him in *utu* (Russell to Superintendent, Otago, October 1862, MA-Na, 1/2).
22. Sewell to Commissioners of Native Reserves, Taranaki, 4 November 1861, MA 4/4.
23. *PD,* 1861-3, p. 610.
24. Bell memo, 6 November 1862, *AJHR,* 1863, A-1, pp. 8-11; *PD,* 1861-3, p. 611.
25. See, for example, his virulent hostility to a syndicate seeking to purchase Stewart Island (Bell to Resident Magistrate, Southland, n.d., early 1863, MA 4/59.
26. Sewell Journal, 9 September and 13 September 1863.
27. Sewell Journal, 3 August 1862. Until amended by Sewell and his supporters in the Legislative Council the Bill allowed the sale of land on the basis of a certificate of title even before its endorsement by the Governor, who was supposed, before giving that endorsement, to satisfy himself as to the provision of adequate reserves for the Maori (see Domett memo, 29 December 1862, PM 1/2, p. 49).
28. Bell to Grey, 5 September 1862, Grey MSS.

29. Bell memo, 5 November 1862, PM 1/2, p. 7.
30. *PD,* 1861-3, pp. 483-513.
31. J. C. Richmond to Mary Richmond, 18 July 1862, Scholefield, *Richmond-Atkinson Papers,* I, p. 771.
32. *The Aucklander,* 22 August 1862.
33. White to Native Minister, 18 November 1863, JC-WG 4.
34. Barstow to Civil Commissioner, Waimate, 14 July 1863, JC Russell 1.
35. There was an ever-present likelihood of drowning while fording New Zealand's swift and boulder-strewn streams. A return of 1870 calculated that 1115 Europeans drowned in rivers (quite apart from those drowned in harbours, swamps, wells and the sea) between 1840 and 1870 (*AJHR* 1870, D-46).
36. Russell to Native Minister, 26 January 1863, MA-Na 1/2.
37. *The New Zealander,* 8 March 1862.
38. This was the outcome as reported to Bell by Heta Tairangi, described as Tamihana's secretary (Bell to Grey, 5 November 1862, Grey MSS.). Other accounts suggest a firm resolution that Waitara should not be investigated, in which Tamihana reluctantly joined.
39. *DSC,* 15 January 1863; for a similar account see *The New Zealander,* 14 January 1863.
40. *Te Pihoihoi Mokemoke,* 10 February 1863.
41. Grey to Newcastle, 6 February 1863, *AJHR,* 1863, E-3, sec. I, pp. 6-7.
42. Grey to Granville, 27 October 1869, ibid., 1870, A-1B, pp. 81-2.
43. See Bell to Mantell, 6 December and 28 December 1862, Mantell MSS., 243.
44. A later account, that of the *Daily Southern Cross* of 27 December 1865, reports a meeting of James Mackay, then Civil Commissioner in the Waikato, and Tamihana, who had not long ceased fighting in the belief that he could have the origins of the war investigated by a parliamentary inquiry. Mackay said, 'as to Thompson's desire to maintain law and order, the Governor had given him an opportunity to do so at the great meeting at Taupiri. The Governor had proposed that the natives should form a runanga, of which the King should be the head, but under another name. They were to make laws and submit them to the Governor for approval. Thompson had rejected this offer, and preferred war.' Thompson then came forward and said the Governor had never made any such offer. Mackay then called on two Maori companions named Raihi and Hakariwhi who, he said, were at the Taupiri meeting, to certify his assertion, which, the *Daily Southern Cross* reports, they did in detail. Apart from his long record of integrity and idealism, which would incline one to accept him as a more credible witness than Mackay's paid assistants, there is the undeniable fact that Gorst's own contemporary account, and the *Daily Southern Cross* show Tamihana to be making substantially the offer that Mackay described, and Grey refusing or evading it. Somehow, in the meantime, Grey had succeeded in having the reverse of the truth accepted in government circles.
45. *Te Hokioi,* 15 January 1863.
46. Maunsell to Society, 23 May 1863, CN/O 64b.
47. Rogan Report, 18 May 1863, UPP, 1865, no. 22.
48. Domett to Mantell, 10 August 1863, Mantell MSS., 270.
49. Ashwell to Venn, 28 July 1863, B. Y. Ashwell, Letters and Journals.
50. *AJHR,* 1863, E-3, sec. I, p. 61.
51. Bell to Mantell, 7 July 1863, Mantell MSS., 244.
52. Maunsell to Society, 20 May 1863, CN/O 64b.
53. *DSC,* 25 August 1865.

54. *DSC,* 14 April 1862.
55. Grey to Cardwell, 4 April 1865, *AJHR,* 1865, A-5, pp. 15-16; Grey to Card-well, 2 February 1866, ibid., 1866, A-1, pp. 65-6.
56. *DSC,* 5 June 1862.
57. Reported in Ashwell to Society, 1 May 1862, CN/O 17.
58. See below, chapters 20 and 21.
59. Bell to Mantell, 7 July 1863, Mantell MSS., 244.
60. A. S. Atkinson, Journal, 5 June 1863; Scholefield, *Richmond-Atkinson Papers,* II, p. 49.
61. Morgan to Browne, 30 December 1863, GB 1/2.
62. *The New Zealander,* 12 January 1864.
63. Maning to McLean, 7 November 1863, McLean MSS., 311.
64. Barstow to Editor, *DSC,* JC-Russell 1.

Chapter 11

1. Petition of Tamihana to the General Assembly, 24 July 1866, *AJHR,* 1866, G-2, p. 6.
2. Related by Dr Pei Te Hurinui Jones, Taumarunui.
3. W. H. Oliver and Jane M. Thompson, *Challenge and Response; a study of the development of the Gisborne East Coast Region,* pp. 86 ff.
4. Related by Dr Jones, Taumarunui.
5. *AJHR,* 1869, A-14; ibid., 1870, A-23 and A-1B, pp. 60-1.
6. See *DSC,* 3, 8 and 11 February 1864 and 12 September 1865; *Weekly News,* 12 April 1864.
7. Fox to Grey, 30 August 1864, *AJHR,* 1864, E-2, p. 87.
8. See R. Firth, 'Rumour in a Primitive Society', in *Tikopia Ritual and Belief,* pp. 141-61.
9. Sewell Journal, 11 June 1865.
10. Parris to McLean, 6 February 1862, McLean MSS., 335.
11. Shortland to Mainwaring, 17 May 1864, MA 4/59.
12. Native Office circular to Waikato Resident Magistrates, 17 June 1864, ibid.
13. Halse to Resident Magistrate, Port Waikato, 4 October 1864 and Shortland to Resident Magistrate, Raglan, 8 July 1864, ibid.
14. Resident Magistrates' Court, Taupo, Court Book, 1863-8.
15. Report of meeting, Waima, 29 August 1863, MA Waimate 6, 63/86.
16. Rev. R. Burrows to Society, 28 November 1863, CN/0 27a.
17. Buller to Col. Sec., 12 May 1864, *GBPP,* 1865, [3425], p. 27.
18. Whitmore to Col. Sec., 13 November 1863, MA-Na 1/2.
19. Gillies to McLean, 22 December 1863, McLean MSS., 228.
20. *DSC,* 30 December 1863, 28 March 1864 and 29 May 1866.
21. Ibid., 2 February, 23-30 March and 14 April 1864; Barstow to Civil Com-missioner, Waimate, 23 January 1864, JC-Waimate 1.
22. Williams to Col. Sec., 17 June 1864, JC-Waimate 1; also MA-Waimate 7, 64/66 and 64/68.
23. Thomas report, 20 February 1865, MA 24/21. Thomas estimated the popula-tion of the Chatham Islands to comprise 312 Maori, 124 Moriori and 83 Europeans.
24. See speeches of Hohepa Poutama, Heremaia and Karaka, *The New Zealander,* 27 February 1864.

Chapter 12

1. Sewell Journal, 6 and 7 January 1865, vol. II, pp. 324-37, vol. III, p. 11; G. Hensley, 'The withdrawal of the British troops from New Zealand, 1864-1870', pp. 38-9.
2. For details of land confiscation see *AJHR*, 1873, C-4B, p. 6 and 1928, G-7. The confiscations were rapacious enough without their being inflated to the exaggerated estimates of 5 million acres and more which some historians have adduced. Confiscations in the Waikato and on both East and West Coasts totalled about 3.3 million acres, of which about 600,000 were returned to Maori claimants and purchase money subsequently paid in respect of about 600,000 more.
3. Weld to McLean, 15 March 1865, McLean MSS., 408.
4. Ormond to Mantell, 26 November 1865, Mantell MSS.
5. Oliver and Thompson, *Challenge and Response,* p. 94.
6. Weld minute, 17 April 1865, Mantell minute, 24 April 1865, IA 65/969.
7. Shortland to Clarke, 30 August and 9 September 1864, MA 4/59.
8. *DSC,* 30 June 1864.
9. Among the first Land Court Assessors named were W. Kukutai, A. Kaihau, H. Tauroa, W. Te Wheoro, H. Matini, H. Nera and T. Tarahau (*NZ Gazette*, 1865, *inter alia*). The offices of Assessor in the Resident Magistrates' Courts and Assessor in the Native Land Court were distinct, though sometimes both were held by the same men. In this book, unless otherwise stated, the term 'Assessor' will still refer to Assessors in the Resident Magistrates' Courts.
10. Fenton to Mantell, 1 December 1879, Mantell MSS., 277.
11. Rolleston to Fenton, 18 December 1865, MA 4/7.
12. H. T. Kemp to McLean, 13 July 1866, McLean MSS., 270.
13. *AJHR,* 1891, sess. II, G-1, pp. 56, 60.
14. Ibid., p. 151.
15. See reports MA Waimate 6, 63/86, and MA Waimate 7, 64/66.
16. MA 13/84, NLP 74/47.
17. James Mackay, *Our Dealings with Maori Lands.*
18. *AJHR,* 1891, sess. II, G-1, p. 145.
19. *PD,* 1864-6, p. 206.
20. *AJHR,* 1888, I-8, p. 92.
21. Ormond to McLean, 13 August 1865, McLean MSS., 326.
22. Ormond to McLean, 26 August 1865, ibid.
23. FitzGerald to J. C. Richmond, 25 August 1865, Scholefield, *Richmond-Atkinson Papers,* II, pp. 178-9.
24. Sorrenson, 'The purchase of Maori lands', and 'Land purchase methods and their effect on Maori population', pp. 183-99.
25. Gillies J. in Mangakahia *v.* NZ Timber Coy, 1881, 2 *NZLR,* SC 345.
26. Martin, 'Notes on best mode of introducing and working "The Native Lands Act" ', 30 June 1865, *AJHR,* 1866, A-1, pp. 74-85.
27. See *Bills Not Passed,* 1865.
28. *PD,* 1864-6, p. 370.
29. Ibid., p. 729.
30. Whitmore to McLean, n.d., early 1865, McLean MSS., 414, no. 3.
31. Rolleston memo, 6 September 1865 and FitzGerald minute, 13 September 1865, MA 24/21.
32. Rolleston to Fenton, 4 November 1865, MA 4/7.
33. Evidence of E. W. Puckey, 29 November 1888, MA 70/2. The evidence was given during an inquiry which arose from the discovery that Judges were taking widely differing courses on the question of whether chiefs were entitled to a

greater share of an award than rank-and-file Maori on account of their greater *mana* (see also *AJHR,* 1887, sess. II, I-30, pp. 6-7).

34. Hugh Kawharu, 'New Zealand', pp. 129-30.
35. Native Lands Act, 1865, s. 30.
36. Rogan J., Judgment on the Papakura block, *NZ Gazette,* 1867, p. 189.
37. *PD,* 1864-6, p. 349.
38. Ibid., p. 347.
39. *DSC,* 2 January 1868.
40. *PD,* 1864-6, pp. 207, 235, 347, 350.
41. Minutes of proceedings of the Representation Committee, 16 November 1863, UPP, 1863.
42. A reference to the 'Maori Electoral Act' and Mantell's and Richmond's minutes on the subject, appear in Mantell MSS., 225.
43. Weld to Grey, 19 July 1865, Grey MSS.
44. *PD,* 1864-6, p. 259.
45. R. C. Mainwaring to Native Minister (reporting conversation with Tamihana), 28 September 1865, *AJHR,* 1865, E-14, p. 3.
46. F. Weld, *Notes on New Zealand Affairs,* p. 32.
47. Native Office circular, 11 October 1865, MA 4/60.
48. Martin to Native Minister, 18 July and 23 December 1865, *AJHR,* 1866, A-1, pp. 67-83. Martin regarded White's administration at Mangonui as a promising model.
49. FitzGerald to McLean, 28 June 1869, McLean MSS., 215.
50. *PD,* 1864-6, pp. 621-4.
51. *DSC,* 5 and 9 October 1865.
52. FitzGerald to McLean, 8 October 1865, McLean MSS., 215; *PD,* 1867, vol. I, part 1, p. 524 (Carleton); ibid., 1868, vol II, part 1, p. 329 (Ormond).
53. FitzGerald to Mainwaring, 22 August 1865 and Mainwaring to FitzGerald, 28 September 1865, *AJHR,* 1865, E-14, pp. 1-3. See also J. C. Richmond to McLean, 25 August 1865; 'Orders have been sent to Mackay and Mainwaring to enter into friendly relations with Thompson' (McLean MSS., 355).
54. *DSC,* 1 August 1865.
55. Sewell Journal, 13 August 1865, vol. III, p. 211.
56. Learning that the military settlers would not be shifted from the Waikato Tamihana said: 'It was like a great rock fixed deep in the earth which could not be moved.' The Ngatihaua retained above 275,000 of their 400,000 acres centred about Matamata. But this was land they had obtained by conquest; the original Ngatihaua land, on the delta between the Horotiu stream and the Waipa river, south of Ngaruawahia, was not restored. (See report of the Maori Petitions Committee, UPP, 1866, and *AJHR,* 1873, G-3, p. 1). In any case Tamihana sought the return of the land of all the Waikato tribes, not just the Ngatihaua.
57. *DSC,* 26 August 1865.
58. FitzGerald to McLean, 8 October 1865, McLean MSS., 215.
59. FitzGerald to Clarke, 1 September 1865, MA 4/60.
60. FitzGerald to Parris, 30 August 1865, MA 4/7.
61. A. S. Atkinson Diary, 30 August 1865, Atkinson family, MSS.
62. FitzGerald to Parris, 8 September 1865, MA 13/15, NO 65/2053.
63. Parris to Native Minister, 5 January 1866, MA 13/15, NO 66/99.
64. Carrington to H. Atkinson, 18 September 1865, Atkinson MSS., 7B; H. R. Atkinson to H. Atkinson, 9 October 1865, ibid., 8; A. S. Atkinson Diary, 9 December 1865, ibid. See also Parris's evidence to the Select Committee on Confiscated Lands, UPP, 1866.

65. FitzGerald minute, 14 October 1865, MA 13/15, NO 65/2053.
66. FitzGerald to Stack, 9 October 1865, MA 4/7.
67. *PD,* 1864-6, pp. 491-3, 610-14. The Government's defeat was admitted by Stafford to be 'accidental'. Colenso had not been expected to push the matter to a vote and Weld had failed to keep a majority in the chamber. The motion was rescinded the next day.

Chapter 13

1. Stafford to McLean, 3 November 1865, McLean MSS., 384.
2. Parris to Rolleston, 7 February 1866, Rolleston MSS., 1.
3. *PD,* 1867, vol. I, part 2, p. 831; *AJHR,* 1868, A-3.
4. *PD,* 1864-6, p. 682.
5. Russell minute, 14 February 1866 and Rolleston draft memo, 15 February 1866, MA 24/21; Rolleston to Parris, 6 and 7 March 1866, MA 4/61.
6. UPP, 1876, no. 58 (return of executions). One other condemned prisoner— a follower of Te Kooti—committed suicide while awaiting execution.
7. Russell to White (Civil Commissioner, Mangonui), 8 February 1866, MA 4/66.
8. *PD,* 1864-6, pp. 813-16; 1867, vol. I, part 1, pp. 414ff and part 2, p. 811; 1868, vol. II, p. 58.
9. Rolleston to Mackay (Civil Commissioner, Auckland), 19 February 1866, MA 4/61.
10. See instructions to Resident Magistrates and Civil Commissioners, December 1865 and January 1866, MA 4/60 and 4/61.
11. Russell to Smith, 19 April 1866, Smith letters.
12. Mackay to Rolleston, 12 October 1866, Rolleston MSS., 1.
13. Rogan to McLean, 13 November 1865, McLean MSS., 360.
14. Williams to Native Minister, 31 October and 28 November 1865 and 23 January 1866, JC Waimate 1.
15. Rolleston to Rogan, 17 November 1866, MA 4/61; *DSC,* 18 and 20 October 1866.
16. Notes of meetings, 23 and 24 May 1866, MA 24/21.
17. Russell to Stafford, 18 August 1866, W. Stafford, MSS., 50.
18. Rolleston memo, 9 May 1866, Rolleston MSS., 1.
19. Mackay to Rolleston, 26 October 1866, ibid.
20. Mantell MSS., 137. 'The ex-sergeant major' seems to refer to Russell's domineering manner rather than his actual career in the British army, which he joined as an ensign (G. Scholefield (ed.), *Dictionary of New Zealand Biography*).
21. *AJHR,* 1866, D-7, p. 6 and D-7a, pp. 16-17.
22. *PD,* 1864-6, p. 895.

Chapter 14

1. Richmond to Matutaera, 8 October 1867 and Grey to Matutaera, 17 October 1867, MA 4/75, pp. 7 and 37.
2. *DSC,* 22 February 1868. The scanty official records neither confirm nor deny this rumour.
3. Searancke to Richmond, 2 November and 11 December 1867, JC-HN 3.
4. See the Governor's speech opening the General Assembly session of 1867 (*PD,* 1867, vol. I, part 1, p. 1).
5. Richmond memo, 23 October 1866, MA 24/21.
6. Native Office circular, 21 November 1867, MA 4/63.

7. Clarke to McLean, 26 July 1869, McLean MSS, 183.
8. Mackay to Rolleston, 26 October 1866, Rolleston MSS, 1.
9. Colenso to Mantell, 6 March 1865, Mantell MSS., 261.
10. *Hawke's Bay Herald,* 23 April 1867.
11. Locke to McLean, 23 January 1865, McLean MSS., 282.
12. See correspondence of Campbell to McLean, 1 September 1866 to 18 August 1869, ibid., 174.
13. White report, 5 September 1868, *AJHR,* 1868, A-4, p. 36. (See also similar reports from Barstow and Nesbitt, ibid., pp. 6, 12).
14. Rolleston to Barstow (Resident Magistrate, Russell), 15 and 30 October 1866, MA 4/61; *AJHR,* 1868, A-4, pp. 3-4.
15. Ibid., p. 36.
16. Rolleston to Resident Magistrate, Waimate, 28 January 1867, MA 4/62.
17. *DSC,* 10 and 11 September 1868; *AJHR,* 1869, A-16, pp. 3-7.
18. Ibid., A-17, pp. 6, 7, 10-11.
19. Mackay to Rolleston, 29 November 1867, Rolleston MSS., 1.
20. *PD,* 1868, vol. III, p. 558.
21. FitzGerald to McLean, 28 July 1867, McLean MSS., 215.
22. *PD,* 1867, vol. I, pp. 336, 459.
23. *PD,* 1868, vol. II, pp. 494. See also Renwick, 'Self-government and protection', pp. 449-52 and W. K. Jackson and G. A. Wood, 'The New Zealand Parliament and Maori representation', p. 384.
24. *DSC,* 2 September 1867.
25. Rolleston to McLean, 17 December 1867, McLean MSS., 362.
26. *DSC,* 3 August 1868; *AJHR,* 1868, E-4, p. 31.
27. Campbell (Resident Magistrate, Waiapu) to McLean, 24 November 1867 and 27 May 1868, McLean MSS., 174; *Hawke's Bay Herald,* 18 April 1868; H. T. Clarke to McLean, 1 October 1869, McLean MSS., 183.
28. Mackay to Rolleston, 13 December 1867, 2 and 10 June 1868, MT-N 1/1; *DSC,* 23 April 1868.
29. *Wellington Independent,* 20 April 1867.
30. *AJHR,* 1867, A-3, p. 1; ibid., 1868, A-6, pp. 6-8; report of the Commission on Religious, Charitable and Educational Trusts, ibid., 1869, A-5 and on Native Educational Trusts, ibid., 1870, A-3, pp. 26-35 and 85. Also John Barrington, 'Maori Education and society, 1867-1940' and T. H. Beaglehole, 'Maori schools, 1816-1880'.
31. Russell to Superintendent, Taranaki, 11 August 1866, MA 4/8.
32. Rolleston to Mackay, 17 January 1868, MA 4/63.
33. Mackay to Rolleston, 13 December 1867 and 3 and 10 February 1868, MT-N 1/1.
34. Bowen to Buckingham, 30 June 1868, *AJHR,* 1868, A-1, pp. 75-6.
35. See Sorrenson, 'Land purchase methods and their effect on Maori population', pp. 183-99.
36. A. S. Atkinson, diary, 5 June 1866, Atkinson MSS.
37. Whitaker to Col. Sec., 19 February 1866, IA 66/627.
38. Sorrenson, 'The purchase of Maori lands', pp. 53ff.
39. G. Maunsell to Smith, 5 September 1868, Smith Letters, p. 203.
40. *DSC,* 27 August 1866.
41. Ormond to McLean, 19 July 1866, McLean MSS., 326.
42. Fenton to McLean, 12 September 1866, ibid., 212.
43. Rolleston to the Rev. R. Taylor, 20 September 1866, *AJHR,* 1866, A-8, p. 9.
44. E.g. *DSC,* 27 February 1867; *PD,* 1867, vol. I, part 1, pp. 268-9. Heavy criticism was also focused on clause 13 of the 1866 Act which exempted Super-

intendents of Provinces from the provisions of the 1865 Act making void any dealings with Maori lands prior to the Court award. This was an attempt to give legality to the negotiations of Whitaker, then Superintendent of Auckland Province, for lands on the East Coast. The clause was repealed in 1867.

45. *PD*, 1867, vol. I, part 1, p. 272.
46. Ibid., p. 279.
47. *DSC*, 28 February 1867.
48. See Rolleston to A. de Bathe Brandon, 11 October 1866, MA 4/10.
49. See report and minutes of the Petitions Committee on the petition of John Topi Patuki, UPP, 1867; see also G. W. Rusden, *A History of New Zealand*, II, pp. 395-6.
50. FitzGerald to Mantell, 15 April 1866, Mantell MSS., 278.
51. Richmond memo, 25 February 1868, MA 17/1, NO 68/441 and attached papers.
52. J. C. Richmond to C. W. Richmond, 13 January 1868, Scholefield, *Richmond-Atkinson Papers*, II, p. 267.
53. Fenton to Native Minister, 11 July 1867, *AJHR*, 1867, A-10, pp. 3-5.
54. Fenton, opinion on the 17th Clause of the 1867 Native Lands Act, 7 April 1868, MA 13/2, NO 71/1153, pp. 99-101; Haultain to McLean, 18 July 1871, *AJHR*, 1871, A-2A, p. 4.
55. *PD*, 1868, vol. IV, p. 231.
56. Fenton memo, n.d., *c.* July 1871, MA 13/2, NO 71/1637.
57. *PD*, 1869, vol. VI, pp. 166-7; *AJHR*, 1871, A-2A, p. 10; Fenton, Judgment, 3 November 1880, on the application for rehearing of the Owhaoko-Kai-manawa block, *Hawke's Bay Herald*, 4 November 1880, cited in *AJHR*, 1886, G-9, p. 13. (For similar views see also Fenton memo, 7 April 1868, MA 13/2, NO 71/1153, pp. 98-101.)
58. Drummond Hay to McLean, n.d., *c.* 1870, McLean MSS., 257, no. 14.
59. The Ngaitahu Reference Validation Act, 1868.
60. Bowen to Buckingham, 7 December 1868, *AJHR*, 1870, A-1, p. 1.
61. *DSC*, 20 May 1868.
62. *PD*, 1869, vol. VI, p. 76; *Weekly News*, 8 July 1865.
63. *AJHR*, 1871, G-42, p. 5; MA 61/7.
64. Schedule to Military Pensions Act, 1866.
65. Cusack memo, *NZ Gazette*, 1868, p. 72; see also Williams report, 1 June 1868, *AJHR*, 1868, A-4, p. 23.
66. Barstow report, 7 March 1868, *AJHR*, 1868, A-4, p. 8.
67. Stack report, n.d., *c.* 1869, ibid., 1870, A-3, pp. 69-70; *Epitome of Official Documents*, Section D, n. 96, p. 48; Reimenschneider to Rolleston, 22 May 1866, *AJLC*, 1866, pp. 49-51.
68. *DSC*, 6 March 1867.
69. Te Rangikaheke to the Duke of Edinburgh, December 1867, ibid., 24 December 1867; Te Wheoro to Bowen, 27 February 1868, ibid., 26 March 1868; *PD*, 1868, vol. II, p. 270.
70. *The Weekly News*, 5 March 1864.
71. *AJHR*, 1869, D-17. European constabulary received an extra two shillings a day while employed on road work. In 1872 the Native Contingent at Te Teko struck for this extra rate (*PD*, 1872, vol. XIII, p. 830).
72. Clarke report, 29 September 1864, UPP, 1864, no. 1.
73. Stack report, *c.* 1869, *AJHR*, 1870, A-3, p. 70.
74. Ibid.
75. H. R. Russell, n.d., cited in Carrington to Col. Sec., 4 October 1865, IA 65/2609.

76. *Taranaki Herald,* 10 October 1868, MA 24/26; Halse to Pollen (Resident Minister, Auckland), 28 July 1869, MA 4/12.

Chapter 15

1. For a detailed description of conditions in eastern Bay of Plenty see MA 68/19.
2. Rolleston minute on H. Govett to Rolleston, 28 November 1866, Rolleston MSS., 1.
3. Richmond to Booth, 13 May 1868, MA 4/63, Appendix, p. 19.
4. Parris to Rolleston, 31 December 1867, Rolleston MSS., 1.
5. *PD,* 1868, vol. II, p. 14; *AJHR,* 1868, A-8, p. 2; Under-Secretary (Cooper) to J. Mackay, 8 July 1868, MA 4/63.
6. Titokowaru to Col. Whitmore, 5 December 1868, *AJHR,* 1869, A-10, p. 36.
7. *Wellington Independent,* 20 April 1867; *Hawke's Bay Herald,* 16 April 1867, MA 24/27.
8. J. W. Harris to McLean, 20 April 1867, McLean MSS., 254.
9. *DSC.,* 2 April 1868.
10. James Cowan is incorrect in his laudatory biography of McLean, in asserting that McLean broke with the Stafford Government because he could not persuade them to release the Chatham Island prisoners earlier (Cowan, *Sir Donald McLean,* p. 92).
11. Copy of proclamation, 23 September 1868, in JC Waimate 9; also J. Mackay to Native Minister, 28 June 1868, AGG-A, 1/3, GA 68/428; and Cooper to Resident Magistrate, Waimate, 8 July 1868, JC Waimate 9.
12. Richmond to Stafford, 26 December 1868, Stafford MSS., 42; James Cowan, *The Adventure of Kimble Bent,* pp. 157, 277.
13. *AJHR,* 1868, A-8, pp. 22-41.
14. See Searancke's reports from July 1868, JC-HN 1.
15. Under-Secretary to the Rev. C. Schnackenburg, 19 February 1869, MA 4/12.
16. Richmond to C. W. Richmond, 26 February 1869, Scholefield, *Richmond-Atkinson Papers,* II, p. 281; Bowen to Matutaera, 8 January 1869, MA 23/22, NO 72/836; Bowen to Granville, 12 March 1869, *AJHR,* 1869, A-1, pp. 56-9.
17. Richmond to Stafford, 13 May 1869, Stafford MSS., 42.
18. Scholefield, *Richmond-Atkinson Papers,* II, p. 264.
19. Deighton to McLean, 22 November 1868, McLean MSS., 203; Halse to Atkinson, 11 November 1868, MA 4/12; Campbell to McLean, 10 January 1868, McLean MSS., 174; Halse to McLean, 30 December 1868, MA 4/12.
20. 'Notes of public meeting, cizca, February 1869', Mitchell Library MS., Sydney.
21. Hensley, 'The withdrawal of the British troops from New Zealand', p. 187.
22. McLean memo, August 1864, PM 1/6; *AJHR,* 1869, A-10, pp. 72-87.
23. Fox to Gisborne, 20 January 1870, IA 70/156.
24. *Wellington Independent,* 25 September 1869.
25. H. T. Clarke to Under-Secretary, 3 February 1871, *AJHR,* 1871, F-6A, pp. 8-9, and 14 February 1872, ibid., 1872, F-3A, pp. 5-8; *AJLC,* 1872, no. 11, p. 7; Ormond to McLean, 28 December 1871, McLean MSS., 329.
26. Vogel, financial statement, 29 July 1869, *AJHR,* 1869, B-2, p. 13; see *PD,* 1869, vol. V, pp. 315, 455 for the Fox Governments policy statements.
27. Te Waru of Wairoa, Hawke's Bay, in fact did not take advantage of the amnesty and died in exile near Opotiki (Under-Secretary to Preece, 2 July 1883, MA 4/26).
28. McLean to Woon, 4 December 1871, MA-WG 1/2.
29. Mair to Clarke, 18 October 1870, *AJHR,* 1871, F-6A, p. 3.
30. *PD,* 1868, vol. II, pp. 185, 204-5, 224, 230, 270.

NOTES TO PAGES 230-8

31. Ibid., vol. III, p. 380.
32. McLean to Minister of Public Works, 8 November 1872, MA 4/66.
33. Clarke to Under-Secretary, 12 June 1871, *AJHR,* 1871, D-1, pp. 19-20; A. C. Turner to J. Blackett, 3 March 1871, ibid., p. 15; McLean to Parris, 18 October 1870, ibid., p. 51.
34. *PD,* 1869, vol. VI, pp. 203-4.
35. McLean memo to Cabinet, 16 September 1870, McLean MSS., 30.
36. McLean note on Martin memo, on 'Relations with the King Party', enclosed in Martin to McLean, 21 February 1870, ibid., 30.
37. *PD,* 1869, vol. VI, pp. 60, 79-80.
38. Journal, 20 November 1869, vol. IV, p. 106, McLean MSS.; McLean to Ministers, 26 October 1869, Native and Defence Department Letterbook, 1869-70, ibid.; McLean memo to Cabinet, 16 September 1870, ibid., 30.
39. Reports of meeting, 9 November 1869, and Mair to McLean, 26 November 1869, MA 24/22, NO 69/337.
40. Brabant to Native Minister, 21 February 1871, *AJHR,* 1871, F-6A, p. 16; ibid., 1873, G-3; ibid., 1877, G-1, pp. 6-7; Hopkins Clarke to Under-Secretary, 15 May 1876, ibid., 1876, G-1, p. 26; Harsant (Resident Magistrate, Raglan) to McLean, 12 September 1876, McLean MSS., 231; T. Jackson (Resident Magistrate, Papakura) to Under-Secretary, 13 May 1880, *AJHR,* 1880, G-4, p. 5.
41. MA 23/2, NO 71/1725.
42. Cracroft Wilson, address to the electors of Auckland City West, 3 February 1871, *DSC* extract, filed McLean MSS., 30; see also *PD,* 1869, vol. VI, pp. 74-5.
43. MA 13/66, NO 69/708 and attached papers.
44. Woon to Native Minister, 7 March 1876, MA-WG 2/2.
45. Chief Justice Arney to Kimberley, 10 April 1873, *AJHR,* 1873, A-1A, p. 18.
46. Cited in *PD,* 1872, vol. XIII, p. 447.
47. *AJHR,* 1873, C-4A, pp. 4-5.
48. Parris to McLean, 23 March 1870, *AJHR,* 1870, A-16, pp. 18-19, and 1 October 1870, ibid., 1871, F-6B, pp. 7-10; *Taranaki Herald,* 15 February 1873, McLean MSS., 34.
49. Parris to McLean, 12 August 1870, ibid., 335.
50. McLean memo, 20 January 1872, *AJHR,* 1879, sess. I, A-8, p. 5; notes of meeting at Putiki, 13 January 1873, MA 13/15; Brown to Under-Secretary, 23 May 1876, *AJHR,* 1876, G-1, p. 31; Fox report 1 July 1882, ibid., 1882, G-5A, p. 2.
51. Brown to McLean, 21 June, 24 July and 21 August 1876, McLean MSS., 155.
52. McLean to Atkinson, 15 January and 6 March 1875, ibid., 101.

Chapter 16

1. Fox to McLean, 9 and 21 October 1869, ibid., 220; Parris to McLean, 23 August and 28 December 1869, ibid., 335; McLean to Parris, King and others, 16 December 1869, *AJHR,* 1870, A-16, p. 29.
2. Mackay to Stafford, 23 August, 7 and 8 October 1872, Stafford MSS., 8; Pollen to Stafford, 12 September 1872, ibid., 40; C. O. Davis to McLean, 3 December 1872 and 3 February 1873, McLean MSS., 198; Mackay to McLean, 3 April 1873, ibid., 294.
3. Mackay to McLean, 23 July 1875, and 7 February 1875, ibid., 294. Mackay boldly went to Tokangamutu to demand the surrender of Sullivan's murderers. He was attacked in his tent by a Waikato man and subsequently protected by

Rewi and the Ngatimaniapoto (*AJHR,* 1873, G-3). He was forced to sever official connection with McLean in 1875 when some discrepancies in his land purchase operations were exposed, but continued to asist McLean privately against
the rising threat from the Grey party (Mackay to McLean, 12 October 1875 *et
seq.,* McLean MSS., 294). Mackay never did attain high office. He was briefly
Special Commissioner in 1879, investigating the origin of Te Whiti's agitation
on the Waimate plains, and the wheel turning full circle, was appointed
by Rolleston as Resident Magistrate (for the Justice rather than the Native
Department) in Nelson and Westland, where he had been Assistant Native
Secretary in 1858-63. But he did earn £10,400 commission as Land Purchase
Officer from 1872-8, £1400 as Special Commissioner in 1873, and various
lesser sums for official duties in addition to a considerable income from private
land agency work (UPP, 1880, Native Affairs Committee, evidence on petition
of J. Mackay no. 326).

4. Vogel to Stafford, 9 December 1872, Stafford MSS., 41.
5. Fergusson to Kimberley, 17 December 1873, *AJHR,* 1874, A-1, p. 21. The
   Rangitikei-Manawatu dispute originated in the conquest by Ngatiraukawa
   coming from Waikato of resident Ngatiapa, Rangitane and Muaupoko. In
   1840 the latter tribes were virtually hunted fugitives in the interior. During the
   1860s the Wellington Provincial Government began to purchase interests and
   found the Ngatiapa very willing to sell the territory conquered by the Ngatiraukawa. In 1869 the Land Court, in a highly contentious judgment, awarded
   the majority of the block to the Ngatiapa on the ground that they were still
   resisting in 1840. The judgment gave little to the conquering Ngatiraukawa
   but was, of course, highly convenient to the Wellington provincial authorities.
   McLean, taking office after the judgment, did not feel it was just but Fox
   persuaded him that it must be accepted (Fox to McLean, 22 September 1870,
   McLean MSS., 111). McLean therefore negotiated concessions by the Ngatiapa
   and Wellington authorities to the Ngatiraukawa. In a later judgment the
   Land Court held that the Ngatiraukawa who had left the Waikato had lost
   all rights there—in effect they were denied a place both in their homeland
   and the district they had conquered (MA 13/16, NO 83/2444).
6. See McLean MSS., 72 (telegram duplicates) and MA 5/1, 5/2, etc. (outward
   telegrams) for instructions on a great variety of routine matters.
7. Halse to Woon, 15 August 1871, MA-WG 1/2.
8. Davis and Mitchell to Under-Secretary, 24 April 1876, *AJHR,* 1876, G-5, p. 2.
9. McLean to Te Wheoro, 21 August 1873, MA 4/80; Woon to McLean, 25 June
   1873, McLean MSS., 437; Under-Secretary to Civil Commissioner, Taranaki,
   13 August 1870, MA 4/65.
10. McLean Journal, 4 January 1870, McLean MSS.
11. For notes on these cases see MA Wanganui 3/2.
12. Woon to Under-Secretary, 21 February 1872, MA-WG 2/1; 24 November
    1873 and 27 September 1875, MA-WG 2/2.
13. Woon to McLean, 28 January 1874, McLean MSS.; Woon to Under-Secretary,
    15 August 1876, MA-WG 2/2; report of Rupuha *v.* Hiroki, MA-WG 3/7 and
    MA-WG 2/1, p. 23.
14. See Woon's 'Plaint Book', MA-WG 3/10.
15. Woon to Under-Secretary, 6 August and 28 December 1872, MA-WG 2/1;
    Booth to Under-Secretary, 4 May 1877, MA 1/8, NO 77/2014.
16. Woon to Under-Secretary, 19 November 1878, MA-WG 1/9; MA 13/22, NO
    78/4147 (Putiki remains an important Maori centre today).
17. Woon to Commissioner of Native Reserves, 1 May 1873, MA-WG 2/1; Woon
    to Under-Secretary, 10 July 1874, MA-WG 2/2. The landing place and

market was granted but not as conveniently near to the centre of the town as Woon desired (Under-Secretary to Woon, 19 April 1880, MA-WG 1/11).

18. Speeches of Perene and Kohumuru, notes of meetings, Russell, 20 March 1873, MA 13/15.

19. Williams to Under-Secretary, 31 July 1878, JC Waimate 2.

20. Hamlin to Dr Bestie, 9 January 1872 and Hamlin to Attorney-General, 3 May 1872, JC Maketu 2.

21. Von Sturmer to Native Minister, 1 to 16 June 1874, JC Hokianga 1.

22. Brabant to McLean, 17 June 1873 to 14 August 1874, McLean MSS., 151.

23. Not the Native Department officer and Land Court Judge of the same name.

24. Under-Secretary to Civil Commissioner, Taranaki, 25 July 1870, MA 4/65.

25. White to McLean, 22 April 1873, *AJHR,* 1873, G-1, p. 2.

26. Jackson to Native Minister, 22 April 1878, ibid., 1878, G-2, p. 4; Aubrey to Under-Secretary, 17 June 1873, ibid., 1873, G-1, p. 23; Woon to Minister of Justice, 3 March 1873, MA-WG 1/3.

27. Perenera Tamataki to Ormond, n.d., *c.* 1872, AGG-HB, 2/1; Von Sturmer to Under-Secretary, 16 December 1871, JC Hokianga 1; Paora Te Rauhihi to Ormond, 18 November 1873, AGG-HB 2/2.

28. Brown to Under-Secretary, 31 January 1877, *AJHR,* 1877, G-1, p. 14.

29. Von Sturmer to Under-Secretary, 11 May 1876, ibid., 1876, G-1, p. 19.

30. Nesbitt (Resident Magistrate, Poverty Bay) to Under-Secretary, 23 June 1874, ibid., 1874, G-2A, p. 3; Campbell (Resident Magistrate, Waiapu) to Under-Secretary, 13 June 1874, ibid., p. 2; Clarke to Native Minister, 18 May 1877, ibid., 1877, G-1, pp. 24-7.

31. White to Under-Secretary, 18 May 1876, ibid., 1876, G-1, p. 18; Williams to Under Secretary, 12 May 1877, ibid., 1877, G-1, p. 3; Von Sturmer to Under-Secretary, 11 May 1876, JC Hokianga 1; and Von Sturmer to Minister of Justice, 21 November 1879, Resident Magistrate's Courts, Hokianga, Letterbook 1878-80.

32. Williams to Native Minister, 12 May 1874, *AJHR,* 1874, G-2, pp. 2-3.

33. McLean to Vogel, 15 March 1876, McLean MSS., 108; Woon to Under-Secretary, 24 May 1879, *AJHR,* 1879, sess. I, G-1, pp. 8-9.

34. Campbell to Under-Secretary, 13 June 1874, ibid., 1874, G-2A, p. 2; Preece to Under-Secretary, 26 June 1882, ibid., 1882, G-1, pp. 6-7.

35. Von Sturmer to Under-Secretary, 27 June 1872, ibid., 1872, F-3, p. 4; Bush to Native Minister, 5 May 1875, ibid., 1875, G-1, pp. 7-8.

36. Draft of Native Council Bill and supplementary notes, *c.* 1872-3, McLean MSS., 31.

37. *PD,* 1872, vol. XIII, pp. 587, 894-9.

38. McLean to Campbell, 5 November 1872, MA 4/66; Under-Secretary to Campbell, 7 February and 22 April 1873, MA 4/67; Campbell to McLean, 29 January 1873, McLean MSS., 177.

39. Draft of Native Councils Bill, *c.* 1873, McLean MSS., 31 and 118; *PD,* 1873, vols. XIV, p. 106 and XV, p. 1514; Fenton to Mantell, 6 November 1872, Mantell MSS., 277.

40. Hamlin to Under-Secretary, 19 June 1874, *AJHR,* 1874, G-2a, p. 1. Other Resident Magistrates who were encouraged to establish local councils with limited judicial authority included Woon, Locke and Watt (Otago).

41. See, for instance, E. G. Schwimmer's description of the founding of a school by two young Northland men ('The Maori Village' in *The Maori and New Zealand Politics,* ed. J. G. A. Pocock, pp. 73-4). Further examples are given in the annual reports of Resident Magistrates in Maori districts.

42. Native Office circular, 14 July 1873, MA 6/1; Under-Secretary to Resident Magistrate, Waiapu, 16 February 1874, MA 4/68.
43. White to Under-Secretary, 8 May 1874, *AJHR*, 1874, G-2, p. 1; Kelly to Under-Secretary, 20 August 1879, JC Mangonui 8.
44. M. P. Kawiti, reported in Williams to Civil Commission, 13 June 1864, MA Waimate 7; McLean memo, 14 May 1872, MA 4/66; Native Office circular, 8 November 1872, MA-WG 1/3.
45. Campbell to McLean, 30 June 1872, *AJHR*, 1872, F-3, p. 12 and 13 July 1873, McLean MSS., 75; Woon to H. Bunny, Provincial Secretary, 23 May 1873, MA-WG 2/11; Brabant to Native Minister, 26 May 1874, *AJHR*, 1874, G-2, pp. 6-7; *PD*, 1878, vol. XXX, p. 947.
46. MA 23/3, NO 81/237.
47. Woon to Native Minister, 7 March 1876, MA-WG 2/2; Mair to Under-Secretary, 20 May 1876, *AJHR*, 1876, G-1, p. 22.

Chapter 17

1. *PD*, 1869, vol. VI, pp. 220, 608. For a copy of the Bill, with revealing annotations, see Maning to Webster, n.d., Maning Autograph Letters, no. 497.
2. *PD*, 1869, vol. VI, pp. 166-7. Fenton's anger at the failure of his move was exacerbated by the passage of the Shortland Beach Act. This provided for the purchase of Maori interests in the Thames foreshore, below high water mark, and seemed to undermine a decision by Fenton in the Land Court, that the lands already belonged to the Crown, by prerogative. McLean took the view that payment was necessary to honour promises made earlier by James Mackay. It was made as compensation and not regarded as a precedent to support subsequent Maori claims to proprietary rights over fisheries in tidal land (MA 1/17, NO 70/1103 and attached papers).
3. Fenton to Mantell, 1 December 1879, Mantell MSS., 277.
4. Report of Select Committee on the Native Reserves Bill, 15 August 1870, *AJLC*, 1870; PD, 1870, vol. IX, pp. 359-60 (Sewell).
5. Ibid., vol. IX, pp. 455, 564.
6. Turton to McLean, 16 December 1871, 18 and 22 June and 17 August 1872, McLean MSS., 399.
7. MA 13/22, NO 78/4908; MA 13/26, NO 80/2030.
8. *PD*, 1886, vol 54, p. 463 (Ballance).
9. *AJHR*, 1872, F-3, p. 16; 1873, G-1, p. 19; 1877, G-3A; 1879, sess. II, G-3A, p. 4.
10. Petition of Renata Kawepo, *AJLC*, 1873, no. 7.
11. H. T. Clarke to McLean, 5 August 1871, McLean MSS., 183; Martin to McLean, 15 September 1871, ibid., 315; *AJHR*, 1871, A-2.
12. Fenton to McLean, 28 August 1871, ibid., A-2A, pp. 10-12; Fenton memo, n.d., *c.* July 1871, MA 13/2, NO 71/1637.
13. See MA 13/2, NO 71/1153 (Haultain's commission) and *AJHR*, 1873, G-7, pp. 1-9 (Hawke's Bay commission).
14. Sorrenson, 'The purchase of Maori lands', p. 127.
15. *PD*, 1873, vol. XIV, p. 606 and vol. XV, pp. 1372-4. See also the evidence of John Curnin, the legal officer who drafted the 1873 Act at McLean's instructions (*AJHR*, 1891, sess. II, G-1, report ix and minutes of evidence, pp. 170-1).
16. W. S. Grahame to McLean, 6 July 1873, McLean MSS., 243.
17. MA 18/2, NO 74/3522.
18. *AJHR*, 1885, G-1, p. 29.
19. J. A. Wilson memo, n.d., *c.* 1880, UPP, 1882, Public Petitions Committee.

20. Maning Autograph Letters, nos. 506 and 508, and Von Sturmer to Under-Secretary, 3 April 1886, *AJHR*, 1886, G-12, p. 3.
21. MA 18/2, NO 74/5058 and 70/16; *AJLC*, 1877, no. 19.
22. Gudgeon to Under-Secretary, 23 April 1880, *AJHR*, 1880, G-4, p. 11.
23. Gilbert Mair to Native Minister, 6 August 1881, Rolleston MSS., 4.
24. E.g., Under-Secretary to J. M. Clarke, 2 August 1870, MA 4/13; Under-Secretary to Douglas, 9 September 1870, ibid.; Under-Secretary to Borlase, 15 December 1873, MA 4/17; Under-Secretary to Hodge, 12 July 1877, MA 4/23.
25. MA 13/67, NO 70/1038 and 71/617.
26. Native Land Sales and Leases Bill, *Bills Not Passed,* 1876.
27. Clarke to McLean, 27 September 1874, McLean MSS., 74.
28. Ibid.
29. *PD,* 1873, vol. XV, p. 1542.
30. See, for example, Under-Secretary to H. Katene, 23 December 1872, MA 4/79; Under-Secretary to Brown, 20 August 1875, MA 4/69; Under-Secretary to Raniera Te Iho, 5 June 1876, MA 4/82.
31. St John to McLean, 6 July 1872, McLean MSS., 42.
32. Woon to Under-Secretary, 24 May 1874, MA-WG 2/2.
33. E.g., Booth to Under-Secretary, 7 June 1873, *AJHR,* 1873, G-1, p. 16; Woon to Native Minister, 16 June 1874, ibid., 1874, G-2, p. 14; Locke to McLean, 4 July 1872, ibid., 1872, F-3A, p. 33.
34. *AJLC,* 1877, no. 2.
35. Fox memo for Cabinet, 5 July 1872, McLean MSS., 111.
36. E. Douglas to Grey, 15 November 1877, *AJHR,* 1879, sess. I, I-4, p. 31.
37. Brown to McLean, 21 June 1875, McLean MSS., 155.
38. Campbell to McLean, 31 August 1872, ibid., 175.
39. *PD,* 1869, vol. VI, pp. 486-7, 870; 1870, vol. IX, pp. 120, 411-18, 455; 1871, vol. XI, p. 374; 1873, vol. XIV, pp. 537-42.
40. Under-Secretary to Kemp (Civil Commissioner, Auckland), 14 September 1874, MA 4/68.
41. *PD,* 1876, vol. XX, pp. 361ff.
42. *AJHR,* 1876, I-4, pp. 19, 27.
43. *PD,* 1876, vol. XXI, pp. 257, 262-3, 267.

Chapter 18

1. For the myth in various forms, see the writings of Raymond Firth, I. L. G. Sutherland, Felix Keesing and, more recently, John Harre, 'The background to race relations in New Zealand'. For more accurate reconstructions of the reality see N. G. Pearce, 'Size and location of Maori population'; M. P. K. Sorrenson, 'The politics of land' in *The Maori and New Zealand Politics,* ed. Pocock, pp. 31ff., and 'The Maori King movement', pp. 48ff.; John A. Williams, *Politics of the New Zealand Maori.*
2. Reports of Governor's visit to Hokianga and Mangonui, May 1874, McLean MSS., 41, nos. 28 and 29; Von Sturmer to McLean, 28 April 1873, *AJHR,* 1873, G-1, p. 3; S. Locke reports, 1870-1, ibid., 1871, F-6; speeches of Kingi Kiipa and Aporo, notes of meetings, Whangaroa, 1870, ibid., 1870, A-7, pp. 12, 16; address of Taupo chiefs to Locke, cited in J. Barrington, 'Maori education and society', p. 1.
3. Ngata to Buck, 15 July 1930, cited in G. V. Butterworth, 'The politics of adaptation: the career of Sir Apirana Ngata, 1874-1928', p. 11.

4. See Annual Reports of Resident Magistrates, *AJHR,* usually paper G-1 for each year. The Ngatiporou flocks were scabby but after they had been bought and boiled down by the Government in 1875-8 the Ngatiporou quickly rebuilt their flocks.

5. G. L. Meredith, *Adventuring in Maoriland in the Seventies,* p. 41.

6. It will be seen that this picture considerably modifies that in W. P. Hargreaves, 'Maori agriculture after the wars'.

7. Campbell to Under-Secretary, 24 May 1875, *AJHR,* 1875, G-1, p. 15.

8. *DSC,* 29 June 1869; prospectus of the Raglan and Waikato Company, *Hawke's Bay Times,* 12 June 1874; also Under-Secretary to Bush, 27 November 1872, MA 4/66.

9. *New Zealand Herald,* 6 October 1879. For further discussion of Maori economic enterprise see C. Lesley Andrews, 'Aspects of development; the Maori situation, 1870-1890'.

10. *AJHR,* 1874, G-2, p. 13, and 1881, G-11.

11. See Sorrenson, 'Land purchase methods and their effect on Maori population'.

12. *AJHR,* 1876, J-4.

13. Notes of meetings, 19 March 1873, MA 13/15.

14. Bush to Native Minister, 5 May 1875, *AJHR,* 1875, G-1, p. 8.

15. See Ashwell to Society, 22 February 1872 and 21 October 1874, CN/O 19.

16. E. B. Clarke to Society, 1 February 1877, CN/O 31.

17. T. S. Grace, *A Pioneer Missionary among the Maoris, 1850-1879,* pp. 244ff.

18. Campbell to McLean, 17 May 1873, McLean MSS., 175.

19. Ashwell to Society, 19 November 1873, CN/O 19.

20. McLean to Superintendent, Otago, 16 March 1872, MA 4/95; McLean to Superintendent, Taranaki, 14 October 1874, MA 4/20.

21. See debate on Provincial Councils Powers Bill, *PD,* 1873, vol. XIV, pp. 94, 514.

22. IA 70/3238; *AJLC,* 1878, no. 20.

23. Wi Katene to Governor, *AJHR,* 1870, A-7, p. 7.

24. Ibid., 1879, sess. II, H-17.

25. Maori elections are extremely difficult to analyse. Voting figures are far from complete, though some may be gleaned from newspaper reports and scattered comments by officials. Some patterns are fairly clear. For example, Hawke's Bay candidates usually dominated the Eastern Maori electorate, because Ngatiporou and Arawa candidates split the remaining votes in a first-past-the-post voting system. In 1876 the voting was Takamoana (Hawke's Bay) 401; Rangipuawhe (Arawa) 373; Hikairo (Arawa) 376; Porourangi (Ngatiporou) 145 (see ibid., 1876, I-3A, p. 2). In Southern Maori, Otago and South Canterbury voters gave Taiaroa a majority over rivals from Kaiapoi and Motueka. Western Maori remained a very open seat with Waikato, Hauraki, Wanganui and Manawatu voters shifting fairly considerably according to the candidate. Northern Maori reflected rivalry between the Rarawa, the Ngatiwhatua and several sections of the Ngapuhi. In 1871 Wi Katene was elected by a combination of Rarawa and Hokianga Ngapuhi (ibid., 1871, F-GA, p. 11). On the other hand Timoti Puhipi, an extremely able Rarawa leader, was so valued by his own tribe that they were said to have refrained from voting in order that he should not be elected and leave the district (White to Under-Secretary, 18 May 1876, ibid., 1876, G-1, p. 18). Such considerations would render largely invalid an analysis of Maori elections according to the normal criteria of psephology.

26. *PD*, 1872, vol. XIII, pp. 156, 579. In both votes Takamoana supported Stafford, and Katene and Taiaroa supported Fox. But Wi Parata, who had turned out Fox, crossed the floor in the second division to leave him in a minority of 35 to 37. The interim had seen an exchange of promises by both parties regarding the confiscated lands (see Stafford memo, n.d., Stafford MSS., 49; R. Pharazyn to Stafford, 30 September 1872, *AJHR*, 1872, C-4A, pp. 18-19; H. T. Clarke to Under-Secretary, 3 December 1872 and 30 January 1873, ibid., 1873, G-1B, pp. 2, 8).

27. *PD*, 1872, vol. XIII, p. 168.

28. See *AJHR*, 1876, H-28 and I-3A, and 1879, sess. I, H-8.

29. *PD*, 1872, vol. XIII, pp. 433, 636, 768; 1875, vol. XIX, pp. 21-34, 319-50; 1876, vol. XXII, pp. 230-40.

30. Jackson and Wood, 'The New Zealand Parliament and Maori representation', pp. 390ff.

31. *AJHR*, 1870, A-7, p. 7, A-16, p. 27; 1872, F-3, p. 11.

32. Notes of interview between the four Maori members and the Governor, 9 December 1879, G 13/7, no. 55; petition of Te Ara, Katene and others, *AJHR*, 1878, I-3, p. 5.

33. *PD*, 1876, vol. XXI, p. 298.

34. *Hawke's Bay Herald*, 11 September 1879.

35. See minute books of the Native Affairs Committee, UPP, 1877-82.

36. See the influence of Native Affairs Committee decisions on disputes regarding land claimed by Harding (MA 13/95) and McCaskill (MA 13/26, NO 77/840) and the draining of Lake Wairarapa (MA 13/97)—all contentious issues of the 1870s and 1880s.

37. Tutekanahau to Ormond, 8 June 1872, AGG-HB 2/1.

38. Williams to McLean, 19 May 1875, *AJHR*, G-1, pp. 5-6.

39. *DSC*, 18 June 1869.

40. See resolutions of the Orakei 'parliament' 1879, *AJHR*, 1879, sess. II, G-8. At the Assembly Arama Karaka stated that the first 'parliament' was held two years earlier at Otamatea (ibid., p. 43). I have seen no other reference to this; but Otamatea, on the Kaipara harbour, is a mingling point of the Ngapuhi and Ngatiwhatua tribes and an early council of the two may well have taken place there.

41. See letters and circulars of Henare Matua, AGG-HB, 2/2, especially circular of 3 November 1874; also the *panui* (proclamation) of 1876 in Porter to McLean, 19 May 1876, McLean MSS., 32B.

42. Williams, *Politics of the New Zealand Maori,* chapters 3 and 4.

43. Brabant to Native Minister, 21 February 1871, *AJHR*, 1871, F-6A, p. 16; Searancke to McLean, 24 June 1871, ibid., p. 15; Bush to Native Minister, 1 April 1875, ibid., 1875, G-1, pp. 1-2; ibid., 1877, G-1, p. 7 and 1878, G-1, pp. 8-9.

44. Under-Secretary to Brabant, 26 September 1876, MA 4/69; Under-Secretary to Locke, 14 March 1877, MA 4/70; Brabant to Native Minister, 10 June 1878, *AJHR*, 1878, G-1, p. 10.

45. McLean to Kemp (Civil Commissioner, Auckland), 6 March 1873, MA 4/17. (McLean was protesting against the closure.)

46. Gill to Under-Secretary, 7 May 1875, *AJHR*, G-2A, p. 11; Willis to Under-Secretary, 19 May 1876, ibid., 1876, G-1, p. 36.

Chapter 19

1. *PD,* 1879, vol. XXXI, p. 37.
2. Ibid., 1877, vol. XXIV, p. 262; Ballance to Vogel, 1 March 1878, J. Vogel, MSS., miscellaneous correspondence.
3. *PD,* 1877, vol. XXVII, pp. 234-9; Stone, 'The Maori Lands question', p. 58.
4. Return of unauthorised expenditure, *AJLC,* 1879, sess. II, no. 6.
5. UPP, 1877, 168a; Grey to Manuhiri, 18 and 19 June 1878, MA 5/5; *AJHR,* 1878, G-1A, p. 2, G-3, pp. 19-20; *PD,* 1879, vol. XXXI, p. 182; Sheehan memo, 5 July 1879, MA 13/66, N & D 78/3921.
6. *AJHR,* 1879, sess. I, G-2, pp. 2-12, 13-15; *PD,* 1879, vol. XXXI, p. 182.
7. Ibid., 1878, vol. XXX, p. 894; 1879, vol. XXXI, pp. 73-88, 102-5, 253-5.
8. Bush to Native Minister, 2 June 1879, *AJHR,* 1879, sess. I, G-1, p. 16.
9. *PD,* 1876, vol. XXIII, pp. 366-7 (Sutton's dispute); *AJLC,* 1877, no. 10 (Harding's dispute); *AJHR,* 1878, I-3, p. 23.
10. Chapman, 'The South Island Maoris and their reserved lands', pp. 100-6.
11. Sheehan to Nelson (Road Supervisor), 29 April 1878, MA 30/2.
12. UPP, 1878, no. 68.
13. Wilson to Sheehan, 4 June 1878, MA 5/5.
14. Under-Secretary to Native Minister, 10 December 1878, MA 5/5.
15. Williams to Under-Secretary, 5 September 1879, JC Waimate 2; Von Sturmer to Under-Secretary, 3 October 1879, *AJHR,* sess. II, G-9, p. 3.
16. *PD,* 1879, XXXII, pp. 361, 366.
17. Stone, 'The Maori lands question', pp. 59ff.
18. Maori Real Estate Act Amendment Act, 1877; Native Land Act Amendment Act, 2 November 1878, ss. 4, 6; some references suggest that the Court of Appeal was to consist of a panel of Maori chiefs (*PD,* 1877, vol. XXVII, p. 237); the Native Lawsuits Bill, 1878, however, proposed a court similar to the Supreme Court, but empowered to decide issues on equity and conscience, rather than technical law. Opposition from Supreme Court Judges seems to have contributed to its defeat (C. W. Richmond to Rolleston, 29 October 1878, Rolleston MSS., 2).
19. *PD,* 1878, vol. XXIX, p. 226.
20. *AJHR,* 1885, G-6, p. 1.
21. Brown to Under-Secretary, 10 August 1878, *AJHR,* 1879, sess. I, C-4, pp. 9-10.
22. Hiroki had been a brave and daring scout for McDonnell in 1869-70; McDonnell did not regard his killing of McLean, the cook, as murder (T. McDonnell, MSS., 18. See also Cowan, *Adventures of Kimble Bent,* p. 311). I have been unable to ascertain whether he was the same Hiroki who acted as 'policeman' for the *runanga* established in the Wanganui district at Henare Matua's suggestion and was prosecuted by Woon.
23. See exchange of telegrams between Grey, Sheehan and Taranaki settlers, in UPP, 1879, sess. II, no. 142, part 2.
24. *PD,* 1879, XXXII, pp. 361-6.
25. Stone, 'The Maori lands question'.
26. Ibid., p. 73 and W. J. Parker, 'John Sheehan, Native Minister and colonist'.
27. Under-Secretary to Woon, 8 April 1878, MA 4/24.
28. Waterhouse to Hall, 5 March 1879, J. Hall, MSS., 37; see also Ormond to McLean, 13 November and 16 June 1873 and 8 May 1875, McLean MSS., 330 (recounting the irritation of Renata Kawepo at Sheehan's winning away from him a girl he coveted).

Chapter 20

1. I am indebted to Mr Don Bryce of Wellington for these recollections.
2. *PD,* 1879, vol. XXXII, pp. 350-60; *AJHR,* 1879, sess. II, G-1, pp. 1-15.
3. Kelly to Under-Secretary, 27 September 1880, JC Mangonui 8.
4. Lewis memo, n.d., *c.* June 1880, MA 4/20, p. 555.
5. *PD,* 1880, vol. XXXV, p. 51; Native Office circular, 2 April 1880, MA 6/1; Under-Secretary to Registrar, Native Land Court, Auckland, 24 August 1881, MA 5/11; Lewis evidence, *AJHR,* 1886, 1-8, p. 67, q. 1462.
6. Kelly to Under-Secretary, 11 June 1880, JC Mangonui 9; Woon to Under-Secretary, 2 October 1880, MA 13/4, NO 80/3660; Preece to Under-Secretary, 13 October 1880, MA 13/95, NO 80/3571.
7. *PD,* 1886, vol. XLVI, p. 344.
8. Proceedings of Paora Tuhaere's second 'parliament', MA 4/12; evidence of Retreat Tapsell, *AJHR,* 1885, G-1, pp. 43-4.
9. Bryce minute, 11 January 1881, MA-WG 1/2, NO 80/3905; Under-Secretary to M. P. Kawiti, 11 January 1883, MA 4/87; Under-Secretary to Wilkinson, 21 April 1884, MA 4/38.
10. Petition of Tamati Te Wera and others, *AJHR,* 1882, I-2, p. 14.
11. The Act affected about 3.5 million acres out of 13 million, by 1883. (Lewis memo, 26 October 1883, MA 4/37).
12. Under-Secretary to Native Minister, 17 February 1881, MA 5/11, p. 102.
13. Tapsell to Native Minister, 20 September 1892, MA 1/13, NO 92/1724.
14. *PD,* 1882, vol. XLI, p. 557 (Whitmore).
15. Maning to Webster, 3 August 1883, Maning Autograph Letters.
16. Under-Secretary to Wilkinson, 7 March 1883, MA 4/36.
17. Rolleston to Mair, 8 June 1881, Rolleston MSS., 4.
18. Pollen to Rolleston, 7 November 1881, Rolleston MSS., 5.
19. *NZH,* 7 October 1879.
20. Hall to Bell, 1 December 1882, Hall MSS., vol. X, p. 354.
21. Bryce to Wahanui, 31 December 1883, MA 4/88; MA 23/4, NO 82/1262.
22. MA 23/5; *AJHR,* 1884, D-5, pp. 3-5.
23. Bryce minute, 20 January 1884, MA 13/93, NO 84/204.
24. Bryce memo, 16 October 1883, *AJHR,* 1884, G-1. By 1886 the Ngati-maniapoto were petitioning against the removal of the troops for this reason. MA 23/4, NO 87/1738.
25. MA 13/93, NO 84/359. This letter and one from Rewi are on sheets of squared graph paper, and were clearly drafted, if not written, by the same author.
26. MA 13/93, NO 84/304.
27. MA 13/43, NO 84/3668 *et seq.*
28. Stone, 'The Maori lands question', p. 72.
29. See his minute, 17 December 1880, MA 1/8, NLP 80/803.
30. Hall to Whitaker, 29 February 1880, Hall MSS., 6.
31. *PD,* 1880, vol. XXXV, pp. 267-74; vol. XXXVI, p. 383; vol. XXXVII, pp. 91ff.
32. *AJLC,* 1882, no. 7; Brabant to Under-Secretary, 14 June 1883, *AJHR,* 1883, G-1A, p. 4; 1883, I-2, p. 5; *PD,* 1888, vol. LXI, p. 183, 1890, vol. LXVII, p. 547; special file 43985, 'Rotorua Township', Department of Lands and Survey, Wellington.
33. Native Land Laws Amendment Act, 1883, s. 7.
34. MA 13/22, 13/23, 13/24, *inter alia.*

35. *PD*, 1880, vol. XXXVI, pp. 3-4, 46. For a fuller exposure see Robert Stout's attack on Fenton in respect of the Owhaoko case, *AJHR*, 1886, G-9, I-8, p. 65 and 1887, sess. I, G-1.

36. Minute of T. W. Hislop on MacDonald memo, 13 March 1888, MA 11/3, NO 88/487.

37. *PD*, 1880, vol. XXXV, pp. 142-4; correspondence on application for a rehearing of the Ngarara block, MA 70/3.

38. MA 23/13, NO 80/328; *AJHR*, 1880, I-2, pp. 1, 9.

39. MA 23/13.

40. Under-Secretary to Registrar, Auckland, 10 September 1885, MA 4/42.

41. Kelly to Under-Secretary, 11 June, 23 July and 2 September 1880, JC Mangonui 8; Kelly to Under-Secretary, 16 May 1881. *AJHR*, 1881, G-8, p. 1. (Kelly, Resident Magistrate's clerk, Mangonui, with the aid of some of the remaining Assessors, quashed the Rarawa attempt at self-government).

42. Von Sturmer to Under-Secretary, 7 May 1880, ibid., 1880, G-4, p. 2.

43. MA 23/1.

44. MA 1/8, NLP 80/151 and attached papers; MA-WG 1/11 and 1/12; *PD*, 1880, vol. XXXVI, p. 397; MA 13/14, NO 80/3418 and attached papers.

45. This is obscure; he was probably referring to his place on the commission into Hawke's Bay land dealing in 1872.

46. Cited in Rusden, *History of New Zealand*, III, p. 355.

47. MA 23/1, NO 82/307.

48. Bryce to Secretary, Aborigines Protection Society, 11 January 1884, MA 23/1, NO 84/166.

49. Rolleston to Whitaker, 23 February 1881, Rolleston MSS., 1881.

50. Hall to Bell, 19 April 1882, Hall MSS., no. 10 (see also Hall to Bell, 6 October 1882, ibid.).

51. The quarrel was occasioned by a telegram from Hall to Whitaker and others, then visiting the Waikato, containing some disparaging remarks about Bryce's overbearing behaviour. The telegram was handed to the group at dinner, and Bryce, who happened to have the Government cipher with him, decoded it and read what was not intended for his eyes (see Hall MSS., 1884).

52. Report of Native Affairs Committee on Petition of Te Rangiwhararua, *AJHR*, 1876, I-4, p. 16.

Chapter 21

1. MA 21/23.

2. *PD*, 1886, vol. LIV, p. 448 (Beetham).

3. MA 4/47, pp. 2-12; pp. 445 and 457ff; MA 4/94, p. 28; MA-NLP 1/20, 86/126 and 86/344.

4. Ballance to Governor, 3 August 1886, MA 4/44; Pardy to Ballance, 17 July 1886 et seq., J. Ballance, MSS., nos. 724-63.

5. Pardy to Commissioner of Police, 28 December 1892, MA 1/21, NO 92/2211.

6. *NZH*, 23 and 26 July 1887; *AJHR*, 1888, G-5, p. 2.

7. Special Powers and Contracts Act, 1884, s. 22; Under-Secretary to Preece (Resident Magistrate, Napier), 26 November 1884, MA 4/40.

8. *PD*, 1884, vol. L, p. 314; MA 13/27, 13/28; *AJHR*, 1884, sess. II, G-5; 1885, G-7, 1886, G-11a.

9. Vogel to Ballance, 8 February 1885, Ballance MSS., nos. 36-7; also memo headed 'Resolution', n.d., Vogel MSS., 1.

10. Letter by 'Nga Puia', 30 September 1887, McDonnell MSS., 40.

11. *AJHR*, 1887, sess. II, G-1, p. 5.

12. Ibid., 1884, sess. II, G-2; see also my unpublished M.A. thesis, 'The history of the East Coast Maori Trust', chapter II.

13. See Wi Pere's Native Land Administration Bill, 1884, *Bills Not Passed*.

14. See *AJHR*, 1885, G-1, and I-2B; 1886, G-2; *PD*, 1886, vol. LIV, pp. 328-30; vol. LV, p. 22.

15. Richard Duncan to Grey, 15 March 1887, Grey MSS.

16. Preece to Under-Secretary, 6 June 1887, *AJHR*, 1887, sess. II, G-1, p. 14; and 18 May 1888, ibid., 1888, G-5, p. 7.

17. The file MA/MLA 5/1, which was opened in respect of the 1886 Act, contains only letters from Maori saying they did not intend to place land under the Act but would deal with it themselves; see also Commissioners' reports, *AJLC*, no. 16. Only one transaction was recorded: 1216 acres sold for £304. £16.5.0 was deducted for fees and £287.15.0 paid to the Maori owners.

18. Heaphy to Woon, 14 December 1878, MA-WG 1/9.

19. In 1960 1.47 million acres of remaining Maori land was being farmed by incorporations (*AJHR*, 1961, G-10, statistical supplement, p. 47). The problems of distrust and recrimination between owners and elected committees, still plague the running of some incorporations, but not usually to a critical degree (see Norman Smith, *Maori Land Corporations*).

20. *PD*, 1884, vol. L, pp. 315-6; *AJHR*, 1885, G-1, pp. 17 and 48-9.

21. Ballance minute, 26 January 1885 and Attorney-General's opinion, 27 February 1885, MA 23/4, NO 85/1961; MA 23/4, NO 86/1101 and attached papers. See also Ballance's reply to Te Wheoro and Paora Tuhaere, *AJHR*, 1885, G-1, pp. 27-9. Topia Turoa, who accompanied Tawhiao to England, was struck off the roll of Assessors. Tawhiao, on the other hand, was tempted through the offer of a seat in the Legislative Council (Under-Secretary to Turoa, 2 April 1885, MA 4/89; MA 23/4, NO 87/1738).

22. Election address of J. D. Ormond, *Hawke's Bay Herald*, 18 July 1887; see also address of James Mackay, *NZH*, 29 July 1887 calling for the abolition of the office of Native Minister and transfer of his duties to the Minister of Lands.

23. *PD*, 1888, vol. LXI, pp. 187 and 693; Maori Relief Bill, Native Land Court Act Repeal Bill and Native Land Administration Bill, *Bills Not Passed*, 1888 and 1889.

24. *PD*, 1888, vol. XLIII, p. 230.

25. Ibid., 1889, vol. LXVI, p. 130.

26. Ibid., 1888, vol. LXIII, pp. 223-4. He added, in something of a reversal from his individualist attitude of 1865: 'I think we ought to take care . . . that all the old institutions of the Maori—the communal institutions—are protected, at all events, for a very considerable time.'

27. MA 1/20, NO 92/2163.

28. MA 13/97.

29. W. H. Grace to Wilkinson, 22 March 1890, MA 13/78, NLP 90/60.

30. Wilkinson to Native Minister, n.d., *c*. March 1890, MA 13/78, NLP 90/76.

31. *PD*, 1890, vol. XLVIII, p. 26. The principal allocations were £2000 (approximately) for Head Office, £2500 for Maori pensioners, £700 for remaining Assessors, £600 for medical care, £152 for grants of food and clothing and £800 for contingencies (*AJHR*, 1890, B-1, p. 22; see also estimates for 1890, ibid., 1890, B-3A).

32. MA 1/9, NO 87/3082; Lewis evidence, *AJHR*, 1889, I-10, p. 9.

33. Lewis minute, 27 February 1891, MA 4/53.

34. Bishop to Under-Secretary, 29 May 1888, *AJHR,* 1888, G-5, p. 1.
35. Puckey to Under-Secretary, 29 May 1880, ibid., 1880, G-4, p. 4.
36. *NZH,* 21 to 31 July 1888; *AJHR,* 1888, G-6; ibid., 1891, sess. II, G-1 (minutes of meetings with natives) p. 17 (evidence of Wi Pomare).
37. *PD,* 1889, vol. LXIV, p. 125; *AJHR,* 1890, G-2, p. 8.
38. *AJHR,* 1891, sess. II, G-5, p. 3; Under-Secretary to Premier, 22 October 1890, MA 23/6.
39. Atkinson to Hislop, 21 February 1889, MA 23/9, NO 89/495.
40. MA 23/9.
41. Goodall *v.* Te Kooti, 9 *NZLR* (1891), CA, p. 27.
42. *AJHR,* 1883, G-1A, pp. 7, 9; G-3, p. 9; 1890, G-2, p. 8.
43. MA 13/64, NLP 90/347 and 90/2280; *NZH,* 6 and 7 November 1890; *AJHR,* 1892, G-3, p. 6.
44. *PD,* 1891, vol. LXX, pp. 59-60.
45. MA 1/4, NO 91/2207, 91/2327 and 91/2482; MA 1/11, NO 92/1243.
46. Cadman memo for Cabinet, 24 February 1892, MA 1/7, 92/531.
47. *PD,* 1893, vol. LXXXII, pp. 911-12. (Kapa, Parata and Taipua voted against the Bill, James Carroll for it.)
48. See Jackson and Wood, 'The New Zealand Parliament and Maori representation'. By law those of less than 50 per cent Maori descent were to vote on the common roll, those of more than 50 per cent Maori descent were to vote for the Maori members (there was no Maori roll until 1949) and the exactly half-Maori, half-European had a choice. Actually mixed-race New Zealanders usually acted according to their sense of identity rather than to their percentage of descent.
49. *AJHR,* 1889, E-2, p. 3.
50. Ibid.; *PD,* 1888, vol. LXII, pp. 109, 204-9, 230-1; 1890, vol. LXIX, pp. 98ff; 1891, vol. LXXIV, p. 462 (W. P. Reeves).
51. In 1960 65.35 per cent of Maori pupils attended the regular state Education Board primary schools, and 27.87 per cent Maori primary schools (Report of Northland Regional Maori Leadership Conference, 1960). The Maori schools were closed or translated into Education Board schools in the late 1960s.
52. Governor's speech, *PD,* 1893, vol. LXXIX, p. 2, and Ballance's financial statements, *AJHR,* 1891, sess. II, B-6, p. 11, and 1892, B-6, p. 8. In fact the Liberals purchased about 3.6 million acres between 1891 and 1911, a rather lower annual average than in the previous twenty years, but including more acres previously under restriction.
53. UPP, 1893, 235G.
54. C. Dufaur to Cadman, 25 September 1894, J 94/1439.
55. Williams, *Politics of the New Zealand Maori,* chapters VII and VIII.
56. R. J. Martin, 'Aspects of Maori affairs in the Liberal period', Appendices 3A and 3C.
57. Von Sturmer to Webster, 2 March 1890, J. Webster, Letters from S. Von Sturmer.
58. *Dominion,* 16 July 1909, filed in MA 10/2. But this criticism could have reflected the opinions of settlers impatient to acquire land, rather than Maori litigants, for in the twentieth century the Maori people came to accept the principles and procedures implemented by the Land Court, particularly the concept of succession by all children, in equal shares and whether absent or resident, as an accurate reflection of traditional custom.

59. Ballance to Wi Mahapuku, 7 October 1886, MA 4/91.
60. *PD,* 1886, vol. LIV, pp. 354-5.
61. Ibid., 1873, vol. XIV, p. 527; vol. XV, pp. 1007-9, 1172-3, 1263-5.
62. See the most recent decision in 'The Ninety-Mile Beach Case', *NZLR* [1963] CA, p. 468. It was also held in 1914 that even if the Treaty of Waitangi should have the force of statute 'it would be very difficult to spell out of its several clauses the creation or recognition of territorial or extra-territorial fishing rights in tidal waters' (Stout C.J. in Waipapakura *v.* Hempton [1914] 33 *NZLR,* 1065).
63. Mangakahia *v.* NZ Timber Coy. 2 *NZLR* [1881-2], *SC,* 345.
64. Opinion of Lord Davey and his colleagues in respect of Nireaha Tamaki *v.* Baker [1901], AC, 561 and Wallis *v.* Solicitor-General [1903], AC, 173, *New Zealand Privy Council Cases,* p. 371, Native Land Act, 1909, s. 84; H. F. Von Haast (ed.), 'The Treaty of Waitangi and its consideration by the courts', p. 12.
65. *PD,* 1890, vol. LXVIII, p. 105. Also ibid., 1889, vol. LXV, p. 482 and Native Lands Administration Bill, 1889, *Bills Not Passed.*
66. In the late 1880s they were held at Waiomatatini (East Coast), Waipatu and Omaahu (Hawke's Bay) and Putiki (Wanganui). Most effective were possibly those at Waitangi in April 1892, and Waipatu, Hawke's Bay (June 1892). See MA 1/5, NO 91/2592; MA 1/12, NO 92/1108, 92/1160; *NZH,* 23 and 28 April 1892. For a clear statement of the aims of 'the Federated Assembly of New Zealand at Waipatu' see UPP, 1893, 134G; see also Williams, *Politics of the New Zealand Maori,* chapters III and IV.
67. See Von Sturmer to Webster, 21 August and 9 September 1892, Webster Letters, reporting the withdrawal of many cases from the Court, and Bush to Native Minister, 3 February 1892, MA 1/3, NO 92/238, reporting *Kotahitanga* 'pickets' at a Bay of Plenty hearing.
68. The reasons for Ratana's outstanding success where many earlier prophets had flourished briefly and died unknown outside their own community, is a subject worthy of closer inquiry (but see J. Henderson, *Ratana*).

Chapter 22

1. W. L. Buller, 'The development of the South Pacific', pp. 9-12.
2. Henry Vickers to Governor, 16 October 1861, G 3/5.
3. Earl Grey to Sewell, 19 October 1870, Mitchell Library MSS.
4. MA 1/14, NO 92/1515.
5. I am indebted to Messrs C. Hare and E. Keating of the Engineers and General Workers Unions, Wellington, for their information on this point. Also to Mr H. Roth, Deputy Librarian of the Auckland University Library, for showing me a copy of the rules of the New Zealand Workers Union printed in Maori (*c.*1892).
6. In the 1891 census 219 European men declared themselves married to Maori women but many more had *de facto* Maori wives (*AJHR,* 1891, sess. II, H-17a, p. 1, note b).
7. Ibid., 1880, G-4, p. 1.
8. Robert Stout, *The Maori as Land Reformer.*
9. *PD,* 1889, vol. LXIV, pp. 144-52, 539-44; vol. LXV, pp. 293-5; vol. LXVI, pp. 84-7.
10. Schwimmer, 'The Maori village', in *The Maori and New Zealand Politics,* ed. Pocock, p. 73.

11. See Pocock, *The Maori and New Zealand Politics*, and Williams, *Politics of the New Zealand Maori*, pp. 160-2.
12. Erik Schwimmer, 'The aspirations of the contemporary Maori', in *The Maori People in the Nineteen-Sixties*, ed. Schwimmer, pp. 9-64.
13. Morpeth to Cadman, 8 August 1892, MA 1/13, NO 92/1346.

A Note on the Primary Sources

The principal sources for this study have been Maori Affairs Department records in the New Zealand National Archives, Wellington. The yearly files showing Under-Secretaries' and Ministers' minutes survive only for the years 1857-63, and 1906 onwards. However, the extant outwards letterbooks and special series of files such as the series MA 13/1 *et seq.* (particular blocks of land) and MA 23/1 *et seq.* (leading figures such as Te Kooti) go far to make up for this. A reading knowledge of 'official' Maori (relatively simple in comparison with many colloquial and literary Maori compositions) is of value in view of the importance of some of the outwards correspondence in the Maori language letterbooks.

The work of the civil officers in the out-districts is revealed in the surviving Maori Affairs files of officers such as Woon, in the extant files from Waimate for the period 1861-5, in the unofficial MSS. of John White and in the letterbooks of other officers collected from various local Magistrates' Court offices and filed in the Justice Courts series.

The shaping of policy at government level is revealed to some extent in Governor's papers, Prime Minister's Department files and other official records, but better still in the unofficial MSS. collections held in the Alexander Turnbull and General Assembly Libraries. Of particular importance are the Mantell MSS. (1861-5), the Rolleston MSS. (including 1865-7 when Rolleston was Under-Secretary in the Native Department), the McLean MSS. (1850s to 1876) and the Hall MSS. (for the period 1879-84). The published *Richmond-Atkinson Papers* (ed. G. H. Scholefield), if supplemented by reference to the MSS. originals, are also very useful.

New Zealand Parliamentary Debates, and *Appendices to the Journals of the House of Representatives* contain a mine of material. The annual 'Reports from Officers in Native Districts' (usually *AJHR,* G-1 for each year after 1870) provide a ready insight into the work of Native Department officers and into Maori social conditions. Important information is also to be found in unpublished parliamentary papers, numbers of which were presented in the House of Representatives each year but not ordered to be printed. These, together with minutes of evidence heard by parliamentary committees, are housed in the Legislative Department, Parliament Buildings, Wellington. Newspapers are useful for expressions of settler opinion on various issues, but are unreliable guides to fact, especially in the 1860s.

Colonial Office records in the series CO 209 are essential to an assessment of British policy about the foundation of the Colony; published House of Commons Papers disclose events and evolution of policy in New Zealand in the 1840s and 1850s.

Maori opinion is recorded in a few published books and articles, but more particularly in the King movement newspaper *Te Hokioi* and in numerous letters, records of meetings, petitions and minutes of evidence filed in the Native Department and other archives, in the unpublished papers of the Native Affairs Committee and published papers in the *Appendices to the Journals of the House of Representatives.*

Bibliography

Agents of the General Government, Archives, New Zealand National Archives, Wellington, AGG-A 1/1-4, AGG-HB 2/1-3.

Anderson, J. C. and Petersen, G. C., *The Mair Family,* Wellington, 1956.

Andrews, C. Lesley, 'Aspects of development; the Maori situation, 1870-1890', M.A. thesis, University of Auckland, 1968.

Appendices to the Journals of the House of Representatives, Auckland and Wellington, 1854-93. Also 1961, G-10, J. K. Hunn, Report on Department of Maori Affairs.

Appendices to the Journals of the Legislative Council, Auckland and Wellington, 1863-93.

Ashwell, B. Y., Letters and Journals, typescript, Auckland Institute and Museum Library.

Atkinson family, MSS., General Assembly Library and Alexander Turnbull Library, Wellington.

Ballance, J., MSS., Alexander Turnbull Library, Wellington.

Banks, Joseph, *The Endeavour Journal of Joseph Banks,* 2 vols., ed. J. C. Beaglehole, Sydney, 1962.

Barnes, J. A., 'Law as politically active, an anthropological view', in Geoffrey Sawer (ed.), *Studies in the Sociology of Law,* Canberra, 1961.

Barrington, John, 'Maori education and society, 1867-1940', M.A. thesis, Victoria University at Wellington, 1965.

Baucke, William, *Where the White Man Treads,* 2nd ed., Auckland, 1928.

Beaglehole, T. H., 'Maori schools, 1816-1880', M.A. thesis, Victoria University of Wellington, 1955.

Beecham, John, *Colonization: Being Remarks on Colonization in General with an Examination of the Proposals of the Association which has been Formed for Colonizing New Zealand,* London, 1838.

Best, A. D. W., *The Journal of Ensign Best 1837-1842,* ed. Nancy M. Taylor, Wellington, 1966.

Biggs, Bruce, *Maori Marriage,* Wellington, 1960.

Billing, Graham, 'The Wairau affray', *New Zealand Heritage,* vol. II, part 17.

Bills Not Passed, Wellington, 1862-93.

Binney, Judith, *The Legacy of Guilt, A Life of Thomas Kendall,* Auckland, 1968.

——, 'Christianity and the Maoris to 1840: a comment', *New Zealand Journal of History,* vol. III, no. 2, October 1969.

Bohannen, Paul, 'The differing realms of the law', *American Anthropologist,* vol. LXVII, no. 6, part 2, 1965.

Bowen, G. C., *Thirty Years of Colonial Government,* ed. S. Lane-Poole, London, 1889.

Buck, Peter [Te Rangi Hiroa], *The Coming of the Maori,* New Plymouth, 1929.

——, *Vikings of the Sunrise,* Christchurch, 1954.

Buddle, Thomas, 'Maori Kingism and the Kopua meeting', MS. of address to YMCA Auckland, 1876, Auckland Public Library.

Buick, T. Lindsay, *The Treaty of Waitangi*, Wellington, 1914.

——, *New Zealand's First War*, Wellington, 1926.

Buller, W. L., 'The development of the South Pacific', reprinted from *The British Empire Review*, January 1901.

——, MSS., Alexander Turnbull Library, Wellington.

Bunbury, T., *Reminiscences of a Veteran*, 3 vols., London, 1861.

Butler, John, *Earliest New Zealand; the Journals and Correspondence of the Reverend John Butler*, ed. R. J. Barton, Masterton, 1927.

Butterworth, G. V., 'The politics of adaptation: the career of Sir Apirana Ngata, 1874-1928', M.A. thesis, Victoria University of Wellington, 1968.

Chapman, R. W., 'The South Island Maoris and their reserved lands, 1860-1910', M.A. thesis, University of Canterbury, 1966.

Church Missionary Society, Letters and Journals of the missionaries working in New Zealand, notably B. Y. Ashwell, Ralph Barker, James Booth, A. N. Brown, Thomas Chapman, Octavius Hadfield, James Hamlin, Robert Maunsell, John Morgan, Richard Taylor and William Williams, microfilm of originals, National Library of Australia, Canberra.

Civil Secretary's Archives, Inwards Letters, 1848-53, New Zealand National Archives, Wellington.

Clarke, George (Senior), Letterbook 1861-5, Auckland Institute and Museum Library.

Coates, Dandeson, *The Principles, Objects and Plan of the New-Zealand Association Examined, in a Letter to the Right Hon. Lord Glenelg, Secretary of State for the Colonies*, London, 1837.

——, *Notes for the Information of those Members of the Deputation to Lord Glenelg, Respecting the New-Zealand Association, who have not Attended the Meetings of the Committee on the Subject*, London, n.d., *circa* 1838.

——, *Documents Exhibiting the Views of the Committee of the Church Missionary Society on the New Zealand Question and Explanatory of the Present State of that Country*, London, 1839.

Colonial Office files relative to New Zealand, CO 209/4-29, CO 201/276, microfilm in State Library of Victoria, Melbourne.

Colonial Treasurers' Archives, Inwards Letters 1857-8, New Zealand National Archives, Wellington.

Compendium of Official Documents Relative to Native Affairs in the South Island of New Zealand, 2 vols., ed. A. Mackay, Wellington, 1872-3.

Cook, James, *The Voyage of the Endeavour 1768-1771*, ed. J. C. Beaglehole, Cambridge, 1955.

Cowan, James, *The Adventures of Kimble Bent*, London and Christchurch, 1911.

——, *Tales of the Maori Bush*, Dunedin and Wellington, 1934.

——, *Sir Donald McLean*, Wellington, 1940.

——, *Tales of the Maori Border*, Wellington, 1944.

Crocombe, R. G., *Land Tenure in the Cook Islands*, Melbourne, 1964.

Cruise, Richard A., *Journal of a Ten Months' Residence in New Zealand* [*1820*], ed. A. G. Bagnall, Christchurch, 1957.

Dalton, B. J., 'Tamihana's visit to Auckland', *Journal of the Polynesian Society*, vol. LXXII, no. 3, September 1963.

——, 'A new look at the Maori Wars of the sixties', *Historical Studies, Australia and New Zealand*, vol. XII, no. 46, April 1966.

——, *War and Politics in New Zealand 1855-1870*, Sydney, 1967.

Davidson, J. W., 'European penetration of the South Pacific 1779-1842', Ph.D. thesis, Cambridge University, 1942.

——, 'New Zealand 1820-70, an essay in re-interpretation', *Historical Studies, Australia and New Zealand*, vol. V, no. 20, May 1953.

Dieffenbach, Ernest, *Travels in New Zealand*, 2 vols., London, 1843.

Earle, Augustus, *Narrative of a Residence in New Zealand; Journal of a Residence in Tristan da Cunha*, ed. E. H. McCormick, Oxford, 1966.

Elias, T. Olewale, *The Nature of African Customary Law*, Manchester, 1956.

Epitome of Official Documents Relative to Native Affairs and Land Purchases in the North Island of New Zealand, ed. H. Turton, Wellington, 1883.

Executive Council Minutes, EC 1/2, New Zealand National Archives, Wellington.

Fargher, R. W. S., 'Donald McLean, Chief Land Purchase Agent 1846-1861, and Native Secretary 1856-1861', M.A. thesis, University of Auckland, 1947.

Fenton, F. D., *Observations on the State of the Aboriginal Inhabitants of New Zealand*, Auckland, 1859.

——, *Important Judgments Delivered in the Compensation Court and Native Land Court 1866-79*, Wellington, 1879.

Fieldhouse, D. K., 'Sir Arthur Gordon and the Parihaka crisis', *Historical Studies, Australia and New Zealand*, vol. X, no. 37, November 1961.

Firth, J. C., *Nation Making*, London, 1890.

Firth, Raymond, *Economics of the New Zealand Maori*, Wellington, 1959.

——, *Tikopia Ritual and Belief*, London, 1967.

FitzGerald, J. E., *Letters on the Present State of Maori Affairs*, Christchurch, 1865.

——, *Speech on the Native Affairs of New Zealand. Delivered in the House of Representatives on 18 August, 1865*, Wellington, 1865.

——, *The Self-Reliant Policy in New Zealand*, London, 1870.

——, MSS., Alexander Turnbull Library, Wellington.

FitzRoy, Robert, *Remarks on New Zealand, in February 1846*, London, 1846.

Foden, N. A., *The Constitutional Development of New Zealand in the First Decade*, Wellington, 1938.

Fox, William, *The Revolt in New Zealand* (letters to the Rev. George Townshend), London, 1865.

Freeman, J. D. and Geddes, W. R. (eds.), *Anthropology in the South Seas*, New Plymouth, 1959.

Geertz, C., 'Religion as a culture system', in William A. Lessa and Evon Z. Vogt, *Reader in Comparative Religion*, New York, 1965.

Gibbons, P. D., 'The Protectorate of Aborigines', M.A. thesis, Victoria University of Wellington, 1963.

Gisborne, William, *New Zealand Rulers and Statesmen*, London, 1886.

Godber, A. P., MSS., Alexander Turnbull Library, Wellington.

Gore Browne papers (memoranda and correspondence relative to Maori affairs) GB 1/2-3,2/3-4, New Zealand National Archives, Wellington.

Gorst, John, *The Maori King*, ed. Keith Sinclair, London, 1959.

Governors' archives (memoranda and inwards correspondence relative to Maori affairs). G 3/5, 13/2, 17/3, 25/89, 35/1-2, 36/3, 41/1-6, New Zealand National Archives, Wellington.

Grace, T. S., *A Pioneer Missionary Among the Maoris 1850-1879, being letters and journals of Thomas Samuel Grace*, ed. S. J. Brittan, G. F., C. W. and A. V. Grace, Palmerston North, 1928.

Graham, George, 'The Ngatipaoa Invasion of Auckland, notes taken from Maku-whara, a participant', Auckland Public Library.

Great Britain, Parliamentary Papers relative to New Zealand; Command Papers in square brackets.

Grey, G., MSS., Auckland Public Library.

Gudgeon, T. W., *The Defenders of New Zealand*, Auckland, 1887.

Hadfield, Octavius, Letters, typescript, Alexander Turnbull Library, Wellington.

Hall, J., MSS., General Assembly Library, Wellington.

Hamilton, Lila, 'Christianity among the Maori', Ph.D. thesis, University of Otago, 1970.

Hargreaves, W. P., 'Maori agriculture after the wars', *Journal of the Polynesian Society*, vol. LXIX, no. 4, December 1960.

Harper, N. D., 'An experiment in Maori self-government, 1861-5', *Report of the Australian and New Zealand Association for the Advancement of Science*, 1932.

Harré, John, 'The background to race relations in New Zealand', *Race*, 1963, vol. V, no. 1.

Harrop, A. J., *England and the Maori Wars*, London, 1937.

Hawtrey, Montagu, 'Exceptional Laws in favour of the Natives of New Zealand', Appendix A in E. G. Wakefield and J. Ward, *The British Colonization of New Zealand; being an account of the Principles, Objects, and Plans of the New Zealand Association; together with Particulars concerning the Position, Extent, Soil and Climate, natural Productions, and Native Inhabitants of New Zealand*, London, 1837.

——, *An Earnest Address to the New Zealand Colonists—with Reference to their Intercourse with the Native Inhabitants*, London, 1840.

——, *Justice to New Zealand, Honour to England*, London, 1861.

Henderson, J., *Ratana*, Wellington, 1963.

Hensley, Gerald C., 'The withdrawal of the British troops from New Zealand 1864-1870: a study in imperial relations', M.A. thesis, University of Canterbury, 1957.

Herron, D. G., 'The franchise and New Zealand politics', *Political Science*, vol. XI, no. 1, March 1960.

Hetherington, Jessie I., *New Zealand, Its Political Connection with Great Britain*, 2 vols., Dunedin, 1926.

Hight, J. and Bamford, H. D., *The Constitutional History and Law of New Zealand*, Wellington, 1924.

Hinds, Samuel, *The Latest Official Documents Relating to New Zealand, with Introductory Observations*, London, 1838.

Historical Records of Australia, vol. XV, Sydney, 1922.

Historical Records of New Zealand, 2 vols., ed. R. McNab, Wellington, 1914.

Hoebel, E. Adamson, *The Law of Primitive Man*, Cambridge (Mass.), 1967.

Hogbin, H. Ian, *Law and Order in Polynesia*, Hamden (Conn.), 1961.

Hooker, M. B., 'An enquiry into the function of the magico-religious as a jural mechanism in primitive Maori society', LL.M. thesis, University of Canterbury, 1965.

Integration of Maori and Pakeha, Department of Maori Affairs special study, Wellington, 1962.

Internal Affairs Department archives (Colonial Secretary's Department); office files, relative to Maori affairs, IA 63/118, 63/2648, 64/2671, 65/46, 65/969, 66/627, 66/629, 66/1919, 66/2957, 70/156, New Zealand National Archives, Wellington.

Jackson, W. K. and Wood, G. A., 'The New Zealand Parliament and Maori representation', *Historical Studies, Australia and New Zealand*, vol. XI, no. 43, October 1964.

Jellicoe, R. L., *The New Zealand Company's Native Reserves*, Wellington, 1930.

Journals of the House of Representatives, Wellington, 1865, 1869-70.

Jurist Reports, Wellington.

Justice Department archives relative to Maori affairs, J 1/22, 62/2618, 63/91, 63/304, 92/1244, 93/378, 93/1740, 94/1439, 94/1502, 97/115 and 115a, 1917/55.

Justice Department Courts archives; files and letter-books of Magistrates' Courts from various centres including

Hamilton	(JC-HN 3, 4 and 5)
Maketu	(JC-Maketu 2 and 3)
Mangonui	(JC-Mangonui 8 and 9)
Russell	(JC-Russell 1 and 2)
Waimate	(JC-Waimate 1 and 2)
Wanganui	(JC-WG 4 and 5)

New Zealand National Archives, Wellington.

Kawharu, Hugh, 'New Zealand', in *Land Tenure in the Pacific*, ed. Ron Crocombe, Melbourne, 1971.

Keesing, Felix, *The Changing Maori*, New Plymouth, 1928.

Kelly, R. A., 'The politics of racial equality', *The New Zealand Journal of Public Administration*, vol. XXIV, no. 2, March 1962.

Ko Nga Ture o Ingarani [The Laws of England], ed. F. D. Fenton, Auckland, 1858.

Kohere, Rewiti T., *The Autobiography of a Maori*, Wellington, 1951.

Lambert, Thomas, *The Story of Old Wairoa*, Dunedin, 1925.

Lands and Survey Department, Head Office, Wellington; special file 43985, 'Rotorua Township'.

Lloyd, Dennis, *The Idea of Law*, Harmondsworth, 1970.

McClean, Sheila, 'Maori representation 1905-1948', M.A. thesis, University of Auckland, 1949.

McDonnell, T., MSS., Alexander Turnbull Library, Wellington.

Mackay, James, *Our Dealings with Maori Lands*, Auckland 1887.

McLean, D., MSS., Alexander Turnbull Library, Wellington.

McLintock, C. H., *Crown Colony Government in New Zealand*, Wellington, 1958.

McNab, Robert, *From Tasman to Marsden, a History of Northern New Zealand from 1642 to 1818*, Dunedin, 1914.

Mair, family, MSS., Alexander Turnbull Library, Wellington.

[Maning, F. E.], *Old New Zealand, a Tale of the Good Old Times*, by 'A Pakeha Maori', Auckland 1922.

Maning, F. E., Autograph letters, Auckland Public Library.

Mantell, W., MSS., Alexander Turnbull Library, Wellington.

Maori Affairs Department Archives; Head Office (MA series):

MA 1/1-3	(memoranda and office files, 1857-63)
1/4-20	(memoranda and office files, 1891-2, 1906)
2/40	(register of inwards correspondence)
4/4-70	(outwards correspondence, letterbooks)
4/71-99	(Maori language letterbooks, outwards correspondence)
5/1-11	(outwards telegrams)
6/1	(Native Office circulars)
10/2	(race relations; memoranda and newspaper clippings)
11/3	(Trust Commissioner's reports)
13/2	(land legislation)
13/22-29	(removal of restrictions on alienation)
13/3-21, 30-99	(files relating to particular blocks of land)
17/1	(Maori reserves)
18/2	(Native Land Court)
19/1	(Medical Officers' returns)
23/1-8	(Leading political questions—Te Kooti, Native Committees under 1883 Act, etc.)
23/10	(Proceedings of the Kohimarama Conference)
23/21-4	(Miscellaneous papers)

24/4   (Sale of liquor)
24/21   (Political and administrative, *circa* 1863-4)
24/26-7   (newspaper clippings)
25/1   (summary of careers of Native Service officials)
30/3   (Ballance's meetings with Maori leaders)
31/24   (land law)
MA/MLA 5/1   (relative to the Native Land Administration Act, 1886)
MA/MLP 1/29   (file of the Maori Land Purchase Department)
MLC 1/2, 10/2 (Maori Land Court)
   District Offices: Outwards Letterbooks and files.
   Collingwood   (MA-Collingwood 2/1)
   Napier   (MA-NA 1/2)
   Wanganui   (MA-WG 1/1-12, 2/1-2, 3/10, 4/9)
   Waimate   (MA Waimate 1-7)
Letterbooks of Commissioners of Maori Reserves (later the Maori Trustee)
   MT-CH 1/1 (outwards letterbooks of Commissioner of Native Reserves, Christ-
             church, Alex Mackay, 1868-76)
   MT-N 1/1-2 (outwards letterbooks of Commissioner of Native Reserves, Nelson,
              James Mackay, 1858-62)
New Zealand National Archives, Wellington.
Markham, Edward, *New Zealand or Recollections of it,* ed. E. H. McCormick,
   Wellington, 1963.
Marsden, Samuel, *The Letters and Journals of Samuel Marsden 1765-1838 Senior
   Chaplain in the Colony of New South Wales and Superintendent of the Mission of
   the Church Missionary Society in New Zealand,* ed. John Rawson Elder, Dunedin,
   1932.
Marshall, William Barrett, *A Personal Narrative of Two Visits to New Zealand in
   His Majesty's Ship Alligator, A.D. 1834,* London, 1836.
Martin, Lady, *Our Maoris,* London, 1844.
Martin, R. J., 'Aspects of Maori affairs in the Liberal period', M.A. thesis, Victoria
   University of Wellington, 1956.
Martin, William and Shortland, Edward, *Memorial on Maori Lands and Suggestions
   for Legislation,* Auckland, 1873.
Matheson, Peter C., 'The views of the New Zealand clergy of 1860 on race relations',
   M.A. thesis, University of Otago, 1959.
Meade, Herbert, *A Ride Through the Disturbed Districts of New Zealand,* ed. R. H.
   Meade, London, 1870.
Meredith, G. L., *Adventuring in Maoriland in the Seventies,* ed. A. J. Harrop, Sydney,
   1935.
Miller, Harold, *New Zealand,* London, 1950.
——, *Race Conflict in New Zealand 1814-65,* Auckland, 1966.
Miller, John, *Early Victorian New Zealand: a study of racial tension and social
   attitudes,* London, 1958.
Morrell, W. P., *The Provincial System in New Zealand, 1856-76,* Wellington, 1964
   (2nd edition).
——, *British Colonial Policy in the Mid-Victorian Age,* Oxford, 1969.
Motte, Standish, *A System of Legislation for Securing Protection to the Aboriginal
   Inhabitants of all Countries Colonized by Great Britain,* London, 1840.
Murray, Janet, 'A missionary in action', in *The Feel of Truth: Essays in New
   Zealand and Pacific History,* ed. Peter Munz, Wellington, 1969.
Murray-Oliver, Anthony (ed.), *Augustus Earle in New Zealand,* Christchurch, 1965.
New Munster Archives, Inwards letters, 1848-53, New Zealand National Archives,
   Wellington.

New Zealand Government Gazette, Auckland and Wellington, 1861-8.

New Zealand Law Reports, Wellington.

New Zealand Law Reports Consolidated Digest, 1861-1902, Auckland and Wellington, n.d.

New Zealand Parliamentary Debates, Wellington, 1854-93.

New Zealand Privy Council Cases, 1840-1932, ed. H. F. Von Haast, Wellington, 1938.

New Zealand Statutes, Wellington, 1856-93.

Ngata, Apirana Turupa, 'Anthropology and the government of native races in the Pacific', *Australian Journal of Psychology and Philosophy,* vol. VI, no. 1, March 1928.

'Notes of Public Meeting', *circa* February 1869, MS. account of a public meeting at Napier to discuss McLean's dismissal, Mitchell Library, Public Library of New South Wales, Sydney.

Oliver, W. H. and Thomson, Jane M., *Challenge and Response; a study of the development of the Gisborne East Coast Region,* Gisborne, 1971.

Oliver, W. H., *The Story of New Zealand,* London, 1960.

Ordinances of the Legislative Council of New Zealand and of the Legislative Council of the Province of New Munster, Wellington, 1871.

Outline of the Laws of England, ed. Sir W. Martin, Wellington, 1867.

Owens, J., 'Christianity and the Maoris to 1840', *New Zealand Journal of History,* vol. II, no. 1, April 1968.

——, 'Religious disputation at Whangaroa, 1823-7', *Journal of the Polynesian Society,* vol. LXXIX, no. 3, September 1970.

Palmer, Pauline B., 'The Native Ministry of Donald McLean', M.A. thesis, University of Canterbury, 1937.

Parker, W. J., 'John Sheehan, Native Minister and colonist', M.A. thesis, University of Auckland, 1963.

Pearce, N. G., 'Size and location of Maori population', M.A. thesis, Victoria University of Wellington, 1952.

Pocock, J. G. A. (ed.), *The Maori and New Zealand Politics,* Auckland and Hamilton, 1965.

Pool, D. I., 'The Maori population of New Zealand', Ph.D. thesis, Australian National University, 1964.

Prime Minister's Department (archives relative to Maori affairs)
    PM 1/1-6 (memoranda and inwards correspondence, 1861-9)
    PM 2/5   (memoranda from Ministers to Governor, 1862-3), New Zealand National Archives, Wellington.

Ramsden, Eric, *Marsden and the Missions; Prelude to Waitangi,* Sydney, 1936.

——, *Busby of Waitangi; H.M.'s Resident at New Zealand, 1833-1840,* Wellington and Dunedin, 1942.

Renwick, W. L., 'Self-government and protection: a study of Stephen's two cardinal points of policy in their bearing upon constitutional development in New Zealand in the years 1837-1867', M.A. thesis, Victoria University of Wellington, 1961.

Report on the Northland Regional Maori Leadership Conference, 1960, duplicated.

Resident Magistrates' Courts, MS. Letterbooks, Hokianga 1878-80 and Wanganui 1874-5 and Court Book, Taupo, 1863-8, Alexander Turnbull Library, Wellington.

Richmond, J. C., *Reminiscences of a Minister for Native Affairs in New Zealand,* Wellington, 1888. Legislative Council Speech of 1 August, 1888.

Richmond, family, MSS., General Assembly Library, Wellington.

Rickard, G. S., *Tamihana the Kingmaker,* Wellington, 1963.

Ritchie, J., *The Making of a Maori,* Wellington, 1963.

Robinson, Wanda M., 'The pacification of the Waikato 1869-76', M.A. thesis, University of Auckland, 1949.

Robson, J. L. (ed.), *New Zealand—the Development of its Laws and Constitution,* London, 1954.

Rolleston, W., MSS., General Assembly Library, Wellington.

Ross, Janet E., 'The missionary work of the Rev. Richard Taylor of Wanganui', M.A. thesis, Victoria University of Wellington, 1965.

Ross, R. M., *'Te Tiriti o Waitangi,* texts and translations', *New Zealand Journal of History,* vol. VI, no. 2, October 1972.

Rusden, G. W., *History of New Zealand,* 3 vols., London, 1883.

——, *Aureretanga: groans of the Maoris,* London, 1888.

Rutherford, J., *Sir George Grey K.C.B. 1812-1898: a study in colonial government,* London, 1961.

Sahlins, Marshall D., *Social Stratification in Polynesia,* Seattle, 1958.

Scholefield, G. (ed.), *A Dictionary of New Zealand Biography,* 2 vols., Wellington, 1940, 1964 (2nd edition).

—— (ed.), *The Richmond-Atkinson Papers,* 2 vols., Wellington, 1960.

Schwimmer, E. G., 'Government and the changing Maori', *The New Zealand Journal of Public Administration,* vol. XXII, no. 2, March 1960.

—— (ed.), *The Maori People in the Nineteen-Sixties,* Auckland, 1968.

Scott, Dick, *The Parihaka Story,* Auckland, 1921.

Searancke, W., MS. Diary, Nan Kivell Collection, National Library of Australia, Canberra.

Sewell, Henry, *The New Zealand Native Rebellion,* London, 1864.

——, Journal, Typescript, Alexander Turnbull Library, Wellington.

Shortland, Edward, *The Southern Districts of New Zealand,* London, 1851.

——, *Traditions and Superstitions of the New Zealanders,* London, 1856.

Shrimpton, A. W. and Mulgan, A. E., *Maori and Pakeha,* Auckland, 1921.

Sinclair, Keith, 'The Aborigines Protection Society and New Zealand: a study in nineteenth century opinion', M.A. thesis, University of Auckland, 1946.

——, 'Maori nationalism and the European economy', *Historical Studies, Australia and New Zealand,* vol. V, no. 18, May 1952.

——, *The Origins of the Maori Wars,* Wellington, 1961.

——, 'Some historical notes on an Atiawa genealogy', *Journal of the Polynesian Society,* vol. 60, no. 1, March 1961.

——, *A History of New Zealand,* Harmondsworth, 1969.

Smith, Norman, *Maori Land Law,* Wellington, 1960.

——, *Maori Land Corporations,* Wellington, 1962.

Smith, T. H., Letters, Typescript, Auckland Institute and Museum Library.

Sorrenson, M. P. K., 'The purchase of Maori lands, 1865-1892', M.A. thesis, University of Auckland, 1955.

——, 'Land purchase methods and their effect on Maori population 1865-1901', *Journal of the Polynesian Society,* vol. LXV, no. 3, September 1956.

——, 'The Maori King movement, 1858-1885', in *Studies of a Small Democracy,* ed. Robert Chapman and Keith Sinclair, Auckland, 1963.

St John, Lieut.-Col., *Pakeha Rambles Through Maori Lands,* Wellington, 1873.

Stafford, W., MSS., Alexander Turnbull Library, Wellington.

Stewart, W. D., *William Rolleston, A New Zealand Statesman,* Christchurch, 1940.

Stone, R. C. J., 'The Maori lands question and the fall of the Grey Government, 1879', *The New Zealand Journal of History,* vol. 1, no. 1, April 1967.

Stout, R., 'The Maori as land reformer', *The Internationalist,* vol. III, September 1908.

Sutherland, I. L. G. (ed.), *The Maori People Today,* Wellington, 1940.

Swainson, W., *New Zealand and its Colonization,* London, 1859.

Symonds, W. C., MS. Journal, Mitchell Library, Public Library of New South Wales, Sydney.

Taiwhanga, S. [Hirini], *Proposals for Colonization and Settlement of Maori Lands,* Wellington, 1888.

Tapp, E. J., *Early New Zealand; a dependency of New South Wales, 1788-1841,* Melbourne, 1958.

Taylor, Richard, *The Past and Present of New Zealand and Its Prospects for the Future,* London, 1868.

——, Journal, Typescript, Auckland Institute and Museum Library.

Te Hurinui [Jones], Pei, *King Potatau, an Account of the Life of Potatau Te Wherowhero the First Maori King,* Wellington, 1960.

Unpublished parliamentary papers; papers laid on the table of the House of Representatives and not ordered to be printed, 1860-93; minutes of and evidence presented to the Native Affairs Committee of the House of Representatives, 1870-93; Parliament Buildings, Wellington.

Vogel, J., MSS., General Assembly Library, Wellington.

Von Haast, H. F. (ed.), 'The effect of the Treaty of Waitangi on subsequent legislation', *The New Zealand Law Journal,* vol. X, 1934.

——, 'The Treaty of Waitangi and its consideration by the courts', *The New Zealand Law Journal,* vol. X, 1934.

Votes and Proceedings of the House of Representatives, Auckland, 1854-6.

Wake, C. H., 'George Clarke and the government of the Maoris', *Historical Studies, Australia and New Zealand,* vol. X, no. 39, November 1962.

Wakefield, Edward Jerningham, *Adventuring in New Zealand from 1839 to 1844,* London, 1845.

Wakefield, E. G. and Ward, J., *The British Colonization of New Zealand,* London, 1837.

Ward, A. D., 'The history of the East Coast Maori Trust', M.A. thesis, Victoria University of Wellington, 1958.

——, 'Tamihana's visit to Auckland', *Journal of the Polynesian Society,* vol. LXXIII, no. 3, September 1964.

Ward, John P., *Wandering with the Maori Prophets Te Whiti and Tohu,* Nelson, 1883.

Wardell, H., MS. Diary, 1858, Alexander Turnbull Library, Wellington.

Wards, Ian, *The Shadow of the Land,* Wellington, 1968.

Webster, J., Letters from S. Von Sturmer, Typescript, Auckland Public Library.

Weld, F., *Notes on New Zealand Affairs: comprising a sketch on its political history, in reference especially to native questions,* London, 1869.

White, John, *Ancient History of the Maori,* Wellington, 1887, 1888, 1890 (6 vols.).

White, John, MSS., Alexander Turnbull Library, Wellington.

White, W. B., 'Reminiscences 1821-1908', typescript by Kate White, Alexander Turnbull Library, Wellington.

Whiteley, John, Journal, Typescript, Alexander Turnbull Library, Wellington.

Whitmore, G. S., MSS., Alexander Turnbull Library, Wellington.

Williams, family, MSS., Alexander Turnbull Library, Wellington.

Williams, Henry, *The Early Journals of Henry Williams,* ed. Lawrence M. Rogers, Christchurch, 1961.

Williams, John A., *Politics of the New Zealand Maori: protest and cooperation, 1891-1909,* Auckland, 1969.

Williams, William, *Christianity Among the New Zealanders,* London, 1867.

Williams, W. Leonard, *East Coast Historical Records,* Gisborne, n.d.

Wilson, Ormond, 'Papahurihia, First Maori Prophet', *Journal of the Polynesian Society,* vol. LXXIV, no. 4, December 1965.

Wohlers, J. F. H., *Memories of the Life of J. F. H. Wohlers,* an autobiography translated from the German by John Haughton, Dunedin, 1895.

Wood, G. A., 'The political structure of New Zealand, 1858-1861', Ph.D. thesis, University of Otago, 1965.

Wright, Harrison M., *New Zealand 1769-1840: Early Years of Western Contact,* Cambridge, (Mass.), 1967.

Young, T. J., 'The political career of John Ballance', M.A. thesis, University of Auckland, 1963.

NEWSPAPERS

The Aucklander, 1862.

The Daily Southern Cross, 1861-8 (Auckland).

The Hawke's Bay Herald, 1860-62, 1867-8, 1871, 1876, 1879, 1887 (Napier).

Te Hokioi, (the first King movement newspaper) 1862-3.

The New Zealand Colonist, October 1842 (Auckland).

The New Zealander, 1862-5 (Auckland).

The New Zealand Gazette and Wellington Spectator, December 1843.

The New Zealand Herald, 1887-8 (Auckland).

Te Paki o te Matariki, (the second King movement newspaper) 1892-4.

Te Pihoihoi Mokemoke, (Gorst's newspaper) 1863.

The Press, July 1861 (Christchurch).

The Weekly News, 1864-5 (Auckland).

The Wellington Independent, June-July 1865, September 1869.

Copies and translations of *Te Hokioi* and *Te Pihoihoi* were located in UPP, 1865, and microfilmed for the General Assembly Library collection; copies of *Te Paki o te Matariki* are to be found in MA 1/13, NO 92/238, MA 1/21, NO 92/2168, J93/1740 and J94/1502.

Extracts from various New Zealand newspapers for the period 1866-8 are filed in MA 24/26 and 24/27.

Index

Alan Ward, Senior Lecturer in History at La Trobe University, Melbourne, served during 1973 as Consultant to a commission of inquiry into the land problems of Papua New Guinea, at its government's request. He is a New Zealander and a graduate of Victoria University of Wellington and the Australian National University.

Text set in 10pt Baskerville and printed on 75 G.S.M. "2275" Printing by Wright and Carman Limited, Trentham, New Zealand.